THE PAPERS OF ALEXANDER HAMILTON

Alexander Hamilton, *circa* 1791. Oil portrait by Charles Willson Peale
Independence National Historical Park Collection

THE PAPERS OF

Alexander Hamilton

VOLUME XI

FEBRUARY 1792–JUNE 1792

HAROLD C. SYRETT, EDITOR

JACOB E. COOKE, ASSOCIATE EDITOR

Assistant Editors

JEAN G. COOKE   CARA-LOUISE MILLER

DOROTHY TWOHIG   PATRICIA SYRETT

 COLUMBIA UNIVERSITY PRESS

NEW YORK AND LONDON, 1966

FROM THE PUBLISHER

The preparation of this edition of the papers of Alexander Hamilton has been made possible by the support received for the work of the editorial and research staff from the generous grants of the Rockefeller Foundation, Time Inc., and the Ford Foundation, and by the far-sighted cooperation of the National Historical Publications Commission. To these organizations, the publisher expresses gratitude on behalf of all who are concerned about making available the record of the founding of the United States.

The New York Foundation, through a special grant, has enabled the Press to publish this volume.

PREFACE

THIS EDITION of Alexander Hamilton's papers contains letters and other documents written by Hamilton, letters to Hamilton, and some documents (commissions, certificates, etc.) that directly concern Hamilton but were written neither by him nor to him. All letters and other documents have been printed in chronological order. Hamilton's legal papers are being published under the editorial direction of Julius Goebel, Jr., George Welwood Murray Professor Emeritus of Legal History of the School of Law, Columbia University. The first volume of this distinguished work, which is entitled *The Law Practice of Alexander Hamilton*, was published by the Columbia University Press in 1964.

Many letters and documents have been calendared. Such calendared items include routine letters and documents by Hamilton, routine letters to Hamilton, some of the letters or documents written by Hamilton for someone else, letters or documents which have not been found but which are known to have existed, letters or documents which have been erroneously attributed to Hamilton, and letters to or by Hamilton that deal exclusively with his legal practice.

Certain routine documents which Hamilton wrote and received as Secretary of the Treasury have not been printed. The documents that fall within this category are warrants or interest certificates; letters written by Hamilton acknowledging receipts from banks, endorsing margins of certificate of registry, and enclosing sea letters; letters to Hamilton transmitting weekly, monthly, and quarterly accounts, or enclosing certificates of registry and other routine Treasury forms; and drafts by Hamilton on the treasurer. Statements of facts from the judges of the District Courts on cases concerning violations of the customs laws and warrants of remission of forfeiture issued by Hamilton have generally been omitted unless they pertain to cases discussed in Hamilton's correspondence.

The notes in these volumes are designed to provide information concerning the nature and location of each document, to identify Hamilton's correspondents and the individuals mentioned in the text, to explain events or ideas referred to in the text, and to point out textual variations or mistakes. Occasional departures from these standards can be attributed to a variety of reasons. In many cases the desired information has been supplied in an earlier note and can be found through the use of the index. Notes have not been added when in the opinion of the editors the material in the text was either self-explanatory or common knowledge. The editors, moreover, have not thought it desirable or necessary to provide full annotation for Hamilton's legal correspondence. Perhaps at this point it should also be stated that arithmetical errors in Hamilton's reports to Congress have not been corrected or noted. Finally, the editors on some occasions have been unable to find the desired information, and on other occasions the editors have been remiss.

GUIDE TO EDITORIAL APPARATUS

I. SYMBOLS USED TO DESCRIBE MANUSCRIPTS

AD	Autograph Document
ADS	Autograph Document Signed
ADf	Autograph Draft
ADfS	Autograph Draft Signed
AL	Autograph Letter
ALS	Autograph Letter Signed
D	Document
DS	Document Signed
Df	Draft
DfS	Draft Signed
LS	Letter Signed
LC	Letter Book Copy
[S]	[S] is used with other symbols (AD[S], ADf[S], AL[S], D[S], Df[S], L[S]) to indicate that the signature on the document has been cropped or clipped.

II. MONETARY SYMBOLS AND ABBREVIATIONS

bf	Banco florin
V	Ecu
f	Florin
₶	Livre Tournois
medes	Maravedis (also md and mde)
d.	Penny or denier
ps	Piece of eight

£	Pound sterling or livre
Ry	Real
rs vn	Reals de vellon
rdr	Rix daller
s	Shilling, sou or sol (also expressed as /)
sti	Stiver

III. SHORT TITLES AND ABBREVIATIONS

Annals of Congress, I, II, and III	*The Debates and Proceedings in the Congress of the United States; with an Appendix, Containing Important State Papers and Public Documents, and All the Laws of a Public Nature* (Washington, 1834–1849).
Arch. des Aff. Etr., Corr. Pol., Etats-Unis	Transcripts or photostats from the French Foreign Office deposited in the Library of Congress.
Archives Parlementaires	*Archives Parlementaires de 1787 à 1860* (Paris, 1868–).
ASP	*American State Papers, Documents, Legislative and Executive, of the Congress of the United States* (Washington, 1832–1861).
Bayley, *National Loans*	Rafael A. Bayley, *The National Loans of the United States from July 4, 1776, to June 30, 1880* (Washington, 1882).
Boyd, *Papers of Thomas Jefferson*	Julian P. Boyd, ed., *The Papers of Thomas Jefferson* (Princeton, 1950–).
Calendar of the General Otho Holland Williams Papers	*Calendar of the General Otho Holland Williams Papers in the Maryland Historical Society* (Baltimore, 1940).
Carter, *Territorial Papers*	Clarence E. Carter, ed., *The Territorial Papers of the United States* (Washington, 1934–).

Clark, *State Records of North Carolina* — Walter Clark, ed., *The State Records of North Carolina* (Goldsboro, North Carolina, 1886–1907).

Davis, *Essays* — Joseph Stancliffe Davis, *Essays in the Earlier History of American Corporations* ("Harvard Economic Studies," XVI [Cambridge, 1917]).

Executive Journal, I — *Journal of the Executive Proceedings of the Senate* (Washington, 1828).

Ford, *Writings of Jefferson* — Paul Leicester Ford, *The Writings of Thomas Jefferson* (New York, 1892–1899).

Freeman, *Washington* — Douglas Southall Freeman, *George Washington* (New York, 1948–1957). Volume VII of this series was written by John Alexander Carroll and Mary Wells Ashworth.

Goebel, *Law Practice*, I — Julius Goebel, ed., *The Law Practice of Alexander Hamilton: Documents and Commentary* (New York and London, 1964–).

GW — John C. Fitzpatrick, ed., *The Writings of George Washington* (Washington, 1931–1944).

Hamilton, *History* — John C. Hamilton, *Life of Alexander Hamilton, a History of the Republic of the United States of America* (Boston, 1879).

Hamilton, *Intimate Life* — Allan McLane Hamilton, *The Intimate Life of Alexander Hamilton* (New York, 1910).

Hamilton, *Life* — John C. Hamilton, *The Life of Alexander Hamilton* (New York, 1840).

HCLW — Henry Cabot Lodge, ed., *The Works of Alexander Hamilton* (New York, 1904).

Hogan, *Pennsylvania State Trials* — [Edmund Hogan] *The Pennsylvania State Trials: Containing*

	the Impeachment, Trial, and Acquittal of Francis Hopkinson, and John Nicholson, Esquires . . . (Philadelphia, 1794).
Hunt, *Calendar of Applications*	Gaillard Hunt, *Calendar of Applications and Recommendations for Office During the Presidency of George Washington* (Washington, 1901).
Hunt, *Writings of Madison*	Gaillard Hunt, ed., *The Writings of James Madison* (New York, 1902).
JCC	*Journals of the Continental Congress, 1774–1789* (Washington, 1904–1937).
JCH Transcripts	John C. Hamilton Transcripts. These transcripts are owned by Mr. William H. Swan, Hampton Bays, New York, and have been placed on loan in the Columbia University Libraries.
JCHW	John C. Hamilton, ed., *The Works of Alexander Hamilton* (New York, 1851–1856).
Journal of the House, I	*Journal of the House of Representatives of the United States* (Washington, 1826), I.
Laws of the State of New York, I	*Laws of the State of New York Passed at the Sessions of the Legislature Held in the Years 1777, 1778, 1779, 1780, 1781, 1782, 1783, and 1784, Inclusive, Being the First Seven Sessions* (Albany, 1886), I.
Laws of the State of New York, II	*Laws of the State of New York Passed at the Sessions of the Legislature Held in the Years 1785, 1786, 1787, and 1788, Inclusive, Being the Eighth, Ninth, Tenth, and Eleventh Sessions* (Albany, 1886), II.
Mayo, *Instructions to British Ministers*	Bernard Mayo, ed., "Instructions to the British Ministers to the United States," *Annual Report of the American Historical As-*

Miller, *Treaties*, II

"Minutes of the S.U.M."

Mitchell, *Hamilton*

Morris, *Diary of the French Revolution*

Naval Records of the American Revolution

New York Assembly *Journal*, 1792

Pennsylvania Statutes

PRO: F.O., or PRO: C.O.

PRO: F.O., or PRO: C.O. (Great Britain)
"Reynolds Pamphlet"

sociation for the Year 1936 (Washington, 1941), III.
Hunter Miller, ed., *Treaties and Other International Acts of the United States of America* (Washington, 1931), II.
MS minutes of the Society for Establishing Useful Manufactures, City of Paterson, New Jersey, Plant Management Commission, Successors to the Society for Establishing Useful Manufactures.
Broadus Mitchell, *Alexander Hamilton* (New York, 1957–1962).
Gouverneur Morris, *A Diary of the French Revolution*, ed. by Beatrix Cary Davenport (Boston, 1939).
Naval Records of the American Revolution, 1775–1788 (Washington, 1906).
Journal of the Assembly of the State of New York. Fifteenth Session (New York, 1792).
James T. Mitchell and Henry Flanders, eds., *The Statutes at Large of Pennsylvania from 1682 to 1801* (Harrisburg, 1896–1908).
Transcripts or photostats from the Public Record Office of Great Britain deposited in the Library of Congress.
Public Record Office of Great Britain.
Alexander Hamilton, *Observations on Certain Documents Contained in No. V and VI of "The History of the United States for the Year 1796," in which the Charge of Speculation against Alexander Hamilton, Late Secretary of the*

	Treasury, is Fully Refuted. Written by Himself (Philadelphia: Printed for John Fenno, by John Bioren, 1797).
Smyth, *Writings of Franklin*	Albert Henry Smyth, *The Writings of Benjamin Franklin* (New York, 1905–1907).
Sparks, *Gouverneur Morris*	Jared Sparks, *The Life of Gouverneur Morris* (Boston, 1832).
Sparks, *Works of Benjamin Franklin*, X	Jared Sparks, *The Works of Benjamin Franklin* (Boston, 1848), X.
1 Stat.	*The Public Statutes at Large of the United States of America* (Boston, 1845).
6 Stat.	*The Public Statutes at Large of the United States of America* [Private Statutes] (Boston, 1856).
Turner, "Correspondence of French Ministers"	Frederick J. Turner, ed., "Correspondence of the French Ministers to the United States, 1791–1797," *Annual Report of the American Historical Association for the Year 1903* (Washington, 1904), II.
Wharton, *Revolutionary Diplomatic Correspondence*	Francis Wharton, ed., *The Revolutionary Diplomatic Correspondence of the United States* (Washington, 1889).

IV. INDECIPHERABLE WORDS

Words or parts of words which could not be deciphered because of the illegibility of the writing or the mutilation of the manuscript have been indicated as follows:

1. ⟨– – – – –⟩ indicates illegible words with the number of dashes indicating the estimated number of illegible words.
2. Words or letters in broken brackets indicate a guess as to what the words or letters in question may be. If the source of the words or letters within the broken brackets is known, it has been given in a note.

V. CROSSED-OUT MATERIAL IN MANUSCRIPTS

Words or sentences crossed out by a writer in a manuscript have been handled in one of the three following ways:

1. They have been ignored, and the document or letter has been printed in its final version.
2. Crossed-out words and insertions for the crossed-out words have been decribed in the notes.
3. When the significance of a manuscript seems to warrant it, the crossed-out words have been retained, and the document has been printed as it was written.

VI. TEXTUAL CHANGES AND INSERTIONS

The following changes or insertions have been made in the letters and documents printed in these volumes:

1. Words or letters written above the line of print (for example, 9th) have been made even with the line of print (9th).
2. Punctuation and capitalization have been changed in those instances where it seemed necessary to make clear the sense of the writer. A special effort has been made to eliminate the dash, which was such a popular eighteenth-century device.
3. When the place or date, or both, of a letter or document does not appear at the head of that letter or document, it has been inserted in the text in brackets. If either the place or date at the head of a letter or document is incomplete, the necessary additional material has been added in the text in brackets. For all but the best known localities or places, the name of the colony, state, or territory has been added in brackets at the head of a document or letter.
4. In calendared documents, place and date have been uniformly written out in full without the use of brackets. Thus "N. York, Octr. 8, '99" becomes "New York, October 8, 1799." If, however, substantive material is added to the place or date in a calendared document, such material is placed in brackets. Thus

"Oxford, Jan. 6" becomes "Oxford [Massachusetts] January 6 [1788]."

5. When a writer made an unintentional slip comparable to a typographical error, one of the four following devices has been used:

    a. It has been allowed to stand as written.

    b. It has been corrected by inserting either one or more letters in brackets.

    c. It has been corrected without indicating the change.

    d. It has been explained in a note.

6. Because the symbol for the thorn was archaic even in Hamilton's day, the editors have used the letter "y" to represent it. In doing this they are conforming to eighteenth-century manuscript usage.

1792

To George Gale [1]

Treasury Department
February 1, 1792

Sir

I have received your letter of the 20th Ultimo,[2] and shall consider the several suggestions contained in it.

The subject of compensation will come into view when the law [3] shall be under revision.

I am, Sir,   with great consideration,   Your Obed. Servant.

Alex Hamilton

George Gale Esq.
Supervisor Maryland.

LS, Northwestern University
1. Gale was supervisor of the revenue for the District of Maryland.
2. Letter not found.
3. In "Report on the Difficulties in the Execution of the Act Laying Duties on Distilled Spirits," March 5, 1792, H recommended an increase in the compensation of supervisors of the revenue beyond that allowed by "An Act repealing, after the last day of June next, the duties heretofore laid upon Distilled Spirits imported from abroad, and laying others in their stead; and also upon Spirits distilled within the United States, and for appropriating the same" (1 *Stat.* 199–214 [March 3, 1791]).

From Isaac Ledyard [1]

[New York, February 1, 1792]

Dear sir

On my arrival here finding that a tide was likely to make strongly for Mr. Burr,[2] I grew more anxious on the grounds which I had the honor to converse with you about in Phia. I talked with several of our common friends, but with none confidentially excepting Genl. Schuyler,[3] who with the same confidence was pleased to inform me of the circumstance of Mr. Yates resigning his pretensions.[4] Mr.

Schuyler concluded to have an interview with you, & to let the determination of Mr. Yates remain a secret 'till his return.[5]

Mr. Yates it is probable will feel much inclined to return the favor which he has recd. from your friends in affording his support to the Candidate which they may propose, but against this it is to be calculated that supporting Mr. Burr will best please most of his antient friends & tend to restore him to their confidence, & also that the Candidate in question has a personal dominion over him. Mr. Schuyler supposes that if Mr Clinton and Mr. Burr were to be the only Competitors & his friends thrown out of the scale it would be doubtful which succeeded. To oppose Mr. B with success, your friends will be necessitated to promote the interest of the Old Incumbent [6] which might be considered a dereliction of sentiment & to cherish the hopes of a third Candidate will probably be to loose a triumph. If B. finally succeeds & you not have the merit of it, it will be an event extremely disagreeable to me. With this impression I have sought repeated interviews with him, untill I could procure from him an *artless* declaration from him of his sentiments both with respect to the Union on present grounds & also with respect to you. He has expressed a sincere regard for the safety & well being of the former, with respect to yourself he expresses an entire confidence in the wisdom & integrity of your designs, & a real personal friendship, & which he does not seem to suppose you doubt of, or that you ever will unless it may arise from medling Interveners. Unless you have grounds of objection which I do not know of, I ardently wish that the result of your interview with Genl. Schuyler may be an adoption of the Candidate.

It is not necessary to say more on this head considering our conversations in Phia. Permit me only to add that I was very sorry to find your real friend honest Troup [7] under impressions of being neglected by you, which he said was also a complaint of some others of your friends. I hope I have removed it in him. May I be permitted to intreat you to silence such complaints, which may have an unhappy tendency as far as your very laborious life will permit. Troup has been innocently led astray in the Bank business & can not now easily get out of the scrape.[8]

I am with entire Respect & Esteem   Your very Obedt. & humble Servt.   Isaac Ledyard

N York 1st Feby 17⟨92⟩

ALS, Hamilton Papers, Library of Congress.

1. Ledyard, a resident of Newtown, Long Island, had served as a surgeon's mate during the American Revolution. In 1784, writing as "Mentor," Ledyard had attacked H's "Phocion" articles. See H's *Second Letter from Phocion*, April, 1784.

2. This is a reference to reports that Aaron Burr was being considered by some Federalists as their party's candidate in the New York gubernatorial election of 1792.

3. Philip Schuyler, who was H's father-in-law, had been elected to the short term as United States Senator from New York in 1789 and was defeated for reelection by Burr in 1791. He was then elected to the fifteenth New York Senate, which met in New York City on January 5, 1792.

4. Robert Yates, Federalist candidate for governor of New York in 1789, had declined the nomination for governor early in 1792.

5. Schuyler was going to Philadelphia to confer with H. He carried with him Ledyard's letter, which was addressed "The Honble Alexr. Hamilton Esquire Favored by the Honble. Genl. Schuyler."

6. Governor George Clinton.

7. Robert Troup, a New York lawyer, had been a close friend of H since before the American Revolution when both had been students at King's College.

8. At this time Troup was one of the leaders in the attempt to form "The Million Bank of the State of New York" and to secure a charter for it. Schuyler had written H on January 29, 1792, that it seemed unlikely that the legislature would incorporate the proposed bank. For further information on the "Million Bank," see H to William Seton, January 18, 24, 1792, and Seton to H, January 22, 1792.

To Baron von Steuben [1]

[*Philadelphia, February 1, 1792.* On February 5, 1792, von Steuben wrote to Hamilton: "Votre lettre du 1 mier me parvient hier." *Letter not found.*]

1. H had become friendly with von Steuben during the American Revolution when the baron was inspector general of the Continental Army. At the close of the war von Steuben settled in New York and engaged in the development of a large tract of land north of Utica which the New York legislature granted to him in 1786.

From Henry Van Schaack [1]

[*Pittsfield, Massachusetts, February 1, 1792.* On April 20, 1792, Hamilton wrote to Van Schaack: "I received your letter of the 1st of February." *Letter not found.*]

1. Van Schaack was banished from New York State during the American Revolution because of his Loyalist sympathies. He moved to Massachusetts, first settling in Richmond and then in Pittsfield. He was a close friend and correspondent of Philip Schuyler, James Duane, and several other New Yorkers who were well known to H.

From Joseph Whipple [1]

Portsmouth, New Hampshire, February 1, 1792. "The Packet herewith enclosed contains the Accts. of the Revenue Cutter Scammel to the 31 of December last. In addition to the payments made to Cap Yeaton [2] for his Wages and Rations from the date of his Commission (the 21st. of March 1791), he claims allowance of Wages & Rations from the 6th. of Octr. 1790 as the time of his appointmt: as Stated in his Account enclosed Marked No. 6—to which Account he has also added Several Articles, which I have declined paying for. The Colours also are still withheld, which though I conceive them necessary I cannot furnish, consistently with a declaration heretofore made to Cap. Yeaton without your Special order. I have desired Capt. Yeaton to keep at the entrance of the harbour at such times as the Weather is too severe to be at Sea, that he may be in readiness to examine Vessels who may take Shelter there."

LC, RG 36, Collector of Customs at Portsmouth, Letters Sent, 1791–1792, Vol. 3, National Archives; copy, RG 56, Letters from the Collector at Portsmouth, National Archives.

1. Whipple was collector of customs at Portsmouth.
2. Hopley Yeaton, captain of the New Hampshire revenue cutter *Scammell.*

To Sharp Delany [1]

Treasury Department, February 2, 1792. Questions two entries in Delany's "account with the United States." States: "The Register of the Ship Blum Hoff Lady has been transmitted to me by the Collector of Burlington.[2] He mentions that this vessel departed from his district without any papers, and that she has since sailed from Philadelphia. I wish to be informed if she brought any goods into your district from Burlington, whether she obtained a new register with a surrender of the old one, and in whose names: also what measures were taken to obtain the delivery of the certificate of Registry, No 101, for which bond was given in your office."

LS, Bureau of Customs, Philadelphia; copy, RG 56, Letters to Collectors at Small Ports, "Set G," National Archives; copy, RG 56, Letters to the Collector at Philadelphia, National Archives.

1. Delany was collector of customs at Philadelphia.
2. The letter which John Ross, collector of customs at Burlington, New Jersey, sent to H has not been found.

Treasury Department Circular
to the Collectors of the Customs

Treasury Department
February 2. 1792.

Sir

In a former letter you were constituted the Agent for the Cutter destined for the Station off Maryland.[1] I have now to inform you that the authority of directing its movements is henceforward committed to you, subject to the instructions which shall be transmitted from this Department.

I shall communicate this arrangement to the Captain of the Cutter on the Maryland Station.[2]

I am Sir   Your obdt. Servant

L[S], to Otho H. Williams, Office of the Secretary, United States Treasury Department; copy, to Otho H. Williams, Circulars of the Office of the Secretary, "Set T," National Archives; copy, to John Lamb, United States Finance Miscellany, Treasury Circulars, Library of Congress.
1. See "Treasury Department Circular to the Collectors of the Customs," June 1, 1791. "New York" was substituted for "Maryland" in the letter sent to John Lamb.
2. See "Treasury Department Circular to the Captains of the Revenue Cutters," February 3, 1792. Simon Gross had been appointed captain of the Maryland revenue cutter in 1790.
In the letter sent to Lamb, "New York Station" was substituted for "Maryland Station."

From James Watson [1]

New York Feby 2d. 1792

Sir

The nature of my business has allowed me but a few liesure moments since my return to this place. I called pretty early, & repeatedly on General Schuyler, but have not had the good fortune to find him at home: [2] If I had I am not sufficiently known to him, to expect his confidential communications on a subject so delicate as that of the approaching Election.[3]

Knowing that truth & the public good engage all your attention, & govern all your actions, it may serve as apology for my suggesting the observations I have made, & the inferences that result. So far then as I have been able to collect opininions, there is some prospect that the gentleman alluded to in our last interview [4] may at all events be prefered to the Government; And in case it was tho't expedient to give him the Federal interest, the probability would be strong.

If that Interest is denied him, & he succeeds; will it not make him an enemy if he is not one now, or increase his enmity if he now has any? If he is refused this support, & fails; will he not return to the senate of the United States, imbittered against the government & its ablest advocates? *a circumstance the more to be regretted in the present irritable State of the Legislature, & Body Politic:* If this aid is given him, & he fails; will it not serve to moderate his conduct, or rather to bind him by the ties of interest & gratitude to his supporters? If it could be possible that he should absolve himself from these ties, would not the ingratitude, & atrocity of the act, diminish his power of doing harm, & make all future opposition to him equally just & popular? You will have the goodness to recollect that these remarks, are founded upon the presumption, that Judge Yates [5] chuses not to be a candidate, & that he will resign his pretensions with most satisfaction to the character in Question.

This I am assured is the fact, without which I should not have troubled you with these remarks.

Whenever I imagine how much easier it is to embarrass, & obstruct the benign operations of Government than to give them the requisite tone, & vigour I am solicitous, to remove talents, perseverance & address as far from the opposition as possible. I have omitted to urge any positive good, that may result from this measure; Altho' I am strongly persuaded that a very great one may accrue.

The absence of evil will continue to be desirable, untill the public mind becomes more quiet, & Federal habits take deeper root. I shall only add that the cautious distance observed by this gentleman, towards all parties, however exceptionable in a politician may be a real merit in a Governor.

I have the honor to be, With perfect truth & Esteem Your Most Humble Servant James Watson

Hone A Hamilton Esqr

ALS, Hamilton Papers, Library of Congress.
1. Watson, formerly a resident of Connecticut, was a New York City merchant and a director of the Bank of the United States.
2. Philip Schuyler was in New York City as a member of the New York State Senate. He had left or was soon to leave for Philadelphia to consult with H. See Isaac Ledyard to H, February 1, 1792.
3. Watson is referring to the approaching election for governor of New York.
4. Watson is referring to Aaron Burr. See Schuyler to H, January 29, 1792, and Ledyard to H, February 1, 1792.
5. The announcement of Robert Yates's refusal to run for governor was withheld until Schuyler's return to New York. See Ledyard to H, February 1, 1792.

From Joseph Nourse [1]

Treasury Department,
Registers Office 3rd. Feb. 1792.

Sir

Having agreeably to your directions examined the Actual payments which have been made, upon the several appropriations of public Monies to 31st. Decemr. 1790 & having compared them with each other a balance of 314.747.29 Dolls. remains stated as ℔: B.

I have not been able yet to ascertain what proportion thereof will form a fund of surpluses which is appropriated by act of Feb. 11th: 1791,[2] for the payment of the expences of Government for that Year, but think it probable that the following will arise Vizt.
Upon the Appropriation of 216.000 Drs: granted by act of 20th. Septr. 1789. for the Civil List 1789 [3] } 35,000.

LC, RG 53, Register of the Treasury, Estimates and Statements for 1792, Vol. "134-T," National Archives.
1. Nourse was register of the Treasury.
2. "An Act making appropriations for the support of Government during the year one thousand seven hundred and ninety-one, and for other purposes" (1 Stat. 190).
3. Nourse is referring to "An Act making Appropriations for the Service of the present year" (1 Stat. 95 [September 29, 1789])

Upon the   do: . . . . 190.000 " by same act for⎫
  discharge of Treasy: Warrts: drawn by the late Gov-⎬ 35,000
  ernmt.   ⎭

Upon the   do: of 141.492..73 Drs. for the Civil⎫
  List 1790. ℔ act 26th. Mar: 1790 [4]   ⎬ 4,000.
                                                       ⎭

do: do: of 147.169..54 Drs. for discharg-⎫
  ing Specific Demands including the building a lighthouse⎬ 40,000
  on Cape Henry ℔ act do.   ⎭

Upon the   do   of 104.327..22 by act 12th Augt:⎫
  1790 for extraordinaries [5]   ⎬ 10,000
                                                        ⎭

Upon the   do: of 96.000 dols: for pay-⎫
  ing pensions to Invalids for the yr: 1789 ℔. act⎬ (little or no
  of 20th: Septr. 1789 [6]   ⎭ surplus will

do: do: of 96.979..72 for pay-⎫ arise on these
  ing pensions to Invalids for 1790 granted by act⎬ appropriations)
  26th Mar: 1790.   ⎭

Estimated Amount of Surpluses which by act of⎫
  11th. Feb. 1791. is appropriated to the paymt.⎬ _____
  of certain sums for the support of Governt. for⎪ 124,000.
  that Year.   ⎭

A more Certain comparison has been made between the sums
appropriated for the services of the year 1791 & the actual payments as ℔ statemt: C: by which it appears there is a surplus fund
of 40,000 after paying all the demands which can probably be made
upon those appropriations.

The Statement A: shews the Ntt. amount of Revenue to 31st:
Decmr: 1790. together with the total amount of Appropriations to
that time.

I have the Honor to be &ca:

Honble: A. Hamilton
Secy: of the Treasury:

4. "An Act making appropriations for the support of government for the year one thousand seven hundred and ninety" (1 *Stat.* 104–06).

5. "A Act making certain Appropriations therein mentioned" (1 *Stat.* 185–86).

6. "An Act providing for the payment of the Invalid Pensioners of the United States" (1 *Stat.* 95 [September 29, 1789]) provided the authorization for payment. The specific appropriation was provided by "An Act making Appropriations for the Service of the present year" (1 *Stat.* 95 [September 29, 1789]).

[ENCLOSURE][7]

A.

Amount of the Ntt Revenue arising on Goods, Wares and Merchandize imported into the United States from the commencement of the Act   [8] to the 31st of December, 1790.   2.805.013.45 ⅓

Tonage for the same period . . . . . .   221.130.85.

                                3.026.144.30 ⅓

Amount of Storage & Interest received by the Collectors during said time . . . . }   66.35.

                                3.026.210.65 ⅓

Deduct Collectors salaries . . . .   140.

                   Dollars.   3.026.070.65 ⅓

Total amount of Appropriations to the 31st. of December 1790. }   1.690.420.51

Deduct for this sum, received of the receivers of Continental Taxes ℈ Act of Septmr: 29th: 1789 [9] and Ledger No. 1. Folio 66 }   3.225.70

                               1.687.194.81.

                   Dollars   1.338.875.84 ⅓

7. LC, RG 53, Register of the Treasury, Estimates and Statements for 1792, Vol. "134-T," National Archives.

8. Space left blank in MS. Nourse is referring to "An Act for laying a Duty on Goods, Wares, and Merchandises imported into the United States" (1 *Stat.* 24–27 [July 4, 1789]).

9. "An Act making Appropriations for the Service of the present year" (1 *Stat.* 95).

B.

Appropriations made by Congress between August 1789 and December 1790.

	Appropriation of Dollars.		Total.	No.	Balance.
39	216.000.	℔ act of Septmr: 20th. 1789 [10]	216.000		38 125.68
69.	190.000. "	ditto	190 000		38.854. 3.
88.	147.169.54/100	" March 26th: 1790 [11]	147 169.54		53 688.30
319	141.492.73/100.	"	141.492.73		4.429.15.
320.	20.000	" July 22nd. 1790 Indian Treaty [12]	20.000	No. 1	13.000. –
336.	104.327.22/100.	" Augst. 12th. 1790 [13]	104 327.22		11.035.35.
	38.892.75/100	" 1. 1790 [14]	38.892.75		209.62
			857.882.24		159.342.13.
57.	96.000 "	" Septmr. 20th. for Invalids in the year [15]	96.000.–		48.482. 4
292.	96.979.72/100	" for Ditto in [16]	96.979.72	No. 2	7.018.72
			192.979.72		55.500.76
85.	10.000 "	" August 4th. 1790 for revenue Cutters [17]	10.000.–		9.430.
329.	10.000 "	" Mar: 26th: 1790 for Contingent expences of Governmt: [18]	10.000		
339.	50.000 "	" Augt. 12th. 1790 [19]	50.000		8.774.30
355	40.000 "	" July 1. 1790, for intercourse with Foreign Nations [20]	40.000.–	No. 3	2.695.51.
357.	40.000 "	" Augt: 12.1790. for the late Qr. Mr. Genls: Departmt [21]	40.000.–		38.766.67
	192 "	" March 26th 1790. for Gefford Dally & J: Mathers. [22]	192.–		38.545.92
	1.500 "	" Augst 10th: 1790 for building. Portland light-house [23]	1.500.–		192.–
			151.692.		1.500.–
	20.000 "	" 20. 1789 for the Indian treaty [24]	20.000.		
	137.000 "	" Septr. 29. 1789. War depart [25]	137.000.–		
	200 "	" Augt: 11.1790. [26]	200.–	No. 4	
74.	155.537.71	" War departt. 1790 [27]	155.537.72		
299.	1.309.71 "	" July 1st: 1790 [28]	1 309.71		
	120 "	" in the year 1790 [29]	120.–		
			314.167.43		99.904.40
81.		Genl Appropriation for Congress &ca: March 26th. 1790 [30]	173.699.12	No. 5	
301.		Appropriation for paying of Interest August 4th. 1790 [31]	1.184.652.87	No. 6	
		" for the reduction of the Public Debt Augt: 12 1790 [32]	699.984.23		
			1.884.637.10		

10. Nourse is referring to "An Act making Appropriations for the Service of the present year" (1 *Stat.* 95 [September 29, 1789]).

11. "An Act making appropriations for the support of government for the year one thousand seven hundred and ninety" (1 *Stat.* 104–06).

12. "An Act providing for holding a Treaty or Treaties to establish Peace with certain Indian tribes" (1 *Stat.* 136).

13. "An Act making certain Appropriations therein mentioned" (1 *Stat.* 185–86).

14. Nourse is referring to "An Act making certain Appropriations therein mentioned" (1 *Stat.* 185–86 [August 12, 1790]).

15. Nourse is referring to "An Act making Appropriations for the Service of the present year" (1 *Stat.* 95 [September 29, 1789]).

16. "An Act further to provide for the Payment of the Invalid Pensioners of the United States" (1 *Stat.* 129–30 [July 16, 1790]) provided authorization for payment. The specific appropriation was provided by "An Act making appropriations for the support of government for the year one thousand seven hundred and ninety" (1 *Stat.* 104–06 [March 26, 1790]).

17. Section 62 of "An Act to provide more effectually for the collection of the duties imposed by law on goods, wares and merchandise imported into the United States, and on the tonnage of ships or vessels" provided: "That the President of the United States be empowered to cause to be built and equipped, so many boats or cutters, not exceeding ten, as may be necessary to be employed for the protection of the revenue, the expense whereof shall not exceed ten thousand dollars, which shall be paid out of the product of the duties on goods, wares and merchandise, imported into the United States, and on the tonnage of ships or vessels" (1 *Stat.* 175).

18. Section 3 of "An Act making appropriations for the support of government for the year one thousand seven hundred and ninety" provided: "That the President of the United States be authorized to draw from the treasury a sum not exceeding ten thousand dollars, for the purpose of defraying the contingent charges of government, to be paid out of the monies arising as aforesaid from the duties on imports and tonnage; and that he cause a regular statement and account of such expenditures to be laid before Congress at the end of the year" (1 *Stat.* 105).

19. "An Act making certain Appropriations therein mentioned" (1 *Stat.* 185–86).

20. "An Act providing the means of intercourse between the United States and foreign nations" (1 *Stat.* 128–29).

21. "An Act making certain Appropriations therein mentioned" (1 *Stat.* 185–86).

22. Section 6 of "An Act making appropriations for the support of government for the year one thousand seven hundred and ninety" reads in part as follows: ". . . the sum of ninety-six dollars to James Mathers and Gifford Dalley, each, for services during the late recess of Congress" (1 *Stat.* 105).

23. "An Act authorizing the Secretary of the Treasury to finish the Lighthouse on Portland Head, in the District of Maine" (1 *Stat.* 184).

24. "An Act providing for the Expenses which may attend Negotiations or Treaties with the Indian Tribes, and the appointment of Commissioners for managing the same" (1 *Stat.* 54).

25. "An Act making Appropriations for the Service of the present year" (1 *Stat.* 95).

26. Section 6 of "An Act for the relief of disabled soldiers and seamen lately in the service of the United States, and of certain other persons" reads as follows: "*And be it further enacted,* That there shall be allowed to Seth Harding, for three months and ten days' services on board the Alliance frigate, during

Recapitulation.

No 1 "   For_____ 159.342.13.
    2 "   "   _____ 55.500.76
    3. "   "   _____ 99.904.40
    4. "   "   _____ 314.167.43.
    5. "   "   _____ 173.699.12
    6 "   "   _____ 1.884.637.10

Mr: O Hara's [33] explanation to

No. 1. I apprehend that most of the demands upon the appropriations of which this is the balance are fully complied with,
but I suppose it wou'd be well to retain 26.000 drs. to answer
any demands that might occur.

2. On this balance demands are and probably will be made in
future.

3. Large demands are expected to be made upon this balance
except Appropriation of 192 dolls: for dally & Mathers
which has been paid by the Secy. of the Senate & Clerk of
the House of representatives.

4. No balance arises here being for the War departmt. & fully
paid up.

---

the late war, at the rate of sixty dollars per month, being the pay of a captain,
to be paid out of the moneys arising from imposts and tonnage" (6 *Stat.* 4).

27. "An Act making appropriations for the support of government for the
year one thousand seven hundred and ninety" (1 *Stat.* 104–06 [March 26,
1790]).

28. "An Act to satisfy the claims of John McCord against the United States"
(6 *Stat.* 2–3).

29. Section 6 of "An Act making appropriations for the support of government for the year one thousand seven hundred and ninety" reads in part as
follows: "*And be it further enacted,* That the sum of one hundred and twenty
dollars, be paid . . . to Jehoiakim M'Toksin, in full compensation for his services as an interpreter and guide in the expedition commanded by Major-general
Sullivan, in the year one thousand seven hundred and seventy-nine" (1 *Stat.* 105
[March 26, 1790]).

30. Section 2 of "An Act making appropriations for the support of government for the year one thousand seven hundred and ninety" provided: "That
all the expenses arising from, and incident to the sessions of Congress, which
may happen in the course of the aforesaid year, agreeably to laws heretofore
passed, shall be defrayed out of the monies arising from the aforesaid duties on
imports and tonnage" (1 *Stat.* 104).

31. "An Act making provision for the (payment of the) Debt of the United
States" (1 *Stat.* 138–44).

32. "An Act making Provision for the Reduction of the Public Debt" (1
Stat. 186–87).

33. Thomas O'Hara was the clerk in the register's office in charge of accounts of receipts and expenditures and of statements of appropriations.

5. Amount paid for the reduction of the public Debt and payment of Interest on Funded & Registered Debt.

6. No balance arises here being appropriated for the Compensation of Congress &ca.

C.

The following sums may probably be deemed as Balances upon the Appropriations for the Year 1791.[34] Vizt:

On the Appropriation of 299.276. $53/100$ Drs. Dollars.

Judiciary—Pennsylvania by the Death of Francis Hopkinson	.289.49
Congress. after paying the Members of Senate & House of Representatives, secy. Clerks &ca. to 31st. Decr. 1791	34.396.12
Treasury Department, comprising the secretarys, Comptrollers, Auditors, Registers & Treasurers Offices	3.041.72
Department of State	146.93
Department of War	1.168. 6
Board of Commissioners	270.45

Contingencies,

Congress, Senate & House of Representatives	3.—
Treasury, comprising all the Offices	97.—
Department of War, Nothing drawn on this fund	600.—
Board of Commissioners for settling the &ca.	6.25
Dollars	40.019. 2

The Appropriation of 50.756. $7/100$ Drs: cannot yet be ascertain'd as there are many Charges against it now depending in the Auditors Office,

The Ditto of 87.463. $60/100$ is still liable to demands, to what amount is yet to be ascertained.

" Ditto of 302.735. $94/100$. for the War Departmt is compleated.

" Ditto of 20.000 Drs. ℔ act of Mar: 3rd: 1791 [35] for renewing the treaty with the Emperor of Morocco. on this 13.000 Drs: has

34. These appropriations were from "An Act making appropriations for the support of Government during the year one thousand seven hundred and ninety-one, and for other purposes" (1 *Stat.* 190 [February 11, 1791]). Detailed estimates of these appropriations were submitted with H's "Report on Appropriations of Money for Certain Purposes," January 6, 1791. These estimates are printed in *ASP, Finance*, I, 83–88.

35. "An Act making an appropriation for the purpose therein mentioned" (1 *Stat.* 214).

been paid whether any further sum will be necessary. rests with the Secy: of state to determine.

Treasury Department Circular to the Captains of the Revenue Cutters

Treasury Department
Feb. 3. 1792

Sir

I have this day written to the Collector of Boston [1] informing him, that in addition to his duty as agent for the cutter under your command, she is henceforward committed to his general direction, subject only to the instructions which shall be from time to time received from this department. You will therefore receive and execute his orders, and you will make your communications to him, whenever the service shall require representation from you.

I am, Sir   Your obedt. servant   Alex Hamilton

LS, to John Foster Williams, Essex Institute, Salem, Massachusetts.
1. See "Treasury Department Circular to the Collectors of the Customs," February 2, 1792. Although the copy of this circular addressed to Benjamin Lincoln has not been found, Lincoln in a letter to H, dated February 15, 1792, refers to H's letter of February 2.

To Benjamin Lincoln

[*Philadelphia, February 4, 1792.* On February 15, 1792, Lincoln wrote to Hamilton: "Your two letters one under the 2d & the [other] under the fourth instant came to hand this evening." *Letter of February 4 not found.*]

To Jeremiah Olney [1]

Treasury Department, February 4, 1792. "I request that You will advance to the Supervisor of the District of Rhode Island [2] the Sum of Two hundred Dollars, to be repaid to You by the said Supervisor, as soon as he shall be in cash. . . ."

LS, Rhode Island Historical Society, Providence; copy, RG 56, Letters to the Collector at Providence, National Archives; copy, RG 56, Letters to Collectors at Small Ports, "Set G," National Archives.
1. Olney was collector of customs at Providence, Rhode Island.
2. John S. Dexter.

To George Washington

Treasury Department, February 4, 1792. Transmits "a Contract between the Superintendant of the establishments on Delaware river,[1] & Thomas Conaroe the elder, for repairing the public Piers adjacent to Reeding Island. . . ." States "that the charge is not disproportioned to what has been usually paid in other similar cases."

LC, George Washington Papers, Library of Congress.
1. William Allibone.

To Joseph Whipple

[*Philadelphia, February 4, 1792.* On February 28, 1792, Whipple wrote to Hamilton: "Your letter of the 4th. instant I had the honor to receive." *Letter not found.*]

From William Heth [1]

[*February 5, 1792.* On June 7, 1792, Hamilton wrote to Heth: "The same cause . . . has postponed the acknowlegement of your three private letters of the 5. 27 & 29th of February." *Letter of February 5 not found.*]

1. Heth was collector of customs at Bermuda Hundred, Virginia.

From Tobias Lear [1]

[*Philadelphia*] *February 5, 1792.* "By the President's command, T. Lear has the honor to return to the Secretary of the Treasury, with the President's approbation annexed, a Contract between the superintendant of the establishments on Delaware River and Thomas

Conaroe, the elder, for repairing the public piers adjacent to Reeding Island in the said River."[2]

ALS, RG 26, Lighthouse Letters Received, "Segregated" Lighthouse Records, Lear, National Archives; LC, George Washington Papers, Library of Congress.
  1. Lear was George Washington's secretary.
  2. See H to Washington, February 4, 1792.

From Baron von Steuben

New: York le 5 de fevrier [1792]

Votre lettre du 1 mier me parvient hier.[1] Vous n'aviez pas besoin mon cher Hamiton, des Excuses pour n'avoir repondue plutot a ma derniere;[2] Votre silence même est Eloquant et je L'ai interpretté a la lettre.

J'ai lue tout les absurditées qu'on a écrit au sujet des Absurditée qu'on a fait, et je me suis préscrit un silence inviolable, je regrette sincerement la honte et la disgrace des Armes Americaine,[3] mais je rend grace au Ciel que je n'en ai plus a repondre.

Il en coute Cher aux E: U: et il en couterat encore plus chere, de Vouloir faire la Guerre sans Ordre et Discipline. Si notre departement de Guerre continue ce train d'administration, il nous fàut quatre departement des finences pour le soutenir. Quelle horrible depense, pour cette misérable Expedition! Si 500 Miserable soldat ont couté pour une Campagne de Seize jours, la somme de   [4] combien couterons 5000. pour une et peut etre pour deux Campagne, mettez cela a la regle de trois, et dites moi, si Vous ne serez pas Efraye du resultat? Ce calculs mon Ami Vous regarde de près et je crois quil merite Votre attention.

Faire des Operation Militaire à un tell prix, Epuserait les trésors des plus grande Royaumes du Monde.

Vous Vous souvenez sans doute d'un Coll: Cochran[5] qui etoit dans la Ligne de N: York. Il vient hier chez moi, il est pauvre et chargé d'une Nombreuse famille, il demande une place d'officier pour son fils Ainé, Agée de Vingt trois Ans et fait je croie pour etre Scalpée. Comme je ne suis en correspondence avec d'autre Ministre d'Etat que Vous, je Promis au pauvre Pere de Vous Ecrire une ligne. La Voila, je le recommende a Votre bon Coeur.

Je ne croyois pas que les politiques du tems mettrais un Obstacles de Vous Venir Voir cet hyver—c'est cependent le Cas, et ma Vanité me porte au point, que mon Vieux personage ne devroit pas paroitre a la Cour avec decence, dans un tems ou on discute sur L'Art, dont jadis J'ai fait profession.

je suis de tout mon Coeur le Votre   Steuben

ALS, Hamilton Papers, Library of Congress.
   1. Letter not found.
   2. See von Steuben to H, January 2, 1792.
   3. This is a reference to the defeat of Major General Arthur St. Clair by the Indians in November, 1791. See "Conversation with George Hammond," December 15–16, 1791, note 2.
   4. Space left blank in MS.
   5. Robert Cochran, who had served as a major in the Third New York Regiment, was appointed lieutenant colonel in the Second New York Regiment in March, 1780, and served until the end of the war.

From William Seton [1]

[New York] 6 Feby 1792

My dear Sir

I have delayed answering your very kind Letter of the 24th till I could have a more ⟨detailed⟩ knowledge of what was going on. Col Duer tells me he has however written you [2] in the mean while. Every Interest is rushing by the phalanx of opposition with our Legislature to grant them a Charter [3]—and it is impossible yet to judge whether they will carry their point or not. The Committee have reported that the prayer of the Petition ought to be granted.[4] Our friends are preparing a Counter Petition to the House, & mean to propose to borrow from the State on Interest all the money they have which will be 1½ Millions.[5] Could we bring them to consent to this, it would effectually prevent their giving the Charter to the others—however should all our efforts be in vain & this heterogeneous mass get into Motion—it will then be more essentially necessary that the Bank of the U S. & this Institution be upon the most confidential footing—for unless we unite against this Host, the 3 [6] acting & operating & at varience might produce a general bankruptcy. From appearance the Bank will soon get into operation here. Coallition or not, it is of the utmost consequence that we should draw together in every point—

otherwise their Speculation will play upon us both, & may drain us of every shilling of Specie. From what I can observe of their intentions, they are aiming at an accumulation of large deposits in the Bank—which we must check by not allowing them any discounts—& watch the funds of payments they have to make to us. I feel the highest satisfaction in being permited to be confidential with you on these subjects, I shall therefore open everything to your advice, and I must candidly say that unless our Directors will act with decided firmness and that we receive from you every possible support, when their Bank is to be set agoing, the consequences may be fatal to us. The Balance on ⟨–⟩ the Bank of the U. S. is 176453—this sum no doubt they will depend upon to receive in Specie—& can do us no harm—but if the balance due the Treasurer of 232,000 was to be drawn for & exported in Specie also—together with the opposition balance that will absolutely be drawn from us—then it would become scarce—& would oblige us to send to Phila. the National Notes we have for exchange in Specie. We have now 230,000 Dolls. of them, & this week & the next the last Amsterdam Bills will be paid for, probably all in that Paper as they amount to 205,000 Dolls more. The fact is we have actually in Specie in the Vaults better than 600,000 Dollars & the balance due us on Discounted Bills is 2,500,000 Doll's—which is full double the amt of all we owe on Deposits. Our Circulating Notes is a trifle only—yet if our Deposits are called for, more suddenly than we can call in our Discounts much temporary Distress must ensue. It is therefore of great consequence to us as well as to the Bank of the US. that the paper we have of theirs should be set against what we owe them & the Public—that neither may be forced to an ⟨interchange⟩ of Specie.

ADf, Bank of New York, New York City.

1. Seton was cashier of the Bank of New York.

2. Letter not found. William Duer had resigned as Assistant Secretary of the Treasury in April, 1790, to return to private business. He soon became one of New York's biggest and most flamboyant speculators.

3. This is a reference to the efforts of various groups in New York City to obtain a charter for a new bank. See H to Seton, January 18, 24, 1792; Seton to H, January 22, 1792; and Philip Schuyler to H, January 29, 1792.

4. On February 4, 1792, "Mr. [Nathaniel] Lawrence [of Queens County], from the committee to whom were referred sundry petitions, praying for the incorporation of a bank, by the name and stile of the President, Directors and company of the State Bank, reported . . . That the committee are in possession of the draft of a bill, which fully delineates the objects of the petitioners; and

contains also certain propositions for opening canals, and effecting that internal navigation which is at present contemplated as so highly interesting to the prosperity of the State. . . ." The bill was introduced and read the first time (New York Assembly *Journal,* 1792, 49).

5. On February 9, 1792, the president and directors of the Bank of New York resolved that ". . . if the legislature of the State of New-York shall think proper to authorize their Treasurer, to place upon loan to individuals and bodies corporate any of the money belonging to the State the directors . . . agree . . . to allow therefor such interest as the State may require, not exceeding six per centum per annum . . ." (New York Assembly *Journal,* 1792, 64).

6. Seton is referring to the New York branch of the Bank of the United States, the Bank of New York, and the proposed "Million Bank."

Treasury Department Circular
to the Collectors of the Customs

Treasury Department,
February 6, 1792.

Sir,

It is my wish that you transmit to this office a return of the public property, exclusive of cash and bonds, in the hands of all the officers of the customs in your district, that is to say, the scales, weights, boats, &c. which may be in the hands or charge of any officer of the customs, from the Collector to the Inspector or Inspectors. This return it will be fit that you also transmit with your quarterly accounts on the 31st of December next, and so for each succeeding year.

Should the Register of the brig Lydia,[1] of Washington, North-Carolina, appear at your office, it is to be detained, proof being before me that the brig has been sold. The certificate is No. 4, of 22d April 1790, James Rhodes owner and master, and states the vessel to be of 98½ tons, square sterned, and without a head. The brig being now in the port of Philadelphia, this instruction is not extended to the vessel, but is confined to the certificate of registry.

It is my desire whenever any person's bond for duties shall be put in suit, by you, that you will transmit information to the Collectors of the several ports within the State in which you reside, in order that further credit may be refused according to law[2] during the default; and should it be common for the importers in your district to use other adjacent ports, or should you know that such defaulter uses any such ports to make his importations, you will give notice in such places also. When the bonds shall be discharged information thereof should be given at such of the Custom-houses as may have been notified of the default.

Ample time having been given to the Commanders of vessels trading to foreign ports, it is my desire that the 9th Section of the Collection Law may hereafter be enforced.[3]

I am, Sir,   Your most obedient servant,   A Hamilton

LS, to Benjamin Lincoln, RG 36, Collector of Customs at Boston, Letters from the Treasury, 1789–1818 (volume unnumbered), National Archives; LS, to Jeremiah Olney, Rhode Island Historical Society, Providence; LS, to William Webb, Mr. F. W. Daniels, Cleveland, Ohio; L[S], to Otho H. Williams, Office of the Secretary, United States Treasury Department; copy, to Otho H. Williams, RG 56, Circulars of the Office of the Secretary, "Set T," National Archives; copy, United States Finance Miscellany, Treasury Circulars, Library of Congress.

   1. See H to Sharp Delany, January 11, 1792.
   2. Section 41 of "An Act to provide more effectually for the collection of the duties imposed by law on goods, wares and merchandise imported into the United States, and on the tonnage of ships or vessels" provided in part: "That no person whose bond for the payment of duties is due and unsatisfied, shall be allowed a future credit for duties, until such bond shall be fully paid or discharged." Section 45 of the same act provided: "*And be it further enacted,* That where any bond for the payment of duties shall not be satisfied on the day it became due, the collector shall forthwith cause a prosecution to be commenced for the recovery of the money thereon, by action or suit in law, in the proper court having cognizance thereof; and in all cases of insolvency, or where any estate in the hands of executors or administrators shall be insufficient to pay all the debts due from the deceased, the debt due to the United States, on any such bond, shall be first satisfied" (1 *Stat.* 168–69 [August 4, 1790]).
   3. Section 9 of the act required masters of vessels from foreign ports to have manifests of their cargo (1 *Stat.* 144 [August 4, 1790]).

From William Ellery [1]

Newport [Rhode Island] February 7, 1792. "Thomas Cotrell,[2] and Joseph Finch[3] are committed to Gaol on the Executions against them. The Brig Three Brothers[4] remains on hand. The cause of Capt. Elliot[5] was tried yesterday, and the Jury found a verdict for the Plts for twenty-five Cents, and Costs. . . ."

LC, Newport Historical Society, Newport, Rhode Island.
   1. Ellery was collector of customs at Newport.
   2. Cotterell was the owner of the sloop *Betsy.* See Ellery to H, August 2, 23, 26, 29, September 19, October 4, 25, November 15, 28, 1791.
   3. Finch was the master of the brig *Seven Brothers.* See Ellery to H, July 11, August 2, 23, October 4, 10, 25, November 15, 28, 1791.
   4. Ellery is referring to the brig *Seven Brothers.*
   5. Joseph Elliott. See Ellery to H, January 9, 1792.

To Jeremiah Olney

Treasury Department
Feb. 7. 1792.

Sir

I think it will be proper for the reasons in your letter of the 23d. ultimo, that you do not pay into the Providence Bank, for the account of the United States the monies you have in hand, and which you shall receive before the 20th. of May next. It is however my desire that you deposit the same in that institution to be passed to the credit of "the Collector of the district of Providence" and that you note at foot of your weekly returns, that the cash appearing on hand is necessary to discharge such demands as may be pending, for fish, distilled spirits, or foreign goods exported as the case may be.

I am, Sir,   Your obedt. Servant   Alexander Hamilton

Jeremiah Olney Esq
Collector Providence

LS, Rhode Island Historical Society, Providence; copy, RG 56, Letters to Collectors at Small Ports, "Set G," National Archives; copy, RG 56, Letters to the Collector at Providence, National Archives.

From Otho H. Williams [1]

Baltimore 8th. February 1792

Sir

I have received your letter of the 2d Instant [2] commiting to me the direction of the future movements of the Revenue Cutter; But you have not yet informed me how the hands ⟨are to⟩ be subsisted. I think that it would be cheapest and best to supply them as on board merchantmen. Any bargain with the Captain might be the cause of discontent among the crew, and to draw rations on shore would be attended with much delay, inconvenience, and trouble. It is expedient that I should be officially informed of the subsistence of Captains &c in the army in order to a settlement with the Officers of the Cutter.

I am Sir Your Most H. Servt.   O. H. Williams

A Hamilton Esqr.

ALS, Office of the Secretary, United States Treasury Department.
  1. Williams was collector of customs at Baltimore.
  2. "Treasury Department Circular to the Collectors of the Customs," February 2, 1792.

From William Allibone [1]

[*Philadelphia*] *February 9, 1792.* "Sometime about the setting in of the winter . . . the Inspector for Port Penn, having discovered that a Large quantity of the filling of the second Pier had been taken out, and several Coasters laying there at the same time, his suspicions led him to challenge them therewith, but as all persisted in denying the fact; And their Hatches being laid he could not make any certain discovery, and did not think himself authorised to Search. Thus as the said Piers are detached from the shore, and are the verry places of safety for those who plunder and ungratefully destroy them, it will be always dificult to make any Effectual discovery, unless it is made the Interest of those who may come at any knowledge thereof to Inform, in aid of which, perhaps it might be made the duty of the Inspectors or other officers of the Revenue, to Search all vessels Suspected of such depredations. . . ."

ALS, RG 26, Lighthouse Letters Received, Vol. "A," Pennsylvania and Southern States, National Archives; copy, RG 26, Lighthouse Letters Received, Vol. "A," Pennsylvania and Southern States, National Archives.
  1. Allibone was superintendent of lighthouses, beacons, buoys, and public piers for Philadelphia, Cape Henlopen, and Delaware.

From Medad Mitchell [1]

[Philadelphia, February 9, 1792]

Sir
    Having been Employed in the Illinois Country last Autumn, beg

ALS, Hamilton Papers, Library of Congress.
  1. Medad Mitchell (who was sometimes called Thomas Mitchell) was a sur-

leave to lay before You some information which I acquaired relative
to the commerce of that Country. Perhaps it woud be Nessesary
first to give you some Idea of the Number of Inhabitants of several
places, since they differ very materialy from the account given by

---

veyor and adventurer. He subsequently became a free-lance agent on the
Spanish-American frontier. It was in this capacity that in 1793 he relayed to
Josef de Viar and Josef de Jaudenes, the Spanish commissioners in Philadelphia,
information he had obtained from French officers in New York concerning the
Clark-Genet negotiations for an expedition against Spanish possessions in Louisiana and was sent by the commissioners to carry news of this plot to the Spanish
governor at New Orleans.

In a statement to Manuel Gayoso de Lemos, commandant at Natchez, pre-
sumably written in the hope of obtaining permanent Spanish employment,
Mitchell gave the following autobiographical information: "I was born in the
State of Connecticut. My father was a farmer, and at the early age of fifteen
I entered the field as a Soldier—here the Baron [von Steuben] took notice of
me. Two Years I was employ'd by him, as an overseer to his house & plantation.
After which time, his Aid de Camps leaving him, he treated me as his com-
panion and gave me an education which might enable me to gain a Livelihood.
. . . Upon Leaving him I entered the service of New York as Surveyor. I
served them seven months—at the expiration of which time, I returned to his
house and practiced drawing Military plans five Months. . . . on the arrival of
the french Emigrants, adventurers in the Scioto Company, Colonel William
Duer whereof was Superintendant, Who Employed me as Agent, to Suply with
provisions & Quarters for said Emigrants, for four Months. . . . I received the
appointment of Comissary—but previous to this I was to have acted as Surveyor to the Company. I continued however in that Capacity Untill the 1st
February 1791 When I resigned it—And returned to New York—for a Settlement Which unluckily I did not get. Colonel Duer then Appointed me Surveyor Genl. to the Scioto Company—And sent me imediately to fort Washington With A Supply of money to his agent, as he was Contractor for the Army,
and t'was much wanted. . . . Resting a few days at fort Washington, I returned up the River to Galipolis, to commence Surveying. But a few days after,
an Order came from Colonel Duer to go to the Illinois Country to Survey one
Million Acres of Land. . . . I did not Compleat the Survey And returned to
Philadelphia by the Ohio as quick as Possible. Made my report accordingly—
discouraged the Attempt of making a Town, or at Least to let it be a Secondary Object. But to push a very Large Store to the Illinois Country as quick as
possibly might be done Sufficient to Supply the whole Trade of the country, of
which I made a Compleat Map. And to put Armed Boats in the Ouisconsing &
Illinois Rivers, to check the Trade of Canada into the Mississippi. But a Want
of knowledge, concerning this Country—And believing the trade not to be so
Valuable as I represented my Plan did not Succeed. I Laid this plan before
Secretary Hamilton in Philadelphia—where I remained Six Weeks by the order
of Colonel Duer Waiting for him—had he been there it most undoubtedly
would have suceeded. At the expiration of Six Weeks I went to New York, in
expectation of meeting with a Liberal reward for all my toil. But the day before I arrived Colonel Duer failed, to the Amount of 500.000. My Situation
now became deplorable. . . . Some few days after, I embarked for England . . .
I was employed by the Vice Governor & directors of the National Manu-
factary. I Compleated my business, and returned in less than Eighty Days. I
then waited in New York near eight Weeks, for a Settlement—but from a

Hutchens description [2] of that country. I shall begin with St Louis on the Spanish Side—it contains about 300 good stone houses—has a small garison—a strong Castle, and a tolerable wall nearly round the Town. The no. of the Militia is computed at 500—it is one of finest inland towns I ever saw. The Situation is delightful—it is nine miles below the confluence of the Missouri & Missisippi—St Genevieve is 60 Miles below St Louis is an inconsiderable Town only famous for its Salt Works—Kaskaskias opposite St Genevieve, it contains about 80 stone buildings and a small Church—about one hundred men and a Large Proportion of Negroes. St Phillips is of little consequence at present. Fort Chartres has been declining—very few inhabitants. Cahokia is a fine Town it is Situated 3 Miles below St Louis on the opposite Side, it contains 100 Stone houses about the same no. of Inhabitants capable of Bearing arms. Belle Fountaine lies 26 Miles from the Mississippie East from Cahokia—it is composed of Americans, about 30 Families.

The commerce of this Country is immense, when we consider the no. of Inhabitants. It is the opinion of Mr. John Edgar [3] at Kas-

---

confusion in every branch of business . . . I was not in that time able to get a Settlement. I got what I coud and set out for this Country. . . . I waited on Colonel Hamilton Secretary of the Treasury And Solicited a Letter to the Spanish Consul. He told me he woud wait upon the Consul himself. By which means I got a Letter to his Excellency Baron De Carondelet. . . . I observed in the former part of my Narrative that I was born in Connecticut. But I did not mention that my Father removed while I was young into the State of Massachusetts Bay" (ADS, Papeles de Cuba, 208A, Archivo General de Indias, Seville).

For a photostat of the document quoted above and for additional information on Mitchell, the editors are indebted to Professor Abraham P. Nasatir, San Diego State College, San Diego, California.

For additional references to Mitchell, see Frederick Jackson Turner, "Selections from the Draper Collection in the Possession of the State Historical Society of Wisconsin, to Elucidate the Proposed French Expedition under George Rogers Clark Against Louisiana, in the Years 1793–94," *Annual Report of the American Historical Association for the Year 1896* (Washington, 1897), I, 1027–32; Abraham P. Nasatir, *Before Lewis and Clark* (St. Louis, 1952), I, 79–80, 84, 150; Louis Houck, *The Spanish Regime in Missouri* (Chicago, 1929), II, 4–8.

2. Thomas Hutchins had been appointed Geographer to the United States of America in 1781 (*JCC*, XX, 475, 738). The description to which Mitchell is referring is contained in *A Topographical Description of Virginia, Pennsylvania, Maryland and North Carolina* (London, 1778).

3. John Edgar, former captain of a British vessel on the Great Lakes, was engaged in trade in 1779 when he was arrested and imprisoned by the British on charges of corresponding with Americans. He escaped from prison in the fall of 1781 and delivered information concerning a Vermont conspiracy to Governor George Clinton of New York, for which he was later rewarded by

kaskias, that the consumtion of English property alone amounts to
250,000 £ annually. The Missouri is navigated near 1200 Miles among
various Tribes of Savages—it employs annually from 50 to 100 boats.
The whole of the Mississippi from the Natches to its source is supply'd by Canadaian Merchts. Ouiscansing [4] & Illinois Rivers are at
this moment have an immense quantity of British merchandize on
their Banks. The Traders were impressed with the Idea that St Clair's [5]
arms were Terrible. They in consequence of it, pushed Large quantities of goods on the Illinois to Supply those who might retreat there
from the fury of the incensed eagle. When we consider the vast No.
of Savages on the Banks of those great Rivers, that are supply'd from
canada and the baneful influence they never fail to gain, wherever
they are permited to have a commercial intercourse—I think every
man interested for his country would wish to put a check to their
progress, and turn the channel of commerce, trifling as it may appear,
to the advantage of the Revenue of the U⟨nited S⟩ or at least to the
citizens of America. I shall next endeavour to show you the method
which I beg leave to propose for putting an effectual stop to a
contraband trade between canada and the Missisisppi River—as there
is only two places by which they can possibly advance into that
country—one by the Illinois & the other by the Ouiscansing both
have 12 Miles Land cariage, an armed boat in each with a small
tender to run in Shallow water woud in my opinion be a sufficient
force to put a final Stop to British Influence in that part of America.
Michlamachina [6] a flourishing Town at the head of Lake Michigan
must be intirely ruined—and shoud a town be erected at the mouth
of Illinois, no doubt woud transfer their property to it.

The Boats that will be Nessesary to answer every purpose for succeeding in an enterprize of the Kind I Lay before You. must be light

Congress with land in Kaskaskia in the Illinois country. According to an
affidavit taken from Edgar by Robert Yates and Richard Morris, several Vermont leaders, including Ira Allen and Jonas Fay, were offering to accept British
rule over Vermont in exchange for food, payment, and clothes for the Vermont troops and a stipulation that the troops would retain their Vermont
officers and would not be deployed outside Vermont (George Clinton, *Public
Papers of George Clinton* [Albany, 1904], VII, 606–07).

At the time this letter was written Edgar was serving as chief justice of the
court of Kaskaskia and as judge of the Court of Quarter Sessions and of the
Court of Common Pleas.

4. The Wisconsin River.
5. Major General Arthur St. Clair.
6. Michillimackinac.

Keel Boats manned with 18 men & 16 oars—plenty of canvass—two ⟨br⟩ass swivels—a few Blunderbusses—and each man a rifle. There must be a cover made for the Men to row under bullet proof—the men must be chosen among the best—aproved courage & Fidelity. Such men can be had for 8 Dollars ₱ Month. A small light rowing Skiff with four oars & a cockswain to run in Shallow water where a Large boat cant swim. A man must be acquainted with inland navigation to be capable of traversing the Mississippi—it is a very dangerous River to those not acquainted with it. There must be a block house built on an Island in each river to prevent being cut off or Surprized. I hope Sir that You'l not be offended at the bold Language which I make use of. I would only wish to be understood as humbly offering my opinion to the first character in America, from whose benevolence many have experienced the smiles of Fortune, That you may Long live To enjoy the confidence of Your country is the Sincere Wish of Your   humble Servt.   M Mitch⟨ell⟩

Alexr. Hamilton Esqr.
Secretary of the Treasury.
Philadelphia
Feby 9th 1792.

NB all dry goods consumed in Illinois country are at present brot from canada the expence of a voyge (being 3 Months) and from New Orleans to St Louis is very considerable and are as high at New Orleans as at Ft Pitt.

To William Seton

Treasury Department February 9th 1792

Sir

It appearing from documents in the Treasury, that there remain at this time a number of draughts unpaid, which were drawn by the Treasurer upon the Collector of Norfolk [1] and others, in the months of April, May, June, July &ca last, and lodged in the Bank of New York for sale; I request that you will cause a statement to be transmitted to this office, of all the Treasurers draughts, which may remain in the Bank undisposed of.

I am sir, with consideration   Your obedt. Servt

Alexander Hamilton

William Seton Esqr
Cashier of the Bank of New York

LS, The Andre deCoppet Collection, Princeton University Library.
1. William Lindsay.

From William Ellery

[*Newport, Rhode Island*] *February 10, 1792.* "On the third of this month the Sloop Hannah William Corey master from Martinico and destined for the District of Providence arrived in this District, but could not enter the first mentioned district on account of the ice. . . . Capt. Corey appeared at the Custom House for the first time & reported on the morning of the 7th. of this month. The reason of his not reporting sooner . . . was owing . . . to his supposing that he might enter his vessel at Providence, and to the obstructions he met with in his progress to Newport. . . . If he had acted conformably to his duty, he might have reported and entered here in season. The Law [1] is violated, and under the circumstances mentioned I submit it to you whether a prosecution should be commenced or not, and thereon request your direcn." [2]

LC, Newport Historical Society, Newport, Rhode Island.
    1. Ellery is referring to Section 16 of "An Act to provide more effectually for the collection of the duties imposed by law on goods, wares and merchandise imported into the United States, and on the tonnage of ships or vessels," which provided in part as follows: "That within twenty-four hours after the arrival of any ship or vessel from any port or place, at any port of the United States established by law . . . the master or other person having charge or command of such ship or vessel, shall repair to the . . . [customs] office, and shall make report to the . . . chief officer of the arrival of said ship or vessel" (1 *Stat.* 158 [August 4, 1790]).
    2. Ellery endorsed this letter "Answered." H's reply has not been found.

To William Seton

Philadelphia
Feby. 10. 179[2] [1]

My Dear Sir
    I have received your letter of the 6th instant. The full and confidential communication you make is equally acceptable and necessary.

I sincerely hope the Petitioners for a New Bank[2] may be frustrated; but I fear more than I hope. General Schuyler will do every thing in his power against them. Every day unfolds the mischievous tendency of this mad scheme. The enemies to Banks & Credit are in a fair way of having their utmost malignity gratified.

It is certainly necessary, that if an independent branch of the Bank of the U States be carried into effect in your City,[3] there should be a good understanding between the two institutions. But I tell you in the *strictest confidence* that there are circumstances which must of necessity postpone this operation, and which are opening the eyes of certain folks to the expediency of a coalition.

I am under a necessity of authorising the Treasurer to draw upon you for One hundred thousand Dollars. It is a necessary aid to the Bank of the U States which feels more than you do the effects of certain machinations.[4] *This* for your *own breast* exclusively. I advance it upon terms which will insure its restoration to you *in specie*, if a branch is established; so that it will not eventually affect your safety. I may be compelled to go further; but it will be on the same conditions.

You will understand that all the money which you may receive for bills or otherwise, on account of the U States, subsequent to the 31st of January last shall be received from you in bills of the Bank of the United States. And that no order shall issue to derange this engagement.

You appear to me to mistake a point, which is, that in the case of an establishment of a branch, you will have to pay the Bank of the U States the amount of their deposit in specie. They certainly cannot make a difficulty about receiving their own Notes. This idea I think you may safely proceed upon. At all events no distress will be permitted to arise to you on this account.

The state of things however requires unusual circumspection. Every existing bank ought within prudent limits to abrige its operations. The superstructure of Credit is now too vast for the foundation. It must be gradually brought within more reasonable dimensions or it will tumble. Adieu My Dear Sir

Most sincerely Yrs   A Hamilton

Wm. Seton Esqr

ALS, Bank of New York, New York City.
1. H mistakenly wrote "1791" in MS.

2. For information on the attempt to organize new banks in New York City, see H to Seton, January 18, 24, 1792; Philip Schuyler to H, January 29, 1792; Seton to H, January 22, February 6, 1792.

3. The board of directors of the Bank of the United States had decided in November, 1791, to establish branch banks in the large cities of the country. The New York branch did not open until April 2, 1792.

4. James O. Wettereau discusses some of the changes which were made in the original plan of the Bank of the United States before the branches had been opened. In the original resolutions of November 8, 1791, which pertained to the branch banks, the regulations concerning discount gave broad discretionary power to the directors of the branch banks. But "on February 6, 1792, before any of the branches were in operation, this [resolution] was rescinded." At the same time it was "stipulated: 'That the amount of Bills and Notes discounted by the respective officers of Discount and Deposit, shall not at any time exceed five times the amount of the Specie Capital apportioned to them respectively'" ("The Branches of the First Bank of the United States," *The Journal of Economic History*, II [December, 1942], Supplement, 88–92). Before the end of February the parent bank had apparently suspended discounts (*The* [New York] *Daily Advertiser*, February 23, 1792).

From Samuel Tredwell [1]

[*February 10, 1792*. On July 13, 1792, Tench Coxe wrote to Thomas Benbury: [2] "In a letter from Mr. Samuel Treadwell, addressed to the Secretary of the Treasury under the date of February 10th mention is made, that Thomas Davis Freeman, Surveyor and Inspector of the port of Plymouth, had left that port, without any intention as was supposed of returning." [3] *Letter not found.*]

1. Tredwell was deputy inspector of the revenue and deputy collector of customs at Edenton, North Carolina.

2. Benbury was collector of customs for the port of Edenton.

3. LC, RG 58, Letters of Commissioner of Revenue, 1792–1793, National Archives.

From Francis Childs [1]

[*New York, February 11, 1792*. On February 27, 1792, Hamilton wrote to Childs: "I duly received your letter of the 11th instant." *Letter not found.*]

1. Childs was editor of *The* [New York] *Daily Advertiser* and printer for the state of New York. He also provided financial support and publication arrangements for the [Philadelphia] *National Gazette*, which had commenced publication on October 31, 1791, under the editorial management of Philip Freneau.

To William Ellery

[*Philadelphia, February 11, 1792*. On February 27, 1792, Ellery wrote to Hamilton and referred to "Your letter of the 11th of this month in answer to mine of the 16th of Jany." *Letter not found.*]

From Tobias Lear

United States 12th. Feby. 1792.

By the Presidents command T. Lear has the honor to transmit to the Secretary of the Treasury a letter from Mr. Baldwin [1] mentioning the death of Mr. Collins the Collector of Sunbury in Georgia,[2] and recommending a Mr. Francis Coddington [3] to fill his place.

The President wishes the Secretary to make such enquiry into the matter as may be proper, previous to the filling said office.

Tobias Lear
S. P. U. S.

LC, George Washington Papers, Library of Congress.
  1. Abraham Baldwin, member of the House of Representatives from Georgia.
  2. Cornelius Collins.
  3. John Lawson, not Francis Coddington, was appointed to the post.

From William Ellery

Newport [*Rhode Island*] *February 13, 1792.* ". . . . On the 11th. of this month I received a letter from the Surveyor of Pawcatuck [1] in which he informs me that he had received the Thermometer, which I had forwarded to him, that on opening it he found the Glass broken, and should return it the first opportunity. It is unfortunate that the Thermometer for this Port,[2] & Pawcatuck should have been broken on their passage. One is much wanted for this Port, and an hydrostatic balance would be useful."

LC, Newport Historical Society, Newport, Rhode Island.
  1. George Stillman.
  2. See Ellery to H, April 25, 1791.

To George Washington

[Philadelphia, February 13, 1792]

The Secretary of the Treasury has the honor to communicate to the President some letters which have recently come to hand [1] respecting the execution of the Excise Law [2] in Kentuckey.

Februy. 13th. 1792.

LC, George Washington Papers, Library of Congress.
  1. Letters not found.
  2. "An Act repealing, after the last day of June next, the duties heretofore laid upon Distilled Spirits imported from abroad, and laying others in their stead; and also upon Spirits distilled within the United States, and for appropriating the same" (1 *Stat.* 199–214 [March 3, 1791]).

To Nathaniel Appleton [1]

[*Philadelphia, February 14, 1792.* On March 5, 1792, Hamilton wrote to Appleton: "In mine of the 14th ultimo, I instructed you to dispose of the draughts." *Letter not found.*]

  1. Appleton was commissioner of loans for Massachusetts.

To John Kean

Treasury Department
February 14 1792.

Sir

You will herewith receive a Warrant upon the Treasurer in your favor for 225 33/100 dollars, for the purpose of paying certain dividends of interest due to non subscribing Creditors. In the doing of which you will be guided by the Abstracts accompanying this, certified by the proper Officers of the Treasury.

I am with great consideration, Sir,   Your Obedt servt
Alexander Hamilton

John Kean Esqr
Cashier of the Bank of the United States.

LS, Ohio Historical Society, Columbus.

To William Short [1]

(Duplicate)   Treasury Department
                                                February 14. 1792
Sir

I have received your several favours of Sept. 23d. Oct. 10th. & Dec. 1st.

It appears to me probable that your movement towards Antwerp produced the appearance of a four per cent loan, and I hope from it in the result good effects.

Inclosed you will find a copy of a letter of the same date with this to the Commissioners in Holland.[2] You will easily comprehend the motives which dictated the turn of it.

As to the charges on the six million loan [3]—though you had a right to insist on the point which you made with the Commissioners, and did right to insist upon it till there was a concession of the principle, y⟨et⟩ it appears upon the whole to be more interest⟨ing⟩ to the United States to keep the Commissioners in good humour, in order to a cheerful cooperation in the more important point of a reduction of interest than to make so small a saving in the charges. I have obtained the consent of the President of the United States to authorise you to allow on the whole loan of six millions the same charges as attended the preceding loan.[4]

With great consideration and esteem, I have the honor to be   Sir Your most obedt. servt.   Alex Hamilton

Wm Short Esq.

LS, William Short Papers, Library of Congress.
    1. Short's appointment as United States Minister to The Hague had been confirmed by the Senate on January 16, 1792.
    2. Willink, Van Staphorst, and Hubbard were the United States bankers in Amsterdam. See H to Willink, Van Staphorst, and Hubbard, February 14, 1792.
    3. For a description of the September, 1791, Holland loan for six million florins, see Short to H, August 31, 1791. For Short's attempt to reduce the commission charges on this loan, see Short to H, August 8, 23, 31, September 3, 23, October 10, 1791.
    4. The Holland loan of March, 1791, had carried charges of four percent. For a description of this loan, see Short to H, February 17, 1791.

To Wilhem and Jan Willink, Nicholaas and Jacob van Staphorst, and Nicholas Hubbard

Treasury Department Febr 14th 1792

Gentlemen

I am just honored with your several favours of Nov 21st & 24th & December 2d.[1]

I learn with regret the disappointment, which has attended your endeavour, to procure a loan for the united states, at the reduced rate of four per cent interest.[2] Your success would doubtless have been as interesting, to the credit of this country, as it would have been pleasing, both to the President of the united States and myself.

But as I rely on the mutual good disposition, both of Mr Short and yourselves, I shall confide that any circumstances which may have taken place, not exactly corresponding with your views of the public interest, will not interfere with a cordial cooperation in the prosecution of it hereafter; and as events will continue to second your efforts, I shall allow myself to hope, that the expectation of reducing the rate of interest on American loans to four per cent, will ere long be realized, notwithstanding the momentary impediment which has happened. The price of the public funds here will satisfy you that it is ceasing to be the interest of the united States to borrow abroad at a higher rate of interest than 4 per cent.

If you are able to bring the matter to that standard, it will effectually obviate the possibility of any future recourse elsewhere, and will secure to all parties the important advantage of permanently concentring the loans of the united States in one great money market, upon terms which will conciliate in a satisfactory degree all interests public and private.

With very great consideration and esteem, I have the honor to be Gentlemen   Your obedt servant   Alexander Hamilton

Messrs W & J Willink
N & J van Staphorst & Hubbard
Amsterdam

Copy, William Short Papers, Library of Congress; copy, Short Family Papers,
Library of Congress.
    1. Letters not found.
    2. When this letter was written, H did not know that William Short had
finally succeeded in negotiating a four percent loan with Willink, Van Staphorst, and Hubbard. For background to these negotiations, see Short to H,
December 1, 15, 23, 28, 1791, January 26, 1792.

To William Ellery

[*Philadelphia, February 15, 1792.* On March 5, 1792, Ellery wrote
to Hamilton: "I . . . received a letter of the 20th. of the last month
from the Assist. Secry . . . and a Letter from you Sir, of the 15th.
of the same month." *Letter not found.*]

From Benjamin Lincoln

Boston Feby 15th. 1792

Sir

Your two letters one under the 2d.[1] & the [other] under the fourth
instant[2] came to hand this evening by the post. To the directions
they contain a strict attention will be paid.

In my last[3] I mentioned to you that empty old rum hogs. when
the certificates could be obtained with them were in demand. Since,
I think, I have discovered the use to be made of them. A few days
pass four hogs. as west India rum were entered here from portland.
On examination it is found to be new England rum put into old west
india Hogs. Perhaps there may be a little west India rum with the
new England. We have taken possession of the rum as New England
rum without proper certificates and shall have it labeled. I think we
shall have little difficulty to prove the fraud.

Secy of the Treasury

LC, Massachusetts Historical Society, Boston; LC, RG 36, Collector of Customs
at Boston, Letter Book, 1790–1797, National Archives; two copies, RG 56, Letters from the Collector at Boston, National Archives.
    1. See "Treasury Department Circular to the Collectors of the Customs,"
February 2, 1792.
    2. Letter not found.
    3. Lincoln to H, January 17, 1792.

From John Nixon [1]

[Philadelphia, February 15, 1792] [2]

Sir

We take pleasure in thanking you for the candid state of the public existing engagements to the holders of Certificates, for monies lent the United States to carry on the late War between September 1777 and March 1778; and also for the proposed provision for 1791 & 1792 to those continuing nonsubscribers.

We find by your Report on the public debt alluded to above,[3] that you conceive the holders of this Class of Certificates should from various motives, be induced, to come into the terms held out for and accepted by so great a portion of the public Creditors; at the same time you would have their choice & election to be free.

We therefore declare our willingness to give up as much as the funding System requires from other Creditors; all we desire is not to relinquish more, which you know would be done, if we relinquish an higher demand for an equal Sum.

As you observe, the interest is payable on the nominal amount of our respective demands, and the terms preceded the Loan; That the depreciation of the principal commenced from the first of September 1777 & not from March 1st 1778 was owing to a small majority in Congress; however in this we acquiesce, whereby 3,459,000 Dolls. are reduced to 2,538,572 Dolls., making a difference of 920,428 Dolls., being a reduction of upwards of one fourth part of the whole, on which an interest is now payable. Both debts are redeemable at pleasure on paying the arrears of interest in Specie, and a direliction of this interest amounting to more than ¼ of the whole for ever, is at least equal to a relinquishment of the interest for 9 years on one third of the Capital of the other creditors. We therefore agree to accept the proposals contained in the funding System established by Act of Congress of August 4th 1790; [4] provided the remaining third of our principal reduced by the Scale is given us in Six p Cent Stock, bearing interest from the time to which the arrears are settled in 3 p Cent Stock; and that this average shall be adapted in the ratio of depreciation to the case of each Creditor, so that where the loss of interest is less than the average aforesaid, a proportionate Sum of the Capital shall be in Deferred debt, and where greater a proportionate Sum of the 3 p Cent Stock shall be augmented to Six p Cent Stock, and by this means do equal Justice to all.

As the subject is now before Congress, you may perhaps think it proper to submit to them these proposals also.

In behalf of ourselves and others we are sir with great respect your most obed servt John Nixon

The Honble Alexr Hamilton Esqr
Secy. Treasy. of the U states

LS, Division of Public Records, Pennsylvania Historical and Museum Commission, Harrisburg.

1. Nixon had been elected president of the Bank of North America on January 10, 1792. For an earlier letter on the same topic also signed by Nixon, see Blair McClenachan et al. to H, March 16, 1791.

2. This letter is not dated, but the endorsement, in the handwriting of John Nicholson, comptroller general of Pennsylvania, reads: "Letter to A Hamilton, Feby 15th 1792."

3. See "Report on the Public Debt and Loans," January 23, 1792.

4. "An Act making provision for the (payment of the) Debt of the United States" (1 Stat. 138–44).

From Oliver Pollock [1]

[Philadelphia, February 15, 1792. "Warrant No. 1566 in favour of Don Joseph De viar and Don Joseph De Jaudennes [2] Commissioners of his most Catholic Majesty dated 28. February 1792 [was issued] agreeably to a Letter of 15 Feby. 1792 from . . . O. Pollock to the Secy. of the Treasury [for] 74.087." [3] Letter not found.]

1. During the American Revolution Pollock had served as an agent at New Orleans for the Continental Congress. In the decade following the war both the Continental Congress and the state of Virginia repeatedly refused to pay the debts which Pollock had incurred in support of the Revolution (James Alton James, Oliver Pollock: The Life and Times of an Unknown Patriot [New York, 1937], 1–20, 269–345). The largest single account that Pollock had charged against Congress was for a loan made to the United States during the war by the Spanish governor of Louisiana, Don Bernardo de Gálvez, for which Pollock was held responsible (JCC, XXI, 1107; XXIV, 234–38, 323, 531–32; letters concerning the Gálvez account may be found in the Papers of the Continental Congress, National Archives). In 1791 Congress passed "An Act making Appropriations for the Support of Government for the year one thousand seven hundred and ninety-two," which provided "For payment of the principal and interest on a liquidated claim of Oliver Pollock, late commercial agent of the United

States, at New Orleans, for supplies of clothing, arms, and military stores, during the late war, one hundred and eight thousand, six hundred and five dollars, and two cents: *Provided,* That the said monies be not paid to the said Oliver Pollock, without the consent of the agents of the court of Spain" (1 *Stat.* 227 [December 23, 1791]). Pollock's accounts may be found in RG 39, Blotters of the Register of the Treasury, 1782–1810, National Archives.

2. Josef de Viar and Josef de Jaudennes were agents for Spanish interests in Philadelphia.

3. D, dated December 31, 1792, Blotters of the Register of the Treasury, 1782–1810, National Archives.

To Tobias Lear

[Philadelphia, February 17, 1792]

Dr. Sir,

If I understood the President aright, in a conversation some days since, it was his pleasure that a Mr. William Alexander [1] of Rowan County in the State of North Carolina should be *nominated* as Inspector in place of Mr. Dowel [2] who declined & whose commission *I* delivered to the President. If he has not mentioned the thing to you, will you ask his orders concerning it? 'Tis of importance the place should be filled.

Yrs.   A: Hamilton

Philada.
17th. Feby 1792.

LC, George Washington Papers, Library of Congress.

1. William Alexander had been in charge of public stores in North Carolina in 1781 and had been nominated for the office of treasurer from the district of Salisbury in 1783.

2. Joseph McDowell, Sr., Revolutionary War soldier, member of the North Carolina House of Commons from 1785 to 1788 and of the North Carolina Senate from 1791 to 1795, had been appointed an inspector of the revenue for North Carolina. See H to the Senate and the House of Representatives, October 31, 1791.

From Isaac Ledyard

N York 17 Feby 1792

Dear sir

I can not see a necessity for Mr. Burrs having cause to consider you as unfriendly to him.[1]

The circumstance of Mr. Jays candidateship [2] he knows is a conclusive objection to your aiding his views & for you to be *publicly* & *declaredly* Mr. Jays advocate here would have questionable consequences with respect to the advancement of his cause. Mr. Burr has reasons to be unwilling to offend even me by offending you on whose account principally he knows I have been his friend, from just before the time Mr. Hazard [3] visited you in Phila. I shall therefore presume to act as a bond of union between you untill I have the honor to hear further from you.

I have just recd. yours [4] & am suddenly leaving Town. I shall do myself the pleasure to write you more fully anon, and am with every sentiment of respect & attachment your   Isaac Ledyard

A Hamilton Esqr

ALS, Hamilton Papers, Library of Congress.
  1. H was opposed to giving Federalist support to Aaron Burr in the New York gubernatorial election. See Philip Schuyler to H, January 29, 1792; Ledyard to H, February 1, 1792; James Watson to H, February 2, 1792.
  2. On February 9, 1792, a meeting of Federalists in New York City had voted to support John Jay as governor and Stephen Van Rensselaer as lieutenant governor (*The* [New York] *Daily Advertiser*, February 17, 25, 1792). The traditional account of Jay's candidacy, repeated by most historians who have written on the subject, is that H persuaded Jay to run and dictated his nomination to the New York Federalists. No letters by H, however, have been found to substantiate this version.
  3. Nathaniel Hazard.   4. Letter not found.

To Benjamin Lincoln

Treasury Department
February 18. 1792.

Sir

It appears from the abstract of unclaimed interest, rendered by the Commissioner of loans of your State,[1] that you have a credit on his books for 337$\frac{50}{100}$ Dollars, being the amount of interest on 15,000, 6 per Cent and 15,000, 3 per Cent Stock, for the quarter ending the 31st of March 1791.

This Stock is supposed to have been purchased by you under the Act making provision for the reduction of the public debt; [2] and as the interest is now payable at the Treasury it is proper, if the supposition be right, that a power be executed by you to the Trustees named in that act for the purpose of receiving it.[3] The power ought to name the Trustees by their proper names, annexing their *official additions*, as they stand in the act. It will be well to let one be prepared by the District Attorney [4] and to transmit it to this Office.

I am, with consideration,   Sir, Your Obed Servant.

Alexander Hamilton

Benjamin Lincoln Esqr.
Boston.

LS, RG 36, Collector of Customs at Boston, Letters from the Treasury, 1789–1808, National Archives; copy, RG 56, Letters to Collectors at Small Ports, "Set G," National Archives; copy, RG 56, Letters to the Collector at Boston, National Archives.

1. Nathaniel Appleton's account of interest paid and unclaimed for this period may be found in RG 217, Miscellaneous Treasury Accounts, 1790–1894, Account No. 1914, National Archives.

2. "An Act making Provision for the Reduction of the Public Debt" provided that the surplus resulting from duties on goods and tonnage was to be applied to the purchase of the public debt (1 *Stat.* 186 [August 12, 1790]). Lincoln had been directed to purchase stock for the sinking fund under a resolution of the commissioners of the sinking fund of January 18, 1791 (*ASP, Finance*, I, 235).

3. The act provided that "the purchases to be made of the said debt, shall be under the direction of the President of the Senate, the Chief Justice, the Secretary of State, the Secretary of the Treasury, and the Attorney General . . ." (1 *Stat.* 186).

4. Christopher Gore.

To John Tayler [1]

Philadelphia Feb. 18. 1792

Dear Sir

Capt Williamson [2] who will deliver you this, was formerly a British Officer. He comes to this Country to take the direction of a settlement about to be made in the Western parts of our State, by a Company of Gentlemen in England, who purchased a tract of land from Mr. Morris.[3] He has I understand become a Citizen of The United States, and is, I am well assured, very friendly to them. He appears to be a Gentleman and a man ⟨of sen⟩se. Under these different titles, ⟨I take⟩ the liberty to recommend him to yo⟨ur at⟩tention and Civility.

With great esteem &   regard D Sir   Your Obedient serv

A Hamilton

John Taylor Esqr

ALS, The Newberry Library, Chicago.
1. Tayler was an Albany merchant and land speculator.
2. Charles Williamson, a land promoter in the Genesee country in western New York, had arrived in the United States late in 1791. Born in Scotland, Williamson came to New York as agent for the Pulteney Associates, a group of British investors associated with William Johnson Pulteney, who was a member of Parliament and one of England's leading land speculators. Pulteney had bought lands in the Genesee country from Robert Morris.
3. Robert Morris.

To Abraham Ten Broeck [1]

Philadelphia, February 18, 1792. Introduces Captain Charles Williamson.[2]

ALS, Davenport Library, Bath, New York.
1. A resident of Albany, Ten Broeck was a lawyer, land speculator, and prominent New York Federalist.
2. The contents of this letter are the same as that of H to John Tayler, February 18, 1792.

To George Washington

[Philadelphia, February 18, 1792]

The Secretary of the Treasury has the honor to communicate for the information of the President a letter which he had just received from the Supervisor of North Carolina.[1] The complexion of things there tho' not pleasing is rather better than worse.

February 18th. 1792.

LC, George Washington Papers, Library of Congress.
1. Letter not found. The supervisor of the revenue for North Carolina was William Polk.

To Charles Lee [1]

Treasury Department, February 20, 1792. "I duly received your letter of the 29th Ultimo, and am of opinion that you may safely accept an entry made under the appointment by Mr Cuthbert[2] transmitted to me in that letter."

LS, RG 56, Letters to and from the Collector at Alexandria, National Archives; copy, RG 56, Letters to Collectors at Small Ports, "Set G," National Archives.
1. Lee was collector of customs at Alexandria, Virginia.
2. William Cuthbert of Norfolk, Virginia.

From Otho H. Williams

Baltimore 20th February 1792

Sir.

Inclosed is a list of bonds taken for duties on Merchze pts. of the payments whereof have been postponed, according to law, upon the Merchandize being exported for drawbacks.[1] The certificates of the landing of these goods in foreign ports are not yet returned, and the bonds ought to be put in suit; but as the ⟨–⟩ Sales of part of them at foreign markets have come to hand and I have good reasons to believe that the arrival of the proper vouchers is prevented by the ice in our river and bay, I have ventured to defer the enforceing the collection of the duties in expectation that the harbour would soon be open. The rigours of the Season must soon abate, and it cannot be long before this excuse of the exporters will be removed. If in the mean time it is indispensably necessary to put the bonds in suit you will please to inform me.

I am, Sir,   O H W

A. Hamilton Esqr.

ADfS, RG 53, "Old Correspondence," Baltimore Collector, National Archives.
1. This letter is in reply to "Treasury Department Circular to the Collectors of the Customs," February 6, 1792.

From Jean Baptiste de Ternant [1]

Philade. 21 fevr. 1792

En consequence des arrangemens pris entre moi et votre gouvernement, je vous addresse cy-jointe la note des sommes à acquitter. Des motifs de prudence tendant à prévenir dans notre comptabilité nationale tout embarras relatif au reversement de ces fonds sur le compte des diverses branches de l'administration me font desirer que vous receviez pour le montant des avances que vous alles faire ainsi que pour celui des armes et munitions envoyés à st. Domingue,[2] une reconnaissance en livres tournois reglée sur le pied du pair intrinsèque entre nos monnoies respectives. Cet arrangement au quel vous avez déja verbalement consenti a besoin d'etre officiellemt adopté, et je ne doute pas que vous ne vous y pretiez, puis qu'il est purement relatif aux convenances de votre administration et ne change rien au fond de l'affaire principale. Ces reconnoissances dont je rendrai compte à ma cour seront alors recues par notre tresor national, dans les remboursemens que les Etats unis auront à y faire successivement.

Copy, *Arch. des Aff. Etr., Corr. Pol., Etats-Unis*, Supplement Vol. 20.

1. Ternant was French Minister Plenipotentiary to the United States. For background to this letter, see Ternant to H, September 21, 1791, and H to Ternant, September 21, 1791.

2. On September 24, 1791, George Washington had written to Ternant that he had dispatched "orders to the Secretary of the Treasury to furnish the money, and to the Secretary of War to deliver the Arms and Ammunition, which you have applied to me for" (*GW*, XXXI, 375). The sum of $8,962 was spent on the arms and ammunition which were received in New York on October 4, 1791, by Antoine René Charles Mathurin de La Forest, who was officially appointed French consul general for the states of New York, New Jersey, Pennsylvania, and Delaware on March 2, 1792, although he had conducted the affairs of the office since June 22, 1785 (copy, RG 217, Miscellaneous Treasury Accounts, 1790–1894, Account No. 2092, National Archives; copy, William Short Papers, Library of Congress). For Ternant's reports on the money secured from the United States, see Ternant to Comte de Montmorin, November 24, December 10, 1791, and February 23, 1792 (Turner, "Correspondence of French Ministers," 76–84, 86–87).

Treasury Department Circular to the Collectors of the Customs

Treasury Department,
February 21st, 1792.[1]

Sir,

In pursuance of arrangements with the Bank of the United States, I have to desire, that after the expiration of a month from the time of the receipt of this letter, you will discontinue the execution of my former instructions concerning the receipt, and exchange for specie, of the Cash Notes and Post Notes of the Banks of North-America and New-York.[2]

The regularity of the service requires that none of the Officers of the Cutters should be absent from them at any time without a *written* leave or furlough, which you will take an opportunity to communicate to them. The propriety or necessity of these absences you will judge of.

It is wished by the Treasurer that the Draughts paid at the Custom-Houses, may be transmitted as soon as possible, after their discharge, to the Treasury. It will be best, therefore, that the Draughts mentioned in your weekly returns of Cash, paid and received, should always be enclosed in them.

I am, Sir,

L[S], to Otho H. Williams, Office of the Secretary, United States Treasury Department; two copies, RG 56, Circulars of the Office of the Secretary, "Set T," National Archives; copy, United States Finance Miscellany, Treasury Circulars, Library of Congress.

1. This letter was presumably sent at a later date. On March 31, 1792, in a letter to Gulian Verplanck H indicated that the circular would be sent out on that date. Jeremiah Olney's acknowledgment of the receipt of this circular indicates that it was not mailed before May 10, 1792. See Olney to H, June 5, 1792.

2. See "Treasury Department Circular to the Collectors of the Customs," September 22, 1789. See also "Treasury Department Circular to the Collectors of the Customs," January 2, 1792.

To Jean Baptiste de Ternant [1]

Treasury Department
February 22d. 1792

Sir

I have the honor to acknowlege your letter of yesterday.

You will find enclosed warrants[2] on the Treasurer for the sums you desire, that is to say, one in favour of yourself for Eight thousand three hundred and twenty five Dollars, the other in favour of Mr. De la forest, Vice Consul General of France for Twenty two thousand Dollars. The amounts of these warrants will be paid by the Treasurer at sight.

These sums will be liquidated into livres, as you desire, and the intrinsic par of the metals in the two countries will govern to operate as a payment on account of the debt due from the U States to your Government.

In making this payment I derive pleasure from the idea of any accomodation which may result from it at the particular conjuncture; and I assure you of a cordial disposition on my part to cooperate in any extension which may be requisite and practicable.

I have the honor to be with sincere sentiments of respect and esteem   Sir   Your obedient servant   Alexander Hamilton

Mr Ternant
Minister Plenipotentiary of France

ALS, *Arch. des Aff. Etr., Corr. Pol., Etats-Unis,* Supplement Vol. 20.
   1. For background to this letter, see Ternant to H, September 21, 1791, and H to Ternant, September 21, 1791.
   2. According to a table of the French debt included in H's "Report on Foreign Loans," which was sent to the House of Representatives on January 3, 1793, the warrants were dated February 21, 1792.

From Jeremiah Olney

Providence, February 23, 1792. ". . . I have deposited in the Providence Bank, agreeable to your directions of the 7th Instant, 4,097 Dollars & 18½ Cents, . . . having retained 40 Dollars for my present private Expences, not doubting it would meet with your approbation, as the Emoluments of my Office afford me little or no Support."

ADfS, Rhode Island Historical Society, Providence.

To George Washington

Treasury Department
23d. Feby. 1792.

The Secretary of the Treasury has the honor respectfully to inclose to the President of the United States, a contract [1] made by the Superintendant of the Lighthouse on the Island of New Castle in the State of Hampshire with Titus Salter [2] for supplying, keeping, lighting, & superintending the occasional repairs of that building.

The terms of this Contract being the same as those in the last agreement for the same supplies and services, and there appearing no circumstances to produce a diminution of the cost of the Keepers supplies for himself or for the Lighthouse, the Secretary is humbly of opinion that it is not disadvantageous to the United States.

LC, George Washington Papers, Library of Congress.
1. This contract, dated January 1, 1792, and signed by Salter and by Joseph Whipple for H on behalf of the United States Government, may be found in RG 26, Lighthouse Letters Received, "Segregated" Lighthouse Records, New Hampshire, National Archives. The following note in Washington's handwriting appears at the end of this contract: "Approved February the 24th 1792 Go: Washington."
2. Salter was commander of Fort William on New Castle Island in Portsmouth Harbor. One of his responsibilities was the maintenance of the lighthouse on the island.

To Tobias Lear

[Philadelphia, February 24, 1792]

Dr. Sir,

The President is right.[1] The person intended is Joseph McDowell the younger; and a more precise designation would be by adding, "*of Pleasant Garden.*" But I imagine it will be well to defer the matter 'till the general nomination of the Officers of Inspection is made to the Senate, & to include this case.[2]

Yrs. &c   A: Hamilton

24th. Feby. 1792.

LC, George Washington Papers, Library of Congress.
1. See H to Lear, February 17, 1792.
2. On March 6, 1792, the President recommended to the Senate that "Joseph M'Dowell, the younger, of Pleasant Garden" be appointed as inspector of Survey No. 5 for North Carolina. Two days later the Senate confirmed the appointment (*Executive Journal*, I, 102, 111).

From Tobias Lear

United States February 24th: 1792

The President of the United States having approved of the Contract made by the Superintendant of the Light House in New Hamp-

shire with Titus Salter for supplying, keeping, lighting and superintending the occasional repairs of that building,[1] it is respectfully
returned to the Secretary of the Treasury by

Tobias Lear.
Secretary to the President
of the United States.

LS, RG 26, Lighthouse Letters Received, "Segregated" Lighthouse Records,
Lear, National Archives; LC, George Washington Papers, Library of Congress.
   1. See H to George Washington, February 23, 1792.

To George Washington

[Philadelphia, February 24, 1792]

The Secretary of the Treasury has the honor to return the President the papers received from Mr. Lear, which he has carefully perused, and will wait on the President tomorrow at ten o'Clock accordingly.[1]

February 24th. 1792

LC, George Washington Papers, Library of Congress.
   1. The papers which H received from Tobias Lear were apparently the same
ones that the President sent to the Secretary of State on February 24, 1792, for
in his letter to Thomas Jefferson of that date Washington instructed Jefferson
to "give the enclosed Papers an attentive perusal" and return them so "that
Colo. Hamilton may have an opportunity of doing it also" (GW, XXXI, 484).
According to John C. Fitzpatrick, the "enclosed Papers" were from Justice
James Iredell of the United States Supreme Court and dealt with "two cases
which have occurred in the judicial department, and which require the interference of the Legislature of the United States to remedy the inconveniences
arising from them" (GW, XXXI, 484, note 90).
   A letter of February 23, 1792, from Iredell to Washington reads as follows:
   "In consequence of the letter you did the Judges of the Supreme Court the
honour to write to them on the 3d. April, 1790, I presume it is not only proper
for a single Judge, but his express duty when he deems it of importance to the
public service, to state any particular circumstances that occur to him in the
course of his personal experience which occasion unexpected difficulties or inconveniences in the execution of a system so new and in many respects unaided
by any former examples. I therefore, Sir, take the liberty to state some circumstances of great moment that occurred in the last Southern Circuit, which was
attended by no other Judge of the Supreme Court but myself.
   "A decision extremely interesting to many Suits in the Circuit Courts, took
place in the Supreme Court in the Term in August last. It was, that a Writ of
Error to remove any Proceeding out of a Circuit Court to the Supreme Court

must be taken out of the Clerk's office of the latter. By the act of Congress that alone concerns that subject a Writ of Error can only operate as a *Supersedeas*, and stay executions in cases where a Copy of it is lodged for the adverse Party in the Clerk's office where the record remains within ten days after the Judgment complained of is given. The above decision therefore made it appear, that after a Judgment was given against a Defendant in the Circuit Court, if the Circuit Court was at such a distance from the Clerk's office of the Supreme Court that it was impracticable to obtain a Writ of Error from that office, and send a copy as directed by the act within the time limited, which was so short that it could avail in very few instances; the Defendant, if desirous to prosecute a Writ of Error, might, without any fault of his own, be subjected to an immediate execution, though he still might prosecute such a Writ, and Judgment be eventually given in his favour. This consequence the Judges of the Supreme Court were aware of when they gave the above decision, and they were persuaded that if the mischief had been foreseen as resulting from the law in question, it would never have existed. But they conceived the principles upon which they were bound to determine rendered such a decision unavoidable, and they were unanimous in the determination that was given. The mischief however was so palpable, that there was no doubt but that the Legislature upon its being made known to them would provide an early remedy. In the mean time it became a subject of very great concern to Parties in Causes then ready for trial in the Circuit Courts. The Courts upon the Southern Circuit, which I had the honour to attend, and where the evil might have existed in every case that was tried in which a Writ of Error could be brought, felt it accordingly, and the Court in each District stated the circumstances to the Bar, hoping that some measure would be adopted by consent to prevent any Defendant from suffering by such an unforeseen consequence of a law, under which it was intended both Parties might have complete relief. But though the Bar seemed generally to acquiesce in the propriety of a continuance of such causes when a Writ of Error might really be desired if Judgment went against Defendant, yet some gentlemen wished to make distinctions which others would not agree to, and the interposition of the Court, if such interposition was proper, became unavoidable. The Court, upon reflexion, although they were fully sensible that in general it was their duty to administer the law as it was, regardless of its policy or consequences, thought that this was so extraordinary a case, the unequal condition of the Parties was so glaring, the intention of the Legislature if it could have been expressed must have been so utterly contrary to any design of making an injurious discrimination between Citizens of the same Government in a point where no locality as to right could at all come in competition with the equal principles of impartial Justice, —that as they did not entertain the smallest doubt but that the Legislature would provide an early remedy for the evil, so it was their duty, by the exercise in this instance of a discretionary power as to the time of trying causes, which they conceived to be vested in them for the purposes of public justice, to prevent any immediate injury by ordering a continuance of all such causes in which the evil I have stated could arise, unless they were brought on by consent. And the Courts accordingly did so in each of the three Southern Districts, in the fullest confidence that a remedy would be provided during the present session; after which undoubtedly no such reason for a continuance could have any effect.

"Another circumstance of great importance, though perhaps not admitting of so easy a remedy, arose in the Circuit Court of Georgia. There were depending there some suits for the recovery of Debts, to which Pleas were put in by the Defendants, not denying the existence of the debts, but shewing (as they con-

ceived) a right in the State of Georgia to recover them under certain Acts of
Assembly of that State passed previous to the Treaty of Peace. The Attorney,
and Solicitor General of the State were directed to interfere in the defence,
but the Counsel for the Defendants refused to permit them. The Attorney and
the Solicitor being dissatisfied with the Pleas, applied to the Court for leave to
interplead on behalf of the State. The propriety of this application, if the law
had admitted of its being granted, and it could have been done with proper
effect, the Court were very sensible of, because it was evident on the face of
the Pleadings, from the statement of the Defendants themselves, that the State
was materially interested in the most effectual defence being made that the
nature of the cases would admit of; and nothing was more desirable than that
in all cases, but particularly in cases of such high importance, all Parties concerned, so far as it was practicable, should have their pretensions fully examined. However, we could find no instance where an Interpleader in a Court
of Law was directed, but on an application of a Defendant, much less against
his consent; and therefore were under the necessity of rejecting the motion.
It was also questionable, if that difficulty had not intervened, whether inasmuch
as by such a Proceeding a State would become a Party, though collaterally to
the principal action, it was not a case which ought to be tried in the Supreme
Court. It did indeed occur, that the State perhaps had a remedy by a Bill of
Interpleader in Equity—But no such Bill had been brought, nor in all probability, if such a bill was proper, could it be brought in the Circuit Court, the
reasons against this method of proceeding being competent in any but the Supreme Court operating, I apprehend, more strongly than in the other case suggested above. I have been thus particular in stating this interesting subject, because it appears to me of the highest moment, although I believe it would be
difficult to devise an unexceptionable remedy. But the discussion of questions
wherein are involved the most sacred and awful principles of public justice,
under a system without precedent in the history of Mankind, necessarily must
occasion many embarrassments which can be more readily suggested than removed.

"I should have taken the liberty to make this representation sooner, but that
I thought it probable before this time a Bill which has long been in contemplation by the House of Representatives for amending the Judicial System would
have been brought in, in which a provision might have been made for the
peculiar cases I have mentioned, but as other important business has hitherto
delayed this, and the time of the Circuits is approaching, it appeared to me that
I could not justify any further delay in communicating the important information which is the subject of the present letter." (ALS, RG 59, Miscellaneous
Letters of the Department of State, National Archives.)

To Francis Childs

Treasury Department
February 27 1792

Sir

I duly received your letter of the 11th instant,[1] inclosing a copy
of the bill before the Legislature of New York for erecting another
Bank,[2] and beg you to accept my acknowledgments for the information.

I am, Sir. Your Mo. Obed Servant.   A Hamilton

Francis Childs Esq.
New York

ALS, from a typescript supplied by Mr. Percy Hamilton Goodsell, Jr., White Plains, New York.
    1. Letter not found.
    2. For information on the attempt to organize new banks in New York City, see H to William Seton, January 18, 24, and February 10, 1792; Seton to H, January 22, February 6, 1792; and Philip Schuyler to H, January 29, 1792.

From William Ellery

[*Newport, Rhode Island*] *February 27, 1792.* "Your Letter of the 11th of this month [1] in answer to mine of the 16th of Jany. did not come to hand until the 24th. of this month. . . . By the inclosed weekly return of monies received and paid, it will appear that the Cash I have on hand is 2186 dolls 93½ cents . . . and [I] will only observe now that at the expiration of this month will be due to Inspectors &c &c to the amount of about sixty dolls., & that there is now due for bounties on fish & salt provision to the amount of about two hundred dolls, which may be demanded, and which should be considered in the provision to be made for the drawback on Spirits which will be due. . . . It gives me Uneasiness to call your attention from the important business about which it is constantly employed; but the regard which I owe to myself and family compells me to urge that the present System may not pass away without an allowance and compensation to me, adequate to the services of my office. I would only add to what I have heretofore observed [2] that the fees have decreased every six months since I first opened my office."

LC, Newport Historical Society, Newport, Rhode Island.
    1. Letter not found.
    2. See Ellery to H, July 18, November 11, 1791.

From William Heth

Shillelah [1] [Virginia] 27th Feby. 1792.

Dear Sir

    The Merchants of Richmond Petersburg & Manchester—by deputation—spent last friday, & saturday, on the Subject of petitioning

Congress for the removal of the office from Bermuda Hundred. The scheme will end as I wishd—nothing will be done. It being acknowledged, pretty unanimously that, if there was only tolerable accommodations at the Hundred, they could have no good cause of complaint; it being unquestionably the most proper place for the general accommodations within the District, to keep the Collectors Office—and as to the safety of the *U States money* & property, it was none of their look out. But, even this objection would be removed, should a branch of the National bank as a State bank be established in Richmond—when the duties would be chiefly paid in Notes. This project thus dropping, I shall only wait your ⟨answer⟩ to the other questions which I took the liberty ⟨of asking in⟩ a private letter sometime in the early part of this Month [2] to determine upon making some little establishment at Bera Hundred.

I am   Dear Sir,   Most sincerely   and Affecy Yrs   W Heth

The Hoble
Alex Hamilton Esqe

ALS, Hamilton Papers, Library of Congress.
    1. "Shillelah" was one of three estates owned by Heth in Virginia.
    2. The letter, which has not been found, was dated February 5, 1792.

Thomas Jefferson to Pierre Charles L'Enfant [1]

[Philadelphia, February 27, 1792]

From your letter in answer to mine of the   [2] and your declarations in conversation with Mr. Lear it is understood that you absolutely decline acting under the authority of the present Commissioners.

If this understanding of your meaning be right I am instructed by the President to inform you that notwithstanding the desire he has entertained to preserve your agency in the business the condition upon which it is to be done is inadmissible and your services must be at an end.

Df, in the writing of H, Thomas Jefferson Papers, Library of Congress.
    1. On July 16, 1790, Congress had passed "An Act for establishing the temporary and permanent seat of the Government of the United States" on the Potomac River (1 *Stat.* 130). Under that law the President was instructed to appoint three commissioners to survey the district where the new capital was to be located. Washington appointed Thomas Jefferson, Daniel Carroll of Maryland, and David Stuart, a Virginian and an old friend of the President.

Major Pierre Charles L'Enfant was appointed to make "a survey of the grounds . . . as may aid in fixing the site of the federal town and buildings" (*GW*, XXXI, 226–27). L'Enfant's refusal to cooperate with the commissioners soon created difficulties. Washington decided with some reluctance that L'Enfant must be dismissed. On February 26, 1792, Washington wrote to Jefferson as follows:

"I have perused the enclosed answer to your letter to Majr L'Enfant. Both are returned. A final decision thereupon must be had. I wish it to be taken upon the best ground, and with the best advice. Send it, I pray you, to Mr Madison who is better acquainted with the *whole* of this matter than any other. I wish also that the attorney General may see, and become acquainted with the circumstances (I can think of no other, at this moment to call in), and wish that all three of you would be with me at half-after Eight o'clock to-morrow—if convenient—at a later hour, to be named, that I may be at home and disengaged." (ALS, Thomas Jefferson Papers, Library of Congress.)

After the meeting of Madison, Jefferson, and Randolph on February 27, 1792, Jefferson sent the letter printed above, with minor changes, to L'Enfant (ALS, Digges-Morgan-L'Enfant Papers, Library of Congress; ALS, letterpress copy, Thomas Jefferson Papers, Library of Congress).

2. Space left blank in MS. In the letter which Jefferson sent to L'Enfant the first line reads: "From your letter received yesterday in answer to my last. . . ."

From Thomas Smith[1]

[*Philadelphia*] *February 27, 1792.* ". . . I have . . . large returns in forwardness which Shall be compleated as soon as the very pressing business of the Office will permit—with out any further addition to the business of this office it will yet take four or five Clerks three or four months at least to Compleat it but Very unfortuneatly the Auditor cannot pass My Acct of Clerks wages for their Services since the first of Octor. so that they remain unpaid. I entreat your assistance sr. in this matter as it is out of my Power to keep them without it."

LC, RG 53, Pennsylvania State Loan Office, Letter Book, 1790–1794, Vol. "615-P," National Archives.

1. Smith was commissioner of loans for Pennsylvania.

Circular Letter from the Officers of the Massachusetts Line of the Late Army[1]

Boston, Massachusetts Feb. 28, 1792.

Sir,

We have had the honour to be appointed a Committee, by the Officers of the Massachusetts line of the late Army, to attend to and prosecute their memorial [2] to the Congress of the United States, on the subject of compensation for the losses sustained by them and the soldiers who served during the war, in consequence of the singular manner in which their services have been acknowledged and requited by the United States.

By a letter bearing date June 1, 1791,[3] you were informed of the measures adopted in pursuing that object, and that a Memorial was presented to Congress on the subject of our complaint.

Finding that no relief has been afforded, or as far as our information extends, contemplated, and convinced that there is a just debt as yet undischarged on the part of Government, our determination is to repeat our application, and reassert our claim, until we obtain consideration and relief; or until it shall be declared by the voice of the United States in Congress, that our claims are visionary and without foundation; and that a hard-earned *bonâ fide* debt can be honourably and justly cancelled by certificates received in the first instance by a kind of compulsion, alienated in most cases from necessity, unsupported by funds, and passing in exchange for only a sixth or an eighth of their nominal value.

To the pursuit of this measure we are urged by a conviction that our request is founded on the immutable principles of reason, equity and justice, by a sense of duty to ourselves and more especially to those faithful companions of the war, who served under our command; whose dispersed and embarrassed circumstances preclude them from application, and in whose behalf we are bound to appear by every principle of affection and gratitude.

Should it be objected that the claim has lain dormant and may have suffered diminution, we would observe, that if America had been conquered by Britain, neither life liberty, or retribution would probably have been the lot of many of the present applicants. To have preferred the application in any of the years of publick embarrassment which succeeded the peace, when the government and finances of the country wanted energy and even existence, would have comported neither with the interests nor character of the army. The records of the old government contain ample and frequent acknowledgments that the services have been faithfully performed on one part, together with an universal disposition to remunerate them. And the publick inability is the true and only source to which the failure on the part of government can be attributed.

The present government was instituted for the establishment of justice among other great objects. To this end they possess the power and ability. And as we have every confidence in the liberality and justice of the existing administration we solicit their final decision on the merits of our cause.

To facilitate the object of our wishes we have judged it expedient to depute an Agent to Congress to attend to and explain the nature of our application. On the twentieth day of March next, he will be in Philadelphia for that purpose; and this communication, which we beg you to take the earliest opportunity to make known to the Officers belonging to your State, is made to acquaint you with our determination, that, if you should think it expedient to adopt correspondent measures, our attempt may receive the aid of your advice and assistance.

To form a Convention of Officers from all the States, in order to consult and agree on a joint application has been a favourite object with many; but taking every consideration into view, we have preferred the mode now adopted, and we hope it will meet with your approbation.

General William Hull,[4] the person whom we have chosen for our Agent, will give his constant attendance in *Philadelphia*, during the present session of Congress; and we beg to recommend him to your attention and assistance.

With sentiments of respect, we are Sir, your most obedient servants,

W Heath
J Brooks
H Jackson
W. Eustis
Jos. Crocker
Thos. Edwards.[5]

LS, Hamilton Papers, Library of Congress.
1. For background to this circular, see James Blanchard to H, May, 1791.
2. The Massachusetts line presented memorials to Congress on August 3, 1790, and March 24, 1792.
An entry in the *Journal of the House* for August 3, 1790, reads as follows: "A petition of the Officers of the late Massachusetts line of the American Army, in behalf of themselves and the Soldiers of the said line, was presented to the House, and read, praying that further and adequate compensation may be made them for military services during the late war.
"*Ordered,* That the said petition do lie on the table." (*Journal of the House,* I, 287.)

An entry in the *Journal of the House* for March 24, 1792, reads as follows: "A petition of the officers of the Massachusetts line of the late Army was presented to the House and read, praying that the subject-matter of a petition presented at the last session, respecting the losses they sustained in the mode of compensation for their military services, may now be taken into consideration, and relief granted.

"*Ordered,* That the said petition do lie on the table." (*Journal of the House,* I, 547.)

3. No letter to H of this date concerning the memorial of the officers of the Massachusetts line has been found, but see Blanchard to H. May, 1791, note 1.

4. Hull rose to the rank of lieutenant colonel during the American Revolution and after the war practiced law in Newton, Massachusetts. In 1792 he served as brigadier general of the First Brigade of the Third Division of the Massachusetts Militia.

5. William Heath had risen to the rank of major general during the Revolutionary War. John Brooks had become a lieutenant-colonel commandant of the Seventh Continental Infantry Regiment. Henry Jackson had been breveted a brigadier general at the close of the American Revolution. William Eustis had been a hospital physician and surgeon during the last three years of the war. Joseph Crocker had served as a captain, and Thomas Edwards had been appointed judge advocate of the Army during the American Revolution.

From Isaac Ledyard

NYork Feby 28th. 1792

Dear sir

The inclosed was left with Mr. Hazard [1] to forward but was carelessly mislaid & forgotten. I do not recollect the contents, but will recollect the impression under which it was written, & that the design must have been to prevent drawn swords. I shall be able in a few days to convince you that on *election grounds* you need not be the enemy of Mr. ———[2] & I hope nothing else will disturb the operation of the *experiment.* I should have admired the candour & firm integrity which dictated your Letter [3] had it been recd. from almost any other person. It afforded me no new subject of pleasure or contemplation comeing from whence it did. It is probable that by next Sunday I may be able to give you the satisfaction herein intimated. I am most respectfully in all things your assured friend & Obedt. Servt.

Isaac Ledyard

ALS, Hamilton Papers, Library of Congress.
1. Nathaniel Hazard. See Ledyard to H, February 17, 1792.
2. Aaron Burr. See Ledyard to H, February 1, 17, 1792.
3. Letter not found.

Report on the Petition of the Executors of Edward Carnes

Treasury Department
February 28th. 1792.
[Communicated on February 29, 1792] [1]

[To the Speaker of the House of Representatives]

The Secretary of the Treasury, pursuant to an Order of the House of Representatives, of the 5th. of February 1790, referring to him a Memorial of the Executors of Edward Carnes, respectfully submits the following Report.[2]

The object of the said Memorial is, to obtain payment of a sum of five hundred and forty four pounds nineteen shillings and eleven pence, money of Massachusetts, claimed as due to the estate of the said Edward Carnes, for supplies furnished, and work done for sundry vessels of the United States, during the late war.

The following are the material facts, which appear in relation to this case.

James Warren, William Vernon, and John Deshon, were Commissioners of the Navy Board, for the Eastern Department.[3]

The United States in Congress assembled, on the 29th. of August 1781, among other things, resolved;

That an agent of Marine should be appointed, and that as soon as

Copy, RG 233, Reports of the Treasury Department, 1791–1792, Vol. II, National Archives.

1. *Journal of the House*, I, 523. The communicating letter may be found in RG 233, Reports of the Treasury Department, 1791–1792, Vol. II, National Archives.

2. On February 4, 1790, "A petition of Joseph Henderson, and John Carnes, jr. of Boston, executors, &c. of Edward Carnes, deceased, was presented to the House and read, praying that payment may be made of a liquidated debt, due to their testator's estate, from the United States."

On February 5, 1790, the House "*Ordered*, That the petition of the executors of Edward Carnes, deceased, which was presented yesterday, be referred to the Secretary of the Treasury, with instruction to examine the same, and report his opinion thereupon to the House" (*Journal of the House*, I, 152–53).

3. To assist the Marine Committee of the Continental Congress, two naval boards had been established, one at Philadelphia and the other at Boston. The Boston board, which was established on April 19, 1777, consisted of James Warren, a political leader in Massachusetts, William Vernon of Newport, Rhode Island, a partner in the mercantile firm of Samuel and William Vernon, and John Deshon, merchant and shipowner of New London, Connecticut.

the said Agent should enter upon the execution of his Office, the functions and appointments of the Board of Admiralty, the several Navy Boards, and all the civil officers appointed under them, should cease and be determined.[4]

On the seventh of September following, they further resolved; That until an Agent of Marine should be appointed, all the duties, powers and authorities, assigned to the said Agent, should devolve upon, and be executed by the Superintendant of Finance, and that as soon as the said Superintendant should take upon him, the execution of those duties and powers, the functions and appointments of the Board of Admiralty, the several Navy Boards, Agents and civil officers under them should cease and determine.[5]

On the twenty first of the same month of September, the Superintendant of Finance wrote to the Navy Board of the Eastern Department,[6] communicating to them the aforesaid resolutions, deputing John Brown [7] to act on his behalf, and requiring them to surrender to him, all the public books, papers or stores in their possession or custody; observing only, that if the Frigates Alliance and Deane, then fitting for sea, should not be completed, when his letter arrived, their equipment should proceed under the direction of the Board, so that their accounts might close with those vessels.

On the twenty sixth of March 1782, the Superintendant of Finance, in a letter to the then late Navy Board, expresses himself thus—"I think you should settle the accounts of the persons, to whom your Department is indebted, and give them certificates of the sums due."

The petitioners produce an account settled between the said Edward Carnes, and William Vernon and James Warren (the said John Deshon having previously resigned his office) [8] which bears date the 25th of July 1782, and states a balance in favor of Edward

4. See *JCC*, XXI, 919–20.
5. For the interim authority granted to Robert Morris, Superintendent of Finance, see *JCC*, XXI, 943. For the unsuccessful attempts to organize an effective Department of Marine and to appoint an agent to administer it, see *JCC*, XIX, 127–28, 133, 203; XX, 724–26, 764–67.
6. LC, Papers of the Continental Congress, National Archives.
7. Brown had served as secretary of the Marine Committee of the Continental Congress.
8. Deshon had resigned from the Navy Board on April 26, 1781. His resignation was accepted on May 7, 1781 (*Naval Records of the American Revolution*, 175).

Carnes of five hundred and forty four pounds nine shillings and eleven pence, lawful money of Massachusetts. The account is signed by the said William Vernon and James Warren.

The Navy Board aforesaid have not settled their accounts with the United States, and the probability of a satisfactory settlement cannot be inferred, from the circumstances which have hitherto appeared.

This leaves the government without adequate means of testing and checking demands of the nature of that, which is the object of the petition under consideration.

The books, however, of the Navy Board, which in August or September 1786, were lodged in the hands of the Commissioner for settling the accounts of the Navy Department,[9] correspond, in this instance, with the account produced.

It does not appear, that this account was ever exhibited, either to the Commissioner charged with the settlement of accounts in the State of Massachusetts,[10] or at the Treasury, within the periods prescribed by the Acts of limitation.[11]

If, therefore, the claim is to be considered as an unliquidated claim, it is barred by those Acts.

But the Secretary is of opinion, that this claim, admitting the adjustment to have taken place, in conformity to the face of the account, does not fall under that description; inasmuch as there appears to have been, prior to those Acts, a formal settlement, and a precise balance struck by persons, who were charged with settling

9. Benjamin Walker was the commissioner of accounts of the Marine Department.

10. Both William Imlay of Connecticut and Royal Flint of New York served as Continental commissioners to settle accounts in Massachusetts.

11. On November 2, 1785, and on July 23, 1787, Congress agreed upon two resolutions which debarred claims not submitted for liquidation before specified dates. Claims for services performed in the military department were to be presented to the commissioners of army accounts on or before August 1, 1786. Claims for the commissary, quartermaster, hospital, clothier, or marine departments were to be presented to the commissioner of accounts of the respective departments on or before March 23, 1788, and other claims against the United States were to be submitted to the comptroller of the Treasury on or before July 23, 1788. These resolutions applied to all claims against the United States arising out of the Revolutionary War with the exception of those connected with the settlement of the state accounts with the United States and some claims for which special circumstances later justified an individual or group waiver of the limitation (JCC, XXIX, 866; XXXIII, 392).

accounts in the department, by the Superintendant of Finance, acting under the authority of Congress, as Agent of Marine.

If this idea be well-founded, a question will still remain, how far such a settlement is to be deemed conclusive upon the public, or liable to revision and re-adjustment.

On the first supposition, there would be nothing more to do than to satisfy the claim. On the last, the revision would be most advantageously made by the Accounting Officers of the Treasury.

The Secretary begs leave to state here, that there are a number of claims upon the Government, the respective amounts of which hav been ascertained and certified by public officers of various descriptions; but which are not admitted by the present practice and course of the Treasury.

A resolution of Congress of the 23d. of February 1785 [12] requires all persons, who have issued certificates of debts due from the United States (Loan office certificates and certificates of final settlement excepted) forthwith to deliver to the Board of Treasury, or to some Commissioner of Accounts in the State where such persons reside, a fair abstract of all the certificates, which they had issued, and directs that copies of those abstracts should be transmitted by the Board of Treasury, to the several Commissioners of accounts, as a guide in detecting frauds.

And another resolution of the same date enjoins it upon those Commissioners, to be careful how they admit charges against the United States, on Certificates not duly supported by the authority of Congress, and the accounts of the officers, who had issued them.

Influenced by the precautions contemplated by those resolutions, and by the great danger of admitting certificates which could not be checked by any return, account or document from the officer who had issued them, it grew into a practice, at the Treasury, to decline the admission of any Certificates, of which there was not such evidence in the possession of the Treasury.

When it is considered, how great a number of persons were charged, during the late war, with issuing Certificates for services and supplies, and that the accounts of a considerable proportion of them are still unsettled, and of many, by deaths, abscondings, de-

12. For this and the resolution mentioned below, see *JCC*, XXVIII, 92–93.

struction of papers and other casualties, never can be settled—It will be readily perceived, that great hazard of abuse and imposition would have attended a contrary practice.

The claims of the individuals concerned are, nevertheless, embarrassing. They urge, that the public are bound, to admit claims founded upon the acts of officers, whom they had entrusted to contract such claims, and to give the evidences of their being contracted, especially where nothing appears to invalidate them.

A medium between a total rejection of such claims, and an implicit admission of them, seems best reconcilable with public justice and public policy.

The Secretary, pursuant to this idea, submits the following arrangement, to the consideration of the House of Representatives.

That provision be made by law, requiring all persons having claims upon the United States, not barred by any Act of limitation, founded upon certificates, or other written documents, from public officers (except Loan-Office certificates, certificates of final settlement, register's certificates, and certificates issued pursuant to the Act making provision for the debt of the United States) [13] to exhibit their respective claims at the Treasury, depositing the documents and vouchers, upon which they are founded, within the term of eighteen months from the passing of the law; and barring all such claims, as should not be exhibited within the term limited: empowering the accounting officers of the Treasury, after the expiration of that term, to admit and adjust, as in similar cases, all such of those claims, as should appear to them proper to be admitted, and requiring them to report to Congress all such as should appear to them objectionable, together with their objections, in order to a final Legislative disposition concerning them, as justice and right may require.[14]

All which is respectfully submitted

Alexander Hamilton
Secretary of the Treasury.

13. "An Act making provision for the (payment of the) Debt of the United States" (1 *Stat.* 138–44 [August 4, 1790]).

14. A law incorporating H's suggestions was passed on February 12, 1793, entitled "An Act relative to claims against the United States, not barred by any act of limitation, and which have not been already adjusted" (1 *Stat.* 301–02).

From Thomas Smith

[Philadelphia] February 28, 1792. ". . . the amount of Certificates
of the assumed debt presented & funded at this office is 674,675
Dollars which deducted from the Quota allotted this State Viz
2.200.000.[1] Dollars leaves 1,525.325 the Interest On Which agreeably
to the statement on the other side amounts to 13982.14 Cts. for the
Quarter ending 31 March 1792."

LC, RG 53, Pennsylvania State Loan Office, Letter Book, 1790–1794, Vol.
"615-P," National Archives.
   1. For the allocation of the total state debt assumption among the states,
see Section 14 of "An Act making provision for the (payment of the) Debt
of the United States" (1 *Stat.* 143 [August 4, 1790]). For this section, see
Smith to H, June 6, 1791.

From Joseph Whipple

Portsmouth, New Hampshire, February 28, 1792. "Your letter of
the 4th. instant [1] I had the honor to receive the 21st. and conformably with your directions I now give you the Name of *Benjamin
Gunnison* as a Suitable person for the first Mate of the Revenue
Cutter Scammel. . . ."

LC, RG 36, Collector of Customs at Portsmouth, Letters Sent, 1791–1792,
Vol. 3, National Archives; copy, RG 56, Letters from the Collector at Portsmouth, National Archives.
   1. Letter not found.

From James Blanchard [1]

Norfolk Virginia February 29. 1792

sir
   When the Funding System was in agitation, those who were not
in the paper Line was in hopes the President would not Sign the
Bill.[2] However he did. Still they were in hopes at next Session he
would recommend some Sort of Justice to be done but they were
disappointed. As soon as the session ended the Circular Letter No. 1,

No. 2. and No. 3 [3] was Sent to every State Society of Officers—and what has been said or done I have not heard—Except in Virginia.

This brought on an Enquiry, and recourse was had to the proceedings of Congress and the Secretaries Report.[4]

The Officers of the virginia Line had a full meeting the 25th of October, but the business being new to the greatest part of them, they observed, they was Sensible they had been CHEATED but for what purpose, could not determine. It was without a doubt you was the Fomenter of the business—and your Rangers (so Called) had been in every Creek and Corner hunting up the defered debt— which was Supposed to be a Scheme of the concern (at some Subsequent Session to make them Six per Cents).

This has been Corroborated by the Mimorial Introduced by Mr. Fitzsimons [5]—and Information Lately received from a *member*, to his Friends here in the paper Line, that you are bringing forward a plan to Fund the residue of the public debt (but to return) as all you have done, or Could possibly do, at Present in Sinking the Public debt, was a mere, *bagatelle*, and could be for no other purpose than a Cloak for private Speculation.

Therefore an application to the Present *Ministry*, was thought, would prove fruitless—and the only remedy would be a True Statement to the people from the Journals of Congress of the principles and Conduct of their representatives and if they see proper to Chuse others in their Stead perhaps, the next would be disinterested. This will be done in a pamphlet to Contain abt. 100. pages and as many Hand bills as are Necessary, adapted to the places where the Elections will be held—and placed in the Hands of those who wish for Other Members.

An Address will be presented to the President, Signed by a number of Officers, Soldiers, and private Gentlemen who he will remember—(the purport of it will be) that they are Sensible of the Injuries done them in the Funding Law—and this Silent digestion of one wrong has provoked a Second—but that they by no means regret their time and advances, as it answered so valuable a purpose —and they had the Honour of his example—but the heavy Taxes (that is Thought to be eclipsed) is every day visible—and an *Incredible*, debt is almost, all they have Left to bequeath to their Posterity—and will, hope the Additional bill may Subside for the present—as an Address will be Laid before the people of the United States on the subject at their Next Election—which he may have an Opportunity of seeing previous to the Circulation.

I am Sir—Your very humble servant   James Blanchard

Alexander Hamilton Esqr.

ALS, Hamilton Papers, Library of Congress.
 1. For background to this letter, see Blanchard to H, May, 1791.
 Blanchard had served as quartermaster and regimental paymaster of the Third New Hampshire Regiment during the American Revolution. In 1791–1792 he was a persistent opponent of the funding system and an advocate of discrimination in favor of those Revolutionary War soldiers who had alienated their certificates.
 2. "An Act making provision for the (payment of the) Debt of the United States" (1 *Stat.* 138–44 [August 4, 1790]).
 3. None of these circulars have been found, but for information concerning one of them, see Blanchard to H, May, 1791.
 4. See "Report Relative to a Provision for the Support of Public Credit," January 9, 1790.
 5. On November 16, 1791, Thomas FitzSimons, a member of the House of Representatives from Pennsylvania, had "called up the petition of a committee of the public creditors who loaned money to the United States, between September, 1777, and March, 1778, and moved that it should be referred to the Secretary of the Treasury, for his opinion. . . ." The petition demanded the payment by the United States of certain bills of credit which according to the petition had not been provided for in the funding system (*Annals of Congress*, III, 191).

From William Heth

Private
Richmond 29th Feby. 1792.

Dear Sir

When at Petersburg the other day, I found an Idea prevailing that, Mr Randolph, the present Marshall,[1] & myself, were about to exchange Offices, at which, I was a good deal surprised—tho' it gave me no *concern*. But, on coming to Town this morning, it was suggested to me that Mr Randolphs *friends* might effect this exchange, without my knowledge or consent, by insinuating to the President that I had been consulted thereon, and that it was agreeable to me. This alarm'd me a good deal, and should such a *scheme*, be actually in contemplation, I know not, how to prevent its taking effect, but by thus assuring *you*, that nothing was ever farther from my intentions or wishes, than such an exchange, and to rely upon your aid and friendship, to prevent my being so greatly injured—by acquainting the President with the *contents* of this—should you think it expedient.

Some time ago, I received a confidential letter from a certain member of Congress, asking me—"if in case, the Office of Marshall should be made Worth from £600 to perhaps £1000 ℔ Ann I would prefer it to the one I now hold." Being somewhat *flatterd* and *complimentd* I answerd him cautiously, and, as delicately as I could declaring my own to be a more agreeable office, and more Suitable to my *genius* & *talents*—but that, I could not determine thereon, until I saw the *new law*[2] and I wishd to *consider more on the Subject.* The same person it seems, wrote at *same time* to Mr Randolph and tho' I cannot suppose him capable, of any double dealing, or any underhanded work, yet, I have been urgd to take this Step, to Secure myself against any *Court Machinations*, which, *may* be forming on this subject.

The *Jealousy*, which has dictated this measure, would not, perhaps have existed, had not Mr Randolphs appointment, with certain circumstances preceding it, occasiond universal astonishment, and what *further his friends* may have in view, cannot be known.

I must therefore, my dear Sir, rely upon you to prevent such an act of imposition and injustice, taking place. Pray favor me with a single line in answer to this, and believe me to be ⟨with⟩ every Sentiment, of respect, friendship & Es⟨teem⟩

D sir, yr mo. Ob sert   Will Heth

The Honble
Alex Hamilton Esquire

ALS, Hamilton Papers, Library of Congress.
   1. David Meade Randolph had succeeded Edward Carrington as marshal of the District of Virginia on November 7, 1791.
   2. Congress at this time was considering legislation concerning the fees of both marshals and customs officers. On May 8, 1792, two acts concerning the fees of these officers were approved by George Washington: "An Act relative to the compensations to certain officers employed in the collection of the duties of impost and tonnage" (1 *Stat.* 273–75) and "An Act for regulating Processes in the Courts of the United States, and providing Compensations for the Officers of the said Courts, and for Jurors and Witnesses" (1 *Stat.* 275–79).

Report on the Petitions of Jabez Bowen and William Gardner

Treasury Department,
February 29th 1792.
[Communicated on March 3, 1792] [1]

[To the Speaker of the House of Representatives]
Pursuant to the Orders of the House of Representatives of the 20th. of December and 31st. of January last, referring to the Secretary of the Treasury, the petition of Jabez Bowen, Commissioner of Loans for the State of Rhode Island and Providence Plantations, and the petition of William Gardner, Commissioner of Loans for the State of New Hampshire,[2] the said Secretary respectfully submits the following Report.

That the following Salaries were established by the Act, intituled "An Act making provision for the debt of the United States,"[3] as compensations for the services of the Commissioners of Loans in the several States.

	Dollars.
To the Commissioner for the State of New Hampshire, . .	650.
To the Commissioner for the State of Massachusetts, . .	1500.
To the Commissioner for the State of Rhode Island, . . .	600.
To the Commissioner for the State of Connecticut, . . .	1000.
To the Commissioner for the State of New York, ...	1500.
To the Commissioner for the State of New Jersey, . . .	700.
To the Commissioner for the State of Pennsylvania, . . .	1500.

Copy, RG 233, Reports of the Treasury Department, 1791–1792, Vol. II, National Archives.
   1. *Journal of the House*, I, 526.
   2. On December 20, 1791, "A petition of Jabez Bowen, Commissioner of Loans in the State of Rhode Island, was presented to the House and read, praying to be allowed the expense of stationery and clerk hire until the first day of October next," and on January 31, 1791, "a petition of William Gardner, praying to be allowed a farther compensation for his services as Commissioner of Loans in the State of New Hampshire" was received. Both petitions were referred to the Secretary of the Treasury (*Journal of the House*, I, 478, 500).
   3. This act was passed August 4, 1790, and the salaries of the commissioners of loans are stated in Section 11 (1 *Stat.* 142).

To the Commissioner for the State of Delaware, ...   600.
To the Commissioner for the State of Maryland, ... 1000.
To the Commissioner for the State of Virginia, ... 1500.
To the Commissioner for the State of North Carolina, . . 1000.
To the Commissioner for the State of South Carolina, . . 1000.
To the Commissioner for the State of Georgia, ...   700.
And that said salaries are declared, by said Act, to be in full compensation for all services and expenses.

That by an Act passed on the third day of March 1791, the said Commissioners were further allowed "such sums, as should appear to have been necessarily expended by them in the purchase of books and stationery, for the use of their several offices, and for the hire of clerks, from the commencement of the same, until the first day of October 1791." [4]

That though an appropriation of money has been made, during the present session, for such expenses, as have been incurred, by the said Commissioners, for books and stationery, to the end of the year 179[2],[5] yet a legislative Act will be necessary to justify the officers of the Treasury, in admitting the accounts for said expenses, so far as they have accrued in the last quarter of the year 1791.

That it will be also necessary, in the event of a renewal of the loans, in the public debt, to extend a similar provision to the end of the present year.

That the compensations, at present established for the Commissioners of Loans, are the same, as were allowed by the resolution of the late Congress, passed on the 23d. of March 1787,[6] (when, on account of the deranged state of the public finances, a general reduction of the salaries of the civil department took place, and when the business in the Loan Offices was considerably less than it had formerly been) except in respect to the Commissioners for New York, and South Carolina, and Georgia, to whose salaries, an addition has been made. That the services, performed by the Commissioners under the late establishment of the Loan-Office Department,

4. See "An Act for making compensations to the Commissioners of Loans, for extraordinary expenses" (1 Stat. 216).
5. "1791" in MS. H is referring to "An Act making Appropriations for the Support of Government for the year one thousand seven hundred and ninety-two" (1 Stat. 226–29 [December 23, 1791]).
6. JCC, XXXII, 128–30.

consisted merely in receiving and remitting to the Treasury, the monies paid by the States, on the requisitions of Congress, and in issuing indents for the payment of interest on the domestic debt; and that, though there is reason to believe, that the salaries, then allowed, were, in most instances, a sufficient compensation for the services, which were performed, yet, when the importance and responsibility of the trusts, at present reposed in the Commissioners, and the laborious nature of their services, are considered, an augmentation of their salaries appears to be advisable.

The following sums are considered, as reasonable compensations, to be allowed, annually, from the first day of the present year.

                                                              Dollars.
To the Commissioner for the State of New Hampshire, . .   900.
To the Commissioner for the State of Massachusetts, . . . 1600.
To the Commissioner for the State of Rhode Island, . . .   800.
To the Commissioner for the State of Connecticut, . . .   1100.
To the Commissioner for the State of New York, ...   1600.
To the Commissioner for the State of New Jersey, . . .   900.
To the Commissioner for the State of Pennsylvania, . . .   1600.
To the Commissioner for the State of Delaware . . . .   700.
To the Commissioner for the State of Maryland . . . .   1200.
To the Commissioner for the State of Virginia . . . . .   1600.
To the Commissioner for the State of North Carolina . .   1100.
To the Commissioner for the State of South Carolina . .   1100.
To the Commissioner for the State of Georgia . . . . .   800.

The charges for Office rent, stationery, and fuel, will, in several of the offices, be so considerable, as to form a great deduction from the salaries of the Commissioners, if borne by them. It is, therefore, proposed, that the accounting officers of the Treasury should be allowed to admit any, or all such charges, as shall be judged reasonable.

The extent of the business, in several of the States, will render it indispensable for the Commissioners of such States, to have one or more clerks. To expect them to provide clerks out of their salaries, would require, that the salaries should be considerably larger, than is proposed, or than it would be expedient to grant. Some separate provision, therefore, for furnishing them with clerks, is conceived to be absolutely necessary. This must be, either by defining the number, that each Commissioner may have, or by vesting a discretionary power, somewhere, to allow so many, as may, in experience, be found requisite, not exceeding a certain limit. The first, in the present stage of the business, is difficult, and indeed, from the variations likely to happen, as to the quantity of business, at different offices, that, which would be, at present, a proper standard, might not long continue to be so. On these accounts, the second mode appears to be preferable. It may be so restricted, that not more than two clerks can be allowed to any one Commissioner.

Occasions frequently occur, in which it is desirable, that there should be an officer, in each State, authorised to act in the capacity of Deputy-Treasurer. For want of it, public monies are confided, where there is no responsibility of sureties: a circumstance, which ought, as much as possible to accompany the receipt and disbursement of public monies. The sums annually paid to invalids may serve, as an example. These are now paid through the Commissioners of Loans; but as the business makes no part of the established duties of their offices, it is presumed, that their sureties would not be answerable for the misapplication of the monies, in this respect, entrusted to them.

This inconvenience would be remedied, by constituting each Commissioner of Loans a Deputy-Treasurer, and making it his duty to receive and disburse all public monies, which should be confided to him.

This will make it proper, that the sums, in which the Commissioners are required to give security, should be enlarged, and that new sureties should be taken; a requisition, which will be the more reasonable, if competent additions are made to their compensations, so as to render them more duly proportioned to the degree of responsibility.[7]

All which is respectfully submitted,

Alexander Hamilton,
Secretary of the Treasury.

7. On May 8, 1792, a law was enacted providing for money to be paid to the commissioners of loans for the purchase of stationery and the hire of clerks from October 1, 1791, until March 1, 1793. The salaries of the commissioners of loans were not increased, nor were H's other recommendations adopted. See "An Act for making compensations to the Commissioners of Loans, for extraordinary expenses" (1 *Stat.* 284).

From Oliver Wolcott, Junior [1]

Treasury Department, Comptroller's Office, February 29, 1792.
Sends report on memorial of Samuel Fowler.[2] States: "Though there
is not any recollection of the particular Certificate presented by Saml
Fowler and defaced at the Treasury, yet from the circumstances now
stated, it is evident that said Certificate was a forgery and not chargeable to the public. That the negligence imputed by the memorialist to
the Commissioner and malconduct of his Clerks, appears to be altogether without foundation."

ADfS, Connecticut Historical Society, Hartford.
   1. Wolcott was comptroller of the Treasury.
   2. An entry in the *Journal of the House* for February 24, 1792, reads as
follows: "A petition of Samuel Fowler, praying that the amount of a certificate
of the late Commissioner of Army accounts, the property of the petitioner,
which has been defaced at the Treasury, as counterfeit, but which the petitioner is prepared to show is authentic and genuine, may be made good to him.
   "*Ordered,* That the said petition be referred to the Secretary of the Treasury, with instruction to examine the same, and report his opinion thereupon
to the House." (*Journal of the House*, I, 519.)
   H made no report on this petition (*Journal of the House*, II, 284).

Notes on Thomas Jefferson's Report of
Instructions for the Commissioners to Spain [1]

[Philadelphia, March 1–4, 1792] [2]

[JEFFERSON'S COMMENTS]	[HAMILTON'S NOTES]
	The General Tenor of the Report appears solid and proper.
	The following observations however on a hasty perusal occur.
The Report is amended in conformity with this observation.	Page 2. Is it to put our Revolution upon the *true* or the best footing to say that the circumstances which obliged us to *discontinue* our foreign Magistrate *brought upon us the*

D, in the writing of H and Thomas Jefferson, George Washington Papers,
Library of Congress; copy, Hamilton Papers, Library of Congress.
   1. After John Jay failed to conclude a treaty with Spain under the Confederation, negotiations were not resumed until the summer of 1790, when
William Carmichael, United States chargé d'affaires at Madrid, attempted

[JEFFERSON'S COMMENTS]   [HAMILTON'S NOTES]

War?[a] Did not the war previously
exist and bring on the *discontinu-
ance?* Was it not rather the *cause*
than the *effect?*

without success to use the Nootka Sound controversy as a lever for obtaining
Spanish concessions on the question of free navigation of the Mississippi River.
On June 1, 1791, William Short, United States chargé d'affaires at Paris, wrote
to Comte de Montmorin, French Foreign Minister, and asked France's support for Carmichael's overtures on the Mississippi question. Short's letter,
which was sent to Madrid, was supported by the French chargé d'affaires
there. Perhaps fearing the results of the settlement of Anglo-American differences, Diego de Gardoqui, Spanish Minister of Finance, reported favorably to
the King on Carmichael's renewed representations and recommended that
Spain reply directly to the United States and offer to resume negotiations on
the free navigation of the Mississippi. As a result, Josef de Jaudenes and
Josef de Viar, the agents representing Spanish interests at Philadelphia, informed Jefferson in December, 1791, that Spain would be willing to resume
negotiations at Madrid. On December 22, 1791, Jefferson wrote to Washington
of this offer (ALS, letterpress copy, Thomas Jefferson Papers, Library of
Congress), and on January 11, 1792, Washington submitted Jefferson's recommendations to Congress, nominating Carmichael and Short, who had been
appointed United States Minister at The Hague, to represent the United
States in these negotiations (*ASP, Foreign Relations*, I, 130–31). The Senate
confirmed the nominations on January 24, 1792.
    Jefferson's instructions to Carmichael and Short were written in the form
of a report to the President and were sent to H for his suggestions. H accordingly made the "notes" printed above in the right-hand column, and Jefferson
in the left-hand column added his comments on H's notes. The draft in
which Jefferson incorporated many of H's suggestions may be found in the
Thomas Jefferson Papers, Library of Congress. The final version of Jefferson's
instructions, dated March 18, 1792, is printed in Ford, *Writings of Jefferson*,
V, 460–81, and in *ASP, Foreign Relations*, I, 252–57. The full contents of the
instructions were not laid before the Senate until December 16, 1793.
    Washington, however, sent the third section, which related to commerce,
to the Senate on March 7, 1792, in support of a request to extend the powers
of the commissioners. His letter of transmittal reads as follows:
    "I submit to your consideration the report of the Secretary of State which
accompanies this, stating the reasons for extending the negotiation proposed
at Madrid to the subject of commerce, and explaining under the form of instructions to the commissioners lately appointed to that court the principles
on which commercial arrangements with Spain might, if desired on her part,
be acceded to on ours; and I have to request your decision, whether you will
advise and consent to the extension of the powers of the commissioners as
proposed, and to the ratification of a treaty which shall conform to those instructions, should they enter into such a one with that court." (*ASP, Foreign
Relations*, I, 133.)
    2. The editors are indebted to Dr. Julian P. Boyd, editor of *The Papers of
Thomas Jefferson*, for assistance in dating this document.
    3. The sentence in the draft which H objected to reads as follows: "Cir-
cumstances obliging us afterwards to discontinue our foreign magistrate, & to
name one within every state, this brought on us a war on the part of the
former magistrate, supported by the nation among whom he resided." Jefferson deleted this sentence and substituted one which incorporated H's
suggestions.

[JEFFERSON'S COMMENTS]

The capture of the army struck out.

[HAMILTON'S NOTES]

Is it *accurate* to say that France aided us in capturing the *whole army* of the enemy? [4] Does this not imply that there was no other enemy army in the country; though there were in fact two others one in New York, another in South Carolina? This last is a mere criticism as to the accuracy of expression. The sense is clear enough.

No conquest of the territory was made, to wit of the island of N. Orleans on the one side, or Louisiana on the other, as both had belonged to Spain before the war. Therefore no change in the right to the water is incident to the territory. This circumstance however is inserted in the Report to make the reasoning the clearer.

Page 11. Are *"naval victories"* the essen⟨tial⟩ [5] means of conquest of a water as seems to be impli⟨ed?⟩ [6] Is not the conquest of a *water* an incident to th⟨at⟩ of Territory? If this idea is not sound, that combined with it is—namely that in no event could Spain be considered as having *conquered the River against* the U States —with whom she not only had no war but was an associa⟨te.⟩

The word *chuse* substituted for *wish* however England could hold that right of common in the water only as incident to Florida, which she then held. When she conveyed Florida to Spain the incident passed by the same conveyance, & she can never have a claim against us on a stipulation the benefit of which she has conveyed to another.

Page 22. [7] May it not be inferred from what is said here that though the U States would not *wish* to insert an express stipulation against other Nations; yet they may be prevailed upon to do it? [8] Would such a stipulation be consistent w⟨ith⟩ the right which G Britain reserved to herself in the treaty with us? If the inference alluded to is intended to be excluded, will it not be adviseable to vary the turn of expression so as render the intention more unequivocal?

4. The sentence to which H is referring reads as follows: "France on our invitation landed a large army within our territories, continued it with us two years, and aided us in recovering sundry places from the possession of the enemy, & finally in capturing their whole army. . . ." Jefferson deleted the last seven words.

5. Material within broken brackets has been taken from the copy in the Hamilton Papers, Library of Congress.

6. Jefferson did not delete the part of the report to which H took exception, but added only the material which he wrote in the margin opposite H's remark.

7. In MS, H mistakenly wrote the number "12."

8. H is referring to the following statement in Jefferson's draft: "If Spain apprehends that other nations may claim access to our ports in the Missisipi under their treaties with us giving them a right to come & trade in all our ports, tho' we would not wish to insert an express stipulation against them, yet we shall think ourselves justified to acquiesce in fact under any regul~s Spain may from time to time establish against their admission." Jefferson substituted "chuse" for "wish," as indicated in the left-hand column of the MS.

[JEFFERSON'S COMMENTS]

Report altered in conformity to this.

⟨The power to alienate the unpeopled te⟩rritory of any ⟨state, is not among the enumerated po⟩wers given by the Constitution to the General government: & if we may go out of that instrument, & *accomodate to exigencies which may arise*, by alienating the *unpeopled* territory of a state, we may accomodate ourselves a little more by alienating that which is *peopled*, & still a little more by selling the *people* themselves. A shade or two more in the degree of exigency is all that will be requisite, & of that degree we shall ourselves be the judges. However may it not be hoped that these questions are forever laid to rest by the 12th Amendment, now made a part of the Constitution, declaring expressly that the "powers not

[HAMILTON'S NOTES]

Page 23. Are there conclusive reasons to make it a *sine qua non* that no phrase shall be admitted which shall express or *imply* a grant? ⁹ Could the negotiation with propriety be broken off on such a point?

Is it not rather one to be endeavoured to be avoided than the avoiding of ⟨it⟩ to be made a *sine qua non?* Page 25. Is it true, that the U States have no right to *alienate an Inch* of the Territory in Question; except in the case of necessity, intimated in another place? ¹⁰ Or will it be useful to avow the denial of such a right?

It is apprehended that the Doctrine which restricts the alienation of Territory to cases of *extreme necessity* is applicable rather to *peopled* territory, than to waste and uninhabited districts. Positions restraining the right of the U States to accomodate to exigencies which may arise ought ever to be advanced with great caution.¹¹

9. H is referring to the following paragraph in Jefferson's draft: "That no phrase be admitted in the treaty which would express or imply that we take this by *grant* from Spain." Jefferson deleted this paragraph and at the end of this section of the draft added the following:

"We might add, as a 5th sine qua non that no phrase should be admitted in the treaty which would express or imply that we take the navigation of the Missisipi as a *grant* from Spain. but, however, disagreeable it would be to subscribe to such a sentiment, yet were the conclusion of a treaty to hang on that single objection, it would be expedient to wave it, and to meet, at a future day, the consequences of any resumption they may pretend to make, rather than at present those of a separation without coming to any agreement."

10. H is referring to the following statement in Jefferson's draft: "We have nothing else to give in exchange: for as to territory, we have neither the right, nor the disposition to alienate an inch of what belongs to any member of our union."

11. A document in Jefferson's handwriting, which is dated March 5, 1792, and is located in the Thomas Jefferson Papers, Library of Congress, is headed: "Notes by A. Hamilton on T:J's Report of instructions for the Commissioners to treat at Madrid. Eight of these notes were conformed to. The two following were not." The "two following" with which Jefferson did not agree are the two preceding paragraphs by H printed above and the material referred to in note 13. In his document Jefferson then copied the two paragraphs by H in question and his own comment, which is also printed above. For the other point on which Jefferson disagreed with H, see note 13.

[JEFFERSON'S COMMENTS]   [HAMILTON'S NOTES]

delegated to the U.S. by the Constitution are reserved to the states respectively"? And if the general government has no power to alienate the territory of a state, it is too irresistable an argument to deny ourselves the use of it on the present occasion.

It is certainly impossible for any nation to have stipulations of this kind & extent, with two others at the same time. However the language of the Report is made more correct & conformable to the words of the French treaty.

If the Secretary of the Treasury will be so good as to particularise the advantages to be asked & the equivalents to be offered, it will be proper to consider of them.

Page 28. Is it true that the stipulation with France respecting the Reception of prizes is exclusive and incommunicable?[12] It is doubtless so as against France, but why is it so as against other Nations?

It is however a stipulation very inconvenient and even dangerous to the U States and one which ought by all means to be excluded.

Though a Treaty of Commerce like that contemplated in the Report ought not to be rejected, if desired by Spain and coupled with a satisfactory adjustment of the boundary and Navigation; yet ought not something more to be attempted if it were only to give satisfaction to other parts of the Union?

Some positively favourable stipulations respecting our Grain flour and Fish even in the European Dominions of Spain would be of great consequence and would justify reciprocal advantages to some of her commodities (say Wines and brandies).[13]

12. Jefferson had written that the stipulations respecting prizes "entered into by the U.S. and France towards each other, is, in it's nature, exclusive & incommunicable to any other." This section of the draft was expanded to include the provision made in the treaty with France.

13. As mentioned in note 11, there is a separate document, dated March 5, 1792, written by Jefferson, stating that he disagreed with H on two points. The first point is discussed in note 11. The second point concerns the two paragraphs by H printed above. To indicate his disagreement on the second point Jefferson copied these paragraphs in the March 5 document, but for his own comment printed above in the left-hand column Jefferson substituted the following more detailed criticism of H's comments:

"Th: Jefferson will be glad if the Secretary of the Treasury will state the specific propositions he would have made to Spain, on the subject of our fish, grain & flour, to wit, what he would ask, & what propose as an equivalent. The following considerations will of course occur to him.

"1. If we quit the ground of the most favored nation, as to certain articles for our convenience, Spain may insist on doing the same, for other articles for her convenience: & apprehend that our Commissioners might soon be out of their depth in the details of commerce.

It seems sufficient to stipulate that the treaty shall be ratified, without saying by what body, or by what individuals it is to be. An instruction however is inserted to allow 16 months for the exchange of ratifications.

This has been decided before.

Will it not be necessary to add an instruction that the usual stipulation respecting the ratification of the Treaty by the U States be varied so as to be adapted to the participation of the Senate?

Last Page. The words "nor inattentive to their rights" have a pencil line drawn through them.[14] Tis certainly best to obliterate them. The less commitment the better.

"2. If we grant favor to the wines &c of Spain, Portugal and France will demand the same, & may create the equivalent, the former by laying duties on our fish & grain, the latter by a prohibition of our whale oils; the removal of which will be proposed as the equivalent." (AL, letterpress copy, Thomas Jefferson Papers, Library of Congress.)

Jefferson apparently sent this statement to Washington (AL, George Washington Papers, Library of Congress), and although a copy of this statement is in the Hamilton Papers, Library of Congress, no evidence has been found that this copy was sent to H by Jefferson.

Jefferson included the paragraphs numbered 1 and 2 in the above statement in the instructions which he sent to William Carmichael and William Short on March 18, 1792, and in the section relating to commerce which Washington sent to the Senate on March 7, 1792.

14. Jefferson had written in the draft: "Should the negociations on the subject of navigation & boundary assume at any time an unhopeful aspect, it may be proper that Spain should be given to understand that if they are discontinued, without coming to any agreement, the government of the U.S. cannot be responsible for the longer forbearance of their Western inhabitants, nor inattentive to their rights." He had crossed out the phrase "nor inattentive to their rights."

To George Washington

Treasury Department
March 1st. 1792.

The Secretary of the Treasury has the honor to submit to the President of the United States the draft of a Report on the subject of the Act concerning distilled Spirits.[1] There are one or two blanks in the draft, to the filling of which some additional examination & enquiry are requisite. The suggestions however to which they relate are true, as they stand, and the sense will be apparent. The Secretary sends the draft before they are filled to save time. He will wait upon the President on Monday for his commands respecting it.

LC, George Washington Papers, Library of Congress.
1. See "Report on the Difficulties in the Execution of the Act Laying Duties on Distilled Spirits," March 5, 1792.

To George Washington

Treasury Department
March 4th. 1792

The Secretary of the Treasury has the honor to inclose the List of appointments of Inspectors of the Revenue, which took place during the recess of the Senate, as well for ports as Surveys.[1] The President will recollect that the Joseph McDowell who was truly contemplated is *"the younger"* of Pleasant Garden, though described in the Commission & in the List as *"the Elder."* [2]

LC, George Washington Papers, Library of Congress.
1. This list consists of the names of the inspectors of surveys and the inspectors of ports which Washington submitted to the Senate for confirmation on March 6, 1792. This list is printed in *Executive Journal*, I, 102–05.
2. See H to Tobias Lear, February 17, 24, 1792.

To George Washington

[Philadelphia, March 4, 1792]

The Secretary of the Treasury has the honor to communicate to the President of the U: States certain resolutions of the Bank of the U: States, in answer to communications from the Treasury.[1] He will ask the President's orders on Monday. The first resolution will particularly require attention.

4th. March 1792.

LC, George Washington Papers, Library of Congress.
1. The reports and letters of the Bank of the United States to the Treasury Department have not been found. It is generally assumed that they were destroyed by the Treasury Department fire of 1814 or 1833. See Burton A. Konkle, *Thomas Willing and the First American Financial System* (Phila-

delphia, 1937), 151, and James O. Wettereau, "New Light on the First Bank of the United States," *Pennsylvania Magazine of History and Biography*, LXI (July, 1937), 265.

To Nathaniel Appleton

Treasury Department March 5th 1792

Sir

In mine of the 14th ultimo,[1] I instructed you to dispose of the draughts, remitted you by the Treasurer towards payment of the present quarters interest, upon either of the Banks of the united States or New York.

And as it will be necessary, lest adequate demands for bills upon those banks should not occur in time, to extend that instruction, with regard to the further disposition of the draughts; I now add, that you may supply the deficiencies, by directing such necessary sums as you shall not find negotiable upon the banks in season, to the bank of Massachusetts, and the collector of Boston;[2] [informing yourself previously of the sum in possession of each on account of the Government.][3]

I am, sir, Your obedt Servt   A Hamilton

Nathaniel Appleton Esqr
Commissioner of loans
Massachusetts

LS, University of Chicago Library.
1. Letter not found.
2. Benjamin Lincoln.
3. The words within brackets are in H's handwriting.

From William Ellery

Newport [Rhode Island] March 5, 1792. "I have received a Letter from the Assist. Secry of the Treasy.[1] in which he informs me that . . . two Thermometers will be forwarded . . . and mentions that it appears proper that you should be informed, in what cases I would find an Hydrostatic balance useful. . . .[2] I have written to the Surveyor of Pawcatuck[3] to send me his broken Thermometer, as soon as I receive I will transmit it by Post to the Treasy. The cases in which I would find an hydrostatic balance useful would be all cases in which I should suspect the gold coin offered in payment for duties and fees was counterfeit, or not of equal fineness, with the gold coins of the Nations specified in the 55 Sec: . . . of the Revenue Law.[4] Some pieces of coined gold of suspicious appearance have been offered to me, and I had no other way to ascertain their quality but by sending them to a person who is possessed of an hydrostatic balance; and gold cobbs[5] have been offered some of which had been received from the bank of Providence, and were manufactured in this town, where the others were made I could not tell. . . . I also received a letter of the 20th. of the last month from the Assist. Secry acknowledging the Receipt of the Bank of Providence for Seven Thousand Dollars, and a Letter from you Sir, of the 15th. of the same month[6] respecting the case of Capt. Elliot,[7] and directing that the attention of the Owners and Commanders of vessels must be drawn to the requisition of the manifest, as made by the Legislature. . . . It is probable that a quantity of sugars will be imported into this District in the course of two or three months. It is very disagreeable to the merchants here that the tare should be taken out of each 112 lb. imported by them, when in New york and Philadelphia it is taken out of each 100 lb. I wish that the mode of deducting the tare from all articles imported might be regulated and made uniform as soon as it can be conveniently done. . . ."[8]

LC, Newport Historical Society, Newport, Rhode Island.
   1. Tench Coxe.
   2. See Ellery to H, February 13, 1792.
   3. George Stillman.
   4. Ellery is referring to Section 56 of "An Act to provide more effectually for the collection of the duties imposed by law on goods, wares and merchandise imported into the United States, and on the tonnage of ships or vessels," which determined the rates at which foreign coin would be receivable in payment of customs charges (1 *Stat.* 173 [August 4, 1790]).
   5. This is an eighteenth-century designation for Spanish-American dollars, distinguishing them from those struck in Spain with greater care and precision.
   6. Letter not found.
   7. See Ellery to H, January 9, February 7, 1792.
   8. See "Treasury Department Circular to the Collectors of the Customs," May 13, 1791.
Ellery endorsed this letter "Ansrd Mr. 21." H's reply has not been found.

To Benjamin Lincoln

Treasury Department, March 5, 1792. "It is probable that Treasury draughts in favour of the commissioner of loans of New Hampshire [1] to the extent of 6000 Dollars will be directed to you, which I request you to pay, together with such sums as shall be presented to you in the like draughts by the Commissioner of Your state,[2] towards payment of the interest for the accruing quarter."

L[S], RG 36, Collector of Customs at Boston, Letters from the Treasury, 1790–1810, Vol. 2, National Archives; copy, RG 56, Letters to Collectors of Small Ports, "Set G," National Archives; copy, RG 56, Letters to the Collector at Boston, National Archives.
  1. William Gardner.
  2. Nathaniel Appleton was commissioner of loans for Massachusetts.

Report on the Difficulties in the Execution of the Act Laying Duties on Distilled Spirits [1]

[Philadelphia, March 5, 1792
Communicated on March 6, 1792] [2]

[To the Speaker of the House of Representatives]

In Obedience to the orders of the House of Representatives of the first & second days of November last, the first directing the Secre-

DS, RG 233, Original Reports of the Secretary of the Treasury, 1791–1792, National Archives.
  1. On January 9, 1790, H proposed to Congress a tax on spirits distilled in the United States in his "Report Relative to a Provision for the Support of Public Credit." He repeated this proposal in his "First Report on the Further Provision Necessary for Establishing Public Credit," December 13, 1790. The excise bill, after going through various stages of debate, conference, and compromise, reached the President on March 1, 1791, and on March 3, 1791, "An Act repealing, after the last day of June next, the duties heretofore laid upon Distilled Spirits imported from abroad, and laying others in their stead; and also upon Spirits distilled within the United States, and for appropriating the same" (1 *Stat.* 199–214) became law.
  In accordance with the provisions of this act, Washington on November 1, 1791, submitted to the Senate and House of Representatives a report on arrangements made "in respect to the subdivisions of the several districts, created by the said act, into surveys of inspection, the appointment of officers for the same, and the assignment of compensations" (*Journal of the House,* I, 445; *Executive Journal,* I, 87–88). See H to the Senate and the House of Repre-

tary of the Treasury to report to the House such information as he
may have obtained, respecting any difficulties which may have
occurred in the execution of the Act "repealing after the last day
of June next, the duties heretofore laid upon distilled spirits imported from abroad and laying others in their stead, and also upon
spirits distilled within the United States, and for appropriating the
same" [3] together with his opinion thereupon; the second directing
him to report to the House whether any, and what alterations in
favor of the spirits which shall be distilled from articles of the
growth or produce of the United States, or from foreign Articles,
within the same can, in his opinion, be made in the Act for laying
duties upon spirits distilled within the United States, consistently
with its main design, and with the maintenance of the public faith.
The said Secretary respectfully submits the following Report

From the several petitions and memorials which have been referred to the Secretary,[4] as well as from various representations
which have been made to him, it appears that objections have arisen
in different quarters against the above mentioned act; which have in
some instances embarrassed its execution, and inspired a desire of its
being repealed, in others have induced a wish that alterations may
be made in some of its provisions.

These objections have reference to a supposed tendency of the

---

sentatives, October 31, 1791. The President's message was considered by the
House in a two-day debate. On November 1, 1791, the House "*Ordered*, That
the Secretary of the Treasury be directed to report to this House, such information as he may have obtained respecting any difficulties which may
have occurred in the execution of the act 'repealing, after the last day of
June next, the duties heretofore laid upon distilled spirits imported from
abroad, and laying others in their stead; and also upon spirits distilled within
the United States, and for appropriating the same;' together with his opinion
thereupon" (*Journal of the House*, I, 446).

On November 2, 1791, the House "*Ordered*, That the Secretary of the
Treasury be directed to report to this House, whether any, and what, alterations in favor of the spirits which shall be distilled from articles of the growth
or produce of the United States, or from foreign articles within the same, can,
in his opinion, be made in the act for laying duties upon spirits distilled within
the United States, consistently with its main design, and with the maintenance
of the public faith" (*Journal of the House*, I, 446).

2. *Journal of the House*, I, 529.

3. 1 *Stat.* 199–214 (March 3, 1791).

4. Several petitions requesting either the repeal or the modification of the
act of March 3, 1791, had been referred by the House of Representatives to
H. See, for example, the petitions mentioned in the *Journal of the House*,
I, 453, 455, 458, 471.

act; 1st. to contravene the principles of liberty; 2ndy to injure morals; 3dly to oppress by heavy and excessive penalties; 4thly to injure industry and interfere with the business of distilling.

As to the supposed tendency of the Act to contravene the principles of liberty, the discussions of the subject which have had place in and out of the Legislature supercede the necessity of more than a few brief general observations

It is presumed that a revision of the point cannot in this respect weaken the convictions which originally dictated the law.

There can surely be nothing in the nature of an *internal duty* on a *consumable* commodity more incompatible with liberty, than in that of an external duty on a like commodity. A doctrine which asserts, that all duties of the former kind (usually denominated excises) are inconsistent with the genius of a free government, is too violent and too little reconcileable with the necessities of society to be true. It would tend to deprive the government of what is in most Countries a principal source of Revenue, and by narrowing the distribution of taxes, would serve to oppress particular kinds of industry. It would throw in the first instance an undue proportion of the public burthen on the merchant and on the landholder.

This is one of those cases in which names have an improper influence, and in which certain preposessions exclude a due attention to facts.

Accordingly the law under consideration is complained of though free from the features, which have served in other cases to render laws on the same subject exceptionable. And though the differences have been pointed out, they have not only been overlooked, but the very things, which have been studiously avoided in the formation of the law, are charged upon it, and that too from quarters where its operation would from circumstances have worn the least appearance of them.

It has been heretofore noticed, that the chief circumstances, which in certain excise-laws have given occasion to the charge of their being unfriendly to liberty, are not to be found in the act, which is the subject of this report; namely 1st. a summary and discretionary jurisdiction in the excise officers contrary to the course of the common law, and in abrigement of the right of trial by jury; and 2ndly. a general power in the same officers to search and inspect *indiscriminately* all the houses and buildings of the persons engaged in the business to which the tax relates.

As to the first particular, there is nothing in the act even to give colour to a charge of the kind against it, and accordingly it has not been brought. But as to the second, a very *different power* has been mistaken for it, and the Act is complained of as conferring that very power of indiscriminate search and inspection.

The fact nevertheless is otherwise. An officer, under the Act in question, can inspect or search no house or building, or even *apartment* of any house or building, which has not been *previously entered* and *marked* by the possessor as a place used for distilling or keeping spirits.

And even the power so qualified is only applicable to distilleries from foreign materials, and in cities towns and villages from domestic materials; that is only in cases in which the law contemplates that the business is carried on upon such a scale as effectually to seperate the *distillery* from the *dwelling* of the distiller. The distilleries scattered over the country, which form much the greatest part of the whole, are in no degree subject to discretionary inspection and search.

The true principle of the objection, which may be raised to a general discretionary power of inspection and search is, that the *domicil* or *dwelling* of a citizen ought to be free from vexations inquisition and intrusion.

This principle cannot apply to a case in which it is put in his own power to seperate the place of his *business* from the place of his *habitation*, and, by designating the former by visible public marks, to avoid all intermeddling with the latter.

A distillery seldom forms a part of the *dwelling* of its proprietor, and even where it does, it depends on him to direct and limit the power of visiting and search, by marking out the particular *apartments*, which are so employed.

But the requisition upon the distiller to set marks on the building or apartments which he makes use of in his business, is one of the topics of complaint against the law. Such marks are represented as a dishonorable badge. And thus a regulation, designed as much to conform with the feelings of the Citizen, as for the security of the revenue, is converted into matter of objection.

It is not easy to conceive what maxim of liberty is violated, by requiring persons, who carry on particular trades, which are made contributory to the revenue, to designate by public marks the places in which they are carried on. There can certainly be nothing more harmless, or less inconvenient, than such a regulation. The thing itself is frequently done by persons of various callings for the information of Customers; and why it should become a hardship or grievance, if required for a public purpose, can with difficulty be imagined.

The supposed tendency of the act to injure morals seems to have relation to the oaths, which are in a variety of cases required, and which are liable to the objection, that they give occasion to perjuries.

The necessity of requiring Oaths is whenever it occurs matter of regret. It is certainly desireable to avoid them as often and as far as possible. But it is more easy to desire than to find a substitute. The requiring of them is not peculiar to the Act in question. They are a common appendage of Revenue laws, and are among the usual guards of those laws, as they are of public and private rights in courts of justice. They constantly occur in jury trials, to which the Citizens of the United States are so much and so justly attached. The same objection in different degrees lies against them in both cases. Yet it is not perceivable how they can be dispensed with in either.

It is remarkable, that *both* the kinds of security to the revenue, which are to be found in the act, the oaths of parties, and the inspection of Officers, are objected to. If they are both to be abandoned, it is not easy to imagine what security there can be for any species of revenue, which is to be collected from articles of consumption.

If precautions of this nature are inconsistent with liberty, and immoral, as there are very few indirect taxes, which can be collected without them, the consequence must be, that the entire or almost entire weight of the public burthens must, in the first instance, fall upon fixed and visible property, houses and lands, a consequence which would be found in experiment productive of great injustice and inequality and ruinous to agriculture.

It has been suggested by some distillers, that both the topics of complaint, which have been mentioned, might be obviated by a fixed rate of duty, adjusted according to a ratio compounded of the capacity of each still and the number and capacities of the cisterns employed with it; but this and every similar method are objected to by other distillers as tending to great inequality, arising from un-equal supplies of the material at different times and at different places, from the different methods of distillation practiced by dif-ferent distillers, and from the different degrees of activity in the business which arise from capitals more or less adequate.

The result of an examination of this point appears to be, that every such mode in cases in which the business is carried on upon an extensive scale, would necessarily be attended with considerable inequalities; and upon the whole would be less satisfactory, than the plan which has been adopted.

It is proved by the fullest information, that, in regard to distil-leries, which are rated in the law, according to the capacity of each still, the alternative of paying according to the quantity actually distilled is viewed in many parts of the United States as essential to the equitable operation of the duty. And it is evident, that such an alternative could not be allowed, but upon the condition of the party, rendering upon oath an account of the quantity of Spirits distilled by him, without entirely defeating the duty.

As to the charge, that the penalties of the act are severe and oppressive, it is made in such general terms, and so absolutely with-out the specification of a single particular, that it is difficult to ima-gine where it points.

The Secretary however has carefully reviewed the provisions of the Act in this respect, and he is not able to discover any foundation for the charge.

The penalties it inflicts are in their nature the same with those which are common in revenue laws, and in their degree compara-tively moderate.

Pecuniary fines from fifty to five hundred dollars, and forfeiture of the article in respect to which there has been a failure to comply with the law, are the severest penalties inflicted upon delinquent parties, except in a very few cases: In two, a forfeiture of the value of the article is added to that of the article itself, and in some others, a forfeiture of the ship or vessel, and of the waggon or other instrument of conveyance, assistant in a breach of the law is likewise involved.

Penalties like these for wilful and fraudulent breaches of an important law, cannot truly be deemed either unusual or excessive. They are less than those which secure the laws of impost, and as moderate as can promise security to any object of revenue, which is capable of being evaded.

There appears to be but one provision in the law which admits of a question, whether the penalty prescribed may not partake of severity. It is that which inflicts the pains of paying on any person who shall be convicted of "wilfully taking a false oath or affirmation in any of the cases in which oaths or affirmations are required by the act."

Precedents in relation to this particular vary. In many of them the penalties are less severe, than for perjury in courts of justice; in others they are the same. The latter are generally of the latest date and seem to have been the result of experience.

The United States have in other cases pursued the same principle as in the law in question. And the practice is certainly founded on strong reasons.

1st. The additional security which it gives to the revenue cannot be doubted. Many who would risk pecuniary forfeitures and penalties would not encounter the more disgraceful punishment annexed to perjury.

2. There seems to be no solid distinction between one false oath in violation of law and right and another false oath in violation of law and right. A distinction in the punishments of different species of false swearing is calculated to beget false opinions concerning the sanctity of an oath; and by countenancing an impression that a violation of it is less heinous in the cases in which it is less punished, it tends to impair in the mind that scrupulous veneration for the obligation of an oath which ought always to prevail, and not only to facilitate a breach of it in the cases which the laws have marked with less odium, but to prepare the mind for committing the crime in other cases.

So far is the law under consideration from being chargeable with particular severity, that there are to be found in it marks of more than common attention to prevent its operating severely or oppressively.

The 43rd. Section of the act contains a special provision (and one which it is believed is not to be found in any law enacted in this country prior to the present constitution of the United States) by which forfeitures and penalties incurred without an intention of fraud or wilful negligence may be mitigated or remitted.

This mild and equitable provision is an effectual guard against suffering or inconvenience in consequence of undesigned transgressions of the law.

The 38th. section contains a provision in favor of persons, who though innocent may accidentally suffer by seizures of their property (as in the execution of the revenue laws sometimes unavoidably happens) which is perhaps entirely peculiar to the law under consideration. Where there has even been a *probable* cause of seizure, sufficient to acquit an officer, the Jury are to assess whatever damages may have accrued from any injury to the article seized, with an allowance for the detention of it at the rate of six per centum per annum of the value, which damages are to be paid out of the public Treasury.

There are other provisions of the act which mark the scrupulous attention of the government to protect the parties concerned from inconvenience and injury, and which conspire to vindicate the law from imputations of severity or oppression.

The supposed tendency of the Act to injure industry, and interfere with the business of distilling, is endeavored to be supported by some general and some special reasons; both having relation to the effect of the duty upon the manufacture.

Those of the first kind affirm generally, that duties on home manufactures are impolitic, because they tend to discourage them; that they are particularly so, when they are laid on articles manufactured from the produce of the country, because they have then the additional effect of injuring agriculture; that it is the general policy of nations to protect and promote their own manufactures; especially those which are wrought out of domestic materials; that the law in question interferes with this policy.

Observations of this kind admit of an easy answer. Duties on manufactures tend to discourage them or not, according to the circumstances under which they are laid, and are impolitic or not, according to the same circumstances. When a manufacture is in its infancy, it is impolitic to tax it; because the tax would be both unproductive, and would add to the difficulties, which naturally impede the first attempts to establish a new manufacture, so as to endanger its success.

But when a manufacture (as in the case of distilled Spirits in the United States) is arrived at maturity, it is as fit an article of taxation as any other. No good reason can be assigned, why the consumer of a domestic commodity should not contribute something to the public revenue, when the consumer of a foreign commodity contributes to it largely. And as a general rule it is not to be disputed, that duties on articles of consumption are paid by the consumers.

To the manufacture itself the duty is no injury, if an equal duty be laid on the rival foreign Article. And when a greater duty is laid upon the latter than upon the former, as in the present instance, the difference is a bounty on the domestic article, and operates as an encouragement of the manufacture. The manufacturer can afford to sell his fabric the cheaper, in proportion to that difference, and is so far enabled to undersell and supplant the dealer in the foreign article.

The principle of the objection would tend to confine all taxes to imported articles, and would deprive the government of resources which are indispensible to a due provision for the public safety and welfare; contrary to the plain intention of the constitution, which gives express power to employ those resources when necessary; a power which is found in all governments, and is essential to their efficiency, and even to their existence.

Duties on articles of internal production and manufacture form in every country the principal sources of Revenue. Those on imported articles can only be carried to a certain extent, without defeating their object; by operating either as prohibitions; or as bounties upon smuggling. They are moreover in some degree temporary; for as the growth of manufactures diminishes the quantum of duty on imports, the public revenue, ceasing to arise from that source, must be derived from articles which the national industry has substituted for those previously imported. If the government cannot then resort to internal means for the additional supplies, which the exigencies of every nation call for, it will be unable to perform its duty or even to preserve its existence. The community must be unprotected, and the social compact be dissolved.

For the same reasons, that a duty ought not to be laid on an article manufactured out of the produce of the country (which is the point most insisted upon) it ought not to be laid upon the produce itself, nor consequently upon the land, which is the instrument of that produce; because taxes are laid upon *land* as the *fund* out of which the *income* of the proprietor is drawn, or, in other words, *on account of its produce*. There ought, therefore, on the principle of the objection, to be neither taxes on land nor on the produce of land, nor on articles manufactured from that produce. And if a nation should be in a condition to supply itself, with its own manufactures, there could then be very little or no revenue, of course there must be a want of the essential means of national justice and national security.

Positions like these, however well meant by those who urge them, refute themselves, because they tend to the dissolution of government, by rendering it incapable of providing for the objects for which it is instituted.

However true the allegation that it is and ought to be the prevailing policy of nations to cherish their own manufactures, it is equally true that nations in general lay duties for the purpose of revenue on their own manufactures; and it is obvious to a demonstration that it may be done without injury to them. The most successfull nations in manufactures have drawn the largest revenues from the most useful of them. It merits particular attention, that ardent Spirits are an article, which has been generally deemed and made use of, as one of the fittest objects of revenue, and to an extent in other countries, which bears no comparison with what had been done in the United States.

The special reasons alluded to are of different kinds.

I. It is said, that the act in question by laying a smaller *additional* duty on foreign spirits, than the duty on home made spirits, has a tendency to discourage the manufacture of the latter.

This objection merits consideration, and as far as it may appear to have foundation ought to be obviated.

The point however seems not to have been viewed in all respects in a correct light.

Before the present constitution of the United States began to operate, the regulations of the different states, respecting distilled spirits were very dissimular. In some of them duties were laid on foreign spirits only, in others, on domestic as well as foreign. The absolute duty in the former instances, and the difference of duty in the latter, was upon an average considerably less than the present difference in the duties on foreign and home made spirits. If to this be added the effect of the uniform operation of the existing duties throughout the United States, it is easy to infer that the situation of our own distilleries is in the main much better, as far as they are affected by the laws, than it was previous to the passing of any act of the United States upon the subject. They have therefore upon the whole gained materially under the system, which has been pursued by the national Government.

The first law of the United States on this head laid a duty of no more than eight cents per gallon on those of Jamaica proof.[5] The second encreased the duty on foreign spirits to twelve cents per gallon of the lowest proof, and by certain gradations to fifteen cents per gallon of Jamaica proof.[6] The last act places the duty at twenty cents per gallon of the lowest proof, and extends it by the like gradations to twenty five cents per Gallon of Jamaica proof, laying also a duty of eleven Cents per Gallon on home made spirits distilled from foreign materials of the lowest proof, with a like gradual extension to fifteen cents per gallon of Jamaica proof; and a duty of nine cents per gallon on home made spirits distilled from domestic materials of the lowest proof, with the like gradual extension to thirteen cents per gallon of Jamaica proof.[7]

If the transition had been immediate from the first to the last law,

5. See "An Act for laying a Duty on Goods, Wares, and Merchandises imported into the United States" (1 Stat. 24–27 [July 4, 1789]). H's figure is incorrect. According to the law, the following duties were to be laid on distilled spirits: "On all distilled spirits of Jamaica proof, imported from any kingdom or country whatsoever, per gallon, ten cents. On all other distilled spirits, per gallon, eight cents" (1 Stat. 25).
6. See Section 1 of "An Act making further provision for the payment of the debts of the United States" (1 Stat. 180 [August 10, 1790]).
7. See Sections 1, 14, and 15 of "An Act repealing, after the last day of June next, the duties heretofore laid upon Distilled Spirits imported from abroad, and laying others in their stead; and also upon Spirits distilled within the United States, and for appropriating the same" (1 Stat. 199, 202–03 [March 3, 1791]).

it could not have failed to have been considered as a change in favor of our own distilleries, as far as the rate of duty is concerned. The mean duty on *foreign Spirits* by the first law was nine cents, by the last the mean *extra* duty on foreign spirits is in fact about eleven cents, as it regards spirits distilled from *foreign* materials, and about thirteen, as it regards spirits distilled from *domestic* materials. In making this computation it is to be adverted to that the four first degrees of proof mentioned in the law correspond with the different kinds of Spirits usually imported, while the generality of those made in the United States are of the lowest class of proof.

Spirits from domestic materials derived a double advantage from the last law, that is, from the encreased rate of duty on foreign imported Spirits, & from a higher rate of duty on home made spirits of foreign materials.

But the intervention of the second law has served to produce in some places a different impression of the business, than would have happened without it. By a considerable addition to the duties on foreign Spirits, without laying any thing on those of home manufacture, it has served to give to the last law the appearance of taking away a part of the advantages previously secured to the domestic distilleries. It seems to have been over looked, that the second act ought in reality to be viewed only as an intermediate step to the arrangement finally contemplated by the Legislature; and that as part of a system, it has upon the whole operated in favour of the national distilleries. The thing to be considered is the substantial existing difference in favor of the home manufacture, as the law now stands.

The advantage, indeed, to the distillation of spirits from the produce of the country arising from the difference between the duties on spirits distilled from foreign and those distilled from domestic materials, is exclusively the work of the last act, and is an advantage which has not been properly appreciated by those distillers of spirits from home produce, who have complained of the law, as hurtfull to their manufacture.

Causes entirely foreign to the law itself have also assisted in producing misapprehension. The approximation of the price of home made spirits to that of foreign spirits, which has of late taken place, and which is attributed to the operation of the Act in question is in a great degree owing to the circumstances, which have tended to raise the price of Molasses in the West India market, and to an extra importation of foreign spirits prior to the first of July last, to avoid the payment of the additional duty which then took place.[8]

It is stated in the petition from salem,[9] that previous to the last act the price of domestic to foreign spirits was as 1/9 to 3/4, of the money of Massachusetts per Gallon, & that since that act it has become as 3/3 to 4/2.

It is evident that a rise from 1/9 to 3/3 per gallon, which would be equal to 20 cents, is not to be attributed wholly to a duty of eleven cents. Indeed if there were a concurrence of no other cause, the inference would be very different from that intended to be drawn from the fact, for it would evince a profit gained to the distiller of more than 80 ℔ Cent [10] on the duty.

It is however meant to be understood, that this approximation of prices occasions a greater importation and consumption of foreign, and a less consumption of domestic spirits than formerly. How far this may or may not be the case, the Secretary is not now able to say with precision; but no facts have come under his notice officially, which serve to authenticate the suggestion. And it must be considered as possible that representations of this kind are rather the effect of apprehension than of experience. It would even be not unnatural, that a considerable enhancement of the price of the foreign article should have led to a greater consumption of the domestic article, as the cheapest of the two, though dearer itself than formerly.

But while there is ground to believe that the suggestions which have been made on this point are in many respects inaccurate and misconceived, there are known circumstances; which seem to render adviseable, some greater difference between the duties on foreign

8. July 1, 1791, was the effective date for duties imposed by "An Act repealing, after the last day of June next, the duties heretofore laid upon Distilled Spirits imported from abroad, and laying others in their stead; and also upon Spirits distilled within the United States, and for appropriating the same" (1 Stat. 199).

9. On November 16, 1791, the House of Representatives received "a petition of the distillers of spirits in the town of Salem, in the State of Massachusetts . . . praying a reduction of duties . . . on spirits distilled within the United States" (Journal of the House, I, 455).

10. The words "more than 80 ℔ Cent" are in H's handwriting.

and on home made spirits. These circumstances have been noticed in the report of the Secretary on the subject of Manufactures,[11] and an alteration has been proposed by laying two cents in addition upon imported Spirits of the lowest proof, with a proportional increase on the higher proofs, and by deducting one cent from the duty on the lowest proof of homemade spirits, with a proportional diminution in respect to the higher proofs.

This alteration would bring the proportion of the duties nearly to the standard, which the petitioner Hendrick Doyer,[12] who appears likely to be well informed on the subject, represents as the proper one to enable the distillation of Geneva to be carried on with the same advantage as before the passing of the Act. He observes that the duty on home made Geneva being 9 cents the additional duty on foreign ought to have been twelve cents. By the alteration proposed the proportion will be as 10 to 8 which is little different from that of 12 to 9.

It is worthy of remark, that the same petitioner states, that previous to the passing of the act, of which he complains, he "could sell his Geneva 16 ¼ ℔ Ct under the price of Holland Geneva," but that "he cannot do it at present, and in future lower than 14 ℔ Cent." If, as he also states, the quality of his Geneva be equal to that of Holland, and if his meaning be, as it appears to be, that he can now afford to sell his Geneva lower by 14 ℔ Cent than the Geneva of Holland, it will follow that the manufacture of that article is in a very thriving train, even under the present rate of duties. For a difference of 14 ℔ Ct. in the price is capable of giving a decided preference to the sale of the domestic article.

II. It is objected that the duty, by being laid in the first instance upon the distiller, instead of the consumer, makes a larger capital necessary to carry on the business, and in this country, where capitals are not large, puts the national distillers under disadvantages.

11. See "Report on the Subject of Manufactures," December 5, 1791.

12. On November 24, 1791, "A petition of Kendrick Doyer, Geneva distiller, in the city of New York, was presented to the House and read, praying that the act, passed at the last session, imposing a duty on distilled spirits, may be so modified and amended, that the duty on Geneva, imported from abroad, may be augmented, and the duty on the said article, distilled within the United States, reduced.

"*Ordered,* That the said petition be referred to the Secretary of the Treasury for his information." (*Journal of the House,* I, 461.)

But this inconvenience, as far as it has foundation, in the state of things, is essentially obviated by the credits given. Where the duty is payable upon the quantity distilled, a credit is allowed, which cannot be less than six and may extend to nine months. Where the duty is charged on the capacity of the still, it is payable half yearly. Sufficient time is therefore allowed to raise the duty from the sale of the article, which supercedes the necessity of a greater capital. It is well known, that the article is one usually sold for Cash or at short credit. If these observations are not applicable to distilleries in the interior country, the same may be said in a great degree of the objection itself. The cause of the business, in that quarter, renders a considerable capital less necessary than elsewhere. The produce of the distiller's own farm, or of the neighboring farms brought to be distilled upon shares or compensations in the article itself, constitute the chief business of the distilleries in the remote parts of the country. In the comparatively few instances, in which they may be prosecuted as a regular business, upon a large scale, by force of capital, the observations which have been made will substantially apply.

The collection of the duty from the distiller has, on the other hand, several advantages. It contributes to equality, by charging the article in the first stage of its progress, which diffuses the duty among all classes alike. It the better secures the collection of the Revenue, by confining the responsibility to a smaller number of persons and simplifying the process. And it avoids the necessity of so great a number of Officers as would be required in a more diffuse system of collection, operating immediately upon purchasers and consumers. Besides, that the latter plan would transfer, whatever inconveniencies may be incident to the collection, from a smaller to a greater number of persons.

III. It is alleged that the inspection of the officers is injurious to the business of distilling, by laying open its secrets or mysteries.

Different distillers there is no doubt, practice, in certain respects, different methods in the course of their business and have different degrees of Skill. But it may well be doubted whether in a business so old and so much diffused as that of the distillation of Spirits, there are at this day secrets of consequence to the possessors.

There will at least be no hazard in taking it for granted, that none such exist in regard to the distillation of Rum from molasses or sugar, or of the spirits from grain usually called whiskey, or of brandies from the fruits of this country. The cases in which the allegations are made with most colour, apply to Geneva, and perhaps to certain cordials.

It is probable, that the course of the business might and would always be such, as in fact to involve no inconvenience on this score. But as the contrary is affirmed, and as it is desireable to obviate complaint as far as it can be done, consistently with essential principles and objects, it may not be unadviseable to attempt a remedy.

It is to be presumed, that if any secrets exist, they relate to a primary process, particularly the mixture of the ingredients; this, it is supposeable, cannot take a greater time each day, than two hours. If therefore, the officers of inspection were enjoined to forbear their visits to the part of the distillery commonly made use of for such process, during a space not exceeding two hours each day to be notified by the distiller, there is ground to conclude that it would obviate the objection.

IV. The regulations for marking of Casks and vessels, as well as houses and buildings, also furnish matter of complaint.

This complaint as it regards houses and buildings has been already adverted to: But there is a light in which it is made that has not yet been taken notice of.

It is said that the requiring the doors of the apartments as well as the outer door of each building to be marked, imposes unnecessary trouble.

When it is considered how little trouble or expence attends the execution of this provision, in the first instance, and that the marks once set will endure for a great length of time, the objection to it appears to be without weight.

But the provision, as it relates to the apartments of buildings, has for its immediate object the convenience of the distillers themselves. It is calculated to avoid the very evil of an indiscriminate search of their houses and buildings, by enabling them to designate the *particular apartments*, which are employed for the purposes of their business, and to secure all others from inspection and visitation.

The complaint, as it respects the marking of casks and vessels, has somewhat more foundation. It is represented (and upon careful enquiry appears to be true) that through long established prejudice, home made spirits of *equal quality* with foreign, if known to be home made, will not command an equal price. This particularly applies to Geneva.

If the want of a distinction between foreign and home made spirits were an occasion of fraud upon consumers, by imposing a worse for a better commodity, it would be a reason for continuing it, but as far as such a distinction gives operation to a mere prejudice, favorable to a foreign and injurious to a domestic manufacture, it furnishes a reason for abolishing it.

Though time might be expected to remove the prejudice, the progress of the domestic manufacture, in the interval, might be materially checked.

It appears therefore expedient to remove this ground of complaint by authorising the same marks and certificates, both for foreign and for home made Geneva.

Perhaps indeed it may not be unadvisable to vest somewhere a discretionary power to regulate the forms of Certificates, which are to accompany and the particular marks which are to be set upon Casks and vessels containing spirits, generally, as may be found convenient in practice.

Another source of objection with regard to the marking of Casks is, that there is a general prohibition against defacing, or altering the marks, and a penalty upon doing it, which prevents the using of the same Casks more than once, and occasions waste, loss and embarrassment.

It is conceived, that this prohibition does not extend to the effacing of old marks and placing of new ones by the officers of the revenue, or in their presence and by their authority. But as real inconveniencies would attend a contrary construction, and there is some room for question, it appears desireable that all doubt should be removed, by an explicit provision to enable the officer to efface Old marks and substitute new ones, when casks have been emptied of their former contents, and are wanted for new use.

V. The requisition to keep an account from day to day of the quantity of spirits distilled is represented both as a hardship and impossible to be complied with.

But the Secretary is unable to perceive that it can justly be viewed either in the one or in the other light. The trouble of setting down in the evening the work of the day in a book prepared for and furnished to the party must be inconsiderable, and the doing of it would even conduce to accuracy in business.

The idea of impracticability must have arisen from some misconception. It seems to involve a supposition that something is required different from the truth of the fact. Spirits distilled are usually distinguished into high wines, proof spirits and low wines. It is certainly possible to express each day the quantity of each kind produced, and where one kind is converted into another to explain it by brief notes, shewing in proper columns the results in those kinds of spirits which are ultimately prepared for sale.

A revision is now making of the forms at first transmitted, and it is not doubted that it will be easy to obviate the objection of impracticability.

On full reflection the Secretary is of opinion, that the requisition in this respect is a reasonable one, and that it is of importance to the due collection of the revenue, especially in those cases, where, by the alternative allowed in favour of Country distilleries, the oath of a party is the only evidence of the quantity produced. It is useful in every such case to give the utmost possible *precision* to the object which is to be attested.

VI. It is alleged as a hardship, that distillers are held responsible for the duties on spirits which are exported, 'till certain things difficult to be performed are done, in order to entitle the exporter to the drawback.

This is a misapprehension. The drawback is at all events to be paid in six months, which is as early as the duty can become payable, and frequently earlier than it does become payable. And the government relies on the bond of the exporter for a fulfilment of the conditions upon which the drawback is allowed.

An explanation to the several Collectors of this point, which has taken place since the complaint appeared, will have removed the cause of it.

The same explanation will obviate another objection founded on the supposition that the bond of the distiller and that of the exporter are for a like purpose. The latter is merely to secure the landing of the goods in a foreign Country, and will often continue depending after every thing relative to duty and drawback has been liquidated and finished.

VII. It is an article of complaint that no drawback is allowed in case of Shipwreck when spirits are sent from one port to another in the United States.

There does not occur any objection to a provision for making an allowance of that kind, which would tend to alleviate misfortune and give satisfaction.

VIII. The necessity of twenty four hours notice, in order to the benefit of drawback on the exportation of Spirits, and the prohibition to remove them from a distillery after sunset, except in the presence of an officer, are represented as embarrassments to business.

The length of notice required appears greater than is necessary. It is not perceived, that any inconvenience would arise, from reducing the time to six hours.

But it is not conceived to be necessary or expedient to make an alteration in the last mentioned particular. The prohibition is of real consequence to the security of the revenue. The course of business will readily adapt itself to it, and the presence of an officer in extraordinary cases will afford due accomodation.

IX. It is stated as a hardship, that there is no allowance for leakage and wastage in the case of spirits shipped from one state to another.

The law for the collection of the duties on imports and tonnage allows two per Cent for leakage on spirits imported. A similar allowance on home made spirits at the distillery, does not appear less proper.

X. It is mentioned as a grievance, that distillers are required to give bond *with surety* for the amount of the duties, and that the sufficiency of the surety is made to depend on the discretion of the chief officer of inspection.

The requiring of sureties can be no more a hardship on distillers than on importing merchants and every other person to whom the public afford a credit. It is a natural consequence of the credit allowed; and a very reasonable condition of the indulgence, which without this precaution might be imprudent, and injurious to the United States.

The party has his option to avoid it by prompt payment of the duty and is even entitled to an abatement, which may be considered as a premium if he elects to do so.

As to the second point, if sureties are to be given, there must be some person on the part of the government to judge of their sufficiency, otherwise the thing itself would be nugatory, and the discretion cannot be vested more conveniently for the party than in the chief officer of inspection for the survey.

A view has now been taken of most, if not all, the objections of a general nature, which have appeared.

Some few of a local complexion remain to be attended to.

The representation signed Edward Cook Chairman, as on behalf of the four most western counties of Pennsylvania,[13] states, that the distance of that part of the country from a market for its produce leads to a necessity of distilling the grain, which is raised, as a principal dependance of its inhabitants; which Circumstance and the scarcity of cash combine to render the tax in question unequal, oppressive, and particularly distressing to them.

As to the circumstance of equality, it may safely be affirmed to be impracticable to devise a tax which shall operate with exact equality upon every part of the community. Local & other circumstances will inevitably create disparities more or less great.

Taxes on consumable articles have upon the whole better pretentions to equality than any other. If some of them fall more heavily on particular parts of the community, others of them are chiefly borne by other parts. And the result is an equalization of the burthen as far as is attainable. Of this class of taxes it is not easy to conceive

13. Cook was chairman of a meeting of representatives of the Pennsylvania counties of Washington, Westmoreland, Fayette, and Alleghany which convened at Pittsburgh on September 7, 1791. At the meeting several resolutions critical of the financial policies of the Federal Government were agreed upon and it was decided to send a representation to Congress embodying these objections. The resolutions do not, however, contain any reference to the problems of grain transport or to a shortage of cash which are mentioned by H.

On November 22, 1791, the House of Representatives received and referred to H "A memorial of the committee of the counties of Washington, Westmoreland, Fayette, and Alleghany, in the State of Pennsylvania . . . stating their objections to an act, passed at the last session, imposing a duty on spirits distilled within the United States, and praying that the same may be repealed" (*Journal of the House*, I, 458).

one which can operate with greater equality than a tax on distilled Spirits. There appears to be no article, as far as the information of the Secretary goes, which is an object of more equal consumption throughout the United States.

In particular districts a greater use of cyder may occasion a smaller consumption of spirits; but it will not be found on a close examination that it makes a material difference. A greater or less use of Ardent spirits, as far as it exists, seems to depend more on relative habits of sobriety or intemperance than on any other cause.

As far as habits of less moderation, in the use of distilled spirits, should produce inequality any where, it would certainly not be a reason with the legislature either to repeal or lessen a tax, which by rendering the article dearer, might tend to restrain too free an indulgence of such habits.

It is certainly not obvious how this tax can operate particularly unequally upon the part of the country in question. As a general rule it is a true one, that duties on articles of consumption fall on the consumers, by being added to the price of the commodity. This is illustrated in the present instance by facts. Previous to the law laying a duty on home made spirits the price of whiskey was about 38 Cents it is now about 56 Cents.[14] Other causes may have contributed in some degree to this effect, but it is evidently to be ascribed chiefly to the duty.

Unless, therefore, the inhabitants of the counties, which have been mentioned are greater consumers of spirits, than those of other parts of the Country, they cannot pay a greater proportion of the tax. If they are, it is their interest to become less so. It depends on themselves by diminishing the consumption to restore equality.

The argument, that they are obliged to convert their grain into spirits in order to transportation to distant markets, does not prove the point alleged. The duty on all they send to those markets will be paid by the purchasers. They will still pay only upon their own consumption.

As far as an advance is laid upon the duty, or as far as the difference of duty between whiskey and other spirits tends to favour a greater consumption of the latter, they as greater manufacturers of

14. The words "38 Cents" and "56 Cents" are in the handwriting of H.

the article, supposing this fact to be as stated, will be proportionably benefitted.

The duty on home made spirits from domestic materials, if paid by the gallon, is 9 cents. From the communications which have been received, since the passing of the act, it appears, that paying the rate annexed to the capacity of the Still, and using great diligence, the duty may be in fact reduced to six cents per Gallon. Let the average be taken at $7\frac{1}{2}$ cents which is probably higher than is really paid.

Generally speaking, then, for every gallon of whiskey which is consumed, the consumer may be supposed to pay [15] $7\frac{1}{2}$ cents; but for every gallon of spirits distilled from foreign materials the consumer pays at least eleven cents, and for every gallon of foreign spirits at least twenty cents. The consumer therefore of foreign spirits pays nearly three times the duty, and the consumer of home made spirits from foreign materials, nearly 50 ₩Cent more duty, on the same quantity, than the consumer of spirits from domestic materials, exclusive of the greater price in both cases, which is an additional charge upon each of the two first mentioned classes of consumers.

When it is considered that $\frac{8}{21}$ parts of the whole quantity of spirits consumed in the United States are foreign, and $\frac{7}{21}$ parts are of foreign materials, and that the inhabitants of the atlantic and midland counties are the principal consumers of these more highly taxed articles, it cannot be inferred, that the tax under consideration bears particularly hard on the inhabitants of the western country.

This may serve as an exemplification of a general proposition of material consequence namely [16] that, if the former descriptions of citizens are able from situation to obtain more for their produce than the latter, they contribute proportionally more to the revenue. Numerous other examples in confirmation of this might be adduced.

As to the circumstance of scarcity of money, as far as it can be supposed to have foundation, it is as much an objection to any other tax as to the one in question. The weight of the tax is not certainly such as to involve any peculiar difficulty. It is impossible to conceive that nine cents per gallon on distilled spirits, which is stating it at the highest, can from the magnitude of the Tax, distress any part of the

15. The words "to pay" are in the handwriting of H.
16. The word "namely" is in the handwriting of H.

Country, which has an ability to pay taxes at all, enjoying too the unexampled advantage of a total exemption from taxes on houses lands or stock.

The population of the United states being about 4.000.000 of persons and the quantity of spirits annually consumed between ten & eleven millions of gallons, the yearly proportion to each family, if consisting of six persons, which is a full ratio, would be about sixteen gallons, the duty upon which would be less than *one dollar and a half*. The citizen who is able to maintain a family and who is the owner or occupier of a farm, cannot feel any inconvenience from so light a contribution, and the industrious poor, whether artisans or labourers are usually allowed spirits or an equivalent in addition to their wages.

The Secretary has no evidence to satisfy his mind, that a real scarcity of money will be found on experiment a serious impediment to the payment of the tax any where. In the quarter, where this complaint has particularly prevailed, the expenditures for the defence of the Frontier would seem alone sufficient to obviate it. To this, it is answered, that the contractors for the supply of the Army operate with goods and not with money: But this still tends to keep at home whatever money finds its way there. Nor is it a fact, if the information of the Secretary be not materially erroneous, that the purchases of the contractors of flour, meat &c are *wholly* with goods. But if they were the Secretary can aver, that more money has in the course of the last year been sent into the western country from the Treasury, in specie & Bank bills which answer the same purpose for the pay of the troops and Militia and for quarter masters supplies than the whole amount of the tax in the four western counties of Pennsylvania and the district of Kentucky is likely to equal in four or five years. Similar remittances are likely to be made in future.

Hence the government itself furnishes and in all probability will continue to furnish the means of paying its own demands, with a surplus which will sensibly foster the industry of the parties concerned, if they avail themselves of it under the guidance of a spirit of œconomy and exertion.

Whether there be no part of the United States, in which the objection of want of money may truly exist, in a degree to render the payment of the duty seriously distressing to the inhabitants, the

Secretary is not able to pronounce. He can only express his own doubt of the fact, and refer the matter to such information as the members of any district so situated may have it in their power to offer to the legislative body.

Should the case appear to exist, it would involve the necessity of a measure in the abstract very ineligible, that is the receipt of the duty in the article itself.

If an alternative of this sort were to be allowed, it would be proper to make it the duty of the party paying, *to deliver the article at the place in each county* where the office of Inspection is kept, and to regulate the price according to such a standard, as would induce a preference of paying in Cash except from a real impracticability of obtaining it.

In regard to the petition from the district of Kentucky,[17] after what has been said with reference to other applications, it can only be necessary to observe that the exemption which is sought by that petition is rendered impracticable by an express provision of the Constitution, which declares, that "all duties, imposts and excises shall be uniform throughout the United States."

In the course of the foregoing examination of the objections which have been made to the law, some alterations have been submitted for the purpose of removing a part of them. The Secretary will now proceed to submit such further alterations as appear to him adviseable, arising either from the suggestions of the officers of the revenue or from his own ref[l]exions.

I. It appears expedient to alter the distinction respecting distilleries from domestic materials in cities, towns and villages, so as to confine it to one or more stills worked at the same distillery, the capacity or capacities of which together do not fall short of four hundred [18] gallons.

The effectual execution of the present provisions respecting distilleries from home materials in cities, towns and villages would occasion an inconvenient multiplication of officers, and would in too great a degree exhaust the product of the duty in the expence of

17. On November 16, 1791, the House of Representatives received "a petition of sundry inhabitants of the District of Kentucky, praying a suspension of the said [excise] act within the said District, until a free navigation of the river Mississippi shall be obtained" (*Journal of the House*, I, 455).

18. The words "four hundred" are in the handwriting of H.

collection. It is also probable that the alteration suggested would also conduce to public satisfaction.

II. The present provisions concerning the entering of stills are found by experience not to be adequate, and in some instances not convenient.

It appears adviseable, that there shall be one office of inspection for each county, with authority to the supervisor to establish more than one, if he shall judge it necessary for the accomodation of the inhabitants; and that every distiller or person having or keeping a still shall be required to make entry of the same at some office of inspection for the county within a certain determinate period in each year. It will be proper also to enjoin upon every person, who residing within the county shall procure a still, or who removing into a County, shall bring into it a still, within twenty days after such procuring or removal, and before he or she begins to use the still, to make entry at the office of inspection. Every entry besides describing the still, should specify in whose possession it is, and the purpose for which it is intended, as whether for sale or for use in distilling; and in the case of removal of the person from another place into the county, shall specify the place from which the still shall have been brought. A forfeiture of the still ought in every case in which an entry is required to attend an omission to enter.

This regulation by simplifying the business of entering stills, would render it easier to comprehend and comply with what is required, would furnish the officers with a better rule for ascertaining delinquencies, and, by avoiding to them a considerable degree of unnecessary trouble will facilitate the retaining of proper characters in the offices of Collectors.

III. It is represented that difficulties have in some instances arisen concerning the persons responsible for the duty. The apparent, not being always the real proprietor, an opportunity for collusion is afforded; and without collusion the uncertainty is stated as a source of embarrassment.

It also sometimes happens, that certain itinerant persons without property, complying with the preliminary requisitions of the law as to entry &c. erect and work stills for a time, and before a half yearly period of payment arrives remove and evade the duty.

It would tend to remedy these inconveniencies, if possessors and proprietors of stills were made jointly & severally liable, and if the duty were made a *specific lien* on the still itself, if also the proprietor of the land, upon which any still may be worked should be made answerable for the duty, except where it is worked by a lawful and bona fide tenant of the land of an estate not less than for a term of one year, or unless such proprietor can make it appear, that the possessor of the still was during the whole time without his privity or connivance an intruder or trespasser on the land; and if in the last place any distiller about to remove from the division in which he is, should be required previous to such removal to pay the tax for the year, deducting any prior payments, or give bond with approved surety, conditioned for the payment of the full sum for which he or she should be legally accountable to the end of the year, to the collector of the division to which the removal shall be, rendering proof thereof under the hand of the said Collector, within six months after the expiration of the year.

As well with a view to the forfeiture of the stills for non entry, as to give effect to a *specific lien* of the duty (if either or both of these provisions should be deemed elegible) it will be necessary to enjoin it upon the officers of the revenue to indentify by proper marks the several stills which shall have been entered with them.

IV. The exemptions granted to stills of the capacity of fifty gallons and under, by the 36th. section of the law appear from experience to require revision. Tending to produce inequality, as well as to frustrate the revenue, they have excited complaint. It appears at least adviseable, that the obligation to enter, as connected with that of *paying duty*, should extend to stills of all dimensions, and that it should be enforced in every case by the same penalty.

V. The 28th section of the Act makes provision for the seizure of spirits unaccompanied with marks and certificates in the cases in which they are required; but as they are required only in certain cases and there is no method of distinguishing the spirits, in respect to which they are necessary, from those in respect to which they are not necessary, the provision becomes nugatory, because an attempt to enforce it would be oppressive. Hence not only a great security for the due execution of the law is lost, but seizures very distressing to unoffending individuals must happen notwithstanding great precaution to avoid them.[19]

19. The word "them" is in the handwriting of H.

It would be, in the opinion of the Secretary of great importance to provide, that all spirits whatsoever, in casks or vessels of the capacity of twenty gallons and upwards should be marked and certified, on pain of seizure and forfeiture, making it the duty of the Officers to furnish the requisite certificates *gratis* to distillers and dealers in all cases, in which the law shall have been complied with.

In those cases in which an occasion at recurrence to the officers for certificates might be inconvenient, blanks may be furnished to be accounted for. And it may be left to the parties themselves in the like cases to mark their own casks or vessels in some simple manner to be defined in the law. These cases may be designated generally. They will principally relate to dealers, who in the course of their business draw off spirits from larger to smaller casks, and to distillers who pay according to the capacities of their stills.

As a part of a regulation of this sort it will be necessary to require, that within a certain period, sufficiently long to admit of time to know and comply with the provision, entry shall be made, by all dealers and distillers, of all spirits in their respective possessions, which shall not have been previously marked and certified according to law, in order that they may be marked and certified as old stock.

The regulations here proposed though productive of some trouble and inconvenience in the outset, will be afterwards a security both to individuals and to the revenue.

VI. At present spirits may not be imported from abroad in casks of less capacity than fifty gallons. The size of these casks is smaller than is desireable, so far as the security of the revenue is concerned, and there has not occured any good objection to confining the importation to larger casks, that is to say, to casks of not less than ninety gallons. Certainly as far as respects rum from the West Indies it may be done without inconvenience, being conformable to the general course of business. The result of examination is that the exception as to this particular in favor of Gin may be abolished. Should any alteration on this subject take place it ought not to begin to operate 'till after the expiration of a year.

VII. There is ground to suppose, that the allowance of drawback without any limitation as to quantity has been abused. It is submitted that none be made on any less quantity than one hundred and fifty gallons.

VIII. There is danger that facility may be given to illicit importations, by making use of casks which have been once regularly marked, and the certificates which have been issued with them to cover other spirits than those originally contained in such casks. Appearances which countenance suspicion on this point have been the subjects of representation from several quarters.

The danger may be obviated by prohibiting the importation in such marked casks, on pain of forfeiture, both of the Spirits and of any ship or vessel in which they may be brought. A prohibition of this sort does not appear liable to any good objection.

IX. The duty of sixty cents per gallon of the capacity of a Still was founded upon a computation, that a still of any given dimensions worked *four* months in the year, which is the usual period of country distillation, would yield a quantity of spirits which at the rate of nine cents per gallon, would correspond with sixty cents per gallon of the capacity of the still. It will deserve consideration, whether it will not be expedient to give an option to country distillers, at the annual entry of their stills, to take out a license for any portion of the year, which they may respectively think fit, and to pay at the rate of 12½ cents, per gallon of the capacity, per month, during such period. This to stand in lieu of the alternative of paying by the gallon distilled. It would obviate in this case the necessity of accounting upon oath, and would leave it in the power of each distiller to cover the precise time he meant to work his still with a license and to pay for that time only. A strict prohibition to distill at any other time, than that for which the license was given, would be of course necessary to accompany the regulation as far as regarded any such licensed distiller.

The only remaining points which have occurred as proper to be submitted to the consideration of the Legislature respects the officers of the revenue.

It is represented, that in some instances from the ill humour of individuals, the officers have experienced much embarrassment, in respect to the filling of stills with water, to ascertain their capacity, which upon examination is found the most simple and practicable mode. The proprietors have in some instances not only refused to aid the officers, but have even put out of their way the means by which the filling might be conveniently accomplished.

It would conduce to the easy execution of the law, and to the very important purpose of retaining and procuring respectable characters as Collectors, if the proprietors and possessors of stills were required to aid them in the execution of this part of their duty, or to pay a certain sum as a compensation for the doing of it.

The limits assigned in the law respecting compensations are found in practice essentially inadequate to the object.

This is so far the case, that it becomes the duty of the Secretary to state, that greater latitude in this particular is *indispensible to the effectual execution of the law.*

In the most productive *divisions* the commissions of the Collectors afford but a moderate compensation. In the greatest part of *them* the compensation is glaringly disproportioned to the service, in many of them it falls materially short of the expence of the officer.

It is believed, that in no country whatever has the collection of a similar duty been effected within the limit assigned. Applying in the United States to a *single* article only, and yielding consequently a less total product than where many articles are comprehended, the expence of collection must of necessity be proportionally greater.

It appears to the Secretary that 7½ per Cent of the total product of the duties on distilled spirits, foreign as well as domestic, and not less will suffice to defray the compensations to officers and other expences incidental to the collection of the duty.[20] This is to be understood as supplemental to the present Custom house expences.

It is unnecessary to urge to the House of Representatives, how essential it must be to the execution of the law in a manner effectual

---

20. Section 58 of "An Act repealing, after the last day of June next, the duties heretofore laid upon Distilled Spirits imported from abroad, and laying others in their stead; and also upon Spirits distilled within the United States, and for appropriating the same" reads in part as follows: "That it shall and may be lawful for the President of the United States from time to time, to make such allowances to the said supervisors, inspectors, and to the deputies and officers by them to be appointed and employed for their respective services in the execution of this act, to be paid out of the product of the said duties, as he shall deem reasonable and proper: *Provided always,* That the aggregate amount of the allowances to all the said supervisors, inspectors and other officers, shall not exceed seven per cent. of the whole product of the duties arising from the spirits distilled within the United States: *And provided also,* That such allowance shall not exceed the annual amount of forty-five thousand dollars, until the same shall be further ascertained by law" (1 *Stat.* 213 [March 3, 1791]).

to the purposes of the Government and satisfactory to the community, to secure by competent, though moderate rewards, the *diligent services* of respectable and trust worthy characters.[21]

All which is humbly submitted   Alexander Hamilton
                                        Secy of the Treasy.

Treasury Department
March 5. 1792.

21. This report was committed to a committee of the whole on March 16, 1792, but debate did not begin until April 13. A "bill concerning the duties on spirits distilled within the United States" was read on April 27. After debate, it was passed by the House of Representatives on May 2. The Senate amended it and the House agreed to the amendments on May 5 (*Journal of the House*, I, 538, 578, 587–94, 598, 606). "An Act concerning the Duties on Spirits distilled within the United States," which became law on May 8, 1792, incorporated many of H's suggestions (1 *Stat.* 267–71).

To William Short

Treasury Department
March 5th 1792

Sir

Since my last of the 14th ultimo I have the pleasure of your two letters of the 8th & 12th of Novemer.

The reimbursement of the Spanish Debt [1] will be perfectly acceptable, but there will be matter for regret, if before this reaches you the sum claimed by the Farmer's General has been paid to them.[2]

There is certainly a million of livres in the pecuniary transactions between the United States and France acknowledged as a subsidy, which remains unaccounted for,[3] with some ground of conjecture that it is the same Million which constitutes the claim of the Farmers General. This affair, though it has heretofore been moved, has never received any satisfactory solution. It is however proper in every view that such a solution should be had. And the documents are preparing, on which to found a regular application, concerning it, to the French Court. In the mean time, the payment to the Farmers General, if not made, ought to be forborne.

I observe that you would have shortly reached the point when by your instructions you would cease to be at liberty to continue the reimbursements to France upon loans made at 4½ ⅌ Cent exclusive of charges.[4] I shall be glad to find that the accomplishment of a loan at 4 ⅌ Cent has prevented that instruction proving an obstacle to further payments.

But if this should not have been the case, and if the rate of exchange shall have been so fixed with France as that it may prove an equivalent for the charges and the additional half per Cent you may proceed in borrowing on the terms of the Antwerp Loan[5] to an extent sufficient to discharge the intire debt to France.

The condition which is here made is deemed necessary to justify the executive in regard to the construction of the law[6] and public opinion. And when it is considered, that immense loss was sustained in realizing here the sums borrowed abroad during the war in many instances to the extent of 40 ⅌ Cent, it cannot appear extraordinary that some attention is paid to conditions of advantageous reimbursement—especially of the part which is not yet due.

It must be proper to unite liberality towards France with an equitable regard to the interest of the United States.

With very great consideration & esteem.   I have the honor to be Sir Your obed servt   Alexander Hamilton

William Short Esquire
&ca. &ca.

ALS, William Short Papers, Library of Congress. A copy of this letter was enclosed in H's "Report on Foreign Loans," February 13, 1793.

1. See Short to H, November 12, 1791. For a description of the Spanish debt, see H to Short, September 1, 1790, note 19.

2. See Short to H, November 12, 1791. For a description of the loan from the French Farmers-General, see H to Short, September 1, 1790, note 26.

3. For an account of the so-called lost million, see the introductory note to Oliver Wolcott, Jr., to H, March 29, 1792.

4. See H to Short, August 1–2, 1791.

5. For a description of the Antwerp loan, see Short to H, November 8, 1791, note 4, and November 12, 1791. See also Short to H, December 1, 1791.

6. Section 2 of "An Act making provision for the (payment of the) Debt of the United States" reads in part as follows: "*Be it further enacted,* That the President of the United States be, and he is hereby authorized, to cause to be borrowed on behalf of the United States, a sum or sums, not exceeding in the whole twelve million of dollars; and that so much of this sum as may be necessary to the discharge of the said arrears and instalments [of the foreign debt], and (if it can be effected upon terms advantageous to the United States) to the paying off the whole of the said foreign debt . . ." (1 *Stat.* 139 [August 4, 1790]).

From Otho H. Williams

Baltimore, March 5, 1792. "The misfortunes which have attended the arms of the U States against the Savages [1] very naturally engage attention. . . . there are perhaps a *few* who, instead of sympathising, as they ought, in the public concern, find for themselves, consolation in the opportunity of censuring the measures of the Executive. . . . The Secretary of War, whose friendship I have no reason to doubt, might nevertheless think the communication of my sentiments officious, and an impertinent intrusion on the perogatives of his Office; to you therefore, in private, I take the liberty of communicating them. The heterogeneous composition of the late Army —The animosities among the Officers, occasioned partly by the different constitution of their corps—The delay in forming them; and the deficiency of supplies, were, most probably the true causes of the defeat of our friend St. Clair. . . . How far the arrangements made for the temporary defence of the frontier [2] will prove effectual will depend upon the fidelity of the friendly Indians. . . . Would it not be good policy to cultivate a firmer connection with the senecas? . . . If Indians are to be faught on their own grounds they must be faught in their own way; experience has perfected them in the art of Bush fighting: and none but our expert Rifle Men (not mere Militia) are a match for them in the woods. . . . The difference between select rifle corps, and the Militia in general you well remember. Great advantages might be obtained, in the present contests, by a well chosen Battalion with a few valiant Indians, under a good partizan Officer. . . . if by means of a few peace offerings reciprocally presented, a trade with them could be commenced, in all probability, the Ustates would soon derive advantages commensurate to all their pecuniary losses by the War. . . . I sincerely believe the danger of disaffection among the Indians now in amity with us, is to be apprehended, and the object of this letter is to awaken that suspicion. . . ."

ALS, Hamilton Papers, Library of Congress; ADf, Maryland Historical Society, Baltimore.

1. This is a reference to the defeat of Major General Arthur St. Clair by the Indians in November, 1791. See "Conversation with George Hammond," December 15–16, 1791, note 2.
2. For the arrangements made by Congress, see "An Act for making farther

and more effectual Provision for the Protection of the Frontiers of the United States" (1 *Stat.* 241–43 [March 5, 1792]).

To Thomas Jefferson

Treasury Department March 6th 1792

Sir,

In consequence of the application of Mr Andw. Ellicot,[1] I have the honor to transmit you the official copy of the Survey of the tract of Land purchased by the State of Pennsylvania from the United States.[2]

As I conceive this as an original paper filed of record in this office in the Execution of an Act of the Legislature,[3] I must ask the favor of your returning it to the Treasury as soon as you shall have caused a copy of it to be made.

I have the honor to be very respectfully [4] Sir, Your most obedt. Servant   Alexander Hamilton

The Honble
The Secretary of State

LS, Thomas Jefferson Papers, Library of Congress.
   1. In the seventeen-eighties Andrew Ellicott, a surveyor and mathematician, had several commissions for running the western and northern boundaries of Pennsylvania. Between 1791 and 1793 he conducted the survey of the ten-mile square that was to become the District of Columbia.
   2. The land which Pennsylvania purchased from the United States was known as the Erie Triangle. Bounded on the east by New York and on the northwest by Lake Erie, the section contained more than two hundred thousand acres. It had been ceded to the United States by New York and Massachusetts in the seventeen-eighties. During the summer of 1788 negotiations between the Board of Treasury and the state of Pennsylvania resulted in a contract for the purchase of the Erie Triangle, and the contract was approved by Congress on September 4, 1788 (*JCC*, XXXIV, 499–500).
   3. "An Act for carrying into effect a Contract between the United States and the State of Pennsylvania" (1 *Stat.* 229 [January 3, 1792]).
   4. The words "very respectfully" are in H's handwriting.

From James Tillary [1]

[New York, March 6, 1792]

sir

When I reflect how long I have been in your Debt I am ashamed, not that I have had any reason to complain of your patience or doubt your generosity.

When Mr Childs [2] was in Phila. about 10 days ago, I expected he would have called & taken up my note. I had actually put him in possession of the ways & means for doing so, except what interest may be due upon it.

He hurried away sooner than he intended, & I believe was obliged to make provision for conducting his business in Phila beyond his expectations of any existing necessities. I need not offer apologies to you, for delaying to take up my note—I am persuaded of your goodness. The Baron whose Note I now have, could not consistently with his arrangements pay me the whole of the rent he owed to me.[3] He is still in my debt, but such is his delicacy & his honor, that I could as soon offend the former, as suspect the later.

But what has that to do with my note for £80?—Nothing. I can pay you with ease, & shall do so with gratitude. Send it to any person you please—or let me know how much it amounts to, & I will pay it into the Bank.

The Bank Mania rages violently in this City,[4] & it is made an engine to help the Governors re-election. Judge Yates' sudden & unexpected resignation, or rather *declination*—Judge Jays sudden & unexpected *acceptation*—The obstinacy of Gov Clinton—The interference of Burr, & the tergiversation of the Chancellor, confound divide & distract the City.[5] If the Conflict was to terminate in the Triumph or defeat of either of the Candidates, it would be of less consequence, but I either see, or fancy I see, the Malignant spirit of Antifederalism hovering over our land & ready to seize the first favorable opportunity of making *a Stand*. Farewell May success attend your measures & happiness yourself.

James Tillary

N. York March 6th
1792

ALS, Hamilton Papers, Library of Congress.

   1. Tillary was a New York City physician and a Federalist politician.

   2. Francis Childs.

   3. Baron von Steuben had rented an apartment from James Tillary at the southeast corner of Broadway and Wall Street.

   4. For information on the attempt to organize new banks in New York City, see H to William Seton, January 18, 1792. See also Philip Schuyler to H, January 29, 1792; H to Seton, January 24, February 10, 1792; Seton to H, January 22, February 6, 1792; and H to Childs, February 27, 1792.

5. Tillary is referring to the gubernatorial election held in New York in the spring of 1792. George Clinton, a candidate to succeed himself, was supported by "the Republican interest" and by Chancellor Robert R. Livingston, a former Federalist. After Robert Yates, the Federalist nominee in 1789, had refused to run again, John Jay was nominated to oppose Clinton. Aaron Burr had hoped to obtain Federalist support as a candidate in the election. See Isaac Ledyard to H, February 1, 28, 1792.

Some indication of the uncertainty concerning the candidacy of Jay and Yates is contained in newspaper reports of the meetings held for the promotion of Jay's campaign. On February 16, 1792, a meeting of New York City Federalists sent a committee to Jay because "some doubts have been expressed whether Mr. Jay would serve." The committee returned to the meeting with the answer that Jay would serve if elected. On the same day in Albany a meeting of Federalists discounted the rumor that Yates had declined the nomination in order to support Burr. The report of the Albany meeting stated that, in New York on February 9 at the meeting which nominated Jay, Yates had said that his refusal to be a candidate "did not arise from a want of confidence in the sincerity of his friends, nor the least diffidence of the issue of his election and that the report which had circulated that he was induced to decline from motives partial to Col. Burr was without foundation" (*The* [New York] *Daily Advertiser*, February 18, 25, 1792). Burr did not finally renounce his candidacy until March 15, 1792.

To Richard Harison [1]

[Philadelphia] March 7. [1792]

My Dear Sir

This will be delivered to you by Mr. Ceracchi,[2] whom I recommend to your attention.

He goes to New York in pursuit of subscriptions towards a Monument of the American Revolution.[3] You have doubtless heared of the Artist and his project. He will explain to you more particularly.

I have prepared him to find difficulties in the *present political* situation of New York.[4] How far they may really stand in his way he will better ascertain on the spot.

While I warmly wish success to the plan I would not embarrass my friends by urging it to the prejudice of public objects.

Yrs. sincerely   A Hamilton

R Harrison Esqr

ALS, New York Society Library, New York City.
1. Harison was United States attorney for the District of New York.
2. On October 31, 1791, a memorial of Giuseppe Ceracchi, a Roman sculptor, was presented to the House of Representatives (George Washington Papers, Library of Congress). In this memorial Ceracchi offered "to execute, on a cer-

tain design, and on certain terms, a monument to perpetuate American liberty and independence" (*Journal of the House*, I, 444). On the same day a similar memorial was presented in the Senate (*Annals of Congress*, III, 20).

On December 6, 1791, the House proposed a joint committee with the Senate to consider means of carrying out the resolutions of the Continental Congress of August 7, 1783, which concerned a monument to commemorate the American Revolution including an equestrian statue of George Washington (*Journal of the House*, I, 468). Although the message from the House of Representatives of December 6 is printed in the Senate *Journal*, no evidence has been found that the Senate acted on this proposal (*Journal of the Senate of the United States of America, Being the First Session of the Second Congress, Begun and Held at the City of Philadelphia, October 24th, 1791; and in the Sixteenth Year of the Sovereignty of the Said United States* [Philadelphia: Printed by John Fenno, No. 69, High Street, 1791], 46).

On March 31, 1792, after seeing Ceracchi's model for the monument, John Jay wrote to Egbert Benson, praising Ceracchi's design and suggesting that payments might be deferred and that ways and means of payment be referred to H (ADfS, Columbia University Libraries). Benson was a member of the committee appointed by the House on April 11, 1792, to consider Ceracchi's memorial of October 31, 1791 (*Journal of the House*, I, 574). After deliberating for a week, the committee reported in favor of implementing the resolutions of the Continental Congress of August 7, 1783, and of appointing the secretaries of State, Treasury, and War as commissioners for that purpose. The report further proposed that Congress at the next session should provide for payments in unspecified amounts for a term not exceeding ten years ([Philadelphia] *Gazette of the United States*, April 25, 1792). On May 7, 1792, the report was recommitted, and in view of a second memorial of Ceracchi which stated the terms upon which he would begin work on the monument (*Journal of the Senate*, 2nd Cong., 1st sess., 176), the committee reported on the same day that "at the present time, it might not be expedient to go into the expenses which the Monument . . . would require, especially with the additional ornaments proposed by the artist" (*Journal of the House*, I, 602).

3. In his letter of March 31, 1792, to Benson, Jay had supported the idea of soliciting subscriptions from individuals or from states to defray the expense of Cerrachi's monument. Although further attempts were made to raise the money needed and some subscriptions were taken in 1795, the monument was never built (*GW*, XXXIV, 136–39).

4. For some contemporary views on the political situation in New York, see Isaac Ledyard to H, February 1, 28, 1792; Philip Schuyler to H, January 29, 1792; H to William Seton, January 18, 1792; James Tillary to H, March 6, 1792.

To John Kean [1]

Treasury Department
March 8. 1792.

Sir

I have desired the Treasurer to transmit to the Bank of the United States a bill or bills on the Bank of New York for the sum of one hundred thousand dollars, which are to be passed, to the credit of the United States.

It is to be understood that the Bank of the United States are to receive the amount in their own notes or in specie at the option of the Bank of New York.

I am, Sir, Your most obedt. servant   Alexander Hamilton

John Kean Esq.
Cashier of the Bank of the United States.

LS, from the original in the New York State Library, Albany.

1. For background to this letter, see H to William Seton, February 10, 1792.

From Jean Baptiste de Ternant

Phile. [8] [1] de mars 1792

J'ai l'honneur de vous envoyer cy jointe une copie de la reponse que je viens de recevoir de Mr. le secretaire d'Etat,[2] sur ma demande du 3 du present, dont vous avez connaissance. Les besoins de st. Domingue me faisant un devoir d'obtenir auplutot les moyens sollicités pour secourir cette colonie; je vous prierai avec instance de vouloir bien me faire connàitre si la somme que j'ai demandée en àcompte de ce que les Et. Un. doivent à la france peut m'etre remise à court delay, et de quelle nature sont les arrangemens que Mr. Jefferson represente dans sa lettre comme necessaires à la conclusion de cette affaire.

J'ai l'hr. d'et. avec resp. et attacht. Mr. &c.

LC, *Arch. des Aff. Etr., Corr. Pol., Etats-Unis,* Supplement Vol. 20; LC, *Arch. des Aff. Etr., Corr. Pol., Etats-Unis,* Supplement Vol. 20.

1. Although the letter book copies of this letter are dated March 7, subsequent correspondence (H to Ternant, March 8, 1792, and Ternant to H, March 10, 1792) indicates that the letter that was sent to H was dated March 8.

2. On March 3, 1792, Ternant asked Thomas Jefferson for four hundred thousand dollars as an advance on the money the United States owed to France (LC, *Arch. des Aff. Etr., Corr. Pol., Etats-Unis,* Supplement Vol. 20). On March 7, 1792, Jefferson replied to Ternant: "I have laid before the President of the U. S. your letter of the 3d. inst. asking a supply of four hundred thousand dollars on account of reimbursements due from us to France, to be applied to releive the distresses of the colony of St. Domingo. . . . I have to assure you that the President feels every disposition which the occasion is calculated to inspire, to do whatever we can for the relief of that colony, and that he hopes your demand may be complied with, under such arrangements as may be mutually convenient & agreeable. For the settlement of these I take the

liberty of referring you to direct conferences with the Secretary of the treasury, which may shorten the business, & save a delay equivalent perhaps in the present case to a denial" (ALS, letterpress copy, Thomas Jefferson Papers, Library of Congress).

To Jean Baptiste de Ternant

Treasury Department
March 8th 1792

Sir

I have the honor of your letter of this date, communicating the copy of one to you from the Secretary of State in answer to your application of the 3d. instant.

Assuring you of the pleasure I shall feel, in executing the views of the President, relatively to the accommodation, which is desired, in as efficacious a manner, as the state of our public resources compared with our public exigencies will admit—I am to inform you that you can have from the Treasury of the United States, on account of your Government the following advances viz 100,000 Dollars immediately, a like sum on the first of June, a like sum on the first of September and a like sum on the first of December next. Provision will be made for the punctual payment of these several sums at the Bank of the United States.

It would be more agreeable, if it were practicable to stipulate shorter periods for these advances, but considering the extrademands, which the operations on foot for the defence of our Western frontier will add to the ordinary demands for the current service,[1] it does not appear adviseable to promise earlier payments.

If however in the progress of things, it shall be found compatible with the general arrangements of the Treasury, to anticipate the periods which have been mentioned, it will without fail be done.

It remains more to explain the principles on which these advances, consistently with the authority vested by law in the President, can be made.

ALS, *Arch. des Aff. Etr.*, *Corr. Pol.*, *Etats-Unis*, Supplement Vol. 20; letterpress copy, Thomas Jefferson Papers, Library of Congress; copy, Columbia University Libraries.

1. See "An Act for making farther and more effectual Provision for the Protection of the Frontiers of the United States" (1 *Stat.* 241–43 [March 5, 1792]).

From the instructions which have been given to Mr. Short, from the known progress of his operations, and from some passages in a letter which I have received from him of the 12th of November last—I conclude with certainty, that he has discharged all the arrears of interest and installments of principal due to France to the end of the year 1791.[2]

The sums now agreed to be furnished therefore will be an anticipation of so much *hereafter to become due.*

The law, which makes provision for the reimbursements to France, contemplates the payment of whatever sums should have *actually become due,* unconditionally, but restrains the discretion of the Executive as to payments, by anticipation, with this condition—that they "can be effected upon terms *advantageous* to the United States." [3]

It is clear then, adopting the most liberal construction of this condition, that such payments can only be made upon terms which will involve *no loss* to the United States.

The fund, from which must arise the advances proposed to be made, is a part of the sums borrowed abroad, pursuant to the law which has been referred to.

These monies have been borrowed at an interest of five per Cent, with charges amounting to four per Cent, and are to be reimbursed in six equal yearly installments, the first at the end of ten years. The time between the receipt of the money in Amsterdam from the lenders, and the placing of it in the Treasury of the United States, cannot be stated at less than six months, during which time an interest has been paid by the United States, for which they have not been compensated by the use of the money. As the money was drawn from Amsterdam by bills of exchange, which were sold upon a credit the transfer was effected at *par,* while private bills, upon that place were at the times of the sales considerably below par in our market.

The United States will consequently avoid loss, and no more, if the advances which shall be made, are so liquidated, as to include an indemnification for the charges of the loan and the interest of

2. See H to William Short, September 1, 1790, April 13, May 9, 1791.
3. See H to William Short, March 5, 1792, note 6.

the money during the time lost in transferring it from Amsterdam to the United States. The quantum of such an indemnification will be merely matter of calculation upon the data above stated.

If however instead of an allowance for the six months interest, you prefer as a rule the rate of exchange between the United States and Amsterdam you are at liberty to make the option.

The sums, which have been mentioned will of course only operate as payments, from the respective times; when they shall be actually paid, so as *thenceforth* to arrest the progress of interest on *equal sums* of the Debt to France.

The intrinsic par of the metals will be the standard of computation, for converting dollars into livres.

When it is considered, that the indemnification, which is sought, is in compliance with an express law, it is hoped that it will obviate all impression of a too minute attention to pecuniary advantage in a case, which is certainly not of great magnitude, and on an occasion, which it is felt claims a liberal treatment.

When also it is considered, that the United States sustained a heavy loss in the first instance, upon their negociations in relation to the aids which constituted their debt to France—on a considerable proportion of not less than 40 per Cent—that by the terms of their contract they are obliged to repay that debt at Paris and consequently were subjected to whatever loss might have been incident to a state of exchange disadvantageous to them—that they in the present case wave the benefit of a state of Exchange highly advantageous to them, and, renouncing gain from that circumstance, are content with merely not suffering loss; it is relied upon, that the terms which have been suggested will appear to you not only equitable but liberal.

Nevertheless, as it is the wish of the President, to obviate all embarrassment on your part and to put the matter upon a footing perfectly satisfactory to your Government and Nation, I am instructed by him to inform you, that if it will be more agreeable to you, he will refer the question of indemnification to a future adjustment with your Court and will cause the necessary instructions for that purpose to be sent to our minister Plenipotentiary there.[4]

4. Gouverneur Morris had been appointed Minister Plenipotentiary for the United States at Paris on January 12, 1792.

With very great respect and attachment I have the honor to
be Sir Your obedient servant   Alexander Hamilton

Mr. Ternant
Minister Plenipotentiary of France

To George Washington

[Philadelphia, March 8, 1792]

The Secretary of the Treasury has the honor to submit to the
President a letter which he has drafted in answer to one from the
Minister Plenipotentiary of France,[1] and which contains such Ideas
as have appeared to him compatible with the Law, with the state
of the Treasury and with a liberal attention to the conjuncture.
He will wait on the President this evening for his orders, as Mr.
Ternant appears urgent.

8th. March 1792.

LC, George Washington Papers, Library of Congress.
    1. See H to Jean Baptiste de Ternant, March 8, 1792.

To John Daves [1]

Treasury Department, March 9, 1792. "You will receive by the
first Vessel, for North Carolina from this Port the several articles
for the use of the Revenue Cutter, which you desire. . . ."[2]

Copy, RG 56, Letters to the Collector at New Bern, National Archives; copy,
RG 26, Lighthouse Letters Received, Revenue Cutter Service Letters Sent, Vol.
"O," National Archives; copy, RG 56, Letters to Collectors at Small Ports, "Set
G," National Archives.
    1. Daves was collector of customs at New Bern, North Carolina.
    2. See Daves to H, November 12, 1791.

From Thomas Marshall [1]

Buck-pond [*Virginia*] *March 9, 1792.* "Permit me to return you
my grateful thanks for your very polite & friendly letter [2] accom-

panying the Commission of Inspector of Revenue for the seventh
survey of the District of Virginia. . . ."

ALS, RG 58, General Records, 1791–1803, National Archives.
1. Thomas Marshall, father of John Marshall, had served in various county
and state offices in Virginia before becoming a colonel in the Continental
Army. After the American Revolution he moved from Virginia and opened a
surveyor's office in Kentucky. As a Federalist he supported the new government and used his influence to keep Kentucky in the Union. His home farm of
"Buck Pond" was a part of the extensive land holdings which he accumulated
in Virginia and Kentucky. For his appointment as inspector of the revenue, see
Tobias Lear to H, August 13, 1791, and H to Lear, August 31, 1791.
2. Letter not found.

From Timothy Pickering [1]

Genl Post Office March 9. 1792.

Sir,
    After much enquiry, I have found a house which would accom-
modate my numerous family, and at the same time give me office-
room. The *greatly extended* business of the department, I think may
be accomplished with the *same help* which has been used since the
time of Mr. Osgoods appointment,[2] to wit, an assistant and clerk.
For these, with their necessary writing desks, table, boxes, cases &
shelves, for a considerable bulk of books & papers, would sufficiently occupy one room; and another room would be convenient
for myself. A servant also will be wanted to keep the rooms in
order, make fires, and perform other services. These services, however, not being constant, I could employ a *domestic* servant, but
one selected with a reference to such public service. If for the two
rooms for the Genl Post Office, a cellar for wood, and the necessary attendance of my domestic servant, I might make a charge of
about 300 dollars, I would then engage the house referred to; but
previous to such engagement I wish to obtain your opinion of the
propriety of the charge.
    I am &c   T. P.

The Secretary of the Treasury.

ADfS, Massachusetts Historical Society, Boston.
1. Pickering had been appointed Postmaster General on August 12, 1791.

2. Samuel Osgood had succeeded Ebenezer Hazard as Postmaster General in 1789. Osgood resigned in 1791 because he was unwilling to move from New York to Philadelphia.

To George Washington

Treasury Department, March 9, 1792. "The Secretary of the Treasury has the honor respectfully to enclose to the President of the United States a petition to the President from Samuel Davis [1] of the State of Rhode Island & providence plantations, together with the papers from the files of the Treasury relative thereto. . . ."

LC, George Washington Papers, Library of Congress.
    1. For background to this letter, see Benjamin Lincoln to H, July 29, September 9, October 7, 1791. At the November, 1791, term of the Circuit Court held in Boston, Davis pleaded guilty to the charge of carrying on board the schooner *Sally* two bales of cotton not recorded in his sworn testimony concerning the cargo. He was fined fifty dollars and sentenced to jail until the fine was paid (Massachusetts Circuit Court Records, Federal Records Center, Boston). A pardon by the President was sent to H on June 21, 1792 ("Register of the Acts of the Federal Congress and Communications Received by the Department of State, 1790–1792," Papers of the Continental Congress, National Archives).

From Joseph Whipple

Collectors Office
District of Portsmo [New Hampshire]
March 9. 1792

Sir

I conceive it to be a duty incumbent on me to mention to you that the ill State of Health of the Judge of this district [1] has prevented his attendance at the two last Courts, in consequence of which two actions brought to that Court on Bonds for Impost duties have failed in their expected issue, and I have been induced to put a third in Suit at the State Court of Common Pleas to avoid the like consequence—it is here Subject [to] the delay of an appeal to the Supreme Court. I find on enquiry there is but little or no prospect that the Judge will ever recover So as to attend business.

Being of opinion that the practice of inserting in bonds given for

Money a penal Sum equal to double the amount of the debt was to Secure all damages that might arise from the delay of payment beyond the term for which the bond was given, and that the Value of the use of Money equal to the legal interest in the Country where the debt exists, should be considered as part of such damage, I have demanded interest at 6 pCt. on bonds Sued but I find it to be the opinion of the Courts in this State that interest should not be recovered on bonds unless Specified in the Obligation. Hence the public is subject to loss—and I do not conceive the law authorizes the insertion of interest in bonds to take place after the expiration of the term of credit allowed. A remedy appears necessary in the law or the practice—if in the latter, be pleased to inform me for my future government.

I have the honor to be &c

Hon. Alex. Hamilton Esquire

LC, RG 36, Collector of Customs at Boston, Letters Sent, 1791–1792, Vol. 3, National Archives; copy, RG 56, Letters from the Collector at Portsmouth, National Archives.

1. John Sullivan, who had served as major general during the American Revolution, had been appointed United States judge of the District of New Hampshire on September 26, 1789. Before his appointment as a Federal judge, he had served in the Continental Congress, as state attorney general, speaker of the state legislature, chairman of the New Hampshire Ratifying Convention, and president of New Hampshire.

Sullivan became ill during the fall of 1791 and was unable to serve as a judge during 1792 sessions of the New Hampshire District Court because of continuing poor health.

From Thomas Jefferson

Philadelphia March 10th. 1792

Sir

The last grant of money for defraying the contingent and other expences of the Department of State having been laid out, and the account thereof and vouchers presented at the Auditor's office for settlement and settled, I have to request the favour of your directing a warrant for the sum of two hundred and fifty dollars to be issued for the payment of such expences as may arise in future.

I have the honor to be with great respect Sir Your most
obedient & most humble Servant   Th: Jefferson

The Secretary of the Treasury.

LS, letterpress copy, Thomas Jefferson Papers, Library of Congress; LC, Papers
of the Continental Congress, National Archives.

Report on Tonnage and Imports
for the Several States

Treasury Department March 10th. 1792
[Communicated on March 12, 1792] [1]

[To the President of the Senate]
Sir,

In obedience to the order of the Senate, of the 8th instant,[2] I
have the honor to transmit thirteen returns exhibiting, as accurately as is practicable, the various descriptions of vessels employed
during the year ending the 30th September, 1790, in the import
trade of each State at that time comprehended in the Union, together with the foreign places from whence they departed for the
United States.[3]

I have also the honor to transmit thirteen returns exhibiting, as
far as the public accounts admit, the various species of Merchandize
imported during the year ending on the 30th day of September,
abovementioned.[4] Two of each sets of those returns, Vizt: those for
North Carolina and Rhode Island, are not for the intire year, as
they were not during a part of it comprehended within the Union.[5]

It is ascertained by the Books of the Treasury, and the fact will
appear from a return now in preparation, that the proportion of
duties accruing on goods imported in foreign ships during the year
ending the 30th of September *last*, is less than one-fourth of the
whole duties [on goods imported.] [6]

Those returns, having been completed prior to the order of the
Senate, do not convey all the information required by their Act,
but as they contain a considerable portion of what is directed, I have
thought it best to transmit them without delay. The remaining in-

formation will be prepared as expeditiously as possible; [7] [though the preparation of a part of it will require very considerable time.]

With the highest respect, I have the honor to be, Sir Your most obedt & most humble Servant   A Hamilton
                                        Secy of the Treasury

The Vice President of
the United States & President of the Senate.

LS, RG 46, Second Congress, 1791–1793, Report of the Secretary of the Treasury, National Archives.

1. *Annals of Congress,* III, 106.
2. The Senate *"Ordered,* That the Secretary of the Treasury be directed to furnish the Senate with returns of the imports of each of the United States for twelve months, specifying the different articles, with reference to the places from whence the imports are made, the kind of vessel or vessels in which they are brought, and to what power said vessel or vessels may belong, at the time of such import or imports. Also, with returns of the exports, in the same form as those of the imports" (*Executive Journal,* I, 110).
3. These statements may be found in *ASP, Commerce and Navigation,* I, 51–63. The statements were signed by Tench Coxe, Assistant Secretary of the Treasury.
4. These returns may be found in *ASP, Commerce and Navigation,* I, 64–102.
5. North Carolina ratified the Constitution on November 20, 1789, and Rhode Island ratified it on May 29, 1790.
6. Bracketed words in this letter are in the handwriting of H.
7. "The remaining information" consists of figures on exports for the year ending September 30, 1791. See "Report on the Return of Exports for the Year Ending September 30, 1791," March 15, 1792.

From Jean Baptiste de Ternant [1]

Phile. [10] [2] mars 1792

J'ai recu votre reponse à ma lettre d'avant hier; et d'après l'assurance que vous me donnez du remboursement total de ce qu'il y a d'exigible sur la dette des Etats unis envers la france, ainsi que de la necessité où la loi met votre gouvernement de ne faire des remboursemens anticipés qu'à des conditions avantageuses, je ne puis qu'accepter l'avance que vous etes disposé de faire, et acceder provisoirement aux termes proposés pour l'effectuer. Quant à l'indemnité à accorder pour couvrir les Etats unis de tout Sacrifice, je préfere puis que le President l'approuve que cet objet soit reglé à Paris, d'après les bases ou l'alternative exprimeés dans votre lettre. Je vais en consequence transmettre cette lettre à ma cour, et lui rendre compte de la maniere avec laquelle le gouvernement des Etats unis s'est preté à la demande que les besoins de st. Domingue m'ont forcé de faire. Il me reste à vous prier de vouloir bien faire payer les quatre cens mille piastres au Vice Consul general de france le Sr. laforest[3] ou à son order, et de devancer les payemens, comme vous me le faites esperer, autant que vos arrangemens interieurs pourront le permettre.

LC, *Arch. des Aff. Etr., Corr. Pol., Etats-Unis*, Supplement Vol. 20; LC, RG 59, Diplomatic and Consular Instructions of the Department of State, 1791–1801, National Archives; letterpress copy, Thomas Jefferson Papers, Library of Congress; copy, Columbia University Libraries.

1. For background to this letter, see Ternant to H, March 8, 1792, and H to Ternant, March 8, 1792.

2. Although the letter book copy of this document is dated March 9, 1792, this date is presumably an error. The other copies of this letter are dated March 10, 1792, and H in his reply of March 12, 1792, refers to Ternant's "letter of the 10th instant."

3. Antoine René Charles Mathurin de La Forest was the French consul general in the United States.

From Oliver Wolcott, Junior

T.D

C. Off March 10. 1792

Sir,

I have examined the papers transmitted to me from your Office and find it duly certified that State Securities were issued in lieu of Certificates of the United States to the amount of . . . . £470,649 . . 17 . . 6.[1]

And that there have been paid in & cancelled in State Certificates which issued particularly for Certificates of the United States the sum of . . . . £91.363 . . . 9 . . 8.

And that Certificates of the United States have been delivered out in exchange for Certificates of the State to the amount of . . . 409.399 . . . 2 . . 4

amounting in the whole to . . . . £500.762 . . 12 . . 0

From this statement it appears that including a sum of State Certificates which issued specifically for Certificates of the United States, which have been paid in & cancelled there has been recovered by the exchange of Certificates of the U:S: for those of the State a greater sum, than were issued for the Certificates of the United States.

It does not appear that the exchanges have been confined to the identical State Certificates which issued for those of the United States, and from the obvious difficulty of making a discrimination between Creditors whose claims were of equal merit, it is probable that no distinction has been observed.

The question for consideration I presume is, whether under these circumstances, the payment of Interest to the Creditors who have subscribed to the Loan in the assumed Debt, should be suspended in consequence of the provisions of the eighteenth Sectn. of the Act making provision for the Debt of the United States.[2]

That the payment of Interest ought not to be suspended is I think evident from the following considerations.

1st. This provision in the Law was intended to prevent the payment of Interest twice on what originally constituted but one debt. The evil intended to be remedied does not exist in the present case, for it is evident that the sum of debt in the State has not been eventually increased by the operations before stated.

2nd The nineteenth Section of the Act directs that the debt of the State which may be subscribed to the Loan shall be charged to the State in account with the United States.[3] By all fair principles of construction, the right to charge the State here assumed by the Law, must be considered as an equivalent or compensation for the Credit admitted by the United States on account of the Loan. If in adition to this compensation the United States, require the providing of another equivalent, to wit the Certificates of the United States, it is evident that an equal Credit must be imediately passed in favour of the State; no use, but much embarassment would attend this mode of conducting the business.

It is therefore my opinion, that as no fictitious capital has been created upon which Interest is liable to be paid, and as it would be improper to charge the State for Certificates issued by them, & at the same time enact a suspending of the consideration for which they became indebted, it may be proper that the payment of Intt. on the assumed Debt be directed to be made.

Hon A H

ADf, Connecticut Historical Society, Hartford.

1. During the seventeen-eighties some states had assumed a part of the Continental debt owed to their own citizens and had issued their own securities in place of Continental certificates. For further information concerning this figure, see "An Account of Continental Securities now in the Treasury of the State of New-York" in "Report Relative to a Provision for the Support of Public Credit," January 9, 1790. The New York State assumption of the Continental debt was carried out under "An Act for emitting the sum of two hundred thousand pounds in bills of credit for the purposes therein mentioned" (*Laws of the State of New York*, II, 253–72 [April 18, 1786]).

2. Sections 17 and 18 of "An Act making provision for the (payment of the) Debt of the United States" read in part as follows: "But as certain states have respectively issued their own certificates, in exchange for those of the United States, whereby it might happen that interest might be twice payable on the same sums: . . . the payment of interest whether to states or to individuals, in respect to the debt of any state, by which such exchange shall have been made, shall be suspended, until it shall appear to the satisfaction of the secretary of the treasury, that certificates issued for that purpose by such state, have been re-exchanged or redeemed, or until those which shall not have been re-exchanged or redeemed, shall be surrendered to the United States" (1 *Stat.* 144 [August 4, 1790]).

3. 1 *Stat.* 144.

To Jean Baptiste de Ternant [1]

[Philadelphia, March 11, 1792]

Dear Sir

I hoped ere this to have sent you the calculation desired.[2] But it happens that the Gentleman of my Office whom I usually employ on such occasions is unwell and I have been too much engaged myself to test by calculation the idea which has been in my mind.

Of this however you are sure that the charges being   4   ⅌ Ct
and the interest for 6 Months   2½   ⅌ Ct
                                             6½   ⅌ Ct

six and a half ⅌ Ct. is the *utmost* extent of the requisite imdemnification.

If there is no fallacy in my view of the matter, it will be less; though it cannot be more. But I am not certain on reflection that there is not some fallacy in the view I had taken of it. Tomorrow or next day will decide.

Yrs. with great attachment   A Hamilton

Sunday March 11
The Minister Plen of France

ALS, *Arch. des Aff. Etr., Corr. Pol., Etats-Unis,* Supplement Vol. 20.
    1. For background to this letter, see H to Ternant, March 8, 1792.
    2. See Ternant to H, March 8, 1792.

From William Duer

New York March 1⟨2⟩th. 1792.[1]

A Hamilton Esqr.

My dear Friend.

I find by a Letter from Colo. Wadsworth [2] that News has arrived there of my hav[in]g skipt Payment.[3] The Fact is that I have been compelled to do it, with Respect to a certain Description of Notes, which were issued by my agent [4] during my absence from this City —the Circumstances are too long and too Painful to detail: you shall know them on my Arrival in Phila. for which Place I will certainly set off to morrow.[5] Colo. Wadsworth writes me that Unless I arrive this day a Suit will Certainly be brought against me.[6]

For Heavens sake, Use for once your Influence to defer this till my Arrival—when it will not be Necessary. My Public Transactions are not blended with my private affairs. Every Farthing will be Immediately accounted for. Of this I pledge my Honor. If a Suit should be brought on the Part of the Public, under my present distrest Circumstances, My Ruin is complete. I despatch this by Express in order that this Step may not be taken—if it is I am sure that those who persue this Measure will in a short Time lament the Consequence.

I am your affectionate but distrest Friend   W Duer.

ALS, Hamilton Papers, Library of Congress.
    1. In MS the date is illegible. In Mitchell, *Hamilton,* II, 175, 615, note 28, this letter is dated March 10; Allan McLane Hamilton dates it March 18 (*Intimate Life,* 272); and Joseph Stancliffe Davis on one page dates it March 11 and on another page March 18 (*Essays,* I, 292, 293). H in answering this letter refers to it as "Your letter of the 11th" (H to Duer, March 14, 1792). In the first sentence, however, Duer refers to a letter Jeremiah Wadsworth wrote to him. Apparently Duer received the Wadsworth letter on March 12, for in a letter clearly dated March 12 he replied to Wadsworth: "I have this Moment received your Letter, to which I answer immediately" (ALS, Connecticut Historical Society, Hartford). Moreover, in both the letter to H printed above and the letter to Wadsworth, Duer writes of leaving New York for Philadelphia "to morrow."
    2. Wadsworth, who during the American Revolution had served as commis-

sary general of purchases and as a representative from Connecticut to the Continental Congress, had widespread business interests. He was a founder of the Bank of North America, the Hartford Bank, and the Hartford Manufacturing Company, and had engaged in a number of speculative enterprises. For several years he had been a member of a Hartford firm which carried on an extensive trade with the West Indies. During the Confederation period H had handled the legal affairs of Wadsworth and his wartime business partner, John B. Church.

3. In December, 1791, Duer, former Assistant Secretary of the Treasury, formed a partnership with Alexander Macomb, a wealthy New York merchant, for speculation in public securities. By using all his available money and borrowing large sums on his personal notes, Duer furnished most of the operating capital of the firm. The extensive purchases of securities by Duer and Macomb were chiefly responsible for the speculative mania of the first months of 1792. Not only in New York, where Duer had his headquarters, but in other large American cities, there was a feverish buying and selling of stocks. The success of Duer's operations depended on a steady rise in stock prices. But after reaching a high point in late January, 1792, security prices declined for the next five weeks, and Duer was ruined. On March 9 he was forced to suspend payments. Duer's failure produced a panic which was accompanied by a further decline in security prices and a corresponding increase in Duer's difficulties. On March 28, 1792, Duer was imprisoned for his debts.

4. Although it cannot be stated with certainty, Duer may at this point be referring to John Pintard. See Mitchell, *Hamilton*, II, 612, note 28.

5. Duer was not able to carry out his plan of going to Philadelphia. See H to Duer, March 14, 1792.

6. On the day Duer wrote this letter, Oliver Wolcott, Jr., comptroller of the Treasury, announced that the Treasury Department intended to bring suit against Duer for a deficiency of two hundred thousand dollars in his account with the United States. For an account of Duers' finances, see Davis, *Essays*, I, 279–91. A statement of Duer's account for indents of interest for 1787–1788 over which this action arose, as well as the relevant vouchers, may be found in RG 217, Miscellaneous Treasury Accounts, 1790–1894, Account No. 3508, National Archives.

To William Ellery

[*Philadelphia, March 12, 1792.* On March 26, 1792, Ellery wrote to Hamilton: "On the 24th of this month I received your letter of the 12th." *Letter not found.*]

To John Kean

[*Philadelphia, March 12, 1792.* On April 18, 1792, Hamilton wrote to Kean concerning the suspension of the sale of bills desired "by my letter of the 12th ultimo." *Letter not found.*]

To Timothy Pickering

Treasury Department
March 12. 1792.

Sir

I have received the communication which you made to me with respect to a a part of the contingent expences of the general post office,[1] and on comparing the sum you mention with the charges for similar objects, which have been necessarily sustained in this department, and in the public service in general I cannot perceive any thing in the arrangement you propose, but what appears consistent with the interest of the United States.

I am, with great esteem,   Sir,   Your most obedt. servt.

A Hamilton

Timothy Pickering Esq.
Post Master General.

LS, Massachusetts Historical Society, Boston.
  1. Pickering to H, March 9, 1792.

To Jean Baptiste de Ternant

Treasury Department
March 12, 1792.

Sir

I have the honor to receive your letter of the 10th. instant, and Mr. de la Forest [1] has applied at the Treasury for the payment of the sum of one hundred thousand dollars at the moment when I was about to request you would take order for the receipt of that sum. A warrant on the Treasurer has in course been executed.

With very great respect & attachment, I have the honor to be Sir   Your obed. servant   Alexander Hamilton

Mr. Ternant
Minister Plenipotentiary of France

LS, *Arch. des Aff. Etr., Corr. Pol., Etats-Unis,* Supplement Vol. 20.
  1. Antoine René Charles Mathurin de La Forest, French consul general in the United States.

From William Allibone

[*Philadelphia*] *March 13, 1792.* "Unpleasant as the task is, to be the Bearer of bad tidings, it has fallen to my lot; and it is no less then the entire loss & destruction of one of the Piers at mud Island,[1] by the Breaking up of the Ice on thursday last, when the whole body thereof moved at once, with the flood tide and a heavy easterly wind, which forced it with great Violence for A long time against the Northeastermost Pier until it was nearly Buried in the Broken Ice, at Length the whole Pier gave way bodily & being forced from its bed, turned Over and Sunk in deep Water and disappeared. . . ."

ALS, RG 26, Lighthouse Letters Received, Vol. "A," Pennsylvania and Southern States, National Archives.
  1. Mud Island was in the Delaware River.

Conversation with Jean Baptiste de Ternant

[Philadelphia, March 13–26, 1792]

Mr. Hamilton, avec qui j'en ai causé ensuite, et qui est plus particulièrement ici l'homme essentiel en finances, m'a paru également bien disposé—"Nos ressources pécuniaires sont extrêmement bornées; mais *nous pourrons cependant quelque chose* si les circonstances l'exigent; et en cas de demande de votre part vous pouvez compter que je ferai tout, pour remplir les vues de votre Gouvernement," ce sont là les propres paroles du Secrétaire de la Trésorerie.—Il a ajouté ensuite que ce qu'il reste à payer pour compléter les remboursemens de l'année courante, et dont le montant est d'environ deux cens mille piastres, pourroit être acquitté à Philadelphie, d'ici à un an, et que quant aux remboursemens subséquents, il prévoyoit encore la possibilité de les faire en Amérique, sinon en totalité, au moins en grande partie, et qu'enfin il se prêteroit sur cela à tous les arrangemens désirés par la Cour, en tant qu'ils pourroient se concilier avec les dispositions de la loi, dont j'ai eu l'honneur de vous parler dans ma dépêche No 26.[2]

Turner, "Correspondence of French Ministers," 98.

1. For Ternant's attempt to obtain a four hundred thousand dollar advance on account of the debt due France, see Ternant to H, March 8, 10, 1792; H to Ternant, March 8, 12, 1792.

2. Ternant's dispatch No. 26 is printed in Turner, "Correspondence of French Ministers," 89–91. See also H to Ternant, March 8, 1792.

From William Ellery

[*Newport, Rhode Island*] *March 13, 1792.* ". . . I wish for a supply of Registers having only seven on hand; and I should be very happy if an allowance and compensation for my services could be made to me before the adjournment of Congress."[1]

LC, Newport Historical Society, Newport, Rhode Island.

1. On April 5, 1792, H submitted to Congress his "Report on Compensation of Officers Employed in the Collection of the Revenue."

To William Rawle [1]

Treasury Department
March 13 1792

Sir

A foreign attachment at the suit of Paulus Kok against Theodosius Gerhardus Bosch was served on the Secretary of the Treasury and on the Register out of one of the Courts of Pennsylvania by William Will, Esquire, Sheriff of the City and County of Philadelphia, with summons, as garnishees.[2] The Defendant was supposed by the Plaintiff to be a Creditor of the United States, which, in fact, is the case. I consider it as important that measures should be taken to ascertain how far the Stock standing on the public books, in the name of a public Creditor, is affected by such proceedures.

It is my wish that the right of parties to attach the public Stock may be seriously examined and contested—and in a way that will finally secure a decision in the Supreme Court of the United States. I deem it of considerable moment that such a right should not appear to exist.

You will be pleased to communicate the matter to the Attorney General, that the United States may avail themselves of his cooperation, and I shall also make the case known to him.

I am, Sir, with great consideration,　Sir, Your Mo. Obed Servant

Alexander Hamilton

Wm Rawle Esquire

LS, Historical Society of Pennsylvania, Philadelphia.
1. Rawle was United States attorney for the District of Pennsylvania.
2. Presumably this action was taken in connection with Bosch's New York debts, for on March 10, 1792, The [New York] Daily Advertiser carried the following notice:

"By order of the honorable John Sloss Hobart, Esquire, one of the justices of the supreme court of the state of New York, Notice is hereby given to Theodorus Gerhardus Bosch, of the city of Utrecht, in that part of the United Netherlands, called Holland, merchant, an absent debtor, and all others whom it may concern, that on application and due proof made to him, the said judge, pursuant to the direction of the law of the state of New York, entitled 'an act for relief against abscondry and absent debtors,' passed the fourth day of April, 1786, he hath directed all the estate, real and personal, within the state of New York, of the said Theodorus Gerhardus Bosch, an absent debtor, to be seized, and that unless the said Theodorus Gerhardus Bosch doth discharge his debts within one year after this public notice of such seizure, all his estate, real and personal will be sold for the payment and satisfaction of his creditors."

To William Duer

Philadelphia March 14. 1792

My Dear Duer

Your letter of the 11th.[1] got to hand this day. I am affected beyond measure at its contents; especially as it was too late to have any influence upon the event you were apprehensive of—Mr. Woolcott's instructions having gone off yesterday.[2]

I trust however the alternative which they present to the Attorney of the _____ [3] and the discretion he will use in managing the affair will enable you to avoid any pernicious éclat; if your affairs are otherwise retrievable.

Be this as it may—Act with fortitude and honor. If you cannot reasonably hope for a favourable extrication do not plunge deeper. Have the courage to make a full stop. Take all the care you can in the first place of Institutions of public Utility and in the next of all fair Creditors.

God bless you and take care of you and your family. I have

experienced all the bitterness of soul, on your account, which a warm attachment can inspire. I will not now pain you with any wise remarks, though if you recover the present stroke, I shall take great liberties with you. Assure yourself in good and bad fortune of my sincere friendship and affection.

Adieu   A Hamilton

Wm. Duer Esqr.

JCH Transcripts.
    1. See Duer to H, March 12, 1792, note 1.
    2. On March 12, Oliver Wolcott, Jr., comptroller of the Treasury, had written to Richard Harison, United States attorney for the District of New York, requesting him to inform Duer that he must either pay the amount of his balance with the United States Government or face legal proceedings. Wolcott's letter is printed in Davis, *Essays*, I, 290–91. The suit concerned Duer's indent account with the United States. Copies of the statements of this account which Wolcott sent to Harison may be found in RG 217, Oliver Wolcott's "Explanation of Accounts, 1792–1794," Comptroller of the Treasury, National Archives.
    3. Space left blank in MS.

From Benjamin Lincoln

Boston March 14th. 1792

Sir

By the 7th. section in the act for registering vessels &c it is provided that when an owner resides out of the district where the ship may be at the time a register is required that such owner may take and subscribe the oath before the collector of the district in which he resides.[1]

A Gentleman from Baltimore came here a few months since and purchased a vessel, loaded her and wished her to sail from this district to a foreign port therefore requested that I would give him a register. I supposed that there would not be any question respecting the propriety of my doing; Although the owner belonged to the State of Maryland. Had he been there & forwarded his Certificate from the Collector[2] that he was the owner, a Citizen &c I must have granted the register. His being upon the spot and taking and subscribing the oath before me was as good evidence at the least as a Certificate would be if forwarded from Maryland. I therefore did not hesitate to administer the usual oath and granted a register.

Since, the Collector has written to me from Baltimore Supposing that the register granting was irregular. I find Mr. Lee of the District of main [3] holds the same ideas. I am not convinced by any reasoning I have heard on the subject that the proceeding was irregular. The law was manifestly calculated for the benefit & ease of the Merchant. If I was wrong in granting the register on the evidence I did, nothing, I think could have healed the defect but the Gentlemans returning to Baltimore & thence sending me his certificate, this must have caused a delay of one month at the least.

Cases often happen that Merchants of one State doing business in an other apply for registers being on the spot. If in your opinion they cannot in such cases be granted untill the purchaser returns home & forwards a certificate from the collector of his district to me, I should be happy to know it.

The late keeper of the Light-Houses on Thatcher Island Mr. Houstin [4] & A number of persons wish to be the keeper of them & have applied for my interest in their favour as will appear by the papers inclosed. From all I learn Capt. Sayward is by far the best qualified for the business.[5] He is an old master of a vessel, is a good pilot himself & will carry on to the Island one or more of his Sons who are also well acquainted with the coast and would in the opinion of our best merchants, interested in that neighbourhood, render very essential services to the trade. I am informed that Capt Sayward could have obtained every certificate he wished had he been a candidate for the office in the first instance but he was not. The people rather sought him than he the office.

As there was some question respecting the allowance to the keeper I hope whoever shall be appointed that his whole allowance be expressed.

LC, Massachusetts Historical Society, Boston; LC, RG 36, Collector of Customs at Boston, Letter Book, 1790–1797, National Archives; copy, RG 56, Letters from the Collector at Boston, National Archives.

1. "An Act for Registering and Clearing Vessels, Regulating the Coasting Trade, and for other purposes" (1 *Stat.* 55–65 [September 1, 1789]).

2. Otho H. Williams was collector of customs at Baltimore.

3. John Lee, collector of customs for the port of Penobscot, District of Maine.

4. Samuel Houston. At this point the other copies of this letter read "is no more."
Thatcher's Island is located off Cape Ann.

5. Joseph Sayward was subsequently appointed lighthouse keeper on Thatcher's Island.

Report on the Return of Exports for the Year Ending September 30, 1791

Treasury Department
March 15. 1792.
[Communicated on March 16, 1792] [1]

[To the President of the Senate]
Sir

In further pursuance of the order of the Senate of the 8th. instant,[2] I have the honor to transmit a return of the exports from the United States for one year ending the 30th. September 1791, exhibiting the islands and countries to which those exports have been shipt.[3]

This document is completed so far as the returns have been received at the Treasury, but an addition is yet to be made of the exports from Charleston in South Carolina, and from some ports of inferior consequence for the two last quarters of the returned year, the papers relative to which have not been received. There is also transmitted a return of outward tonnage for one year ending March 31st. 1791.[4]

In regard to the remainder of the statements required by the Senate; it is very uncertain whether the delay of the returns from certain of the Custom houses, and the length of time they will require, will not prevent the completion of them before the end of the session.

I have the honor to be, Sir   Your most obedient & most humble servant   Alexander Hamilton
Secy of the Treasy

The Vice President of the United States
and President of the Senate.

LS, RG 46, Second Congress, 1791–1793, Reports of the Secretary of the Treasury, National Archives.
   1. *Annals of Congress*, III, 108.
   2. The Senate "*Ordered*, That the Secretary of the Treasury be directed to furnish the Senate with returns of the imports of each of the United States for twelve months, specifying the different articles, with reference to the places from whence the imports are made, the kind of vessel or vessels in which they are brought, and to what power said vessel or vessels may belong, at the time of such import or imports. Also, with returns of the exports, in the same form as those of the imports" (*Executive Journal*, I, 110).

3. The enclosure, signed by Tench Coxe, Assistant Secretary of the Treasury, is entitled "A General Statement of Goods, Wares, and Merchandise, exported from the United States, from the 1st day of October, 1790, to the 30th September, 1791" and is printed in *ASP, Commerce and Navigation*, I, 104–38.

4. A footnote to this sentence in MS reads: "This statement is not now to be found." There is a crossed-out footnote to the same sentence which indicates that the statement had been returned to the Treasury Department for use in another compilation.

From William Allibone

[*Philadelphia*] *March 16, 1792.* "Having Particularly Inspected the Condition of the Piers at mud Island, I have the honor to report, that the Pier destroyed by the Breaking up of the Ice, was not Removed intirely from its bed as at first Represented,[1] But that all the upper part thereof Below low water mark was Torn away and now lays sunk. Just against the back part or upper side of what remains in its old bed, only pressed a little farther in Shore. However the Pier is as Effectually destroyed, And I am of Opinion that the part which remains, will be of no advantage in erecting another. . . . From a view of the Prices and estimates of Building Peirs heretofore with some allowance for the General advance of Wages, I am of Opinion that it will require an appropriation of not less than two thousand Dollars. . . ."

ALS, RG 26, Lighthouse Letters Received, Vol. "A," Pennsylvania and Southern States, National Archives.

1. See Allibone to H, March 13, 1792.

Report on Claims of the Lutheran and Calvinist Churches in Chester County, Pennsylvania, and the Public Grammar School of Wilmington, Delaware

[Philadelphia, March 16, 1792
Communicated on March 17, 1792] [1]

[To the Speaker of the House of Representatives]

The Secretary of the Treasury, to whom was referred the petition

Copy, RG 233, Reports of the Treasury Department, 1792–1793, Vol. III, National Archives.

1. *Journal of the House*, I, 538. The communicating letter, dated March 16, 1792, may be found in RG 233, Reports of the Treasury Department, 1792–1793, Vol. III, National Archives.

of the Minister and Trustees of the Lutheran Church in Pikeland [2] Township Chester County in the State of Pennsylvania: The petition of the Wardens of the Calvinist church in Vincent Township, in the County and State aforesaid; [3]—and the petition of the Corporation of Trustees of the public Grammar School of Wilmington in Delaware State,[4] respectfully submits the following Report thereupon.

The two first mentioned petitions seek an indemnification for damages alledged to have been done to two several places of religious worship in the County of Chester in the State of Pennsylvania, in consequence of their having been made use of, during certain periods of the late war, as military hospitals for the accommodation of the Troops of the United States.

The facts stated in the said several petitions are no otherwise authenticated to the Secretary, than by the certificates which accompany them respectively, and which are stated to be from persons appointed by General Greene,[5] to appraise the damages which were sustained. Nevertheless, the Secretary does not perceive any ground to doubt the truth of the allegations, which are contained in the said petitions.

There is no evidence of any application for an adjustment of either of these claims, in the manner, or within the periods, prescribed by the Acts of limitation: [6] Wherefore, they are to be considered, as barred by those Acts:

2. In MS, "Rheland."

3. On February 12, 1791, the House received "The petitions of the ministers and trustees of the Lutheran Church, Pikeland Township, Chester county, and of the wardens of the Calvanist Church, in Vincent Township, Chester county, in the State of Pennsylvania, respectively praying compensation for damages done to their churches, by the Army of the United States, during the late war.

"Ordered, That the said petitions . . . be referred to the Secretary of the Treasury, with instruction to examine the same, and report his opinion thereupon to the House." (Journal of the House, I, 376.)

4. On December 21, 1790, "A petition of the corporation of trustees of the public grammar school and academy of Wilmington, in the State of Delaware, was presented to the House and read, praying that compensation may be made for the use of, and the injuries done to, the buildings of the said academy, by the troops of the United States, during the late war.

"Ordered, That the said petition be referred to the Secretary of the Treasury, with instruction to examine the same, and report his opinion thereupon to the House." (Journal of the House, I, 340.)

5. Nathanael Greene was involved because at the time he had been quartermaster general of the Continental Army.

6. See JCC, XXIX, 866; XXXIII, 392.

The last mentioned petition, namely, that from the Trustees of the public Grammar School and Academy of Wilmington, seeks an indemnification for the occupation and injury, by the troops of the United States, of the Building in which that School and Academy were kept.

The material facts alledged in the said petition, with respect to the occupation and injury of the building in question, and the several applications for indemnification, are satisfactorily established; as will be seen by the documents herewith transmitted, No. I, II, III.[7]

There are two precedents, among the files of the Treasury, of allowances for the occupation and injury of public institutions; one of the fourteenth of January 1783, which is an account settled at the treasury, with the proprietors of the Pennsylvania Hospital, for the rent of a house and Elaboratory, occupied by the Apothecary of the United States, from the first day of August 1778, to the first day of August 1781: another, of the twenty seventh of May 1784; which is an account settled with the Managers of the House of employment in Philadelphia, for damages done to that building, while occupied as a general Hospital.

It appears also, that the Reverend Doctor John Witherspoon [8] stands charged in the books of the Quarter Master's department, with the sum of 19.040 dollars received by him in the year 1779, for the purpose of repairing the College at Princeton, which had been damaged by the troops, for which he has signed a receipt, promising to be answerable, if the advance was not approved of by Congress. But it does not appear, that any farther proceeding has been had upon the subject.

A question arises, whether the claim of the petitioners is barred by any Act of limitation.

Considering that this claim was duly exhibited prior to the existence of those Acts, was referred by Congress to the Board of Treas-

7. These documents may have been attached after the petition had been submitted to H, for on January 29, 1792, "The Trustees of the Academy of Wilmington in Delaware" were charged for "an authenticated copy of three petitions they presented to the old Congress, praying an indemnification for the injury done said Academy by the continental troops" (D, Papers of the Continental Congress, National Archives). For background to this petition, see E. Miriam Lewis, ed., "The Minutes of the Wilmington Academy, 1777–1802," *Delaware History,* III (September, 1949), 193, 195, 197, 200, 205, 217–18, 220.

8. Witherspoon was president of the College of New Jersey (Princeton).

ury, to be filed among similar papers, and a decision thereon specially referred by that body to the termination of the war, to be then taken into consideration in common with other applications of a similar nature, The Secretary is of opinion, that these circumstances amount to a virtual exception of the case out of the Acts of Limitation.

But, in whatsoever light this may be viewed, it appears to him most consistent with the justice and liberality of the government, to authorize the allowance of a reasonable compensation, in all cases, in which any place of religious worship, or any Seminary of learning has been occupied, or injured, for or by the troops of the United States; the Acts of limitation notwithstanding.

An innovation or relaxation in this particular will, it is conceived, be sufficiently discriminated by the nature of the object, so as essentially to obviate all difficulty on the score of precedent.

If it should appear to the legislature advisable, to authorize a compensation in such cases, the Secretary is of opinion, that it will be expedient to leave the quantum to be ascertained, upon due proof, by the accounting officers of the Treasury, as in other cases of claims against the United States.[9]

All which is humbly submitted.   Alexander Hamilton,
                                              Secy. of the Treasy.
Treasury Department,
March 16th 1792.

9. On March 23, 1792, this report was referred to a committee consisting of John Vining of Delaware, John F. Mercer of Maryland, and John B. Ashe of North Carolina. On March 30 the committee reported and the House agreed to that part of the report which called for the appropriation of an unspecified sum for the grammar school and academy of Wilmington (*Annals of Congress*, III, 473, 481, 498, 538). "An Act to compensate the corporation of trustees of the public grammar school and academy of Wilmington, in the state of Delaware, for the occupation of, and damages done to, the said school, during the late war" became law on April 13, 1792 (6 *Stat.* 8).

Report Relative to the Additional Supplies for the Ensuing Year

Treasury Department
March 16, 1792.
[Communicated on March 17, 1792] [1]

[To the Speaker of the House of Representatives]

The Secretary of the Treasury pursuant to a Resolution of the House of Representatives of the 8th instant directing the said Secretary to report to the House his opinion of the best mode of raising the Additional Supplies requisite for the ensuing year,[2] respectfully submits the following report.

The sum which is estimated to be necessary for carrying into effect the purposes of the Act for making further and more effectual provision for the protection of the Frontiers of the United States [3] beyond the provision made by the Act making appropriations for the support of Government for the year 1792 [4] is Dollars 675.950.8

The returns which have been received at the Treasury subsequent to the Secretarys Report of the 23rd. of January last,[5] among which are those of some principal ports afford satisfactory ground of assurance, that the quarter ending the last of December was considerably more productive than it was supposed likely to prove; authorizing a reliance that the revenues to the end of the year 1791 will yield a

DS, RG 233, Reports of the Treasury Department, 1792–1793, Vol. III, National Archives.

1. *Journal of the House*, I, 538. The communicating letter may be found in RG 233, Reports of the Treasury Department, 1792–1793, Vol. III, National Archives.

2. After some debate, the House on March 8, 1792, "*Resolved,* That the Secretary of the Treasury be directed to report to this House his opinion of the best mode for raising the additional supplies requisite for the ensuing year" (*Journal of the House*, I, 530–31).

3. This act provided for raising three additional regiments for the protection of the country's frontiers (1 *Stat.* 241–43 [March 5, 1792]).

4. Section 4 of "An Act making Appropriations for the Support of Government for the year one thousand seven hundred and ninety-two" had appropriated $37,339.48 for the protection of the frontiers (1 *Stat.* 228 [December 23, 1791]).

5. See "Report Relative to a Provision for the Support of Public Credit," January 23, 1791.

surplus of 150.000 dollars which may be applied in part of the sum of 675.950 dollars and eight Cents above stated to be necessary.

Provision remains to be made for the residue of this sum namely 525.950 Dollars & 8 Cents.

Three expedients occur to the option of the government for providing this sum.

One, to dispose of the Interest, to which the United States are intitled in the Bank of the United States. This, at the present market price of Bank Stock, would yield a clear gain to the Government much more than adequate to the sum required.

Another, to borrow the money; upon an establishment of funds, either merely commensurate with the interest to be paid, or affording a surplus which will discharge the principal by installments within a short term.

The third is to raise the amount by taxes.

The first of these three expedients appears to the Secretary altogether unadviseable.

First. It is his present opinion, that it will be found, in various respects, permanently the interest of the United States to retain the Interest to which they are intitled in the Bank. But

Secondly—If this opinion should not be well founded, it would be improvident to dispose of it at the present juncture—since upon a comprehensive view of the subject, it can hardly admit of a doubt, that its future value, at a period not very distant, will be considerably greater than its present—While the Government will enjoy the benefit of whatever dividends shall be declared in the Interval. And

Thirdly—Whether it shall be deemed proper to retain or dispose of this Interest, the most useful application of the proceeds will be as a fund for extinguishing the public debt. A necessity of applying it to any different object, if it should be found to exist, would be matter of serious regret.

The second expedient would in the judgment of the Secretary be preferable to the first.

For this the following Reason, if there were no other, is presumed to be conclusive—namely, That the probable increase of the value of the Stock may itself be estimated as a considerable, if not a sufficient fund, for the repayment of the sum which might be borrowed.

If the measure of a Loan should be thought eligible, it is submitted as most adviseable to accompany it with a provision, sufficient not only to pay the interest, but to discharge the principal within a short period. This will, at least, mitigate the inconvenience of making an addition to the public debt.

But the result of mature reflection is, in the mind of the Secretary, a strong conviction, that the last of the three expedients, which have been mentioned, is to be preferred to either of the other two.

Nothing can more interest the National Credit and prosperity, than a constant and systematic attention to husband all the means previously possessed for extinguishing the present debt, and to avoid, as much as possible, the incurring of any new debt.

Necessity alone therefore can justify the application of any of the public property, other than the annual Revenues, to the current service, or to the temporary and casual exigencies of the Country— or the contracting of an additional debt, by loans, to provide for these exigencies.

Great emergencies indeed might exist in which loans would be indispensible. But the occasions which will justify them must be truly of that description.

The present is not of such a nature. The sum to be provided is not of magnitude enough to furnish the plea of necessity.

Taxes are never welcome to a community. They seldom fail to excite uneasy sensations more or less extensive. Hence a too strong propensity, in the Governments of Nations, to anticipate and mortgage the resources of posterity, rather than encounter the inconveniences of a present increase of taxes.

But this policy, when not dictated by very peculiar circumstances, is of the worst kind. Its obvious tendency is, by enhancing the permanent burdens of the people, to produce lasting distress, and its natural issue is in National Bankruptcy.

It will be happy, if the Councils of this country, sanctioned by the voice of an enlightened community, shall be able to pursue a different course.

Yielding to this impression, The Secretary proceeds to state for the consideration of the House the objects, which have occurred to him as most proper to be resorted to, for raising the requisite sum by taxes.

From the most careful view, which he is able to take of all the circumstances, that at the present juncture naturally enter into consideration, he is led to conclude, that the most eligible mode, in which the necessary provision can at this time be made, is by some additional duties on imported articles.

This conclusion is made with reluctance, for reasons which were noticed upon a former occasion, and from the reflection, that frequent and unexpected alterations in the rates of duties, on the objects of Trade, by inducing uncertainty in mercantile speculations and calculations, are really injurious to Commerce and hurtful to the interests of those who carry it on.

The stability of the duties to be paid by the merchants is in fact of more consequence to them than their quantum; if within reasonable bounds.

It were therefore much to have been wished that so early a resort to new demands on that class of Citizens could have been avoided— and especially that they could have been deferred, until a general Tariff could have been maturely digested, upon principles, which might with propriety render it essentially stationary.

But while there are these motives to regret, there are others of a consoling tendency; some of which indicate, that an augmentation of duties, at the present juncture, may have the effect of lessening some public evils, and producing some public benefits.

It is a pleasing fact, if the information of the Secretary be not very erroneous—that the improved state of the credit of this country enables our Merchants to procure the supplies, which they import from abroad, upon much more cheap, and advantageous terms than heretofore; a circumstance which must alleviate to them the pressure of somewhat higher rates of duty; and must contribute at the same time to reconcile them to burthens, which being connected with an efficacious discharge of the duty of the government, are of a nature to give solidity and permanency to the advantages they enjoy under it.

It is certain, also, that a spirit of manufacturing prevails at this time, in a greater degree, than it has done at any antecedent period; and as far as an increase of duties shall tend to second and aid this spirit, they will serve to promote essentially the industry, the wealth, the strength, the independence and the substantial prosperity of the country.

The returns for a year, ending with the 30th of September last, an abstract of which is in preparation to be communicated to the Legislature, evince a much increased importation, during that year, greater far than can be referred to a naturally increasing demand, from the progress of population, and announce a probability of a more than *proportional* increase of consumption; there being no appearance of an extraordinary abundance of goods in the Market. If happily an extension of the duties shall operate as a restraint upon excessive consumption, it will be a salutary mean of preserving the community from future embarrassment, public and private. But if this should not be the case, it is at least prudent in the government, to extract from it the resources necessary for current exigencies, rather than postpone the burthen to a period, when that very circumstance may cause it to be more grievously felt.

These different considerations unite with others, which will suggest themselves to induce, in the present state of things, a preference of taxes on imported articles to any other mode of raising the sum required.

It is therefore respectfully submitted.

That the existing duties [6] on the Articles hereafter enumerated be repealed and that in place of them the following be laid—Vizt.

		Cents
Wines.		
Madeira of the quality of London parti∽ ℔ Gall.		56
ditto . . . . . London Market ℔ ditto		49
Other Madeira Wines . . . . . . ℔ ditto		40
Sherry . . . . ℔ ditto		33
St. Lucar . . . . ℔ ditto		30
Lisbon . . . . ℔ ditto		25
Oporto . . . . ℔ ditto		25
Teneriffe & Fayal . . . . . . ℔ ditto		20

All other Wines 40 ℔ Centum ad valorem.

Spirits.		
Those distilled wholly or chiefly from Grain.		
Of the first class of proof . . . . ℔ Gallon		28
Of the second . . ditto . . . ℔ ditto		29

6. The existing duties on wines and spirits were imposed by "An Act repealing, after the last day of June next, the duties heretofore laid upon Distilled Spirits imported from abroad, and laying others in their stead; and also upon Spirits distilled within the United States, and for appropriating the same" (1 *Stat.* 199–214 [March 3, 1791]). The existing duties on the remaining articles had been imposed by "An Act making further provision for the payment of the debts of the United States" (1 *Stat.* 180–82 [August 10, 1790]).

Of the third class of proof . . . . . . ℔ Gallon   31.
Of the fourth   ditto . . . . . . ℔ ditto   34
Of the fifth . . . . . ditto . . . . . ℔ ditto   40
Of the sixth . . . . . ditto . . . . . ℔ ditto   50.

Other distilled Spirits.

Of the second class of proof & under . ℔ Gall.   24
Of the third . . . . . ditto . . . . . ℔ ditto   27
Of the fourth . . . . . ditto . . . . . ℔ ditto   31
Of the fifth . . . . . ditto . . . . . ℔ ditto   37
Of the sixth . . . . . ditto . . . . . ℔ ditto   45

Beer, Ale and Porter . . . . ℔ Gallon   8
Steel . . . . ℔ Cwt.   100
Nails . . . . ℔ lb.   2
Cocoa . . . . ℔ do.   2
Chocolate . . . . ℔ do.   3
Playing Cards . . . . ℔ pack   25
Shoes & Slippers of silk   20
Shoes & Slippers of stained or colored ⎤
   Leather (other than black) for Men ⎬   10
   & Women   ⎦
   ditto . . . . . ditto . . . . . for Children   7
All other Shoes & slippers for (men & women)
   clogs & goloshoes   10
All other Shoes & slippers for children   7

Articles ad valorem.
China Wares . . . .
Looking Glass, Window and other glass and all manufactures
   of Glass, black quart bottles excepted . . . .
Muskets . . . .
Pistols . . . .
Swords, Cutlasses, Hangers & other fire & side Arms . . .
Starch . . . .
Hair Powder . . . .
Wafers . . . .
Glue . . . .

15. ℔ Centum advalorem.

Cast Slit and rolled Iron, and generally all manufactures of Iron,
Steel, Tin, Pewter, Copper, brass or of which either of these
Metals is the Article of chief value (not being otherwise par-
ticularly enumerated)

Cabinet wares . . . .

Leather tanned and tawed and all manufactures of Leather, or
of which leather is the article of chief value (not being otherwise particularly enumerated) . . . .

Medicinal drugs, except those commonly used in dying . .

Hats, Caps and Bonnets of every sort . . . .

Gloves and Mittens . . . .

Stockings . . . .

Millinary ready made . . . .

Artificial flowers, feathers and other ornaments for womens
Head dresses.

Fans.

Dolls dressed and undressed.

Toys

Buttons of every kind

Carpets & Carpeting, Mats and floor Cloths

Sail Cloth

Sheathing & Cartridge paper

All powders, pastes, balls, balsams, ointments, oils, waters,
washes, tinctures, essences liquors, or other preparation or
composition, commonly called *sweet-scents, odours, perfumes*
or *cosmetics* . . . .

All Dentifrice, powders, tinctures, preparations or compositions
whatsoever for the teeth or gums.

Printed Books, except those specially imported for a College,
Academy or other public or incorporated Seminary of Learning or institution which shall be wholly Exempted from duty.

10 ⅌ Centum advalorem.

The foregoing duties to be permanently established and to be appropriated in the first place to the payment of the interest of the
public debt, in the second to such other grants and appropriations as
have been heretofore made, and in the third to the purposes of the
Act for making further and more effectual provision for the protection of the frontiers of the United States.

An addition of two & half ℔ Cent advalorem to be made to the duty on all goods heretofore rated at five ℔ Centum ad valorem.

This addition to be temporary, and accordingly to be so established as that it shall not continue longer, than till the present Indian War shall terminate, and the expences of carrying it on shall have been defrayed, which will of course include the reimbursement of any sums, that may have been borrowed by way of anticipation of the product of the duties.

It is represented that the present duty on Salt operates unequally from the considerable difference in weight in proportion to quantity of different kinds of Salt, a bushel weighing from about 56 to upwards of 80 Wt. It would have an equalizing effect if the bushel were defined by weight; and if 56 pounds were taken as the standard, a valuable accession to the revenue would result.

This regulation is therefore submitted as a resource upon the present occasion. The rate of duty to remain as it is.

It will be a reasonable accomodation to Trade, if it is made a part of this arrangement, to extend the credit for the duty on salt to a longer term. It is an article which from the circumstances of its importation frequently lies on hand for a considerable time; and in relation to the Fisheries is usually sold upon a credit of several Months.

Some remarks may be proper in regard to the proposed duties.

Those on Spirits and Wines may appear high. They are doubtless considerable. But there are precedents elsewhere of much higher duties on the same Articles. And it is certainly in every view justifiable to make a free use of them for the purposes of Revenue.

Wines generally speaking are the luxury of classes of the community who can afford to pay a considerable duty upon them.

It has appeared adviseable to adhere to the idea of a specific duty ℔ Quantity on all the species of wines in most common consumption in the Country, and those most susceptible of precise designation; as affording greatest certainty to the Revenue. And to adopt a general ad valorem rate for other kinds, proportioned to the specific duties. This rate is 40 ℔ Cent.

The distinction has proceeded from the difficulty of a precise enumeration of all the other kinds of Wine, which are and may be imported, and of such an adjustment of specific rates, as will bear some reasonable proportion to the value of the Article. The

present lowest rate of duty on Wines amounts to 200 and 300 ℔
Cent on the value of certain kinds; which may be considered as
equivalent to a prohibition.

While therefore ideas of proportion will be better consulted than
heretofore, by the proposed arrangement, it is probable, that the
revenue will be benefitted, rather than injured, by a reduction of
the duties on low priced Wines.

The considerations which render Ardent Spirits a proper object
of high duties, have been repeatedly dwelt upon. It may be added
that it is a familiar and a just remark that the peculiarly low price
of Ardent spirits in this Country is a great source of Intemperance.

To bring the price of the Article more nearly to a level with the
price of it in other markets by an increase of duty, while it will
contribute to the advancement of the revenue, cannot but prove in
other respects a public benefit. The rates proposed will be still moderate compared with examples in other Countries; and the Article is
of a nature to enable the Importer, without difficulty, to transfer
the duty to the consumer.

A discrimination is suggested in respect to duties on spirits distilled from Grain. To this, there have been two inducements—One,
that the difference in the duty is conformable to the difference
[between] [7] the cost of the grain Spirits usually imported and [that]
of West India Rum. Another, that it is in a particular manner the
interest of the United States to favor the distillation of its own
grain, in competition with foreign spirits from the same material. In
the second division of Spirits, the first class of proof is dropped;
because none of it comes from the West Indies; and because any
other Spirits usually imported which may be of so low a proof are
higher priced, even than some of the higher proofs of West India
Spirits. The dropping of that class of proof therefore in this case
is favorable to the Revenue and favorable to equality.

Several of the other specific duties which are proposed, besides
the inducements to them as items of revenue are strongly recommended by considerations which have been stated in the Report of
the Secretary on the subject of manufactures.[8] The same Report
states inducements to a 15 ℔ Cent duty on some of the Articles,
which are mentioned, as proper to be comprized under that rate.

7. Material in brackets in this document is in the handwriting of H.
8. "Report on the Subject of Manufactures," December 5, 1791.

With regard to China and Glass there are two weighty reasons for a comparitively high duty upon them. The use of them is very limited except by the wealthier classes. And both their bulk and liability to damage in transportation are great securities against evasions of the Revenue. It will however merit consideration whether for the accommodation of Importers a longer term of credit ought not to be allowed on these Articles.

A duty of two Cents ℔ lb on Cocoa is less in proportion to value than the present duty on Coffee. As an extensive article of consumption it is a productive one of Revenue.

The Duty on playing cards can give rise to no question except as to the practicability of a safe Collection. In order to this it will be proper to supperadd certain precautions, which will readily occur in regulating the details of a bill for the purpose. A similar attention will be requisite in regard to the duties on Wines. The employment of marks and certificates may advantageously be extended to this Article.

The rate of 10 ℔ Centum ad valorem it is hoped will not be deemed immoderate in relation to the Articles to which it is proposed to apply it. It is difficult to assign rules for what ought to be considered as a just standard. But after the best consideration, which the Secretary has been able to bestow upon it, he cannot discover, that any real inconvenience is likely permanently to result from the extension of that rate to the cases proposed.

The addition of 2½ ℔ Cent to the duty on the mass of articles now rated at 5 will constitute an important, though not an excessive augmentation. Nevertheless, it is proposed, that it shall be only temporary—and there is reasonable ground of expectation, that the cause for having recourse to it will not be of very long continuance.

It will not have escaped the observation of the House that the duties which were suggested in the Secretary's report, on that subject, as encouragements to Manufactures, are for the most part included among the objects of this report.

It may tend to avoid future embarrassment, if such abolitions and drawbacks, as shall be deemed expedient, with a view to promoting manufactures, shall accompany the establishment and appropriation of whatever further duties may be laid, for the object in contemplation.

And it may be found convenient to qualify the appropriation of the surplus which is to be applied to that object, so as to let in such other appropriations during the session as occurrences may suggest.

An estimate of the additional revenue which may be expected from the proposed duties is subjoined.

It will occur to the house, that the Credit allowed for the duties will require an anticipation of their product by a temporary loan for which provision in the law will be requisite.[9]

[All which is humbly submitted   Alexander Hamilton
                                                  Secy of the Treasury]

Estimate of probable additional Revenue
from the proposed duties

Madeira Wine 300 000 Gallons average increase 12 Cents ⅌ Gallon	36.000
Other Wines 700.000 Gs. average increase 3 Cents ⅌ Gallon	21.000
Distilled Spirits 3.600 000 Gallons average increase, allowing for proposed deduction from the duties on domestic Spirits 2 Cents	72 000.
Salt, from the equalizing regulation proposed will probably yield ⅙ more or 2 Cents ⅌ bushell on 2.000 000 bush.	40.000.
Malt liquors 200.000 Gallons at 2 ½ Cents	5.000
Nails & Spikes 1.800.000 lb at 1 Cent	18 000
Cocoa 800.000 at 1 Cent	8 000
Playing Cards 20.000 at 15 Cents	3 000
Other enumerated Articles ad valorem at 15 ⅌ Cent	10 000.
Increased duty on articles rated permanently at 10 ⅌ Cent ad valorem computed at 2 Millions of Dollars in value at 3 ⅌ Cent	60.000
Temporary addition at 2½ ⅌ Cent on the Articles now rated at 5 computed on 10.000.000 of dollars	250 000.
Dollars	523.000

9. Early in April, 1792, the House considered H's report, and between April 17 and April 21 debated and passed a bill that followed H's suggestions. Before the end of April the Senate and the House agreed to a bill with minor amendments (*Journal of the House*, I, 563, 566–69, 575, 580–84, 591–93, 595). See "An Act for raising a farther sum of money for the protection of the frontiers, and for other purposes therein mentioned" (1 *Stat.* 259–63 [May 2, 1792]).

To George Washington

Treasury Departt. March 16th. 1792

The Secretary of the Treasury has the honor to submit to the President the draft of a report on the subject of *ways & means* for carrying into execution the Military bill.[1]

He will wait on the President tomorrow morning for his orders; as it is interesting there should be no avoidable delay.

LC, George Washington Papers, Library of Congress.
   1. See "Report Relative to the Additional Supplies for the Ensuing Year," March 16, 1792.

From Joseph Whipple

Portsmo. New Hamp. March 16. 1792

Sir   (private)

On the 9th. of June last I had the honor to write you on the Subject of my emoluments as Collector of the Customs for the district of Portsmouth and transmitted you a Statement of them for one Year in Conformity with your Circular direction of the 14th. of April.

The Many important public matters which continually arrests your attention I imagine would hardly admit of your reporting on every Subject to which you had extended your intention of producing a reform—among those of the least importance to the public is possibly that which is the Subject of this letter. On this consideration, it is with difficulty that I can prevail on myself to address a private letter to you, but having conceived that further delay would be extremely injurious to my interest, and that an application to Congress was necessary as a ground of inquiry, and having transmitted a petition [1] to be presented in which I have refered to the above mentioned Statement of emoluments, I have considered it as expedient to the purpose of my petition to request your obliging attention to it and that you will be pleased to make such remarks on the emoluments and the duties of the office, as shall appear on your examination to be requisite in order to obtain a just allowance. Indeed my principal reliance must be on your report—as but few members of the Legislature can be competent judges of the Value of the Services. I will not presume to remark on the mode—but only to observe that should such compensations as may be allowed, only look forward to future Services—the part time of more than two years and an half will remain uncompensated.

I intreat you to excuse this application & to believe me to be with Sentiments of respect & esteem   Sir   Your Mo. Ob: & hume serv

The Hon. Alex. Hamilton Esqr.

LC, RG 36, Collector of Customs at Portsmouth, Letters Sent, 1791–1792, Vol. 3, National Archives.
1. On February 27, 1792, the House received "A petition of Joseph Whipple, Collector of the Customs . . . in the State of New Hampshire, praying that the compensation allowed him by law for his services, may be augmented. . . .
"*Ordered*, That the said petitions be referred to the Secretary of the Treasury, with instructions to examine the same, and report his opinion thereupon to the House." (*Journal of the House*, I, 521.)

To the President and Directors of the Bank of the United States [1]

Treasury Department
March 17. 1792

Gentlemen

When lately I furnished you with drafts upon the Bank of Massachusettes for 50.000 Dollars I mentioned to the Committee of your Board, on whose application, the operation was made, That it might happen, that I should want an equal sum there, at the end of the present Quarter, for payment of the Quarters Interest; in which case I should rely upon the aid of the Bank.

It does happen that the *specie* at my command, in that state, is short Thirty thousand Dollars of the requisite sum.

It is very probable that this deficiency will in time be supplied from public sources; but of this I cannot be sure. And it will not answer to leave the least uncertainty upon so delicate a point.

I am therefore under the necessity of requesting that you will furnish me with a Credit for 30 000 Dollars upon whatever specie funds you may have in the state of Massachusettes; to be used or not as occasion may require.

The advanced stage of the quarter requires dispatch.

With perfect consideration I have the honor to be   Gentlemen Your obedient servant   Alexander Hamilton

The President Directors & Company
of the Bank of the U States

ALS, Mr. Otto Madlener, Hubbard Woods, Illinois.
1. Thomas Willing was president of the Bank of the United States.

From Otho H. Williams

[*Baltimore, March 18, 1792.* On June 5, 1792, Hamilton wrote to Williams: "I have before me your letters of the 18th of March, 18th of April, 8th & 27th of May." *Letter of March 18 not found.*]

To the President and Directors of the Bank of the United States

[*Philadelphia, March 19, 1792.* On April 10, 1792, Hamilton wrote to the president and directors of the Bank of the United States: "the operation suggested in my letter of the 19th ultimo continues to be desirable." *Letter not found.*]

From James Brice [1]

[Annapolis] State of Maryland
In Council March 19th. 1792.

Sir.

We are informed by our agent resident in Philadelphia [2] that there are between nine and ten thousand dollars appropriated for the discharge of the arrears of pay due the late Maryland line for the year 1783.[3] As it would be more convenient for the claimants to recieve their money in this State if it can be done with propriety, we shall be obliged to you to pay the money so appropriated to

William Campbell [4] Esquire the Bearer of this, to be by him delivered to our Treasurer,[5] and by him paid over to the respective Claimants.

We have the honor   to be with great respect &c   James Brice.

The Honorable
The Secretary of the Treasury of the U. S.

LC, RG 56, Letters 2d Comptroller, 2d Auditor, Executive of Maryland and Georgia, 1789–1833, National Archives.

1. Brice, president of the Governor's Council of Maryland, became acting governor after the death of George Plater on February 10, 1792. He served as acting governor until April, 1792, when a special session of the General Assembly elected Thomas Sim Lee as governor.

2. The "agent resident in Philadelphia" for Maryland was Christopher Richmond, who was employed in settling the state's accounts with the United States.

3. "An Act making Appropriations for the Support of Government for the year one thousand seven hundred and ninety-two" appropriated "for pay of the late Maryland line, for which no appropriations have been made, ten thousand four hundred and ninety dollars, and thirty-six cents" (1 Stat. 228 [December 23, 1791]).

4. Campbell was a prominent Baltimore merchant.

5. Benjamin Harwood.

From William Ellery

Newport [Rhode Island] March 19, 1792. "By the last Post I received a Letter from the Comptroller,[1] inclosing a Statement of my Account from the first of July to the 30th. Septr 1791, by which I find that my charge for Scales & weights for the Port of Bristol . . . was rejected being unauthorized by you. Scales & Weights were absolutely necessary for that Port. . . . Please, Sir, to signify your assent to that purchase in such a manner that I may obtain a credit for it in the books of the Treasy. I now send by the Post directed to you the Thermometer from the Port of Pawcatuck. . . .[2] The President has pardoned Joseph Finch [3] late master of the Brig Seven Brothers, and Thomas Cottrell [4] late Owner of the Sloop Betsy, and remitted to each of them the fines of four hundred Dollars, recovered against them, and for which they were committed to Gaol, so far as the United States have any claim, title or Interest therein. Capt. Finch is discharged from Gaol, and the Brig Seven Brothers is sold to her former Owner John Topham for five hundred Dollars,

for the Price she was put up and struck off at, at Publick Auction
in Novr. last. Mr. Cottrell is not yet discharged from Gaol, no
advice having yet been received from the Informer against
him. . . ."

LC, Newport Historical Society, Newport, Rhode Island.
    1. Oliver Wolcott, Jr.
    2. See Ellery to H, April 25, 1791; February 13, March 5, 1792.
    3. See Ellery to H, July 11, August 2, 23, October 4, 10, 25, November 15,
28, 1791; February 7, 1792.
    4. See Ellery to H, August 2, 23, 26, 29, September 19, October 4, 25, November 15, 28, 1791; February 7, 1792.

To John Lamb

[*Philadelphia, March 19, 1792.* On March 19, 1792, Hamilton
wrote to William Seton, cashier of the Bank of New York, enclosing
a letter to Lamb, collector of the customs for New York City.
Letter not found.]

To William Seton

[Philadelphia] March 19. 1792

My Dear Sir
    It is strongly represented here, that you have restricted your
operations so as absolutely to afford no accommodation in the present distress of the City.[1] Knowing the disposition of the Directors,
I am persuaded, that every thing is done which is prudent. And I
dare say, there is much exaggeration.
    This is therefore barely to observe, That as far as you may have
been influenced by any apprehension of being distressed by the
establishment of a branch of the Bank of The U States[2] and a want
of *cooperation*, you may relinquish your apprehensions, as I have
good evidence from a variety of conversations that it will be enjoined upon the Directors of the Branch to maintain the most perfect & confidential communication with your institution & to co-
operate in mutual & general accommodation.
    You may therefore act on this Idea and do as much as would be
otherwise prudent. In giving you this intimation I will add that
should not the course be pursued which I have good ground to

expect by the Bank of the U States I will decidedly aid your Institution so as to preserve it from harm in consequence of any greater latitude which may have been taken upon this intimation.

At the same time I am far from wishing to encourage an imprudent extension of accommodation at such a crisis. Perhaps however it may be worth considering how much more can be done in favour of parties who can pledge *public Stock* as collateral security. This foundation of Credit you are sure is a good one.

The Merchants of New York have to pay considerable sums in duties in this and the next Month. You may boldly accommodate them under an assurance that the money shall in no event be drawn out of your hands in less than three Months, unless perfectly agreeable to you.

You know the Collector will receive *bank* notes, which have thirty days to run. I send you inclosed a letter [3] directing him to furnish you, if required, with a list of the names and sums of those who have bonds which will fall due to the end of April in order that you may if you please make a *special* operation for their accommodation, under the above assurance.

Yours sincerely   A Hamilton

Wm. Seton Esquire Cashier

ALS, Bank of New York, New York City.
1. The failure of William Duer had precipitated a financial panic in New York City. See Duer to H, March 12, 1792, and H to Duer, March 14, 1792.
2. The directors of the Bank of the United States had resolved that as soon as possible after the first Monday in January, 1792, a branch of the Bank of the United States (Office of Discount and Deposit) should be opened in New York City. It opened for deposits on April 2, 1792, and commenced discounting on April 19.
3. H's letter to John Lamb has not been found.

From Robert Troup [1]

NYork 19 March 1792

My dear friend

Ever since the recipt of your last letter [2] I have been kept in such

ALS, Hamilton Papers, Library of Congress.
1. Troup, a New York City lawyer, had been a close friend of H since the period immediately preceding the American Revolution when both had been undergraduates at King's College.
2. Letter not found.

a state of distraction that I have not been able to compose my mind sufficiently to write to you. Courts have been sitting day after day & it so happens that I have had business in all of them, but, as was the case with you, instead of being simple it is of the most perplexing kind.

I now am forced to write to you by an event which has called into action all my feelings & overwhelmed me with grief, the bitterness of which can only be conceived by an heart like yours. Before I enter upon this painful subject I must inform you that before Genl Schuyler went to Philadelphia I had totally withdrawn myself from a⟨ll⟩ engagements with the friends of the new bank [3] & had left the thing to its fate. After mature reflection upon the subject I saw that it would be productive of real evil—and it was manifest to me that there was mingled with the motives of some of the leaders of the association a large portion of personal enmity to you & of rooted hatred of the government. Upon this ⟨conviction⟩ I requested Genl. Schuyler to get a letter from you to Col. Lewis [4] who I understood was an advocate of the measure. You will not censure my heart for my connexion with this project. It has ever felt the liveliest emotions for your fame & the public good. I condemn myself however for one thing—I am ashamed that any thing said about the friends of the measure should ever have irrated me. It was unworthy of me and of that rectitude which I am upon every occasion anxious to observe. At present I consider the bill [5] as lost. If no *other* cause existed to prove the ruinous tendency of the establishment of another bank the present convulsion in this City furnishes the dearest evidence of it. This convulsion is immediately owing to the event above alluded to—Our friend Duer's failure.[6] This poor man is in a state of almost complete insanity; and his situation is a source of

3. For information on the attempt to organize new banks in New York during the first months of 1792, see H to William Seton, January 18, 24, February 10, 1792; Seton to H, January 22, February 6, 1792; and Philip Schuyler to H, January 29, 1792.

4. Morgan Lewis, the attorney general of New York State.

5. For the bill for the incorporation of the "Million Bank," see H to Seton, January 18, 1792.

6. For an account of William Duer's failure and the subsequent financial panic in New York, see Duer to H, March 12, 1792, and H to Duer, March 14, 1792.

inexpressible grief to all his friends. On Saturday night his friends met at his house & staid with him till near 12 o'Clock when we broke up in confusion without being able to agree upon a single measure. An effort was made on Sunday to collect another meeting at my house which was effected. All we could do was to draw up a notification & sign it—by which we said that from the magnitude & variety of Duer's operations he would not be able to ⟨make⟩ any specific propositions to his creditors till next saturday when we requested a meeting of the creditors. I find this has composed the public mind which had been much irritated and threatned to break forth into acts of violence. What will be the result God only knows. The truth is that the notes unpaid amount to about half a million of dollars & Duer has not a farthing of money or a particle of stock to pay them with. All the property he has in the World is ⟨some⟩ land in the Province of Maine upon which there is a heavy encumbrance of purchase Money due. You will ask what has become of his money & Stock. His answer is & he calls God to witness the truth of it that every iota of money & stocks has been applied by him to the satisfaction of engagements personally made with him upon a confidence in his honor and friendship. Such is the state of things. We all see the absolute necessity of supporting his character & extricating him if possible from his embarrassments. For this purpose we are endeavoring to open a loan upon his land—for nothing but money will satisfy the voracious appetites of his note holders. If we fail in this attempt & there is nothing offered but land I fear his reputation will be eternally blasted & that his person will be endangered. Widows, orphans, merchants mechanicks &c are all concerned in the notes. And in the large number are some low & turbulent spirits. We shall also attempt the loan in Philadelphia. If your friends in Philadelphia view the subject in the light we do here, they will suppose that Duer's total bankruptcy will affect the public interest by bringing the funding system into odium. I am strongly impressed with the mischiefs that will result from it myself and I am striving day & night to put Matters upon the best footing I can. My heart bleeds for Duer and My purse shall flow for him as far as prudence will warrant. This letter is for your own eye only. Communicate Duer's situation to our friends & give us your advice by the earliest opportunity. I am exceedingly thankful for your last letter & shall ever regard it as the most unequivocal testimony of your friendship.

The Moment Jay came forward I abandoned all ideas of Burr [7] & have constantly been doing every thing in my power to promote Jay's election. If we can carry it the state will be blessed. He is one of the worthiest of men—& independent of his character I owe him obligations which my heart tells me I never can discharge. With regard to Burr's election I have a secret to tell you which I cannot communicate till I see you. I have reason to suspect that we have both been abused. No good can result from any explanations at present; and therefore I shall be quiet. This hint is most confidentally communicated.

God bless you Yours   Rob. Troup

A Hamilton Esqr

7. This is a reference to the candidacy of John Jay for the governorship of New York. Before Jay had received the support of New York Federalists, Aaron Burr had expressed his willingness to oppose George Clinton, the incumbent. See Schuyler to H, January 29, 1792, and Isaac Ledyard to H, February 1, 17, and 28, 1792.

To John Adams

[Philadelphia, March 20, 1792]

Mr. Hamilton presents his respectful Compliments to the Vice President. He may have heared that the Treasurer was in the Market last night [1] and may be at a loss concerning his authority. The ground of the operation is an Act of the Board of the 15th of August last appropriating a sum *between* three & four hundred Thousand Dollars, which Mr. Hamilton considers as *any* sum *short* of 400.000 Dollars; [2] leaving still a sum to be expended within the terms as to price prescribed by that Act. This is merely by way of information.

Tuesday March 20th. 91 [3]

AL, Adams Family Papers, deposited in the Massachusetts Historical Society, Boston.

1. Samuel Meredith, treasurer of the United States, was purchasing Government securities for the Government. The object of these purchases was to maintain or restore the price of Government securities in the face of the panic precipitated by William Duer's failure. See Duer to H, March 12, 1792; H to Duer, March 14, 1792; H to William Seton, March 19, 1792; Robert Troup to H, March 19, 1792.

According to Meredith's statement of March 31, 1792, between March 21 and March 27, 1792, he purchased deferred stock in the amount of $16,118.74 of assumed state debt and $17,236.89 of domestic debt; during the same period he purchased three percent stock in the amount of $1,165.28 of assumed debt and $12,316.56 of domestic debt. The total specie expended from the sinking fund amounted to $28,915.52 (*ASP, Finance*, I, 163).

2. The resolution of August 15, 1791, authorized the purchase of Government stock by Seton at New York and by Meredith at Philadelphia of an amount ranging "between three and four hundred thousand dollars." See "Meeting of the Commissioners of the Sinking Fund," August 15, 1791.

3. H misdated this letter, for this should read "92."

To Thomas Jefferson

[*Philadelphia*] *March 20, 179*[2.] [1] Explains why the "Treasurer was in the Market last night." [2]

AL, Thomas Jefferson Papers, Library of Congress.
1. H misdated this letter "Tuesday March 20 1791."
2. This letter is the same as H to John Adams, March 20, 1792.

John Adams to John Jay [1]

Philadelphia
March 21. 1792

Sir

A difference of opinion having arisen among those of the Trustees of the Sinking Fund, who are now in this City, respecting the construction of their authority under the Act making provision for the Reduction of the Public Debt, by which they are equally divided,[2] your presence here towards settling the principle which is in question, in order to the future conduct of the business, has become indispensable.

The Board at a Meeting this day have accordingly come to a resolution to request your attendance here as speedily as possible; which on their behalf I now do.

I have the honor to be very respectfully Sir Your most
Obedient ser   John Adams

The Chief Justice of The United States

LS, in the writing of H, Columbia University Libraries; Df, in the writing of
H, Essex Institute, Salem, Massachusetts.

1. Jay was the Federalist candidate for governor of New York in 1792. At the
time this letter was written, he was in New York City in his capacity as judge
of the Circuit Court.

A note, signed by Charles Francis Adams, which appears at the top of the
draft, reads as follows: "This is an Autograph of Alexander Hamilton, Secretary
of the Treasury—A copy of a letter written by him to John Jay, Chief Justice
of the United States, as a Trustee of the Sinking fund, furnished to John
Adams, as Vice president and likewise a Trustee."

For background to this document, see H to Adams, March 20, 1792, and H to
Thomas Jefferson, March 20, 1792.

A letter written by Edmund Randolph to Jay on March 21, 1792, reads in
part as follows:

"The four trustees of the sinking fund, who are here, having been divided on
two occasions, very interesting to the United States, I am instructed to request
your attendance, as soon as it may be convenient to you.

"They are aware, how much their desire to see you here may interfere with
your arrangements for the ensuing circuit; but in truth they cannot justify
themselves in forbearing to represent to you the urgency of the case." (ALS,
Columbia University Libraries.)

2. The questions dividing the commissioners concerned Section 1 of "An Act
making provision for the Reduction of the Public Debt," which reads in part as
follows: "That all such surplus of the product of the duties . . . as shall remain after satisfying the several purposes for which appropriations shall have
been made by law to the end of the present session, shall be applied to the
purchase of the debt of the United States, at its market price, if not exceeding
the par or true value thereof" (1 *Stat.* 186 [August 12, 1790]).

The differences in the interpretation of this section which arose at the March
21, 1792, meeting of the commissioners of the sinking fund were later summarized by the commissioners and forwarded to Jay for his opinion. Randolph's
transcription of that summary reads as follows:

"The following questions have been approved by the Vice President, the
secretary of State, the secretary of the treasury, and the attorney general of the
U. S, as comprehending the points, on which the board was divided.

"1. Do the words, '*if not exceeding the par or true value thereof,*' in the first
section of the act, making provision for the reduction of the public debt, restrict the purchase of any part of the debt of the United States, (whether *subscribed,* and bearing an immediate interest of six per centum, or an immediate
interest of three per cent, or a future interest of six per cent.; or *unsubscribed;*)
so long as the market-price of the same shall not exceed twenty shillings in the
pound?

"2. If those words do restrain the purchase of any species of the public debt
within limits, narrower than twenty shillings in the pound; what rate of interest
shall be adopted, as the rule for computing the value of each kind of stock at
this day?" (ADS, Columbia University Libraries.)

Above Randolph's summary in this document are minutes of the meeting of
the commissioners of the sinking fund of March 28, 1792, signed by Randolph

and sent by him to Jay in a letter dated March 29, 1792 (ALS, Columbia University Libraries).

From William Duer [1]

[*New York, March 21, 1792.* The calendar summary of this letter reads as follows: " 'Your letter of the 14th has been Balm to my Soul. . . .[2] You shall never blush to call me your friend.' Sends letter by the surveyor of Gallipolis.[3] Recommends that settlement." *Letter not found.*]

1. Letter listed in "Calendar Summary of Philip Church and Alexander Hamilton Papers," Personal Miscellaneous, Box 6, Schuyler, MS Division, New York Public Library.
2. For information on Duer's bankruptcy, see Duer to H, March 12, 1792; H to Duer, March 14, 1792; and Robert Troup to H, March 19, 1792.
3. Presumably this is a reference to Medad Mitchell. See Mitchell to H, February 9, 1792.

To William Ellery

[*Philadelphia, March 21, 1792.* On April 9, 1792, Ellery wrote to Hamilton: "I have received your letter of the 21st. of this last month." *Letter not found.*]

From Benjamin Lincoln

Boston [March] [1] 21 1792

Sir

I shall pay particular attention to your directions [2] respecting the payment of the drafts of the treasurer in favour of the Loan officer of New Hampshire & Mr Appleton of this State. You will learn by the inclosed return that a large proportion of the money on hand is in the bills of the bank of the united States issued in Philadelphia which are now sold here at a discount of one ⅌ Cent. From what I hear of the price of stock with you, which is much under what they are sold for in this Town I think the bank bills issued in Philadelphia will soon be up at par at the least.

Secy of the Treasury

LC, Massachusetts Historical Society, Boston; LC, RG 36, Collector of Customs at Boston, Letter Book, 1790–1797, National Archives; two copies, RG 56, Letters from the Collector at Boston, National Archives.
   1. Lincoln mistakenly wrote "May." The copy in the Massachusetts Historical Society and one of the two copies in RG 56, Letters from the Collector at Boston, National Archives, are dated May 21, 1792. In the Lincoln letter book in the Massachusetts Historical Society, however, this letter appears after a letter of March 21, 1792, addressed to Nathaniel Appleton, commissioner of loans for Massachusetts, on the same topic as that discussed in Lincoln's letter to H printed above. The next letter in the letter book is dated March 31, 1792.
   2. See H to Lincoln, March 5, 1792.

From Gouverneur Morris [1]

London 21 March 1792

Dear Hamilton

A Vessel just going to New York presents me an Opportunity of saying that I thank you for your Exertions to effect my Appointment. I know you too well my good Friend to make long Speeches on that Subject. I shall acknowlege the Services of my Friends properly on proper Occasions and till then be silent. In patronizing this Appointment you have incurred more Trouble than you was perhaps aware of for you must water the Tree which you have planted. In plain English I beg you to favor me with your Correspondence and to give me Information, *which otherwise I may not obtain.* In Return I will apprize you of what is doing on this Side of the Water *confidentially* which I will not do to *every Body.*

The other Day at an Auction of the late Marquis de la luzerne's [2] Effects his various Orders were put up and among them those of the Cincinnati. These I bought out of Respect to that Society But as I have not the Honor of belonging to it they are useless to me and therefore if you know any worthy Member to Whom they may be acceptable I will with much Pleasure deliver them to your order.

   I am truly yours   Gouv Morris

ALS, Hamilton Papers, Library of Congress; LC, Gouverneur Morris Papers, Library of Congress.
   1. The Senate had confirmed Morris's appointment as United States Minister Plenipotentiary to France on January 12, 1792.
   2. Anne César, Chevalier de La Luzerne, French Minister to the United

States during the American Revolution, was appointed French Ambassador to Great Britain in January, 1788, where he remained until his death on September 14, 1791.

From William Seton

[New York, March 21, 1792]

My Dear sir

Your very kind favor of the 19 I recd yesterday & this day as it contained matters of the utmost importance to this Institution laid it before our board. You may be assured that so far from restricting our operations so as not to offend any accomodation in the present distress, we have gone as far & perhaps farther than prudence would have dictated. It is true no new Loans have very lately been made, but the reductions required of the old, have been very trifling compard to the Security the Bank had a right to have in this time of suspention & distrust—had it not been for the great drain of Specie we have had, & the dread that it might be followd, by a further one from the captiousness of our dealers & the hint of opposition—no doubt we should have gone on loaning with the same confidence as we did but in this failure of our friend Duer [1] so many were tainted it is next to impossible to say whom can be counted on again in advance.

The Interview that our directors have already had with that of the Branch; [2] & the improved genl intention of both, drive away all idea of any apprehension of our being distressed by that Institution. With certainy the two Directions are perfectly disposed to assist each other in case of Emergency & I trust such confidential Communication will be kept up as to occasion a mutual accomodation. It is what I have pressed & pointed out from the first,—the prosperity of both depends upon it. I delivered your Letter to the Collector [3] & have requested him to furnish us between this & Friday with a list of the Names of & Sums that the Merchants have to pay for duties between this and the last of April. The Board will do any thing to Accomodate their payments. We are now in a much better situation than we were—our balance of actual Specie exceeds the balance due to our depositors not taking in the money due the

Public, & the Treasurer of the State of New York [4]—the latter
debt which now amounts to 379 M dollars, we had reason to suppose as the Treasurer was a Director of the Branch might be taken
from us to place in their Vaults—& altho we ⟨command an item⟩ of
actual Specie for it having ⟨discounted⟩ for those who had to pay the
Treasurer upon the presumption it could not be called for in any
month & then only by installments—which discounts are now outstanding & obliged to be secured from inability to pay up. Yet it is
a debt we owe & must take into our consideration in the present
state of affairs.

We have now about 100,000 Dollars ⟨National⟩ Notes, & they are
increasing daily. By the deposits of the Collector & from our receiving them of those who have no other manner to pay us & each
other—the State of Credit is so deranged, and the evil resulting from
the Creating of this Mass of artificial credit supported only by
usurious Loans is so universal that there is no forming a judgment
of the evil situation of individuals. If Duer is not able to satisfy his
Creditors by what he is to say to them on Saturday, the day appointed for their Convention—the Consequence will be awfull &
I shall tremble for him. Stocks rose a little yesterday in consequence
of the Intelligence of the Treasurer having entered the Market at
Phila. [5]—but today they are down again. Perhaps a purchase for the
public if consistent with ⟨policy⟩ might be of good Consequence
here, & one or two hundred thousand Dollars of the Balance we
owe the Public thrown into Circulation in this way would not injure us as it would pass from hand to hand & merely fill up the
vacuum of drooping Credit without draining us of Specie.

The letter you enclosed ⟨me⟩ in yours of the 1⟨9⟩th. I delivered.

I am with the Sincerest truth   My dear sir   Your Obliged Obdt.
Ser.

ADf, Bank of New York, New York City.
1. For information on the bankruptcy of William Duer, see Duer to H,
March 12, 1792; H to Duer, March 14, 1792; and Robert Troup to H, March
19, 1792.
2. Seton is referring to the branch of the Bank of the United States at New
York. See H to Seton, March 19, 1792, note 2.
3. Letter to John Lamb not found. See H to Seton, March 19, 1792.
4. Gerard Bancker.
5. See H to John Adams, March 20, 1792; H to Thomas Jefferson, March 20,
1792.

To William Short

Treasury Department March 21st. 1792

Sir,

As the discharge of the arrears of interest and instalments of principal of the French debt, which are due, may have occasioned your power to borrow for that object to be suspended, until you can obtain a loan at a rate of interest and Charges sufficiently reduced, it is my wish, that as soon as it shall be proper after the receipt of this letter you would proceed to borrow the sum of three Millions of florins on the terms of the Antwerp loan,[1] to be applied to the purposes mentioned in the Act of the 12th August 1790 for the reduction of the public debt.[2]

I shall wish for the earliest advices upon this subject to enable me to direct the draughts, and I request your particular attention so to manage the operation, that no loss of interest, which can be avoided may take place.

I have the honor to be   with great consideration & esteem   Your most obedt Servant   Alexander Hamilton

Wm Short Esqr
Minister Resident
at the Hague

LS, Hamilton Papers, Library of Congress.
1. For a description of this loan, see Short to H, November 8, 1791, note 4, and November 12, 1791.
2. Section 4 of "An Act making Provision for the Reduction of the Public Debt" reads as follows: "*And be it further enacted,* That the President of the United States be, and he is hereby authorized to cause to be borrowed, on behalf of the United States, a sum or sums not exceeding in the whole two millions of dollars, at an interest not exceeding five per cent., and that the sum or sums so borrowed, be also applied to the purchase of the said debt of the United States, under the like direction, in the like manner, and subject to the like regulations and restrictions with the surplus aforesaid: *Provided,* That out of the interest arising on the debt to be purchased in manner aforesaid, there shall be appropriated and applied to a sum not exceeding the rate of eight per centum per annum on account both of principal and interest towards the repayment of the two millions of dollars so to be borrowed" (1 *Stat.* 187 [August 12, 1790]).

To Nathaniel Appleton

Treasury Department
March 22. 1792.

Sir

You will find enclosed an open letter for the Directors of the Office of Discount and Deposit (or the Branch of the Bank of the United States) at Boston,[1] by which you will perceive that you are to obtain from them the sum of thirty thousand Dollars, if you shall have occasion for it, to pay the quarter's interest.[2]

You are first to avail yourself of all the specie in the hands of the Collector of Boston, excepting only the sum of 6,000 Dollars, which is to be retained by him, to meet certain bills of the Commissioner of Loans in New Hampshire, which he is authorized to direct to the Collector.[3] The remaining specie the Collector is to deposit in the Boston Branch of the Bank of the United States, for the purpose of paying the interest on the public debt. He is also to pay in all the notes of the Bank of the US to be deposited in such way or form as the said Branch shall determine to receive the paper of the Bank of the United States.

You are further to avail yourself of all the monies received, when this reaches you, or to be received on or before the 2d of April, by the Bank of Massachusetts,[4] taking the greatest care so to manage and conduct the receipt of this money as to produce to them no avoidable inconvenience or derangement. The sum they held in specie at the last return, on the 24th of February, was 31,197. $^{5}\!\%_{100}$ Dollars, and in the Bills or notes of the Bank of the United States 620 Dollars. Since that, further sums have no doubt been transmitted, and additions may be made before the expiration of the 2d of April.

The monies in your hands, arising from the sales of the Treasurers Bills, and whatever may remain of the former Quarters will be deposited with the Branch Bank, with which you are hereafter to make your deposits. You will also apprize the Branch Bank of the sum you possess in the Treasurer's bills, and the places or persons, on which you are at liberty to fill up their direction, in order that both you and they may have the chance of disposing of them, if there be need and opportunity.

Any of the public Creditors, who may incline to receive their interest in notes of the Bank of the United States, may be so paid as far as the notes are at command.

No use is to be made of the Treasurer's Bills, or other means in your power, or in the power of the Branch Bank further than what may be necessary to the discharge of the interest that will be payable the 1st of April, including any balances on former quarters.

Whatever monies (part of the 30,000 Dollars mentioned in the letter from the President of the Bank of the United States) shall be expended in the payment of the interest is to be finally covered by the Draughts of the Treasurer, of which you are possessed so far as they shall be finally unsold, which will be in lieu of my draughts for that sum mentioned in the letter. Should these draughts be insufficient to cover the 30,000 Dollars, my letter will be sufficient present Authority, and all due formality will be given to the transaction, on advice.

The payment of the quarter's interest is to be conducted by the Branch Bank in the manner pursued here. That is to say—You are to possess them of the Dividend Book, with the unsigned receipts, which it is necessary for you to have as vouchers, and they are to make the payments and take the receipts in Bank. Your particular information and some extraordinary attention to the course of their payments the first time will be prudent, and may save future trouble. But should the Branch Bank [5] not be in operation yet, so as to render it practicable for them to perform on the day the business of the payment of the interest, you are to pursue the former method, and to proceed in the payments, yourself, as no remission of the usual and perfect punctuality is on any account to occur.

I am with great consideration   Sir   Your obedient serv [6]

Alexander Hamilton

Nathaniel Appleton Esqr
Commissr of Loans
Boston

PS   It will be proper to govern yourself entirely by the judgment of the President and Directors of the Branch Bank in the receipt of the monies and United States Bank notes which are to be paid to you by the Massachusetts Bank.

LS, The Bostonian Society, Boston.
1. This enclosure was a letter from Thomas Willing, president of the Bank of the United States, to the directors of the Boston branch bank, as stated in paragraph seven of the letter printed above.
2. See H to the President and Directors of the Bank of the United States, March 17, 1792.
3. See H to Benjamin Lincoln, March 5, 1792, and Lincoln to H, March 21, 1792.
4. Massachusetts Bank of Boston, a private bank chartered by the state in 1784.
5. The Boston branch of the Bank of the United States commenced discounting on March 26, 1792.
6. The closing is in H's handwriting.

From William Duer [1]

[*New York, March 22, 1792.* The calendar summary of this letter reads as follows: "Similar letter of appreciation." [2] *Letter not found.*]

1. Letter listed in "Calendar Summary of Philip Church and Alexander Hamilton Papers," Personal Miscellaneous, Box 6, Schuyler, MS Division, New York Public Library.
2. See Duer to H, March 21, 1792.

To Benjamin Lincoln

Treasury Department
March 22. 1792.

Sir

The Commissioner of Loans will receive by this post my instructions relative to the quarter's interest on the public debt.[1] After retaining the sum of six thousand Dollars, in specie, to pay certain Bills of the Commissioner of Loans in New Hampshire,[2] you will be pleased to pay into the Boston Branch Bank the remaining specie and notes of the Bank of the United States which will be in your hands, for the purpose of discharging the interest abovementioned. You will hereafter make your deposits, once in every week, in the

Boston Branch Bank, taking duplicate receipts, and transmitting one of them to this Off⟨ice.⟩ [3]

Benjamin Lincoln Esqr
Collector Boston.

⟨P. S. My meaning is that the⟩ specie you have in hand after retaining the above mentioned six thousand Dollars should be paid to the order of the Commissioner of Loans upon drafts of the Treasurer in his favour in order to being deposited in the Branch-Bank.[4]

L[S], RG 36, Collector of Customs at Boston, Letters from the Treasury, 1772–1818, National Archives; copy, RG 56, Letters to the Collector at Boston, Vol. 6, National Archives; copy, RG 56, Letters to Collectors at Small Ports, "Set G," National Archives.

  1. See H to Nathaniel Appleton, March 22, 1792.
  2. See H to Lincoln, March 5, 1792, and Lincoln to H, March 21, 1792.
  3. Material within broken brackets has been taken from one of the copies in the National Archives.
  4. The postscript is in H's handwriting.

To Philip Livingston [1]

[*Philadelphia, March 22, 1792.* On March 24, 1792, Livingston wrote to Hamilton: "Upon the receipt of your Letter of the 22d. Inst." *Letter not found.*]

  1. Livingston, a New York City Federalist, was a lawyer, businessman, and politician. He was a director of the Bank of New York, a stockholder of the Society for Establishing Useful Manufactures, and first president of the New York branch of the Bank of the United States. In 1792 he was a member of the New York Senate.

From John Page [1]

[Philadelphia] March 22d. 1792

Dear Sir
  I have snatched a few Minutes from my Business to scribble an answer to the Author of the Letter which I delivered to you in the

Presence of Col. Hartley.[2] I have inclosed it for your perusal according to my Promise & hope it will serve as a Proof to you that I disdain to be an accomplice in a Cabal against you & convince Mr. Blanchard that he has mistaken my Character. I am dear Sir with real Esteem & perfect Respect

Your most obedt Servant   John Page

ALS, Hamilton Papers, Library of Congress.
    1. Page was a member of the House of Representatives from Virginia.
    2. Thomas Hartley was a member of the House of Representatives from Pennsylvania. The letter which John Page delivered to H was undoubtedly from James Blanchard, who had written a scurrilous letter to H on February 29, 1792.

To William Seton

[*Philadelphia, March 22, 1792.* The dealer's catalogue description of this letter reads: "On financial matters." *Letter not found.*]

ALS, sold at Parke-Bernet Galleries, February 10, 1959, Lot 69.

From Otho H. Williams

[*Baltimore, March 22, 1792.* On March 29, 1792, Hamilton wrote to Williams: "I have received your letter of the 22d instant." *Letter not found.*]

To William Duer [1]

[Philadelphia, March 23, 1792] [2]

My Dear Duer

Five minutes ago, I received your Letter of yesterday.[3] I hasten to express to you my thoughts; as your situation does not permit delay.

I am of opinion that those friends, who have lent you their money or security from personal confidence in your honor, and without being interested in the operation in which you may have been engaged, ought to be taken care of absolutely and preferably to all other Creditors. In the next place, public institutions ought to be secured. On this point the Manufacturing Society [4] will claim peculiar regard. I am told the funds of that Society have been drawn out of both banks. I trust they are not diverted. The public interest & my reputation are deeply concerned in this matter.

Your affairs with the Government as connected with your office as Assistant to the Board of Treasury [5] will deserve your particular attention.

Persons of whom you have made actual *purchases* and whose property has been delivered to you would stand next after public institutions. But here perhaps some arbitration may be made. It would certainly be desireable to distinguish between the price of the Stock at the time of purchase and enhanced price upon time.

With regard to contracts merely *executory* and in regard to which differences would be to be paid, no stock having been delivered—I postpone claims of this nature to all others. They ought not to interfere with any claim which is founded on value actually given.

As to the usurious Tribe—these present themselves under different aspects. Are these *women* or *ignorant* people or Trustees of Infants? [6] The real principal advanced & legal interest would in such cases stand in my mind on high ground. The *mere* veteran *usurers* may be taken greater liberties with. Their *real principal* & *interest* however abstracted from usurious accumulation would stand better than claims constituted wholly by profits from speculative bargains.

But the following course deserves consideration. Take care of Debts to friends who have aided you by their money or credit disinterestedly and public institutions.

Assign the rest of your property for the benefit of Creditors generally. The Law will do the rest. Wherever usury can be proved the contract I take it will be null. Where it cannot be proved the parties will be obliged to acknowledge on oath & *then their principal & Interest only will be due.*

Wherever a fair count can be stated and all the sums borrowed & paid can be set against each other, it is probable it will be found that more has been paid than on a computation of legal interest was ever received. Here I presume the demand would be extinguished & possibly the parties would be compelled to disgorge.

These are rather desultory thoughts than a systematic view of the subject. I wish I had more time to form a more digested opinion but as I have not you must take what I can give.

Adieu My unfortunate friend God bless you & extricate you with reputation. Where is Lady Kitty?[7] Give my love to her. Again Adieu.

Be honorable calm & firm.   A Hamilton

March 23d.
Wm. Duer Esqr.

JCH Transcripts.
1. Duer had been forced to suspend payments on his many obligations on March 9, 1792. For an account of his financial difficulties, see Duer to H, March 12, 1792; H to Duer, March 14, 1792; and Robert Troup to H, March 19, 1792. On the date on which H wrote this letter, March 23, Duer was imprisoned for debt.
2. This letter is dated May 23, 1792, in JCHW, VIII, 245–47; HCLW, IX, 510; Hamilton, History, IV, 289.
3. Letter not found.
4. Duer was at this time governor of the Society for Establishing Useful Manufactures.
5. Duer had served as secretary to the Board of Treasury from April, 1785, until the Board concluded its operations in 1789. H is presumably referring to the two charges for indents of interest during 1788 and 1789 for which Duer had not accounted. These charges formed the basis of the Government's case in the suit which was instituted against Duer. See H to Duer, March 14, 1792.
6. In a notice of March 26, 1792, from New Prison, Duer requested "All widows, trustees of orphans, mechanics or tradesmen" who held his notes to present them to William S. Livingston "in order that the same may be registered and reported on previous to provision being made for the same" (The [New York] Daily Advertiser, March 28, 1792).
7. "Lady Kitty" was Duer's wife and the daughter of the late William Alexander of Basking Ridge, New Jersey. While in England before the American Revolution, Alexander had tried without success to establish his claim to the title of Earl of Stirling. In America, however, he was generally known as "Lord Stirling."

From John Jay [1]

New York 23 March 1792

My good Friend

By the post I recd. this afternoon Letters from the Vice Presidt.[2] & Atty. Genl.[3] calling me to the Board of Trustees. My answers to both are necessarily very concise, having been engag'd by Company, and now being pressed for Time, they are enclosed.[4]

I regard my Duty to attend the Courts as being in point of legal Obligation *primary*, and to attend the Trustees as *secondary*—and yet I can concieve that the Order would be sometimes inverted, if only the Importance of the occasion was considered.

My answr. to the Vice presidt. proposes in a few words, that the Question in agitation be stated to me. It appears from his Letter to be a meer law Question. In that Case my opinion shall without Delay be formed and transmitted. This Letter will go by an Express who I am told will set out at 10 OCk.

You doubtless have heard more than I can tell you of the nature and extent of our friend Duers misfortunes.[5] I sincerely regret these Consequences to him and to the very many who are and will be affected by them. They have affected all money operations here, and I believe it is still doubtful whether any favorable change *likely to last*, will soon take place.

Why cannot I give my opinion on a Law Question in the city of New York as well as in the City of Pha? [6]

Yours very Affy.   John Jay

The Honb. A. Hamilton Esqr

ALS, Hamilton Papers, Library of Congress.
1. For background to this letter, see H to John Adams, March 20, 1792, and the letter which H wrote for Adams to Jay on March 21, 1792.
2. Adams to Jay, March 21, 1792.
3. See Adams to Jay, March 21, 1792, note 1.
4. Jay to Adams, March 23, 1792 (ADf, Columbia University Libraries).
5. For the misfortunes of William Duer and their repercussions in the New York financial scene, see Duer to H, March 12, 1792; H to Duer, March 14, 23, 1792; Robert Troup to H, March 19, 1792; H to William Seton, March 19, 1792; Seton to H, March 21, 1792.
6. The commissioners of the sinking fund decided that Jay should be permitted to submit his opinion in writing. See "Meeting of the Commissioners of the Sinking Fund," March 26, 1792.

To Nicholas Low [1]

[*Philadelphia, March 23, 1792.* On April 10, 1792, Low wrote to Hamilton: "I am duely favord with yours of 23. 29 & 31 Ulto." *Letter of March 23 not found.*]

1. Low, a New York City merchant and land speculator, was a director of the Bank of New York, the New York branch of the Bank of the United States, and the Society for Establishing Useful Manufactures.

Contract with Peter Nagle and Philip Zieber

[*Philadelphia*] *March 24, 1792.* "Articles of agreement between Alexander Hamilton Secretary of the Treasury, on behalf of the United [States] of America, and Peter Nagle & Philip Zieber of the Borough of Reading in the County of Berks Hatters. . . . That the said Peter Nagle and Philip Zieber shall furnish & Delive⟨r⟩ to the order of the Secretary for the department of War four Thousand Six hundred & eight hats . . . at the price of five Shillings & nine pence pennsylvania Currency, or Seventy Six & two thirds Cents each hat."

Copy, RG 217, Miscellaneous Treasury Accounts, 1790–1894, Account No. 2878, National Archives.

From Philip Livingston

New York 24th. March 1792

Dear Sr

Upon the receipt of your Letter of the 22d. Inst.[1] I called upon Mr. Jay, who I find is of opinion that, he cannot go to Philadelphia & return in time, for his Court & that he can give his opinion in writing.[2] Mr. Gulian Verplanck[3] seems disposed that the New York Bank shoud give every aid in their power consistent with safety, & on Tuesday they will assist the Dealers in some degree.

I have seen Low,[4] He thinks the Stock of the Manufacturing Society[5] safe, except 10,000 Drs in the hands of Duers Agents a Mr. Ingram,[6] to be safe.

Schuyler, & myself think, Mr. Jay's opinion, if the Trustees, who may be oposed to it, object, will not decide the business—that his vote must be viva, voce. I sat with Low & Schuyler two Hours last night. Stock's continue depressed & Things Gloomy. Duer comes forward to day, with some propositions,[7] but I hope not in person as he cannot make any propositions that will be satisfactory & his Creditors will be enraged.

As Mr. Jays opinion in writing may be received, & enable you to come into the Market again, & you would not receive it by Post untill Tuesday afternoon I thought best to send it off by express.[8] I am with great regard   Your's   Ph: Livingston

The Honbe. A Hamilton Esqr.

ALS, Hamilton Papers, Library of Congress.

1. Letter not found.

2. H wished John Jay to return to Philadelphia to vote as one of the commissioners of the sinking fund on the proposition that the sinking fund should be used to maintain the price of Government securities during the panic. See H to John Adams, March 20, 1792; the letter which H wrote for Adams to Jay on March 21, 1792; and Jay to H, March 23, 1792.

3. Verplanck was president of the Bank of New York.

4. Nicholas Low.

5. The Society for Establishing Useful Manufactures.

6. Francis Ingraham, a Philadelphia merchant, arranged stock contracts for Duer with Jonathan Williams, Robert Morris, and other stock purchasers.

7. On March 24, the day after he went to jail, Duer wrote a public letter "To the holders of engagements under the signature of the Subscriber" ([Philadelphia] National Gazette, March 29, 1792). This letter, which was reprinted in several newspapers, described Duer's plans for paying his debts.

8. See Jay to the Commissioners of the Sinking Fund, March 31, 1792.

To Richard Morris [1]

[Philadelphia, March 24, 1792. On April 13, 1792, Morris wrote to Hamilton: "Your favour of the 24th. Ulto. is duly Recd." Letter not found.]

1. Morris had been appointed supervisor of the revenue for the District of New York on March 8, 1792.

From James Reynolds [1]

[Philadelphia] Sunday Evening 24th March. 1792

Sir

On my entering the Room the last evening. I found Mrs Reynolds in a setuvation little different from distraction and for some time could not prevail on her to tell me the Cause. at last She informed me that you had been here likewise of a letter she had wrote you in a fright. which she need not have don as I Never intended doing any thing I told her but did it to humble Her. for the imprudent languge

she made youse of to me. and You may Rest ashured sir. that I have
not a wish to do any thing that may give you or your family a
moments pain I know not what you may think of me. but suppose
yourself for a moment in my setuvation. that your wife whom you
tenderly love. should plase her affections on another object and
here her say. that all her happiness depends intirely on that object.
what would you do in such a Case. would you have acted as I have
don. I have Consented to things which I thought I never could have
don. but I have dun it to make life tolerable. and for the sake of a
person whose happiness is dearer to me than my own. I have another
afliction aded to the Rest that is almost insupportable. I find when
ever you have been with her. she is Chearful and kind. but when you
have not in some time she is Quite to Reverse. and wishes to be alone
by her self. but when I tell her of it. all her answer is she Cant help
it. and hopes I will forgive her. shurely you Cannot wonder if I
should Act ever so imprudent. though at present if I could take all
her Grief upon myself I would do it with pleashure. the excess of
which alarm me untill now. I have had no idea of. I have spent this
day at her bed side in trying to give her the Consolation which I
myself stand in need of. she also tell me. you wish to see me tomorrow evening and then I shall Convince you. that I would not
wish to trifle with you And would much Rather add to the happiness of all than to disstress any
    am sir Your   James Reynolds

Mr. Alexr. Hamilton

"Reynolds Pamphlet," August 31, 1797.
    1. This letter is printed as document No. XI in the appendix of the "Reynolds
Pamphlet," August 31, 1797.
    For background to this letter, see Reynolds to H, December 15, 17, 19, 22,
1791, January 3, 17, 1792; H to Reynolds, December 15, 1791; Maria Reynolds
to H, December 15, 1791, and January 23–March 18, 1792.

From Maria Reynolds [1]

[Philadelphia, March 24, 1792]
Sunday Night one OClock
Reade this all
My dear friend
    In a state of mind wich know language can paint I take up the

pen but alas I know not what I write or how to give you an idea
of the anguish wich at this moment rends my heart yes my friend
I am doomed to drink the bitter cup of affliction Pure and unmixed
but why should I repine why pour forth my wretched soul in fruitless complainings for you have said It you have commanded and I
must submit heaven tow Inexorable heaven Is deaf to my anguish
and has marked me out for the child of sorrow oh my dear friend
wether shall I fly for consolation oh all all consolation is shut against
me there is not the least gleme of hope but oh merciful God forgive
me and you my friend Comply with this Last Request   Let me once
more se you and unbosom Myself to you perhaps I shal be happier
after It I have mutch to tell wich I dare not write And wich you
ought to know oh my dear Sir give me your advice for once In an
affair on wich depends my Existence Itself   Think not my friend
that I say this to make you come and se me and that I have nothing
to tell you for heaven by wich I declare knows that I have woes
to relate wich I never Exspected to have known accept by the name
Come therefore to-morrow sometime or Els In the Evening do I
beg you to come gracious God had I the world I would lay It at
your feet If I could only se you oh I must or I shall lose my senses
and It is not because I think to prevail on you to visit me again no
my dear Col Hamilton I do not think of It but will when I se you
do just as you tell me so doant be offended with me for pleadeing
so hard to se you If you do not think it proper to come here Let
me know by a line where I shal se you and what hour you need not
put your name to It or mine Either Just direct Mr or Els leve It
blank   adieu my Ever dear Col hamilton you may form to yourself
an Idea of my destress for I cant desscribe It to you Pray for me and
be kind to me Let me se you death now would be welcome Give

"Reynolds Pamphlet," August 31, 1797.
1. This letter is printed as document No. XII in the appendix of the "Reynolds Pamphlet," August 31, 1797.
For background to this letter, see James Reynolds to H, December 15, 17, 19,
22, 1791, January 3, 17, March 24, 1792; H to Reynolds, December 15, 1791;
Maria Reynolds to H, December 15, 1791, and January 23–March 18, 1792.

From William Short

Paris March 24. 1792

Sir

It has been some time since I have had the honor of writing to you, owing to no material event having taken place—& to my being in constant expectation from day to day that there would be occurences which would render it necessary for me to trouble you.

Being very much indisposed I took the liberty of asking the Secretary of State to communicate to you from his letter the intelligence respecting the Antwerp loan, & the delay of the assembly here, in voting the succours to the islands, towards which the minister of Marine had proposed applying the American debt.[1] The delay still continues, but a decision must inevitably take place ere long.

I have formerly mentioned to you that the Antwerp loan would be continued to be paid here as fast as recieved—as well as the manner in which these payments were paid, & my reasons for consenting

ALS, letterpress copy, William Short Papers, Library of Congress.

1. For a description of the Antwerp loan, see Short to H, November 8, 1791, note 4, and November 12, 1791. For the plan to apply portions of the French debt on supplies for Santo Domingo, see Short to H, December 28, 1791, and January 26, 1792.

On February 29, 1792, Short wrote to Jefferson on these matters as follows: "There has been daily expectation of the National Assembly allowing a part of our debt to be employed in advances to the sufferers in St. Domingo & I have for that reason as yet suspended the payment of the sums arrising on the last loan at Amsterdam in hopes of its being employed in that manner. The Antwerp loan is paid here as fast as received. I have already receipts from the French Agent at Antwerp for near 1,800,000 florins & that sum will be compleated by to day agreeably to the engagement of the undertaker of the loan. I will ask the favor of you to communicate these circumstances to the Secy. of the Treasury, who I hope will excuse my not writing by the present conveyance, my last to him was by the way of Havre & I shall write to him again by the same way very shortly." (LC, RG 59, Despatches from United States Ministers to France, 1789–1869, January 16, 1791–August 6, 1792, National Archives.)

A copy of this section of Short's letter was sent to H by Jefferson on May 30, 1792 (AL, letterpress copy, Thomas Jefferson Papers, Library of Congress).

On March 15, 1792, Jean de Lacoste had been appointed French Minister of Marine. Short, however, is probably referring not to Lacoste but to a former Minister of Marine, Antoine François, Marquis de Bertrand de Molleville. Bertrand was among the chief proponents of the plan for using the American debt to France to send supplies to Santo Domingo.

to the reciepts given at Antwerp being expressed in florins,[2] their value in livres tournois being to be regulated in future, viz the indemnity which you purpose allowing for the depreciation on the assignats. You authorize me in your letter to fix this indemnity by the rate of exchange in specie.[3] I have thought it most advisable, however to leave this indemnity open to future consideration, as no inconvenience could arise to the U.S. from this circumstance, & as it left the discussion to the person who, being to be named here in a permanent character,[4] would necessarily have a greater degree of the confidence of the government of the U.S., than if in a temporary one only, & of course do this business as well as every other of a delicate nature more satisfactorily both to them & to himself.

As you informed me that you had on M. de Ternant's application mentioned to him that the U.S. did not intend taking advantage of the depreciation of the assignats,[5] & as I was sure he would inform ministry of this intention I thought it proper in every account to make them the same communication.[6] I have been fully satisfied since that he had no authority for making such an application to you. You will probably find that there were several motives for this volunteer step.

The Antwerp loan as you have been informed was to be paid at the rate of 600,000 florins monthly. M. de Wolf [7] had assured me & authorized me to assure you also that it would be paid much sooner. I found however it began to go more slowly owing probably to the sum being too large for the market. I had frequently mentioned to him my desire that it should be stopped at 1,500,000 or two millions, but he always replied that this did not depend on him, without the consent of the undertakers & that I might rest assured that the loan would be completed in the time agreed on. Fearing however he might be too sanguine & judging that it would be more advantageous for the credit of the U.S. to have a loan opened there at a reduced

2. See Short to H, January 26, 1792.
3. See H to Short, September 2, 1791.
4. Gouverneur Morris's appointment as United States Minister Plenipotentiary to France had been confirmed by the Senate on January 12, 1792 (*Executive Journal*, I, 96).
5. See H to Short, September 2, 1791.
6. See Short to H, November 22, 1791.
7. Charles John Michael de Wolf, the banker of the United States at Antwerp. See Short to H, December 1, 1791, and January 26, 1792.

rate of interest as he had always assured me was practicable,[8] I made
him the offer of authorizing him to open a loan there at 4. p. cent
interest, for the amount of the sum he could suppress of the present
loan [9]—& in order to induce the undertakers as well as himself to
come into the plan I added that I would consent for this diminution
of the interest to increase the premium—without fixing this increase
I knew it would be a very small one, which would be much more
than compensated by the reduction of the interest, besides that it
wd. have the advantage of preventing the risk of the present loan
going more slowly than was agreed on, from its being too heavy for
the market. I could not help having my fears on this subject notwithstanding the positive assurances of M. de Wolf to the contrary. I
considered myself sufficiently warranted in these fears from what
had passed & particularly from the payment of the month of febry
not being fully completed until the 5th of this month.

In answer to my offer he informed me [10] that he had found means
of suppressing 700,000 florins of the present loan & had hopes of
suppressing 300,000 more so as to stop it at two millions. He was
taken ill a few days after as he informed me by one of his clerks,
being confined to his bed & his life considered as in danger by the
physicians, he has done nothing further in this way. I hope however
it will be stopped at two millions in which case there will remain
only the trifling sum of 200,000 florins to be disposed of.

You will readily concieve that the first time of opening a loan at
any place whatever, there are several circumstances depending on
locality which cannot be known & for which reliance must necessarily be placed on the banker. A short experience persuaded me that
it would have been better to have opened a smaller loan at Antwerp,
but it was then too late. I had been guided in this business by M. de
Wolf, recommended to me & supported with much warmth by Mr.
Morris as having a perfect acquaintance with him, & by Mr. Morris
himself who having resided some time at Antwerp, had an opportunity of knowing the place.

I have frequently mentioned to you that the increasing credit &

---

8. See Short to H, December 30, 1791.
9. Short to De Wolf, February 27, 1792 (ALS, letterpress copy, William
Short Papers, Library of Congress).
10. De Wolf to Short, March 5, 1792 (ALS, letterpress copy, William Short
Papers, Library of Congress).

confidence in the administration of the U.S. would present them necessarily to their choice a variety of alternatives for liquidating & ameliorating the conditions of their foreign debt. I have good reason to believe since my return from Amsterdam that the debt to France might be immediately paid off by one stroke by a contract with the first banking house in Paris, Boyd & Kerr,[11] who would engage to pay into the public treasury the amount of the balance of the American debt to France as well due as to become due & recieve in payment the obligations of the U.S. at 4. p. cent interest, either in London or Amsterdam, according to the rate of exchange at present.

The advantages of such an operation would be considerable—1. it would place the U.S. beyond any future reproach on account of delay & would reduce the interest of this debt from five to four p. cent. 2. the sum on which they would have interest to pay would be but more than half what it is at present, as the exchange is about that rate. 3. they would be still more perfectly masters of the indemnity they purpose offering to France, & even if they were in future to add the half gained at present by way of exchange, still they would in the mean time avoid the interest on that half, because the debt to France being considered as completely discharged at the moment of the nominal amount in assignats being delivered here. An interest of course would be expected on the additional sum which the U.S. should prefer to give in future as an indemnity for the depreciation of assignats. 4. their obligations for this operation being given payable in London, would leave the Amsterdam market free for other purposes & particularly for immediately reducing the interest on all their bonds there to 4. p. cent. The banking house here wch. would make this contract having in their hands & at their disposition the funds of La Borde,[12] the richest individual in France, & being connected closely in their operations with Hope of Amsterdam [13] & his correspondent in London & becoming thus stock holders in the American funds to so great an amount would be powerful auxiliaries enlisted in support of their credit.

The only possible objection I see to such an operation is that

11. Walter Boyd, an English financier, was the chief member of this Paris banking firm.

12. Jean Joseph, Marquis de Laborde, banker to Louis XV.

13. Henry Hope of the Amsterdam banking house of Hope and Company. See Short to H, December 2, 1790, note 8.

which was formerly made by the commissioners at Amsterdam, when Mr. Morris & Mr. Parker had an idea of purchasing up the French debt [14]—viz. that it would be dangerous for the U.S. to have so large a sum in the hands of a few individuals, as it would render their credit dependent, on the speculations & resources of those individuals. This objection however loses its force in the present instance in a very great degree, as the sum due now is considerably smaller & as the value of obligations would be in reality not more than half the amount of the nominal balance remaining—& also as the contractors in the present instance are fully masters in themselves of such sums whereas the others were to raise them by such aid as they should find or by future speculation, & of course might have been found to make sacrifices on these bonds injurious to the credit of the U.S.

I am aware that it would have been a matter of much delicacy to have settled the rates of exchange, at which these sums should have been paid to the contractors by the obligations of the U.S. as they would not probably have furnished the whole amount in assignats at once & as the exchange varies daily. It was this consideration alone which prevented my pressing an operation which appeared to me to promise so many advantages to the U.S. & made me desirous that it should remain open if time & circumstances would admit of it, until the will of the government of the U.S. should be more completely represented here, determining however if it became absolutely necessary to act, not to let pass so favorable an opportunity of serving their interests. I considered my powers fully competent thereto, as it was in fact nothing more than borrowing in London a certain sum, much within my limits, to pay off the French debt.

Under these circumstances I learned through the public papers & also from Mr. Morris in London, that the President had nominated him, to represent the U.S here as minister plenipotentiary. I expected of course that he would arrive here without delay in that character—& consequently determined on no consideration to act further, previously to his arrival. Although I learned afterwards

14. In 1789 Gouverneur Morris had formed a combination with Daniel Parker to purchase the French debt. See Short to H, November 30, 1789, and January 28–31, 1790. Parker, in association with John Holker, William Duer, and others, had been among the most important of the contractors for supplying the Continental and French armies in the United States during the American Revolution.

that the Senate had not yet confirmed the nomination, yet you will no doubt, Sir, readily concieve that delicacy & propriety forbad my proceeding after having learned that the President's will was thus pronounced in favor of another, & as by his instructions to you, of which you sent me a copy,[15] arrangements respecting the French debt were to be made by the person resident here. I still remain in daily expectation of the delay to the Senate's confirmation ceasing, & of Mr. Morris's arrival here. I dont doubt that he will consider the plan abovementioned in the same light that I have done & that he will pursue the interests of the U.S. with more intelligence, efficacity & success in this as well as every other instance, than has fallen to my share.

As it is probable that their general interests have been less advanced in this country, whilst confided to my care, than might have been hoped for, I flatter myself you will excuse me, for taking the liberty to arrest your attention an instant on the peculiarly unfavorable circumstances which seem to have begun with the moment of my having been employed & to have ceased also with the expiration of my term.

The revolution here carried with it a spirit of innovation in the whole organisation of their system, & of hostility to every thing that existed under the former government. The moment for organizing their commercial system came soon after I was charged with the affairs of the U.S. & was taken absolutely into the hands of the committee of the assembly, where the influence of the ministry was not only without weight, but their opinions in favour of any plan were prejudicial to it. They were constantly in favor of treating the productions of the U.S. with marked favor & on the most liberal footing. My letters will have shewn how the nature of the revolution, private intrigues & private interests formed a current against such a system which unquestionably no person here from the U.S. of what talents, virtue & merit soever could have resisted. I have never ceased announcing that changes such as we wish would be made in time, & as soon as the government should be formed & really in action. Although that term is not yet arrived, yet the present state of ministry is such as to give the fullest hopes

15. See Washington to H, August 28, 1790.

of the change being now possible. The majority of the assembly have by various means at length obtained a ministry of their choice, & in whom they place their confidence—the plans of ministry will accordingly be adopted, & the minister who will have the direction of all commercial matters M. Claviere [16] is a man much known for his writings in favour of a liberal system of commerce & particularly of encouragement to that with the U.S. He published a work express[ly] on the subject some years ago [17] & will now attempt to realize his ideas. This accidental circumstance takes place at the moment of my being withdrawn from hence & leaves Mr. Morris nothing to do but to call the attention of government to this object in order to affect the changes desired by the U.S. I mention this by no means with the intention of taking from the merit of the efforts which will certainly be made by that gentleman, but merely to explain the circumstances, that government may not attribute absolutely to me, a commercial system which begun as it were & will end with the term of my being employed. I may flatter myself with a just & enlightened administration, well acquainted with the principles of this revolution & weighing their influence in the present case, ascribing the effects to their true causes. I have no right to hope that the public who judge of actions by the event, should make an exception in my favor; & of course as it has been my misfortune to reside here during the adoption of a system of commerce prejudicial to the U.S. & as it will cease with the time of my residence, I must submit to the fault being in their mind attributed to me & will sincerely rejoice in a change, by whomsoever effected, that I am persuaded will be advantageous to the United States. I have now Sir only to beg your pardon for so long & tedious a digression, into which I have been involuntarily led by the high value I place on your opinion with respect to my conduct in every instance—& if I have been wrong in thus troubling I hope you will consider the motive as a sufficient excuse & allow me to add assurances of the

16. This is a reference to the Girondist Ministry under the control of Charles François Dumouriez and Jean Marie Roland de La Platière which came into power in March, 1792. Etienne Clavière was appointed Minister of Finance in the new ministry.

17. Etienne Clavière and J. P. Brissot de Warville, *De la France et des Etats-Unis, ou de l'importance de la Révolution de l'Amérique, pour le bonheur de la France, des rapports de ce royaume et des Etats-Unis, des avantages réciproques qu'ils peuvent retirer de leurs liaisons de commerce, et enfin la situation actuelle des Etats-Unis* (London, 1787).

profound respect with [which] I shall ever have the honor to be, Sir, your most obedient & most humble servant   W: Short

The Honble.
Alexander Hamilton Secretary of the Treasury, Philadelphia

From Robert Troup [1]

[*New York, March 24, 1792*. The calendar summary of this letter reads as follows: " 'My heart is nearly broken with the distress of poor Duer.' [2] Brockholst Livingston [3] and others gloating over Duer." *Letter not found.*]

1. Letter listed in "Calendar Summary of Philip Church and Alexander Hamilton Papers," Personal Miscellaneous, Box 6, Schuyler, MS Division, New York Public Library.
2. For information of William Duer's bankruptcy, see Duer to H, March 12, 1792; H to Duer, March 14, 1792; Troup to H, March 19, 1792; and Philip Livingston to H, March 24, 1792.
3. Livingston was a prominent New York speculator, businessman, and lawyer.

To George Washington

[Philadelphia, March 24, 1792]

The Secretary of the Treasury has the honor to communicate to The President a letter which he has just received from Mr. Short.[1] It communicates the agreeable information of a Loan at four per Cent.

24th. March 1792

LC, George Washington Papers, Library of Congress.
1. H received two letters from William Short announcing the Holland loan of December, 1791. See Short to H, December 23, 28, 1791.

From Nicholas Low [1]

[*New York, March 25, 1792*. The calendar summary of this letter reads as follows: "On the affairs of the Manufacturing Society (Paterson, N.J.) [2] as left by Duer's failure." [3] *Letter not found.*]

1. Letter listed in "Calendar Summary of Philip Church and Alexander Hamilton Papers," Personal Miscellaneous, Box 6, Schuyler, MS Division, New York Public Library.
2. This is a reference to the Society for Establishing Useful Manufactures. Low was a director of the society. See Philip Schuyler to H, March 25, 1792.
3. For background on William Duer's bankruptcy, see Duer to H, March 12, 1792; H to Duer, March 14, 1792; Robert Troup to H, March 19, 1792; and Philip Livingston to H, March 24, 1792.

From Philip Schuyler

New York March 25th 1792

My Dear Sir

Mr. Philip Livingston, afforded me the perusal of a letter from you, to him.[1] The closing paragraph give me so much uneasiness, that I requested Mr Low [2] to meet Mr Livingston & me, at my room on friday evening, where Mr Low detailed the state of the funds of the Manufactoring society, the result of which was that ten thousand dollars thereof were under such arrangements of Mr Duer, that they would be probably lost,[3] that fifty thousand were in the hands of one of the Company for the purpose of importing Cloaths from Europe,[4] that 20000 Dollars would be properly Accounted for by Mr Walker,[5] and that the residue was on loan to Mr McComb,[6]

ALS, Hamilton Papers, Library of Congress.
1. H's letter to Livingston, which has not been found, was dated March 22, 1792. See Livingston to H, March 24, 1792.
2. Nicholas Low.
3. William Duer had been elected first governor of the Society for Establishing Useful Manufactures. For an account of Duer's financial difficulties in March, 1792, see Duer to H, March 12, 1792; H to Duer, March 14, 23, 1792; Robert Troup to H, March 19, 1792; and Livingston to H, March 24, 1792.
4. In January, 1792, the directors of the Society for Establishing Useful Manufactures had appropriated fifty thousand dollars for procuring materials and workmen for the society ("Minutes of the S.U.M.," 14-15).
5. Benjamin Walker, who was closely associated with Duer in stock speculation, was a director of the Society for Establishing Useful Manufactures. During the American Revolution Walker had served as aide-de-camp to Baron von Steuben and at the time this letter was written was naval officer of the port of New York.
6. Alexander Macomb, like Low and Walker, was a director of the Society for Establishing Useful Manufactures. Macomb's position as one of New York City's wealthiest merchants was founded on his activities as a fur trader, land speculator, and supplier of the troops during the American Revolution. In December, 1791, Macomb had formed a secret partnership with Duer for speculation in public securities.

who besides his bond, was to deposit or had deposited, a sufficiency of deffered debt as a collateral security. Mr Low promised me to write you on the Subject,[7] but least he should forget, or that his letter may miscarry, I deemed It best to give the above detail. If my recollection serves, I think he mentioned, that Mr Duer had drawn in favor of Mr Ingram [8] of Philadelphia, for the ten thousand,[9] and that Duer said they were not *Appropriated*. Would It not be proper to converse with Mr Ingram, and If the money is still in his hands, and not appropriated by Mr Duer, I conceive that the latter Gentlemen would on your Application draw in favor of Mr Walker on Mr Ingram.

Early on friday Morning I was sent for to Mr.   [10] in the broad way. I went, he informed me that he was involved in Mr Duers misfortunes, that he had sent for me to afford my advice. It would be needless particularly to state what passed, If Your opinion had not been quoted, and If I had not subsequently been informed that he intends, If he has not already, to apply to you for advice. "I have", says he "indorsed, Duers notes, they are now daily payable, and If I discharge them, or must Discharge them, It will absorb my whole estate."—to which Amount have you indorsed, "One hundred and Sixty thousand pounds,"—without any Security, "No I have some but not Adequate to cover my endorsements. For Gods sake, My Dear Sir try If you cannot prevail on Mr Duer to secure me, he has bills on England I will take them." It is delicate for me to interfere, why not apply in person. "He thinks I am secured and storms when I speak to him." I cannot ask of Mr Duer any thing that would be improper. I will go to him, and converse with him about his affairs, and try to learn what propositions he intends to make to Morrow. I have several days ago called on him, he took It kind. If I am permitted to communicate any thing that passes between him and me, I will advise you thereof, that you may

7. See Low to H, April 10, 1792.
8. Francis Ingraham. See Philip Livingston to H, March 24, 1792.
9. As governor of the Society for Establishing Useful Manufactures, Duer had been allotted ten thousand dollars for confidential expenditures. See Davis, *Essays*, I, 407.
10. Space left blank in MS. Schuyler's subsequent remarks make it clear that the person to whom he is referring is Walter Livingston, a New York City lawyer and former member of the Board of Treasury. Livingston had become involved in various stock speculations as an associate of Duer and Macomb.

take your Measures. Mr Duer had taken Shelter at Baron Steubens.
I went, saw him, found him exceedingly distressed and agitated,
Not prepared to come forward with any specific proposition to his
Creditors, Complained that some who had pretended friendship had
deserted him, that they pressed him for partial security, that he had
afforded It in two instances, the effects of which he already felt.
After this It was unnecessary to say any thing on the Subject of the
person who had requested me to see him, If even I had conceived it
proper, which I did not. He Duer told me he expected a letter from
you,[11] that he would wish to see me after he should have received
it, assured me that he would be able to convince the candid, that he
had not acted dishonestly by any, however his fortune might be
lost. I returned to the other person—mentioned generally what had
passed. Observed that I did not believe Mr Duer would be able to
pay. "What then is to be done" was the question put to me. I answered prepare a statement of all the indorsements by you, exhibit
an Account of all the debt, Bank Stock &c that has been transferred
to you to cover your indorsements, and If as you assert, you are
merely an indorser out of friendship to Mr. Duer, the holders of
the indorsed notes may consider you as an Unfortunate Creditor of
Mr Duer and they may possibly be contented with the property that
has been transferred, or assigned to you. "But If I do that, they will
still fall on my Estate." So they may in any event, but unless you
make such a statement, and Account for every farthing that has been
covered and how, you will add a sacrifice of reputation, to that of
property, and you will sour minds instead of conciliating them. A
near relation of his was present, accorded with me in opinion. But
I found great reluctance in the debtor to such an exhibit, he would
"rather go to Goal than give up his estate." "Many of the notes,"
says he, "have been due some days, and yet are not protested, and
I am informed that *Colo. Hamilton* has given an opinion that the
indorser in such case is *not liable*." I question it, but If it is so, that
would be an improper action for the forbearance of the holders.
*"By God I will not give up my estate. I cannot give it up. It is not
mine, I have conveyed it.*[12]

11. The anticipated letter was probably that which H wrote to Duer on
March 23, 1792.
12. According to George Dangerfield, Walter Livingston managed to convey his portion of the manor estates to his brother and his son-in-law, Henry
and Philip Henry Livingston, "with an adroitness which his creditors did not

I walked out, and have not seen him since. I forgot to mention that the person to whom I have attended, informed me that Mr Duer had conveyed to him about eighty thousand acres of land in this state, a large tract or tracts in Vermont, that the lands and Stocks are he estimated at about Sixty thousand pounds, but Observed that Mr Duer *owed him much money by notes of hand.*

I do not like the complexion of this business, either as It regards the conduct of Mr Duer, or the other person. And permit me to add that I believe It will be most prudent, If Your opinion should be required, either as a Gentleman of the law, or otherwise, to wave It.

Just before I finished the last sentence Mr. Cochran [13] came in, informed me that he was well informed, that a number of persons who hold notes indorsed as abovementioned, were determined to discover what stock had been transferred by Duer to the person in question, and that If he (Cochran) did not suffer an inspection of the books, they would Obtain It by force, and beged my advice. I gave It as follows. That he should request a written order from the person to him to permit the holders of the notes or some particular one or more of them to inspect the Account of that person, that If he refused to give this order, he should state his information in writing to the Attorney of the United States for the district,[14] intreating his advice, what course to pursue in case any force should be attempted. That as he supposed the holders would come in a body to his office, during office hours, that he ought to refuse complying with their request to see the Accounts of the person. That If they seized the books by force, he should inform them that having done his duty, in the refusal, and not able to oppose the force, he had only to intreat them not to take the books out of the office, and not to inspect any other than the Account in question. Immediately after Cochran left me I was informed by several Gentlemen, that the Animosity against Duer is transferring to the other person, and to

---

relish and which the manor tenants, when they heard of it, celebrated with lawsuits and riots . . ." (George Dangerfield, *Chancellor Robert R. Livingston of New York, 1746–1813* [New York, 1960], 280).

13. Presumably John Cochran, commissioner of loans for the state of New York. Under the terms of "An Act making provision for the (payment of the) Debts of the United States" (1 *Stat.* 140–41 [August 4, 1790]), all stock transfers had to be recorded on the books of the commissioners of loans.

14. Richard Harison.

a neighbour of his, who are both believed to have coluded with him, to very unjustifiable purposes. Heaven only knows what will be the ultimate result of all this confusion; suspicion increases and every man seems afraid of his neighbour.

You may have seen a publication in Childs daily Gazette [15] of the 21st Instant, that I was appointed one Amongst others to produce a memorial to Congress on the claims of the late Army. I was not at the Meeting was not advised with, have never declared my sentiments on the Subject. Gen: Clinton was not there and I find that Coll. Cortlandt named me as a proper person. I have tasked him for taking the liberty, without giving my sense on the Subject.

Adieu I am Dr Sir   Most Affectionately Yours &c &c

Ph: Schuyler

I wish Mr King [16] was here. I have urged him to come, persuaded that he would do much good, and prevent evils which a set of unprincipled villains contemplate. I hope you will think It proper to second my request to King.

Hone Alexander Hamilton Esq.

15. On March 21, 1792, in *The* [New York] *Daily Advertiser*, Francis Childs printed the "Circular Letter from the Officers of the Massachusetts Line of the Late Army," dated February 28, 1792. Below the circular the following appeared: "In consequence of the foregoing letter (we are informed) a meeting was held on Monday evening last, agreeable to notice given by the late officers of this state, and who have chosen Gen. Schuyler, Gen. [James] Clinton, Gen. [Philip Van] Cortland, Col [Marinus] Willet, and Col. M. Hughes, to prepare a memorial to Congress in like manner to that presented by their fellow officers, from the state of Massachusetts."
16. Rufus King, United States Senator from New York.

To William Seton

Phila. 25th March 1792

Private

If six per Cents should sink below par, you may purchase on account of the United States at par to the extent of Fifty thousand Dollars. You will not however declare on whose account you act, because tho there is, as to a purchase on that principle, no difference of opinion among the Trustees, the thing is not formally aranged and this is Sunday.[1]

It will be very probably conjectured that you appear for the Public; and the conjecture may be left to have its course but without confession. The purchase ought in the present state of things to be at Auction and not till tomorrow evening. But if the purchase at Auction will not tend as well to the purpose of relief as a different mode—it may be departed from. The usual Note must be made of persons, time &c. You will consider whether done all at once, or a part now and a part then will best answer the purpose—in the state of this Market, the latter mode is found preferable. I have just received a Letter from Mr. Short[2] our Minister Resident dated Amsterdam 28th December, by which he informs me that he has effected a loan for Three Millions of Florins at 4 ℔ Cent Interest on account of the United States. This may be announced; and as in the present moment of suspicion some minds may be disposed to consider the thing as a mere expedient to support the Stocks, I pledge my honor for its exact truth. Why then so much despondency among the holders of our Stock? When Foreigners lend the United States at 4 ℔ Cent will they not purchase here upon a similar scale making reasonable allowance for expence of Agency &c? Why then do Individuals part with so good a property so much below its value? Does Duers failure[3] affect the solidity of the Government?

After paying the present Quarters Interest I shall have near a Million of Dollars in Cash, and a Million more in Bonds from the Duties of last year. All this is truly so much before hand. The Duties for the Current year being fully adequate to the objects of the year. Except a *further* sum of about Five hundred thousand Dollars for the Western Expedition for which the ways and means have been proposed.[4] Is the Treasury of Great Britain comparatively in so good a State? Is the Nation comparatively so equal to its debt. Why then so much depression? I shall be answered—the immediate necessity for Money. But if the Banks are forbearing as to the necessity of paying up—cannot the parties give each other *mutual credit* and avoid so great a press? If there are a few *Harpies* who will not concur in the forbearance, let such be paid and execrated, and let others forbear. The necessity of great sacrifices among your Dealers cannot affect the Nation; but it may deeply wound the City of New York; by a transfer to Foreigners and Citizens of other States of a large Mass of property greatly below its value. The face of your affairs may undergo for a considerable time a serious change. Would not the plan I suggested to you in my last [5] be a means of securing more effectually the debts due to the Bank—by accepting in part payment the *Credits on your Books?*

While I encourage due exertion in the Banks, I observe, that I hope they will put nothing to risk. No calamity truly *public* can happen while these Institutions remain sound; they must therefore not yield too far to the impulse of circumstances.

Yours &ca

Copy, in the writing of Seton, Hamilton Papers, Library of Congress; ALS, sold by Paul C. Richards, Catalogue No. 1, Lot 192.

1. Following William Duer's suspension of payments on March 9, 1792, and the ensuing financial panic, a meeting of the commissioners of the sinking fund was held to decide what action should be taken to bolster the prices of government stock. See H to John Adams, March 20, 1792; H for Adams to John Jay, March 21, 1792; Jay to H, March 23, 1792; and Philip Livingston to H, March 24, 1792. For the formal authorization given to H, see "Meeting of the Commissioners of the Sinking Fund," March 26, 1792.

2. William Short.

3. For information on Duer's financial failure, see Duer to H, March 12, 1792; H to Duer, March 14, 23, 1792; Robert Troup to H, March 19, 1792; Philip Livingston to H, March 24, 1792; and Philip Schuyler to H, March 25, 1792.

4. By "An Act for making farther and more effectual Provision for the Protection of the Frontiers of the United States" (1 *Stat.* 241-43 [March 5, 1792]) Congress provided for raising three additional regiments. On March 8, 1792, the House of Representatives requested H to submit an opinion on the best method for raising the revenue necessary for supporting the additional troops. For H's proposals, see "Report Relative to the Additional Supplies for the Ensuing Year," March 16, 1792.

5. Letter not found.

From William Ellery

[*Newport, Rhode Island*] *March 26, 1792.* "On the 24th of this month I received your letter of the 12th.[1] respecting an application to the Bank of Providence for the Sum of Six hundred and ten dollars. This Sum, with the Sum of Nineteen Hundred and fifty five dolls. sixty eight ninetieths to be provided for drawbacks which will be due the 10th of April . . . and the further sum of five hundred and three dollars, twenty three cents will . . . pay off all the drawbacks which will be due by the 26th of April next. . . . I am happy to be informed that there is a probability of your reporting in time on the Emoluments of the Offs of the Customs. . . ." [2]

LC, Newport Historical Society, Newport, Rhode Island.
1. Letter not found.
2. See Ellery to H, July 18, November 11, 1791; February 27, March 13, 1792.

Meeting of the Commissioners of the Sinking Fund [1]

[Philadelphia, March 26, 1792]

At a meeting held at the house of the Vice President on the 26th of March 1792:

Present: The Vice President, the Secretary of State, the Secretary of the Treasury, and the Attorney General.

This Board having been equally divided, at their former meeting,[2] on the construction of the act establishing the Board,[3] and a letter having been written, by their order, to the Chief Justice,[4] desiring his immediate attendance in the city of Philadelphia, and he having requested that the points on which the said division took place should be stated to him in writing; and, it appearing to the Board, that the question turns upon the mere words of the law; that his attendance as a trustee of the sinking fund, would interfere with his attendance as a judge, on the circuit courts now near at hand;[5] and that it is necessary to operate immediately, if at all.

Resolved, (the Secretary of State dissenting) That the said question be stated in writing, and forwarded to the Chief Justice, with a request that he transmit his opinion thereupon, as soon as convenient.[6] But this resolution being dictated by special circumstances, is not to be interpreted so as to form a precedent for obtaining the vote of an absent member on any other occasion.

Resolved, that the Secretary of the Treasury be authorised to cause to be applied, either at the city of Philadelphia, or New York, a sum not exceeding one hundred thousand dollars, to the purchase of that part of the funded debt which bears an immediate interest of six per centum per annum, at the rate of twenty shillings in the pound. And, that the said purchases be made, if at the city of Philadelphia, by the Treasurer of the United States; if at New York, by the cashier of the Bank of New York.

ASP, Finance, I, 236.
1. For background to this document, see H to John Adams, March 20, 1792; H for Adams to John Jay, March 21, 1792; Jay to H, March 23, 1792.
2. The minutes of the meeting of March 21, 1792, have not been found. However, see H for Adams to Jay, March 21, 1792, note 2.
3. "An Act making provision for the Reduction of the Public Debt" (1 *Stat.* 186–87 [August 12, 1790]).
4. See H for Adams to Jay, March 21, 1792.
5. See Jay to H, March 23, 1792.
6. For the questions which Edmund Randolph submitted to Jay appended to a signed transcription of the minutes of this meeting of the commissioners of the sinking fund, see H for Adams to Jay, March 21, 1792, note 2. The only substantive difference between the version of the minutes which Randolph sent to Jay and those which were included in a report presented to Congress on February 23, 1793, is the omission of the final resolution from Randolph's transcription (*ASP, Finance,* I, 236).

To William Seton

Philadelphia
March 26. 1792

Dear Sir

I send you an Official Order for 50 000 Dollars subject to the directions in my private letter of yesterday.

Yrs. sincerely   A Hamilton

You will only present the inclosed [1] when necessary.

Wm. Seton Esqr

ALS, Mr. Pierce Gaines, Fairfield, Connecticut; copy, on the writing of Seton, Hamilton Papers, Library of Congress.
1. H to Gulian Verplanck, March 26, 1792.

From William Seton

New York 26th March 1792

My dear sir

I had the pleasure to receive your kind Letter of yesterday, this day at 10 o'Clock. We have no public Sales of Stocks now in the Evenings—therefore I can not go into the Market till tomorrow, and altho the sum is small, yet be assured it will be a relief. The Collector [1] has furnished the List of Names of those who have duties to pay between this and the first of May, and our Directors have given out that they will discount on a Deposit of Stock. The Large Dealers in Stock are to have a meeting this Evening and it is reported will enter into an absolute agreement not to draw out any Specie from the Banks for 3 Months to come—So that from tomorrow I hope the prospect will brighten. I have made as public as possible the New Loan obtained in Amsterdam,[2] it gives most universal satisfaction. The January Packet arrived this day—the orders for the purchase of 6 ℔ Cents at 22/ are very extensive if Bills could be sold at par—but the present consternation and want of Confidence in each other have ordered Bills to 10 ℔ Cent under par—that the orders cannot be executed.

I am writing in such a bustle of business that I hardly know what I say—shall have the pleasure of writing you again tomorrow. Meanwhile have the honor to be with the greatest esteem & respect

Dear sir   Your obliged Obed Hume Servt   Wm Seton

Alexander Hamilton Esqr.

ALS, Hamilton Papers, Library of Congress.
    1. John Lamb, collector of customs at New York City.
    2. See H to Seton, March 25, 1792, and William Short to H, December 23, 28, 1791.

To Gulian Verplanck [1]

Treasury Department
March 26, 1792

Gentlemen:

You will please to pay to William Seton Esquire cashier of your institution, fifty thousand dollars to be applied by him towards purchases of the public debt on account of the United States—which shall be covered by a warant in due form. With great consideration,

I have the honor to be, gentlemen,   Your obd't serv't
                                         Alexander Hamilton
                                         Sec'y of the Treasury

Gulian Verplanck, Esq.
Cashier of the Bank of New York [2]

ALS, from typescript supplied by Mr. Arthur P. Morgan, Princeton, New Jersey.
1. This letter was enclosed in H to William Seton, March 26, 1792. Verplanck was president of the Bank of New York.
2. This is a mistake, for Seton was the cashier of the Bank of New York.

From William Allibone

[Philadelphia, March 27, 1792]

Sir

I have the Honor to Enclose a statement [1] of what mony will be wanted in discharge of the engagments in the Office of Superintendant of the Delaware Light House &c for the present quarter up to the thirty first Instant and am with Highest Respect your most Obedient.

Humble Servant   Willm Allibone

Honble Alexander Hamilton
Esquire Secretary
of the Treasury
March 27th. 1792

ALS, RG 26, Lighthouse Letters Received, Vol. "A," Pennsylvania and Southern States, National Archives.
1. "Statement of Money that will be wanted to discharge the engagements for the present quarter up to the thirty first Instt. in the Office of Superintendant of the Delaware Light House &c. &c.," March 27, 1792 (ADS, RG 26, Lighthouse Letters Received, Lighthouse Estimates, Delaware, National Archives).
Allibone estimated that the amount required would be $384.06¼.

From Isaac Ledyard

NYork 27th. Mar: 1792

Dear sir

The Petition which you was so good as to shew a friendly concern for (to benifit by the final provision from which I was strangely precluded) is as you advised referred to the Secy of War.[1] I fear this information may come too late for your benevolence to be exercised toward me as you designed.

Yesterday I was informed to my great disappointment & grief that an application of mine to Congress praying leave for the Offices of the Treasury Depart. to revise my account with the public in which there was an error acknowledged by the Comr. who settled it of several hundred pounds to my disadvantage, was rejected by the House of Representatives after having passed the Senate.[2] This fatality happening to my *least disputable* Claim has nearly destroyed my hopes in the others,[3] what remain rest intirely on your friendship.

Had only one of my Claims succeeded, its aid with careful nursing might have rendered my situation tolerable, without it I must abandon Society & former pursuits. I pray you my dear and honored friend to be assured that nothing but necessity could induce me to give you the trouble of this Letter, & that with a gentleman not less proud for being poor the necessity must be very great that induces to the acknowledgement. A Wife and Infants out of the question, for myself alone I could soon close the unvarying scene of my disappointments & mortifications, As it is I am—unhappy.

Pitty & forgive what your firmer mind sees wanting in my philosophy. I have left the happiness to be most respectfully and affectionately your Obedient & hunble Servt. Isaac Ledyard

PS The prospect of Mr. Jays success brightens very considerably so that now a fair hope may be entertained.[4]

ALS, Hamilton Papers, Library of Congress.
1. On March 10, 1792, Ledyard presented to the House of Representatives a petition requesting "compensation for services in the Military Hospital of the United States, during the late war." This petition was referred to Henry Knox, Secretary of War, for an opinion (*Journal of the House*, I, 532).
2. On January 9, 1792, "The petition of Isaac Ledyard, of the State of Connecticut, for the re-settlement of his account, for reasons stated in his petition was read" in the Senate. The petition was referred to a committee composed of Aaron Burr of New York, Caleb Strong of Massachusetts, and Pierce Butler of South Carolina. On January 26, 1792, the committee reported a bill, but the Senate postponed consideration of it pending a decision on a bill sent from the House of Representatives, which was entitled "An act for the relief of certain widows, orphans, invalids, and other persons" and which had been referred to the same committee on January 10 (*Annals of Congress*, III, 56, 76, 57).
On March 1, 1792, the Senate committee reported the House bill with amendments, among which the following was agreed to:
"Section 2. *And be it further enacted,* That the officers of the Treasury be,

and they are hereby, authorized to re-examine the accounts of Isaac Ledyard, late assistant deputy director, and John Berrien, late commissary of the hospital department; and if any error has taken place in the settlement of the said accounts, to correct the same." (*Annals of Congress,* III, 98.)

On March 7, 1792, the House agreed to some of the Senate amendments but apparently disagreed on the section concerning Ledyard. The Senate did not insist on its amendment to the second section of the bill (*Journal of the House,* I, 530, 540). For the act as approved by the President on March 27, 1792, see "An Act for the relief of certain Widows, Orphans, Invalids, and other persons" (6 *Stat.* 607).

In answer to a petition from his heirs, Ledyard's claim was finally settled on March 2, 1833, when "An Act for the relief of the heirs of Doctor Isaac Ledyard, deceased" was approved. The act included payment of both commutation and the balance due after revision of the hospital accounts equivalent to the amount which would have accrued if the certificates for both amounts had been subscribed under the Funding Act in 1791 (*Resolutions, Laws, and Ordinances, Relating to the Pay, Half Pay, Commutation of Half Pay, Bounty Lands, and Other Promises Made by Congress to the Officers and Soldiers of the Revolution; to the Settlement of the Accounts Between the United States and the Several States; and to the Funding the Revolutionary Debt* [Washington, 1838], 100).

3. In addition to the claim referred to in note 1, on February 16, 1792, Ledyard petitioned the House "praying the liquidation and settlement of claims against the United States." This petition was referred to the Secretary of the Treasury (*Journal of the House,* I, 380). H reported on it in November ("Report on the Petition of Joseph Ball and Isaac Ledyard," November 21, 1792), and the House rejected it on March 2, 1793 (*Journal of the House,* I, 625, 733).

4. John Jay was the Federalist candidate for governor of New York. For Ledyard's earlier advocacy of Aaron Burr, see Ledyard to H, February 1, 17, 28, 1792.

From William Maxwell [1]

[*Greenwich, New Jersey, March 27, 1792.* On June 26, 1792, Hamilton wrote to Maxwell: "Your Letter of the 27 of March was duly received." *Letter not found.*]

1. Maxwell, a resident of New Jersey, had served as a brigadier general in the Continental Army from October, 1776, to July, 1780.

To John Kean

[*Philadelphia, March 28, 1792.* Letter listed in dealer's catalogue. *Letter not found.*]

ALS, sold by Charles F. Heartman, May 19, 1927, Lot 154.

Report on a Return of Imports and Tonnage Duties, and a Statement of Exports for the Year Ending September 30, 1791

Treasury Department
March 28th. 1792.
[Communicated on March 28, 1792]

[To the Speaker of the House of Representatives]
Sir,

In pursuance of the order of the House of Representatives of the 10th. day of November last,[1] I have the honor to transmit returns of duties arising on Imports and Tonnage within the United States, for the year ending the 30th. day of September last:[2] also a return of Exports within the same year, excepting two quarters of the district of Charleston in South Carolina, and a few quarters of some of the small ports.[3] These documents would have been transmitted earlier, but the delay of the returns from Charleston, arising from the death of the late Collector of that district,[4] has rendered it impossible.

I have the honor to be, With the greatest respect, Sir Your most obedient, and Most humble servant, Alexander Hamilton.

The Honorable
The Speaker of the House of Representatives.

Copy, RG 233, Reports of the Treasury Department, 1792–1793, Vol. III, National Archives.

1. The House "*Ordered,* That the Secretary of the Treasury do report to this House the amount of the exports from the several districts within the United States respectively; also, of duties arising on imports and tonnage, from the twenty-ninth of September, one thousand seven hundred and ninety, to the thirtieth of September, one thousand seven hundred and ninety-one" (*Journal of the House,* I, 452).

2. The returns, given by states, are printed in *ASP, Commerce and Navigation,* I, 140–42.

3. The return of exports, entitled "Abstract of Goods, Wares, and Merchandise, exported from the United States, from the 1st October, 1790, to the 30th September, 1791," is printed in *ASP, Commerce and Navigation,* I, 143–46.

4. George A. Hall was the "late collector" of the customs at Charleston. Isaac Holmes succeeded him on November 7, 1791.

Report on the Petition of William Smith

[Philadelphia, March 28, 1792
Communicated on March 29, 1792] [1]

[To the Speaker of the House of Representatives]

The Secretary of the Treasury, to whom was referred the petition of William Smith of Baltimore Town in the State of Maryland,[2] respectfully submits the following Report:

The resolutions of the United States in Congress assembled, which respect the issuing of the Certificates commonly called Loan Office Certificates, make it necessary, that they should be previously countersigned by certain officers, denominated Commissioners of Loans, who were to be appointed under the authority of the particular States.[3]

After diligent inquiry within the State of Georgia, no evidence has been obtained, either of the appointment of E. Davies,[4] (the person by whom the certificates in question were countersigned) to the office of Commissioner of Loans for that State, or that he was ever known or reputed to have acted in that capacity. The reverse of this, indeed, appears, from various communications to the Treasury, copies of which are contained in the Schedule herewith submitted.[5]

It is to be remarked, that E. Davies does not even stile himself, Commissioner of Loans, but, instead of this, adds to his signature, the words "by order of J. A. Frutler,[6] Governor of Georgia."

The Certificates, however, are signed, by the proper officer, and all such as have appeared are genuine; and interest, as alleged in the petition, has been paid upon them by the late Treasurer of the United States,[7] as in other cases.

A number of those Certificates have been offered to the present Commissioner of Loans for the State of Georgia, to be subscribed, pursuant to the Act making provision for the debt of the United States,[8] and upon a reference to the Treasury by that officer, have been directed to be refused.

The reasons for this direction are substantially, as follow.

The certificates in question having been irregularly issued, and without the requisites prescribed by the Acts of Congress, were of course, in the first instance, not obligatory upon the United States.

The subsequent payment of interest upon them, by an executive officer, without the sanction of any order or resolution of Congress, could not confer validity upon a claim, originally destitute of it; it might occasion hardship to individuals who, upon the credit of that payment, may have been induced to become possessors of those certificates for valuable consideration.

There are examples of the payment of interest, by the mistakes of public officers upon counterfeit and forged Certificates. It seems to be clear, that such payments cannot render valid, or obligatory, certificates of that description. And yet a similar hardship to that which has been mentioned, would attend those, who may have afterwards become possessed of them for valuable consideration. Nor does there occur any distinction between the effect of such payment in the one and in the other case.

Between individuals, the payment of interest by an Agent, upon the presumed, but not real obligation of his principal, either through mistake or otherwise, without special authority of the principal, could certainly give no new validity to such an obligation. And the same rules of right, which govern cases between individuals, appear to be proper guides in cases between the public and individuals.

These considerations were deemed conclusive against the admission of these certificates under the powers vested in the officers of the Treasury. It remains for the Legislature to decide, how far there are considerations strong enough to induce a special interposition in their favor.

In making this decision, the following circumstances will, it is presumed, appear to deserve attention.

The present is not a case of mere informality. There is no evidence that the certificates were issued for any purpose of the United States. The contrary, indeed, is stated to be the fact.[9]

Their amount is not positively ascertained, no account of issues having ever been rendered, though there is no appearance of any considerable sums being afloat.[10]

All which is respectfully submitted.   Alexander Hamilton,
                                             Secy. of the Treasy.
Treasury Department
March 28th: 1792.

Copy, RG 233, Reports of the Treasury Department, 1792–1793, Vol. III, National Archives.

1. *Journal of the House*, I, 554. The communicating letter, dated March 28, 1792, may be found in RG 233, Reports of the Treasury Department, 1792–1793, Vol. III, National Archives.

2. On December 26, 1791, "A petition of William Smith, of the town of Baltimore, was presented to the House and read, praying that he may be allowed to fund certain Continental Loan Office Certificates, which were issued in the State of Georgia, some difficulty in receiving them having arisen with the Comptroller of the Treasury.

"*Ordered,* That the said petition be referred to the Secretary of the Treasury, with instruction to examine the same, and report his opinion thereupon to the House." (*Journal of the House*, I, 481.)

Smith, who was a merchant, had been a member of the Continental Congress during the American Revolution. He served as a Federalist member of the House of Representatives from Maryland during the First Congress.

3. A resolution of Congress of October 3, 1776, for establishing the loan offices reads in part as follows: "That for the convenience of the lenders, a loan office be established in each of the United States, and a commissioner, to superintend such office, be appointed by the said states respectively, which are to be responsible for the faithful discharge of their duty in the said offices . . ." (*JCC*, V, 845).

On January 17, 1778, Congress "*Resolved,* That ten millions of dollars be borrowed on the credit of the United States, at an annual interest of six per cent. and that loan office certificates of the following denominations be forthwith struck, under the direction of the Treasury Board, (signed by Michael Hillegas, Esqr. treasurer, or Samuel Hillegas, and countersigned by the respective commissioners who shall borrow the money) . . ." (*JCC*, X, 59).

4. Edward Davies had served as deputy postmaster in Savannah. See Jonathan Burrall to H, March 26, 1791.

5. For the enclosures to this report, see Richard Wylly to H, May 17, June 13, 1791. The third enclosure was an extract of a letter from Wylly, who was commissioner of loans for Georgia, to William Simmons, principal clerk in the auditor's office, dated August 31, 1791 (copy, RG 233, Reports of the Treasury Department, 1792–1793, Vol. III, National Archives).

6. John Adam Treutlen was governor of Georgia during the year 1777. In May, 1780, a fire destroyed the official records of the executive and treasury departments of Georgia for the period from May, 1777, to January, 1778.

7. Michael Hillegas had served as treasurer of the United States from 1776 until the new Treasury Department was organized in 1789 (*ASP, Claims,* I, 465).

8. "An Act making provision for the (payment of the) Debt of the United States" (1 *Stat.* 138–44 [August 4, 1790]).

9. According to one contemporary, Davies was a temporary agent of Georgia for the purchase of Indian goods (*ASP, Claims,* I, 174).

10. On May 10, 1792, at a meeting of the agents of the Ohio Company in Philadelphia, it was resolved: ". . . that it be intirely in the Direction of the Treasurer to sell or retain the Loan Office Certificates Countersigned E. Davis as he shall think most condusive to the Interest of the Company—Provided always that the Sale of the said Certificates, Shall be made on such conditions as not to subject the Company to refund the proceeds of such Sale if the Certificates shall not prove obligatory on the U. States." The question of the certificates signed by Edward Davies was finally settled in 1870, when the Supreme Court decided against the treasurer of the Ohio Company in a case he had brought for the Ohio Company against the United States (Archer

Butler Hulbert, *The Records of the Original Proceedings of the Ohio Company* [Marietta, 1917], I, cxxxvi; II, 133–34.)

From Thomas Smith

Loan Office [Philadelphia] Penna. March 28th 1792.

Sir,

The amount of Stock on the books of this office subject to Interest for the Quarter ending the 31st March 1792 is as follows Viz.

Amot. of 6 ⅌ Ct. Funded Stock	4201.79	
Interest from the 1st Octr. 1791.		126. 5
Amot. of Ditto	1203686.55	
Interest on Do. from Jany. 1. 1792		18055.29
Amot. of 3 ⅌ Ct. Stock	361.55	
Interest on Do. from Octr. 1. 1791		5.42
Amot. of Do	582,824.25	
Intt on do from Jany 1. 1792		4371.18
Amot. of 6 ⅌ Ct Stock assumed Debt	299.404.95	
Intt. from Jany. 1. 1792.		4491. 7
Amot of 3 ⅌ Ct. Do Do	239,737.22	
Int. from Jany. 1. 1792.		1798. 2
	Total Dollars	28.847. 3

exclusive of the Interest to the State of Pennsa. which amounts as ⅌ my Letter the 28th of Febuary last to 13.982 Dollars 14 Cents.

From the importunate necessity of my Clerks, who have not received their Wages for two Quarters past I am under the necessity of praying your attention for the payment of their Salarys. I flatter myself that after a few months the greater part of their services may be dispensed with.

I have the honor to be with the greatest respect   Sir   your most obedt Hble servt   Thomas Smith Com Loans

Honble. Alexander Hamilton
Secty Treay. United States

ALS, RG 53, Pennsylvania State Loan Office, Letter Book, 1790–1794, Vol. "615-P," National Archives.

To Otho H. Williams

Philadelphia
March 28. 1792

My Dear Sir

An uncommon press of business has prevented my thanking you sooner for your private letter of the   .[1]

Your ideas of the manner of conducting a certain business have a remarkable correspondency with my own. I think one might venture to ensure success, humanly speaking, on such a plan, and every other will be precarious and critical.

I flatter myself the general principles of it will govern future instructions; but how they may be executed must depend on who is to execute them. This point is not yet decided and is not without embarrassment. In confidence I say to you that you have been in conversation [2]—But the state of your health for some time past is supposed to be a serious objection. I am sorry to find an unfavourable allusion to it in your letter. Why do you admit so troublesome an inmate in your tenement?

My official letter of [to]day [3] will have announced to you my desire that no relaxation may be admitted into the course of payments of the duties. Exact punctuality in this respect is essential to the whole system of public Credit and Finance. I must risk all ill consequences in maintaining punctuality.

I hope however the Bank will prevent any occurring upon the present occasion. You see the latitude I give. That institution may lend its aid boldly—And I trust will. But be this as it may coercive measures if necessary must proceed without delay.

The Bank of Maryland need not fear in this instance to extend its operations on the score of the establishment of a Branch of the National Bank.[4] This event must be suspended for a time & my forbearance will at all events render the extension in this instance without danger to them.

Yrs. with great regard   A Hamilton

Otho H Williams Esqr.

ALS, Maryland Historical Society, Baltimore.

1. Space left blank in MS. H is referring to Williams to H, March 5, 1792.

2. On April 5, 1792, Williams wrote to H: "I am much gratified by your intimation that my name has occurred in conversation about a successor to the unfortunate St. Clair."

3. As the postmark on this letter reads "30 Mr" and the subject of punctuality in the payment of duties is discussed in H to Williams, March 29, 1792, presumably H is referring to that official letter.

4. The Bank of Maryland, which was located in Baltimore, had been granted a charter by the state legislature on December 14, 1790. On February 6, 1792, the directors of the Bank of the United States elected directors and a cashier for the Baltimore branch of the Bank of the United States.

To Nicholas Low

[*Philadelphia, March 29, 1792.* On April 10, 1792, Low wrote to Hamilton: "I am duely favord with yours of 23. 29 & 31 Ulto." *Letter of March 29 not found.*]

To John Miller [1]

Treasury Department, March 29, 1792. "I am desirous to avail the United States of your knowledge of the various species of Merchandize . . . for the Infantry and Cavalry of the United States, which are to be furnished, by contract, by Messrs Charles Young and Thomas Billington. . . ." [2]

Copy, RG 217, Miscellaneous Treasury Accounts, 1790–1894, Account No. 3269, National Archives.

1. Miller was a Philadelphia merchant.

2. Young and Billington were Philadelphia tailors.

On June 6, 1792, Tench Coxe wrote to Miller: "The Secretary of the Treasury has intmiated to me his wish that you would take an early occasion to Inspect all *the Woolen Cloth* now in the hands of the Contractors, and not made up. He understands that they have recently procured a considerable supply. You will be pleased to let me hear from you as soon as you shall have gone the Examination of these Cloths" (LC, RG 58, Letters of Commissioner of Revenue, 1792–1793, National Archives).

Miller submitted a bill for his services on November 1, 1792, on which H wrote:

"The service was performed by my direction and upon a stipulation of four Dollars for each day of employment as per my Letter.   A Hamilton" (ADS, RG 217, Miscellaneous Treasury Accounts, 1790–1894, Account No. 3269, National Archives).

To Jeremiah Olney

Treasury Department, March 29, 1792. "There is due to William Peck, Marshall for the District of Rhode Island upon a settlement made at the Treasury, the sum of two thousand, one hundred & five Dollars and twelve Cents, which sum I request you will pay to the said Marshall. . . . This transaction is of course not to be brought into your accounts, but merely to be noted at foot of your weekly return."

LS, Rhode Island Historical Society, Providence; copy, RG 56, Letters to the Collector at Providence, National Archives; copy, RG 56, Letters to Collectors at Small Ports, "Set G," National Archives.

To Otho H. Williams

Treasury Department
March 29 1792.

Sir

I have received your letter of the 22d instant,[1] and am extremely sorry to perceive the difficulties you mention. It is not in my power to authorise your dispensing with the execution of the laws, as explained by your standing instructions from the Treasury; but as I have always a desire to give every convenient and prudent facility to commerce, I have made an eventual engagement to the Bank of Maryland to leave in their hands a sum of public money, equivalent to any Notes they may discount for importers, to discharge the duties which shall fall due in your Office on or before the 15th day of April next. Should they require a list of the Bonds, exhibiting as well the names of the Obligors as the sums due, and the times of payment, You will furnish it to them.

I am, Sir,   Your Mo. Obedt Servant   A Hamilton

PS—I hope the arrangement desired will produce the requisite accomodation to the Merchants; because it is indispensable that punctuallity should be enforced if necessary.[2]

Otho H Williams Esqr.
Baltimore

LS, Columbia University Libraries.
1. Letter not found, but see Williams to H, February 20, 1792.
2. The postscript is in the handwriting of H.

From Oliver Wolcott, Junior

Introductory Note

This letter concerns the problem of the so-called lost million. As early as September, 1775, Pierre August Caron de Beaumarchais, the French writer and courtier, had attempted to persuade the French government of the desirability of aiding the American colonies in their revolt against England. When, in the spring of 1776, the French government agreed to send supplies from France to the colonies, Beaumarchais secured the appointment as agent and opened negotiations with Arthur Lee and Silas Deane, American agents in Paris. To protect France's neutrality it was intimated to the Americans that the transaction should be presented as a private business undertaking between the United States and Beaumarchais through the fictitious Spanish firm of Roderigue Hortalez et Cie. Arms, ammunition, and uniforms were to be sent to the United States and, in order to retain the appearance of a business transaction, certain payments in supplies were to be sent to Beaumarchais by the American states.[1]

In addition to the supplies secured through Beaumarchais, Benjamin Franklin and Silas Deane negotiated a loan on March 24, 1777, with the Farmers-General of France. Article 5 of this agreement provided that "The Farmers-General oblige themselves for the discharge of the amount of five thousand hogsheads [of tobacco], to remit at the disposal of Congress, and to pay into the hands of the banker who shall be appointed by Messrs. Franklin and Deane, or to direct their receiver-general at Paris to accept the bills which shall be drawn upon him by Messrs. Franklin and Deane as far as a million of livres tournois, in the course of the ensuing month, and another million the instant of the arrival of the first ships loaded with tobacco, which shall be delivered to them; the said two millions making the balance an entire payment for the five thousand hogsheads, or five million weight of tobacco, mark weight, sold by Congress at the price of eight sols per pound, before agreed upon."[2]

ADf, Connecticut Historical Society, Hartford.
1. Beaumarchais's ambiguous position caused difficulties from the beginning of the negotiations. It was not clear to Congress whether the supplies were in reality being provided as a gift to the American states by the French government using Beaumarchais's firm as a disguise to protect its neutrality, or whether the transaction was to be regarded as a straightforward business undertaking between Beaumarchais and the United States. Even the American commissioners in Paris were divided in their opinions on this subject. For an account of this divergence of views, see Wharton, *Revolutionary Diplomatic Correspondence*, I, Introduction, § 62.
2. Wharton, *Revolutionary Diplomatic Correspondence*, II, 300.

Soon after the signing of this contract the sum of one million livres was paid to Deane and Franklin by the Farmers-General. The American agents then deposited this sum with the banker of the United States in Paris, Ferdinand Le Grand, and, as agreed to in the contract, shipments of tobacco were made from the United States to the Farmers-General.

On February 21, 1783, Franklin and Charles Gravier, Comte de Vergennes, the French Foreign Minister, signed a contract with the French government which summarized and explained the various loans that Franklin had obtained from France. According to the contract, there had been "Aids and Subsidies furnished to the Congress of the United States, under the title of gratuitous assistance, from the pure generosity of the King, three millions of which were granted before the treaty of Feby. 1778. . . ." [3]

Le Grand's accounts showed that he had received only two million livres from the French government in the form of gratuities, and the search for the "lost million" began. At first it was supposed that the advance of one million livres from the Farmers-General might constitute the missing million, and on July 11, 1786, Franklin wrote to Le Grand as follows:

"I send you enclosed some letters, that have passed between the Secretary of Congress and me,[4] respecting three million of Livres, acknowledged to have been received, before the Treaty of February 1778 as *Don gratuit* from the King, of which only Two Millions are found in your accounts; unless the million from the Farmers-General be one of the three. I have [been] assured, that all the money received from the King, whether as Loan or Gift, went through your hands; and as I always looked on the million we had of the Farmers-General to be distinct from what we had of the Crown, I wonder how I came to sign the Contract acknowledging three millions of gift, when, in reality, there was only two, exclusive of that from the Farmers. . . .

"It is possible, that the million furnished ostensibly by the Farmers, was in fact a gift of the Crown, in which case . . . they owe us for the two Ship Loads of Tobacco, which they received on account of it. I most earnestly request of you to get this matter explained, that I may stand clear before I die, lest some enemy should afterwards accuse me of having received a million not accounted for." [5]

Inquiry was made repeatedly of the French government on this matter, but the royal administration refused to provide the commissioner with a statement of account. On January 27, 1787, Franklin wrote to Charles Thomson, secretary of the Continental Congress, as follows:

"You may remember, that in the correspondence between us in June last, on the Subject of a Million *free gift* of the King of France, acknowledged in our contract to have been received, but which did not appear

3. Smyth, *Writings of Franklin*, X, 383–84.
4. On May 15, 1786, Charles Thomson wrote to Franklin concerning the missing million livres (Edmund C. Burnett, ed., *Letters of Members of the Continental Congress* [Washington, 1921–1938], VIII, 361–62). Franklin replied on June 18, 1786 (Smyth, *Writings of Franklin*, IX, 517–18).
5. Smyth, *Writings of Franklin*, IX, 527–28.

to be accounted for in our Banker's accounts, unless it should be the same with the million said to be received from the Farmers-General, I mentioned, that an explanation might doubtless be easily obtained by writing to Mr. Grand, or Mr. Jefferson. . . . I wrote myself to Mr. Grand a letter upon it, of which I now enclose a Copy, with his answers, and several letters from M. Durival, who is *Chef du Bureau des Fonds . . . des Affaires Etrangères.*[6]

"You will see by these letters that the million in question was delivered to somebody on the 10th of June 1776, but it does not appear to whom. It is clear that it could not be to Mr. Grand nor to the Commissioners from Congress; [7] for we did not meet in France till the end of December 1776, or beginning of January 1777, and that Banker was not charged before with our affairs.

"By the Minister's [reserve] in refusing him a Copy of the Receipt, I conjecture it must be money advanced for our use to M. de Beaumarchais, and that it is a *mystère du cabinet,* which perhaps should not be further enquired into, unless necessary to guard against more demands than may be just from that agent: For it may well be supposed, that, if the Court furnished him with the means of supplying us, they may not be willing to furnish authentic proofs of such a transaccion so early in our dispute with Britain. . . ." [8]

It was not until 1794, after the fall of the royal government, that Gouverneur Morris, United States Minister Plenipotentiary to France, was able to obtain a definite account of the missing million, and Franklin's surmise was proved to be correct. In reply to an inquiry by Morris, Philibert Buchot, French Minister of Foreign Affairs, sent to Morris a "Copie d'une quittance dattée du 10 juin 1776. Qui parait être celle dont le gouvernement des Etats-unis a besoin pour regler Ses Comptes" [9] (LS, Columbia University Libraries). The receipt reads as follows:

"J'ai recu de Monsieur Du Vergier, Conformément aux ordres de Monsieur Le Comte de Vergennes en date du 5. courant que je lui ai remis. La Somme d'un million, dont je rendrai compte à mondit Sieur Comte de Vergennes. à Paris ce 10. juin 1776.

"Caron de Beaumarchais.

"Bon pour un million de Livres Tournois." [10]

6. Le Grand's letter to Franklin, dated September 9, 1786, and the enclosures from Jean Durival, dated August 30 and September 5, 1786, are printed in Sparks, *Works of Benjamin Franklin,* X, 269–72.

In his letter of September 5, 1786, Durival assured Le Grand that the gift from the French government had "nothing to do with the million, which the Congress may have received from the Farmers-General in 1777; consequently [the Comte de Vergennes] . . . thinks, that the receipt, which you desire may be communicated to you, cannot satisfy the object of your view, and that it would be useless to give you the copy which you desire" (Sparks, *Works of Benjamin Franklin,* X, 270).

7. Benjamin Franklin, Silas Deane, and Arthur Lee.

8. Smyth, *Writings of Franklin,* IX, 553–54.

9. Buchot to Morris, July 7, 1794 (Sparks, *Gouverneur Morris,* II, 446).

10. Copy. Columbia University Libraries. For an account of the subsequent claims of Beaumarchais and his heirs against the United States, see Wharton,

T. D

C. Off March 29. 1792

Sir,

On examining the subsisting contracts, between the United States, and the Government of France, and the Farmers General and a comparison thereof with the foreign accounts and documents transmitted to the Treasury the following facts appear.

That previous to the Treaty of February 1778, the sum of Three millions of Livres had been advanced by the government of France, to the agents of the United States under the title of gratutious assistance for which no reimbursement was to be made.

That the payments which composed the before mentioned sum of Three millions of Livres are stated in a Letter of Mr. Durival to Mr. Grand dated in 1786,[11] to have been made on account of one Million of Livres which they contend was advanced in June 1777 in consequence of a special contract, with Messrs. Franklin & Deane, to be repaid by the delivery of Tobacco at certain stipulated prices. And the advance made by the Farmers General is said to be the same money as is credited by Mr. Grand on the 4th. of June 1777.

After a careful examination of the foreign accounts it is found that no more than Three millions of Livres have been credited by any agents of the United States.

An opinion was entertained by the late Officers of the Treasury, that the sum claimed by the Farmers General composed a part of the sum supplied as a gratutious aid by the Government at the following periods—

One million delivered by the Royal Treasury the 10th. of June 1776, and two other millions advanced also by the Royal Treasury in 1777 on four Rects. of the Deputies of Congress of the 17th. of January 3d. of April 10th. of June & 15th. of Oct. of the same year.

Revolutionary Diplomatic Correspondence, I, Introduction, §§ 69, 70, 71; Charles J. Stillé, *Beaumarchais and the "Lost Million"* (n.p., n.d.), 34–38; *ASP, Claims,* I, 343–46.

11. Durival to Le Grand, August 30, 1786 (Sparks, *Works of Benjamin Franklin,* X, 269–70).

In the accounts of Mr. Ferdinand Grand Banker of the United States, the following sums are credited—viz

1777.	January 31st.	Livres	500.000.
"	April 28th		500.000
"	June 4th.		1000.000
"	July 3d		500.000
"	Oct. 10th		500.000
Amounting in the whole to Livres			3.000.000

The Farmers General of France claim a large balance from the United States. Subsequent explanations have however rendered it probable that including the claim of the Farmers General the sum of Four millions of Livres was in fact recd.—it is however indispensible that it should be known to whom the money was paid.

The most direct mode of obtaining this information, will be, to call for copies of the Rects. mentioned in Mr. Durivals Letter of 1786. and more particularly a copy of that said to have been given on the 10th. of June 1776.

I herewith transmit copies of such documents as will enable you to form an opinion of the State of this business & request that such measures may be taken to procure the necessary information as you shall judge most important and effectual.

A H

To William Seton

[*Philadelphia, March 30, 1792.* Letter listed in dealer's catalogue. *Letter not found.*]

LS, sold at Parke-Bernet Galleries, May 12, 1947, Lot 258.

To Gulian Verplanck

Treasury Department March 30th 1792

Sir

As it will be convenient to you to be apprized of the alterations in the business of the Treasury, which take place from time to time in consequence of arrangements with the Bank of the united States, I think it expedient to inform you, that the receipt and exchange for Specie of the Bank notes and Cash notes of the Institution over which you preside, will be discontinued in the Custom houses out of the City of New York in a few weeks after the receipt of a circular letter written this day.[1]

I have the honor to be   Sir   Your most obedt Servt

Alexander Hamilton
Secy of the Treasy

The President of the Bank
of New York

LS, The Andre deCoppet Collection, Princeton University Library.

1. See "Treasury Department Circular to the Collectors of the Customs," February 21, 1792, note 1.

Conversation with George Hammond [1]

[Philadelphia, March 31, 1792] [2]

In consequence of the information and instructions, contained in your Lordship's dispatch No 2, I waited upon Mr Hamilton on Saturday last, and, in the course of a general conversation on several matters, I took occasion to enquire of him, as if accidentally, whether the object of the commission, assigned to Messrs Short and Carmichael, was really such as it had been publicly stated to be; [3] (and as I mentioned to your Lordship in my dispatch No 8) [4] viz. "to negociate a treaty or convention with the court of Spain, relative to the navigation of the Mississippi." Mr Hamilton answered in the affirmative, and added that this and other points of a similar nature had been subjects of frequent disagreement and discussion between the two governments; but he now hoped that they were in a train of being adjusted to their mutual satisfaction.

I then said, that I must take the liberty of reminding him that a free participation in the navigation of the Mississippi was secured to Great Britain by treaty,[5] as well with the Court of Spain as with the United States, and I trusted that, whatever might be the result of this negociation, this government would not consent to any stipulations which might militate against her rights and interest in this or any other respect. Mr Hamilton assured me that this government was far from entertaining any such intention, as neither their interest nor inclination would prompt them to adopt any measures which might affect the rights, to which I had alluded.

In this place I must remark that I am rather inclined to believe this declaration of Mr Hamilton to be sincere. For, from combining it with some accidental observations, that he fomerly threw out on the subject of the Mississippi, in one of our earliest conversations,[6] I am led to infer that this government esteems the participation of Great Britain in the navigation of that river, as an object of benefit, rather than disadvantage, inasmuch as it involves the two countries in one common connexion of interest against any attempt of the Court of Spain, to exclude both or either of them from the navigation of that river, at any future period.

As I did not wish to manifest to Mr Hamilton too great a degree of anxiety upon this subject, I did not press it much farther. But in another part of our conversation, upon my affecting to speak lightly of the general politics of the Court of Spain, he said, with some degree of quickness, that "it is indeed very singular that they have never proposed any thing which has not been clogged by some strange absurd impediment or other". I cannot pretend to conjecture to what he immediately alluded, but I presume that this sentiment had some sort of reference to the present discussions.

D, PRO: F.O. (Great Britain), Series 4, Vol. 14, Part IV.
1. This conversation has been taken from Hammond to Lord Grenville, April 5, 1792, Dispatch No. 15.
2. Hammond informed Grenville that he "waited upon Mr Hamilton on Saturday last." Since Hammond's letter was written on April 5, 1792, a Thursday, "Saturday last" was March 31, 1792.
3. For an account of the mission of William Carmichael and William Short, see "Notes on Thomas Jefferson's Report of Instructions for the Commissioners to Spain," March 1–4, 1792, note 1.
Grenville's Dispatch No. 2, dated January 5, 1792, stated: "Lord St. Helens' [the British Ambassador to Spain] having communicated to me the confidential Information which His Excellency had received from Mr. Carmichael, respecting a Negotiation actually going on for a Treaty of Alliance between Spain and the United States of America, I think it necessary, ir order that You may be apprized of this Circumstance, to transmit to You an Extract of his Letter on this Subject, and to desire that You will be very assiduous in watching the Progress of such Negotiation and that You will acquaint me with all the Particulars You may be able to learn concerning it; but You will take no public Steps to counteract any arrangements which may be concerted between the two Countries, any further than by expressing to the American Ministers your Persuasion that they will enter into no engage-

ment with the Court of Madrid, which may be prejudicial to the interests of Great Britain" (Mayo, *Instructions to British Ministers*, 21–22).

In the extract referred to by Grenville, dated November 25, 1791, "St Helens stated that Carmichael, through Anthony Merry of the British Embassy, had informed him that Count Florida Blanca had suddenly expressed a desire to accommodate differences with the United States, had admitted the American navigation and boundary claims, but had insisted upon certain articles intended to serve as the basis of a regular treaty of alliance between the United States and Spain. Carmichael told Merry that he would forward these Spanish proposals for an alliance to his government, but intended to delay sending them as long as he decently could. Carmichael said that he much preferred a connection between the United States and Great Britain, and, since Hammond's mission to America seemed to indicate that such a connection might be in view, he had thought it fitting to apprise Lord St. Helens of the state of his negotiations with Spain" (Mayo, *Instructions to British Ministers*, 22, note 11).

4. Hammond's Dispatch No. 8 to Grenville was dated February 2, 1792 (MS Division, New York Public Library).

5. Article VIII of the treaty of peace (1783) between the United States and Great Britain provided that "the Navigation of the River Mississippi, from its source to the Ocean shall forever remain free and open to the Subjects of Great Britain and the Citizens of the United States" (Miller, *Treaties*, II, 155).

6. If H and Hammond discussed the Mississippi question "in one of our earliest conversations," Hammond did not forward these remarks to Grenville, for they are not in any of his dispatches to Grenville of 1791 or 1792.

John Jay to the Commissioners of the Sinking Fund [1]

[New York, March 31, 1792]

The Chief Justice of the United States, presents his compliments to the Attorney General, and requests the favor of him to lay before the Board of trustees, the opinion herewith enclosed, on the question stated in their act of the 26th instant; a copy of which the Chief Justice yesterday received, enclosed in the letter which the Attorney General did him the honor to write on the 29th instant.[2]

New-York, March 31, 1792.

Question. 1. Do the words *"if not exceeding the par or true value thereof,"* in the act making provision for the reduction of the public debt, restrain the purchase of any part of the debt of the United States (whether subscribed, and bearing an immediate interest of six per cent. or an immediate interest of three per cent. or a future interest of six per cent. or unsubscribed) so long as the market price of the same shall not exceed 20 shillings in the pound?

Question 2. If these words do restrain the purchase of any species of the public debt, within limits narrower than 20 shillings in the pound, what rate of interest shall be adopted, as the rule for computing the value of each kind of stock at this day?

The meaning of the word *par* is well ascertained. When cash, equal in amount to the sum specified in a bill of exchange, is paid for it, that bill is said to have been bought and sold *at par*.

When stock is bought and sold for more or less than what the public have engaged to pay, that stock is said to have been bought and sold above and below *par*. Bank notes usually pass, in the vicinity of the bank, for the sums they promise, that is, at *par*.

The *true value* of stock considered as merchandise, is the market price. The true value of stock, considered as evidence of *money due from debtor to creditor*, is regarded, by the law, as being precisely so much cash as was contracted to be paid. Hence, it seems, that the value of stock is of two kinds—the one, commercial, and fluctuating; the other, legal, and fixed. The act adverts to and recognises both; the former in restraining the trustees from giving more than the *market price*, though below par, the latter in restraining them from purchasing at prices above *par*.

Is there not a kind of value distinct from either? I think there is; and that it is the one alluded to in the second question above stated. It is the result of comparison, combination, and calculation, and governed by some principle assumed as a standard. It differs, therefore, from the *legal* value, which always is the exact sum promised to be paid; and it differs from the *market* price, which has no *standard*, but depends on momentary and fluctuating circumstances.

Is the *true value*, mentioned in the act, of this latter, or third kind? I think not.

As this is not the ordinary sense of the word value, and as a standard to ascertain it is neither indicated by the act, nor very easy to find; it seems singular that the Congress, if they really contemplated that kind of value, should omit not only to declare this meaning, particularly and expressly, but also to fix the standard whereby the trustees should be regulated.

As the act distinguishes the market value from the legal value, so, also, the value, in question, if intended, would probably have been distinguished from both, and not confounded, as it now is, with the *legal* value, by so connecting the words *the par*, with the words *true value*, by the particle *or*, as naturally and grammatically to exclude the idea in contemplation: for the particle *or*, placed as it is, appears, to me, to be precisely equivalent to—*that is to say; in other words, to wit:*

No other than the legal value can, accurately, be called the *true* value in *general* terms. The laws of morality, and of the land, oblige the debtor to pay the sum promised, and they entitle and direct the creditor to receive it. Debtors and creditors are the only persons strictly interested in the value of debts. Whatever is the true value between *them*, must be seen as being so by others, as well as by them; and, therefore, when laws, or persons, and especially laws, speak of the *true value* of a debt, they are, in my opinion, always to be understood as intending the sum due, or *legal* value, unless they use additional expressions to particularise their meaning.

For these reasons I am of opinion that the words "*if not exceeding the par or true value thereof,*" do not restrain the purchases of any part of the debt of the United States, so long as the market price of the same shall not exceed the sum actually due from, and payable by, the United States, in discharge of those debts.   John Jay.

31st March, 1792.

ASP, Finance, I, 236; copy, in the handwriting of Thomas Jefferson, Thomas Jefferson Papers, Library of Congress.

  1. For background to this letter, see H to John Adams, March 20, 1792; H for Adams to Jay, March 21, 1792; Jay to H, March 23, 1792; "Meeting of the Commissioners of the Sinking Fund," March 26, 1792.

  2. Edmund Randolph to Jay, March 29, 1792 (ALS, Columbia University Libraries). See H for Adams to Jay, March 21, 1792, note 2, and "Meeting of the Commissioners of the Sinking Fund," March 26, 1792, note 6.

  The copy in the Thomas Jefferson Papers does not include this letter of transmittal.

From Benjamin Lincoln

Boston March 31st. 1792

Sir

As you have often expressed a wish to establish uniformity among all the officers commissioned in different districts to perform similar duties I am induced to mention an instance wherein from the want of similarity questions arise which leaves us quite at a loss how to determine the length of Vessels from the registers some inserting therein the real length & some the length after the deduction of three fifths of the Beam. Our practice has been to insert the real length others we find practice differently. Would it not be well when you shall address a circular letter to the collectors to express your opinion on the subject?

Secy of the Treasury

LC, Massachusetts Historical Society, Boston; LC, RG 36, Collector of Customs at Boston, Letter Book, 1790–1797, National Archives; two copies, RG 56, Letters from the Collector at Boston, National Archives.

To Nicholas Low

[Philadelphia, March 31, 1792. On April 10, 1792, Low wrote to Hamilton: "I am duely favord with yours of 23. 29 & 31 Ulto." Letter of March 31 not found.]

To George Washington

[Philadelphia, March, 1792.] Sends list of names of persons recommended for positions of director of the Mint and treasurer of the Mint.[1]

AD, George Washington Papers, Library of Congress.
   1. On verso H wrote: "Names which have occurred as for Director or Treasurer." There are forty names in this list arranged by states.
   On April 13, 1792, Washington nominated David Rittenhouse of Pennsylvania to be director of the Mint, and on May 3, 1792, he nominated Tristram Dalton of Massachusetts to be treasurer of the Mint. The names of both men are on H's list.

From William Ellery

[Newport, Rhode Island] April 2, 1792. "This letter will be accompanied by a weekly return of monies received and paid . . . and also a Statement of the case of the Brig Chance,[1] and papers respectg. the same. I shall refrain from prosecuting Capt. Corey."[2]

LC, Newport Historical Society, Newport, Rhode Island.
   1. The brig Chance was owned by John Innis Clarke and Joseph Nightingale, Providence merchants. On July 26, 1792, a part of the penalty incurred

under "An Act to provide more effectually for the collection of the duties imposed by law on goods, wares and merchandise imported into the United States, and on the tonnage of ships or vessels" (1 *Stat.* 145–78 [August 4, 1790]) was remitted by H (DS, Columbia University Libraries).
2. See Ellery to H, February 10, 1792.

From Meletiah Jordan [1]

Frenchman's Bay [District of Maine] April 2, 1792. ". . . The difficult situation of this District of which I have already informed you [2] has obliged my purchasing a small Boat. . . ."

LC, RG 56, Letters to Collectors at Gloucester, Machias, and Frenchman's Bay, National Archives.
1. Jordan was collector of customs at Frenchman's Bay, District of Maine.
2. See Jordan to H, July 1, 1791.

To Nathan Keais [1]

[Philadelphia, April 2, 1792. On April 26, 1792, Keais wrote to Hamilton: "I this Day was Honored with the Receipt of your Letter of the 2nd Instant Covering A Commission . . . as Inspector of the Revenue for this port." *Letter not found.]*

1. Keais was collector of customs for the port of Washington, North Carolina, and superintendent of stakage in Pamlico and Albemarle sounds.

To Philip Livingston [1]

Philadelphia April 2d
1792

My Dear Sir
I thank you for sending by express the Chief Justice's Letter.[2] It will enable me to enter the Market more advantageously for the support of the Debt. I detained the express 'till today, in expectation of being able to forward by him the result. But certain indispensable engagements of some of the Trustees prevent a Meeting 'till tomorrow. The arrangement will be conveyed by express.
I observe that certain characters continue to sport with the Market & with the distresses of their fellow Citizens.[3] 'Tis time there should be a line of separation between honest Men & knaves; between respectable stockholders and dealers in the funds, and mere unprin-

cipled Gamblers. Public infamy must restrain what the laws cannot. This spirit must be cultivated among the friends of good government and good principles. The relaxations in a just system of thinking, which have been produced by an excess of the spirit of speculation must be corrected. And Contempt and Neglect must attend those who manifest that they have no principle but to get money.

Yrs. with great regard   A Hamilton

P. The monies which you will have paid for the two expresses will be reimbursed at the Treasury. Be so good as to take Receipts for what you pay & make out a little account against the Secretary of the Treasury charging for so much paid at each time to express A or B to carry a letter from the Chief of the United States to the Trustees of the Sinking fund. Send this to Mr. Kean.[4]

P. Livingston Esqr.

ALS, MS Division, New York Public Library.
   1. For background to this letter, see H to John Adams, March 20, 1792; H for Adams to John Jay, March 21, 1792; Jay to H, March 23, 1792; Livingston to H, March 24, 1792; and "Meeting of the Commissioners of the Sinking Fund," March 26, 1792.
   2. Jay to the Commissioners of the Sinking Fund, March 31, 1792. See also Livingston to H, March 24, 1792.
   3. For information on the financial panic in New York in the spring of 1792, see William Duer to H, March 12, 1792; H to Duer, March 14, 23, 1792; Philip Livingston to H, March 24, 1792; Philip Schuyler to H, March 25, 1792; William Seton to H, March 21, 1792; H to Seton, March 19, 25, 1792; Robert Troup to H, March 19, 1792.
   According to Joseph Stancliffe Davis, Edward, Brockholst, and J. R. Livingston "were actively speculating on the 'bear' side of the market and were due to *deliver* most of the New York bank stock which Duer was to *receive* in May. It is probable that the Livingstons were chiefly concerned with lowering the price of stocks, especially that of the Bank of New York" (Davis, *Essays*, I, 283).
   4. John Kean, cashier of the Bank of the United States.

To William Short

Treasury Department
April 2. 1792

Sir

I am to acknowlege the receipt of your several letters of the 22d of November 23d 28th and 30th of December.

The accomplishment, thus early, of a loan at 4 per Cent exceeds expectation as much as it does credit to your exertions.[1] The intelligence of it was received with great satisfaction by the President as well as by myself, and has given no small pleasure to the public at large.

You will perceive, by my letter of the 14th of February, the impression I entertained of the effect of your operation at Antwerp. The event is a confirmation of the good policy of opening to the United States more than one Market.

I observe what you say with regard to the relative state of Exchange and Depreciation in France.[2] I shall be glad to be informed that a rule for liquidating the payments by the United States has been adopted. It will be better to have it settled now than to leave it to future discussion. Embarrassments may hereafter arise in fixing a rule which may be as advantageous to the United States as a very moderate regard to their interest would render desireable. The moment of commencing payments, by anticipation, of sums not already due, has been or will be a very favourable one for a right adjustment of this point.

You desire my ideas concerning the comparative expediency of making loans at Amsterdam or Antwerp on equal terms of interest and charges in the event of a tax being laid by the States General as has been expected.[3] This you will be better able to determine than myself, when I explain to you the ground of the preference heretofore signified by me. It was founded on a supposition, that the course of Trade & money transactions will render remittances from this Country to Amsterdam more easy and less disadvantageous than to Antwerp. Now, the general course of exchange between Amsterdam and Antwerp will decide whether it be more advantageous to pay the tax than to remit *through* Amsterdam to Antwerp, which I presume, generally speaking, must be the case. If exchange be against Antwerp in a degree sufficient to counterballance the Tax, the preference will be due to Amsterdam: If otherwise, to Antwerp.

The explanations you desire respecting the State of the Debt due to France shall be forwarded by the next opportunity,[4] as shall the contracts for the two last loans ratified by the President. An unusual press of business on the Executive departments occasions unavoidably this delay.

It is impossible for me to agree to an alteration of the terms of the six milion loan in particular suggested.[5] It would be a renunciation of an advantage really important in itself and still more so in the public opinion of this Country.

The readiness, which appeared, in the first instance, to accede to the right of redeeming at pleasure was more agreeable than expected. The change of views on this point is a natural result of the circumstances which have been experienced.

The terms of the last loan [6] supersede the necessity of the latitude contemplated in mine of the 21 of March.

The treasurer will draw upon our Commissioners in Holland [7] for Five hundred thousand florins so as to arrive and be payable in June. I fear, under the instructions that have been given, to risk drafts for a greater sum; though I consider it as for the interest of the United States to prosecute purchases of the public debt with monies borrowed upon the terms of the last loan, and mean, as fast as I perceive it can be done with safety, to draw for a further sum of two Millions and a half of florins to complete the three Millions intended by my last mentioned letter. Your future letters will determine me whether to extend my drafts upon the loans already made or to wait for a reservation by you out of some future loan.

With very great and real consideration & esteem   I have the honor to be   Sir Your Obedient servant   Alexander Hamilton

PS. If the terms of the last loan can be rendered stationary; it will be of the happiest consequence. Perhaps it will conduce to this, to let it be understood that the loans will be confined to Amsterdam & probably extended for domestic operations, if things can be kept in the same posture. Something like this has been hinted by me.[8]

William Short Esquire
&c &c

ALS (photostat), William Short Papers, Library of Congress; LS, William Short Papers, Library of Congress. A copy of this letter was enclosed in H's "Report on Foreign Loans," February 13, 1793.

1. For a description of the December, 1791, Holland loan, see Short to H, December 23, 28, 1791.
2. See Short to H, November 22, December 1, 1791.
3. See Short to H, December 30, 1791.
4. See Short to H, December 30, 1791.

5. See Short to H, December 30, 1791.
6. See note 1.
7. Willink, Van Staphorst, and Hubbard.
8. See H to Willink, Van Staphorst, and Hubbard, February 14, 1792.

From James Reynolds [1]

Philadelphia 3d, April, 1792.

Sir

I hope you will pardon me in taking the liberty I do In troubling you so offen. it hurts me to let you Know my Setivation. I should take it as a protickeler if you will Oblige me with the loane of about thirty Dollars. I am in hopes in a fue days I shall be In a more better Setivation. and then I shall Be able to make you ample Satisfaction for your Favours shewn me. I want it for some little Necssaries of life for my family. sir you granting the above favour this morning will very much Oblige your most Obediant and humble Servant

James Reynolds

Alex. Hamilton Esqr.

NB   the inclose is a Receipt for Ninety dollars. that is if you Can Oblige me with the thirty. that including Boath Sums

[ENCLOSURE]

Receipt from James Reynolds

[Philadelphia, April 3, 1792]

Received philadelphia 3d. April. 1792 of Alexander Hamilton Esqr. Ninety dollars which I promise to pay on demand

James Reynolds

90, Dollars

"Reynolds Pamphlet," August 31, 1797.
1. This letter and the enclosed receipt are printed as document No. XIII in the appendix of the "Reynolds Pamphlet," August 31, 1797.
For background to this letter, see Reynolds to H, December 15, 17, 19, 22, 1791, January 3, 17, March 24, 1792; H to Reynolds, December 15, 1791; Maria Reynolds to H, December 15, 1791, January 23–March 18, March 24, 1792.

To James Brice

Treasury Department April 4th 1792

Sir,

I was duly honored with your letter relative to the arrears of pay due to sundry Officers and Soldiers of the Maryland line of the late Army.[1] The payments of arrears due to the lines of Virginia and North Carolina were made in the States under the special injunction of an Act of Congress which did not extend to Maryland or any other State.[2] This circumstance will prevent the allowance of any Commission for the duty to any person in Maryland. It was expected to be performed at the Seat of Government by the Officers of the Treasury, but as it is desired by the executive of the State and it will be more convenient to the Claimants to receive their monies at Annapolis, I have written to the Commissioner of Loans[3] to know whether it will be agreeable to him to receive the Money and to pay it as it shall be applied for. Mr. Campbell[4] suggested that he was only intended to be the Bearer of the Money and that he understood it was afterwards to be placed in the hands of the Treasurer of Maryland[5] who acts with his brother in his Office of Commissioner of Loans. I therefore hope that if the Commissioner undertakes the business your views will be satifactorily executed, while the monies of the United States will be placed in the hands of an officer duly responsible to them.

I have the honor to be with perfect respect Sir, Your most obedt Servt

A Hamilton

His Excellency James Bryce Esqr.
Governor of Maryland
Annapolis

LS, Hall of Records of Maryland, Annapolis; copy, RG 56, Miscellaneous Letters Sent, "Set K," National Archives; copy, RG 56, Letters 2d Comptroller, 2d Auditor, Executive of Maryland and Georgia, 1789–1833, National Archives.
1. Brice to H, March 19, 1792.
2. H is referring to three joint resolutions of Congress, adopted on May 24, 1790, regarding the payment of arrears to the late officers and men of the Virginia and North Carolina lines (*Journal of the House*, I, 217–18, 221;

Journal of the Second Session of the Senate of the United States of America Begun and Held at the City of New-York, January 4th, 1790; and in the fourteenth Year of the Independence of the Said States [New York, 1790], 79–81). The second of these resolutions reads as follows: *"Resolved*, That the President of the United States be requested to cause the Secretary of the Treasury to take the necessary steps for paying (within the said States, respectively,) the money appropriated by Congress, on the twenty-ninth day of September, one thousand seven hundred and eighty-nine, for the discharging the arrears of pay due to the troops of the lines of the said States respectively" (*Journal of the House*, I, 217).

3. Letter not found. Thomas Harwood was commissioner of loans for Maryland.

4. William Campbell.

5. Benjamin Harwood.

To Nathan Keais

[*Philadelphia, April 4, 1792.* On April 26, 1792, Keais wrote to Hamilton: "I this Day was Honored with the Receipt of your Letter . . . of the 4th." *Letter not found.*]

Meeting of the Commissioners of the Sinking Fund [1]

[Philadelphia, April 4, 1792]

At a meeting of the Trustees of the Sinking Fund, at the house of the Vice President of the United States, on the 4th day of April, 1792,

Present: The Vice President, the Secretary of State, the Secretary of the Treasury, and the Attorney General.

Resolved, That the Secretary of the Treasury be authorised to cause to be applied so much of the sum of one hundred thousand dollars, directed to be expended by the act of this Board, of the 26th day of March last, as may remain in hand, to the purchase of three per cent. and deferred stock, upon a computation of interest at the rate of five per centum.

From this resolution, the Secretary of State dissents.[2]

ASP, Finance, I, 236.

1. For background to this document, see H to John Adams, March 20, 1792; "Meeting of the Commissioners of the Sinking Fund," March 26, 1792; John Jay to the Commissioners of the Sinking Fund, March 31, 1792.

2. Jefferson's position, stated in an undated fragment in Jefferson's handwriting in the Thomas Jefferson Papers, Library of Congress, reads as fol-

lows: "The Secretary of State continuing to dissent from any estimate of [the par of the sixes at more than 20/ the pound, of] the ⟨true⟩ value of the three percents at more than 10/ the pound [and of that of the defferred sixes at such a sum as at a compound interest of 6 per cent would produce 20/ at the term of paiment.]" Jefferson inserted the brackets in the preceding statement.

To William Seton

Philadelphia
April 4th 1792

My Dear Sir

The post of this day brought me a letter from you.[1] I am pained, beyond expression, at the picture you and others give me of the situation of my fellow Citizens—especially as an ignorance of the extent of the disorder renders it impossible to judge whether any adequate remedy can be applied.[2]

You may apply another 50 000 Dollars to purchases at such time as you judge it can be rendered most useful.[3] The prices may be 20/ for 6 per Cents 12 for three's and 12/6 for deferred. The law [4] & the object require that it should be known you purchase for the public. I shall by the next post send an Official authorisation.

I have doubt however whether it will be best to apply this immediately or wait the happening of the crisis which I fear is inevitable. If as is represented a pretty extensive explosion is to take place—the depression of the funds at such a moment will be in the extreme and then it may be more important than now to enter the market in force. I can in such case without difficulty add a hundred thousand Dollars probably a larger Sum. But you who are on the spot being best able to calculate consequences I leave the proper moment of operating to your judgment. To relieve the distressed and to support the funds are primary objects.

As it may possibly become adviseable for the Bank to receive *payments* in Stock from embarrassed persons, it may not be amiss that you should know as a guide That there are at this moment orders from a respectable Dutch concern to purchase 6 ℔ Cents at 24/ if bills can be sold at par. Of this I have the most *unequivocal* evidence. This is a proof that foreigners will be willing to give that price.

How vexatious that imprudent speculations of Individuals should lead to an alienation of the National property at such under rates as are now given!

I presume your greatest embarrassments arise from the contracts to pay and deliver not yet at issue. Is it possible to form any conjecture of their extent?

Affectionately Yrs   A Hamilton

P. S. I will thank you for a memorandum, *in confidence*, of how much *remains unexpended in Bank* of the sums which have been passed to the Credit of the Commissioner of Loans [5] at different times,

William Seton Esqr.

ALS, Bank of New York, New York City; copy, in the writing of Seton, Hamilton Papers, Library of Congress.
    1. Letter not found.
    2. This sentence refers to the financial crisis in New York City in the spring of 1792. See William Duer to H, March 12, 1792; H to Duer, March 14, 23, 1792; Philip Livingston to H, March 24, 1792; H to Livingston, April 2, 1792; Philip Schuyler to H, March 25, 1792; Robert Troup to H, March 19, 1792.
    3. H previously had authorized Seton to "purchase on account of the United States at par to the extent of Fifty thousand Dollars" (H to Seton, March 25, 1792). For authorization of further purchases of Government securities, see "Meeting of the Commissioners of the Sinking Fund," April 4, 1792.
    4. A proviso regarding sinking fund purchases in Section 2 of "An Act making Provision for the Reduction of the Public Debt" reads as follows: "*Provided*, That the same be made openly, and with due regard to the equal benefit of the several states" (1 *Stat.* 186 [August 12, 1790]).
    5. John Cochran was commissioner of loans at New York.

To George Washington

Introductory Note

The completion of the census of 1790 offered Congress its first opportunity to reapportion representation to conform to the population. The Constitution provided that each state should have at least one representative, that the membership of the House of Representatives should "not exceed one for every 30,000," and that for purposes of representation the

ALS, George Washington Papers, Library of Congress; JCH Transcripts.

slave population should be counted as three-fifths of the white population. According to the first census, the nation's population was 3,893,000. If the three-fifth's ratio were applied to the country's 697,000 slaves, the population for purposes of representation would be about 3,614,000. Thus, if there were to be one representative for each 30,000 in the population, the maximum number of representatives would be 120. The first Congress, however, had only 65 members; the admission of Vermont raised this total to 67.

There were two methods by which reapportionment could be accomplished. On the one hand, the total population could be divided by 30,000, with each state being assigned its proportionate share of representatives. On the other hand, the population of each state could be divided by 30,000 with the quotient in each case being the number of representatives for that particular state. The first apportionment bill was introduced in the House of Representatives on November 18, 1791, and was passed on November 24. The Senate amended the bill, but, when the House and Senate were unable to agree on the proposed amendments, the measure was dropped.[1] The second apportionment bill was passed by the Senate in February, 1792, and by the House in March of the same year.[2] Entitled "An act for an apportionment of Representatives among the several States, according to the first enumeration," [3] the measure provided for the total population of the United States (not the population of each state separately) to be divided by 30,000 to determine the number of representatives. The number obtained by this division was then to be apportioned among the several states according to their relative population. This measure was presented to President Washington on March 26, 1792.

After holding the bill for approximately a week, Washington asked Attorney General Edmund Randolph for an opinion of the bill and requested him to secure the opinions of the other Cabinet members by April 4. Both Randolph and Thomas Jefferson argued that the measure was unconstitutional. Henry Knox agreed with Hamilton that the bill was constitutional.[4] Washington accepted the views of the Attorney General and the Secretary of State, and on April 5 he sent his first veto message to Congress.[5] A motion to pass the bill over the President's veto failed, and the House quickly passed a revised bill in which the Senate concurred the day on which it was received.[6] On April 14, 1792, "An Act for apportioning Representatives among the several States, according to the first enumeration" became law. It provided in part that "the House of Representatives shall be composed of members elected agreeably to a

---

1. *Journal of the House*, I, 456, 459, 462, 470, 472, 475, 476, 478; *Annals of Congress*, III, 32, 41–43, 46, 47–49, 50–52.
2. *Annals of Congress*, III, 111–12; *Journal of the House*, I, 545.
3. *Journal of the House*, I, 551.
4. A digest of the four opinions in the writing of Tobias Lear is in the George Washington Papers, Library of Congress.
5. *GW*, XXXII, 16–17.
6. *Journal of the House*, I, 565–66, 569, 570–71, 572, 577, 579; *Annals of Congress*, III, 120.

ratio of one member for every thirty-three thousand persons in each state, computed according to the rule prescribed by the constitution."[7]

Philadelphia
April 4 1792

The Secretary of the Treasury presents his respects to the President of the United States. He was informed yesterday, by the Attorney General, that his opinion concerning the constitutionality of the Representation Bill was desired this morning. He now sends it with his reasons but more imperfectly stated than he could have wished—through want of time. He has never seen the bill, but from the accounts he has had of it he takes it for granted that he cannot have misconceived its contents so as to cause any material error in the process of his reasoning.

The President desires an opinion, whether the Act intitled "An Act for an apportionment of Representatives among the several states according to the first enumeration" be constitutional, or not.

It is inferred from the provisions of the Act—That the following process has been pursued.

I   The aggregate numbers of the United States are divided by 30000, which gives the total number of representatives, or 120.

II   This number is apportionned among the several states by the following rule—As the *aggregate* numbers of the *United States* are to the *total number* of representatives found as above, so are the *particular numbers of each state* to the number of representatives of such state. But

III   As this second process leaves a residue of Eight out of the 120 members unapportioned, these are distributed among those states which upon that second process have the largest fractions or remainders.

As a ratio of 30000 appears to have been adopted as a guide—The Question is whether this ratio ought to have been applied, in the first instance, to the aggregate numbers of the United States or to the particular numbers of each state.

I am of opinion that either of these courses might have been constitutionally pursued—or in other words that there is no criterion by which it can be pronounced decisively that the one or the other is

7. 1 *Stat.* 253.

the true construction. Cases so situated often arise on constitutions and Laws.

The part of the constitution in question is thus expressed—"*Representatives* and *direct taxes* shall be *apportioned* among the several states according to their *respective numbers.*"

Tis plain that the same rule is to be pursued with regard to *direct taxes* as with regard to *Representatives.*

What is the process which would naturally be followed in relation to the apportionment of direct taxes?

Clearly this—The *total sum* necessary would be first ascertained.

This total sum would then ⟨be⟩ [8] *apportioned* among the several states by the following rule—viz—

As the *aggregate* numbers of the United States are to the *whole sum* required so are the *particular numbers* of a *particular state* to the proportion of such state. Which is, so far, the exact process that has been followed by the Bill, in the apportionment of representatives.

And hence results a strong argument for its constitutionality.

If there had been no ratio mentioned in the constitution 'tis evident that no other course could have been well purused. No doubt at least of the propriety of that which has been pursued could have been then entertained.

Does the mention of a ratio necessarily alter it?

The words of the constitution in respect to the ratio are these "The number of representatives shall not exceed one for every 30000, but each state shall have at least one representative."

This provision may naturally be read and understood thus—"The whole number of the representatives of the United States shall not exceed one to every 30000 of the aggregate numbers of the United States; but if it should happen that the proportion of the numbers of any state to the aggregate numbers of the United States should not give to such state one representative—such state shall nevertheless have *one.* No state shall be without a representative."

There is nothing in the form of expression to confine the application of the ratio to the *several* numbers of the states. The mode of expression equally permits its application to their joint or *aggregate numbers.* The intent of inserting it is merely to determine a propor-

8. The word "be" has been taken from the JCH Transcripts.

tional limit which the number of the house of representatives shall not exceed. This is as well satisfied by resorting to the collective as to the separate population of the respective states.

There is therefore nothing in the last recited clause to controul or direct the sense of the first.

If it be said that the further process which apportions the residue among the states having the greatest remainders is the circumstance that renders the bill unconstitutional because it renders the representation not *strictly* according *to the respective numbers* of the states it may be answered—

That this is but a necessary consequence of the first principle.

As there would commonly be left, by the first process, an unapportioned residue of the total number, to be apportioned, it is of necessity that that residue should be distributed among the several states by some rule and none more equal or defensible can be found than that of giving a preference to the greatest remainders.

If this makes the apportionment not mathematically "according to the *respective numbers* of the several states" so neither would the opposite principle of construction.

Fractions more or less great would in this case also, and, in a greater degree, prevent a conformity of the proportion of representatives to numbers. The same objection would lie in this respect against both principles of construction; against that in the bill least.

Upon the whole then, The Bill *apportions* the Representatives among the several states *according to their respective numbers;* so as that the *number of representatives* does not *exceed* one for every 30000 persons *each state having at least one member.* It therefore performs every requisition of the constitution; and it will not be denied that it performs this in the manner most consistent with *equality*.

There appears therefore no room to say, that the bill is unconstitutional, though there may be another construction, of which the constitution is capable. In cases where two constructions may reasonably be adopted, and neither can be pronounced inconsistent with the public good, it seems proper that the legislative sense should prevail. The present appears to the Secretary clearly to be such a case.

Philadelphia April
4th 1792
Alex. Hamilton

To Joseph Howell, Junior [1]

[*Treasury Department, April 5, 1792.* The dealer's catalogue description of this letter reads: "Requesting that certified payrolls of the balances due the officers of the Maryland line be furnished him." *Letter not found.*]

LS, sold by Stan V. Henkels, Jr., June 27, 1927, Lot 133.
1. For background to this letter, see James Brice to H, March 19, 1792; H to Brice, April 4, 1792.
Howell was acting paymaster general of the United States.

From Stephen Moylan [1]

Philadelphia, April 5, 1792. "I will not take up your time for the trouble I am about to give by apologizing for it. . . . I never received my commutation certificate the reasons are, first I was under a necessity of living very retired since the peace the Limitation Act [2] never came to my Knowledge until May 89 when I went to New York—the other is, an impossibility of my being able to close my Regimental Accounts [3]—Such as I coud make out were transmitted to the proper office. The reason of my inability in this matter proceeds from the loss of a part of my most essential papers. . . . If you can put me in the way of getting what is so justly due to me for long and some essential services renderd the public it will place me in a very different situation to that I now stand in—it will place me above Want. . . ."

ALS, Hamilton Papers, Library of Congress.
1. During the American Revolution Moylan, a resident of Pennsylvania, had served as an aide-de-camp to George Washington, as quartermaster general, and as colonel in the Fourth Continental Dragoons.
2. On November 2, 1785, Congress "*Resolved,* That all persons having claims for services performed in the military department, be directed to exhibit the same for liquidation to the commissioners of army accounts, on or before the first day of August, ensuing the date hereof, and that all claims, under the description above mentioned, which may be exhibited after that period, shall forever thereafter be precluded from adjustment or allowance, and that the commissioner of army accounts give public Notice of this resolve in all the states for the space of six Months" (*JCC*, XXIX, 866).
3. Moylan's accounts had come to the attention of the Continental Congress in connection with the petition of Moore Faunt Le Ray, one of the officers in Moylan's regiment (*JCC*, XXXIV, 120–21).

Report on Compensation of Officers Employed in the Collection of the Revenue

[Philadelphia, April 5, 1792
Communicated on April 5, 1792] [1]

[To the Speaker of the House of Representatives]

Pursuant to the Order of the House of Representatives of the 18th of January, 1791, directing the Secretary of the Treasury to report his opinion whether any and what farther compensation ought to be made to the respective Officers employed in the collection of the revenue,[2]

The said Secretary respectfully submits the following Report.

The paper marked (A) herewith transmitted, contains an Abstract of the emoluments of the several officers of the customs, for one year, as far as returns have been received at the Treasury, and suggests in a column, for the purpose, such additions as, in certain cases, appear advisable.

These additions are founded upon a combined estimate of various circumstances; the quantity of business to be performed, the probability or otherwise of an increase of emolument under the existing provisions, the expense of living at different places, and the comparative importance of the respective parts to the revenue.

The apportionment is, of course, in many instances, rather matter of arbitration, than of precise calculation, and will probably require correction from the superior local information of the members of the House.

The Secretary takes this occasion to observe, that hitherto there has been no prohibition, by law, of officers of the customs being engaged in trade. Such a prohibition appears indispensible for obvious

Copy, RG 233, Reports of the Treasury Department, 1792–1793, Vol. III, National Archives.

1. *Journal of the House*, I, 564. The communicating letter may be found in RG 233, Reports of the Treasury Department, 1792–1793, Vol. III, National Archives.

2. The House "*Ordered*, That the Secretary of the Treasury be directed to report to this House his opinion whether any, and what, further compensation ought to be made to the respective officers employed in the collection of the revenue" (*Journal of the House*, I, 357).

reasons—while it will be a reason for rendering their emoluments more competent.

The report of the Secretary lately made in respect to the Act laying duties on distilled spirits,[3] submits a farther provision for compensating the officers employed in the execution of that Act, in the only mode, which is presumed to be practicable. Hence it becomes unnecessary to include them in the present report.

All which is respectfully submitted,   Alexander Hamilton
                                            Secry. of the Treasy.
Treasury Department
April 5th 1792.

3. See "Report on the Difficulties in the Execution of the Act Laying Duties on Distilled Spirits," March 6, 1792.

A.

Statement of Emoluments of the Surveyors of the Customs, in the United States, for the year 1790, except in the cases of North Carolina and Rhode Island, which are stated from the time of the operation of the offices in those States, in 1790, to the same period in the year following, so as to embrace likewise one entire year.

Ports	Amount received.	Clerk hire charged	Rent, Fuel, Stationery &c	Nett amount of Emoluments.	Salary allowed by the Collection law.[4]	Additional Salaries proposed.
Portsmouth	344.96					60.
Newbury port	309.88					100.
Gloucester	177.99				50	
Salem	395. 1		73.40	321.61.		50.
Beverly	65.14		25	40.14		80.
Ipswich	26.26		4 80	21.46		80.
Boston						
Portland	269. 5		21	248. 5		50.
Newport	406.11		39.50.	366.61.		80.
North Kingston	1.88.					80.
East Greenwich	9.48		8	1.48		80.
Warren						80.
Bristol	2447.		10.	14.47.		80.
Pawcatuck river	6.86.					80.
Providence	379.11.		65. 9	314. 2		80.
Patuxet	2.32					80.
New London	452.10.		84	368.10.		
Stonington	186. 1.		47.12.	138.89.	50.	50
Middletown	219.39.					50
New-Haven						
New York,					50.	
Hudson,	30				50.	20.
Albany						
Little Egg Harbor	11.10		5.40	5.70	80	20
Philadelphia	1848.56	400.	354.67	1093.89		

[illegible]	6[?].75					80.
Saint Mary's	20.20		13.50	6.70	50	80.
Lewellensburg,						
Norfolk,	815.48	180	66.66	562.82	80	20
Suffolk,	4.85				80	20
Smithfield,	10.25					
Bermuda Hundred,	202.98		40.	162.98		100
Petersburg,	68.12		84.75	76.81	80	20
Richmond,	112.31		35.50			20
Westpoint,	13.50		30.82			20
Urbanna,	80.56		46.17		80	20
Port Royal,	58.82			34.39	50	20
Fredericksburg,					80	
Alexandria,	336.94		56.67	280.27	80	100
Wilmington (N.C.)	328.31		7.50	320.81		100
Beaufort,	26.43				50.	80.
Swansborough,						30.
Hertford,						80.
Winton,						80.
Bennet's creek,						80.
Plymouth,	20					80.
Windsor,	11		13.50			80.
Shewarkey,	3					80.
Murfreesborough,	25.50					80.
Nixonton	30.20					80
Indian Town	27.76		2.	25.76		80.
Curretuck Inlet,						80.
Pasquotank river bridge						80.
Newbiggen Creek						
Charleston						
Savannah	454.17		42.85.	411.32		50.

Treasury Department,
April 4th 1792.

Alexander Hamilton
Secretary.

4. "An Act to provide more effectually for the collection of the duties imposed by law on goods, wares and merchandise imported into the United States, and on the tonnage of ships or vessels" (1 *Stat.* 145–78 [August 4, 1790]).

Statement of Emoluments of the Collectors of the Customs in the United States, for the year 1790, except in the cases of North Carolina and Rhode Island, which are stated from the time of the operation of the offices in those States in 1790, to the same period in 1790, to embrace likewise one entire year.

Ports	Amount received.	Clerk-hire charged.	Rent, Fuel Stationery &c.	Nett amount of Emoluments.	Annual Salary allowed by the Collection law	Additional allowance proposed — Annual Salary.	Additional allowance proposed — Percentage on duties collected.
Portsmouth	556.82	169.	91.	296.82		100.	½ per cent.
Newbury-port	647.13.	333.33	57.33	256.47			½
Gloucester	402.20		39	363.20		50	½
Salem & Beverly	831.56	200	73. 5	558.51		50	¼
Marblehead (9 months)	343.25	90.	68.50	184.75			½
Boston & Charlestown							
Plymouth	311.30		30.	281.30		50.	½
Barnstable	147.50		50.13.	97.37		50.	½
Nantucket & Sherburne	298.21		29.20	269. 1.		50.	½
Edgar Town	106.70		17.	89.70	50.		½
New Bedford	275.60		100.	175.60		50.	½
Dighton	203.97					50.	½
York	128.62		21.65	106.97		50.	½
Biddeford and Pepperelborough	471.81	78	35	358.81		50.	½
Portland	602.35	200.	49	353.35		50.	½
Bath	321.38	10	25.33	286. 5.		50.	½
Wiscassett	300		59.	241.			½
Penobscot	115.16		10.35	104.81	60.	50.	½
Frenchman's Bay	498.78.		30.	468.78.	50		½
Machias	123.23		30.50	91.73.			½
Passamaquody					100.		
Newport	621.91	500	73.48	48.43		50.	½
Providence	650.27	575.	131.35				½
New London	1699.52		95.	1604.52			½

Place							
Fairfield	282.73		140	142.73.		50.	½
Allburgh	75.45.		39.10.	36.35	100.	100	½
Sagg Harbour							
New York	196.48				50	50	½
Perth Amboy	61.86.		30.	31.86	50		½
Burlington	105.76		16.4	89.72		50	½
Bridge town						50	½
Great Egg Harbour.							
Philadelphia		1166.66	150.	328.			½
Wilmington (Delaware)	478.		318.68	843.70		50.	
Baltimore	2328.98						
Chester	77.33		9.57	107.6.	100	50.	½
Oxford	116.63						½
Vienna		40	35.98	64.42		50	½
Snow Hill	140.40.		21.56	53.34	50	100	½
Annapolis	74.90	100.	45.	156.95	100	100.	½
Nottingham	201.95.		91.33		100.		½
Cedar point	126.92					50.	½
George town (of Maryland)	401.55.	240.	82	79.55.		50.	½
Hampton	63.45		194.66		50.	50.	½
Norfolk	1567.45	633.33	270.75	739.2			
Bermuda Hundred	1426.	328.50	70.	826.75		100.	½
York Town	135.67	133.33	186.54	65.67	100		½
Tappahannock	586.41		42.50	266.54			
Yeocomico river	24	65.15	107.72				½
Dumfries	172.87					100.	½
Alexandria					100.		
Foley-landing					100.		
Cherrystone					100.		
South Quay	7.		15.50				
Louisville						150.	
Wilmington (N.C)	478.43	300.	49.95	128.48		50.	½
New Bern	907.20	260.	119.	528.20			½
Washington	474.85	200	36	238.85		50.	½
Edenton						50.	½

Ports	Amount received.	Clerk-hire charged.	Rent, Fuel Stationery &c.	Nett amount of Emoluments.	Annual Salary allowed by the Collection law	Additional allowance proposed	
						Annual Salary.	Percentage on duties collected.
Plankbridge							
George Town (S:C:)	229.40		36,50	192.90		50.	½
Charleston.					100.	50.	½
Beaufort.							
Savannah	866.53	270	79,67	518.86	60.		½
Sunbury					100.		
Brunswick	18,38		10.	8,38	100.		
St. Mary's							

Emoluments of Naval Officers for one year—stated as before mentioned.

Ports	Amount received.	Clerk Hire charged.	Rent, Fuel Stationery &c	Nett amot of Emoluments.	Annual Salary allowed by the Collection law.	Annual Salary proposed.
Portsmouth	378.28		61.68	316.60		100 dollars.
Newburyport	427.97		29.10	398.87		50
Salem	566. 7		65.90	500.17		
Boston						
New York						
Philadelphia						
Baltimore	1337.11	400.	114.36	822.75		
Norfolk	944.85		127.42	817.43		100.
Wilmington (N:C:)	340.42	300.	61.54	278.88		
Charleston	1231.40		137.39	794.1		
Savannah	550.58		58.31.	492.27		50.
Newport	494.36		61.	433.36		50.
Providence	416.65		114.10	302.55		50.

Treasury Department,
April 5th. 1792.
Alexander Hamilton, Secy.

To George Washington

Treasury Departmt. 5th. April 1792.

The Secretary of the Treasury has the honor respectfully to represent to the President of the United States, that an application has been made at the Treasury by the honble Mr. Muhlenberg of Pennsylvania [1] in behalf of the Administratrix of Nicholas F. Westphal [2] deceased, for the discharge of a Claim due to the Estate of her late husband in virtue of the last clause of "An Act for the relief of certain widows, Orphans, Invalids and other persons," [3] of which a copy is enclosed. The Secretary begs leave to suggest that this claim being payable out of the unexpended appropriations to the contingent charges of Government, it appears to require a special order of the President. A. Hamilton

Secy. of the Treasury

LC, George Washington Papers, Library of Congress.
1. Frederick Muhlenberg, a member of the House of Representatives from Pennsylvania, was the Speaker of the House in the first and third Congresses.
2. On February 6, 1791, the House of Representatives received "A petition of Nicholas Ferdinand Westfall . . . praying a gratuity of lands and other advantages, promised by the late Congress to those who should quit the British service, in consideration of his having left that service and joined the American Army, during the late war" (*Journal of the House*, I, 380).
3. The last section of "An Act for the relief of certain Widows, Orphans, Invalids, and other persons" reads as follows: "*And be it further enacted,* That there be granted to Nicholas Ferdinand Westfall, who left the British service and joined the army of the United States, during the late war, one hundred acres of unappropriated land in the western territory of the United States, free of all charges, and also the sum of three hundred and thirty-six dollars, out of any money appropriated to the contingent charges of government" (6 *Stat.* 7 [March 27, 1792]).

From Otho H. Williams

Baltimore 5 April 1792

My Dear Sir

Your official letter respecting the punctual collecting of duties shall have my particular attention.[1]

The advantages expected from your eventual agreement with the bank of Maryland have not been realized by the merchants, owing I understand, to some want of concert among the directors;[2] But I have reason to expect that all will be settled this Week.

I am much gratified by your intimation that my name has occurred in conversation about a successor to the unfortunate St. Clair[3]—and I thank you for your concern about my health. I am so happy as to tell you that my health is much restored; But, my Dear friend, if I had the best health, and all the best qualifications for such a command, what is there in it to excite ambition, or to gratify any other passion?

Happy in my family, and possessing a decent sufficiency, what should induce me to hazzard the fate of Harmar,[4] or the more hapless st. Clair—Or even if I were prosperous and Should even prove myself as great as Greene I might, like him, be traduced in my grave: while my family might beg, in vain, for protection.[5]

I regret extremely the mortifications to which our friend St. Clair is exposed; but he, *unfortunately* shall I say, lives to face his accusers.

Greene, poor fellow, is gone, and as it would seem has left scarcely an advocate behind him. The shameful speech of Genl. Sumpter upon Mrs Greenes petition[6] excited my indignation, and I resolved upon saying some thing to the public in reply to it. But diffidence suspended the execution of my purpose; I have taken up my paper again, and after scratching a great deal almost persuade myself that it ought to appear.[7]

Peruse it, and if you *can* approve let it appear, all at once, in one of the Philadelphia papers—Ours would divide it into two or three scraps, and dissipate the little force it has.

If there is any more brawling in Congress about the unmerited abuse or neglect of the s. Carolina Militia, or the NC Militia,[8] I will take occasion to give a detail of occurrences which shall place their merits in a proper light. The Vanity of puffing the southern Militia has, more than once disgraced the Ho: Rep——, and the insolent vulgarity of some of its members deserves public reproof.

I am with great Esteem and Confidence Dr. sir, Your most Obt
O. H Williams

Coll Hamilton

ALS, Hamilton Papers, Library of Congress; ADfS, Maryland Historical Society, Baltimore.

1. See H to Williams, March 28, 29, 1792.
2. See H to Williams, March 28, 29, 1792.
3. Major General Arthur St. Clair had resigned from the United States Army on March 5, 1792, because of widespread complaints following the defeat of the troops under his command by Indians on November 4, 1791. For an account of this defeat, see "Conversation with George Hammond," December 15–16, 1791, note 2.
4. Brigadier General Josiah Harmar had led an unsuccessful campaign against Indian tribes in the West in September and October, 1790.
5. Major General Nathanael Greene had died in 1786 leaving various accounts pending at the Treasury. For an account of Green's financial difficulties, see "Report on the Petition of Catharine Greene," December 26, 1791.
6. In a debate on January 9, 1792, on the petition of Catharine Greene, widow of Nathanael Greene, for indemnification by the United States, Thomas Sumter, Representative from South Carolina, argued that the petitioner had no valid claim (*Annals of Congress*, III, 321–23).
7. In response to a suggestion of Henry Lee, Williams had prepared a defense of Greene, addressed "To the Citizens of the United States" and signed "Vindicator." After Lee and Edward Carrington had modified and corrected Williams's draft, they returned it with the suggestion that Williams have it published in Philadelphia. The undated draft, partially in Williams's handwriting, contains an account of Greene's southern campaign (Hamilton Papers, Library of Congress). For Williams's correspondence with Lee and Carrington, see *Calendar of the General Otho Holland Williams Papers*, 250, 252–56.
8. In the debate of January 9, 1792, on the petition of Catharine Greene, Sumter "closed the debate in sundry remarks on extracts from letters wrote by General Greene during the late war, inserted in Gordon's History of the American Revolution, which extracts contain unfavorable reflections on the militia of South Carolina, and the patriotism of the inhabitants of that State" (*Annals of Congress*, III, 326–27). In a debate of March 9 on the same subject, John Steele, Representative from North Carolina, "adverted to the letters which he [Greene] wrote, abusing the people South of the Potomac, at the very time he was experiencing their munificence and liberality" (*Annals of Congress*, III, 455).

From Thomas Digges [1]

Belfast (Ireland) Apr 6. 1792

Sir.

I stand in need of Your forgiveness for intruding myself upon You, but I hope that my motive for so doing (an ardent desire to promote manufactures in America) will in some measure appologize for me.

ALS, Hamilton Papers, Library of Congress.
1. Digges, a native of Maryland, encouraged several British and Irish mechanics to emigrate to the United States in the early seventeen-nineties. For a discussion of Digges's career, see Lynn Hudson Parsons, "The Mysterious Mr. Digges," *The William and Mary Quarterly*, XXII (July, 1965), 486–92.

A Vessel sailing this day from hence from Boston, and the opportunity of inclosing this Lettr to Mr Tho' Russel[2] of that place (who I am sure will forward it safe) induces me to write to You on the subject of Manufactures & Machinery, which I am happy to see begins now to be tookd up & pratonized in our Country.

I have not the pleasure to be personally known to You 'tho well acquainted with Your worth & the benefits our Country is likely to derive from Your assiduity & ability. My home & soil is at Digges's Landing on Potowmac nearly fronting the Presidents, to whom & many of the Gentlemen about Him & yourself I am known, and am but a casual Resident in this manufacturing quarter of Ireland in order to get over some Tennantry, and among them Artists, to fix on lands I possess both in Virginia & Maryland not far from the new Federal Town.

It was with much pleasure & attention I very lately read Your Report to Congress on the Subject of Manufactures,[3] wch. I found published in the New York Papers in Numbers compleated to the end. In this quarter American Books are very rarely to be met, & when sent as presents, little read & not attended to. This induc'd me to take the liberty with your book of having it republishd at my Expence 1000 Copys price 1/—by Byrne Book sellers in Dublin[4] in order to distribute it with ease, & for disseminating its information among many Manufactoring Societys here as well as in England, (where I will take 3 or 400 Copys in a few days) and by so getting it read, induce artists to move towards a Country so likely to very soon give them ample employ & domestic ease. I hope You will not be offended with me for so doing, & I am confident the distribution of it, in the way I intend, will induce many to move towards the manufactoring parts of America. Sorry I am to say it that mine is still backward in the encouragement of manufactorys or artists, but I trust it will soon get better as the Slavery by blacks decreases & by Emigration from these Countrys we get betterd as to a free tennantry.

2. Russell was a Boston businessman and a director of the Boston branch of the Bank of the United States.

3. See "Report on the Subject of Manufactures," December 5, 1791.

4. *Report of the Secretary of the Treasury of the United States, On the Subject of Manufactures. Presented to The House of Representatives, December 5, 1791* (Dublin: Re-printed by P. Byrne, No. 108, Grafton-Street, 1792).

I was very lucky in being the means of sending Wm. Pearce [5] to Philaa. last June, where I hope He has succeeded & been encouraged in obtaining a Pattent or Premium for His new invented double loom. I gave him recommendatory Lettrs. to the President, to Mr Jefferson, Goverr. Dickinson,[6] Mr Seton,[7] Conyngham & Nesbit [8] & others, & I am to hope He has made His way to You. He is a Man deserving to be cherish⟨ed⟩ as an uncommon ingenious Artist in the fixing Mill Machinery, Looms, &ca. and before He went explained to me the principle of a Mill for weaving Cloth by force of steam or Water, as well as One for Spinning Flax thred nearly on the same plan of facility & numbers of threads that the Cotton Mules can spin, wch. is from 80 to 180 threads at once, & attended by one man & two small children to each mule. Mr Thos McCabe [9] of this Town (to whom the introduction of Cotton fabricks in Ireland is much indebted) is a partner in the Loom scheme with Mr Wm Pearce, and has now in His possession the compleat drawings & specifications of a machine for spinning the thread which I now inclose you (a description of which you have in the paper covering the thread). It is the first effort in England & spoke highly of as to the benefits of reducing manual labor, for one man & a small boy tends the machine wch spins 80 threads at one throw of the machine. I have seen the Work & got copys of the drawings, and I have Mr McCabes possitive promise of sending it to You or the President by the first Passenger Ship wch. will be the Wilmington Cap Jefferies for Phia & She will sail in May.

I go from hence in a few days to spend the summer among manufacturers & artists in Lancashire & Yorkshire, a Country I have before known, & where many are ready to move for America, but the difficultys of so doing are very great. By the laws of England they

5. See "Receipt from William Pearce," August 20, 1791.
6. John Dickinson had been governor of Delaware in 1782 and 1783.
7. William Seton was cashier of the Bank of New York.
8. David H. Conyngham and John M. Nesbitt were Philadelphia merchants.
9. In 1777 Robert Joy and Thomas McCabe proposed that the children of the Belfast poorhouse be employed in spinning cotton yarn as a means of enabling the children to earn money as well as forming a first step toward the introduction of cotton manufacture into the district. In 1784 the first cotton spinning mill in Ireland to be driven by water was built by Joy and McCabe at Belfast. By 1790 cotton spinning and weaving had become a major industry in Belfast (D. J. Owen, *History of Belfast* [Belfast and London, 1921], 149–50).

can stop an artist from migration, & the smallest particle of machinery, tools &ca will stop the Ship if informed against—the person attempting to inviegle away an artist is subject not only to very rough treatment, but a fine of 500 £ & 12 months imprisonment. In this Country they, are not so nice, & by some art, & very little expence I have been the means of sending 18 or 20 very valuable artists & machine makers in the course of last year. It subjects You however to unpleasant circumstances of jealousy from acquaintances, & private sensure.

There will be a considerable emigration this Spring from this place, Derry & Newry, I dare say not less than 10,000 people, and in every family there are spinners & often weaver's—almost wholly a protestant body, sober, & industrious & very different from the Southern & western Irish, where manufactures have not yet found their way & the people in consequence, idle, distressd, & extremly poor. Such is the encreasing commerce & manufactories of Antrim & Down (by far the fulest peopled Countys in Ireland) that in the Course of the last 12 months not less than 12 or 15,000 £'s worth of machinery for spining Cotton only, has been imported from Liverpool into this port. The Mules, Billys, Brush Rollers & all other of the machinery comes in the frame bulk nearly ready to work, & is of such bulk that very few vessels can admit them, particularly the *mules*, into the hold—of course, abstracted from the risque of shipping them direçt from Engd. to America, the getting 'em across the atlantic would be attended with vast difficulty. The only way to counteract this will be to get over the two men who make each of these machines vist. the Brass, Clockwork movements of them, & the frame & wood-work makers. I mean to make an attempt at this, and will trust to yours & other patronage to such Men as may go to fix in America. The beauty & benefits of *machinery* is such, & has so much reduced the manufacture of various articles, by the reduction of manual labour, as to make it incredible to those who have not seen and contemplated machinery. You have now the man in America, *Wm. Pearce*, who invented first the famous wheel machinery for Sir R. Arkwrights famous spining Mill in Manchester; and He also had a hand in the Mill at Doncaster, wch by force of an Ox *weaves* Broad Cloth by Machinery. He also knows the principle on wch the thread wch I now send you is so quickly & beneficially spun without going thro the usual form of the Finger. His double Loom, wch I hope you have by this time seen at work is also an admirable peice of simple art, and without applying other force than the hand, wch He can do to throw the Shuttle, weaves in proportion of three yards to one in the common way. I look upon Him somewhat like a second Archimedes. His pride, tho an ignorant & low bred man prompted Him to move from Hence on being disapointed, by an il-timed party in the House of Commons here, of getting the Sum that He & Mr McCabe askd for the discovery of the loom. He has I understand quarrelled with Jameson, & Hall [10] (two working artists whom I sent out in the Ship with Him) and I am sure Jameson is in fault, for he *here* made a vile tho' faint attempt to discover Pearce's secret because He had been employd by Pearce to erect the Loom.

I am sure it woud have a tendency to good to have some plan fixd in America for the encouragement of ingenious artists & manufa~rers going there, something like a premium or reward to be publickly advertis'd & held out in the American Papers, & those papers carefully got distributed here & about Liverpool & Manchester, for in these Countrys they hardly ever will publish any favourable acco~ of America or insert a Paragraph wch. may lead the people to Emigration. I think too a small bounty pr head on every Emigrant landing (suppose only one Dollar pr. head for every one that goes in a Vessel carrying more than 100 adults; and to exempt the vessel so carrying them from the Tonnage or other Fees for that voyage, may have a good tendency to induce more to go, for here a few Shillings makes a difference in the price of passage money, that retards many from going. Such are the wants of a people even in a very full peopled Country & possessing a most beneficial staple manufactory of Linen & rapidly rising in the Cotton one.

I hope You will excuse Sir the length of my letter & loose suggestions. I have much at heart & wish most earnestly to see manufactures *begin* even in my Country. I am very confidant our high price of labour will be no obstruction when the facility & cheapness with which we can Errect mill work, & I trust machinery too, will be put

10. In 1791 Digges wrote from Belfast that Jameson and Hall were migrating to America. He described them as "two ingenious workmen . . . , who can make most kinds of machinery such as spinning Jennys, Billys, Mules Carding Machines &c" (Digges to Thomas Jefferson, April 28, 1791, ALS, Papers of Thomas Jefferson, Library of Congress). William Hall became superintendent of the calico printing department of the Society for Establishing Useful Manufactures. Nothing has been found, however, concerning Jameson's career in the United States.

in counterpoise to manual labour. Already there is a Mill in England which can twist from a small cord, up to the largest Cable for a Ship by force of water, & by which in the making of a Cable the labour of about sixty persons is saved. At Manchester too a man whom I well know (Mr Grimshaw) [11] lately erected a Mill at the Expence of 14,000 £, which by force of steam wove some hundreds of ps./s of cotton at once, under one roof & with but little attendance, of only dressing the Looms & loading the Shuttles, but the misguided multitude, fearing it would ruin the working weavers maliciously burnt down the mill after it had begun to work. From the encreasing spirit of the English towards discovery of machinery in various ways, it is impossible to tell or guess what lengths the human genius may not go. I hope it will take a flight across the Atlantic, & by way of expediting it I shall be extremely happy for any hints from you, or from any Gentlemen Engaged in the promotion of Amn. Manufactures, & who may have more leisure to write.

My stay in England will be a full twelvemonth from this period, and my direction is to the care of *Joshua Johnson Esqr Consul Gen~ for US in London.* I shall be happy to execute any Commands for You & am with great esteem & respect

Sir Yr Obt Hle Servt   Thos Digges

You will please to Excuse this hasty letter wch in truth, as the Captn. is about to move, I have not time to read over.

11. Nicholas Grimshaw proposed a mill for carding and spinning cotton to the Belfast Charitable Society in 1778. The mill was erected in 1784 (James Adair Pilson, *History of the Rise and Progress of Belfast* [Belfast, 1846], 145). In 1790 "Messrs. Grimshaw, of Gorton, erected a factory at Knot Mill for the introduction of power-looms into Manchester, which was burnt down before they commenced work" (*The Manchester Historical Recorder* [Manchester, n.d.], 59).

From Archibald Mercer [1]

New Brunswick [New Jersey] April 6th: 1792.

Sir!

The Directors of the Manufacturing Society held their quarterly meeting at this place on Tuesday last. All the Gentlemen from Jersey met,[2] but none of the Directors from New York appearing, it was thought of the utmost importance, considering the advanced season of the Year, the confusion our affairs appeared to be in, and the necessity of restoring the public confidence that a full board should be obtained if possible and the situation of our funds investigated & known. We therefore sent to New York requesting some of the Gentlemen to come forward with every information in their Power.[3] To this Mr: Walker [4] replied "That in this critical moment when every hour brings its misfortunes and the property of every man at hazard none of them can possibly leave town; wishing us to adjourn to New York." By way of accomodation and in order that the business of the Society may not be wholly neglected this board have adjourned to the 17th: Inst: to meet at Powles Hook.[5] From the best information we can obtain there is no Money at Command nor are we wholly satisfied with the application of it, but for want of full information we can only give you this hint. Mr: Peirce [6] called upon the board on Tuesday with a letter, which he said was from you. We did suppose it contained some communications for the inspection of this Board but it being directed to Mr: Low,[7] we concluded to send it forward by Pearce, who has not since returned.

Mr: Hubbard [8] we are informed by Mr. Flint,[9] has resigned his appointment as Superintendant General, but in such a Manner as to preserve our confidence in him as a suitable Person for the appointment.

It is natural for us in the present situation of the business, to look up to you as the founder of the institution & from the communications we have received from you, we have no doubt but you have the good of the Society at Heart. Hitherto we have depended on our Governor for the necessary plans to be pursued and which he promised to lay before us, but as a great deal of time has been spent to little purpose, and the critical situation of his private affairs [10] will and must prevent his attention to this business, we take the liberty of requesting in the Name of the Society that you will be kind enough to furnish us with your Idea's and advice on the Subject and assist us in our operations as far as in your power.

At present we think it advisable to confine our attention to the Cotton branches alone, and have at this meeting dismissed several applications for other branches that have been kept in some measure in suspence. At our last meeting the Governor informed us that some steps had been taken by you, & himself, with regard to the procuring of Workmen from Europe, and that the probable expence would be about 20'000 Dollars. We take the liberty to inclose you the resolutions of the board on that Subject,[11] and would be glad to know whether you have or can take any measures to accomplish that object—and whether you would recommend any other branch of Manufacture besides the Cotton, to be adopted. We are very apprehensive that from the delay that has taken place, the whole year will be lost with regard to the Printing of Callicoes, and a very great expence and to no purpose, as the fashions may totally Change, and the long-cloaths sent for, lay upon hand til next year.

Mr: Lowrey [12] is appointed to wait on you with this letter, and to take in Charge your communications on the Subject. In behalf of the Society for establishing useful Manufactures, I am with perfect respect. sir Your most obedt: and very hum: Servant

Archibald Mercer D.G.

Alexander Hamilton Esqr:
Secretary of the Treasury

ALS, Hamilton Papers, Library of Congress.

1. A resident of Somerset County, New Jersey, Mercer was a lawyer and businessman. He was elected deputy governor of the Society for Establishing Useful Manufactures at its first meeting on December 9, 1791.

2. The directors from New Jersey who were present at the April 3, 1792, meeting were Mercer, John Bayard, John Neilson, Moore Furman, and Thomas Lowrey ("Minutes of the S.U.M.," 22).

3. At the April 3, 1792, meeting of the directors of the Society for Establishing Useful Manufactures the following resolution was adopted: "Resolved, That the Deputy Governor of this Society do write to Elisha Boudinot Esqr: and to Benjamin Walker Esqr. requesting their immediate attendance at this board at their present meeting with the Papers in their possession that relate to the Proceedings of former meetings, with the State of the Society's accounts" ("Minutes of the S.U.M.," 22).

4. Benjamin Walker, a director of the Society for Establishing Useful Manufactures.

5. Jersey City, New Jersey, was formerly called Powles Hook.

6. William Pearce.

7. Letter to Nicholas Low not found.

8. Nehemiah Hubbard of Middletown, Connecticut, had been elected superintendent general of the works of the Society for Establishing Useful Manufactures on January 21, 1792 ("Minutes of the S.U.M.," 19).

9. Royal Flint, a director of the Society for Establishing Useful Manufactures, was at this time involved in the failure of William Duer, for whom he had served as agent and business associate in the Scioto Company and with whom he had been associated in various security speculations.

10. For the financial problems of William Duer, the first governor of the society, see Duer to H, March 12, 1792; H to Duer, March 14, 22, 1792; Robert Troup to H, March 19, 1792; Philip Livingston to H, March 24, 1792; Philip Schuyler to H, March 25, 1792.

11. At the society's meeting on January 21, 1792, the directors voted that twenty thousand dollars "be applied under the direction of the Governor, with the advice of the Secretary of the Treasury" ("Minutes of the S.U.M.," 20–21).

12. Thomas Lowrey was a director of the Society for Establishing Useful Manufactures.

From Gouverneur Morris [1]

London 6 April 1792

Dear Hamilton.

A friend ask'd me some Days ago to calculate for him the true Value of our public funds. I did so and you will find in answer to the Queries No: 1. 2. & 3 the result of my first Enquiries. But my Mind being once in this Train I determined on greater Accuracy at the Expence of a little more Attention, and the Questions I propounded to myself with the Answers are contained in the enclosed Paper under the Heads 4. 5. & 6. Lastly as I had assumed for one Basis the Interest of 4 p % which we pay in Europe, and as a Commission is allowed on the Negotiation, I thought it well to enquire what additional Interest accrued from that Circumstance. This appears in the Question No. 7. You will observe that I communicated only the Answers to the three first Questions.

About the same Time a Newspaper was put into my Hand containing your Report of the 23d of last January,[2] and that led me to consider in what Way Money could be most advantageously employed in Diminution of the public Debt, and after sundry Estimates one Operation appear'd to me so advantageous that I thought it worth while to trouble you with this Letter and with the Calculations above referred to. I beleive that on Examination you will find them to be exact. And altho the Answer to Question 5 may seem to be exhorbitant yet the Result would in fact be still greater if the Party receiving his Annuity of two per Quarter should apply it in discounting Notes which have three Months to run at the low Rate of 1 p%: a fortiori at 1½ the legal Rate now going in America. I need not remark to *you* on the Difference between Discount and

Interest which in the Case put is that between 1/99 & 1/100 or 1 in 9.900.

I ought to apologize for writing this Letter but I will not because if it does not carry its' own Excuse none which I can make will be worth a farthing. farewell

I am truly yours   Gouv Morris

Alexander Hamilton Esqr

[E N C L O S U R E] [3]

Qu: 1. In what Time will an Annuity of 8 pay 100. Int: at 6 p %.
         Ansr. 23.7913 Years or 23 Years 288 Days.

Qu: 2. What is the present Value of an Annuity of 8 for 23.7913 Years Int: at 4 p %.
         Ansr. 121.3342

Qu: 3. What principal Sum will in ten Years amount to 121.3342 Int: at 4 p %.
         Ansr. 81.96914

Qu: 4. In What Time will a quarterly Payment of 2 pay 100. Int: at 1¼ p % quarterly.
         Ansr: 23.277875 Years or 23 Years 101 Days

Qu: 5. What is the present Value of a quarterly Payment of 2 for 23.277875 Years Quarterly Interest at 1 p %
         Ansr: 150.

Qu: 6. What principal Sum will in ten Years amount to 150 Int: at 4 p %
         Ansr. 101.3347.

Qu: 7. What is the Rate of Interest paid by the Borrowers when a Commission of 4 p % is allowed on a Loan for 20 Years bearing 4 p % Interest.
         Ansr. 4.2943274.

Value of the deferred Debt by Qu: & Ansr. No. 3.
                                    viz
                    C   C
to July 92 . 86.9609 say $86.97 . to July 94 . 94.0655 say $94.07
to Jany. 93 . 88.6911 .   . 88.70 . to Jany 95 . 95.9283 .   . 95.93

to July 93 . 90.4476 . . 90.45 . to July 95 . 97.8281 . . 97.83
to Jany 94 . 92.2388 . . 92.24 . to Jany 96 . 99.7655 . . 99.77
   25 January 1796 100

Redemption of deferred Debt.

From July 92 to Jany 93 Value 87.80
 Suppose the Price p % . . . . 75.
 Commission on borrowing 75 at 4 p % . . . 3.
                  ———
                  78.
       Remains . . . 9.80
       Multiply by . . . 8
                 78.40

The gain is then at least one eighth of the Money applied to this Operation.

ALS, Hamilton Papers, Library of Congress; LC, Gouverneur Morris Papers, Library of Congress.
 1. Morris, who had been appointed United States Minister Plenipotentiary to France in January, 1792, did not arrive in Paris until May 6, 1792.
 2. See "Report on Public Debt and Loans," January 23, 1792.
 3. AD, Hamilton Papers, Library of Congress.

To Jonathan Trumbull

Treasury Department
April 6th 1792.

Sir,

 I have the honor, pursuant to the order of the House [1] on that subject, to transmit herewith sundry petitions [2] for personal services in the Army and Navy, which have been heretofore referred to me, and to be, with perfect respect, Sir Your most obedient, and Humble Servant   Alexander Hamilton.

The Honorable
The Speaker of the House of Representatives.

Copy, RG 233, Reports of the Treasury Department, 1792–1793, Vol. III, National Archives.
 1. An entry in the *Journal of the House* for March 27, 1792, reads as follows: "*Ordered*, That the Secretary of the Treasury, and the Secretary of

War, return the petitions presented to this House, by invalids and others, whose cases are comprehended in the provision of any act of the present session, with the papers accompanying the said petitions, which have been referred to them, and are now in their respective offices; and that the several petitioners have leave to withdraw their petitions" (*Journal of the House*, I, 552).

2. The following note appears at the bottom of this letter: "List of petitions referred to in the foregoing letter—viz.

John Carlile,	Laurence Furlong,
Richard Dale,	Ichabod Johnston and others,
William Delaney,	Andrew Ohe,
Abigail Earle	Darby Oram."

From George Washington [1]

[*Philadelphia*] *April 6, 1792.* ". . . you will cause to be paid to Nicholas Ferdinand Westfall the sum of three hundred and thirty six Dollars out of the fund of Ten thousand Dollars appropriated for defraying the contingent charges of Government. . . ."

LC, George Washington Papers, Library of Congress.

1. This letter was written in reply to H to Washington, April 5, 1792.

From George Washington

United States 6. April 1792.

Sir,

You will lay before the House of Representatives such papers from your Department as are requested by the enclosed resolution.[1]

G: W.

NB. The papers alluded to are such as relate to the Expedition under Genl. St. Clair.

LC, George Washington Papers, Library of Congress.

1. On April 4, 1792, the House of Representatives "*Resolved*, That the President of the United States, be requested to cause the proper officers to lay before this House such papers of a public nature, in the Executive Department, as may be necessary to the investigation of the causes of the failure of the late expedition under Major General St. Clair" (*Journal of the House*, I, 561).

For a description of the expedition referred to in this resolution, see "Conversation with George Hammond," December 15-16, 1791, note 2.

From Jonathan Dayton [1]

Thursday noon [April, 7–8, 1792]

Dr. Sir,

I herewith enclose a letter which I have received from Messrs. Mackay & Dixey.[2] The subject appears to be of some moment, and the objects may probably be attained, by an alteration in the bill about to be brought forward pursuant to your report on ways & means,[3] if you do not dissaprove of it. I am still confined to my lodgings and shall be happy to speak with you on the subject.

Another letter respecting the claim of Perry & Hayes,[4] is also enclosed. Be so good as to inform me whether you have yet made, or prepared, your re⟨port⟩ on that matter.

With very sincere esteem   Yours   Jona: Dayton

P.S. Be pleased to return the letters.

ALS, MS Division, New York Public Library.

1. Dayton was a Federalist member of the House of Representatives from New Jersey.

2. Mackay and Dixey was a Staten Island firm that specialized in taking orders for printing and bleaching cloth. The Dayton family firm in Elizabeth, New Jersey, was in the same business (Rita Susswein Gottesman, "The Arts and Crafts in New York, 1777–1779," *Collections of the New-York Historical Society*, LXXXI [New York, 1954], 300).

3. This is a reference to H's "Report Relative to the Additional Supplies for the Ensuing Year," March 16, 1792. On April 7, 1792, the House of Representatives adopted several resolutions concerning this report and appointed a committee to bring in a bill (*Journal of the House*, I, 567–69). Although the bill in question was concerned with securing increased revenues to supply the western expedition, Dayton hoped that it might be amended in such a fashion as to allow the importation of foreign cotton. Such an amendment was actually proposed, but it was defeated (*Journal of the House*, I, 570, 575, 584; *Annals of Congress*, III, 560–62; 1 *Stat.* 259–63).

4. On February 17, 1790, "A petition of James Perry and Thomas Hayes, subjects of the King of Great Britain, was presented to the House and read, praying to receive compensation for sundry articles of property, which were seized and taken from them in the State of New Jersey, during the war, for the use of the Army of the United States.

"*Ordered,* That the said petition be referred to the Secretary of the Treasury, with instruction to examine the same, and report his opinion thereupon to the House." (*Journal of the House*, I, 160.)

H did not report on this petition (H to Frederick A. C. Muhlenberg, January 5, 1795).

From James Reynolds [1]

Philadelphia 7th, April. 1792.

Sir

I am sorry to inform you my setivation is as such. I am indebted to a man in this town about 45. dollars which he will wate no longer on me. now sir I am sorrey to be troubleing you So Offen. which if you Can Oblige me with this *to day*. you will do me infenate service. that will pay Nearly all I owe in this town except yourself. I have some property on the North River which I have Wrote to my Brother sell which as soon as it Come in my hands. I pay you every shilling with the strictest Justice you Oblige me with. the inclose is the Receipt. for the amount

I am sir with due Regard. your humble servant   James Reynolds

Alexr. Hamilton Esqr.

[ENCLOSURE]

Receipt from James Reynolds

[Philadelphia, April 7, 1792]

Received philadelphia. 7th. April. 1792. of Alexander Hamilton Esqr. Forty five dollars which I promise to pay on demand

James Reynolds

45 dollars

"Reynolds Pamphlet," August 31, 1797.
1. This letter and the enclosed receipt are printed as document No. XIV in the appendix of the "Reynolds Pamphlet," August 31, 1797.
For background to this letter, see Reynolds to H, December 15, 17, 19, 22, 1791, January 3, 17, March 24, April 3, 1792; H to Reynolds, December 15, 1791; Maria Reynolds to H, December 15, 1791, January 23–March 18, March 24, 1792.

To James Reynolds [1]

[Philadelphia, April 7, 1792]

To-morrow what is requested will be done. 'Twill hardly be possible *to-day*.

"Reynolds Pamphlet," August 31, 1797.
1. This letter was in reply to Reynolds to H, April 7, 1792. It was explained by H in the "Reynolds Pamphlet," when he wrote that the letters from Reynolds were "a persevering scheme to spare no pains to levy contributions upon my passions on the one hand, and upon my apprehensions of discovery on the other. It is probably to No. XIV [Reynolds to H, April 7, 1792] that my note . . . was an answer. . . . A scarcity of cash, which was not very uncommon, is believed to have modelled the reply" ("Reynolds Pamphlet," August 31, 1797).

[Detector] [1]

[Philadelphia, April 9, 1792]

[Philadelphia] *National Gazette*, April 9, 1792.
1. According to Philip Marsh, this article may have been written by H ("Further Attributions to Hamilton's Pen," *The New-York Historical Society Quarterly*, XL [October, 1956], 352). Since the views expressed by "Detector," however, were contrary to H's position on the Representation Bill, it is unlikely that H was the author.

From William Ellery

[*Newport, Rhode Island*] *April 9, 1792.* "I have received your letter of the 21st. of this last month.[1] As you are apprehensive that the expence of an hydrostatic balance for each of the Custom Houses would be found too great, I have no longer a wish for one.[2] I have received two Thermometers covered with a common wrapper directed to me; but not attended by any letter. On the particular wrapper of one of the Thermometers is a direction to me, on the other is a direction to Zachariah Rhodes Esqr of Patuxet.[3] There is I conceive a mistake in the last direction, and that the Thermometer with this superscription was intended for George Stillman Esqr. Surveyor for Pawcatuck, for I am informed Mr. Rhodes resigned his

Offe. sometime ago, and a Letter I received from the Assist. Secry sometime agoe, gave me a reason to expect that two Thermometers would be sent to me, and one of them for Mr. Stillman. I wish to have this matter explained. . . ."

LC, Newport Historical Society, Newport, Rhode Island.
1. Letter not found.
2. See Ellery to H, February 13, March 5, 1792.
3. Rhodes was surveyor of Patuxet.

From Jeremiah Olney

Providence, April 9, 1792. "Agreeable to your request of the 29th of March, I have, on receiving an Order and the enclosed Assignment, paid to the Marshall of Rhode-Island District,[1] 2105 Dollars and 12 Cents; which sum, as you direct, shall be noted in my Weekly Returns until it is replaced. I beg leave to observe, on this Occasion, that in my last Quarter's Accots., transmitted the 5th Instant, will be found 701 Dolls. & 93 Cents, paid for Drawbacks on Wine exported in the President Washington to the East-Indies, which was not included in my Estimate of Monies that would probably be demandable out of this Office by the 14th of May next; and which added to that now paid the Marshall, makes 2,807 Dollars & 5 Cents, which Sum I expect to be in want of in One Month from this Time. . . ."

ADfS, Rhode Island Historical Society, Providence.
1. William Peck.

From Nicholas Romayne [1]

New York. April 9th. 1792

Dear Sir,
    Mr. Dodge who officiated sometime in the Custom-house Department in this City, I am informed was deranged on account of some neglect of Duty. Circumstances I am told have been so much in his favour that the penalty incurred has not been exacted—with the particulars of which I presumed you are acquainted.[2]
    He has served in the Armies of the United States during the late war, and his engagements there prevented him from acquiring a

trade or profession—he has a large family—his numerous connections in this place are soliciting his being replaced & I am sensible if it be otherwise not against the good of the public service, they will gratefully acknowledge any kindness you may please to extend towards [him] as well as myself.

I have the honour to be   Your Obt. Servt.   Nics. Romayne

The Honble. Alexander Hamilton Esqr

ALS, Hamilton Papers, Library of Congress.
1. Romayne, a prominent New York physician, had resigned in February, 1792, from his post as professor of the practice of physic at Columbia College (*The* [New York] *Daily Advertiser*, March 2, April 11, 1792).
2. On February 21, 1791, Samuel Dodge, an inspector of customs at New York, had been convicted of unloading molasses from the *Hudson Packet* after sunset and without a special license from John Lamb, the collector of that port. Judgment was deferred twice, the first time until the April, 1791, session of the Circuit Court, the second time until the October, 1791, session (H to Richard Harison, March 18, 1791). A pardon was finally issued by Washington in June, 1792.

From William Seton

[New York] Monday 9 April 1792

My dear sir

I did not answer your kind favour of the 4th. this morning as I wished to take in the occurrences of this day, in hopes something better would take place in the State of Credit from the arrival of the East India Ships and other large and valuable property but I am sorry to say it has not had the wished for effect, and every thing still is going down Hill. The extent of the evil, or the amount of Contracts &ca, it is impossible to form a judgement of but I understand from everybody that this week will be the most distressing period of any. I therefore deemed it best agreeably to the lattitude you give me, not to enter into the Market to purchase till Wednesday, before which many must make a settlement on differences between one another—& from inability of all parties they must have forbearance—purchases afterwards will be a real relief, and as 50,000 would be but a small sum to invest I feel a hope from what you say that tomorrow I may receive orders from you to extend the purchases.[1] The Bank continues to discount twice a week on a deposit of Stock & has very considerably by this means extended its loans—but so many failures are daily happening that I fear many of our old Loans are in jeopardy. Before the last credit of 100,000 was put to the account of the Commissioner of Loans, there was a ballance due to him on our Books of 13,561 Dollars. He mentioned to me yesterday that he expected to give the Bank credit for 16,000 Dollars that would not be wanted.

The whisper of the day is very unfavorable, for should the report prove true that Mr. M——— cannot or will not comply with his engagements, the distress already experienced is but a trifle to what is yet to be expected.[2]

I am with the sincerest respect & esteem　Dear sir　Your obliged Obed Servt　　　　　　　　　　　　　　　　　　　　　　　Wm Seton

Alexr. Hamilton Esqr.

ALS, Hamilton Papers, Library of Congress.
　1. The commissioners of the sinking fund had approved the purchase of public securities with Government money to maintain the price of the securities. For H's instructions to Seton on this subject, see H to Seton, March 25, April 4, 1792.
　2. The "whisper of the day" was correct. Alexander Macomb, an associate of William Duer in extensive stock speculations in the early months of 1792, was forced to suspend payments on April 12.

From Thomas Jefferson

Philadelphia April 10. 1792.

Sir

Permit me to request the favor of you, to cause a warrant to be issued on the Treasurer of the United States payable to George Taylor Junr.[1] to the amount of five hundred dollars, for defraying the contingent expenses of the department of State. I have the honor to be with sentiments of the highest respect and esteem &c.

Th: Jefferson.

LC, Papers of the Continental Congress, National Archives.
　1. Taylor was chief clerk of the State Department.

From Nicholas Low [1]

New York 10 April 1792

my dear sir

The Failure of John Dewhurst [2] may be attended with a total Loss to the Manufacturing Society of the Money intrusted to him [3]—he remitted the Money to a Mr. Hill of London his partner subject to the order of a Mr. King [4] of Liverpool to whom Mr. Hall [5] sent the Order for the Goods. The Intelligence of Dewhurst's Failure goes by the British packet saild yesterday to call at Halifax. Walker Duer Macomb [6] & myself with the privaty of Mr. Hall have determined without communicating our plan to any other of the Directors to dispatch a pilot Boat to land a confidential Messenger at the first convenient port she can make in England with a Letter to Mr. King requesting him to repair immediately to London and secure the Money in the Hands of Hill, the Boat will be dispatched in two or three Days at farthest. We trust she will arrive Time enough before the packet to secure our object and have conceived it our Duty to adopt this as the only Chance of saving so large a Sum. This to your private Ear & I hope the Expedient will meet your approbation. The Directors are to meet here on the 17 Instant. We shall be glad to have such Communications as you may think proper for us. I fear Macomb will not be able to go thru all his Engagements. [7] If he stops an almost universal Stoppage of Payment will ensue. I am duely favord with yours of 23. 29 & 31 Ulto. [8]

Yours very sincerely

Nich Low

Alexr. Hamilton Esq
Secretary of the Treasury

ALS, Hamilton Papers, Library of Congress.
1. Low, a New York City merchant and land speculator, was a director of the Society for Establishing Useful Manufactures.
2. Dewhurst, a New York City businessman and a director of the Society for Establishing Useful Manufactures, was a close associate of William Duer, Alexander Macomb, and other New York speculators.
3. The society appropriated fifty thousand dollars for procuring materials and workmen from Europe. A committee consisting of Macomb, Low, Dewhurst, Benjamin Walker, and Elisha Boudinot was established to superintend

the expenditure of this money. The committee, in turn, entrusted the actual spending of the money to Dewhurst ("Minutes of the S.U.M.," 20, 28).

The amount of money spent by Dewhurst is described as follows in the committee's report: ". . . a Warrant was issued in favor of Alexander Macomb Chairman of the Committee for 50000 Dollars the amount of which was delivered to him [Dewhurst] by Mr. Macomb in Bills of Exchange drawn by Mr. Macomb on his Correspondent in London amounting to £ 10,975:12.2. Sterling and Mr: Dewhursts receipt for the Bills filed with Mr. Walker. The particular application of these monies by Mr. Dewhurst, will be seen by his Letters annexed to this Report" ("Minutes of the S.U.M.," 28–29).

4. Joseph King.

5. William Hall, an English artisan, was in charge of the printing business for the Society for Establishing Useful Manufactures.

6. Walker, Duer, and Macomb were all officials of the Society for Establishing Useful Manufactures.

7. Macomb was forced to suspend payments two days after this letter was written.

8. Letters not found.

From Gouverneur Morris

London 10 April 1792.

Dear Hamilton.

I din'd the Day before Yesterday tête a tête with the Russian Minister Count Woranzow [1] who is a very sensible and well inform'd Man. In the Course of an Interesting Conversation after Dinner your Name was Mention'd and he exprest a Desire to see your various Reports to Congress. These he means to transmit to his Brother who is the Minister of Commerce in Russia in Order to undeceive him with Respect to the United States. You will not only oblige me but do a very useful Thing if you will transmit those Reports with any other useful Information in an Envelope directed to the Count de Woranzow Minister plenipo: from the Court of Russia. You can send it to the American Consul here to be deliverd *but chuse a private Ship for the Conveyance.*

The Count to shew the Importance of spreading such Information told me that when he came to this Country [2] beleiving as he did in Mr Pitts Integrity he readily adopted the State given to him of our Country which was as poor and despicable as need be. He says that he is cur'd of his Confidence in Mr. Pitt having detected him in asserting most seriously upon his Honor and laying his Hand upon his Breast things which were absolutely false. But that the Impressions made with Respect to America still exist to our Preju-

dice in many Places. He says that Mr Pitt had at one time he be-
leives some Disposition to make a commercial Treaty with us but
that the Arguments used by Lord Sheffield [3] and the Indisposition
of some of his Colleagues had changed this Intention. That he may
have return'd lately towards his former Mode of thinking in Consequence of our prosperous Situation but that we should be very
much on our Guard and especially against Corruption which is one
of his usual Weapons. He says that Mr Pitt in the late Armament [4]
finding that he would not basely betray the Interest of his Sovereign
had the Insolence to threaten him (thro a third Person) with the
Loss of his Place. He replied in the same Way that he considered
his Flatteries and Threats as equally contemptible That as to the
Charge of intriguing with Opposition [5] he neither avowd nor disavow'd any Thing being amenable only to his own Sovereign. But
that supposing a british Minister to be so weak and vain as to compromise in the Parade of useless Armament the essential Interests of
his Country and that Peace and good Understanding which he had
been sent to cultivate between the two Nations it would best fulfill
the Objects of his Appointment to counteract the Measures of such
a Minister. The End of this curious kind of second Hand Dialogue
was an Apology from Mr Pitt disavowing the first Message but in
such Way as confirmd the Belief of it & therefore only shew'd the
poorness of the Denial. Expede Herculem. This Anecdote will I
think not be useless to you.

Adieu   I am always yours   Gouv Morris

ALS, Hamilton Papers, Library of Congress; LC, Gouverneur Morris Papers,
Library of Congress.
    1. At this time the Russian Ambassador to the Court of St. James's was
Count Semen Romanovich Woronzow. For Morris's account of his interview
with Count Woronzow, see Morris, *Diary of the French Revolution*, II, 409–10.
    2. Woronzow was in England as early as 1785.
    3. Lord Sheffield was the author of an influential defense of England's naviga-
tion laws entitled *Observations on the Commerce of the American States with
Europe and the West Indies including the several articles of import and export;
and on the tendency of a bill now depending in Parliament* (London: J. Debrett,
1783). This book went through two editions in 1783 and four in 1784.
    4. After William Pitt failed in his attempt to use diplomacy to check Russian
aggression against the Ottoman Empire, he ordered an increase in the British
navy. This increase was known as "the Russian Armament."
    5. Pitt's proposal to commission additional ships for the British navy en-
countered opposition in Parliament. It is probably this "opposition" to which
Woronzow referred in his conversation with Morris.

From William Seton

[*New York, April 10, 1792.* On April 12, 1792, Hamilton wrote
to Seton: "I have your letters of the 10th & 11th." *Letter of April
10 not found.*]

To William Short

Treasury Department
April 10. 1792.

Sir.

My last letter to you was of the 2nd instant.

It is proper that you be informed that a sum of eight thousand,
three hundred and twenty five Dollars was paid here on application
of Mr. de Ternant the Minister of France to himself and twenty
two thousand Dollars to Mr. de la forest the Vice Consul General
on the 21st. of February last, and the sum of one hundred thousand
Dollars on the 12th. of March.[1] Three further payments of 100,000
Dollars each are engaged to be made here in like manner, on the
1st. of June, on the first of September and on the first of December
next, or before if convenient.[2] All these are payments on account of
the debt due to France.

I have the honor to be with great consideration Sir Your most
obed. servt. Alex Hamilton

P.S. An account against the Government of France has been
settled at the Treasury for arms, amunition &ca. amounting to
Eight thousand Nine hundred and sixty two Dollars.[3] of which a
certified Copy is here enclosed.[4] This is also on account of the
debt due to France.

LS, William Short Papers, Library of Congress; two copies, signed by H and
marked "Duplicate" and "3rd," William Short Papers, Library of Congress. A
copy of this letter was enclosed in H's "Report on Foreign Loans," February 13,
1793.
    1. For information on the advances of money made to Jean Baptiste de
Ternant and Antoine René Charles Mathurin de La Forest, see Ternant to H,
February 21, March 8, 10, 1792; H to Ternant, February 22, March 8, 12, 1792.

2. See H to Ternant, March 8, 1792.
3. See Ternant to H, February 21, 1792, note 2.
4. Copy, William Short Papers, Library of Congress.

To the President and Directors of the Bank of the United States

Treasury Department April 10th. 1792

Gentlemen,

I am induced by circumstances which have come within my knowledge to inform you, that the operation suggested in my letter of the 19th ultimo [1] continues to be desirable in relation to those, who have payments to make at the Custom house in the course of the current Month. You will consider it as it concerns the convenience of the Bank of the United States.

I have the honor to be, with great consideration Gentlemen, Your most obedt Servt   Alexander Hamilton

The President, Directors & Co of
the Bank of the United States

LS, from the original in the New York State Library, Albany.
1. Letter not found.

From Charles Lee

[*Alexandria, Virginia, April 11, 1792.* On July 4, 1792, Hamilton acknowledged the receipt of Lee's letter of April 11, 1792. *Letter not found.*]

From William Seton [1]

New York 11 April 1792

Dear sir

I find upon enquiry from those who are most conversant in the nature and extent of the Stock Contracts, that Monday the 15th of this month is the day which will probably produce the greatest distress, of course the day on which relief will be the most essential. What is called here the Company, of which Mr Macomb is the ostensible person,[2] have on that day to take Stock or pay differences on half a Million. If they do not comply, then all other Contracts are a float, & the sacrifices must be very great. If they only pay the differences & dont take the Stock, this may be calculated at the rates that the distress will cause the price of Stock to be at, which will go near to ruin them, so that it is of infinite consequence to the Community that the Company should not be too much oppressed if they mean to comply with their Engagements, or that the Public should have immediately relief, if they do not mean to comply. Therefore if it was possible that I could go into the Market for you in force that day, and that it was known I should do so, it would in all probability save the City from utter ruin. Perhaps such a day may never occur again. I take the liberty of mentioning this to you, as your answer can reach me on Saturday which would be time enough.

I am with the most sincere respect & esteem   Dear sir   Your obliged Obe Servt   Wm Seton

A. Hamilton Esqr.

ALS, Hamilton Papers, Library of Congress.
    1. For background to this letter, see H to Seton, March 19, 25, April 4, 1792; Seton to H, March 21, April 9, 1792.
    2. By "the Company, of which Mr. Macomb is the ostensible person," Seton is presumably referring to the secret partnership formed by Alexander Macomb and William Duer late in 1791 for speculation in public securities.

To George Washington

[Philadelphia, April 11, 1792]

Mr. Hamilton presents his respects to the President. Herewith are testimonials in favor of two candidates for the Office of Treasurer of the Mint, Wm. A McCrea [1] who has been mentioned by Mr. Foster [2] of the Senate, and James Abercrombie [3] who is recommended by a number of respectable characters.

April 11th. 1792.

LC, George Washington Papers, Library of Congress.

1. McCrea, a resident of Delaware, applied for appointment as treasurer of the Mint on March 27, 1792. His letter of application, supported by nine letters of recommendation, is described in Hunt, *Calendar of Applications*, 80. McCrea, however, did not receive the appointment, and on April 11, 1792, the day on which H wrote this letter to Washington, he was appointed a surgeon's mate in the Army (*Executive Journal*, I, 119).

2. Theodore Foster was a Senator from Rhode Island.

3. Abercrombie, like McCrea, failed in his application for appointment as treasurer of the Mint. In 1793 he was an unsuccessful applicant for appointment as naval officer at Philadelphia (Hunt, *Calendar of Applications*, 1).

From Bacler de Leval [1]

[New York, April 12, 1792.]

Sans doute Monsieur vous ete dans de bien grandes inquietudes Sur L'existence presente de votre malheureux ami et Sa respectable femme.[2] Je Soufre autans que vous que Les circonstances vous obligent a rester a philadelphie dans un moment ou votre presente Leur est Si necessaire. Ils vous attende avec bien de l'impatience mais en attendans votre arrivée rendé leur un bien grand Service: engagè M de Casenove [3] a partir aussi tot pour aider notre pauvre ami a Sortir d'un embaras cruel. Je lui ecris de leur part, ils l'attende avec La plus vive impatience. Au nom de L'amitie qu'il ne differe pas d'un jour, Vous m'aves dit qu'il vous ecrirois je devois vous porter Sa Lettre mais tout a coup Les affaires ont pris une tournant Si Sinistre que je ne puis pas quiter cette respectable famille. Les affaires a new york Sont dans une Confusion affreuse èt elles empire tous Les jours par de nouvelle bancroute. Tranquilises vous cependant Sur votre ami, il Se tira encore mieux d'affaire que Les autres mais pour cela il faut quil Sois Secondé par Les Conseils et L'experience d'un veritable ami et il ny a pas un moment a perdre. Engagè donc Monsieur M de Casenove a tous quiter pour venir Sauver notre ami. Il espere tout de Sa presence icy, il L'attens Lundy. Vous voyes qu'il faut que Le tems presse bien pour Lui en Laisser aussi peu, et j'espere tous Si il vient, je crains tout, Seulement Si il differe. Voila Monsieur notre Situation presente. M de La roche [4] a pris le partie de ne pas quiter Duer ny jour ny nuit. Il couche dans Sa chambre a La prison et n'en Sortira que Lors que notre ami Sera plus tranquil et que vous Seres tous icy. Je vous prie de me croire Monsieur avec Les Sentiments que vous inspires Votre tres humble Servante

Bacler deLeval

le 12 avril 1792

ALS, Hamilton Papers, Library of Congress.
1. Mme Bacler de Leval was a native of France and a member of the "Company of the Twenty-four" (Société des Vingt-Quatres). Each member of this group agreed to purchase one thousand acres of land in the Ohio country from William Duer's Scioto Company and to provide four laborers who were to be used for clearing and cultivating the land. The "Twenty-four" came to this country in 1790. For a variety of reasons the French settlement in Ohio was not successful, and in 1792 Mme de Leval with other members of the "Twenty-four" contracted to buy some lands in Maine that were owned by Duer and Henry Knox.
2. This is a reference to Duer and his wife, Catharine Alexander Duer, daughter of William Alexander (Lord Stirling). Duer had been imprisoned for debt on March 23, 1792.
3. Théophile Cazenove, who had come to the United States in 1790 as agent for Dutch investors in American state and Federal securities, had settled in Philadelphia. He had been attempting to interest Amsterdam bankers in purchasing American lands.
4. Jean Baptiste La Roche was a member of the Société des Vingt-Quatres.

To the President and Directors of the Bank of New York [1]

Treasury Department
April 12. 1792

Gentlemen

Since my official letter to you authorising an advance to your Cashier of Fifty Thousand Dollars [2] to be applied to the purchase of public debt on account of the United States I have authorised that Gentleman to apply for another fifty thousand Dollars and to make the like use of it.[3] I now confirm this direction and add my desire that he may be furnished with a further sum of fifty thousand Dollars,[4] making in the whole One hundred and fifty thousand, the whole for the purpose above mentioned.

With great consideration I ha⟨ve the honor to be⟩

The President Directors & Comp⟨any⟩
of the Bank of NYor⟨k⟩

AL[S], Bank of New York, New York City; copy, in Seton's handwriting, Hamilton Papers, Library of Congress.

1. This letter was enclosed in H to William Seton, April 12, 1792.
Gulian Verplanck was president of the Bank of New York.
2. H to the President and Directors of the Bank of New York, March 26, 1792.
3. H to Seton, April 4, 1792.
4. See "Meeting of the Commissioners of the Sinking Fund," April 12, 1792.

Report on the Petition of Daniel Ellis and John How

[Philadelphia, April 12, 1792
Communicated on April 17, 1792] [1]

[To the Speaker of the House of Representatives;

The Secretary of the Treasury, pursuant to an Order of the House of Representatives of the 17th. of January 1791, referring to him the petition of Daniel Ellis and John How, Executors of Samuel How, late of the City of Burlington, deceased,[2] respectfully reports.

That it appears by the Petitioners own shewing, that the subject of their claim, which is payment for supplies furnished to a Pennsylvania row-galley, has been originally regarded by Congress, as a charge proper for the consideration of the State. And that the Comptroller General of Pennsylvania,[3] who appears to be the proper Officer to decide on the said claim, has rejected it.

The Secretary does not, therefore, perceive, that the case is of a nature to claim relief from the United States.

All which is humbly submitted,   Alexander Hamilton
                                                  Secry. of the Treasy.
Treasury Department
April 12th 1792.

Copy, RG 233, Reports of the Treasury Department, 1792–1793, Vol. III, National Archives.
1. *Journal of the House*, I, 580. The communicating letter, dated April 16, 1792, may be found in RG 233, Reports of the Treasury Department, 1792–1793, Vol. III, National Archives.
2. "A petition of Daniel Ellis and John How, executors of Samuel How, late of the city of Burlington, deceased, was presented to the House and read, praying to receive payment for a quantity of port which was impressed from the said Samuel How, for the use of the Army of the United States, during the late war. . . .
"*Ordered*, That the said . . . [petition] be referred to the Secretary of the

Treasury, with instruction to examine the same, and report his opinion thereupon to the House." (*Journal of the House*, I, 355.)
3. John Nicholson.

Report on the Petition of Ezra Stiles

[Philadelphia, April 12, 1792
Communicated on April 17, 1792] [1]

[To the Speaker of the House of Representatives]
The Secretary of the Treasury, pursuant to an Order of the House
of Representatives of the 5th. of April 1790, referring to him the
petition of Ezra Stiles, on behalf of the President and fellows of
Yale College in Connecticut,[2] respectfully reports.

That the Act making provision for the debt of the United States,
exempts, in future, Philosophical Apparatus from the duties on importation.[3]

That it will, therefore, be agreeable to the spirit of that Act, if
the Legislature should think proper to direct restitution, in this
case, of the duties which have been paid, as set forth in the petition,
to be made to the parties. And that, to the Secretary it appears
expedient, from a consideration, that it will be conductive to the
interests of learning.

All which is humbly submitted,   Alexander Hamilton
                                         Secry. of the Treasy.

Treasury Department,
April 12th 1792.

Copy, RG 233, Reports of the Treasury Department, 1792–1793, Vol. III, National Archives.
   1. *Journal of the House*, I, 580. The communicating letter, dated April 16,
1792, may be found in RG 233, Reports of the Treasury Department, 1792–
1793, Vol. III, National Archives.
   2. On January 27, 1790, "A petition of Ezra Stiles, in behalf of the President
and Fellows of Yale College, in Connecticut, was presented to the House and
read, praying that the impost duties arising on a philosophical apparatus lately
purchased and imported from London, for the use of the said College, may be
remitted.
   "*Ordered*, That the said petition . . . lie on the table." (*Journal of the
House*, I, 148.)
   On April 5, 1790, the House "*Ordered*, That the petition of Ezra Stiles, on
behalf of the President and Fellows of Yale College, in Connecticut . . . be referred to the Secretary of the Treasury, with instruction to examine the same,
and report his opinion thereupon to the House" (*Journal of the House*, I, 188).

3. See Section 1 of "An Act making further provision for the payment of the debts of the United States" (1 *Stat.* 180–81 [August 10, 1790]).

Report on a Petition of Philip Verplank

[Philadelphia, April 12, 1792
Communicated on April 17, 1792] [1]

[To the Speaker of the House of Representatives]

The Secretary of the Treasury, pursuant to an Order of the House of Representatives, of the 14th of July, 1790, referring to him the petition of Philip Verplank,[2] respectfully reports;

That by reference to the accounts of William Barber, esquire, late Commissioner for the State of New York,[3] it appears, that an account was exhibited to him, for wood, grain, and other supplies, taken by the American Army, as also for the use of the estate of the petitioner, at Verplank's point, during the late war, the estimated value of which was £4238.18.3, New York Currency.

That, of this Account, the Commissioner admitted the sum of 7970. $\frac{81}{90}$ dollars, and rejected the remainder, as being, in his opinion, unauthorized by law.

That, as the claim of the petitioner has already been under the consideration of a Commissioner, who was vested with ample and final authority, a revision of it, in order to a farther allowance, would, in the opinion of the Secretary, be a precedent full of danger. The compensation already made bears so large a proportion to the sum claimed, that there is no appearance of extraordinary loss or signal hardship, to call for a special interposition of the Legislature.

All which is humbly submitted,   Alexander Hamilton
                                              Secry. of the Treasy.
Treasury Department,
April 12th. 1792.

Copy, RG 233, Reports of the Treasury Department, 1792–1793, Vol. III, National Archives.

1. *Journal of the House*, I, 580. The communicating letter, dated April 16, 1792, may be found in RG 233, Reports of the Treasury Department, 1792–1793, Vol. III, National Archives.

2. On July 14, 1790, "The several petitions of John R. Livingston, Philip Verplank, and Peter Pray Van Zandt, were presented to the House, and read,

respectively praying the liquidation and settlement of a claim against the United States.

"*Ordered,* That the said petitions be referred to the Secretary of the Treasury, with instructions to examine the same, and report his opinion thereupon to the House." (*Journal of the House,* I, 269.)

3. Barber was Continental commissioner for settling the accounts of the United States in New York State.

Report on the Petition of Simon Nathan

[Philadelphia, April 12, 1792
Communicated on April 17, 1792] [1]

[To the Speaker of the House of Representatives]

The Secretary of the Treasury, pursuant to an Order of the House of Representatives of the 30th July, 1790, referring to him the memorial of Simon Nathan, of the City of New York,[2] respectfully reports;

That the subject of the Memorialist's application, from his own statement, appears to relate wholly to the State of Virginia, and not to the United States.

The Secretary is, therefore, of opinion, that if, in justice, the case of the said Memorialist should require relief, it cannot, on this ground, be reasonably expected to be afforded by the United States.[3]

All which is humbly submitted,   Alexander Hamilton,
                                                   Secry. of the Treasy.

Treasury Department.
April 12th 1792.

Copy, RG 233, Reports of the Treasury Department, 1792–1793, Vol. III, National Archives.

1. *Journal of the House,* I, 580. The communicating letter, dated April 16, 1792, may be found in RG 233, Reports of the Treasury Department, 1792–1793, Vol. III, National Archives.

2. On July 30, 1790, a petition of Simon Nathan was "presented to the House and read . . . praying the liquidation and settlement of a claim against the United States.

"*Ordered,* That the said . . . [petition] be referred to the Secretary of the Treasury, with instruction to examine the same, and report his opinion thereupon to the House." (*Journal of the House,* I, 285.)

3. During the American Revolution Nathan had advanced the state of Virginia fifty-two thousand dollars in specie at Havanna for Colonel George Rogers Clarke's drafts. In addition, during 1780 he loaned Virginia three hundred thousand Continental dollars without interest for clothing for the soldiers at Fort Pitt. During the seventeen-eighties Nathan drew bills on the state of

Virginia for these and other advances he had made to the state. Virginia, however, refused to honor these bills. Nathan brought suit twice against the state, and in the second suit, which concerned goods he had imported from France for Virginia during the Revolution, Nathan attached some of Virginia's property in Pennsylvania. The courts, however, decided that property of a sovereign state was exempt from judicial procedure in another state (David De Sola Pool, *Portraits Etched in Stone* [New York, 1952], 414–18).

Report on the Petition of May Wooster

[Philadelphia, April 12, 1792
Communicated on April 17, 1792] [1]

[To the Speaker of the House of Representatives]

The Secretary of the Treasury, pursuant to an Order of the House of Representatives, of the 25th of March 1790, referring to him the petition of May Wooster,[2] respectfully reports:

That the State of Connecticut having settled the allowance of seven years half pay with the petitioner, in the same manner, as has been customary in like cases, and charged it to the United States, and adjustments at the Treasury having proceeded on a similar principle, the Secretary is of opinion, that a departure from the rule, by granting the interest claimed by the said petition, would operate partially, with regard to many other claims of the same nature, which have been heretofore adjusted, or, if extended to them, would involve the inconvenient precedent of unsettling an established rule.

All which is humbly submitted   Alexander Hamilton
                                              Secry. of the Treasy
Treasury Department
April 12th 1792

Copy, RG 233, Reports of the Treasury Department, 1792–1793, Vol. III, National Archives.

1. *Journal of the House,* I, 580. The communicating letter, dated April 16, 1792, may be found in RG 233, Reports of the Treasury Department, 1792–1793, Vol. III, National Archives.

2. On March 25, 1790, "A petition of May Wooster was presented to the House and read, praying to be allowed interest on the pension granted her by the former Congress, as widow of the late General Wooster. . . .

"*Ordered,* That the said [petition] . . . be referred to the Secretary of the Treasury, with instruction to examine the same, and report his opinion thereupon to the House." (*Journal of the House,* I, 182.)

Meeting of the Commissioners of the Sinking Fund [1]

[Philadelphia, April 12, 1792]

At a meeting of the Trustees of the Sinking Fund, on Thursday, the 12th of April, 1792,

Present, The Vice President, the Secretary of State, the Secretary of the Treasury, and the Attorney General.

Resolved, That the Secretary of the Treasury be authorised to expend, in the purchase of stock, a further sum, not exceeding two hundred thousand dollars, on the principles of the resolution of the 15th day of August, 1791.

From so much of the above resolution as relates to the purchase of three per cent. and deferred stock, the Secretary of State dissented.

ASP, Finance, 236–37.

1. For background to this document, see H to John Adams, March 20, 1792; "Meeting of the Commissioners of the Sinking Fund," March 26, April 4, 1792.

From Philip Schuyler

New York, April 12, 1792. "Isaac Van Wyck Esqr. of Fish Kill in Dutchess county has requested me for an introductory line to you. He repairs to Philadelphia to Solicit a contract for carrying the mail between this and Albany. I have known Mr Van Wyck from his infancy, and to me has always appeared to deserve the character which he Generally sustains, That of an honest man, punctial in his dealings, and of marked Attention to his business. . . ."

ALS, Hamilton Papers, Library of Congress.

To William Seton

Philad. April 12. 1792

My Dear Sir

I have your letters of the 10th [1] & 11th and more to my distress than surprise I learn by other letters a confirmation of what you apprehended namely Mr. Macombs failure.[2] This misfortune has I fear a long tail to it.

The inclosed[3] you will perceive gives you additional latitude. The terms as heretofore, for six ℔ Cents 20/ three per Cents 12/ & deferred 12/6.

You must judge of the best mode & manner of applying the sum. The operations here not being extensive, I have found it best to eke out my aid. I doubt whether this will answer with you. My reason was to keep up men's spirits by *appearing often* though not much at one time. All is left to you.

You will doubtless be cautious in securing your *transfers* before you pay.

Some time since in a private letter[4] I suggested a plan of relief something like the following.

All parties concerned to agree to *liquidate* all contracts not executed by stating Stock at a liberal value say 22/6. for 6 ℔ Cents 12/ for three's 13 for deferred—to adjust all differences according to the actual differences between these rates and the sums stipulated & to pay and receive those differences in Stock at the above prices.

Many good consequences would have arisen from such a plan. I think it might have parried the misfortune. I fear it is now too late but something like it may perhaps break the force of the Evil.

Yours affecty   A Hamilton

Wm. Seton Esqr

ALS, Bank of New York, New York City; incomplete copy, in Seton's handwriting, Hamilton Papers, Library of Congress.

1. Letter not found.
2. Alexander Macomb, a leading New York speculator and partner of William Duer, went into bankruptcy on April 12, 1792.
3. H to the President and Directors of the Bank of New York, April 12, 1792.
4. Letter not found. See, however, H to Seton, March 25, 1792.

To George Washington

[Philadelphia, April 12, 1792]

The Secretary of the Treasury has the honor to communicate to the President a resolution of the Trustees of the Sinking Fund as of this morning.[1] A particular piece of urgent business prevents personally waiting on the President with it. It is very much to be desired that the resolution may receive the immediate decision of the President. It is upon the same principles with the last.[2]

12th. April 1792.

LC, George Washington Papers, Library of Congress.
   1. See "Meeting of the Commissioners of the Sinking Fund," April 12, 1792.
   2. See "Meeting of the Commissioners of the Sinking Fund," April 4, 1792.

From Richard Morris

New York 13 April 1792

Sir

Your favour of the 24th. Ulto. is duly Recd.[1] I am Sorry at giving you so much trouble in this business but I am Certain Youl Excuse me from the Consideration that I am in Some measure to derange before I can properly Arrange. Had I come to the Office[2] in the first instance, I should have thought the Law, and your Instructions, perfectly Sufficient, and Directory, and taken at once a Decided part, but when I thought it Necessary to make Alterations in the Arrangement of my predecessor I doubted my own Judgement and wished your Sentiments. I am Much Obliged for your Decision in the Business.

Mr Matthew M Clarkson who Mr Smith[3] Appointed I Just now Mett in my way to the Office. I informed him I was about makeing my Quarterly Return and wanted the Necessarys from his Office, amongst Others the Money. It produced Some Little Altercation tho very decent and Good Humour'd it Concluded with my informing him that he was only a Collector and that Amongst them there was no Distinction of Sub and Superior. He mentioned his being then on his way to the Ferry boat in his way to Philadelphia where he Should See You. What his Representations may be I know not. His own Sence may inform him that his Office is Useless and Really is an Embarrasment in the Department. However he may wish to have an Establishment, that may be his Errand, if it is I wish him Disappointed at least untill the deposit is properly Arranged. Then if an Appointment in his present Line is Necessary I shall perhaps be as happy as any one in Seeing a Clarkson fill it. This

I write not as a Publick Letter but hearing Mr Clarkson was going for Philadelphia I thought it my duty to say thus much to you for private Information. I therefore Send you on my Own Scral in the Draft without Copying. My Respectfull Compliments to Your Lady and be Assured I am with Real Regard and perfect Esteem.[4]

Your Obliged Hume Servt   Rd Morris

I mean to Answer Your Last letter to Me.[5]

Alexr Hamilton Esqr.

ALS, Hamilton Papers, Library of Congress.
  1. Letter not found.
  2. Morris had been appointed supervisor of the revenue for the District of New York on March 8, 1792.
  3. William S. Smith had been Morris's predecessor.
  4. On the endorsement H wrote: "Supervisor of New York. Private. Answered by a private letter. Mr. Clarkson was referred to him." H's private letter to Morris has not been found.
  5. Letter not found.

Report on Additional Appropriations

[Philadelphia, April 13–16, 1792
Communicated on April 17, 1792] [1]

[To the Speaker of the House of Representatives]
The Secretary of the Treasury respectfully reports to the House of Representatives, an Estimate of certain Sums, amounting together to thirty four thousand four hundred and ninety seven dollars, ninety Cents, for which an appropriation is requisite, in addition to the provisions heretofore made.[2]
The funds in the power of the legislature, for this purpose, are the surplus of the duties on imports and tonnage to the end of the year 1791; certain unexpended surpluses on former appropriations,

Copy, RG 233, Reports of the Treasury Department, 1791–1792, Vol. III, National Archives.
  1. The communicating letter, dated April 16, 1792, may be found in RG 233, Reports of the Treasury Department, 1791–1792, Vol. III, National Archives.
  2. "The provisions heretofore made" were by "An Act making Appropriations for the Support of Government for the year one thousand seven hundred and ninety-two" (1 Stat. 226–29 [December 23, 1791]).

and certain sums, which have been paid into the treasury, in consequence of settlements with individuals.

The Secretary takes this opportunity to observe, that the only fund, which has been heretofore appropriated for satisfying the purposes of the Act, for raising and adding another regiment to the military establishment of the United States, and for making farther provision for the protection of the frontiers,[3] is the product to the end of the year 1791, of the duties on spirits distilled within the United States, and of the additional duties laid by the same Act, which imposes those duties on imported spirits; which fund will not prove adequate to the object. A farther provision is therefore necessary, and may be made out of the unappropriated surplus of the duties on imports and tonnage to the end of the year 1791.[4]

All which is humbly submitted   Alexander Hamilton,
                                        Secry. of the Treasy.
Treasury Department,
April 13th. 1792.

Estimate of sums necessary to be appropriated in addition to those provided for by the Act passed the 23d Decr. 1791.

                                                    dollars. cents.
For the discharge of a balance due Benjamin Haw-
   kins and other Commissioners appointed under an
   Act of Congress of 15th March 1785,[5] for treating with the Southern Indians, which balance the

---

3. H is referring to "An Act for raising and adding another Regiment to the Military Establishment of the United States, and for making farther provision for the protection of the frontiers" (1 *Stat.* 222–24 [March 3, 1791]) and "An Act for making farther and more effectual Provision for the Protection of the Frontiers of the United States" (1 *Stat.* 241–43 [March 5, 1792]). The second of these two acts provided for raising three additional regiments.

4. The "farther provision" was made by "An Act making certain appropriations therein specified" (1 *Stat.* 284–85 [May 8, 1792]).

5. The resolution providing for instructions and pay for the commissioners was agreed to on March 15, 1785 (*JCC*, XXVIII, 160–62). On March 21, 1785, "Congress proceeded to the election of three Commissioners to treat with the Cherokees, and all other Indians southward of them, within the limits of the United States, pursuant to the act of the 15th of the present Month, and, the ballots being taken, Benjamin Hawkins, Esqr was elected, having been nominated by the delegates of North Carolina; Daniel Carroll, Esqr having been nominated by Mr [James] McHenry; William Peery, esqr having been nominated by Mr. [Gunning] Bedford" (*JCC*, XXVIII, 183).

Comptroller of the Treasury [6] admitted 5th. January 1792 . . . .   2787.88.
For the first Clerk to the general Board of Commissioners, his additional salary provided for by a clause in the Act for extending the time for settling the accounts between the United States and the individual States, from the 23d January to 31st December 1792,[7] at 200 dollars per annum . . .   187.91.
For defraying the expense which will attend the stating and printing of the public accounts at the Treasury, in compliance with the order of the House of Representatives, dated the 30th December 1791 [8] . . . .   800.

Clerks of Courts, Jurors, Witnesses &c.
The fund arising from fines, forfeitures and penalties, having last year proved insufficient for the discharge of the accounts of Clerks of Courts &c to which they were appropriated: [9] a sum for the present year is estimated in order to provide

6. Oliver Wolcott, Jr.
7. Section 3 of "An Act to extend the time limited for settling the Accounts of the United States with the individual States" reads in part as follows: ". . . from and after the passing of this act, the pay of the principal clerk of the said board shall be the same as the pay of the principal clerk in the auditor's office" (1 *Stat.* 229 [January 23, 1792]).
8. On December 30, 1791, the House "*Resolved*, That it shall be the duty of the Secretary of the Treasury to lay before the House of Representatives, on the fourth Monday of October in each year, if Congress shall be then in session, or if not then in session, within the first week of the session next following the said fourth Monday of October, an accurate statement and account of the receipts and expenditures of all public moneys, down to the last day inclusively of the month of December immediately preceding the said fourth Monday of October, distinguishing the amount of the receipts in each State or District, and from each officer therein; in which statements shall also be distinguished the expenditures which fall under each head of appropriation, and shall be shown the sums, if any, which remain unexpended, and to be accounted for in the next statement, of each and every of such appropriations" (*Journal of the House*, I, 484).
9. Section 1 of "An Act providing compensations for the officers of the Judicial Courts of the United States, and for Jurors and Witnesses, and for other purposes" reads in part as follows: ". . . And a sum arising from the fines and forfeitures to the United States, and equal to the amount thereof, is hereby appropriated for the payment of the above accounts" (1 *Stat.* 217 [March 3, 1791]).

against a similar contingency, of . . .   10.000.
And also for the discharge of certain accounts, actually settled to the 31st December,
1791, in addition to the sums heretofore appropriated . . . .   7.000.   17.000.
To rectify a mistake in the Register's estimate [10] for
the enumeration of the inhabitants of Virginia, he
having stated the Marshal's account at   4253.90
Whereas it ought to have been 7553.90,
the difference is. . . . .   3300.
For the Marshall of the district of South Carolina,
his accounts settled; for the enumeration of the inhabitants of that State, amount to . .   4395.59
The sum estimated was only . . . . .   3000.

Remains to be appropriated . . . .   1395.59.
For so much short estimated for the discharge of
sundry accounts against the Treasury Department. The accounts brought in for payment to
31st December 1791, exceeding the said estimate,
by, ...   1355.61.
For defraying the incidental expenses of furnishing
the Supervisors of excise with screw-presses, stamp
seals, and other articles . . . .   600.

For the Commissioner of Army Accounts,
his additional estimate for 1792, Vizt.
For Lieut: John Freeman, of the late Maryland line
for balance of subsistence, for the years 1782 &
1783 . . . .   41.75.
Salary of a Clerk on extra hours, from the first of
May 1791, to the 1st of April 1792 . . .   229.16
Salary of two clerks in addition to those allowed by
the last appropriation, as he finds it impossible with
the present assistance to conduct the business with
that dispatch and propriety required . . .   1.000
Contingencies   100   1370.91.

10. This estimate and that for the marshal of South Carolina are given in
"Report on the Estimate of Expenditures for 1792," November 4, 1791.

For an additional estimate of the Clerk of the House
of Representatives, to enable him to pay the doorkeepers for their respective services during the recess of the House, in conformity with the Act of
Appropriation,[11] passed at the present Session, and
of a resolution of the House of the 24th instant [12] .   700.
For the discharge of such demands on the United
States, not otherwise provided for, as shall have
been ascertained and admitted, in due course of
settlement at the treasury, and which are of a nature, according to the usage thereof, to require
payment in specie . . . .   5000.

Dollars, ...   34.497.90.

Treasury Department
Register's Office, 16th April 1792.

Joseph Nourse, Register.

11. See "An Act for fixing the compensations of the Doorkeepers of the
Senate and House of Representatives in Congress" (1 *Stat.* 252 [April 12, 1792]).
12. Nourse meant "the 24th Ultimo." On March 24, 1792, "The House proceeded to consider the report of the committee to whom was referred the petition of Thomas Claxton: Whereupon,
"*Resolved,* That there be allowed and paid to the said Thomas Claxton, the
sum of one hundred dollars, to be included in the account of the Clerk of this
House, when rendered, for the contingent expenses of the present session."
(*Journal of the House,* I, 549.)

From Oliver Wolcott, Junior

T. D
C. Off Apl. 13. 1792

Sir

I take the liberty to request that the opinion of the Attorney
General of the United States, may be taken on the following questions which have arisen respecting the construction of an Act passed
during the present session intittled "an Act [providing for the
settlement of the claims of persons under particular circumstances
barred by the limitations heretofore established."] [1]

Whether the provisions of said Act will justify the Officers of the Treasury in admitting any other military claims, than those of Officers & soldiers of the battallions raised to serve for three years as during the late War. And in case other claims are admissable, to what description of claims, the Act is to be construed to intend. Whether claims for bounties for inlisting into the service, the gratuities granted to such soldiers as should continue in service to the end of the War, the allowance of one years pay to super-numerary deranged Officers, Commutation in lieu of half pay for life—the allowances for milage forage or Cloathing—or either of them can be admitted as being included in the descriptions of claims for personal service.

I have &

Hon A H—Esqr.

AL, Connecticut Historical Society, Hartford.
1. The words within brackets are in the handwriting of H.
This act, which became law on March 27, 1792, provided that limitations im-posed by resolutions of the Continental Congress on claims of men and officers of the Revolutionary War Army for personal services would be suspended for two years (1 *Stat.* 245).

To the Governor and Directors of the Society for Establishing Useful Manufactures [1]

Philadelphia
April 14. 1792

Gentlemen

Among the disastrous incidents of the present juncture, I have not been least affected by the temporary derangement of the affairs of your Society. If however no real misfortune shall have attended any considerable part of your funds, the mere delay will be no very serious evil. It will not be difficult to put the business in Train with more promising prospects.

The following appears to me to be the course proper to be pursued.

1 To appoint the principal Officers of the Institution and reg-ulate their duties. I mean a Superintendent, an Accountant, and a Cashier, especially the first. Tis impossible that any thing can pro-

ceed with vigour or efficiency till this is done. An infinite deal depends on the qualifications of the Superintendant. If Mr. Hubbard was recoverable, no pains should be spared to effect it.[2] If this is to be despaired of, some *efficient* man of *clear integrity*, ought without delay to be sought in his place.

The Cashier ought also to be of a character and *in a situation* to inspire the most thorough confidence.

No time ought to be lost in determining upon the place and contracting for the land and commencing the buildings. Under present circumstances I would advise that the latter be begun upon a moderate scale yet so as to be capable of extension.

I would also advise that the Society confine themselves at first to the cotton branch. The printing business to commence as early as possible. A complication of objects will tend to weaken still further a confidence already too much impaired.

If a loan should be wanted I would if requisite cooperate to endeavour to procure one on favourable terms.

Means should be taken to procure from Europe a *few essential* workmen; but in this too there ought to be *measure* and circumspection. Nothing should be put in jeopardy.

The lottery must be postponed to a better opportunity.[3]

At my present distance, I can only offer these general suggestions. I am not sufficiently apprised of particulars to enter into detail. I will only add this general observation that nothing scarcely can be so injurious to the affairs of the Society as a much longer suspension of operation.

With great consideration I remain   Gentl: Your Obed ser

A Hamilton

The Governor & Directors
of the Society for establishing useful Manufactures

ALS, Historical Society of Pennsylvania, Philadelphia.

1. The governor of the Society for Establishing Useful Manufactures was William Duer, who had been imprisoned for debts on March 23, 1792. At this time the society's affairs were being conducted by Archibald Mercer, the deputy governor.

An entry in the minutes of the directors of the Society for Establishing Useful Manufactures for April 17, 1792, reads: "The Deputy Governor laid before the board a letter from Colo. Hamilton in answer to the letter written by order of the Board" ("Minutes of the S.U.M.," 25). For the "letter written by order of the Board," see Mercer to H, April 6, 1792.

2. On January 21, 1792, the directors of the Society for Establishing Useful Manufactures had elected Nehemiah Hubbard of Middletown, Connecticut, superintendent general of the works of the society. See Mercer to H, April 6, 1792.

3. On January 21, 1792, the directors of the society had resolved "That a Committee of five, (to be appointed by ballot) be empowered, with the concurrence of the Governor, to form and carry into execution a Plan for raising by Lottery or Lotteries the Sum of One Hundred thousand dollars, granted to the Society by the Act of Incorporation . . ." ("Minutes of the S.U.M.," 17).

Report on Sundry Petitions

[Philadelphia, April 16, 1792
Communicated on April 17, 1792] [1]

[To the Speaker of the House of Representatives]
The Secretary of the Treasury, to whom the House of Representatives were pleased to refer the several petitions enumerated in the lists herewith transmitted, marked, A, B, and C, respectfully submits the following Report:

The petitions in the list A. prefer claims for various supplies to the United States, during the late war: Those in the list B, for transportation of articles by land and water, for the use of the United States, during the same period. Those in the list C, for property taken and damages occasioned by the army of the United States, during the same period: All which claims are barred by the several Acts of limitation,[2] passed at different times, by the United States in Congress assembled.

Copy, RG 233, Reports of the Treasury Department, 1792–1793, Vol. III, National Archives.

1. *Journal of the House*, I, 580. The communicating letter, dated April 16, 1792, may be found in RG 233, Reports of the Treasury Department, 1792–1793, Vol. III, National Archives.

2. Among the statutes of limitation concerning Revolutionary War claims passed by the Continental Congress, those most frequently referred to are the resolutions of November 2, 1785, and July 23, 1787. On November 2, 1785, Congress resolved: "That all persons having claims for services performed in the military department, be directed to exhibit the same for liquidation to the commissioners of army accounts, on or before the first day of August, ensuing the date hereof, and that all claims, under the description above mentioned, which may be exhibited after that period, shall forever thereafter be precluded from adjustment or allowance, and that the commissioner of army accounts give public Notice of this resolve in all the states for the space of six Months" (*JCC*, XXIX, 866). On July 23, 1787, Congress resolved: "That all persons having unliquidated Claims against the United States pertaining to the late Com-

The situation of the United States, in the course of the late war, necessarily occasioned much want of order and regularity in the conduct of public business. The institutions for carrying it on, frequently devised in moments of hurry and confusion, almost always without the requisite lights from experience, were unavoidably in many cases, either faulty in principle, or deficient in some provisions, checks and guards, which were indispensible to their safe and efficacious execution. The commencement of a more orderly system is not of earlier date, than February 1781, when the executive departments were established.

But during the whole of the time, and even after the institution of these departments, the state of the public finances obliging the

---

missary's Quartermaster's, hospital Cloathier's or marine department shall exhibit particular abstracts of such claims to the proper commissioner appointed to settle the accounts of those departments within eight Months from the date hereof; And all persons having other unliquidated claims against the United States shall exhibit a particular abstract thereof to the Comptroller of the treasury of the United States within one year from the date hereof; And all accounts not exhibited as aforesaid shall be precluded from settlement or allowance" (*JCC*, XXXIII, 392).

In this report H also refers to the earlier resolutions of March 5, 1779, August 23, 1780, and March 17, 1785. On March 5, 1779, Congress resolved to restrict the acceptance of certificates of the quartermaster general, commissary general of purchases, and clothier general so that "no certificate given before this date shall be paid, unless the same be presented for payment within six months from this day; and no certificate hereafter given shall be paid, unless presented to the proper officer within three months after the date thereof" (*JCC*, XIII, 278). The resolutions of August 23, 1780, specified the conditions, other than the time of settlement, under which a certificate of the quartermaster's or commissary's department would constitute a claim upon the United States (*JCC*, XVII, 761). On March 17, 1785, Congress resolved: "Whereas it must conduce to the preservation of public credit, and the equal distribution of Justice, that the Amount of the National debt be ascertained with the utmost expedition; and as delay in the settlement of accounts, tends to render them obscure, and to encourage frauds, by preventing the means of detecting them:

"*Resolved*, That all persons having unliquidated claims against the United States, be, and they are hereby required, within twelve Months from the date hereof, to deliver a particular abstract of such claims to some Commissioner in the State in which they respectively reside, who is authorised to settle accounts against the United States; And any person or persons, neglecting to deliver their claims as aforesaid, shall be precluded from any adjustment of the same, except at the board of treasury: Provided that in those states where there is no Commissioner of Accounts, the citizens of such state or states, shall be allowed one year for delivering their claims, from the time when a Commissioner shall have been appointed and enter on the duties of his office.

"That all persons who shall neglect to deliver in a particular abstract of their claims as aforesaid, shall be excluded from the benefit of settlement or allowance." (*JCC*, XXVIII, 168–69.)

Government to rely essentially on operations of credit and sometimes even on coertion, for the means of carrying on the war; an
unexampled number of persons were, of necessity entrusted to bind
the Government by their contracts, and with a latitude of discretion,
which rendered a due supervision of their conduct, and a regular
accountability, impracticable.

In different stages of the war, almost every officer of the army,
whether in the departments charged with procuring supplies, or
otherwise, had it in his power to contract debts legally or equitably
obligatory on the United States. Not only the most subaltern
agents in the departments alluded to, but officers of companies (as
well as those of higher grade) on detachments, and in other situa-
tions, could exercise by authority, or toleration, that delicate and
dangerous power.

Congress, during the war, passed sundry resolutions for regulating and limiting the public responsibility in such cases, and since
the peace, they prescribed periods, within which, claims of certain
descriptions, and finally all unliquidated claims, were to be exhibited for settlement, or to be for ever after barred.

Of the first description, are the resolutions of March 5th 1779,
and August 23d. 1780.

The following have been passed since the peace.

By an act of the 17th March 1785, all persons having unliquidated
claims against the United States are required, within twelve months,
to exhibit particular abstracts of such claims to Commissioners, who
were sent and empowered to adjust all such claims, within such
State; on condition, that accounts not so presented should thereafter
be settled only at the treasury.

By the Act of November 2nd 1785, all persons having claims for
services performed, in the military department, were directed to
exhibit the same for liquidation, to the Commissioner of Army accounts, before the first of August ensuing, under the penalty of
being thereafter precluded from settlement or allowance.

And by the Act of the 23d. of July 1787, all unliquidated claims
pertaining to the Commissionary's, Quarter Master's, Hospital,
Cloathing, or Marine departments, were to be exhibited to the Commissioners appointed to settle the accounts of said departments,
within eight months; and all other accounts were to be exhibited at

the Treasury, within one year from the date of the said Act, or to be precluded from settlement and allowance.

The justice, as well as policy of Acts of limitation, under such circumstances, cannot be doubted. It was essential to the public administration, that the extent of just demands upon the Government should be within a reasonable period definitely ascertained. It was essential to the public safety and to right, in relation [to] the whole community, that all unsettled claims should be made known, within a time when there were yet means of proper investigation, and after which, the public responsibility should terminate. And the possibility of charging the Government by collusive and fictitious contracts should be at an end.

The situation of no country ever presented a more clear necessity for, or a more competent justification of precautions of that nature.

And all the reasons for adopting them operate to recommend unusual caution in departing from them; with the additional force of this circumstance, that the subsequent lapse of time has increased the difficulty of a due examination.

When it is considered, that the final bar to unliquidated claims did not take effect till the middle of April 1788, several years after the re-establishment of peace, it is natural to infer, that the cases are not numerous, in which the want of opportunity, to bring forward claims for liquidation, can be justly pleaded as an excuse for the omission.

And when to this it is added, that the account of a considerable number of Officers, who had it in their power to bind the public by their contracts, and who were entrusted with large sums of money for fulfilling their engagements, remain unsettled: that some of these are dead; that others have absconded; that the business has been conducted by others, with so little order, as to put it out of their power to render a proper statement of their transactions; that the books and papers of others, who had extensive trusts, have been destroyed, so as to preclude the possibility of settlement; it must appear, that the Government would be, in a great number of cases, destitute of the means of repelling unfounded, and even satisfied claims, for want of documents and vouchers, which could only have resulted from a due settlement with those officers, and from the possession of their books and papers.

It might be inferred, without proof, and it has appeared in the course of the business of the Treasury, that it was a practice with certain public officers, on obtaining supplies, to give receipts and certificates for them, and when they made payment, either partially or totally, to take distinct receipts from the parties, without either endorsing the payments upon the original vouchers, or requiring a surrender of them.

Hence it would often happen, that parties could produce satisfactory vouchers of their having performed services, and furnished supplies, for which, though satisfaction may have been made, the evidence of it would not be in the possession or power of the Government.

And hence, from relaxations of the limitation Acts, there would be great danger of much more injustice to the United States, than justice to individuals.

The principles of self defence, therefore, require and justify an adherence to these Acts, with very few exceptions, and those founded upon such clear evidence, as shall avoid all danger of imposition, and such special reasons, as shall effectually discriminate them from that mass of claims, which it would be so dangerous to admit.

The laws of the present Session have removed the obstacle arising from the limitation Acts, to a description of claims of a nature peculiarly meritorious, those for personal services in the army and navy,[3] and for the allowance of halfpay to widows of Officers who died in service.[4]

As the records and vouchers of the public Offices will afford good guides, as to the propriety of claims of this nature, it was practicable to consult the dictates of public justice with regard to them without hazard of public injury.

If it ought not to be pronounced, that there are no other claims barred by the Acts of limitation, in respect to which, it would be proper to grant relief, it must, at least, be inferred, from a due

---

3. "An Act providing for the settlement of the Claims of Persons under particular circumstances barred by the limitations heretofore established" (1 *Stat.* 245 [March 27, 1792]).

4. "An Act to provide for the settlement of the Claims of Widows and Orphans barred by the limitations heretofore established, and to regulate the Claims to Invalid Pensions" (1 *Stat.* 243–45 [March 23, 1792]).

attention to the considerations, which have been stated, that instances of such relief ought to be founded on reasons of a very special and peculiar nature.

No reasons, sufficiently special or peculiar, appear to the Secretary in relation to the petitions specified in the several lists above mentioned, (and which are herewith returned) to induce an opinion on his part, that the Acts of limitation ought to be superseded in favor of the petitioners.

All which is respectfully submitted,   Alexander Hamilton
                                         Secry. of the Treasy.

Treasury Department,
April 16th 1792.

A.

List of petitions for compensations for supplies furnished during the late War.[5]

Petition of Lewis Van Woert, Petition of John Holbrook,
    Jacob Green and   Ludwig Kuhn,
    others surviving   Levy Bartleson,
    partners of Na-   Abiel Smith,
    thaniel Green &   William Harris,
    Co.   Webb and White,
Benjamin Van Fos-   John Crumpton, and
    san, Administrator   Griffith Jones.
    of Peter Van Fos-
    san.
Thomas Hart.

B.

List of petitions for compensation for transportation during the late War.[6]

Petition of Christian Knipe.   Petition of Nathaniel Tracy, and
    John Smyth   Roger McLean

5. For receipt of these petitions by the House of Representatives and their referral to H, see *Journal of the House*, I, 489, 478, 507, 267, 142, 380, 476, 364, 362, 278, 359, 363, 494.

6. For receipt of these petitions by the House, see *Journal of the House*, I, 391, 518, 374, 503.

C.

List of petitions for compensation for damages done and property taken by the Army of the United States, during the late war.[7] Petition of Abraham Darlington. Petition of Peter Miller,

John Wilson.	John Jones,
John Franklin,	Adolphus Brower,
Mary McCullen,	John Harly,
Christian Harner,	William Walton,[8]
William Lane.	and Richard Green.

7. For receipt of these petitions by the House, see *Journal of the House*, I, 483, 206, 456, 244, 391, 360, 376, 369, 179, 478, 510.

8. Presumably there is an error concerning the name of this petitioner. The name of Henry Walton appears in the *Journal of the House* (I, 580) as one of the petitioners whose claim was considered in the report printed above. There is no record in the *Journal of the House* of the referral of a petition of William Walton to H, but on January 24, 1792, "A petition of Henry Walton, in behalf of himself and Anne Walton, and Elizabeth Walton, devisees of Jacob Walton, late of the city of New York, deceased, was presented to the House and read, praying compensation for damages sustained in the property of their testator, by the American Army, during the late war.

"*Ordered,* That the said petition be referred to the Secretary of the Treasury, with instruction to examine the same, and report his opinion thereupon to the House." (*Journal of the House*, I, 495.)

From William Seton

New York 16 April 1792.

My dear sir

I received your Letter [1] by the Express on fryday Morning, previous to which I had been relieving a few by purchases of Stock upon the Strength of the second extention of fifty thousand Dollars.[2] At Noon I went into the Market, but the applications were so numerous & so vastly beyond my expectation, I found it necessary to declare I could take but very small sums from each. However notwithstanding this, every one pressed forward & were so eager, that I could only take down names, upon a declaration that I would average the whole. This I did, that no one might be left without some relief—so that the investment of the 100,000 Dollars, goes to upwards of 80 Persons, from which you may form a judgment that your orders for purchase were well timed—at the same time it is an evidence of the great and universal distress which prevails, & which I am sorry to say is such that it would be utterly impossible to make purchases equal to the relief. However it cannot now be worse, and when the public mind calms down a little, it is to be hoped that good will arise out of evil—that the spirit of Industry, instead of Gambling will revive, and that the Stocks will come to their proper and real value.

I am with the highest esteem and respect Dear sir. Your Obliged Obed Hu Servt   Wm Seton

Alexr. Hamilton Esqr

ALS, Hamilton Papers, Library of Congress.
1. H to Seton, April 12, 1792.
2. See H to Seton, April 4, 1792.

To William Short

Treasury Department April 16th 1792

Sir,

The fluctuation of the price of the Stocks in the United States is a circumstance that cannot have failed to attract your attention nor to excite a temporary feeling in the minds of foreigners.[1] Tho' I doubt not it will be well explained by the Agents of those Citizens of other Countries who have vested their Monies in our funds, I think it necessary that some ideas should be communicated to you on which you can found a true opinion either for your own satisfaction or that of persons interested in our National Welfare, with whom you may have occasion to confer.

The moderate size of the domestic debt of the United States appears to have created the most intemperate ideas of speculation in the minds of a very few persons, whose natural ardor has been encreased by great success in some of the early stages of the melioration of the market value of the Stock. To combinations of private Capitals thus acquired or increased, Sums of specie, obtained as well at the most extravagant rates of premium as at common interest, were added, and to these were joined purchases of stock on credits for various terms so as to create a delusive confidence, that the concentration of so much Stock in a few hands would secure a very high Market rate. This expectation was increased by comparing the Market values of the several species of our funds with those of the same species of Stock in Great Britain, the United Netherlands and other parts of Europe, without due allowance for the deductions which should have been made on account of the great difference in the value of Money and the objections arising from our Distance from those European Money holders, whose capitals they expected to attract and other relative circumstances. At the time when many heavy engagements thus formed were becoming due, some contentions among the dealers in and proprietors of the debt took place, and counter combinations were formed to render the crisis of payment and speculation as inconvenient and disadvantageous as possible. By these means, those eventual contracts, it was probably hoped, could be more cheaply complied with, and moreover that a reduced Market would afford further opportunities of beneficial speculation. The extreme indiscretion of the first mentioned speculations and the distress, which, it was manifest, they must produce, excited perhaps and animated the movements of the other party and brought on a scene of private distress for money both Artificial and real which probably has not been equalled in this Country. It happened in the Winter Season when the influx of Cash articles of trade, as returns from abroad, is nearly suspended, and when quantities of specie were sent from the Sea ports to the interior Country for the purchase of produce, to supply the demand for the Spring exportation.

The Banks, who can always perceive the approach of these things, were influenced to limit their operations, and particularly the Bank of the United States, which was then preparing for the opening of its Branches, or offices of discounts and deposit in Boston, New york, Baltimore and Charleston.

The United States, you would presume, could not be insensible of so fit a moment to make purchases of the public Stock, and the Treasurer was accordingly authorized to buy; but tho' the appearances of private distress for money were so great he could not obtain for several days the sum of fifty thousand Dollars, at the highest rates at which the public purchases had before been made. The holders who were free from engagements were averse to selling—the principal persons, who were under engagements, they could not comply with, were obliged or disposed to place their effects in the hands of their Creditors, who did not chuse to add to their own disappointments of great profits actual losses, by unseasonable sales of the Bankrupts property.

The Stock in the Market therefore was really made scarce. A quarters interest has just been paid. Some of the cautious monied people have begun to purchase. The specie is returning from the Country and the heaviest private engagements having now fallen due, the declension of Stock may be considered as arrested. There is little doubt that the difficulty for money among the dealers in the debt will be at no time so great as it has been, after the present week, and that changes of a favorable complexion are to be confidently expected. At first moderate perhaps, afterwards such as will carry the funds up to their due value.

Should you be of opinion that the State of things in France will render some intimation of these events useful there, you will be good enough to communicate them to Mr Morris our Minister at that Court.[2]

I have the honor to be with great consideration   Sir   Your most obedt Servant   Alexander Hamilton

Willm Short Esqr

LS, Hamilton Papers, Library of Congress; LC, William Short Papers, Library of Congress.
1. The "fluctuation of the price of the stocks" followed the panic precipitated by William Duer's business failure in early March, 1792. For background to the panic, see Duer to H, March 12, 1792, note 3; H to Duer, March 14, 23, 1792; Robert Troup to H, March 19, 1792; Philip Livingston to H, March 24, 1792; Philip Schuyler to H, March 25, 1792; William Seton to H, March 21, 1792.
2. Gouverneur Morris had been appointed United States Minister Plenipotentiary to France in January, 1792; however, he did not arrive in Paris until May 6, 1792.

From William Ellery

Newport [Rhode Island] April 17, 1792. "I should have been very happy to have received by the last Post your direction to borrow of the Providence Bank the Sum . . . wanting on the 10th of this month to pay the drawbacks which would then be due on distilled Spirits exported from this District.[1] They who were entitled to receive drawbacks at that time have frequently applied for payment, and complain that it is hard they should be prosecuted if their bonds are not paid on the day they become due, and that their drawbacks should not be discharged with equal punctuality. In my letter of the 26th. of March I mentioned the Sums which . . . would be requisite to pay off all the drawbacks on distilled Spirits, which would be due by the 26th of this month. Inclosed is a more accurate Statement. . . . In my Letter of the 5th of the same month I mentioned the uneasiness of the merchants here occasioned by the difft. mode of taking the tare out of casks of sugar here, and at New York & Philadelphia. Vessels are daily expected here with that article. I wish therefore to receive directions from you on this subject as early as may be. The bond of John Cook[2] . . . is sent to the Distt. Attorney[3] to be put in suit. Caleb Gardner's[4] bond will I expect be paid this day. This would lessen the Sum stated to be provided for. . . ."

LC, Newport Historical Society, Newport, Rhode Island.
1. See Ellery to H, January 16, February 27, March 26, 1792.
2. Cooke was a member of the Board of Assistants of Rhode Island.
3. William Channing.
4. Gardner was a resident of South Kingstown, Rhode Island, and a member of the state Board of Assistants.

Report on the Erection of Public Piers at New Castle, Delaware

Treasury Department
April 17th 1792.
[Communicated on April 19, 1792][1]

[To the Speaker of the House of Representatives]

The Secretary of the Treasury, to whom was referred by the House of Representatives the petition of the Merchants of the City of Philadelphia,[2] respectfully [makes the following Report.][3]

The building of piers at [the town of] New Castle in the Delaware [State] appears to be in the course of improvements and establishments of that nature, which have been long since commenced and pursued at considerable expence by the State of Pennsylvania.

There are commodious piers at two stations in the first eighteen miles below Philadelphia, and none in the next twenty eight miles, wherefore it seems probable, that the improvement now desired will be of great service in the prevention of injury to vessels trading to and from the River Delaware, and in the dispatch of those vessels in the winter season when they are often unable to proceed to their port of destination.

[It is represented that a distance of about 15 Miles is that which a Vessel going up or down the River can conveniently accomplish by force of the Tide when there is either no wind or the wind is unfavorable. An intermediate station at New Castle will nearly correspond with this distance which will enable vessels to make a progress with safety to a situation which from the settings of the River and comparative width is a better point of departure to go down the River than the station above and to go up the River than the Station below. Hence in the winter when sudden frosts create obstructions in the course of twenty four hours, the completion of a voyage may depend on being able to reach the station proposed. It is said to be almost always practicable to find an opportunity of proceeding from thence to Sea and sometimes more easy from local position to get to it in coming up the River, than the station below. It would also in emergencies be more convenient to load vessels there for sea than lower down.]

From an estimate [4] which has been communicated to the Treasury there is reason to presume that the building of the proposed piers will cost about eight thousand dollars, which will be less expensive. as it is represented that the proprietors of the ground proposed for this site of them are willing to transfer a sufficient portion of it without any pecuniary consideration.

The Secretary therefore respectfully suggests, that if there shall not appear to the house any objection to improvements of the nature contemplated at [the present juncture,] the national commerce and revenue will be [likely to be benefitted] by granting the prayer of the petitioners.

All which is humbly submitted.

Df, RG 26, Lighthouse Letters Received, Lighthouse Estimates, Delaware, National Archives; copy, RG 233, Reports of the Treasury Department, 1792–1793, Vol. III, National Archives.

1. *Journal of the House*, I, 581.
2. On February 3, 1791, the House received "A petition of the Merchants of Philadelphia, praying that public piers may be erected at Newcastle, in the State of Delaware, for the better accommodation of the trade in the port of Philadelphia.
"*Ordered*, That the said [petition] . . . be referred to the Secretary of the Treasury, with instruction to examine the same, and report his opinion thereupon to the House." (*Journal of the House*, I, 369.)
3. All material within brackets in the body of this report is in H's handwriting.
4. The estimate was furnished by Thomas Davis, a wharf builder from the District of Southwark, a southern suburb of Philadelphia, on December 28, 1790, and may be found in RG 26, Lighthouse Letters Received, Lighthouse Estimates, Delaware, National Archives.

Report on Exports for the Year Ending September 30, 1791

Treasury Department, April 17, 1792.
[Communicated on April 17, 1792] [1]

[To the Speaker of the House of Representatives]
Sir:

In obedience to an order of the House, of the 2d instant,[2] I transmit an abstract of the goods, wares, and merchandise, exported from each State, from the 1st October, 1790, to the 30th September, 1791.[3]

Alexander Hamilton, Secretary of the Treasury.

The Speaker of the House of Representatives.

ASP, *Commerce and Navigation*, I, 147.
1. *Journal of the House*, I, 580.
2. On April 2, 1792, the House "*Ordered*, That . . . the Secretary of the Treasury be directed to report to this House, in the course of this session, the quantity and value of the exports from each State, any thing in the order of the tenth of November last to the contrary notwithstanding" (*Journal of the House*, I, 556).
3. The abstract of exports, dated April 12, 1792, and signed by Tench Coxe, may be found in ASP, *Commerce and Navigation*, I, 148–55.

Report on Marine Hospitals

[Philadelphia, April 17, 1792
Communicated on April 17, 1792] [1]

[To the Speaker of the House of Representatives]
The Secretary of the Treasury, to whom were referred certain pap-

ers concerning a marine Hospital at the town of Washington in the State of Virginia,[2] and a memorial of the Marine Society of Boston, on the subject of marine Hospitals,[3] respectfully submits the following Report:

The establishment of one or more marine Hospitals in the United States is a measure desirable on various accounts. The interests of humanity are concerned in it, from its tendency to protect from want and misery, a very useful, and, for the most part, a very needy class of the Community. The interests of navigation and trade are also concerned in it, from the protection and relief, which it is calculated to afford to the same class; conducing to attract and attach seamen to the country.

A fund for the purpose may, it is presumed, be most conveniently derived from the expedient suggested in the abovementioned Memorial, namely, a contribution by the mariners and seamen of the United States, out of their wages to be regulated by law.

The rate of the contribution may be ten cents per month for each mariner or seamen, to be reserved, pursuant to articles, by masters of vessels, and paid to the collectors of districts, to which the vessels respectively belong. Effectual regulations for this purpose may, without difficulty be devised.

The benefit of the fund ought to extend, not only to disabled and decrepid seamen, but to the widows and children of those who may have been killed or drowned, in the course of their service as seamen.

It will probably be found expedient, besides the reception and accomodation of the parties entitled, at any hospital which may be instituted to authorize the granting pensions, in aid of those who may be in condition, partly to procure a subsistence from their own labor. There may be cases, in which this mode of relief may be more accommodating to the individuals, and, at the same time, more œconomical.

The Hospital, or if more than one, each Hospital, and its funds, must be placed under the management of a competent number of directors. It is presumed, that for so charitable a purpose, persons will be found, who will be willing without emolument, to execute the trust, but in order to this, it must be rendered as little troublesome as possible, and for this purpose, the number of directors must be considerable. Twenty five, of whom five to be competent to ordinary business, may be an eligible number. Various options will occur to the legislature, as to the mode of constituting the directors, who must, of course, have the power to appoint and compensate certain necessary officers, attendants and servants.

It is suggested in the memorial from the marine Society of Boston, as expedient, to have three Hospitals. But it is not obvious, that one would not for a considerable time, at least, answer the purpose. More would be productive of a greater expense, in the first establishment, and in the subsequent maintenance of it. A plurality would, however, have some advantages arising from the operation of local considerations and feelings.

Preliminarily to a decision, how far it may be expedient to embrace the offer of the marine Hospital at the town of Washington in Virginia, the general principles of the establishment, including the questions of number and locality, will require to be decided by the Legislature.

Should Congress think fit to adopt an arrangement, which will include the town of Washington, as an eligible situation, it will, in the opinion of the Secretary, be advisable, to vest somewhere a power to contract for the building already there. This will probably be found the best mode of reconciling all the considerations which ought to enter into such an arrangement.[4]

All which is respectfully submitted,   Alexander Hamilton
                                        Secretary of the Treasury.
Treasury Department,
April 17th 1792.

Copy, RG 233, Reports of the Treasury Department, 1792–1793, Vol. III, National Archives.

   1. *Journal of the House*, I, 580.
   2. On November 14, 1791, "A member, in his place, produced certain papers respecting the sale and disposition of the Marine Hospital in the State of Virginia; which were read, and ordered to be referred to the Secretary of the Treasury, with instruction to examine the same, and report his opinion thereupon to the House" (*Journal of the House*, I, 453).
   3. On January 27, 1791, the House received "A memorial of the Boston Marine Society, in the Commonwealth of Massachusetts . . . praying that Congress will establish three Marine Hospitals in the United States, for the care and support of disabled seamen; one for the Southern, one for the Middle, and one for the Eastern States" (*Journal of the House*, I, 364). On February 8, 1791, the House "*Ordered*, That the petition of the Marine Society of Boston, which lay on the table, be referred to the Secretary of the Treasury, with instruction to examine the same, and report his opinion thereupon to the next session of Congress" (*Journal of the House*, I, 371).

4. It was not until 1798 that H's proposals in this report were translated into law. See "An Act for the relief of sick and disabled Seamen" (1 *Stat.* 605–07 [July 16, 1798]).

From James Reynolds [1]

Philadelphia 17th. April. 1792.

Sir

I am sorry to be the barer of So disagreeable. an unhappy information. I must tell you Sir that I have bin the most unhappiest man, for this five days in Existance, which you aught to be the last person I ever Should tell my troubls to. ever Sence the night you Calld and gave her the Blank Paper. She has treated me more Cruel than pen cant paint out. and Ses that She is determed never to be a wife to me any more, and Ses that it Is a plan of ours. what has past god knows I Freely forgive you and dont wish to give you fear or pain a moment on the account of it. now Sir I hope you will give me your advise as freely as if Nothing had eve passed Between us I think it is in your power to make matter all Easy again. and I suppose you to be that Man of fealling that you would wish to make every person happy Where it in your power I shall wate to See you at the Office if its Convenant. I am sir with Asteem yours   James Reynolds

Alexr. Hamilton Esqr.

"Reynolds Pamphlet," August 31, 1797.
1. This letter is printed as document No. XV in the appendix of the "Reynolds Pamphlet," August 31, 1797.
For background to this letter, see Reynolds to H, December 15, 17, 19, 22, 1791, January 3, 17, March 24, April 3, 7, 1792; H to Reynolds, December 15, 1791, April 7, 1792; Maria Reynolds to H, December 15, 1791, January 23–March 18, March 24, 1792.

To Wilhem and Jan Willink, Nicholaas and Jacob Van Staphorst, and Nicholas Hubbard

Treasury Department.
April 17th: 1792.

Gentlemen,

The Treasurer of the United States has my authority to draw upon you, at thirty days sight, for 500,000 Guilders in favor of John

Kean Esquire, Cashier of the Bank of the United States, to which you will please to give due honor.

I am &c.   Alexander Hamilton.

Messrs. Willink, Van Staphorst & Hubbard.
Amsterdam.

Copy, RG 233, Reports of the Treasury Department, 1792–1793, Vol. III, National Archives. This letter was enclosed in H's "Report on Foreign Loans," February 13, 1793.

To John Kean

Treasury Department April 18th 1792

Sir

The bills drawn by the Treasurer on the 11th of February upon the Collectors of New London,[1] New Haven [2] and Fairfield,[3] the sale of which I desired to be suspended, by my letter of the 12th ultimo,[4] may now be disposed of.

I am, with consideration   Sir,   Your obedt Servant   A Hamilton

John Kean Esqr
Cashier of the Bank
of the United States

LS, Pierpont Morgan Library, New York City.
    1. Jedediah Huntington.   2. Jonathan Fitch.   3. Samuel Smedley.
    4. Letter not found.

From John Nicholson

[Philadelphia] April 18, 1792. "Major McCowan [1] informs that it is conceived by you that he must settle with Pennsa. his Accot for monies advanced. . . . If you signify this as your opinion his Accot will be taken up, but the monies advanced him have gone forward in our Accounts with the United States, and the fixing such a principle might tend to delay the settlement thereof with the United States."

LC, Division of Public Records, Pennsylvania Historical and Museum Commission, Harrisburg.

1. During the American Revolution John McGowan had served in the first battalion of a Pennsylvania rifle regiment and had subsequently been captain and brigade major of the Fourth Pennsylvania Regiment.

Report on Sundry Petitions

[Philadelphia, April 18, 1792
Communicated on April 21, 1792] [1]

[To the Speaker of the House of Representatives]

The Secretary of the Treasury, to whom were referred by the House of Representatives, the several petitions specified in the list herewith, praying the renewal of certain Certificates, which are alleged to have been destroyed or lost, respectfully makes the following Report thereupon.

The said Secretary, in a report heretofore made to the House of Representatives on a petition of Jacob Rash [2] (a copy of which is annexed) has stated his opinion concerning the propriety of renewing Certificates, which have been destroyed or lost; and concerning the precautions, which ought to accompany relief, in cases, in which it may be deemed proper to grant it.

The paper B contains an abstract of the several petitions specified in the list, and of the proof, where any is produced, which accompanies them, with brief observations on the respective cases.

It, however, merits consideration, whether any certificate ought to be renewed, till the course of the public operations shall have called in all the old ones, which are still outstanding, and till an arrangement now in execution at the treasury, whereby it will be easy to ascertain, what certificates may have been taken in and cancelled, from the earliest period, shall have been completed.

It can rarely happen, that the proof adduced is more than strongly circumstantial, and the cases numbered 18 and 23, in which, Certificates sworn to have been destroyed, have been presented or taken up at the treasury, serve to evince the necessity of peculiar circumspection.

Copy, RG 233, Reports of the Treasury Department, 1792–1793, Vol. III, National Archives.
  1. *Journal of the House,* I, 583. The communicating letter, dated April 20, 1792, may be found in RG 233, Reports of the Treasury Department, 1792–1793, Vol. III, National Archives.
  2. See "Report on the Petition of Jacob Rash," August 5, 1790.

The renewal of any kind of paper, which is negociable to bearer, is in the nature of the thing, liable to considerable danger, and it is to be doubted, whether it may be conformable to usage in similar cases. It is, therefore, though equitable, discretionary on the part of the Government, and it is reasonable, that the doing of it should be accompanied with every precaution necessary for the public safety.

The taking of security, to idemnify the Government from future claims, is a safeguard; but, for obvious reasons, it can never be considered as one which can altogether be relied upon.

All which is humbly submitted   Alexander Hamilton
                  Secry. of the Treasy.

Treasury Department
April 18th 1792.

A.

List of sundry Petitions for the renewal of Certificates reported on to the House of Representatives, April 20th: 1792.

No. 1 Petition of Josias Clapham		No. 13. Petition of Daniel Schermerhorn.
2	" John Higby.	14 " John Craine.
3	" John Elias Moore	15 " Peter Huber.
4	" William Arnold	16 " John Hays.
5	" William Albaugh and ⎱ Margaret Cowell ³ ⎰	17 " Daniel Robbins.
6	" Daniel Freer.	18 " John Pollhemus.
7	" Laurana Richardson &c.	19 " Thomas Donnellan,
8	" Elizabeth Mark.	20 " Stephen Remington
9	" Henry Lee,	21 " Daniel Skillman,⁴
10	" William Graham junr.	22 " John Hayden.
11	" William Baker.	23 " Job Kittredge &c.
12	" William Jones.	24 " William Robinson.

B.

Abstract of the subjects of sundry petitions praying the renewal of Certificates, and Observations thereon.

No. 1.

The petition of Josias Clapham referred 18th November, 1791,[5] sets forth.

That he was possessed of two Certificates issued from the Loan Office of Virginia,

3. Margaret Crowell. 4. Samuel Skillman.
5. *Journal of the House,* I, 457. In the *Journal of the House* Clapham's first name is incorrectly spelled "Josiah."

No. 12, dated 16th. October 1786, for 1632 $\frac{38}{90}$ dollars, in his own name,

231, " 1st. January 1778 . . . 1000. " in the name of Isaac Zane.

One Certificate issued from the Loan Office of Pennsylvania, May 9th. 1778, for 1000 dollars.

Two others issued from the Loan Office of Maryland,

February 12th. 1779, for 500 dollars,

March 23d. 1779, for 200 "

And about 200 dollars in Indents. All of which, he alleges to have been destroyed by the burning of a house in Richmond, on the 2nd. day of January 1788. This he attests by his own oath, and corroborates it, by the oath of Leven Powell, and by a Cerficate of John Hopkins, Commissioner of Loans, as to the burning of the House.

The existence of the first mentioned two Certificates, No. 12 and 231, is proved by the said Commissioner; but nothing is said about the others, being not sufficiently described.

It does not appear, that any proceedings have been had, pursuant to the resolution of Congress, of the 10th. of May 1780.[6]

6. On May 10, 1780, Congress "*Resolved*, That loan office certificates, destroyed through accident, be renewed at the office where they first issued, and delivered to the persons who shall appear to have been the holders of them at the time they were destroyed, on the following terms, viz.

"1. That all certificates so destroyed, be advertised immediately in the news papers of the State where the accident happened; and, if they have been taken out at the loan office of a different State, in the news papers of such State also; and in every case where no news papers are printed in a State, then in one or more of those which circulate most generally therein; which advertisement shall be continued six weeks, and shall contain the numbers, dates, sums, names in which the certificates were taken out, and the time when, the place where, and the means by which they were destroyed.

"2. That a copy of the advertisement be lodged in the loan office whence the certificates issued, together with such testimony as can be procured, ascertaining the time when, the place where, and the means by which the destruction happened; which copies and testimonies shall be duly certified by the loan officer, to be laid by the party claiming the renewal before the Board of Treasury, who shall finally decide on the sufficiency thereof.

"3. That the party claiming the renewal enter into bond to such loan officer on behalf of the United States, with two or more sufficient freeholders, as securities, in double the amount of the value of the certificates claimed to be renewed, with condition to indemnify the United States against the holders of the certificates said to be destroyed, should any such afterwards appear.

"4. That no certificates be renewed before the expiration of three months after the publication of the advertisement above mentioned.

"5. That where a demand is made by virtue of a letter or warrant of attor-

A certificate from the Auditor of the State is produced, intended (as is presumed) to shew, that the State has renewed certain certificates and warrants, which were lost by the same accident. The fact of the destruction is as well proved, as can generally be expected under such circumstances, and relief seems proper in the particular case, if on the general principle, any ought immediately to be granted; accompanying it with the precautions contemplated by the abovementioned resolution. This, however, is only intended to apply to the certificates, the existence of which is, or can be officially ascertained.

No. 2.

The petition of John Higby New York, referred 21st. November 1791,[7] sets forth:

That he was possessed of a Loan Office Certificate, issued from the Loan Office of the State of New York, No. 10,211, dated April 20th. 1779, for three hundred dollars, in his own name.

That the said Certificate was destroyed by fire, in his dwelling-house, on the night of the 16th. of October 1780, when he was taken prisoner by a party of British, and carried to Canada.

No proof whatever is produced, except of the existence of the Certificate, which is established by the public records.

Without more proof, relief could not be granted with propriety.

No. 3.

The petition of John Elias Moore, Charleston, referred 21st. November 1791,[8] sets forth:

That his father, John Moore held, in his own name, the following Loan-Office Certificates of South Carolina, Viz:

No. 96,6744,6745, dated August 12th. 1779, amount, Dollars   2200.

---

ney, such letter or warrant be first legally proved and recorded, and an authenticated copy lodged in the loan office where the demand is made.

"6. That the renewed certificates be of the same tenor and date with those destroyed, and that the payments of interest, where any have been made, be regularly endorsed, as they appear on the loan office books; and that they bear a mark to distinguish them from the originals, which mark shall be entered in the loan office books.

"*Ordered*, That the Board of Treasury prepare and forward to the respective loan officers the form of a bond, with the necessary instructions, to direct them in the execution of the aforesaid resolution; and that they state the sum to be paid by the applicants to the United States for certificates renewed, and the fees to be taken by the loan officer." (*JCC*, XVII, 420–21.)

7. *Journal of the House*, I, 458.   8. *Journal of the House*, I, 458.

1674,1675,1676, " January 14th. 1780, 3 at 1000, each,   3000.

6758, to 6790, " ditto   ditto, 33 at 600, each   19800.

                                                             22.800.

That the said Certificates were taken away, or destroyed by the British in April 1780.

The only proof produced is the oath of the said John Moore.

The existence of the Certificates for the first mentioned 2200 dollars, with a difference of date (being 9th. August 1780,) and of the other sums above stated amounting to 22.800 dollars, appears by the public records.

Relief, in this state of things, cannot safely be given; The oath of an interested party, not corroborated by collateral proof, is an insufficient foundation.

The non appearance, hitherto, of the Certificates is not conclusive proof that they may not appear hereafter; a considerable part of the public Certificates being still unsubscribed.

No. 4.

The petition of William Arnold, Rhode Island, referred November 24th, 1791,[9] sets forth.

That he was possessed of a Loan Office Certificate of Massachusetts, No. 1207, dated October 25th. 1777, for 600 dollars, in the name of Christopher Clarke.

That the said Certificate was burnt with his house and store on the 27th. December 1787, at East Greenwich. The proof of this, is the oath of the party, corroborated as to the burning of the House and Store, by two witnesses.

The existence of the Certificate is proved by official documents.

The Commissioner of Loans of Massachusetts certifies that proceedings under the resolution of Congress have been had, and are deposited in the Loan Office of Massachusetts.

By the Newport Herald it appears, that it has been advertised from the 10th. of October to the 25th. November 1790, and by N. Appleton's certificate, that it has been advertised in one of the Boston papers, the Columbia Centinel, No. 700.

It was not, however, advertised immediately as the resolution requires.

9. Journal of the House, I, 461.

Relief, however, appears proper in the particular case, if, on the general principle, any ought immediately to be granted.

No. 5

The Petition of William Albaugh, and Margaret Crowell, executors of Henry Crowell, of Maryland, referred November 28th. 1791 [10] sets forth:

That the Testator was possessed of the following Certificates, issued from the Loan Office of Maryland, in his name, Viz:

No. 1296. dated April 27th 1779, for 600 dollars,

1299	" do	"	600.	"
1297	" September 3d "		600	"
1298	" do	"	600	
1947	" do	"	500.	

That after the said Certificates were included in the inventory of the estate of the deceased, they were returned into the possession and care of the said Margaret Crowell, widow of the said deceased, since which those three Certificates, dated in September, have been lost or destroyed, and a piece of one of the others dated in April, is torn away and lost, (the other part is produced.) It is suggested, that they have probably been destroyed by the children of the family.

The proof is the oaths of the parties, and that they have not been sold or conveyed, and certified by George Murdock, Register of Frederick County, that the parties stood charged with the said Certificates.

The existence of the Certificates is proved by official vouchers.

No proceedings under the resolution of Congress appear to have been had.

The circumstances appear to be too inconclusive to authorize relief at present. Better evidence may hereafter result from the calling in of all outstanding certificates. This, however, with the exception of the Certificate, part of which is produced; in regard to which, relief appears proper.

No. 6.

The Petition of Daniel Freer, Ulster County, New York, referred, January 5th. 1792,[11] sets forth.

10. *Journal of the House*, I, 464.   11. *Journal of the House*, I, 487.

That he held, in his own name, the following Office Certificates, issued from the Office of New York;

No. 10.298, dated May 27th. 1779, for 300 dollars,

     6.072,   .   "   .   "   .   600.   "

That in the month of June, 1781, his house, furniture and papers, among which were the said Certificates, were destroyed by fire.

The only proof is the oath of the party.

The existence of the Certificates is proved by official vouchers. No proceedings appear to have been had under the resolution.

The proof thus far is defective, no collateral evidence being produced, even of the burning of the house.

No. 7.

The petition of Laurana Richardson, Administratrix of George Richardson deceased, referred January 10th. 1792,[12] sets forth:

That her testator was possessed of a Loan Office certificate, dated 26th. February 1779, for five hundred dollars.

That on the invasion of the State by the enemy, he buried the said Certificate with some other things—that he could not find the certificate, and suggests, that it must have been destroyed by the earth.

No proof is produced.

The evidence of the Certificate is ascertained by official vouchers.

There appears not sufficient ground for relief in this case.

No. 8.

The petition of Elizabeth Mark, widow of George Mark, referred 15th December 1791,[13] sets forth:

That the said George Mark was, in his lifetime, possessed of a Certificate issued from the Loan Office of Pennsylvania,

No. 189, dated January 1st, 1781, for $345 \frac{44}{90}$ dollars.

That William Mark, son of the petitioner, in the month of February 1783, received the said Certificate from his mother, for the purpose of drawing the interest due upon it. That he went from Reading to Philadelphia, in a boat upon the Schuylkill, and that he lost a pocket-book on the way, which contained the said Certificate.

12. *Journal of the House*, I, 490.
13. *Journal of the House*, I, 474. In the *Journal of the House* the surname of both is given as "Marx."

This is attested by the oath of the said William Mark, and is corroborated by the deposition of George Gardner and Peter Steighter. The existence of the Certificate appears by official record.

The propriety of relief in this case will, therefore depend on the determination of the general question, "whether any shall be granted in the case of lost Certificates."

No. 9.

The petition of Henry Lee, of Pennsylvania, referred, January 17th. 1792,[14] sets forth:

That he was possessed of the following Loan Office Certificates, issued from the Office of Pennsylvania, in his own name, Viz:

No. 2593 dated June 11th. 1779 for 1000 dollars.

  589 . "   .   .   .   . " . . 400. "

That about the month of July 1782, he took the said certificates to Philadelphia, in order to draw the interest, but received none. That on his return home, the said Certificates having got wet, he laid them by the fire to dry; that they were attracted by the heat, and instantly burnt.

The proof adduced is the oath of the party, corroborated by the testimony of Jacob Lee his son.

The existence of the Certificates is proved by official vouchers.

No proceedings appear to have been had, pursuant to the resolution of Congress.

The proof is as can be expected in any similar case, and relief appears to be proper, if, on the general principle, any ought immediately to be granted, accompanying it with the precautions contemplated by the above mentioned resolutions.

No. 10.

The petition of William Graham junior, Philadelphia, referred January 31st. 1792,[15] sets forth.

That he was possessed of the following Loan Office Certificates—

No. 194 dated October 13th. 1779, for 10.000. dollars, payable to

Francis Lee of Philadelphia

---

14. *Journal of the House*, I, 492. In the *Journal of the House* the surname is given as "Ley."
15. *Journal of the House*, I, 500.

519 " March 8th. 1779, 600 dollars, payable to Edmund Custis Virginia.

That on the 20th. November 1779, he placed the said Certificates into the hands of William Graham, of Philadelphia, merchant, as per receipt produced, to be by him delivered to Samuel Montgomery Brown, at Saint Eustatia, for which place, the said William Graham was to sail, in the ship Lady Washington. That the said ship did sail on the 26th. of November, and on the 4th. December, was captured by the Roebuck.

That the said Certificates, being in a leather saddle-bag, got wet and were destroyed.

The proof adduced is the oath of the said William Graham, made the 19th. of January last.

The existence of the Certificates is proved by official vouchers.

The great distance of time between the fact and the proof, is a material objection to it. The objection too is strengthened by the responsibility of the deponent for the Certificates entrusted to him.

It would not appear proper to grant relief in such a case; at least till the calling in of all outstanding Certificates shall have furnished a confirmation.

No 11.

The petition of William Baker, New Jersey, referred, 22d February 1792,[16] sets forth:

That on the 11th. of February 1779, he received two Loan Office Certificates, issued in his name by Joseph Borden;

No. 2120, for 300 dollars.

4768 " 600 dollars.

That on the same day, he delivered them into the hands of his mother, Judith Baker, to take care of them. That she put them in a Cupboard drawer. That some time in the month of October 1781, the said Judith discovered that the Certificates above mentioned, and other papers, were entirely destroyed by rats or other vermin.

The proof adduced is the oath of the said Judith Baker, of the 7th. of February 1792, which testifies the delivery of the Certificates to her, her having put them in the Cupboard, and the destruction by

16. *Journal of the House,* I, 517.

vermin of the papers, which were in the drawer, but admits that there were no remains of the Certificates left to distinguish them from other papers.

The existence of the Certificates is proved by James Ewing; and that they had not been presented on the 4th. of February 1792: The same is proved by records in the Auditor's office.

A certificate of Isaac Collins, printer, of an Advertisement having been inserted six weeks, is also produced.

The proof in this case, though not conclusive, is so strong as to justify relief, if on the general principle, it is deemed advisable to grant immediate relief.

No. 12.

The petition of William Jones, Maryland, referred, March 12th. 1792,[17] sets forth:

That he was possessed of the following Loan Office Certificates, issued from the Office of Maryland; Viz:

No. 4564, dated February 15th. 1779, for 600 dollars, issued to Thomas Graham.

1094 1095	"	August 24th. 500 dollars each, 1000.
2012	"	November 24th . . . . 500.
3339	"	ditto 1000

3100 dollars.

That on the 26th March 1782, his house was consumed by fire, and with it the said Certificates.

The proof adduced is the oath of the party, corroborated by the deposition of Michael Jenifer Stone, as to the good character of the party, and the burning of the house.

The existence of the Certificates is proved by an official Certificate of the Commissioner of Loans.

No proceedings appear to have been had under the resolution of Congress.

The proof in this case is as satisfactory, as can well be expected in a similar case, and relief will be proper, if, on the general principle, immediate relief in any such case, is deemed advisable.

17. *Journal of the House*, I, 534.

No 13.

The petition of Daniel Schermerhorn, New York, referred November 22d. 1791,[18] sets forth.

That he purchased of one David Root a final settlement Certificate, signed by John Pierce, No. 29.158, for 80 dollars. That children got hold of some papers, and the said Certificate not being found among them, it is supposed to have been thrown in the fire, of which no other proof, than the oath of the party, is produced.

The existence of the Certificate appears by official records. No proceedings appear to have been had under the resolution of Congress.

The evidence here is too vague and inconclusive to justify relief without further light.

No. 14.

The petition of John Craine, Virginia, referred November 22d. 1791,[19] sets forth.

That he was possessed of a final settlement Certificate, issued the 13th. of August 1784, in the name of James Swart, No. 80.314, for 100 dollars. That the Certificate was destroyed in his waistcoat pocket, when in the wash, about two years ago.

The proof adduced is the oath of the party, corroborated by no collateral evidence.

The existence of the Certificate appears by official records.

The evidence here does not appear sufficient. The final calling in of outstanding Certificates may afford further light.

No. 15.

The petition of Peter Huber, Pennsylvania, referred November 23d. 1791,[20] sets forth.

That he was possessed of a certain Certificate, signed by Benjamin Stelle, which was upwards of twenty pounds, but the number and exact sum he does not remember. That the said Certificate with others, got wet in crossing Perkioming Creek, and was burnt in the

18. *Journal of the House*, I, 458.   19. *Journal of the House*, I, 458.
20. *Journal of the House*, I, 459.

attempt of drying it, at the house of Jacob Meisinger at Philadelphia. No proof of this, nor of its existence. No ground for relief.

No. 16.

The petition of John Hays, Virginia, referred December 15th. 1791,[21] sets forth:

That he received from the Commissioner of Accounts in Virginia, two Certificates; the one for 1000 dollars, and the other for 1910. $21\frac{1}{90}$ dollars, as part of his commutation.

That on the first Tuesday in March 1791, his house was burned, and among other valuable papers, the said Certificates.

The proof is the oath of the party, corroborated by the oaths of three different persons.

The existence of the Certificates is proved by an Official voucher.

The proof is as full as can be expected in similar cases, and relief is proper, if it is deemed advisable, on the general principle, to grant relief immediately in any such case.

No. 17.

The petition of Daniel Robbins junior, Massachusetts, referred November 3d. 1791,[22] sets forth.

That he was possessed of a final settlement Certificate in the name of Jacob Hart, dated January 1st. 1781, for 80 dollars. That on the 4th. of June 1788, his house was consumed by fire, and the said Certificate burnt in it.

The facts alleged are proved by the oath of the party, and corroborated by a Certificate of George Comings and Jonathan Whiting, selectmen of Winthrop; but the Certificate alleged to have been burnt is not sufficiently identified. And its existence is not proved by any official document. There is, therefore, not sufficient ground for relief.

No. 18.

The petition of John Polhemus, New Jersey, referred 31st. January 1792,[23] sets forth.

21. *Journal of the House*, I, 474.   22. *Journal of the House*, I, 457.
23. *Journal of the House*, I, 500.

That on the 24th. of July 1786, he received a final settlement certificate, issued in his name by John Pierce, No. 94.167, for 284 $^{2}\%_{90}$ths dollars, on interest from the 1st. September 1777.

That some time after, he trusted the said Certificate in the hands of Captain Daniel Baldwin, to draw the interest on the same, at the proper office in New York. That interest was paid up to the 31st. December 1784. That some time in February 1787, the said certificate was accidentally destroyed by fire, while in possession of said Daniel Baldwin. Proof is made by the oath of Daniel Baldwin, that it was burnt, but how, or where, is not stated.

The existence of the Certificate appears from Pierce's register, in the Auditor's office; and on the register it is noted by Guilian Mc.Evers, formerly a Clerk in the Office, that it has been presented since by George Service.

There appears, therefore, to have been a misrepresentation, and no ground for relief.

No. 19.

The petition of Thomas Donnellan, Baltimore, referred February 3d. 1792,[24] sets forth.

That a Certificate was issued to him by the late Quarter Master General, for 308 dollars.

That the said Certificate was accidentally burnt with the dwelling house of the petitioner, and all his effects in the month of December 1788.

There is no proof of the fact, nor any of the existence of the Certificate. Therefore no ground for relief, independent of any objection to the kind of Certificate.

No. 20.

The petition of Stephen Remington, of Providence, referred February 20th. 1792,[25] sets forth.

That in the month of November 1786, he was possessed of a final settlement certificate, issued by John Pierce in the name of Philip Slew, No. 27.340, dated March 1st. 1784 for 80 dollars.

That the said Certificate in the said month of November, was

24. *Journal of the House*, I, 501.   25. *Journal of the House*, I, 511.

taken out of his desk, by one John Whitby, while in liquor, by whom it was thrown into the fire, with sundry other papers, and consumed.

The proof adduced is the oath of the party, corroborated by that of Rufus Humphrey.

The existence of the certificate appears by record in the Auditor's Office, where it stands dated 20th. January 1784.

The proof is as fully as could be expected from the nature of the case. Relief, therefore, on the usual conditions, would be proper, if, on the general principle, it is deemed, at present, advisable in any such case.

No. 21.

The memorial of Samuel Skillman, New Jersey, referred 22d February 1792,[26] sets forth.

That he received a Certificate for services signed by Benjamin Thompson, Commissioner New Jersey, No. 1787, dated 23d. December, 1784, for 588 dollars.

That in the month of August 1785, his house was burnt with all his property, and the Certificate.

The proof adduced is the oath of the party, corroborated by a certificate of sundry persons.

The existence of the Certificate is proved by the Commissioner and Treasurer of the State, and by record in the Auditor's Office.

The proof is as satisfactory, as can be well expected in a similar case; and relief will be proper, on the usual conditions, if, on the general principle, it is deemed advisable at present in any such case.

No. 22

The petition of John Hayden, Pennsylvania, referred 23d. February 1792,[27] sets forth.

That some time in the year 1784, or 1785, he purchased a certificate issued by Jonathan Burrall, to George Emmell, No. 55, for 267 dollars.

---

26. *Journal of the House,* I, 517. In the *Journal of the House* the petitioner is cited as "John Skillman."
27. *Journal of the House,* I, 518.

That the said Certificate was destroyed by accident, on the 26th. day of August 1785.

The proof consists of a certificate of George Emmell, testifying the sale of the certificate in question to the petitioner, and of a deposition of William Nixon, stating that the deponent and petitioner were working in a field; that the petitioner had laid off his jacket; that some cattle being in the field, one of them got hold of the jacket, and eat the pocket, in which was a pocket book containing the said certificate, as was, at the time of the accident, asserted by the petitioner. That, on examination, they found a small piece of the pocket book, the other part being destroyed.

The existence of the Certificate appears from official records.

Further light in this case, from the final calling in of outstanding Certificates, appears to be necessary towards granting relief with safety.

No. 23.

The petition of Job Kittredge, Ebenezer Whittemore and Martha Whittemore, heirs of William Kittredge deceased, referred February 27th. 1792,[28] sets forth:

That the said William Kittredge was, in his life time, possessed of a final settlement certificate, issued to John Paris, dated March 1st. 1784, No. 33.162 for 80 dollars. That the said Job Kittredge was owner of another final settlement certificate, issued to Palfrey Down, bearing the same date, No. 32.627 for 90 dollars, and another final settlement certificate, issued to Benjamin Baldwin, dated May 1st. 1784, No. 58.892, for 26 dollars, and an indent, issued by Nathaniel Appleton, for 20 dollars.

That all these Certificates were burnt on the 25th. of April 1788, with the dwelling house of the deceased.

No proof is produced of the facts alleged.

The existence of the Certificates, except the indent, appears by official records. But it appears, that the first mentioned Certificate No. 33.162, was taken up by the late Board of Treasury, and a Register's certificate given for it. Therefore, there appears to be misrepresentation, and no ground for relief.

28. *Journal of the House*, I, 521.

No. 24.

The petition of William Robinson, Connecticut, referred January 11th. 1792,[29] sets forth.

That he obtained from Captain Simeon Spalding, on certain conditions, as stated in the receipt therewith produced, bearing date, 18th. September 1783, a final settlement certificate, issued by John Pierce, to said Simeon Spalding, for 760 dollars, interest from the 22nd. March 1783.

That the petitioner delivered the said Certificate into the hands of Captain John Cady, who was going to New York, for the purpose of buying goods, with said Certificate for the petitioner.

That he purchased, however, no goods, returned by water, and accidentally fell overboard, and was never afterwards found; and that his pocket book, with all his papers, and the note aforesaid, were lost with him.

The facts alleged are circumstantially proved by the Oaths of the petitioner, of Robert Lightfood, and Joanna Cady.

The existence of the Certificate appears by official records.

There are various possibilities in this case, which would render it particularly unsafe to renew the Certificate, without farther light from the final calling in of outstanding Certificates.

No. 25.

The petition of Henry Bass,[30] Boston, referred July 26th: 1790,[31] sets forth.

That he was owner and possessor of a Continental Loan Office Certificate, issued by Derick Ten Broek, Commissioner for the State of New York, dated March 13th. 1778, for 600 dollars, number not ascertained.

That in the year 1781, he delivered the said Certificate to John Waite, for the purpose of receiving at New York, the interest due thereon.

That the said John Wait lost the said Certificate with a pillow

29. *Journal of the House*, I, 491.
30. This petition is not among those listed in list "A" of this report and is not mentioned in the *Journal of the House*, I, 583, as being among the petitions in this report.
31. *Journal of the House*, I, 279.

case, in which it was kept, with some other papers at Tarrytown. The proof adduced is the affidavit of John Wait.

The Certificate not being sufficiently identified, by the description, its existence cannot be ascertained.

It appears from the register of the Commissioner in the Auditor's office, that no such Certificate was ever issued to Henry Bass, himself.

In this uncertainty, there is no ground for relief. It can never be determined, (taking the loss alledged for granted) that the Certificate may not have been found, and either taken up and cancelled, or exist a claim against the United States.

From Joseph Whipple

Portsmouth [New Hampshire] April 18, 1792. "I have to inform you of a Seizure that has taken place in this district of a Small quantity of Coffee, unladed contrary to Law from the Sch Adventure Edward Tredick Master from St Martins. The discovery was made by the officers of the Scammel then laying in the harbour about one Mile within the light house—who observed a boat go alongside of the Adventure when a Mile without the harbour. The boat was followd on her return by the Master of the Cutter [1] who took possession of three Small boxes or parcells of Coffee which had been landd from her. The Coffee on inquiry appears to have belonged to one of the Seaman. . . ."

LC, RG 36, Collector of Customs at Portsmouth, Letters Sent, 1791–1792, Vol. III, National Archives; copy, RG 56, Letters from the Collector at Portsmouth, National Archives.
1. Hopley Yeaton was captain of the revenue cutter Scammell.

From Otho H. Williams

[Baltimore, April 18, 1792. On June 5, 1792, Hamilton wrote to Williams: "I have before me your letters of the 18th of March, 18th of April, 8th & 27th of May." Letter of April 18 not found.]

To Thomas Jefferson

[Philadelphia, April 19, 1792]

Mr. Hamilton requests Mr. Jefferson to inform him whether he has received from Mr. Hamilton's Office copies of the correspondence between Mr. Ternant & him concerning the advance of the 400.000 Dollars.[1] These copies were prepared sometime since & it is not ascertained whether they have been mislaid or forwarded to Mr. Jefferson. A line in answer will oblige.

April 19

AL, Thomas Jefferson Papers, Library of Congress.
    1. See Jean Baptiste de Ternant to H, February 21, March 8, 10, 1792; H to Ternant, March 8, 11, 12, 1792.
    For information on the advance of four hundred thousand dollars, see H to William Short, April 10, 1792.

To Thomas Jefferson

[Philadelphia, April 19, 1792]

The following are the material facts in relation to the case of Rutgers agt. Waddington,[1] as far as they are now recollected, and a confidence is entertained, that the statement is substantially accurate.

The suit was brought in the Mayor's court of the City of New York,[2] for the occupation and injury of a brewhouse in that City, during the possession of it by the British army founded upon an act of the State of New York, entitled "An act for granting a more effectual relief in cases of certain trespasses"[3] which gives remedy by action of trespass, to all citizens who had resided without the enemy's lines, against those who had resided within those lines, wherever the property of the former had been occupied, injured, destroyed, purchased, or received by the latter, declaring "that no defendant should be admitted to plead in justification, any military order or command whatever of the enemy, for such occupancy, injury, destruction, purchase or receipt, nor to give the same in evidence on the general issue." This act was passed subsequent to the provisional, but prior to the definitive treaty.

The fact was that the defendant had occupied the brewhouse in question, under regular authority of the British army, proceeding for a part of the time, immediately from the commander in chief,[4] and for another part of it, from the Qr. Master General,[5] and had even paid rent for the use of it.

Several pleas were pleaded, for the different portions of time, corresponding with the State of the fact, one alledging the occupation, under the immediate order of the commander in chief, the other under that of the Quarter Master General.

The particulars of the pleas appear to be accurately stated in Mr Hammond's memorial.[6]

The court allowed the plea, which alledged the occupation, under the immediate authority of the commander in chief, and overruled the other, giving judgement for the plaintiff for the portion of time covered by the latter. The ground of distinction, was that it could not be in the course of service, for a Quarter Master General to let out Brew houses. The force of the treaty to overrule the inhibition against pleading a military order, was admitted by the decision, which allowed in fact the validity of such an order, when proceeding from the commander in chief.

But a writ of error was brought by the defendant to reverse the judgement in the supreme Court, and pending that writ, a *voluntary compromise* between the parties took place, which superceded its prosecution to a final decision. A sum of money was paid by the defendant, in consequence of this compromise.

It is however but candor to acknowledge, that from the uncertainty of the event, the desire of the defendant to compromise, as a prudential course, was not discouraged by his Counsel.

It is not recollected that any decision ever took place, in the Supreme Court of the State, giving effect to the inhibition above mentioned. It is believed that none ever did. The exceptionable clause was repealed by the Act of the 4th. of April 1787;[7] which put an end to the question.

I acted as Attorney and Counsel for the defendant.[8]

Alexander Hamilton.

Philadelphia April 19. 1792:

Letterpress copy, Thomas Jefferson Papers, Library of Congress; copy, Adams Family Papers, deposited in the Massachusetts Historical Society, Boston.

1. Shortly after George Hammond presented his credentials as British Minister to the United States, Jefferson proposed that he and Hammond begin negotiations by each specifying the fashion in which the other's country had violated the peace treaty of 1783 (see "Conversation with George Hammond," January 2–9, 1792). On March 5, 1792, Hammond wrote a letter to the Secretary of State which contained a detailed indictment of the refusal of the United States to fulfill its treaty obligations (*ASP, Foreign Relations*, I, 193–200). Among the court decisions which Hammond considered as contravening the treaty was the New York case of *Rutgers* v *Waddington*. As H had represented Joshua Waddington in the case brought by Elizabeth Rutgers, Jefferson asked H for information on the case to be used in his reply to Hammond. H's recollection of *Rutgers* v *Waddington* appears as Item No. 46 in the letter Jefferson wrote to Hammond on May 29, 1792, which was among the documents submitted by Washington to Congress on December 5, 1792 (*ASP, Foreign Relations*, I, 141–246).

2. The Mayor's Court in New York City was convened late in February, 1784. *Rutgers* v *Waddington* was one of the first cases brought before the court.

3. *Laws of the State of New York*, I, 552 (March 17, 1783).

4. Sir Henry Clinton.

5. H is referring to the commissary general, who was Daniel Wies.

6. See note 1.

7. "An Act to repeal part of an act, entitled 'An Act for granting a more effectual relief, in cases of certain trespasses'" (*Laws of the State of New York*, II, 496 [April 4, 1787]).

8. H's account of *Rutgers* v *Waddington* should be compared with the account in Goebel, *Law Practice*, I, 282–419, and in Richard B. Morris, ed., *Select Cases of the Mayor's Court of New York City, 1674–1784* (Washington, 1935), 57–59, 302–27.

From Thomas Jefferson

Philadelphia Apr. 19. 1792.

Sir

In consequence of letters received from mr William Short on the subject of his property invested in the public funds, I am to desire that no transfer may be permitted of any stock standing in his own name, or in the name of any other for his use.[1]

I have the honor to be with perfect esteem & respect Sir Your most obedient & most humble sert.   Th: Jefferson

The Secretary of the treasury.

ALS, letterpress copy, Massachusetts Historical Society, Boston; copy, Thomas Jefferson Papers, Library of Congress.

1. On April 24, 1792, after describing the financial panic, Jefferson wrote to Short: ". . . I have been unable to refrain from interposing for you on the present occasion. . . . Under the impulse therefore of the general panic, I ventured to enter a caveat in the treasury office against permitting the transfer of any stock standing in your name or in any other for your use. This was on the 19th of April . . ." (Ford, *Writings of Jefferson*, 511).

Report on the Petition of Eliphalet Ladd

[Philadelphia, April 19, 1792
Communicated on April 20, 1792] [1]

[To the Speaker of the House of Representatives]
The Secretary of the Treasury to whom was referred the Memorial of Eliphalet Ladd,[2] respectfully makes the following Report thereupon.

It has been made a question, whether under the laws of the United States, as they now stand, duties are payable on goods imported in vessels which have suffered shipwreck in the act of transportation. A suit, in which this question is involved, is depending in one of the Courts of the United States.

But the terms of the law have rendered it the duty of the Officers of the customs to advance the claim, which has been done on all the occasions that have hitherto occurred.

The casualty of shipwreck is so affecting a calamity, and is usually attended with such considerable loss to the concerned, that the exacting from the sufferers, the public dues on the articles which escape, is apt to be regarded as partaking of severity and oppression.

The provision for the case of damaged goods is not always a sufficient remedy. It may happen that the goods saved are not damaged, though a large proportion may have been entirely lost.

It would seem, upon the whole, expedient, either entirely to remit the duties in every case of shipwreck, or to vest somewhere a power, either to remit, or abate, according to the circumstances of each case.

The last would best consist with a due apportionment of the degree of relief, to the degree of suffering. From the rareness of the casualty, the loss to the revenue, from either arrangement, could not be very material.

The case stated in the petition appears to be a strong one for relief.[3]

All which is humbly Submitted,   Alexander Hamilton.
Secry. of the Treasy.

Treasury Department
April 19th 1792.

Copy, RG 233, Reports of the Treasury Department, 1792–1793, Vol. III, National Archives.

1. *Journal of the House,* I, 583. The communicating letter, dated April 19, 1792, may be found in RG 233, Reports of the Secretary of the Treasury, 1792–1793, Vol. III, National Archives.

2. On April 16, 1792, the House received "A petition of Eliphalet Ladd, praying a remission of the duties on a small quantity of goods saved from the wreck of a ship, the property of the petitioner, which was lost on the coast of Massachusetts in March last.

"*Ordered,* That the said petition be referred to the Secretary of the Treasury, with instruction to examine the same, and report his opinion thereupon to the House." (*Journal of the House,* I, 578.)

3. In accordance with H's recommendation, on May 1, 1792, the House of Representatives passed "An Act to authorize the remission of certain duties." The measure was, however, rejected by the Senate (*Journal of the House,* I, 586, 593, 596).

To George Washington

Treasury Department April 19th. 1792.

The Secretary of the Treasury has the honor to transmit to the President a copy of his letter of the 8th. of March to the Minister plenipotentiary of France, on the subject of an advance of money, and another of the Minister's answer;[1] in order that the President may be pleased to cause the necessary instructions to be sent through the proper Department to the Minister plenipotentiary of the United States, at the Court of France.[2]

Copy, Columbia University Libraries; letterpress copy, Thomas Jefferson Papers, Library of Congress; LC, RG 59, Diplomatic and Consular Instructions of the Department of State, National Archives.

1. H to Jean Baptiste de Ternant, March 8, 1792, and Ternant to H, March 10, 1792.

2. Gouverneur Morris.

To Henry Van Schaack

Treasury Department April 20th 1792

Sir,

I received your letter of the 1st of February [1] shortly after its date, and have duly noticed the remarks it contained on the subject of manufactures, which will not fail to recur when the Legislature shall have time to go into the Consideration of the proposed arrangements.[2] The business yet to be transacted will not admit of their further attention to my report than the giving such modification to the ways and means recently required, as will encourage this interesting branch of the national industry.[3] The bill has nearly made its progress thro the house of Representatives in a form calculated as well to produce that effect as the necessary supplies.

The specimens of carpeting [4] which were very acceptable were immediately placed in the Committee room of the house of Representatives among a Collection of specimens of American manufactures transmitted to the Treasury from several of the States.

I am, Sir, with great consideration & Esteem [5] Your most obedt Servant   A Hamilton

H. V. Schaack Esqr.
Pittsfield
Massachusetts

LS, Mr. Hall Park McCullough, North Bennington, Vermont.
   1. Letter not found.
   2. This is a reference to H's "Report on the Subject of Manufactures," December 5, 1791.
   3. This is a reference to H's "Report Relative to the Additional Supplies for the Ensuing Year," March 16, 1792. The report and the congressional act based on it provided for an increase of three and one-half percent on ad valorem duties imposed on carpets and carpeting (1 Stat. 260 [May 2, 1792]).
   4. According to Van Schaack's nephew, "The first domestic carpeting manufactured in Berkshire county was made under the direction of Mrs. Van Schaack, and a parcel forwarded to the secretary of the treasury" (Henry Cruger Van Schaack, Memoirs of the Life of Henry Van Schaack [Chicago, 1892], 176).
   5. The words "& Esteem" are in the handwriting of H.

Report on the Petition of Robert Neill

[Philadelphia April 21, 1792
Communicated on April 21, 1792] [1]

[To the Speaker of the House of Representatives]

The Secretary of the Treasury to whom was referred the petition of Robert Niel,[2] respectfully makes the following report thereupon.

It is stated by the petitioner, that pursuant to an order which he received from Clement Biddle, Deputy Quarter Master General, in the month of April 1777, a capture was made of a number of horses and cattle, for the use of the armies of the United States. That fifteen of the horses and ten of the cattle were actually carried to Head Quarters, and placed in the yard of the deputy Quarter General.

That the said petitioner, agreeably to the instructions he received from General Stevens,[3] and to the usage of the army, caused the horses and cattle to be appraised, and the amount thereof to be paid to the officers of the party who captured them.

That he exhibited an account to the proper officers of the Treasury, for the sum of six hundred pounds, or thereabouts, paid to the officer aforesaid, accompanied with vouchers, as set forth in the said petition, and that the account was rejected by the Auditor [4] and Comptroller of the Treasury.

Copy, RG 233, Reports of the Treasury Department, 1792–1793, Vol. III, National Archives.

1. *Journal of the House*, I, 585. The communicating letter may be found in RG 233, Reports of the Treasury Department, 1792–1793, Vol. III, National Archives.

2. On January 20, 1791, the House received "A petition of Robert Neill, praying relief against the determination of the Auditor and Comptroller of the Treasury on a claim which he has exhibited against the United States. . . .

"*Ordered*, That the said . . . [petition] be referred to the Secretary of the Treasury, with instruction to examine the same, and report his opinion thereupon to the House." (*Journal of the House*, I, 358.)

3. H mistakenly wrote "Stevens" for "Stephen." H is referring to Adam Stephen of Virginia, who was appointed a major general on February 19, 1777, and dismissed from the service on November 20, 1777

4. Oliver Wolcott, Jr., was appointed auditor of the Treasury in September, 1789. On November 7, 1791, he succeeded Nicholas Eveleigh as comptroller of the Treasury. Eveleigh died in April, 1791.

The petitioner, conceiving himself aggrieved by the said determination, of the Officers of the Treasury, therefore, prays that relief may be afforded him by the Legislature.

The following reasons, which guided the late Comptroller of the Treasury, in the decision of this case, have been stated to the Secretary, to wit: In the settlement of the accounts of the said Robert Niel as Assistant Quarter Master, he has obtained credit for sundry disbursements, including his pay from the 15th day of February to the 15th day of August 1777, in the sum of 7935. $^{68}/_{100}$ths dollars, and stands charged for cash received by him at sundry times, to the amount of 7885. $^{15}/_{100}$ dollars, leaving a balance due to the said Robert Niel, of 50. $^{53}/_{100}$ dollars, with interest, at 6 $\mathcal{P}$ cent per annum, from the 15th day of June 1777. Among other credits claimed by him, is that which is the subject of his petition. The circumstances connected with this claim are as follow.

The claim itself is for 15 horses, and ten head of cattle, taken from the enemies lines in April 1777, and delivered to the order of Colonel Biddle, Deputy Quarter Master General, for the use of the army, at the appraised price of 1500 dollars, which sum is represented to have been paid to the captors by order of General Stevens. The evidence produced in support of this claim being judged inconclusive and unsatisfactory, it was not admitted. The reasons, which particularly operated against the admission, were, that no receipt has been produced by Mr. Niel, from the Deputy Quarter Master General's department, for the delivery of the cattle, nor has any appraisement appeared of their value. Receipts have been produced for the payment of 2075. $^{17}/_{100}$ dollars, to several officers, for the dividend of the troops who were captors, which receipts specify, that the monies arose from the sales of property taken, as above stated. But there is no regular account of the property taken, nor has Mr. Niel shewn how far the monies paid by him were received from the sales made by himself. The proof adduced to shew the delivery of the cattle and horses, to Colonel Biddle, consists of affidavits recently taken.

By a paper found among the vouchers to Colonel Biddle's accounts, it appears, that on the 5th of April 1777, nine horses were appraised, by his direction, and that the appraisement amounted to £245: subjoined to the statement thereof, is an order, signed C.

Biddle, D. Q. M. G. for payment of the amount to Captain William Briton, one of the captors. A circumstance, which strongly indicates, that those horses were taken on the same expedition, to which this charge is referred by Mr. Niel. It does not appear that any cattle were paid for by Colonel Biddle, but, as he was not in the Commissary's department, it was not in the line of his duty to pay for them.

It is observable, that the entry, made in Mr. Niel's books, of this transaction, appears, from the color of the ink, and difference of characters, to have been written lately. It is out of its proper place, immediately preceding an entry of the 19th of March, whereas the transaction itself did not take place, till about the 10th of April.

From a conference between the Comptroller and Colonel Biddle, on the subject of this claim, the following information results.

That it was the general practice, whenever any captured cattle or horses were brought to the Quarter Master or Commissary, for the use of the army, to give a receipt for them to the party delivering the same, and to have a certified appraisement made of them immediately, and also to pay the amount of such appraisement to the captors, if they had money, or to give some certificate, that such amount was due, if they had none. That in the spring 1777, the time of this capture, there was plenty of money in the hands of the proper officers for the purpose; and that if Mr. Niel had presented his account, he would, upon application, most assuredly have obtained payment.

That, upon the whole, it appeared highly improbable, that an individual should have paid 1500 dollars, equal to specie, on account of the United States, without a previous receipt of the amount from the proper officers, or without subsequent application for reimbursement, when the means of obtaining the former, or of successfully urging the latter, were so clearly within his power. And although it had been represented, that Mr. Niel conducted himself, as Assistant Quarter, with much zeal and activity; although the inexperience of the period, in which the transaction happened, might palliate for some deviation from forms, yet, considering that Mr. Niel, in support of his claim, had produced no invoice of the property captured, no receipt for the delivery, either from the Quarter Master, or Commissary department, no instrument of Appraisement

—When it was considered, that the advance was greater than an individual would probably make without a voucher, and without immediate application for reimbusement (which, in the opinion of Colonel Biddle, would have been obtained, if it had been applied for) When, along with these circumstances, the suspicious appearance of the entry had been taken into consideration by the late Comptroller, he had been induced to decide against the claim.

Under this representation of the case, the Secretary is of opinion, that the reasons for not admitting the claim of the petitioner, were good and sufficient, and that no special interposition of the Legislature in his favor is advisable.[5]

All which is humbly submitted,   Alexander Hamilton
                                                 Secry. of the Treasy.
Treasury Department
April 21st 1792.

5. H's report was received by the House on April 21, 1792. On April 24, 1792, "The House proceeded to consider the report of the Secretary of the Treasury on the petition of Robert Neil: Whereupon, *Resolved*, That the prayer of the petitioner, praying relief against the determination of the Auditor and Comptroller of the Treasury, on a claim which he has exhibited against the United States, cannot be granted" (*Journal of the House*, 586).

To William Duer

[Philadelphia] April 22, 1792

My Dear Duer

I hoped ere this to have seen you, to have afforded you whatever of aid could have resulted from my advice after knowing your real situation.[1] But the session protracts itself & I can scarcely say when it will finish. Lest the information contained in my last[2] should induce you to postpone any arrangement with your Creditors, in the hope of speedily having an opportunity of consulting me I have thought it best to apprise you of the degree of delay which may attend my proposed visit to New York. Indeed I can hardly flatter myself that my advice could be of any real importance to you.

How are you? How are your family? At a moment of composure I shall be glad to hear from you.

Eliza joins me in affectionate remembrances to Lady Kitty.[3] Farewell   A Hamilton

JCH Transcripts.
1. This is a reference to Duer's bankruptcy. Duer suspended payments on March 9, 1792, and was imprisoned for debt on March 23, 1792.
2. H to Duer, March 23, 1792.
3. "Lady Kitty" was Duer's wife, Catharine, and the daughter of the late William Alexander of Basking Ridge, New Jersey. See H to Duer, March 23, 1792, note 6.

From William Short

Paris April 22. 1792.

Sir
Since my last of the 24th. ulto. the decree which I then, announced to you as being soon to take place, with respect to the supplies for S. Domingo, has been passed. Instead of adopting the proposition of the former minister of Marine, M. de Bertrand,[1] they confined themselves to vote six millions of livres to be applied as relief for S: Domingo, by the Minister of that department.[2] He has determined that a certain sum should be employed in purchases in the U.S. & has therefore applied to me to know if I could take on me to stipulate for our government that they would furnish the money in America on account of our debt to France.

After this decree had been so long delayed I had hoped it would not be passed before the arrival of Mr. Morris,[3] & particularly as I had learned that the Senate had confirmed the nomination of the President, & of course expected him here daily, having written to him how much I was averse to acting in a place after having learned that it was the will of Government that it should be confided to another.[4]

The ministry having made this application to me however, & the business not admitting of delay, I considered it my duty to act in it, on account of the advantage it presents to the U.S. of converting a part of this debt into a fund to be employed in the purchases of their own productions. I could have no doubt of the expediency of the measure as the last loan had been detained in the hands of the bankers of the U.S.[5] in the expectation of its being employed in this way, & as this was conformable to the desire of Mr. Morris, who is now to act in the business & of course if here would take the measures which I have done in compliance with the wishes of the ministry.

It was an inconvenience in fixing the sum to be furnished by the U.S. in livres, as I wished to avoid regulating the rate of exchange. Accordingly in my answer to the minister I engaged that a certain sum, which has been since fixed at 800,000 dollars should be held by you at the disposition of France for the purchase of supplies in America for S. Domingo—the exchange to be regulated hereafter between the two countries. In consequence thereof I have since had a meeting with two of the ministry where it was agreed that I should deliver a credit on you for that sum to the commissaries of the treasury, & that they should pass it to the credit of the U.S. With them there was difficulty on account of the sum being expressed in dollars, as it could not enter in that form into their comptability. These circumstances have occasioned the delay of some days as every thing of the kind has to be sent backward & forward through a variety of hands. In expectation of Mr. Morris's coming on here daily I had hoped from this delay that he might arrive here before the mode of carrying the measure into execution was finally adopted. I have just recieved a letter from him however informing me that although he has recieved his credentials, he is delayed by some business but shall leave London soon; [6] & also one from the Minister of the Marine desiring me to meet him tomorrow to give the finishing hand to this business, as not admitting of further delay.[7]

It is for that reason Sir, that I send off this letter by the post of to-morrow morning, to give you notice that the credit abovementioned will be furnished on you, to answer which the value will be kept in the hands of the bankers at Amsterdam out of the late loan [8] at present existing. You may therefore in all safety begin your draughts for that sum, 2100 bonds having been already delivered. I have not mentioned to this government or to any body that you would have to draw on Amsterdam, lest it might affect the exchange in the course of your operation, nor do the bankers know in what manner the sum in their hands is to be applied. Should this business be finally settled, as I don't doubt, to-morrow, I will inform you of

it by the succeeding English post, & also by the way of Havre. In
the mean time I have the honor to be Sir, most respectfully your
obedt. servant   W: Short

The Honble.
Alexander Hamilton Secretary of the Treasury. Philadelphia

ALS, letterpress copy, William Short Papers, Library of Congress.
 1. Antoine François, Marquis de Bertrand de Molleville, had been appointed
Minister of Marine in 1791. In March, 1792, when the Girondists took office he
was replaced by Jean de Lacoste. For a discussion of Bertrand's plan for the
relief of Santo Domingo, see Short to H, December 28, 1791, January 26, 1792,
March 24, 1792, note 1.
 2. On March 28, 1792, "L'Assemblée nationale désirant venir au secours de la
colonie de Saint-Domingue, met à la disposition du ministre de la marine une
somme de 6 millions, pour y faire parvenir des subsistances, des matériaux de
construction, des animaux et des instruments aratoires" (Archives Parlemen-
taires, XL, 578).
 3. Gouverneur Morris had been appointed United States Minister Plenipotentiary to France in January, 1792, but did not arrive in Paris until May.
 4. Short to Morris, April 11, 1792 (ALS, Columbia University Libraries).
 5. See Short to H, January 26, 1792. Short is referring to the Holland loan of
December, 1791. For a description of this loan, see Short to H, December 23,
28, 1791.
 6. Morris to Short, April 17, 1792 (ALS, William Short Papers, Library of
Congress).
 7. Lacoste to Short, April 21, 1792 (LS, William Short Papers, Library of
Congress).
 8. The December, 1791, Holland loan. For a description of this loan, see
Short to H, December 23, 28, 1791.

From Charles Williamson [1]

[Baltimore, April 22, 1792]

Sir
 I beg pardon for the trouble I am giving but I trust when you
consider the object you will excuse me. In the Course of many
applications I have lately had for Lands in the Genesee I have before
me a Letter from a friend of mine who is to embark in the first ship
for Britain to bring out a considerable number of Highlanders from
Scotland probably 3. or 4 ship load. Mr Steuart [2] informs me that
he has met with a Capt Steuart of the Nancy bound for Ireland—
who is engaged to bring out 200 people from the North of Ireland
to settle in this Country that they are all able to pay their own pas-

sage and mostly all of them worth money besides. Capt. Steuart has desired me to send him my terms for settlements in the Genesee which I have done. As these people come from a part of Ireland where 9/10ths of the country live by the manufactoring of fine Linnen, & come voluntarily without expence to the publick—I think it well worth the attention of Legislature of this Country if it should not be so of individuals to adopt some measures that would at once introduce the manufactory of fine Linnen and Cambrick into a Country certainly better calculated for it than any part of America on this side of the Ohio—as in the Genesee the same as in Ireland every farmer may grow and manufacture his own Flax.

It appears to me that only few points are necessary to accomplish this end vizt. to keep the Irish in one body, to give them Lands capable of growing flax in perfection, and to induce them to occupy as small farms as possible. To give them Lands capable of bearing flax in perfection is in my power—and In the terms I Offer, I have given every inducement to make it their interest to take small Lotts. As I have written more fully to Mr. Morris [3] on the subject I shall tresspass no more on your time. To him as to further particulars I beg leave to refer you—but it appears evident to me that if the object is desirable no opportunity ever occured by which it could be so easily attained.

If manufactories are bribed to come into a Country in all probabillity you get the most dissolute—but those who emigrate voluntarily and pay their own expence must have been industrious to be able to do it.

I have the Honor to be with great Esteem   Sir   Your   very humble Sert   C. Williamson

Baltimore 22d April 1792

ALS, Hamilton Papers, Library of Congress.

1. Williamson was the American agent of the Pulteney Associates, a group of Englishmen who had purchased from Robert Morris more than a million acres in the Genesee Valley in western New York. Soon after Williamson's arrival in the United States in November, 1791, he interviewed H who wrote letters of introduction for Williamson to John Tayler and Abraham Ten Broeck of Albany (H to Tayler, February 18, 1792, and H to Ten Broeck, February 18, 1792). Williamson had made a trip to the Genesee lands in the winter of 1791–1792, returning to Baltimore in April.

2. Donald Stewart was an assistant of Williamson and had accompanied him

to the United States. Stewart was principally responsible for inducing Scottish immigrants to settle on the lands of the Pulteney Associates.

3. Robert Morris, from whom the Pulteney Associates had purchased their land in the Genesee country, owned extensive tracts of land in western New York and was interested in the rapid settlement of the region.

From William Ellery

[*Newport, Rhode Island*] *April 23, 1792.* "I have written so fully already respecting the Provision necessary for the payment of drawbacks,[1] that I have only to add to what I wrote on the 17th instant, that John Cooke's & Caleb Gardner's bonds are both paid. I have not had the pleasure of receiving a line from you by the two last Posts. I hope next friday to receive authority from you to obtain from the Bank of Providence a sufficient sum to discharge the drawbacks which have been some time due, and which will be due on the 26th. of this month. . . ."

LC, Newport Historical Society, Newport, Rhode Island.
1. See Ellery to H, January 16, February 27, March 26, April 17, 1792.

From James Reynolds [1]

Philadelphia 23d. April. 1792.

Sir

I am sorry I am in this disagreeable sutivation which Obliges me to trouble you So offen as I do. but I hope it wont be long before it will be In my power to discharge what I am indebted to you Nothing will give me greater pleasure I must Sir ask the loan of thirty dollars more from you, which I shall asteem as a particular favour. and you may Rest ashured that I will pay you with Strickest Justice. for the Reliefe you have aforded me, the Inclosed is the Receipt [2] for the thirty dollars. I shall wate at your Office. Sir for an answer I am sir your very Humble Servant   James Reynolds

Alexr. Hamilton Esqr.

"Reynolds Pamphlet," August 31, 1797.
1. This letter is printed as document No. XVI in the appendix of the "Reynolds Pamphlet," August 31, 1797.
For background to this letter, see Reynolds to H, December 15, 17, 19, 22,

1791, January 3, 17, March 24, April 3, 7, 17, 1792; H to Reynolds, December 15, 1791, April 7, 1792; Maria Reynolds to H, December 15, 1791, January 23–March 18, March 24, 1792.
2. Receipt not found.

To George Washington

[Philadelphia, April 23, 1792]

The Secretary of the Treasury has the honor to present his respects to the President of the United States, and to submit to him the inclosed communications respecting an instance of misconduct in the Collector of Newbury Port.[1]

23d April 1792.

LC, George Washington Papers, Library of Congress.
1. The collector of customs at Newburyport, Massachusetts, was Stephen Cross. On May 4, 1792, Cross was succeeded by Edward Wigglesworth.

To George Washington

Treasury Department, April 24, 1792. "The Secretary of the Treasury has the honor respectfully to submit to the President of the United States, a Contract lately made between the Superintendant of the Delaware Lighthouse,[1] and Joseph Anthony & Son of Philadelphia, for a quantity of Oil. . . ."

LC, George Washington Papers, Library of Congress.
1. William Allibone.

To William Ellery

[Philadelphia, April 25, 1792. On May 7, 1792, Ellery wrote to Hamilton: "I have received your letter of the 25th of the last month." Letter not found.]

From Tobias Lear

Philadelphia, April 25, 1792. "By the President's command T. Lear has the honor to transmit to the Secretary of the Treasury, a Contract lately made between the Superintendent of the Delaware Light-house, and Joseph Anthony & son of Philadelphia for a quantity of Oil, which has received the President's Approbation." [1]

ALS, RG 26, Lighthouse Letters Received, "Segregated" Lighthouse Records, Lear, National Archives; LC, George Washington Papers, Library of Congress.
    1. See H to George Washington, April 24, 1792.

To Jeremiah Olney

Treasury Department
25th April 1792

Sir

On application to the Supervisor of the Revenue for Rhode Island [1] he will furnish your Office on a temporary loan with the Sum of two thousand eight hundred & seven Dollars for the purpose of discharging the drawbacks &c as ℔ the statement transmitted to me.[2] You will receipt for this money as to be returned by you & pay it accordingly out of the Duties of import & tonnage.

It will be necessary hereafter that you regularly note in your weekly return the drawbacks & allowances which will become due on the exportation of Goods from your District for the Month which will follow the rate of each Weekly Return in order that due provision for the payment of the same may be constantly made. This is meant as a temporary measure as I shall communicate to you a particular arrangement, as soon as I have leisure to devise it. It may be well to observe to the Merchants who are entitled to these Drawbacks that the delay has occured only by reason of the extraordinary amount of them.

I am Sir   Your most obedient Servant   Alex Hamilton

Jeremiah Olney Esqr.
Collector at Providence

LS, Rhode Island Historical Society, Providence; LC, RG 56, Letters to Collectors at Small Ports, "Set G," National Archives; copy, RG 56, Letters to the Collector at Providence, National Archives.
    1. John S. Dexter.
    2. See Olney to H, April 9, 1792.

To William Seton

[*Philadelphia, April 25, 1792.* On April 29, 1792, Seton wrote to Hamilton: "I received your official Letter of the 25th." *Letter not found.*]

From William Short

Paris April 25. 1792

Sir

I had the honor of writing to you on the 22d. & then informed you that I was the next day to have a meeting with the Minister of the Marine by his desire in order to terminate the mode of carrying into execution the measure agreed on of furnishing 800,000 dollars in America for the purchase of supplies for S. Domingo. I considered the business as so far fixed that I thought it proper to give you that previous notice that you might commence your draughts on Amsterdam in order to have the sum at your disposition in America. At our meeting the next day, after my letter had been sent off by the post, it was suggested to the minister by one of his assistants that having already recieved advice that bills would arrive from S. Domingo to the amount of twelve millions of livres, it would be proper to submit the matter to the assembly to know whether their intention still was that the six millions voted should be exclusive of the twelve millions which the colony had drawn for. The minister considered this as indispensable for prudence sake, but told me he was absolutely sure that the decree for the six millions would remain untouched. In this situation of the business therefore I send this letter after my last in hopes of its overtaking it in London, merely to make you acquainted with the circumstance, that your draughts for the 800,000 dollars may be suspended until the present delay shall be removed of which you will be immediately informed.

I thought it right that no appearance of delay on the part of the U.S. should be shewn in this business, & have recieved the thanks of the minister for our readiness to comply with the wishes of France for the relief of so important a colony. But as there still remained some difficulty between the department of marine & the commissaries of the treasury, arising probably from a kind of rivality or misunderstanding & as the application to the assembly would necessarily take up some days during which I had every reason to believe that Mr. Morris [1] would arrive here, I observed to the minister that it wd. be more agreeable to me under those circumstances that the matter should be finally settled by him. The affair stands thus suspended for a few days only.

I know that Mr. Morris has a full idea of the advantage resulting to the U.S. from this mode of paying a part of their debt, as he had been active in it before he was thus publicly employed; & of course that he will approve the measure. But as it is possible he may have some other plan for carrying it into execution, I cannot be sorry under present circumstances, that a delay not proceeding from the U.S. should leave the subject open for him. His experience in matters of commerce may perhaps enable him to discover some other mode of remitting this money as more conducive to the public interest.

Your letters of Feb. 14. & March 5. were recieved yesterday forwarded to me from Amsterdam. The last which I have recieved before them was of Nov. 1. 91.[2]

I have the honor to be with the most perfect respect   Sir   your most obedient & most humble servant   W Short

P.S.   It is proper to inform you that neither the Spanish debt nor that to the Farmers general [3] have been yet touched, & that therefore the intended reclamation mentioned in your letter of March. 5. stands on whole ground. You will see by the state of the debt furnished me by the commissaries of the treasury & forwarded to you in a former letter [4] that the government have taken on their acct. the debt to the farmers-general.

The Honble
Alexander Hamilton Secretary of the Treasury Philadelphia

ALS, letterpress copy, William Short Papers, Library of Congress.
1. Gouverneur Morris had been appointed United States Minister Plenipotentiary to France in January, 1792, but did not arrive in Paris until May.
2. H had also written to Short on November 30, 1791, and January 28, 1792.
3. See Short to H, November 12, 1791; H to Short, March 5, 1792.
4. This statement was forwarded in Short's letter to H of January 26, 1792.

From Nathan Keais [1]

Port Washington [North Carolina] April 26, 1792. Acknowledges "the Receipt of your Letter of the 2nd Instant [2] Covering A Commission from the President of the United States to me as Inspector of the Revenue for this port Likewise yours of the 4th [3] which is now before me." Writes "Respective the Stakage of the Shoals in this State."

ALS, RG 26, Lighthouse Letters Received, "Vol. A," Pennsylvania and Southern States, National Archives.

1. Keais, who had been appointed collector at the port of Washington, North Carolina, on February 9, 1790, was appointed inspector of the revenue for the same port on March 8, 1792.
2. Letter not found.
3. Letter not found.

From Oliver Wolcott, Junior

T.D

C. Off April 26. 1792

Sir,

The inclosed documents were lodged in this office by the assignees therein named for the purpose of obtaining transfers of all the Stock in the books of the Treasury to the Credit of John M. Taylor & Andrew Summers.[1]

The business has been hitherto suspended for the purpose of ascertaining whether any of the provisions in the Bankrupt Law of Pensylvania, would render it unsafe or inexpedient to permit the transfers desired.

No caveat against the transfers of the Stock has been lodged in this Office, & no act of Bankruptcy has to my knowledge been committed by either Messrs. Taylor or Summers, unless the assignment of their property for the benifit of their Creditors, herewith transmitted should be deemed an act of that nature.

At the special request of the assignees I now transmit the instruments of Assignment, for the purpose of obtaining the opinion of the Attorney General of the United States, on the question, whether a general Assignment of the effects of a trader, for the benefit of his Creditors, ought to be considered as an Act of Bankruptcy—and also whether the Offices of the Treasury are bound to suspend the allowance of transfers, by a reputed bankrupt, unless notice of some clear act of bankruptcy shall have been formally communicated by a Creditor.

I have the honor to be with the greatest respect &c

Alex Hamilton

ADf, Connecticut Historical Society, Hartford.
    1. Taylor and Summers were Philadelphia brokers.

From William Allibone

[Philadelphia] April 27, 1792. Encloses "a Coppy of an Invoice of Oil, which has been delivered this day by Joseph Anthony & Son, agreeably to Contract." [1]

ALS, RG 26, Lighthouse Letters Received, Vol. "A," Pennsylvania and Southern States, National Archives.
    1. See H to George Washington, April 24, 1792, and Tobias Lear to H, April 25, 1792.

From Tobias Lear

United States, April 27th 1792.

By the President's command T. Lear has the honor to transmit to the Secretary of the Treasury a letter from the Supervisor of the District of South Carolina [1] requesting leave of absence from his office for about three months.

The President refers this request to the Secretary of the Treasury whose knowledge of the duties to be performed by the Supervisor will enable him to say whether it can be granted consistent with the good of the public service. If it can, the President observes, that he can have no objection to indulging the Supervisor.

Tobias Lear.
S.P.U.S.

LC, George Washington Papers, Library of Congress.
    1. Daniel Stevens.

Report on the Petition of Joseph Henderson

[Philadelphia, April 27, 1792
Communicated on April 30, 1792] [1]

[To the Speaker of the House of Representatives]

The Secretary of the Treasury, to whom was referred the petition of Joseph Henderson,[2] respectfully submits the following Report thereupon.

The Marine Committee of Congress, by a letter to the Navy Board for the eastern department, dated the 19th day of June 1778,[3] authorised that Board to appoint some proper person to the office of Naval Paymaster, observing that Congress had not yet fixed a salary for the Officer contemplated; but that, when it was done, they presumed it would be adequate to the importance of the office.

In consequence of this direction, the Navy Board, on the 5th of August following, appointed the petitioner to act in the above mentioned capacity, in which he appears to have acted, till some time in the year 1782, but when, is not clearly ascertained.

By an account settled between the Board and the petitioner, dated the 1st of August 1782, it appears that he was allowed by the Board, four hundred and three pounds ten shillings, for "his services posting books, from May 1779 to May 1782," which James Warren, one of the Board, avers to have had reference merely to his services as an assistant, or Clerk to the Board, and not to his services as paymaster.

It does not appear, that Congress ever assigned any salary or allowance to the office or appointment in question, or that the petitioner ever received any other compensation than as abovementioned.

From this state of facts, it results, that the petitioner has a claim to a farther compensation, unless there be some other circumstance of sufficient force to controul it.

As well from the nature of the office, as from express instructions, it was the duty of the petitioner, to keep regular and fair books of accounts with all persons belonging to the vessels of war within the department.

But it is represented to the Secretary, that the accounts of the petitioner were not kept agreeably to his instructions, whereby settlements with individuals have been delayed and embarrassed.

How far this circumstance ought, upon the whole, to bar the claim of the petitioner, is respectfully submitted. To the Secretary, it would rather appear to be the most proper course of public proceeding, to allow a moderate yearly compensation. The quantum may reasonably be regulated with an eye to the collateral compensation, which was enjoyed by the petitioner, and to the appearances of defective execution.[4]

No impediment arises on the score of the Acts of limitation.[5]

All which is humbly submitted   Alexander Hamilton,
                                                 Secry of the Treasy.
Treasury Department
April 27th 1792.

Copy, RG 233, Reports of the Treasury Department, 1792–1793, Vol. III, National Archives.
    1. *Journal of the House*, I, 592. The communicating letter, dated April 28, 1792, may be found in RG 233, Reports of the Treasury Department, 1792–1793, Vol. III, National Archives.
    2. On April 6, 1790, "A petition of Joseph Henderson was presented to the House and read, praying compensation for services rendered to the United States during the late war as a Paymaster in the Navy.
    "*Ordered,* That the said petition be referred to the Secretary of the Treasury, with instruction to examine the same, and report his opinion thereupon to the House." (*Journal of the House*, I, 189.)
    3. LC, Papers of the Continental Congress, National Archives.
    4. "An Act to authorize the adjustment of a claim of Joseph Henderson against the United States" passed the House on February 6, 1793 (*Journal of the House*, I, 692) and became law on February 22, 1793 (6 *Stat.* 11).
    5. See "Report on Sundry Petitions," April 16, 1792, note 2.

Report on the Petitions of Richard Blackledge

[Philadelphia, April 28, 1792
Communicated on April 30, 1792] [1]

[To the Speaker of the House of Representatives]
The Secretary of the Treasury, to whom were referred by the House

Copy, RG 233, Reports of the Treasury Department, 1792–1793, Vol. III, National Archives.
    1. *Journal of the House*, I, 592. The communicating letter, dated April 28, 1792, may be found in RG 233, Reports of the Treasury Department, 1792–1793, Vol. III, National Archives.

of Representatives, two petitions of Richard Blackledge, one bearing date the 20th of December 1790, the other bearing date the 19th: of January 1791,[2] respectfully submits the following report thereupon.

The first of the said petitions seeks compensation for some Coffee and Sugar, which appear to have been supplied by the petitioner, to officers and soldiers of the North Carolina line and militia, in captivity, during the late war.[3] By the petitioner's own shewing, the supply was originally intended to be on the credit of the State of North Carolina, induced by a particular measure of that State, without any agency whatever of the United States, to authorize or invite it. However meritorious, therefore, the claim of the petitioner, it can only be properly addressed to the before mentioned State. An admission of it, as a charge against the United States, in favor of the individual, would be contrary to the course of the transaction, and could not be done, without an interference with the Acts of limitation.[4]

The second of the said petitions seeks compensation for a quantity

2. On January 19, 1791, the House received "A petition of Richard Blackledge, praying compensation for a quantity of coffee and sugar supplied to the troops of the late North Carolina Line and militia in Continental service.

"*Ordered*, That the said . . . [petition] be referred to the Secretary of the Treasury, with instruction to examine the same, and report his opinion thereupon to the House." (*Journal of the House*, I, 358.)

On the same day, the House received "A petition of Richard Blackledge, praying compensation for a quantity of leather furnished for the service of the United States, during the late war.

"*Ordered*, That the said petition . . . be referred to the Secretary of War, with instruction to examine the same, and report his opinion thereupon to the House." (*Journal of the House*, I, 358.)

On February 8, 1791, the House "*Ordered*, That the Secretary of War be discharged from considering the petition of Richard Blackledge, which was referred to him on the nineteenth of January last; and that the said petition be referred to the Secretary of the Treasury, with instruction to examine the same, and report his opinion thereupon to the House" (*Journal of the House*, I, 371).

On October 31, 1791, "A petition of Richard Blackledge was presented to the House and read, praying compensation for a quantity of leather furnished for the service of the United States, during the late war.

"Ordered, That the said petition be referred to the Secretary of the Treasury, with instruction to examine the same, and report his opinion thereupon to the House." (*Journal of the House*, I, 444.)

3. A report, dated December 13, 1790, on a petition which Blackledge made to the legislature of North Carolina gives some of the details of this transaction (Clark, *State Records of North Carolina*, XXI, 1044–45).

4. See "Report on Sundry Petitions," April 16, 1792, note 2.

of leather, sold to the late Governor Caswell [5] of North Carolina, in February, April and May 1778, and for fifty sides of leather sold and delivered to Edward Hall,[6] a Quarter Master, in July 1781.

It appears by a resolution of Congress of the 25th. of November 1777,[7] that Governor Caswell, by the description of "Governor Caswell," was requested and empowered to purchase leather for the use of the United States, for the payment of which, he was authorised to draw on the Treasury, and was desired to transmit accounts of his proceedings, to the Board of War, and Clothier General.[8]

A question is made, whether Governor Caswell was, by that resolution, constituted an agent to Congress, in his private or public capacity. If there be any ambiguity on this point, in the wording of the resolution, the contemporary transactions explain, at least, the intention.

It appears by the Treasury books, that warrants have been drawn, to a considerable amount, for satisfying the drafts of the late Governor Caswell (some of them having express relation to his agency,) all which have been charged to the State of North Carolina.

It further appears, from the books of the then Clothier General, (extracts from which, marked A, are herewith sent) that considerable quantities of leather, and some shoes, amounting in nominal value to £7.720.15. were delivered at Lancaster in Pennsylvania, in April, June, August and November 1778, and were credited in these books, to the State of North Carolina.

These circumstances explain the light, in which the agency in question was considered at that time.

The particular transaction, on which the claim of the petitioner is grounded, is an evidence, that he himself considered Governor Caswell, as contracting in his official character, and even that the credit given was to the State of North Carolina. The document, that establishes the purchase, is an account acknowledged by Governor Cas-

5. Richard Caswell, who had been governor of North Carolina from 1777 to 1780, had died in November, 1789.
6. Hall is described as an assistant quartermaster in the report of December 13, 1790, made to the legislature of North Carolina on Blackledge's petition (Clark, *State Records of North Carolina*, XXI, 1043).
7. JCC, IX, 965–66.
8. James Mease was clothier general from 1776 to 1779.

well, which is headed thus "Richard Caswell for the public of North Carolina to the Executors of Richard Blackledge Dr." It may be inferred from this, that the course of the business was understood to be that Governor Caswell purchased, as on account of the State of North Carolina, and that an adjustment was to be made between the United States and that State.

There is a presumption (though it does not appear from the entries) that the leather supplied by the petitioner was a part of that, for which credit is given on the books of the Clothier General.

After a careful examination, it has not been found that Governor Caswell ever rendered an account of his transactions, according to the requisition of the resolution, under which he acted.

With respect to the charge for leather delivered to Edward Hall, there is no other trace of it, than in the documents which accompany the memorial.

The whole claim, as on behalf of the petitioner against the United States, if there were no other objection to it, would be barred by the Acts of limitation.

In this state of things, the only practicable mode of doing justice to the petitioner, without contravening the course of the transaction, and the Acts of limitation, is for the State of North Carolina to adjust and satisfy the demand, as far as regards the leather sold to Governor Caswell, on the consideration of a reciprocal credit in the accounts of that State with the United States.

There are appearances to induce a supposition, that an uncertainty as to such a credit has been heretofore an obstacle to the settlement by the State.[9]

On this point the Secretary can only observe, that there is, in his opinion, no cause to doubt that the State of North Carolina can obtain a credit, in conformity to the entries in the books of the late Clothier General, in the settlement of the accounts of that State with the United States.

With regard to the part of the claim, which relates to the leather

---

9. According to the report of December 13, 1790, to the North Carolina legislature on Blackledge's petition, Blackledge had indicated his willingness to submit his claim to the commissioners for settling the accounts between the states (Clark, *State Records of North Carolina*, XXI, 1043).

delivered to Edward Hall, an admission of it could not, in the opinion of the Secretary, be allowed, but upon a principle, which would entirely unsettle the Acts of limitation.

All which is humbly submitted,   Alexander Hamilton
Secry. of the Treasy.

Treasury Department
April 28th: 1792.

Report on the Petition of Alexander Contee Hanson

[Philadelphia, April 28, 1792
Communicated on April 30, 1792] [1]

[To the Speaker of the House of Representatives]
The Secretary of the Treasury, on the petition of Alexander Contee Hanson, referred to him by the House of Representatives on the 25th of January 1791,[2] respectfully makes the following Report.

It appears that Congress, by their Act of the 14th of September 1786,[3] appointed nine Judges (of whom the petitioner was one) to constitute a Court for hearing and determining a controversy of boundaries between the States of South Carolina and Georgia.

That this Court was directed to be holden at the City of New York, on the third Monday of June 1787.[4]

That the Commissioner, in consequence of his appointment, attended at New York, at the time prescribed, without previous knowledge of a compromise, which had taken place between the parties, which prevented the necessity of a judicial decision.

That the petitioner was sixteen days absent from home upon his journey, having remained some days in Philadelphia (as he alleges) partly for the purpose of endeavoring to procure compensation, and partly on account of indisposition.

That no compensation has been made to him for trouble or loss of time.

It further appears, that no compensation was established by Congress, for the service, and that in no similar case, has any been made by the United States.

It is understood, that compensations have in other cases of similar controversy, been made by the States concerned.

Upon this state of facts, the following observations occur.

Here was a service performed by the petitioner, on the requisition and appointment of the government of the United States.

It seems, therefore, just and regular, that a compensation should be made by the same authority, unless some different mode was originally provided, as resulted from the course of the business.

No different mode was originally provided, and the compromise of the dispute prevented any award or adjustment of costs, by the Court.

It was and still is reasonable that the States concerned should have made the requisite compensation between them; but it appears a well founded expectation, that the United States should either see this done, or should themselves make the compensation.

It is therefore submitted as in the opinion of the Secretary proper, that the Legislature should make provision for the one or the other; defining, at the same time, the quantum of the compensation.

All which is respectfully submitted   Alexander Hamilton
Secry. of the Treasy.

Treasury Department
April 28th 1792.

Copy, RG 233, Reports of the Treasury Department, 1792–1793, Vol. III, National Archives.

1. *Journal of the House*, I, 592. The communicating letter, dated April 28, 1792, may be found in RG 233, Reports of the Treasury Department, 1792–1793, Vol. III, National Archives.

2. On January 25, 1791, the House received "A petition of Alexander Contee Hanson, praying compensation for expenses incurred in consequence of an appointment of the late Congress.

"*Ordered*, That the said . . . [petition] be referred to the Secretary of the Treasury, with instruction to examine the same, and report his opinion thereupon to the House." (*Journal of the House*, I, 362.)

3. JCC, XXXI, 650–52 (September 13, 1786).

4. JCC, XXXI, 654 (September 14, 1786).

From Joshua Mersereau [1]

[Elizabeth, New Jersey, April 29, 1792]

The Honble. Alexr. Hambleton

Sir

I take the liberty of asking, What Success Colo. Harper [2] has Met with in respect to his appointment. You will please to Excuse the Liberty I have taken as I am antious to hear of his appointment—as I am Confident it will tend greatly to the happyness of our part of the Country—as the Indians put full Confidence, in the Col. and Wish much for his appointment saying he never Deceivd. them as others have, in their Translations. Please to Make my respectfull Comps. acceptable To your Lady and accept the same   from Your Obedt. Hum: Servt.   Joshua Mersereau

Elizabeth Town
April 29 1792

NB: I expect our Election is Very *Tight*.[3] Mr. Jays being one of the Emancipation Committee [4] opperates much against him. With our Old Copper heads.

ALS, Hamilton Papers, Library of Congress.
1. Mersereau, who had been deputy commissary of prisoners during the American Revolution, was a resident of Staten Island, New York, and a member of the New York Assembly from 1777 to 1786.
2. As a boy, John Harper attended Eleazar Wheelock's Indian Charity School during the time when Joseph Brant, the Mohawk leader, was also a pupil (Francis Whiting Halsey, *The Old New York Frontier* [New York, 1901], 120–21). Harper became fluent in the Mohawk dialect, and during the seventeen-eighties became an Indian interpreter. During the American Revolution he served as a colonel in command of the Fifth Regiment of New York Militia.
3. This is a reference to the campaign for governor of New York. The candidates were John Jay and Governor George Clinton.
4. Jay was a member and ex-president of the New York Society for Promoting the Manumission of Slaves.

From William Seton

New York 29. April 1792.

My Dear sir

Before I received your official Letter of the 25th.[1] extending a Credit to the Commissioner of Loans for 30 M Dollars, Dr. Cochran[2] had called upon me and mentioned how disagreably he was situated from an error his Clerks had made in the former requisition to you—he said he had sent on one of his Young Men to you, and hoped in the Meanwhile his Checks would be paid, should he be obliged to over draw his Account in Bank, as he expected the State Treasurer & the Amsterdam Agents might call upon him before your answer arrived. I made his mind easy on that subject—but he was not called upon, & therefore did not draw. His balance in Bank was then 21,000 Dollars.

In consequence of a private Letter from you,[3] he again called upon me in great distress—and requested I would come to his Office & examine into the Books & management of the business. I was there yesterday for two hours on this subject, the result of which I beg leave now to mention to you. Mr. Hill[4] who is his principal clerk I find had ommitted in his Estimate or requisition, the ballance of one Ledger, which caused the Error. I am convinced it was mere accident for he appears to be clever and attentive; there are no less than Sixteen Clerks who are constantly employed, and yet they cannot keep the business up. The System of their Books is very complex & voluminous, but they say it is to comply with the forms pointed out to them. They have Six Ledgers & Six Journals which appear to be nearly posted up—and an infinity of other Books, which perhaps are requisite. Where they seem to be the most behind hand, is in the Returns—the Monthly ones they have been pretty regular in, but the general Returns such as the GA &ca are not begun, and without more Clerks will never be rendered. This I mentioned to Mr. Cochran, but he is afraid the expence would fall upon himself. The House is so small and inconvenient, that neither the Clerks or the persons attending on business have room to stir—this impedes their work, and creates delay. They have no place of safety whatever for their papers or Books. Of course there is great confusion amongst them, great risk to the officer & to the Public. I have of late been almost daily at the office & the Clerks appear to me to be trustworthy and attentive. Dr. Cochran says he never has had reasons to suspect any of them, and would be very loth to change them. The pressure of the business in this office I conceive must be nearly double to what it is at any of the other Loan Offices. The Transfers are innumerable to be sure, and they cannot issue the New Certificates as rapidly as they ought. To alter the present system of their Books & the mode of conducting the business would throw every thing into worse confusion—but he certainly wants two or three Competent Persons to bring up the back work, that the Returns might be made & that he might know how he stands himself. He is certainly a worthy honest Man, but for the conducting such an intricate and extensive system, it requires more ability and actual knowledge of Official rotine, to plan execute and overlook than he is equal to. Of course he must rely upon others, & his friends should endeavour to annex to him some body equal to the task. Unless this is done speedily, everything will go wrong—& perhaps become irritrievable.

I mention this to you in confidence trusting that you well know, I have no other motive, than to give you such information as may be requisite for your attention to the public good. I truly am   My dear sir   Your ever obliged Obed Hue Serv   Wm Seton

Alexr. Hamilton Esqr

Mrs. Hamiltons Letter was immediately delivered to Mr. Boulton.[5]

ALS, Hamilton Papers, Library of Congress; ADf, Bank of New York, New York City.
 1. Letter not found.
 2. John Cochran was commissioner of loans for New York.
 3. Letter not found.
 4. James Hill was chief clerk in Cochran's office.
 5. This letter has not been found.

From William Allibone

[Philadelphia] April 30, 1792. "Since delivering the estimates and observations for Building a Pier at mud Island.[1] I have made careful

Enquiry into the vallue of the articles estimated. The result whereof is that the Smiths ask from 6d to 6d ½ for that kind of Iron work, And the Price of Building Stone of Inferiour quality is 5/4 at the whaves & that of Superiour is 6/10. the Delaware paving Stone is 10/6 the load. but would not answer so well for packing in a Pier in that exposed situation. Ships Ballast may be had considerably Lower but could not be depended on, as it might not be to be had when wanted, and could not be waited for. And there would be the addition of freight from hence. . . ."

ALS, RG 26, Lighthouse Letters Received, Vol. "A," Pennsylvania and Southern States, National Archives.
1. See Allibone to H, March 13, 16, 1792.

Conversation with George Hammond [1]

[Philadelphia, April 30–July 3, 1792]

It is somewhat remarkable that in my last conversation with Mr Hamilton on these points,[2] he said that this government would, he doubted not, consent to grant to the subjects of the crown a free intercourse of commerce with the Indians dwelling within the American territory, provided that a similar intercourse with the Indians residing in the territory of Canada should be allowed to the citizens of the United States. Within three days after this conversation I received from Governor Simcoe [3] a memorial of the merchants of Montreal,[4] a copy of which I have the honor of inclosing and from which your Lordship will perceive that those Gentlemen imagine that the evils, resulting from the surrender of the posts, would be considerably alleviated by the permission, to the subjects of the two countries, of this reciprocity of commerce with the Indians residing within their respective dominions.

D, PRO: F.O., Series 4, Vol. 16, Part I.
1. This conversation has been taken from Hammond to Lord Grenville, July 3, 1792, Dispatch No. 26.
2. Hammond is referring to the problems concerning the western posts, the Indians, and the fur trade.
3. John Graves Simcoe, lieutenant governor of Canada, was appointed first governor of Upper Canada, a province which had been formed by the British government in May, 1791.
4. There were two memorials sent to Simcoe by the merchants of Montreal,

one dated December 9, 1791, and the other dated April 23, 1792. The latter
dealt with the "reciprocity of commerce with the Indians" mentioned by Hammond. Both memorials are printed in E. A. Cruikshank, ed., *The Correspondence of Lieut. Governor John Graves Simcoe with Allied Documents Relating
to His Administration of the Government of Upper Canada* (Toronto, 1923),
I, 91–94, 133–37.

From Archibald Mercer

Millstone [New Jersey] April 30 1792

Sir

I am requested to acknowledge rect. of your favour of 14th Inst.
to the Governor and Directors of the Society for establishing useful
Manufactories.

It is with pleasure I inform you that your observations in general
conincide with the opinion of the board of Directors, and that they
will esteem as a favour any communication you may be disposed to
favour them with from time to time.

It is with regret I inform you the affairs of the Society are as much
deranged as they well can be. At present we can only count upon
70,000 Dols in Deferred Stock transferred on the Books of Coch-
rans[1] Office in the Name of the Society at 14/ in the pound, and
this was not done until some time after the Loan, the propriety of
which I leave you to Judge as the money was all wanted; the residue
of the first payment except some necessary advances we consider in
Jeopardy, tho measures have been taken to secure about Eleven
Thousand pounds Stg committed to Mr Duhurst[2] for the purpose of
procureing plain cotton linens to begin the printing business. Should
that Money, or the proceeds be safe, I have no doubt the business
may soon be put in Train with more promising prospects, and at all
events, if we have men of *clear integrity* to conduct the business in
future the institution may yet flourish. A special meeting of the
Board of Directors is called to meet at New Ark the 15th of May, as
the Permanent seat of the Manufactory is then to be fixed on, and
the principal officers of the institution appointed and their duties
regulated. It is the wish of all the directors that you attend the meeting, as every thing depends upon a good beginning. For my part I
confess myself perfectly ignorant of every duty relating to the
Manufactoring business. As it is a favourite design of yours, you

have no doubt considered the subject and as we all have a full confidence in you your presence will be absolutely necessary.

I have the Honour to be sir   Your obt Hume Servt

Archibald Mercer D. Govr.

S U M

Alexander Hamilton Esq

ALS, Hamilton Papers, Library of Congress.
1. John Cochran was commissioner of loans for New York.
2. John Dewhurst was a director of the Society for Establishing Useful Manufactures. For information on the money entrusted to Dewhurst, see Nicholas Low to H, April 10, 1792.

To George Washington

Treasury Department
April 30. 1792

The Secretary of the Treasury has the honor respectfully to communicate to the President authenticated copies of the Contracts for the three last loans made in Europe; that for 6000000 of Florins at Amsterdam bearing date the 14 of December 1791 [1] at a rate of 5 ⅌ Cent Interest, that for 3000000 of Florins at Antwerp at a rate of 4½ ⅌ Cent Interest bearing date the 30th day of November 1791 [2] and the last for 3000000 of Florins at Amsterdam at 4 per Cent Interest bearing date the 24 of December 1791; [3] of which respective contracts a Ratification by The President as heretofore is requisite.

AL, RG 59, Records Relating to Foreign Accounts, 1782–1797, Bills of Exchange and Loan Ratifications, National Archives.
1. This loan was negotiated at Amsterdam in September, 1791. For a description of the Holland loan of September, 1791, see William Short to H, August 31, 1791.
2. For a description of the Antwerp loan, see Short to H, November 8, 1791, note 4, and November 12, 1791.
3. This is a reference to the Holland loan of December, 1791. For a description of this loan, see Short to H, December 23, 28, 1791. The December, 1791, loan was negotiated for three million rather than six million florins. In late 1791, however, Short learned that the Dutch government was considering the imposition of a tax on foreign loans negotiated in Holland. In order to circumvent the payment of this tax on an anticipated United States loan in 1792, Willink, Van Staphorst, and Hubbard, the bankers of the United States in Amsterdam, suggested to Short that the contract of the December, 1791, loan be made for six million florins, leaving the extra three million florins available for 1792 (see Short to H, December 30, 1791).

From John Mathews [1]

[*May 1, 1792*. On July 10, 1792, Tench Coxe wrote to Mathews: "I have before me your Letter of the 1st: of May to the Secretary of the Treasury, and I feel great pleasure in observing that the little duty, which has accrued under the Act of March 1791 [2] is likely to be collected without legal compulsion." [3] *Letter not found.*]

1. Mathews was supervisor of the revenue for the District of Georgia.
2. "An Act repealing, after the last day of June next, the duties heretofore laid upon Distilled Spirits imported from abroad, and laying others in their stead; and also upon Spirits distilled within the United States, and for appropriating the same" (1 *Stat.* 199–214 [March 3, 1791]).
3. LC, RG 58, Letters of Commissioner of Revenue, 1792–1793, National Archives.

From Joseph Nourse [1]

Registers Office [Philadelphia] 1st. May 1792

Sir,

I have the honor to enclose the several papers, upon which I have attempted to form a Conjectural Estimate of the Monies due to the War Department for the year 1791.[2] A. Estimate of the Rations issued by the Contractors 1791.[3] with subordinate vouchers No. 1 a 11— [4]

B. do. at Brunswick, Philadelphia, Carlisle and óther places on the Rout to Fort Pitt together with the probable Expence of transporting the Baggage of the Troops and supplies of Quarter Mrs. Stores.[5]

Together with the following papers viz.

Jos: Howell Acting Pay Mr. his Account of monies paid to Mr. Duer.[6]

do. his Conjectural Estimate of monies due the war Department 1791 [7]

Extract from a Claim filed in the Auditors Office [8]

I have attempted but without Effect to obtain a return of the provisions which remained on hand at the several Posts on the 31st.

Decemr. 1791. All which are submitted. Being with great Respect
Sir Your most obedt: Sert.   J. N.

Hon: Alexr. Hamilton Esqr.
Secty. of the Treasury

ALS, RG 53, Register of the Treasury, Estimates and Statements for 1792,
Vol. "134-T," National Archives.

1. This letter concerns contracts for Army rations made with the War
Department. On October 28, 1790, Theodosius Fowler, a New York City
merchant and speculator in land and securities, contracted to supply rations
to several western Army posts during the year 1791 (see "Contract for Army
Rations," October 28, 1790). On January 3, 1791, Fowler assigned his contract
to William Duer (see H to Duer, April 7, 1791). On March 26, 1791, a
separate "contract was entered into by William Duer with the Secretary of
War, for supplying the troops with provisions until their arrival at Fort
Pitt . . ." (ASP, Military Affairs, I, 42, which gives the date incorrectly as
April 26, 1791). This contract was authorized by "An Act for raising and
adding another Regiment to the Military Establishment of the United States,
and for making farther provision for the protection of the frontiers" (1 Stat.
222–24 [March 3, 1791]). After the defeat by the Indians in November, 1791,
of the United States troops under the command of Major General Arthur
St. Clair, the House of Representatives on March 27, 1792, appointed Thomas
FitzSimons, William Branch Giles, John Steele, John Francis Mercer, John
Vining, Abraham Clarke, and Theodore Sedgwick a committee "to inquire
into the causes of the failure of the late expedition under Major General St.
Clair . . ." (Journal of the House, I, 552). On April 4, 1792, the House requested three members of the committee to deliver to the President a resolution of that date requesting papers relevant to the inquiry which were in the
possession of the executive branch of the Government (see George Washington to H, April 6, 1792). On April 24, 1792, H and Henry Knox appeared
before the committee for two hours. In an undated letter which Knox wrote
to the committee in either January or February, 1793, he described this meeting as follows: ". . . A considerable portion of this time was employed with
the Secretary of the Treasury relatively to the assignment of the Contract
by Theodosius Fowler to William Duer—that a conversation took place relatively to the due bills issued by the contractors the Clothing of the levies and
the time the Money was forwarded for their payment. Neither the Secretary
of the Treasury nor myself recollect that any other objects were then mentioned than those here specified" (copy, Massachusetts Historical Society,
Boston).

On February 15, 1793, a House committee with a somewhat different membership issued a revised report. Two errors in the original report that had
cast suspicion on Duer's contractual relations with the Government were
corrected. First, the original report had stated that Duer's contract stipulated
that he provide supplies for the troops en route to Fort Pitt and at Fort Pitt.
The revised report made it clear that Duer was not responsible for supplies
for the troops at Fort Pitt. Second, the revised report revealed that the Government had paid Duer $5,437.91 rather than the $15,000 which the committee had stated in the original report. In connection with this second point,
on January 7, 1793, Samuel Meredith, treasurer of the United States, had
written to the committee as follows:

"I do certify that the within warrant No. 949 for 15000 dollars was made payable to Joseph Howell for the use of the department of War, the transcript of expenditures on account of said department transmitted to the Honorable Thomas Fitzsimons the 6th April 1792 mentioning that it was paid to Joseph Howell for William Duer being a mistake occasioned by this and a number of other warrants paid by the direction of the Secretary of the Treasury at the Bank of North America without my drafts (and remaining in the said bank as their vouchers for payment) there being no comptroller in that time to countersign them." (Copy, Massachusetts Historical Society, Boston.)

2. The estimated amount of money due the War Department for 1791 was $58,698.10¾ (D, RG 53, Register of the Treasury, Estimates and Statements for 1792, Vol. "134-T," National Archives).

3. The enclosure, entitled "An Estimate of Rations issued to the Troops of the united States in the Year 1791 under the Contract of Theodosius Fowler," showed a total of $70,385.32¾ (D, RG 53, Register of the Treasury, Estimates and Statements for 1792, Vol. "134-T," National Archives).

4. The eleven vouchers, which Nourse enclosed with this letter, were the returns for the troops stationed at Fort Franklin, Fort Harmar, Fort Washington, Dunlaps Station, Covalt Station, Fort Hamilton, Fort Jefferson, Fort Knox, Fort Steuben, the Rapids of Ohio, and Fort Pitt (D, RG 53, Register of the Treasury, Estimates and Statements for 1792, Vol. "134-T," National Archives).

Between the first and second vouchers there is a two-page "Estimate of Rations supplied the Troops from the places of their respective Rendezvous to Fort Pitt, at Fort Pitt and for their Subsistence down the River Ohio." Although this estimate was marked as being erroneous and its total was not used in the summary of these vouchers, it was apparently included in the material transmitted to H, for a note in H's handwriting on the second page of the estimate reads: "(erronius) vide seperate Return for this object."

5. This estimate, totaling $17,861.20, is entitled "Estimate of Rations supplied the Troops on the Road to Fort Pitt and probable Expence of transporting their Baggage and Quarter Masters Stores" (D, RG 53, Register of the Treasury, Estimates and Statements for 1792, Vol. "134-T," National Archives).

6. This enclosure, entitled "William Duer, Esquire, to the united States, Dr: For Cash recd: of Jos: Howell, Acting P. M. Gl," states that Duer had been advanced $5,437.91 (D, RG 53, Register of the Treasury, Estimates and Statements for 1792, Vol. "134-T," National Archives).

7. The amount that was estimated as due to the War Department from the contractor and his agents was $17,948.69 (D, RG 53, Register of the Treasury, Estimates and Statements for 1792, Vol. "134-T," National Archives).

8. This extract is entitled "A Claim is filed in the Auditors Office on Behalf of the Contractor, for sundry supplies to the Army, stated to have been furnished between the 14 Augt. and 20 Nov. 1791" and states that during that period the value of supplies furnished the Army amounted to $55,951.56 (D, RG 53, Register of the Treasury, Estimates and Statements for 1792, Vol. "134-T," National Archives).

To George Washington

[*Philadelphia, May 1, 1792.* On May 2, 1792, Hamilton wrote to Washington: "The case was here before the Secretary's letter of yesterday was sent to the President." *Letter not found.*]

To Benjamin Lincoln

Treasury Department May 2d 1792

Sir

In my letter of the 22d of march I communicated my desire, that you would pay weekly into the Boston branch of the Bank of the united States, the monies arising in Your office, which it was my intention to have passed immediately to the credit of the Treasurer of the united States. I find it necessary to observe however, that the public service will require Your retaining a sufficiency to defray the weekly and in general the contingent expences and disbursements to be made by Yourself; particularly a sum adequate to the discharge of Bounties & Drawbacks. You will therefore keep in Your command the requisite monies, and you will open an account with the Branch Bank in the quality of a depositor. The sums to fall due for drawbacks and Bounties, are to be noted regularly in your weekly returns.

I am with great consideration   Sir   Your obedt. Servt.

A Hamilton

Benjamin Lincoln Esqr.
Collector Boston

LS, Montague Collection, MS Division, New York Public Library; LC, RG 56, Letters to the Collector at Boston, National Archives; LC, RG 56, Letters to Collectors at Small Ports, "Set G," National Archives.

Receipt from George Parkinson [1]

[Philadelphia, May 2, 1792]

Received May 2d. 1792 of Alexander Hamilton One hundred Dollars on account of The Society for establishing useful manufactures.

Geo: Parkinson

D, in the writing of H and signed by Parkinson, Hamilton Papers, Library of Congress.

1. Parkinson had arrived in the United States in 1790. On December 7, 1791, H wrote to the directors of the Society for Establishing Useful Manufactures recommending Parkinson's employment by the society.

From James Reynolds [1]

Philadelphia 2d. May. 1792.

Sir

I must now for ever forbid you of visiting Mrs. R any more I was in hopes that it would in time ware off, but I find there is no hopes. So I am determed to put a finell end to it. if its in my power. for I find by your Seeing her onely Renews the Friendship, and likewise when you Call you are fearful any person Should See you am I a person of Such a bad Carector. that you would not wish to be seen in Coming in my house in the front way. all any Person Can say of me is that I am poore and I dont know if that is any Crime. So I must meet my fate. I have my Reasons for it for I cannot be Reconsiled to it. for there is know person Can tell the pain it give me except the[y] were plased in my sutivation I am shure the world would despise me if the[y] Onely new what I have bin Reconsiled to, I am in hopes in a short time to make you amends for your favour Rendered me I am Sir your humble Servant   J. Reynolds

Alexr. Hamilton Esqr.

"Reynolds Pamphlet," August 31, 1797.
    1. This letter is printed as document No. XVII in the appendix of the "Reynolds Pamphlet," August 31, 1797.
    For background to this letter, see Reynolds to H, December 15, 17, 19, 22, 1791, January 3, 17, March 24, April 3, 7, 23, 1792; H to Reynolds, December 15, 1791, April 7, 1792; Maria Reynolds to H, December 15, 1791, January 23–March 18, March 24, 1792.
    H described this letter as follows: "The letter No. XVII is a master-piece. The husband there forbids my future visits to his wife, chiefly because I was careful to avoid publicity. It was probably necessary to the project of some deeper treason against me that I should be seen at the house. Hence was it contrived, with all the caution on my part to avoid it, that [Jacob] Clingman should occasionally see me.
    "The interdiction was every way welcome, and was I believe, strictly observed." ("Reynolds Pamphlet," August 31, 1797.)

To George Washington

[Philadelphia, May 2, 1792]

The Secretary of the Treasury has the honor of enclosing herewith the draft of a Passport for the President's signature intended for the brigantine Lily, now at Baltimore. The case was here before the Secretary's letter of yesterday [1] was sent to the President, and was overlooked.

2d. May 1792.

LC, George Washington Papers, Library of Congress.
1. Letter not found.

To Nehemiah Hubbard

Philadelphia May 3d. 1792

Sir

I heared with much regret, though under the appearances which must have struck you, not with much surprize, of your determination to decline the appointment of Superintendant of the Manufacturing Society.[1] This institution has presented itself to my mind as of such real public importance, that I feel myself much interested in its success; and I acknowlege that I continue to entertain a conviction of the practicability of insuring that success by judicious management. To this end a fit person as Superintendant is undoubtedly an essential mean. And my repeated reflections have proved to me that it is far from easy to find a choice of proper characters. Hence I feel a peculiar anxiety that you should reconsider your resolution and still consent to undertake the business.

Those characters in the Direction who were too much invelopped in Speculation to pay proper attention to the trust will henceforth be out of the Question and I entertain no doubt that the next Election will supply their places in a manner which will inspire confidence.[2] I am also persuaded that the Superintendant, if a competent and trust worthy person, will be cloathed with such a portion of discretionary authority as will enable him to fulfil the objects of the Society. To this I may add, that subordinate characters, to be placed at the head of the several branches (I mean of the Cotton Manufactory) of whose competency there is satisfactory evidence are actually engaged, and that a considerable progress has been made in preparation.

The Society meet on the 15th. instant.[3] It is my intention to meet them—and I feel a confidence that I shall be able to give such a di-

rection to their measures as will recover the ground that has been
lost by delay & indecision. If I can by that time announce that you
are willing to serve the Company, it will give me particular satisfaction.

I will however observe that in such case it is of moment you
should be able to enter promptly on the business. The spot must be
fixed upon and the buildings commenced. Let me, I pray you, previous to that time hear from you on the subject.

I am aware that the Step proposed to you is of consequence. I will
only add that if the event shall not answer expectation, I should feel
myself bound to endeavour to render it not injurious to you by any
source which might be in my power.

I am with esteem   Sir   Your Obed servant   A Hamilton

N Hubbard Esq

ALS, The Huntington Library, San Marino, California.
   1. On January 21, 1792, the Society for Establishing Useful Manufactures
had elected Hubbard "Superintendent-General of the works of the Society"
at a salary of two thousand dollars a year ("Minutes of the S.U.M.," 12, 19).
See Archibald Mercer to H, April 6, 1792, and H to the Governor and
Directors of the Society for Establishing Useful Manufactures, April 14, 1792.
   2. On October 1, 1792, a general meeting of the stockholders of the Society
for Establishing Useful Manufactures elected eight new directors to a board
of thirteen. Among those directors who were not re-elected were William
Duer, John Dewhurst, Royal Flint, and Alexander Macomb, all of whom had
been prominent in the speculative bubble of January and February, 1792.
   3. Mercer, deputy governor of the society, had invited H to attend the
meeting of the board of directors of the Society for Establishing Useful
Manufactures at Newark, New Jersey, on May 15. See Mercer to H, April
30, 1792.

From Jeremiah Olney

Providence, May 3, 1792. ". . . I beg leave Sir to recall your attention to my Letter of the 9th of April; and to express my anxiety for
the replacing the Sum therein mentioned by the 12th instant; otherwise, should the 9,253 Dollars, due that Day, for Drawbacks on Teas
exported, be then demanded, it will not be in my power to observe
that punctuality, which, as Collector, the Law obliges me to require
from Individuals indebted for Duties. . . ." [1]

ADfS, Rhode Island Historical Society, Providence.
   1. See H to Olney, April 25, 1792.

Report on the Petition of Simon W. Wilson

[Philadelphia, May 3, 1792
Communicated on May 8, 1792][1]

[To the Speaker of the House of Representatives]
The Secretary of the Treasury to whom was referred the petition of Simon W. Wilson,[2] respectfully submits the following Report.

The petition seeks reimbursement of certain expenses, incurred by way of salvage and otherwise, in relation to a certain schooner,[3] which is alleged to have been ordered into the public service, during the late war, by the President of Delaware,[4] and in consequence of it captured by the enemy, and recaptured by a vessel of the United States.

An affidavit is produced, which states the declaration of the fact by one of the owners of the vessel, now deceased, and an acknowledgment of the President of the State of Delaware, having reference to that declaration, that "what he had done was as a public officer; —that the parties ought to be paid for the vessel by the public, and that he should endeavor to get it done."

It is stated, that repeated applications have been made by the legislature of Delaware, for relief, but to no effect; they alleging that the charge was a Continental one, and did not lie before them. But it does not appear, that any application has been made to the United States, within the limits of the Acts of limitation,[5] and no special reason is assigned for the delay.

Compensations in similar cases, are of a delicate nature, and would always require careful examination, under circumstances that could afford full light. At this late day, a satisfactory investigation is perhaps not very easy. If the vessel, for example, was merely hired for public use, without a special guarantee, there would be no good claim for compensation in the case stated. If she was impressed into the public service, the consequence might be different. It is alleged that the vessel was ordered into the public service, but the nature of this order does not appear. It may have been to procure vessels, and may have been executed by a voluntary contract; or it may have been executed in a manner, that had the force of an impressment.

The latter is probable, from the circumstances stated; but it is not unequivocally ascertained.

Under all these circumstances, the Secretary does not perceive any reason sufficiently special and discriminative to induce a relaxation in the acts of the Legislature in favor of the petitioner.

All which is humbly submitted   Alexander Hamilton
                                     Secry. of the Treasy.

Treasury Department
May 3d. 1792.

Copy, RG 233, Reports of the Treasury Department, 1792–1793, Vol. III, National Archives.

1. *Journal of the House,* I, 604. The communicating letter, dated May 3, 1792, may be found in RG 233, Reports of the Treasury Department, 1792–1793, Vol. III, National Archives.

2. On July 17, 1790, "A petition of Simon Wilmer Wilson, of Kent county, in the State of Delaware, was presented to the House and read, praying the liquidation and settlement of a claim against the United States.

"*Ordered,* That the said petition be referred to the Secretary of the Treasury, with instruction to examine the same, and report his opinion thereupon to the House." (*Journal of the House,* I, 272.)

3. On January 30, 1787, the Delaware House of Delegates took "into consideration the Auditor's report of the 5th of February 1785, upon the petition of Simon W. Wilson and Peter B. Fury, praying compensation for losses sustained by the capture of their vessel, the Dover Packet, while employed in the public service during the late war;

"*Resolved,* That the petitioners be referred, for an adjustment of their claim, to the Commissioners that have been, or may be, appointed by the United States for such purposes." (*Votes and Proceedings of the House of Assembly of the Delaware State, At a Session commenced at Dover, on Monday, the eighth Day of January, in the Year of our Lord One Thousand Seven Hundred and Eighty-Seven* [Wilmington: Printed by Frederick Craig & Co. in Market-Street, 1787], 32, Microfilm Collection of Early State Records, Library of Congress.)

4. Thomas Collins.

5. For H's discussion of relevant statutes of limitation, see "Report on Sundry Petitions," April 16, 1792.

To George Washington

[Philadelphia, May 3, 1792]

Mr. Hamilton presents his respects to the President. Colo. Wigglesworth's christian name is Edward.[1]

3d May 1792.

LC, George Washington Papers, Library of Congress.
1. On the same day that this letter was written Washington nominated Wigglesworth collector of customs at Newburyport, Massachetts (*Executive Journal*, I, 121). See H to Washington, April 23, 1792.

From Oliver Wolcott, Junior

T D Co May 3d 1792

Sir,

The inclosed Letters of Administration granted to Catharine Jones on the estates of John Hanholt George Hollman, Bernard Brulbiner, James Burt John Geroir, & Atonia Lasambert late Soldiers of Genl Hazens [1] Regt. were some time since presented at this Office with a power of Attorney from the said Catharine Jones, to Alexander Power of the City of Philadelphia, Broker for the purpose of obtaining the balances due by the United States to the persons above named.

It so happened, that while the papers were under consideration powers of Attorney were presented by Benjamin Mooers [2] Esq who served as an Officer in the Regt. lately commanded by Genl. Hazen for the pay of John Geroir and Antoine Lasambert two of the persons on whose estates Catharine Jones, had administered. On conversing with Mr. Mooers I recd. the most positive assurance, that the persons whose powers he produced were living a few months since, near St Johns in Canada.

The suggestion on which Catharine Jones appears to have obtained Letters of Administration, is that of being a Creditor of the persons before named. On being desired to shew the nature of her demand, she delivered the inclosed Account.

Under these circumstances, I did not hesitate to direct a Certificate to be issued on the power of Atty produced by Mr. Mooers in favr of Antoine Lasembert and to receive a caveat from him in behalf of John Geroir whose power of Attorney was not admitted having been informally executed—And I have declined admitting the authority of Catharine Jones to receive any part of the sums claimed by her as Administratrix.

I conceive it to be my duty to observe, that though no instance has fallen under my observation, when the deception was so apparent as in the present case, yet I have had frequent cause for suspicion that Letters of Administration have been obtained on unfounded suggestions.[3]

As the right to receive the Certificates is contended for in behalf of the Administratrix, and as the interests of the United States & their Creditors are concerned in ascertaining the most proper line of conduct for me to pursue in this & similar cases, I have taken the liberty to request you to state the case to the Attorney General of the United States for his opinion.

I have the honor to be &c

ADf, Connecticut Historical Society, Hartford.
1. Moses Hazen was brevetted a brigadier general on June 29, 1781. During the American Revolution he commanded the Second Canadian Regiment.
2. Mooers served as adjutant for Hazen's regiment.
3. The use of fraudulent letters of administration in settling unclaimed credits was a serious problem for officials at the Federal and state treasuries. See Hunt, *Writings of Madison*, VI, 47; *The* [New York] *Daily Advertiser*, January 24, 1792; and *Journal of the House of Commons. State of North Carolina. At a General Assembly, begun and held at Newbern, on the fifteenth Day of November, in the Year of our Lord one thousand seven hundred and ninety-two, and of the Independence of the United States of America the sixteenth: It being the first Session of this Assembly* (Edenton: Printed by Hodge and Wills, n.d.), 18.

From Oliver Wolcott, Junior

T D
C. Off May 4. 1792

Sir,

The following occurrence took place a few days since in this Office, which I take the liberty to state, that a rule may be established to govern in future or similar occasions. Solomen Marks Jr[1] appeared at the Office with John McCulloh[2] and in his presence wrote a transfer to said McCulloh on a Certificate for One hundred & eighty one Dolls & sixty one Cents. six ⅌ Cent Stock.

Before the transfer was recorded and before it had been presented for my approbation, Marks returned to the Office and in McCulloh's presence revoked the transfer. Marks has also appeared sundry times since and has formally forbid the transfer to be made. Mr. McCulloh has also appeared and demanded that the transfer be not suspended.

The question submitted to your consideration is, whether after a transfer is written on a Certificate & delivered into the Office & before it has been admitted by the Comptroller of the Treasury, it can be revoked.

In the present case I have retained the Certificate & suspended allowing the transfer.

I am &c

Hon A H.

ADf, Connecticut Historical Society, Hartford.
1. Marks was a Philadelphia haberdasher.
2. McCulloch was a Philadelphia merchant.

From ――――

[*May 5, 1792*. On May 28, 1792, Hamilton wrote to an unknown correspondent: "Your letter of the 5th instant has been received at the Treasury." *Letter not found.*]

From Israel Ludlow [1]

Philadelphia, May 5, 1792.

Sir:

The unexpected delays that have attended my executing the surveys of the Ohio and Miami Companies,[2] together with your letters, which I have received from time to time,[3] urging my speedy exertions to effect the business, induces me to explain to you the cause of the delay.

In November, 1790, I was honored with your letter of instruction at this place.[4] I proceeded immediately to Fort Harmar, being possessed of General Knox's letter, or order to the Commandant for an escort. On my way, at Fort Pitt, I saw Maj. Doughty,[5] who, after becoming acquainted with my business, informed me that there was no doubt but an escort would be furnished on my arrival at Fort Harmar, upon which I supplied myself with chain-carriers and other hands necessary, pack-horses, corn, provision, and camp equipage for the coming cold season.

On my arrival at Fort Harmar, I found no escort could be obtained. Maj. Ziegler,[6] who commanded, gave me his answer in writing, which was that he did not consider the troops then under his command more than sufficient to guard the settlement of Marietta, the Indians having shortly before that defeated and broken up one of their frontier stations. Of course, he could not comply with the order of Gen. Knox and my request (a copy of that letter I inclosed to you). Upon that information, from necessity I gave up the pursuit at that time, and proceeded to Fort Washington, supposing I could execute the Miami survey.

Discharging my hired men and pack-horses, I applied to Gen. Harmar,[7] who then commanded, for protection while surveying the Miami tract. He informed me he did not consider his whole command a sufficient escort for my purpose (a copy of his answer I forwarded to you). On the arrival of Gen. St. Clair,[8] in May following, I made an official application for fifteen men or more, should it be convenient, to accompany me as an escort while surveying the Miami and Ohio tracts. He assured me that he considered the execution of this survey a matter of the highest interest and importance to the United States, and that he would make every effort to assist me with a sufficient guard, but that it was then impracticable (his letter I will forward to you). Thus the business was again put off until the 20th of October following, when I was favored with the services of fifteen men, commanded by a sergeant, with whom I proceeded to execute the Ohio Company's survey. I succeeded, and returned to Fort Washington, but with the loss of six of the escort, and leaving in the woods all of my pack-horses and their equipage, and being obliged to make a raft of logs to descend the Ohio as far as Limestone, from opposite the mouth of the Great Sandy River.

On my arrival at Fort Washington, I again applied for protection to proceed in the Miami survey. That assistance was refused by Maj. Ziegler, who then commanded (his letter I will produce). My reputation, as well as the public good, being in some measure affected by the delay of the business, I was constrained to have recourse to an effort which my instruction did not advise, viz.: to attempt making the survey by the aid of three active woodsmen, to assist as spies, and give notice of any approaching danger. My attempts proved unsuccessful. After extending the western boundary more than one hundred miles up the Miami River, the deep snows and cold weather rendered our situation too distressing, by reason of my men having their feet frozen, and unfit to furnish game for supplies. In consequence, we returned to Fort Washington. The cold weather abating, I made another attempt, extending the east boundary as far as the line intersected the Little Miami River, where we discovered signs of the near approach of Indians, and, having but three armed men in company, induced me to return again to Fort Washington, which I found commanded by General Wilkinson,[9] to whom I applied for an escort, which was denied me (his letter I have the honor to inclose to you with the others).

I now have the satisfaction to present to you the whole of the survey of the Ohio and part of the Miami purchases, executed agreeably to instructions.[10]

I am, sir, yours respectfully,   Israel Ludlow.

Hon. Alex. Hamilton,
Sec. of the Treasury.

Henry Benton Teetor, *Sketch of the Life and Times of Col. Israel Ludlow, One of the Original Proprietors of Cincinnati* (Cincinnati, 1885), 50–52.

1. Ludlow, a native of Morristown, New Jersey, had served as an assistant surveyor of the western country under Thomas Hutchins during the Confederation period.

2. On November 20, 1790, H requested Ludlow to complete the survey of the Ohio tract. H's letter to Ludlow is printed in Arthur St. Clair to H, May 25, 1791, note 2.

3. Letters not found.

4. See note 2.

5. John Doughty, who remained in the Army after service during the American Revolution, was responsible for the construction of Fort Harmar and Fort Washington.

6. David Zeigler, who had been a major in the First Infantry Regiment, had resigned from the Army on March 5, 1792.

7. Brigadier General Josiah Harmar was commander of the troops in the West from 1784 to 1791.

8. Arthur St. Clair was governor of the Northwest Territory.

9. James Wilkinson was brevetted brigadier general in the Continental Army on November 6, 1777. He resigned on March 6, 1778, to serve first as secretary to the Board of War in 1778 and then as clothier general in the Continental Army from July, 1779, to March, 1781. In 1782 he became brigadier general in the Pennsylvania Militia. After the Revolution Wilkinson settled in Lexington, Kentucky. From Kentucky he traded with the Spanish in Louisiana, and on October 22, 1791, he rejoined the Army as lieutenant colonel commandant of the Second United States Infantry. He became a brigadier general on March 5, 1792.

10. On May 20 and August 14, 1792, Ludlow submitted bills for his services

(DS, RG 217, Miscellaneous Treasury Accounts, 1790–1894, Account No. 2472 and 2870, National Archives). On May 22 and August 15, 1792, H certified on these bills that Ludlow's services were performed at his direction and according to congressional resolutions (ADS, RG 217, Miscellaneous Treasury Accounts, 1790–1894, Account No. 2472 and 2870, National Archives). In addition to H's certification on the bill of August 15, 1792, there is a second statement signed by H and dated August 15 which reads as follows:

"I certify that Mr. Ludlow was employed to calculate and delineate on a Plot or map the Surveys or tracts of Country granted to the agents of the directors of the Ohio Company by an Act of the last session.

"Mr. Ludlow has Also executed a Map delineating the extremities of the tract of Country contracted for by the Agents of the Scioto Company.

"For the first mentioned service he is clearly intitled to a quantum meruit. As to the last the Accounting Officers will judge how far it is or it is not a part of any service for what he has been otherwise compensated." (DS, with additions in H's handwriting, RG 217, Miscellaneous Treasury Accounts, 1790–1894, Account No. 2870, National Archives.)

From Jeremiah Olney

Providence, May 5, 1792. "I have received your favor of the 25th of April 1792.[1] I shall apply to the Supervisor for the Sum you mention, in a few Days; and repay it as soon as I have the Money to spare. . . ."

ADfS, Rhode Island Historical Society, Providence.
1. See also Olney to H, April 9, May 3, 1792.

To William Seton

[*Philadelphia, May 5, 1792.* On May 28, 1792, Seton acknowledged the receipt of Hamilton's "orders on the 5th May instant." Letter not found.]

From Tench Coxe

[Philadelphia, May 6, 1792]

Dear Sir

The bill relative to the debt having passed thro the House [1] I hope an handsome conclusion will be made to the business of the

ALS, Hamilton Papers, Library of Congress.
1. "An act supplementary to the act making provision for the debt of the United States" passed the House of Representatives on May 7, 1792 (*Journal of the House*, I, 601). It became law on May 8, 1792 (1 *Stat.* 281–83).

Departments.[2] I should not have troubled you again upon [it], but that I am well informed that a Member of the Senate, who opposed the bill in its present Shape said *a week ago* that "the whole of the Treasury clauses except the Compensations[3] would be struck out in the House" and one of the Eastern gentlemen told the Auditor that the bill would certainly be taken up and passed "at least so far as regarded the Compensations." The delays which have been made since the bill came from the Senate, which is now near two weeks,[4] are a painful comment on the observations abovementioned. Permit me, Sir, to say a few words upon this subject before it be too late to remedy the public & personal Evils such a conclusion of the business will produce.

The state of the public business will remain in its present perplexing form—there will be no provision for the settlement of accounts audited by Mr. Wolcot[5]—there will be no provision for the temporary execution of the duties of the Executive offes. of the government. I, and my family will be left without an Establishment —as will Mr. Meyer & Mr. Jones.[6] After so much consideration & discussion this matter cannot fail to be ascribed to causes irritating to and inconsistent with the national interests. It will appear to some members, I *know*, from every part of the Union as a most unde-

2. Coxe is referring to "An Act making alterations in the Treasury and War Departments." On April 3, 1792, a committee of the Senate was appointed to consider what alterations, if any, should be made in the Treasury and War departments. The committee reported on April 10, and the bill passed the Senate on April 17 (*Annals of Congress*, III, 116, 120, 125). After the House had proposed some amendments and these had been altered by the Senate, the bill became law on May 8, 1792 (1 *Stat.* 279–81). Coxe was particularly interested in this bill because he was assistant to the Secretary of the Treasury, and the bill provided: "That the present office of assistant to the Secretary of the Treasury, be abolished, and that instead thereof there be an officer in the department of the treasury, to be denominated Commissioner of the Revenue . . ." (1 *Stat.* 280). Coxe was appointed commissioner of the revenue on May 8, 1792.

3. The act provided an additional allowance for the comptroller, auditor, treasurer, and register of the Treasury (1 *Stat.* 281).

4. Although the bill passed the Senate on April 17, it was not taken up by the House until May 7 (*Journal of the House*, I, 601).

5. Oliver Wolcott, Jr., comptroller of the Treasury. Coxe is referring to Section 7 of "An Act making alterations in the Treasury and War Departments" which provided that ". . . in every case of an account or claim not finally adjusted, upon which the present comptroller of the treasury, as auditor, may have decided, it shall be the duty of the commissioner of the revenue, and of the auditor of the treasury, finally to adjust the same, and in case of disagreement between the said commissioner and auditor, the decision of the attorney general shall be final" (1 *Stat.* 281).

6. Edward Jones and John Meyer were Treasury Department clerks.

served ill turn done to me by a respectable part of the federal interest, a circumstance, which will have, I may say, an astonishing and very unpleasing Complexion to all the sincere friends of the general Government considering the part I have borne in regard to it from the Annapolis Convention to the present time.

The clause relative to the deposit of the Customs is viewed among many good & judicious men as inconsistent with the office of Comptroller of the Treasury.[7] I have good reason to believe that Mr.

7. There was no "clause relative to the deposit of the Customs" in the act that was passed by Congress. The plan to which Coxe is referring, however, was proposed by William Loughton Smith, a member of the House of Representatives from South Carolina, in a report presented to the House on February 29, 1792. The resolutions contained in Smith's report that did not become part of the final act read as follows:

"5th. In relation to the Treasury Department. That it shall be the duty of the Comptroller of the Treasury to superintend, under the head of the Department, the collection of the duties on imports and tonnage. . . .

"7th. That in every case of a claim against the United States not finally adjusted, upon which the present Comptroller of the Treasury, as Auditor, may have decided, and in which his decision is not controverted by the claimant, the said Comptroller be empowered and directed finally to adjust the same; and that in every such case in which the decision of the said Comptroller, as Auditor, is controverted, it shall be lawful for the Secretary of the Treasury, on behalf of the United States, to submit the points in controversy to referees, who shall be three in number; one of whom to be appointed by the Secretary of the Treasury, one by the claimant, and the third to be agreed upon between the Secretary and the claimant; or, in case of disagreement, to be chosen by the two referees who shall have been appointed as aforesaid; and the decision of the said referees, or a majority of them, shall have the like force and effect with an award of arbitrators between individuals. But if any claimant shall refuse to join in a reference, then it shall be lawful for the Comptroller of the Treasury to proceed to an adjustment of the claim as in other cases. That each of the said referees be allowed ―――― dollars per day while actually employed in the reference.

"8th. That in case of the death, absence from the seat of Government, or sickness of the Secretary of the Treasury, whereby he cannot perform the duties of his office, the Comptroller of the Treasury may perform the said duties until a successor be appointed, or until such absence or inability by sickness shall cease; and all warrants which shall be signed by the said Comptroller in place of the said Secretary shall be countersigned by the Commissioner of the Revenue.

"9th. That in case of the death, absence from the seat of Government, or sickness of the Comptroller of the Treasury, whereby he cannot perform the duties of his office, the Commissioner of the Revenue may perform the said duties until a successor be appointed, or until such absence or inability by sickness shall cease.

"10th. That in case of the death, absence from the seat of Government, or sickness of the Auditor of the Treasury, whereby he cannot perform the duties of his office, the first clerk of the said Auditor may perform the said duties until a successor be appointed, or until such absence or inability by sickness shall cease.

Morris's [8] vote in the Senate against it was founded on an opinion that the director of the Collectors conduct ought not to sit in Judgment upon their accounts. Mr. Cabot [9] told me in the most explicit terms that he disapproved of the annexing of the Customs to the office of Comptroller. The first remark I ever heard upon the *first* Report was from Mr. Delany,[10] who called upon me to know, if you were in your office, & finding you were engaged mentioned to me his alarm at the Union of those two duties. He wished to represent it to you, and I earnestly intreated and almost insisted, that he should not, observing that as He was a Pennsylvanian, I should be suspected of moving him to do so. On Saturday, I spoke to Mr. Findley [11] for the first time, on the bill generally, when he told me a Number of the Members & he among them had deter-mined to oppose that clause with decision—and for the reason abovementioned. Now, Sir, I can prove to you that I mentioned to one of the House, whom I once asked to call up the report of Mr Smith [12] &c. (in fact to Mr Murray) [13] that tho I thought ye clause improper I hoped nothing would prevent the arrangement taking effect, as it was necessary for me to get an Establishment for my family, and I was sure the first Session would produce an alteration of the business of the Customs from a general conviction of its impropriety.

I hope & trust, Sir, that the mere circumstance of leaving the Customs in your hands, and the not adding that power to an office, which members of the new & old Congress sought in Competition with Mr. Wolcot, will not influence to unkindness and injustice to

---

"11th. That in case of the death, absence from the seat of Government, or sickness of the Register of the Treasury, whereby he cannot perform the duties of his office, the first clerk of the said Register may perform the said duties until a successor be appointed, or until such absence or inability by sickness shall cease. . . .

"15th. That the restriction on the clerks of the Department of the Treasury, so far as respects the carrying on of any trade or business, be abolished." (*ASP, Miscellaneous,* I, 47.)

8. Robert Morris, Senator from Pennsylvania.

9. George Cabot, Senator from Massachusetts.

10. Sharp Delany, collector of customs at Philadelphia.

11. William Findley, a member of the House of Representatives from Pennsylvania.

12. For the relevant sections of Smith's report, see note 7.

13. William Vans Murray, a member of the House of Representatives from Maryland.

me. The Eastern Gentlemen are not aware of the deep impolicy & impression, which will attend a unfavorable issue to this business. For my own part I know not which way in such an Event to turn from the most painful feelings. In your office and in your domestic circle I shall meet with the Authors of my unmerited dishonor and sufferings. I must exhibit to the gentlemen who are in and above the government a contemptible appearance of good will and harmony with those members of the legislature from whose hands I shall have recd the most unhandsome treatment—or I must avoid (so far as my office will permit) those scenes where they so often are. In short, Sir, I must seek in the bosom of my family, that comfort wch this Event will deprive me of in every other Scene. I do not mean, Sir, to talk of a resignation for tho I own the dignity of my public & personal Character would be better preserved by that measure it is unhappily not in my power at this Moment.

It may be suggested perhaps that all the Sensibility I now feel is the mere workings of Ambition, but to you, Sir, that will not appear to be possible when you remember that I was willing to have left all the prospects of the Treasury for the post office [14] and the connected opportunity of a life employed at pleasure in the investigation of the great interests of my Country. I believed I had some of that talent, which would have enabled me to lead a generous intelligent people, by the light of unknown but interesting truth into the true road to wealth and happiness. Excuse me, Sir, for this last effort to avoid a course of things out of which many evils will arise which I forbear to particularize, & Believe me when I *devoutly* pray, with an aching heart, for the consummation of your noble Scheme of national Happiness *with confidence in its success*, and for a greater portion of personal felicity to you and your family than, I fear, will result from all your exertions & Services.

Yr. respectful Servt.   T. Coxe

May 6th. 1792

14. Coxe had applied for the office of Postmaster General in 1789. He was not, however, appointed.

From Israel Ludlow

[*May 6, 1792. Letter not found.*] [1]

1. This letter is listed as Item No. 23 in "List of Papers: Contract with John Cleves Symmes" (Carter, *Territorial Papers*, II, 391–93).

From William Ellery

[*Newport, Rhode Island*] *May 7, 1792.* "I have received your letter of the 25th of the last month [1] and have borrowed and received of the Supervisor [2] Two thousand, three hundred and thirty three dollars, which will be sufft. to pay all the drawbacks which are due.[3] To preclude the possibility of any delay the Surpervisor on the Receipt of your letter dispatched his Clerk to this place for the purpose of receiving from the Collectors the monies in their hands, to advance it to me. I still wish for an explanation respectg. the Thermometer which I mentioned in my letter of the 9th. of April, and beg leave to call your attention to that Part of my letter of the 5th. of March last which relates to the taring of sugars &c. . . ."

LC, Newport Historical Society, Newport, Rhode Island.
1. Letter not found.
2. John S. Dexter.
3. For a similar problem, see H to Jeremiah Olney, April 25, 1792.

From William Seton

[*New York, May 7, 1792.* On May 10, 1792, Hamilton wrote to Seton: "I received your letter of the 7th instant." *Letter not found.*]

To William Short

Treasury Department May 7th 1792

Sir

The President having ratified the three last loans, namely one of six millions of florins at five per Cent interest; [1] one of three Millions at four per Cent[2] and that which has been negociated at Antwerp,[3] I herewith transmit you the instrument of ratification concerning the latter. The two former I have thought best to enclose directly to the Commissioners in Amsterdam[4] under an impression that this at the time of its arrival may possibly[5] not find you at the Hague.

I have the honor to be with great consideration Sir Your Obedt. Servant   A Hamilton

William Short Esqr.
Minister Resident of the
United States at the Hague

LS, William Short Papers, Library of Congress; LS, marked "2nd," William Short Papers, Library of Congress.
    1. The Holland loan of September, 1791. For a description of this loan, see Short to H, August 31, 1791.
    2. The Holland loan of December, 1791. For a description of this loan, see Short to H, December 23, 28, 1791.
    3. For a description of the Antwerp loan, see Short to H, November 8, 1791, note 4, and November 12, 1791.
    4. H's letter to Willink, Van Staphorst, and Hubbard has not been found.
    5. The word "possibly" is in the handwriting of H.

To Benjamin Walker [1]

Philadelphia
May 7. 1792

Dear Sir

The bearer of this Mr. George Parkinson[2] is an ingenious Mechanic who has been engaged by me in the service of The Society for establishing useful manufactures. I have advised him to go to New York to assist Mr. Marshall[3] to whom I have given him a letter[4] & to whom I am persuaded he will be useful.

I take this occasion to make him known to you that he may receive any little pecuniary aid of which he may stand in need, as far as you may be authorised.

With great regard Yrs   A Hamilton

B Walker Esqr

ALS, Bibliothèque Municipale, Nantes, France.
1. Walker was a director of the Society for Establishing Useful Manufactures.
2. For Parkinson, see H to the President and Directors of the Society for Establishing Useful Manufactures, December 7, 1791, and "Receipt from George Parkinson," May 2, 1792.
2. Thomas Marshall, an Englishman with experience in the construction of cotton mills, had been hired by the Society for Establishing Useful Manufactures.
4. Letter not found.

From George Washington

[Philadelphia, May 7, 1792]

For carrying into execution the provisions in that behalf made by the Act intitled, "An Act for raising a farther sum of money for the protection of the Frontiers, and for other purposes therein mentioned," [1] I do hereby authorise you the said Secretary of the Treasury to agree and contract with The President Directors & Company of the Bank of the United States, with any other body politic or corporate within the United States, or with any other person or persons, for a loan or loans to the United States of any sum or sums not exceeding in the whole Five hundred and twenty three thousand five hundred Dollars to be advanced & paid in such proportions and at such periods as you shall judge necessary for fulfilling the purposes of the said Act. Provided that the rate of interest of such loan or loans shall not exceed five per centum per annum, and that the principal thereof may be reimbursed at the pleasure of the United States. And I hereby promise to ratify what you shall lawfully do in the premises.[2]

In testimony whereof I have hereunto subscribed my hand at the City of Philadelphia the seventh day of May in the year one thousand seven hundred and ninety two.   Go: Washington

LC, George Washington Papers, Library of Congress.
1. 1 Stat. 259-63 (May 2, 1792).
2. The loan was ratified on June 5, 1792 (D, Register of Acts of the Federal Congress and Communications Received by the Department of State, 1790-1795, Papers of the Continental Congress, National Archives).

To George Washington

[*Philadelphia*] *May* 7, *1792.* "The Secretary of the Treasury . . .
has the honor to enclose a copy of the Authorisation which the
President signed this morning." [1]

LC, George Washington Papers, Library of Congress.
1. See Washington to H, May 7, 1792.

To Wilhem and Jan Willink, Nicholaas and Jacob Van Staphorst, and Nicholas Hubbard

[*Philadelphia, May* 7, *1792.* On July 26, 1792, Hamilton wrote to
Willink, Van Staphorst, and Hubbard: "You will herewith receive
triplicates of my letters of the 7th. of May and 20th. ultimo." *Letter
of May* 7 *not found.*]

From Timothy Pickering

Philadelphia May 8. 1792.

Dear Sir,

The Indians of the Five Nations who lately visited Philadelphia,
received their invitation from *me*,[1] in the manner described in the
inclosed copy of a letter to the President.[2] Mr. Kirkland, the bearer
of my message, received his instructions from the Secretary of War,
to whom he from time to time transmitted information of his pro-

ALS, Hamilton Papers, Library of Congress; copy, Massachusetts Historical
Society, Boston.
1. In May, 1791, Henry Knox, Secretary of War, instructed Pickering to
invite the leaders of the Five Nations to meet with Government officials in
Philadelphia "for the purpose of cementing existing friendships" (*ASP, Indian
Affairs,* I, 165). After the defeat by the Indians of the United States troops
under the command of Major General Arthur St. Clair in November, 1791,
Knox on December 20, 1791, instructed Samuel Kirkland, a missionary to the
Indians and founder of Hamilton College, to renew Pickering's invitation
(*ASP, Indian Affairs,* I, 226). This invitation, dated December 19, 1791, is
printed in *Michigan Pioneer and Historical Society Collections,* XXIV (1894),
370–71.
2. See enclosure.

ceedings. Of this I was ignorant until after the arrival of the Indians, when Mr. Kirkland referred to them as matters well known to me, but of which not a syllable had been communicated to me. Nor did I know they were coming, till they had arrived at Nazareth. This I heard from a Moravian of that place. The same day, as I was passing up Chesnut Street, the Secy. of War crossed over and told me the Indians were at Bethlehem, and said—"I believe I must get you to negociate with them: Do think of it." I heard no more of them until one of his clerks came and told me they were arrived at Odlers's Hotel; & that the Secretary of War wished me to see them immediately. I walked up, to bid them welcome. The next day, March 15th, they delivered their formal speeches in answer to my invitation. On the 16th. I replied; and at the close of my speech, used these words.

"Brothers,

I have now finished what I had to do. In behalf of the United States I invited you to their Great Council Fire, to settle the plan of introducing among you the knowledge of husbandry and a few of the most useful arts. You have come. We have taken each other by the hand, and spoken together as friends and brothers. All further proceedings on the subject will be conducted in such manner as the Great Chief of the United States shall direct."

I heard no more from the Secretary of War on the business of negociation, until the 22d. of March, the morning after I had sent the letter before mentioned to the President; when a clerk from the war office came with the compliments of the Secretary, who desired to see me. From the stile of my letter, and an explicit declaration, *that I did not wish to appear in the matter;* I thought the president would have put my letter in his pocket; tho' I did expect it would occasion a material alteration in the intended speech. But when I arrived, I found my letter on the Secretary's table. He looked it up, *and said my sentiments were very just.* He then shewed me the Speech, with the most exceptionable parts crossed out; and after some other alterations had been proposed and agreed to, and he had got to the close of the speech, he asked me if I would permit him to introduce my name with his own, that I might assist in the negociations with the Indians. I consented; and expressed my reason —That having suggested to the Indians ideas of civilization, I felt a solicitude to see a plan formed for the purpose, and a fair experiment made to carry it into effect: and that I would therefore give what assistance I could. You heard the speech, in which the President named me with the Secretary of War as the persons with whom the Indians were to negociate.[3] I suppose it is well known that almost the whole burthen of the business has fallen upon me; and really it has been very burthensome. All the proceedings in *writing* would fill a considerable volume. But besides *formal speeches*, a multitude of *conversations* were inevitable. The Indian speeches were taken in haste from the mouths of the Interpreters; were legible only to myself; and needing corrections, too, I was obliged to transcribe them with my own hand. To give you an exact idea of my labour, I must go into a still more tedious detail; but I will only add That the business has engaged my close attention for more than thirty entire days. I frequently wrote at night; and even Sundays seldom gave me any rest.

You see the conclusion: Am I entiled to any compensation? I have not said a word about it to the Secretary of War: and he also has been silent. Yet he knows that he did not negociate with the Creeks for *nothing;* altho' the business pertained to his department.[4]

More than one reason will occur, why I give *you* the trouble of this communication. Suffer me to submit the ⟨ma⟩tter entirely to your judgment. If you think something should be allowed me, you will have the goodness to put the matter in train. The quantum I should wish you and the Secretary of war to determine. I think you know that I am not mercenary nor extravagant. If it should be thought proper not to make any allowance, I shall acquiesce. In that case I would thank you to return this letter, as I have taken no copy [of] it. I may keep it as a memorandum of facts.[5]

3. The section of Washington's speech to the chiefs and representatives of the Five Nations on March 23, 1792, to which Pickering is referring reads as follows: "I shall not enter into further particulars with you at present, but refer you to General Knox, the Secretary of War, and Colonel Pickering, who will communicate with you upon the objects of your journey, and inform me thereof" (*ASP, Indian Affairs,* I, 229).

4. Knox had acted as commissioner to negotiate the peace treaty signed at New York on August 7, 1790, between the United States and the Creek Nation.

5. On the last page of this letter H wrote: "gave my opinion verbally that no compensation ought to be sought."

With the truest respect & esteem I am, dear sir, Your most obed. servant   Timothy Pickering.

P.S. On Thursday I expect to leave town, to bring my family to this city.

[ENCLOSURE]

Timothy Pickering to George Washington [6]

Philadelphia, Wednesday Evening, March 21. 1792.

Sir,

The manner in which I have been employed to effect the present visit of the Chiefs of the Five Nations, renders me peculiarly interested that the negociations with them should conform with the direct object of the invitation. This object is indelibly impressed on my mind; it having been the main argument offered by me, to convince them of the real friendship of the United States. I feel interested in its accomplishment, *because it involves* the *good faith of the United States.* For, agreeably to my instructions, "I informed them how desirous you were that the Indians should have imparted to them the blessings of husbandry and the arts:" [7] And I repeated to them your words "That the United States will be true and faithful to their engagements." [8]

Having assured them of the assistance of the United States to introduce among them the knowledge of husbandry and a few other important arts connected with it, I invited a small number of the principal chiefs to come to Philadelphia, after the last Corn Harvest, to negociate the plan for their introduction. The visit too,

6. ADfS, Massachusetts Historical Society, Boston; copy, Hamilton Papers, Library of Congress.

7. Knox's instructions to Pickering, dated May 2, 1791, read in part as follows: "You will, also, inform the Indians how desirous the President of the United States is, that the Indians should have imparted to them the blessings of husbandry, and the arts, and of his willingness to receive the young sons of some of their principal chiefs, for the two-fold purpose of teaching them to read and write, and to instruct them fully in the arts of husbandry" (*ASP, Indian Affairs,* I, 166).

8. This statement appears at the conclusion of Washington's address to Cornplanter, Half-Town, and Great Tree on December 29, 1790 (*ASP, Indian Affairs,* I, 143).

independently of its principal object, might make useful impressions. They delayed coming. The destructive defeat of our army took place.[9] This sad event might *prevent* their coming. Good policy dictated a fresh invitation. And that it might not seem to flow from fear or discouragement—I thought the renewal of the invitation should appear to proceed wholly from me. The idea was liked by General Knox. I wrote a message to be sent by Mr. Kirkland. As I recollect, the General informed me that it was approved by you.

In the message I reminded them of my former invitation to come to the *Great Council Fire of the United States*, "in order to fix the time and manner of introducing among them the knowledge of farming—of smith's & carpenter's work—of spinning & weaving— and of reading and writing:" these being the arts I had before expressly mentioned.

I added—"That I was impatient for their arrival, that they might receive strong proofs, that the words I spoke to them were true— that they came from my heart—and that the United States are faithful to their engagements."

The invitation was confined to *this single object*. Permit me, therefore, to express my opinion, That until the entire arrangement relative to it be formed, to their full satisfaction—no other object should be brought into view. But this being adjusted; with such strong proofs before them of the candor—the truth—the justice & the liberality of the United States—they will be convinced that we are *really their friends:* and thus they may be led to entertain a belief that we are heartily disposed to be *the friends* of the *other tribes* now in arms against us: and impressed with this belief —they may listen to overtures to become mediators between us. But if the latter be proposed in the first instance—the natural order of things will be reversed; and, I fear, every object of their visit defeated.

If the secretary of war had asked me in a single question on the subject, I should freely have suggested to him these ideas. This evening I chanced to hear that he (doubtless not adverting to the terms of the invitation) is preparing a speech, to be delivered to-

9. Pickering is referring to the defeat by the Indians of the troops under St. Clair's command on November 4, 1791.

morrow,[10] in which the disposition of the Five Nations to become mediators, is to be sounded. I have therefore thought it *my duty*, without loss of time, to submit them to your consideration. I have no desire to appear in the matter: having nothing in view but to prevent a *serious mischief*.

There is an additional reason for the caution here suggested, which I beg leave to mention.

Last Thursday, when the Indians gave me their formal answers to my invitation, they stated many causes of their delay. Among other things they told me that Brant [11] had been the means of detaining them. "Brant (said they) who knows as much as white people know, told us that the real design of the invitation was not *on* the paper—but *behind* it." That is, the *avowed object* of the invitation was merely *ostensible:* while the *real object* was *kept out of sight*.

There is another reason, which I ought not to conceal. Indians have been so often deceived by White people, that *White Man* is, among many of them, but another name for *Liar*. Really, Sir I am unwilling to be subjected to this infamy. I confess I am not indifferent to a good name, even among Indians. Besides, they viewed, and expressly considered *me*, as "*your Representative*;" and my promises, as the promises of "*the Town Destroyer*." Sir, for you honour & the honour & interest of the United States, I wish them to *know* that *there are some white men who are incapable of deceiving*.

I acknowledge, Sir, that my feelings have been excited: and if I have expressed myself in a state unusual in addressing you, I trust you will ascribe it to the true cause—the interesting situation in which I stand.

10. Presumably Knox was preparing Washington's speech to the Five Nations of March 23, 1792 (*ASP, Indian Affairs*, I, 229). On March 22, 1792, Knox wrote to Tobias Lear enclosing the draft of a speech to the Indian deputation, and the following day Lear replied that Washington would give the speech and would like to have another copy prepared for his use. Both letters may be found in the George Washington Papers, Library of Congress.
11. Knox had made a special effort to induce Joseph Brant, the Mohawk chief and wartime leader of the Iroquois Confederacy, to come to Philadelphia with the other Indian leaders. Brant eventually made a separate visit to Philadelphia in June, 1792.

With great respect   I am, sir,   Your most h'ble & obedt. servt.

T.P.

The President
Of the United States.

From Otho H. Williams

[*Baltimore, May 8, 1792*. On June 5, 1792, Hamilton wrote to Williams: "I have before me your letters of the 18th of March, 18th of April, 8th & 27th of May." *Letter of May 8 not found.*]

From Philip Schuyler

Albany May 9th 1792

Dear Sir

Mrs. Rensselaer's [1] health is so much impaired that It is thought advisable that she should go to N York for better medical assistance, and to try the Effects of a change of Air, I shall accompany her and we shall leave this on friday the 11th Instant at farthest. Cannot you my Eliza and Cornelia [2] make arrangements to meet us at N York towards the close of next week. Pray drop a line to be left at Mrs. Daugbineys [3] until called for best under cover to her.

If all the votes taken for Mr. Jay are to be returned and fairly canvassed, I have reason to believe he would prevail, but I apprehend much foul play in the returning officers at least.[4]

Adieu we all Join in love to you and all with you.

I am Dr Sir Yours affectionately   &c &c   P Schuyler

Honb Alexr Hamilton Esqr

ALS, Union College, Schenectady, New York.
    1. Margaret (or Margarita) Van Rensselaer was the daughter of Philip Schuyler, the wife of Stephen Van Rensselaer, and the sister of Elizabeth Hamilton.
    2. Cornelia Schuyler was the daughter of Philip Schuyler and sister of Elizabeth Hamilton.
    3. Mrs. Mary Daubigny was the proprietor of a boardinghouse at 15 Wall Street, New York City.
    4. Schuyler is referring to the recent New York gubernatorial election in which John Jay was defeated by the incumbent, George Clinton. Soon

after Schuyler's letter was written, accusations concerning the manner in which the April 13, 1792, election had been conducted appeared in the New York press. The "returning officers" in New York State were the members of the joint committee appointed by the legislature to canvass the votes and report the results of the election. A majority of the canvassers who sat from May 29, 1792, until June 11 reported that Clinton had been elected by a majority of fewer than one hundred and fifty votes. A minority of the canvassers reported that Jay would probably have won the election if the ballots of Otsego, Clinton, and Tioga counties had not been disallowed on technicalities. Jay's supporters stated that he had a majority of five hundred in Otsego County alone. Although the ballots from the three counties which had been rejected by the majority of canvassers were burned shortly after the canvassers gave their reports, criticism of the legal grounds on which the majority report of the canvassers was based continued until the legislature concluded its investigation in January, 1793.

The technicalities on which the majority of the canvassers disallowed the votes of the three counties were all related to the fact that the law stated that the ballots in each county had to be delivered to the sheriff and transmitted by him to the secretary of state. In Otsego County it was charged that the ballots had been delivered to and transmitted by a man whose term as sheriff had expired. In Tioga County the charge was that the sheriff turned over the ballots to a special deputy who became ill and entrusted their transmittal to a clerk. In the case of Clinton County it was charged that the sheriff entrusted the transmittal of the box of ballots to a man who was not the sheriff's deputy.

To George Washington

Treasury Department 9th. May 1792.

Sir,

I have the honor to send herewith an adjustment at the Treasury concerning the quantity of Acres in Warrants for army bounty rights, which ought to be deemed an equivalent for the 214,285 Acres of land mentioned in the second enacting clause of the Act intitled "An Act authorising the grant and conveyance of certain Lands to the Ohio Company of associates"; [1] and a Certificate of the delivery of the requisite quantity of Warrants in conformity to that adjustment.[2]

It is with regret I find myself required by Law to discharge an official duty in a case in which I happen to be interested as a party,[3] and which is capable of being regulated by different constructions.

Thus circumstanced I have conceived it proper to repose myself on the judgment of others; and having referred the matter to the accounting Officers of the Treasury, with the opinion of the Attorney General, which was previously obtained, I have governed myself by the determination of those Officers.

I submit it nevertheless to the President whether it will not be adviseable to require as a condition to the issuing of the Grant that the parties give bond to pay any deficiency which there may be in the quantity of Warrants delivered, if the Legislature at the ensuing Session shall decide that the construction which has been adopted is not the true one, or to surrender the Letters Patent for the Tract in question.

With the highest respect,   I have the honor to be &c.

Alexander Hamilton

LC, George Washington Papers, Library of Congress.

1. 1 Stat. 257–58 (April 21, 1792).

2. The Treasury Board had made the original contract with the Ohio Company under a resolution of the Continental Congress of July 23, 1787, which provided in part that no more than one-seventh of the land contracted for might be paid for in rights to bounties of land granted to the late Army and that the minimum price of the land should be one dollar per acre, with an allowance of a maximum of one-third of a dollar per acre for bad lands, incidental charges, and other circumstances (JCC, XXXIII, 400).

Section 2 of "An Act authorizing the grant and conveyance of certain Lands to the Ohio Company of Associates" stipulated that 214,285 acres of land granted to the Ohio Company might be paid for in bounty rights, "Provided, That the said . . . [Ohio Company] shall deliver to the Secretary of the Treasury within six months, warrants which issued for army bounty-rights sufficient for that purpose, according to the provision of a resolve of Congress of the twenty-third of July, one thousand seven hundred and eighty-seven" (1 Stat. 257).

According to the Treasury statement concerning this transaction, one-third of a dollar per acre, as the deduction for bad lands, incidental charges, and other circumstances, was subtracted from the minimum price of a dollar per acre. The payment was in land warrants which were valued at $142,856.66⅔, that is, 214,285 acres at 66⅔ cents an acre (copy, RG 217, Miscellaneous Treasury Accounts, 1790–1894, Account No. 2396, National Archives).

3. H owned five and one-half shares in the Ohio Company.

To George Washington

Treasury Departmt. 9th. May 1792.

The Secretary of the Treasury has the honor to transmit a fair copy of the Draft approved by the President this morning respecting the Port of Entry & Delivery in the District of Vermont.[1]

LC, George Washington Papers, Library of Congress.

1. This enclosure, dated May 9, 1792, reads in part as follows: "I have appointed, and by these presents do appoint the Island of South Hero in Lake

Champlain to be the Port of Entry and Delivery within and for the District of Vermont" (LC, George Washington Papers, Library of Congress).

Authorization for Washington's determination of a port of entry for the District of Vermont was given by Section 19 of "An Act for raising a farther sum of money for the protection of the frontiers, and for other purposes therein mentioned." This section reads in part as follows: ". . . the President of the United States . . . is authorized to appoint such place within the district of Vermont to be the port of entry and delivery within the said district, as he may deem expedient, any thing in the act, intituled 'An act giving effect to the laws of the United States within the state of Vermont,' to the contrary notwithstanding" (1 Stat. 263 [May 2, 1792]).

From George Washington

[Philadelphia, May 9, 1792]

For carrying into execution the provisions of the Eleventh section of the Act intitled "An Act to incorporate the subscribers to the Bank of the United States,"[1] I do hereby authorise you the said Secretary of the Treasury to subscribe by one or more subscriptions, on behalf and in the name of the United States, for such number of shares of and in the capital stock of the said Corporation as together shall amount to two Millions of Dollars, and the same to pay for out of any monies which shall have been or shall be borrowed by virtue of either of the Acts, the one intitled: "An Act making provision for the Debt of the United States,"[2] and the other intitled, "An Act making provision for the reduction of the public Debt":[3] and I do further authorise you to borrow of the said Corporation for and on account of the United States an equal sum, namely, Two Millions of Dollars to be applied to the purposes for which the said monies shall have been procured, and to be reimbursable in Ten years by equal annual installments, or at any time sooner or in any greater proportions that the Government may think fit. Provided that the interest on the said sum so by you to be borrowed, shall not exceed the rate of six per centum per annum, hereby empowering you to enter into and conclude with the said Corporation such contracts and Agreements as shall be necessary for fulfilling the purposes aforesaid, and promising to ratify whatever you shall lawfully do in the premises.

In testimony whereof I have hereunto subscribed my hand at the City of Philadelphia the Ninth day of May in the year of our Lord one thousand seven hundred and ninety two.   G: Washington

LC, George Washington Papers, Library of Congress.

1. Section 11 of "An Act to incorporate the subscribers of the Bank of the United States" reads as follows: "*And be it further enacted,* That is shall be lawful for the President of the United States, at any time or times, within eighteen months after the first day of April next, to cause a subscription to be made to the stock of the said corporation, as part of the aforesaid capital stock of ten millions of dollars, on behalf of the United States, to an amount not exceeding two millions of dollars; to be paid out of the monies which shall be borrowed by virtue of either of the acts, the one entitled 'An act making provision for the debt of the United States;' and the other entitled 'An act making provision for the reduction of the public debt;' borrowing of the bank an equal sum, to be applied to the purposes, for which the said monies shall have been procured; reimbursable in ten years, by equal annual instalments; or at any time sooner, or in any greater proportions, that the government may think fit" (1 *Stat.* 196 [February 25, 1791])

2. Section 2 of this act authorized the President to borrow twelve million dollars to be applied to the discharge of the foreign debt (1 *Stat.* 139 [August 4, 1790])

3. Section 4 of this act authorized the President to borrow two million dollars to be applied to the purchase of the debt of the United States (1 *Stat.* 187 [August 12, 1790]).

From Sylvanus Bourne [1]

Boston May 10th 1792

Sir

I am in this moment favoured with a letter from Mr Bourne [2] informing of my having lost my Object in the mint Department & I'll assure you my Dr Sir the impression on my feelings is severe indeed—as I presume you had not the least doubt of my success from your conversation last had with me. I have on the strength made arrangments which will result injuriously to me—such as borrowing some money &c & with freedom inform you that I am totally destitute of other plans or expectations but feel some relief from a clause in Mr Bourne's letter where he mentions his opinion that I should obtain some other appointment. Of this you will please to inform me if within your cognizance, or give me a clerkship within your department—where I shall hope by my behaviour to merit your future notice to a better place.

My respected Sir—Suffer me to rest my hopes on your friendship & the incense of my gratitude shall never cease to burn.

I anxiously wait your answer & am with sentiments of respect & permit me to add personal attachment   Your Obedt Servt

Sylva Bourne

Excuse my innaccuracies which arise from an agitated mind.

ALS, Hamilton Papers, Library of Congress.

1. Bourne, who had been United States consul at Hispaniola from June, 1790, to September, 1791, hoped that he would be appointed treasurer of the Mint. But this post was given to another candidate, and Bourne subsequently became a clerk in the Treasury Department.

2. Shearjashub Bourne was a member of the House of Representatives from Massachusetts.

To Sylvanus Bourne

[*Philadelphia, May 10, 1792.* On May 24, 1792, Bourne wrote to Hamilton: "I had the honour to receive your favr of the 10th Inst." *Letter not found.*]

From Henry Glen [1]

[*May 10, 1792.* On June 26, 1792, Hamilton wrote to Glen: "Your letter of the 10th of May duly came to hand." *Letter not found.*]

1. Glen, a Schenectady, New York, merchant, had been a member of the Provincial Congress, a deputy quartermaster during the American Revolution, and had served in the New York Assembly in 1786 and 1787.

From Jeremiah Olney

Providence, May 10, 1792. "The Second Section of the Coasting Act [1] requires all Vessels of the United States to be registered by the Collector of the District to which they respectively belong; the Seventh Section [2] provides for registering them at other Districts: different constructions having occasioned different practices, I beg the favor Sir, of your Opinion, whether it is expedient that Vessels, registered in conformity to the sd. Seventh Section, be registered anew on their arrival at the District to which they belong, no alteration in them, nor transfers of Property, having been made? . . ."

ADfS, Rhode Island Historical Society, Providence.

1. Section 2 of "An Act for Registering and Clearing Vessels, Regulating the Coasting Trade, and for other purposes" reads in part as follows: "*And be it further enacted,* That the person or persons claiming property in any such ship or vessel, in order to entitle her to the benefits aforesaid, shall cause the same to be registered, and shall obtain a certificate of such registry from the collector of the district to which such ship or vessel belongs, in manner hereinafter directed . . ." (1 *Stat.* 55 [September 1, 1789]).

2. Section 7 of "An Act for Registering and Clearing Vessels, Regulating the Coasting Trade, and for other purposes" reads as follows: *"Provided always, and be it further enacted,* That whenever the owner or owners of such ship or vessel, usually resides or reside out of the district within which such ship or vessel may be at the time of granting the certificate of registry, that such owner, or where there are two or more owners, any one of them may take and subscribe the said oath or affirmation, before the collector of the district within which he usually resides, omitting in the said oath or affirmation, the description of such ship or vessel, as expressed in the certificate of the surveyor, and inserting in lieu thereof, the name of the port and district within which such ship or vessel may then be; and the collector before whom such oath or affirmation may be taken and subscribed, shall transmit the same to the collector of the district where such ship or vessel may be, upon the receipt whereof the said collector shall proceed to register such ship or vessel, in like manner as though the usual and regular oath or affirmation had been taken and subscribed before him" (1 *Stat.* 56–57).

To William Seton

Treasury Department
May 10th 1792.

Dear Sir,

I received your letter of the 7th instant, covering an account of Stock purchased by you for the United States.[1]

I observe that you have exceeded the sum which was limitted by me to the amount of one thousand and ninety eight Dollars, eighty nine Cents. But so small a difference is not very material, and I am willing that the whole should remain on account of the United States.

In order to a winding up of the business, I have now to request that you will as soon as it can conveniently be done, cause all the stock to be transferred in the names of the Trustees[2] as heretofore, and, that you will then procure from the Commissioner,[3] and forward to me, the necessary certificates, for transferring the Stock from the Books of the Commissioner to those of the Treasury.

You will please to accept of my best acknowledgment for this additional mark of your zeal for the public service, and believe me to be,

With very great consideration & regard[4]   Dear Sir   Your obedt Servant   Alex Hamilton

Willm Seton Esqr
Cashier of the Bank of New York

LS, Bank of New York, New York City; copy, in the handwriting of Seton, Hamilton Papers, Library of Congress.

1. Letter not found, but see H to Seton, March 26, April 4, 16, 1792. Presumably this letter covered the account, dated May 5, 1792, in the amount of $141,098.89 for purchases of Government stock made by Seton between April 2 and April 17, 1792 (copy, RG 217, Miscellaneous Treasury Accounts, 1790–1894, Account No. 2617, National Archives).

2. The trustees of the sinking fund.

3. John Cochran, commissioner of loans for New York.

4. The words "& regard" are in the handwriting of H.

Treasury Department Circular
to the Collectors of the Customs

Treasury Department, May 10, 1792.

Sir,

It is my wish, that in your official correspondence with the Secretary of the Treasury, you will henceforth make it a rule, to designate your *office* and the *place* where it is kept, upon the outside of your letters.

When weekly returns are transmitted which require no particular remarks, it will be agreeable to me, and save trouble to you, if for the future they be simply put under blank covers and directed in the form of a letter.

I inclose you a form of an account of Bonds remaining uncancelled, taken in your district for securing the bonding of duties in some other district, upon goods reported at your office, to be intended to be landed in such other district. This return you will make, in the first instance, on the receipt of the form, and afterwards with your quarterly accounts from time to time.

It is my desire that application be made by letter to the obligors, who may reside in your district, in all cases wherein bonds heretofore executed now remain uncancelled, if dated three months since, and that all such as now are, or shall be uncancelled at the end of four months from their date, be put in suit.

I am, Sir, ⟨Your obedient Servant,⟩

P S. Some Acts of the last session of Congress will accompany this.

L[S], to Benjamin Lincoln, RG 36, Collector of Customs at Boston, Letters from the Treasury, 1789–1807, Vol. 4, National Archives; LS, to Jeremiah

From Joseph Nourse

Treasury Departmt.
Registers Office 11 May 1792.

Sir

I have the honor to enclose a list of the Clerks engaged in this Office, with a note of the Objects on which they were employd and the Rate of their respective Compensations. Being with the greatest Respect   Sir   Your mo: ob: hb: Servt.   J. N. Regr.

The Honble: Alexr. Hamilton Esqr
Secy. of the Treasury

[ENCLOSURE]

remarks A [1]

The Register in the Arrangement of Salaries has been governd by the following Principals.

1st. He has endeavoured to compensate those from whose Abilities he has derived the greatest Assistance, and from whose Characters the same might be made with general Approbation.

2. To employ as many Clerks beyond the number estimated for as the Fund appropriated for their payment (consistent with the foregoing) wou'd admit, and also consistent with

3. The Retention of a Sum for the payment of such Clerks from the nature of whose Employment, Extra Services are frequently required; particularly at the Books of the various public Stocks and

ALS, RG 53, Register of the Treasury, Estimates and Statements for 1792, Vol. "134-T," National Archives.
1. DS, RG 53, Register of the Treasury, Estimates and Statements for 1792, Vol. "134-T," National Archives.

other pressing Business, some of whom have been employ'd from 6 in the Morning untill 10 at night. In these Cases an Extra Compensation, seemed indispensable. But throughout the Register has strictly conformed himself to the 3d Section of the Act, supplemental to the Act for establishing the Treasury Departmt. dated the 3rd. March 1791.[2]

4. The Sum appropriated for the payment of the Clerks in the Registers Office for the year 1792 is as follows

26 Clerks @ 500 drs.	Dollars 13.000
3 do. for arranging public Securities	1.500
Total appropriated for the Payment of Clerks	14.500
Deduct 1st. Quarter received 31st. March 1792	3,599:62
Leaves for 9 Months Clerks Salaries	10,900.38.
9 months for 33 Clerks on the Salaries as stated in the foregoing Schedule amounts to	10,987:50.

But as it is probable that some may be absent with leave on a deduction of Salary, the above Sum of 10,900.38 may be sufficient.

The Opening of the Loan Office[3] and other additional Business, flowing from the Acts passed last Session may require One or Two more Clerks. In that Case it will be a question whether they shoud be taken from the Supernumary, engaged in the Arrangement of the public Securities, or others appointed.

With respect to the Supernumary: Clerks employed in the arangeing the public Securities, it has been with a view to expedite that Business and also to render any further Appropriation of Monies for that Object the least possible. It may be observed that the Salaries to the persons employ'd are low, excepting the Super-

---

2. Section 3 of "An Act supplemental to the act 'establishing the Treasury Department,' and for a farther compensation to certain officers" reads in part as follows: "That it shall and may be lawful for the principal in any of the offices of the United States, who is authorized by law to appoint clerks under him, to allow to each clerk such compensation for his services, as he shall, in the opinion of such officer, deserve for the same: *Provided*, That the whole sum to be expended for clerks in any such office (except the chief clerk) shall not exceed a sum equal to five hundred dollars per annum for every clerk employed therein" (1 *Stat.* 215).

3. See "An Act supplementary to the act making provision for the Debt of the United States" (1 *Stat.* 281–83 [May 8, 1792]).

intendant who is active in the Business and will it is expected complete the Arrangement, to answer the Object of Enquiry as accurately as so extensive an Examination will admit.

33 is the Actual Number of Clerks now employed which
@ 500 Dollar amounts to 16.500
Their Salaries as arranged amounts to　　　　　14.650
If 500 Dollars equal to one Clerks Salary be added⎫
　　　　　　　　　　　　　　　　　　　　　　　⎬　500
for Services of an Extraordinary Nature　　　　⎭
There will remain a Difference between the Salaries agreeably to the Act of 3rd. March 1791
in favour of the Treasury Arrangement for the
Registers Office 1 350
　　　　　　　　　　　　　　　　　　　　　　16.500

The Register woud take this Opportunity of suggesting for future Consideration. That if from the Decrease of Business in his Office, the number of Clerks shou'd be lessened so as not to admit of an Allowance to the Superintending Clerks, adequate to their Services and the Confidence which from long and faithful Attention they might be deemed to merit, whether some permanent additional Salary might not become a Subject of Consideration.

All which is very respectfully Submitted.

> Treasury Department
> Registers Office 11th May 1792
> **J. N. Regr.**

A List of the Clerks engaged in the Registers Office with a note of objects on which they are employed and the Rate of their respective Compensations.

Division of the Treasury Records	Names	Salary	Employment
Revenue arising from Impost, Tonnage and Excise.	Joshua Dawson	700	Superintends and Examines the Accounts of Impost Tonnage and Excise. He also corrisponds with, and forwards to, the several Commissioners of Loans Certificates for the public Debt. He forwards to the several Collectors of the Customs blanks for registering vessels. He registers Bills of Exchange drawn by the Treasurer on the Collectors and certifies on the Bill a Record of the same. He arranges and prepares the Annual Return, for Congress, of the Duties arising from Impost, Tonnage & Excise. He is also deputed by the Register to pay the Contingent Expences of the Treasury Department.
	Edward OHara	400	Under Mr. Dawson—Registers the Accounts of the Collectors in the Impost Book, and occasionally assists in other Branches of the Business.
	William James	350	Keeps the Tonnage Books and those of the Excise.
Receipt and Expenditures of Public Money	Thos. OHara	600	Copying the Auditors and Comptrollers Certificates of Balances found due in Specie, on Settlement at the Treasury, in Order that the Secy. may issue his Warrant therefor. Registering all Specie Warrants drawn upon the Collector of the Duties on Goods, wares and Merchandize—On the Supervisors of the Duties on distilld Spirits. Likewise all Warrants drawn (in Specie) on the Treasurer for monies for use of the Departmt of War, Civil List, for payment of Interest on the Funded Debt &c. Journalizing the above and posting it into the Ledger, which contains the Treasurers, Secretary of War, paymaster Genl. Contractors, Commissioners of Loans for paymt of Interest & Invalids Accts. with various others.

4. DS, RG 53, Register of the Treasury, Estimates and Statements for 1792, Vol. "134-T," National Archives.

Division of the Treasury Records	Names	Salary	Employment
Genl and Particular Loan officer Accts.	Miles F. Clossy	700	Likewise the Statemt: of ye different appropriations. To Certify to the Auditor and Comptroller the Advances made to Individuals—such as the Commissioner of Loans for the Payment of Interest. And of Invalids. To the Contractors for Supply of Provisions Clothing, Quarter Masters Stores &c and of the different Officers of Government for their Contingent Expence. Filing and keeping the Statements and vouchers of the Expenditures in Specie.
	Stewart Cummins	300	On the Journal and Ledger of the Domestic Debt, Ledger of the Assumed Debt and Ledger of the General Account of Interest. Also engaged in examining the Quarterly Accts. Currt. of the several Commissioners and in furnishing Quarterly Statements of their Accounts as they stand on the Books of the Treasury. And generally superintending.
	Michael Kennedy	350	On the Journals of the Assumed Debt and General Account of Interest and in making Enteries from a Blotter into a Book preparatory for journalizing the Warrants of Transferr of the Assumed Debt. Under the Direction of do.
	David Rittenhouse	200	Making Waste Book Enteries of the Warrants of Transfer of the Domestic and Assumed Debts, and also in making fair Enteries of the Warrants of the domestic debt into a Book preparatory to the Journal. Under the Direction of do.
Issuing Certificates of the Domestic and Assumed Debt	Jos: Stretch	700	Making fair Copies into Books opened for the purpose, of the Dividend Accounts of the Treasury, the Accounts of unclaimed Interest, and the Quarterly Abstracts rendered from this Office of the Accounts with the Loan offices. Under the Direction of do. Superintending Clerk. Employd in examining the several Certificates with the original Transferrs or Warrants and deleniating the Checks for the same. He also ocassionally makes out Certificates for deferred Stock and prepares the Receipts for Signature.

Name	Salary	Duties	
Saml M. Frauncis	350	Employd in the Delivery of Certificates and filling Receipts for the same.	On the Books and records which relate to the several Creditors on the Domestic and Assumed Debt.
Jno. Matthews	350	An Assistant in making out Certificates of the above 6 ⅌ Cent Stock.	
Charles Wilson	350	Employd in making out Certificates of 3 ⅌. Cent Stock & Transfer from and to the Books of the General and particular Loan Offices.	
Jacob S. Howell	600	Keeps the Journal and Ledger of the Domestic 6 ⅌. Ct. Stock of public Creditors on the Books of the Treasy.	"
Chas. Tompkins	550	do. 3 ⅌. Cent do.	"
Mattw Walker	500	do. the Deferred Ledger. He also keeps an alphabitical Arrangement of all the old Certificates issued on the Register'd Debt and likewise of the Interest arising thereon.	
Wm. Story	500	Keeps the Journal and Ledger of the Evidences of the Debt funded which shews the various Certificates &c upon which said Debt is founded.	"
John Finley	550	Keeps the 6 ⅌. Cent 3 ⅌ Cent & deferred Assumed Debts.	"
William Shepherd	300	Assistant to the Clerks on the 6 and 3 ⅌. Cent domestic & assumed Debts.	"
Geo. Mitchell	266.60	Employd in arranging the files of the several Description of Stock.	Books and records which relate to the several Creditors on the domestic and Assd Debt Registd Debt, the paymt. of its Intt: and the Enteries of Record from the Statem. and vouchers on which said Debt is founded.
John Litle	500	Keeps the Journal and Ledger of Register'd Debt Sett No. 1. Superintends the Issuing of Certificates and prepares Checks for the Signature of the Register for the Payment of Interest on the registerrd debt.	

Division of the Treasury Records	Names	Salary	Employment
Registerd debt, the payment of its Intt. and the Enteries of Record from the Statement and vouchers on which said Debt is founded.	Gabriel Nourse	500	Fills up Certificates for registerd Debt for Signature, also the Receips for Signature of the public Creditors and files and Endorses the Vouchers.
do.	Jno. Hindman	500	Journalizes and posts the Books of Registerd Debt No. 2
The Books and Records of the Old Govern:	Armit Brown	500	Makes the Blotter Enteries and journalizes the Accots. of the late Governmt.
"	Wm. L. Gardner	500	Posting the Accounts and ballancing the Books of the old Governmt.
"	Geo: Tibbald	400	Recording the Accots. of the Old Governmt.
The Arrangment of public Securities	Jno. Woodside	650	Superintending Clerk is employd in Arrangeing the several Species of Certificates cancell'd at the Treasury under the old and prest. Government.
"	Simeon Reynolds	400	Selects from the vouchers and arranges the Certificates loaned at the Office of the Commissioner of Loans for State of Connecttt.
"	Saml Clendennon	300	Selects from the vouchers and arranges the Certificates loand at the office of the Commissioner of Loans for Pennsylvania
"	James Stewart	266.60	do. those taken up by the late Board of Treasury.
"	Archd. Woodside	350	do. those of Rhode Island.
"	Elias B. Woodward	266.60	do. those of Maryland.
"	Harman Stout	400	do. those of Massachusetts.
Filing and Enrolement of Ships Registers	Jno. Woodward	500	Registering of Shipping &c.
Total Amot. in . . . . Dollrs.		Vide Remarks A 14,650	

Treasury Department
Registers Office 11th. May 1792
J. N. Regr.

From Josiah Parker [1]

Philadelphia May 11th. 1792

Sir

The Surveyors place of the customs at Smithfield will be vacated by the present officer being elected a Member of the Assembly.[2]

I take the liberty to recommend Copland Parker [3] of Smithfield for that office, he served as a deputy in my office at Norfolk, and is well acquainted with the duties, his youth perhaps prevented his obtaining an appointment at the first establishment of the Customs. He is now 23 years of age & will be glad of the appointment; with respect.

Your Mo. Ob servt.   J: Parker

ALS, George Washington Papers, Library of Congress.
   1. Parker, a member of the House of Representatives from Virginia, had been a colonel during the American Revolution and later was naval officer and collector for the District of Elizabeth River from December 20, 1783, until his election to Congress in February, 1789.
   2. James Wells.
   3. Commissions as inspector and surveyor of Smithfield were issued to Copland Parker, Josiah Parker's brother, on June 30, 1792.

To William Allibone

[*Philadelphia, May 12, 1792.* On May 18, 1792, Tench Coxe wrote to "A Committee of the Merchants of the City of Philadelphia" and referred to a letter "from the Secretary of the Treasury of the 12th: instant" to Allibone.[1] *Letter not found.*]

   1. LC, RG 58, Letters of Commissioner of Revenue, 1792–1793, National Archives.

From William Barton

Office of Inspection
Port of Providence May 12th. 1792.

Sir,

There was shiped some time past from this place five chests of Souchong and one Chest of Hyson tea to Messrs. Sam Ward and

Brothers of New York; [1] the tea was imported in the Ship Genl Washington in June last, and for which certificates have regularly been granted from this Office.[2] The Messrs Wards acknowledge to have received the certificates with the tea, but are willing to make affidavit to the same being lost or mislaid; on which account they have applied to this office for new certificates. Tho satisfied in my own mind that there is no intention of fraud in the application, I did not think it my duty to grant the certificates, but have taken the liberty to give you this information; that I might receive such directions in this case as shall be proper.[3] I am Sir with great respect Your most obedient humble servant. Wm. Barton Inspector

of the Revenue

The Secretary of the Treasury.

ALS, RG 58, "Special Cases," Customs, 1792–1842, National Archives.

1. Samuel Ward operated a store at Crane Wharf, New York City.

2. The certificates mentioned in this letter are described in Section 4 of "An Act making farther provision for the collection of the duties by law imposed on Teas, and to prolong the term for the payment of the Duties on Wines." This section reads in part as follows: "*And be it further enacted,* That all teas which, after the first day of April next, shall be imported into the United States from any foreign port or place, shall be landed under the care of the inspectors of the revenue for the ports where the same shall be respectively landed; and for that purpose every permit which shall be granted by any collector, for landing the same, shall, prior to such landing, be produced to the said inspector, who by an endorsement thereupon under his hand, shall signify the production thereof to him, and the time when; after which, and not otherwise, it shall be lawful to land the teas mentioned in such permit. And the said inspector shall make an entry of all such permits, and of the contents thereof; and each chest, box or package containing any teas, shall be marked by the officer under whose immediate inspection the same shall be landed, in legible and durable characters, with progressive numbers, and with the name of the vessel in which the same shall have been imported. And the said officer shall grant a certificate for each such chest, box or package, specifying therein the name or names of the importer or importers, the ship or vessel in which the same shall have been imported, and the number thereof to accompany the same wheresoever it shall be sent" (1 *Stat.* 220 [March 3, 1791]).

3. On May 26, 1792, Tench Coxe wrote to Barton that H had referred Barton's letter to him for reply and that in the future communications should be addressed to John S. Dexter, supervisor of the revenue for the Rhode Island District (LC, RG 58, Letters of Commissioner of Revenue, 1792–1793, National Archives). On the same day Coxe wrote to Dexter that new certificates might be issued under certain conditions when the statement of those conditions was written and sworn to before an officer qualified to administer oaths (LC, RG 58, Letters of Commissioner of Revenue, 1792–1793, National Archives).

To Sharp Delany

Treasury Department,
May 12th. 1792

Sir.

It has been represented to me by a Committee of the Merchants of Philadelphia, that the Delaware Pilots have entered into a combination [1] very inconvenient to the movements of their vessels, and which may produce injury to the National commerce and Revenue. The officers of the Revenue Cutter being acquainted with the River and bay of Delaware, and the chief mate Mr. Roach [2] being a Pilot of the first Class it will be proper that you will immediately apprize Captain Montgomery [3] of these circumstances, and that you communicate to him my desire that he should do every thing in his power by means of the officers and seamen under his command to aid and accomodate the vessels going out and coming in, during the present difficulty.

It may be well to apprize Capt. Montgomery that there are apprehensions that some of the Pilots may be so indiscreet as to attempt the removal or injury of the buoys and beacons. It will be proper therefore, that he or the person employed by the superintendent should have an intimation of this, and in order to the more perfect attention to the business, it may be well for you to confer with Wm Allibone Esqr [4] the superintendent to whom I shall also write.[5]

I am Sir, Your Obedt. Servt.   Alexander Hamilton.

LC, RG 26, Lighthouse Letters Received, Revenue Cutter Service Letters Sent, Vol. "O," National Archives; LC, RG 56, Letters to Collectors at Small Ports, "Set G," National Archives; LC, RG 56, Letters to the Collector at Philadelphia, National Archives.

1. On May 14, 1792, ". . . a letter was received at the Coffee-house, from the convention of Pilots assembled at Marcus-Hook, dated May 12th, . . . enclosing a copy of seven resolutions they have agreed to. . . . A respectable meeting of Merchants took up these resolutions, and resolved, unanimously, that no further notice should be taken of them" ([Philadelphia] *Gazette of the United States,* May 16, 1792). On the same day, Governor Thomas Mifflin of Pennsylvania met to consider a similar complaint with the Board of Wardens of the Port of Philadelphia, under whose authority the pilots operated (*Pennsylvania Archives* [n.p., 1931], 9th ser., I, 390–91). On May 17, 1792, "immediate employment and good encouragement" was offered to prospective pilots by Nathaniel Falconer, master warden of the port. On May 22 the

pilots returned to their jobs (*Gazette of the United States*, May 19, 26, 1792).

2. Isaac Roach.

3. James Montgomery was captain of the revenue cutter *General Greene*.

4. Allibone was superintendent of beacons, buoys, and public piers for Philadelphia, Cape Henlopen, and Delaware.

5. H's letter to Allibone has not been found. On May 18, 1792, Tench Coxe wrote to David H. Conyngham, Robert Waln, and Thomas Murgatroyd, "A Committee of the Merchants of the City of Philadelphia," as follows:

"In Consequence of your Application this morning Enquiry has been made of the Collector of the port of Philadelphia and of the Superintendent of the Delaware Lighthouse, Buoys &c., concerning the measures which have been taken by them in Consequence of the letters from the Secretary of the Treasury of the 12th: instant. It appears that Mr [Michael] Dawson [a pilot] was dispatched on the following day with a letter from the Collector to the Captain of the Revenue Cutter, containing a copy of the Letter from the Treasury, and instructions to Captain Montgomery to make every exertion in his power to aid the Trade and Revenue in the present Difficulty by employing the officers under his Command and the Cutter in that service.

"The attention of Mr Dawson was directed by the Superintendent to the Objects of his immediate legal duty an examination of the Buoys and beacons, and both he and Captain Montgomery were generally authorized and instructed to give their assistance according to their best Judgment on the occasion. By a letter of the 15th: from the Captain of the Cutter to the Collector it appears that he was then possessed of the letters sent by Dawson and gave the strongest assurances of his best exertions. Since that time it is understood that Mr Dawson was to ply with his boat at the mouth of the Bay and is to bring up from thence to Bombay Hook all the inward bound Vessels with which he may fall in, and that the Cutter was to ply between Bombay Hook and New-Castle to receive from Mr. Dawson the inward bound Vessels, which Capt. Montgomery was to conduct to New Castle, and there to take Charge of the outward bound Vessels and to exchange them in like manner with Mr. Dawson at Bombay Hook. The desire of the Merchants in regard to the outward bound fleet was stated to the Collector and Superintendent, who will write letters to Captain Montgomery and Mr. Dawson instructing them to employ the pilots on board their two vessels, to assist the pilots provided by the Merchants in leading the fleet safely to Sea by means of several of the largest Ships. If your Committee will give Notice to the Collector and Superintendent a few hours before the departure of your dispatch boat, their letters will be prepared accordingly and delivered to you. The Superintendent is also ready to give every Assistance in his power in the placing the new buoys and leding marks, according to your desire, and for that purpose it will be proper that early notice be given to him of the time when the boat will sail on that service." (LC, RG 58, Letters of Commissioner of Revenue, 1792–1793, National Archives.)

To Thomas Jefferson [1]

Treasury Department
May 12th 1792

The Secretary of the Treasury presents his Compliments to The Secretary of State and requests that he will be pleased to cause the

Patent for 214.285 acres when sealed & recorded to be delivered to the bearer The Rev Mr Cutler.[2]

AL, RG 59, Miscellaneous Letters, National Archives.

1. For background to this letter, see H to George Washington, May 9, 1792.

2. Manasseh Cutler, a director of the Ohio Company, at this time was in Philadelphia attending a three-day meeting of the board of directors of the company. He received the patent on the day this letter was written (D, Register of Acts of the Federal Congress and Communications Received by the Department of State, 1790–1795, Papers of the Continental Congress, National Archives).

From Benjamin Lincoln

Boston, May 12, 1792. "I have received your Letter of the 2d. instant. The manner in which you have directed the lodgment of the money will obviate all the difficulties which I supposed might take place under your first order. . . . I wish to know how I shall settle the price of goods imported from France. Their paper seems to be in a depreciated state and the goods charged proportionately high. . . ."[1]

LC, Massachusetts Historical Society, Boston; LC, RG 36, Boston Collector, Letter Book, 1790–1797, National Archives; two copies, RG 56, Letters from the Collector at Boston, National Archives.

1. Section 17 of "An Act for raising a farther sum of money for the protection of the frontiers, and for other purposes therein mentioned" provided "That so much of the act, intituled 'An act to provide more effectually for the collection of duties imposed by law on goods, wares, and merchandise imported into the United States, and on the tonnage of ships or vessels,' as hath rated the livre tournois of France at eighteen and an half cents, be and the same is hereby repealed" (1 *Stat.* 262–63 [May 2, 1792]). The act had not, however, substituted any value or rule for accepting French currency.

From Oliver Wolcott, Junior

Philadelphia, May 12, 1792. Submits "forms for regulating the payment of Interest on the Funded Stock in the Loan Offices of Massachusetts, New York, Pensylvania, Maryland & So Carolina."

ADf, Connecticut Historical Society, Hartford.

To George Washington

Bristol [Pennsylvania] May 13. 1792.

Sir,

I left the City of Philadelphia this Morning on my way to Newark [1] as I mention'd to you previous to your departure.[2] Nothing new had occurred.

Mr. Belli [3] was furnished with the requisite sum for the purchase of Dragoon Horses in Kentucke, in conformity to an arrangement, which I understand [from] the Secretary at War, was made pursuant to your direction. The Quarter Master General [4] also has had an advance commensurate with the objects he is immediately to provide for; so that every thing is in proper train as far as pecuniary supply is concerned.[5]

With the most perfect respect and truest attachment,   I have the honor to be &c.   A: Hamilton

LC, George Washington Papers, Library of Congress.
   1. H was going to Newark, New Jersey, to attend a meeting of the directors of the Society for Establishing Useful Manufactures. See Archibald Mercer to H, April 30, 1792.
   2. Washington had left Philadelphia on May 10 for Mount Vernon.
   3. John Belli, deputy quartermaster general of the United States Army.
   4. James O'Hara.
   5. After the defeat of Major General Arthur St. Clair by the Indians in November, 1791, plans had been made for a new campaign against the western tribes. "An Act for making farther and more effectual Provision for the Protection of the Frontiers of the United States" (1 Stat. 241–43 [March 5, 1792]) had increased the forces on the frontier and provided for a virtual reorganization of the Army. In April, 1792, Major General Anthony Wayne was appointed commanding officer to superintend the reorganization and training of the Army in preparation for the new campaign. Belli and O'Hara were engaged in provisioning the troops stationed at Pittsburgh and at the forts along the Ohio and Great Miami rivers.

From William Short

Paris May 14 1792

Sir

I recieved the day before yesterday your letter of the 21st. of March expressing your wish that a loan should be opened at the

ALS, letterpress copy, William Short Papers, Library of Congress.

same rate with that of Antwerp.[1] It found me in correspondence
with our bankers[2] with respect to the charges on one to be made
as soon as a proper moment should occur at 4. p. cent interest—the
rate of the last opened in Amsterdam, of which you had not recieved our letters of notification at the date of yours.[3]

I had desired them to fix the charges at 4 ½ p. cent which I am
persuaded would leave them the same clear profits as on the first
loan,[4] & with which of course they should be satisfied. I was apprehensive however they would insist on higher, & was not therefore
surprized on recieving their answer[5] the day before yesterday covering your letter of March 21st. in which they say that the charges
cannot be lower than 5. p. cent, & that they were not sure of success
at this moment, but would use their utmost endeavour whenever
the instant should be favorable. I have informed them[6] that I supposed the 5. p. cent was asked on the footing of their being obliged
to give more to their undertakers & therefore consented to it—
authorizing them to open the loan as soon as the moment would
admit of it. The present warfaring appearance of Europe may force
a rise in the rate of interest perhaps, but nothing shall be left undone
to procure a loan at the present rate of 4. p. cent. If it can be
effected at all it may be for the charges allowed as well, as if they
were more considerable; & of course I think it improper to propose
an augmentation, although it would be much better to increase
them than to allow an increase of interest. You may rest assured of
being informed without delay of the opening of a new loan, as well
as the prospects which may precede it if there should be delay.

I had the honor of informing you in my two last letters[7] of what

1. The Antwerp loan had been opened in December, 1791, for three million
guilders at four and one-half percent interest and four percent charges. For
a description of the loan, see Short to H, November 8, 1791, note 4, and
November 12, 1791.

2. Willink, Van Staphorst, and Hubbard.

3. For a description of the Holland loan of December, 1791, see Short to
H, December 23, 28, 1791.

4. This is a reference to the Holland loan of 1790. For a description of this
loan, see Willink, Van Staphorst, and Hubbard to H, January 25, 1790; H to
Willink, Van Staphorst, and Hubbard, November 29, 1790. The bankers'
charges on this loan were four and one-half percent.

5. Willink, Van Staphorst, and Hubbard to Short, May 7, 1792 (LS, Short
Family Papers, Library of Congress).

6. Short to Willink, Van Staphorst, and Hubbard, May 12, 1792 (ALS,
letterpress copy, William Short Papers, Library of Congress).

7. See Short to H, April 22, 25, 1792.

had been done here with the minister of marine.[8] Mr. Morris [9] has
since arrived here (on the 7th. of this month) of which I immediately informed the Minister of Marine.[10] Having not yet an answer from him, I should imagine he had not yet obtained of the
committee the explanation he expected from them with respect to
the six millions mentioned in my last. Your letter of the 21st. shewing your intention to employ further sums for the purchase of the
public funds, & your disposition to give even an high rate of interest
for monies to be thus applied, has suggested that it would be agreeable to you if the monies at present in the hands of our bankers
arising on the last loan [11] shd. be put at your disposition for that
purpose instead of going to the minister of marine for succours to
St. Domingo.[12] I have shewn your letter to Mr. Morris who is of
opinion as well as myself to do this. I therefore wish to inform you
that the last loan (of December) at 4. p. cent interest shall be held
to answer your draughts. Its amount was three millions of florins no
part has been paid to France. Of course, there is only to be deducted
the amount of applications known to you—& wch. will appear from
the bankers accounts transmitted to you in which should be included the payments for interest in february & march & the same for
the 1st. of next month. Should the minister of marine obtain from
the committee a report according to his wishes, & come forward in
the promise made to hold the 800,000 dollars [13] at his disposition in
America, Mr. Morris proposes to answer it by informing him that
he has already learned from the government that 400,000 have been
furnished [14] & does not know but that the monies at your disposition

8. Jean de Lacoste.
9. Gouverneur Morris had been appointed United States Minister Plenipotentiary to France in January, 1792.
10. Short to Lacoste, May 8, 1792 (ALS, letterpress copy, William Short
Papers, Library of Congress). According to Morris's diary he arrived in Paris
on Sunday, May 6, 1792. His first interview with Short was on May 7 (Morris,
Diary of the French Revolution, II, 424-25).
11. See note 3.
12. See Short to H, December 28, 1791, January 26, March 24, April 22, 25,
1792.
13. Short had written to H on April 22, 1792, that in his correspondence
with the Minister of Marine he had "engaged that a certain sum, which has
been since fixed at 800,000 dollars should be held by you at the disposition of
France for the purchase of supplies in America for S. Domingo."
14. On the application of Jean Baptiste de Ternant, Minister of France to
the United States, the United States had agreed to advance four hundred

may have been already applied that way. I apprehend however the assembly will include the six millions voted in the twelve millions drawn for,[15] although the minister was formerly persuaded of the contrary, & that the affair will take that turn. Should he delay the renewal of his application it will be an additional reason to give him, that the monies had been in the interval otherwise employed.

Mr. Morris has recieved here under cover to him & delivered to me the triplicate of your letter of Jan 28. for me—neither the first or second has come to my hands, & of course I have not recd. your report therein mentioned.[16] Nor have I recd. your letter of the 30th. Novr mentioned there also. All the others which you have announced have been recd. My late letters to you have been of January 26. March 24. April 22. & 25.

I have formerly informed you of the footing on wch. the payments made here on the Antwerp loan stood [17]—as well as the cogent reasons for having them made at Antwerp instead of being remitted by bills of exchange. Mr. Morris has recieved a letter from the Sec. of State, by which he apprehends it to be the intention of government to transfer to France the loss by depreciation on the assignats.[18] He of course waits for further instructions before settling the rate at which the U. S. are to be credited for the payments made from Antwerp. In consequence of your letter to me of Sep. 2. I informed the minister here & the commissaries of the treasury, of

thousand dollars on "account of the debt due to France." See H to Short, April 10, 1792. Thomas Jefferson had informed Morris of Ternant's application in a letter of March 10, 1792 (ALS, letterpress copy, Thomas Jefferson Papers, Library of Congress).

15. See Short to H, April 25, 1792.

16. In his letter to Short of January 28, 1792, H had enclosed his "Report on Receipts and Expenditures," January 23, 1792.

17. See Short to H, January 26, March 24, 1792.

18. Short is referring to the letter which Jefferson had written to Morris on March 10, 1792. In discussing the French debt, Jefferson wrote: "The Secretary of the Treasury has reason to believe that the late loan at Antwerp has paid up all our arrearages to France both of principal & interest, & consequently that there is no part of our debt exigible at this time. However the legislature having authorized the President to proceed in borrowing to pay off the residue, provided it can be done to the *advantage* of the U.S. it is thought the law will be satisfied with *avoiding loss* to the U.S. This has obliged the Secretary of the Treasury to require some conditions which may remove from us that loss which we encountered, from an unfavorable exchange, to pay what was *exigible,* and transfer it to France as to payments not exigible" (ALS, letterpress copy, Thomas Jefferson Papers, Library of Congress).

the intention of the U. S. not to take advantage of this depreciation. I did not include the payments previously made although your letter authorized it, supposing it best to leave this for your future consideration.[19] Of course no indemnity will be made for them. My letters announced this intention of the U. S. only to begin with the Antwerp loan. The rate of exchange & the current difference between Specie & paper here, being known, will furnish the basis for regulating this business finally, which Mr. Morris will do on recieving your further instructions. I hope they will arrive ere long & that the business will be finally settled by him to your satisfaction. I shall give him the letters which have passed on that subject.

I have mentioned to Mr. Morris what I communicated to you with respect to the proposals of Boyd & Kerr.[20] Since then a very great rise having taken place in the exchange (it was with Amsterdam as low as 27 ½. & rose to 35. & is now 30) has suspended their ideas on this subject, as such a rise would have proved ruinous to them. They consider it however only a suspension, although it is probable they will be more timorous now, the game being much less sure than they expected. Should they come forward again Mr Morris will no doubt do what so advantageous an operation for the U. S. would dictate. These advantages I mentioned to you in my letter of March 24.

I shall not have the honor of writing to you again from hence as I shall set out for the Hague towards the end of the month.[21] I am now much busied & hurried in my preparations of departure, having never known until the 7th. of this month whether I was to go there or to Madrid first,[22] & of course was not able to conform

19. See Short to H, January 26, 1792.
20. See Short to H, March 24, 1792.
21. Short had been appointed United States Minister to The Hague in January, 1792.
22. On January 24, 1792, the Senate had confirmed the appointment of "William Carmichael, present Chargé des Affaires of the United States, at Madrid, and William Short, present Chargé des Affaires of the United States, at Paris, to be Commissioners for negotiating and concluding, with any person or persons, who shall be duly authorized by his Catholic Majesty, a convention, or treaty, concerning the navigation of the river Mississippi, by the citizens of the United States, saving to the President and Senate their respective rights as to the ratification of the same" (Executive Journal, I, 99). See also "Notes on Thomas Jefferson's Report of Instructions for the Commissioners to Spain," March 1–4, 1792, note 1.

my preparations thereto. Until then I had only learned through Mr Morris & the gazettes in general terms that I was appointed to the Hague, & joined in a commission at Madrid. I have the honor to be Sir, most respectfully your obedient & humble servant   W Short

Alexander Hamilton   Secretary of the Treasury, Philadelphia

From Edward Carrington

[*Richmond, May 17, 1792*. On July 11, 1792, Tench Coxe wrote to Carrington: "In your letter of the 17th. of May last, addressed to the Secretary of the Treasury, you acquaint him of the Resignation of Mr. James Wells . . . I presumed you are informed, that Mr. Cowpland Parker [1] has been appointed surveyor and consequently Inspector for that port." [2] *Letter not found.*]

   1. See Josiah Parker to H, May 11, 1792; William Lindsay to H, May 20, 1792.
   2. LC, RG 58, Letters of Commissioner of Revenue, 1792–1793, National Archives.

From Sheftall Sheftall [1]

Philadelphia, May 17, 1792. Inquires concerning action taken on petition of his father, Mordecai Sheftall.[2]

ALS, Mr. B. H. Levy, Savannah (on deposit at American Jewish Archives, Cincinnati, Ohio).
   1. During the American Revolution, Sheftall Sheftall, a resident of Savannah, served as assistant commissary general of issues for the state of Georgia under his father, who was deputy commissary general of issues. In 1778, both father and son were imprisoned by the British. After his exchange as a prisoner in 1780, Sheftall Sheftall was appointed by the Board of War as flag master on a ship which took supplies and money through the British blockade to the prisoners at Charlestown, South Carolina. When this letter was written, Sheftall was a prominent merchant and tobacco inspector at Savannah.
   2. Mordecai Sheftall petitioned Congress for the first time on June 28, 1780. Although he was unable to obtain the necessary records in support of his petition because of the British occupation of Savannah, Congress at that time made a partial settlement of his account (Memorial of Mordecai Sheftall, June 28, 1780, ADS, Papers of the Continental Congress, National Archives; Memorial of Mordecai Sheftall, August 21, 1780, ADS, Papers of the Continental Congress, National Archives; Mordecai Sheftall to Samuel Huntington, November 21, 1780, ALS, Papers of the Continental Congress, National

Archives; *JCC*, XVIII, 1113). On March 29, 1792, the House of Representatives referred Sheftall's second petition "praying a settlement of his accounts as deputy commissary general of issues, during the war" to H (*Journal of the House*, I, 554). It was not until February 27, 1794, that H reported that the acts of limitation barred Sheftall's petition (see "Report on Several Petitions Barred by the Acts of Limitation," February 27, 1794). On March 15, 1802, Sheftall's widow petitioned Congress for a reconsideration of her husband's petition of March 29, 1792 (*Journal of the House*, IV, 136).

From Abishai Thomas [1]

Philadl. 18 May 1792

Sir

I am directed by a Resolution of the General Assembly of the State of North Carolina to "Inform myself by what means this State obtained a Credit with the United States for a quantity of Leather received of Richard Blackledge," and to "transmit to the next General Aseembly such vouchers or other information as I may deem proper to give the necessary information to the General Assembly." [2] To enable me to comply with the said Resolution, I am to solicit the favor of you to cause the proper Officer to furnish me with a Certified transcript from the Books of the Treasury department, or those of the late Clothier General,[3] of the Credit, or Credits which may exist thereon for account of Leather as aforesaid, or generally, designating if practicable such circumstances relative to the delivery as may enable me, or the General Assembly to trace whether it be the same which was purchased from Mr. Blackledge.

I am Sir   very respectfully   yr. mo. obt. Serv.   Ab. Thomas

Secretary of the Treasury

Copy, North Carolina Department of Archives and History, Raleigh.

1. Thomas was an agent for the state of North Carolina to support its claims in the final settlement of accounts between the states. For background to this letter, see "Report on the Petitions of Richard Blackledge," April 28, 1792.

2. This resolution was passed by the North Carolina House of Commons on December 19, 1789 (*Journal of the House of Commons. State of North-Carolina. At a General Assembly, begun and held at Fayetteville, on the Second Day of November, in the Year of our Lord One Thousand Seven Hundred and Eighty-nine, and in the Fourteenth Year of the Independence of the United States of America: Being the First Session of this Assembly* [Edenton: Printed by Hodge & Wills, Printers to the State, n.d.], 63, Microfilm Collection of Early State Records, Library of Congress).

3. James Mease was clothier general from 1776 to 1779.

From Joseph Hiller [1]

[*Salem, Massachusetts, May 19, 1792.* On June 27, 1792, Hamilton wrote to Hiller: "I have yet to reply to your letter of the 19th Ultimo." *Letter not found.*]

1. Hiller was collector of customs at Salem, Massachusetts.

From Jeremiah Olney

Providence, May 19, 1792. "Having been under the disagreeable necessity of putting in suit another of Welcome Arnold Esquire's Bonds,[1] . . . I wish to be informed, whether the directions, contained in your Letter of the 6th of July 1791, to notify other Collectors of his delinquency, was intended as Instructions for my conduct thereafter on similar occasions; or whether I am to omit giving the Notice, on putting any Bond in Suit, until I receive your Orders to do it? . . ."[2]

ADfS, Rhode Island Historical Society, Providence.
1. For an earlier case regarding one of Arnold's bonds, see Olney to H, June 21, July 19, 29, 1791; H to Olney, July 6, 22, October 7, 1791; Arnold to H, July 15, 1792; H to Arnold, July 22, 1791.
2. See H to Olney, July 22, 1791.

From Robert Ballard [1]

[*Baltimore, May 20, 1792.* On May 31, 1792, Hamilton wrote to Ballard and acknowledged "your letter of the 20th. instant." *Letter not found.*]

1. Ballard was appointed inspector of the revenue for the port of Baltimore on March 8, 1792.

From Tench Coxe

[Philadelphia, May 20, 1792]

Dear Sir.

I understand from Mrs. Hamilton that you do not expect to return from Newark for several days from which I conclude that you

mean to make a complete arrangement of the Business of the Manufacturing Society.[1] I am heartily glad of this tho I could have wished
you were returned as I have gone thro the preparation of all the
instructions, forms &ca. which are rendered necessary by the
Alterations in the Excise System.[2] Could I have passed them under
your Eye on Friday when they were completed the greater part of
them might have gone forward on Monday. Mr. Barton entered
with me on Saturday, and I am satisfied he will prove an Acquisition.[3] I find that Mr. Rittenhouse [4] & his other friends have advised
him to it.

The contractors have delivered 33,000 Drs. worth of clothing &
have recd. 43,000 drs. in Money [5] including Smiths Bill accepted
by you, which I should rather have said was recd. by Smith. I find
they have about 5000 Drs. worth of goods on hand not made up,
and are really going on well.

I do not perceive any inconvenience which has occured from
your absence except that the preparations for the opening of the
new loan can not go on.[6] I had a pretty full conversation with
the Comptr. in the first part of the Week and gave him a copy of
the law [7] which I advised him to transmit it to you with some of the
Remarks, wch. struck us. There is no provision in the law for the
payment of the Interest, but I believe the other acts will be found
to provide for it tho I have not yet examined them. I hope you had
time to write the Comptr. by Saturday's mail.

A letter was recd. by the Georgia Mail for the President which I
transmitted to Mt. Vernon.[8]

You some time ago mentioned your wish that I should partake in
the Management of the New Jersey Manufg. Society.[9] As I conceive the *legal* impropriety not to exist, if the Stock is not composed
of the debt of the U. S. nor of any State I mention to you that I
shall not hesitate to take a concern. My wish to aid so salutary a
plan, which has been devised by you & therefore will interest your
feelings will render me perfectly disposed to use my best Endeavours to promote it, if I take but a single Share. The interdiction of
commerce is not applied to the Commr. of the Reve. The Objects
forbidden are "the funds or debts of the U. S & of any state and
every kind of public property of either." [10] & no others.

Receipts for 38,000 Drs. have been recd. from the supervisor of
Masstts.[11]

Letters from Mr. Marshall to Col Carrington & from the latter to you [12] shew an uneasiness about the Revenue law to exist in part of Kentucky. The new Act [13] will diminish their opposition, because it is so much more favorable to them than the former, & because it proves that there is no Idea of a Repeal.

I have the Honor to be with respectful Attachment, dr. sir, yr most obedt & hum. servt.   Tench Coxe

Philada Sunday Night 11 OClock.

The defect in the new law in regard to the return of Spirits distilled in the U.S. which have been exported to foreign Countries appears to be in a considerable degree cured by the prohibition to import any distilled Spirits in *marked* Casks.[14] They might be shifted into other Casks, but the proof of their identity might be made very difficult and they could not be moved without being marked & certified, nor marked & certified without paying duty. This is a hasty View of the Matter, which will require further Examn., but the door of danger is not so open as it at first appeared.[15]

ALS, Hamilton Papers, Library of Congress.

1. H had left Philadelphia on May 13, 1792, to attend a meeting in Newark, New Jersey, of the Society for Establishing Useful Manufactures and returned to Philadelphia on May 20. See H to George Washington, May 13, 21, 1792.

2. Coxe is referring to "An Act concerning the Duties on Spirits distilled within the United States" (1 *Stat.* 267–71 [May 8, 1792]).

3. William Barton commenced his duties as clerk in the office of the commissioner of revenue in the early summer of 1792.

4. In 1790 Barton's uncle, David Rittenhouse, had supported Barton's applications for the posts of assistant to the Secretary of the Treasury and chief clerk in the Department of State. See H to Thomas Jefferson, May, 1790; Barton to H, August 9, 1790.

5. Thomas Billington and Charles Young were clothing contractors for the Army. An "Account Clothing, delivered into the Public Stores—by Billington and Young," which lists the items delivered by the contractors between April 12, 1792, and May 29, 1792, may be found in the Hamilton Papers, Library of Congress.

6. Coxe is referring to the loan from the Bank of the United States authorized by Section 16 of "An Act for raising a farther sum of money for the protection of the frontiers, and for other purposes therein mentioned" (1 *Stat.* 262 [May 2, 1792]). See George Washington to H, May 7, 1792.

7. See note 6.

8. On May 16, 1792, Coxe wrote to Washington, who was at Mount Vernon: "The Secretary of the Treasury having gone to New Jersey to attend an important meeting of the directors of the society for the promotion of useful Manufactures in that State, I most respectfully take the liberty to enclose to you a letter which I found on opening one of the dispatches for him by the

last Georgia Mail" (LS, RG 59, Miscellaneous Letters of the Department of State, 1790–1799, National Archives).

9. Coxe is referring to the Society for Establishing Useful Manufactures.

10. Coxe is quoting from Section 12 of "An Act making alterations in the Treasury and War Departments" (1 *Stat.* 281 [May 8, 1792]).

11. Nathaniel Gorham was supervisor of the revenue in Massachusetts.

12. Letters not found. Edward Carrington was supervisor of the revenue for the District of Virginia and Thomas Marshall was inspector of the revenue for the District of Kentucky.

13. See note 2.

14. Section 12 of "An Act concerning the Duties on Spirits distilled within the United States" provides: "that after the last day of June next, no distilled spirits shall be brought into the United States, from any foreign port or place in any cask or vessel, which shall have been marked pursuant to any law of the United States concerning distilled spirits, on pain of forfeiture of the spirits so brought, and of the ship or vessel in which they shall be brought" (1 *Stat.* 270).

15. At the end of this letter H wrote: "Note I returned on the afternoon of the day this Letter was written & on Monday Morning gave my opinion of the papers prepared."

To Thomas Jefferson

Introductory Note

On March 5, 1792, George Hammond, the British Minister to the United States, submitted to Jefferson a detailed account of the failure of the United States to abide by the provisions of the treaty of peace of 1783. On May 29, Jefferson wrote an extensively documented reply to Hammond's charges.[1]

Jefferson had completed the draft of his letter to Hammond by May 15, 1792, but he delayed sending it until James Madison, Edmund Randolph, and Hamilton had read and approved it. On May 16, 1792, Jefferson wrote to George Washington that "Mr Madison has favored me with some corrections for my Letter to mr H_____ it is now in the hands of the Attorney General, and shall then be submitted to Colo. Hamilton." [2] Jefferson probably submitted to Hamilton the draft of his letter to Hammond on or after May 20, the date on which Hamilton returned to Philadelphia from Newark, New Jersey, where he had been attending a meeting of the Society for Establishing Useful Manufactures.[3] Hamilton presumably sent to Jefferson his observations on Jefferson's letter to Hammond a few days before May 29, for in the draft Jefferson incorpo-

AL, Thomas Jefferson Papers, Library of Congress; copy, Hamilton Papers, Library of Congress.

1. The letters by Hammond and Jefferson are printed in *ASP, Foreign Relations,* I, 193–237.

2. Copy, RG 59, Copybooks of George Washington's Correspondence with Secretaries of State, 1789–1796, Vol. 21, National Archives.

3. See H to Washington, May 21, 1792.

rated some of Hamilton's criticisms and answered others. Both men supported their views by citing legal sources.[4]

Jefferson's comments on H's suggestions are given in the notes. The clerk's copy from which Jefferson's comments have been taken may be found in the Adams Family Papers, deposited in the Massachusetts Historical Society, Boston. Another copy of these notes may be found in the James Madison Papers, Library of Congress. On June 1, 1792, Jefferson wrote to Madison explaining the purpose of the notes: "I send you . . . a copy of Hamilton's notes, finding that the letter would not be ready to be delivered before the Pr's return, I made notes corresponding with his, shewing where I agreed, where I did not, and I put his & mine into the Pr's hands, to be perused at his leisure. The result was that he approved the latter; remaining as it was, particularly on the article of Debts, which he thought a subject of justification & not merely of extenuation" (ALS, James Madison Papers, Library of Congress). The draft of Jefferson's letter to Hammond, which is partly in Jefferson's handwriting and which contains Jefferson's corrections, may be found in the Thomas Jefferson Papers, Library of Congress.

[Philadelphia, May 20–27, 1792][5]

Mr. Hamilton presents his respectful Compliments to The Secretary of State. He has perused with as much care and attention as time has permitted the draft of a letter in answer to that of Mr. Hammond of March 5th.

Much *strong* ground has been taken and *strongly* maintained, particularly in relation to—

1 The recommendatory clauses of the Treaty [6]
2 The previous infractions by G Britain as to *Negroes* & *Posts*.[7]
3 The Question of Interest.[8]

4. Both Jefferson and H referred to Emeric de Vattel, *The Law of Nations; or Principles of the Law of Nature: Applied to the Conduct and Affairs of Nations and Sovereigns* (London, 1759–60), Vol. II, Book IV, Ch. III. Jefferson also cited Christian Wolff, *Institutiones Juris Naturæ et Gentium in Quibus Ex Ipsa Hominis Natura Continuo Nexu Omnes Obligationes et Jura Omnia Deducuntur,* Sections 1220, 1229 (Magdeburg, 1754).

5. In *JCHW,* IV, 141, this letter is dated "March, 1791" and in *HCLW,* IV, 354, it is dated "March, 1792."

6. The treaty of peace of 1783 between the United States and Great Britain provided that the states should place no impediments in the way of the collection of debts owed to British merchants and that Congress should earnestly recommend to the states the restitution of confiscated Loyalist property.

7. H is referring to Negroes taken by the British at the conclusion of the American Revolution and to British retention of the western posts in violation of the terms of the peace treaty. These infractions, Jefferson had argued, occurred before the American violations of the treaty.

8. Jefferson had denied the British contention that interest on American debts to British merchants should be paid for the years of the War of Independence.

And many of the suggestions of the British Minister concerning particular acts and adjudications, as far as can be judged without consulting the documents, appear to be satisfactorily obviated.

But doubts arise on the following particulars—

1. The expediency of the retaliation in the 1. 2 & 3d. Pages.[9] Much of the propriety of what is said depends on the question of the original *right* or *wrong* of the war. Should it lead to observations on that point, it may involve an awkward and irritating discussion. Will it not be more dignified as well as more discreet to observe concisely and generally on the impropriety of having deduced imputations from transactions during the war, and alluding *in the aggregate* and without *specification* to the instances of Legislative Warfare on the part of the British Parliament which might be recriminated, to say, that this is foreborne as leading to an unprofitable and unconciliating discussion? [10]

2 The soundness of the doctrine (page 4) that all Governmental acts of the *States* prior to the 11 of April are out of the discussion.[11] Does not the term *"sujets,"* to whom, according to Vatel, notice is necessary, apply merely to Individuals? Are not *states* members of a *fœderal league* the "parties contractantes" who are bound by the treaty itself from the time of its conclusion; that is, in the present case, from the time the provisional treaty took effect by the ratification of the preliminary articles between France & Britain? [12]

3 The expediency of so full a justification of the proceedings of

---

9. To prove that "legislative warfare" was begun by the British, Jefferson had cited a list of acts passed by Parliament before the American Revolution. Among these acts, Jefferson cited 16 Geo. III, C. 5 (1776), which made American ships on the high seas legal prizes in Britain. Jefferson called this act "confiscation, by wholesale," whereas American acts, which Hammond had maintained were violations of the peace treaty, Jefferson believed "retaliated but on the small scale of individual confiscation."

10. Jefferson's comment on H's objection reads as follows: "1. The retaliating clause is struck out, and only a general allusion to the instances of legislative warfare by the British parliament, as here proposed."

11. Jefferson had stated that, while Congress on March 24, 1783, received "informal intelligence from the Marquis de la Fayette that Provisional articles were concluded," it was not until April 11 that Congress received "an official copy of these articles from Doctor Franklin, with notice that a Preliminary treaty was now signed between France, Spain & England." These facts, Jefferson wrote Hammond, "place all acts preceding the 11th. of April out of the present discussion, & confine it to the treaty itself, and the circumstances attending it's execution.

12. Jefferson made the following comment on H's objection: "2. The reason of the rule will guide it's application to particular cases, and prove the 11th. of

certain states with regard to Debts.[13] In this respect, *Extenuation* rather than *Vindication* would seem to be the desireable course. It is an obvious truth and is so stated that Congress alone had the right to pronounce a breach of the Treaty and to fix the measure of retaliation. Not having done it the states which undertook the task for them contravened both their Fœderal duty and the Treaty. Do not some of the Acts of Congress import that the thing was viewed by that body in this light? Will it be well for the Executive now to implicate itself in too strong a defence of measures which have been regarded by a great proportion of the Union and by a respectable part of the citizens of almost every state as exceptionable in various lights? May not too earnest an apology for installment and paper-money laws, if made public hereafter, tend to prejudice somewhat the cause of good government and perhaps to affect disadvantageously the character of the General Government?

To steer between too much *concession* and too much *justification* in this particular is a task both difficult and delicate—but it is worthy of the greatest circumspection to accomplish it.[14]

April to be the true time after which acts of the state legislatures inconsistent with the treaty became wrongful. *Notice* alone of a law, renders an action against that law criminal in pure theory but as the proof of *individual notice*, would, in most cases be impossible, societies have been obliged to adopt the rule that *promulgation* is *individual notice*. This then fixes the point of time at which a law or a treaty becomes a rule of action for *subjects*, or those who have no other means of knowing it. But the Executives of the two nations have a knowledge of the transaction from it's first embryon to it's perfection. They are the 'parties contractantes' of Vattel, and the 'paciscentes' of Wolf cited. §48. though they do not transact the Business in person, but by Plenipotentiaries, at some distance from themselves, yet the correspondence with these Plenipotentiaries through the whole is understood to be so constant, and every proposition which passes is so immediately communicated, that, tho' at a distance, they know in fact what is doing, and hence their real knowledge is dated from the signature, and their acts must conform to it from that instant, though the formal knowledge may come to them some days later. But our State legislatures had no such constant communication of the progress of the negotiation; they had no privity with it at all. As to matters of treaty, the State governments were mere subjects. Their actions, like those of corporations in England, or like any other individuals, can only be governed by the promulgation, which, therefore, is the term for their conformity. They are the '*sujets*' of Vattel and '*subditi*' of Wolf in the passages before referred to."

13. H is referring to Jefferson's defense of various state laws which hindered collection of debts owed to British creditors. Jefferson's vindication of these laws rested on the precedent set by British infractions of the treaty of peace.

14. On this objection, Jefferson commented as follows: "3. the 1st: question is Whether this Ground is defensible? the 2nd. Whether it ought to be abandoned? It cannot be disputed that Great Britain has been guilty of the first

4 The expediency of risking the implication of the *tacit appro-bation* of Congress of the "retaliations of the four states" by saying that they neither *gave* nor *refused* their sanction to those retaliations? Will not the national character stand better if no ground to suspect the connivance of the National Government is afforded? Is not the

───────────

infractions; that these infractions have been highly injurious to us, that when one party has witheld execution of any article of a Treaty, the other has a right to retaliate by equivalent inexecutions. Had Congress after the first re-fusal to evacuate the posts, (the holding of which with an armed force, was, and is, a continuance of the war on that part of our territory) declared firmly, that they would withold the execution of the article for opening the Courts of Justice, in all the States, till all the States should be completely evacuated, it would have been justifiable. Can a part of the act then be less justifiable than the whole? If a refusal to open the courts in every State would have been right, can a refusal in a few States be wrong, and even in these, not an absolute refusal, but a permission under modifications? It was a refusal in fact to such Creditors only, as did not chuse to prosecute under those modifications. Whether this partial retaliation has been by Congress, by the States, or by Individuals, which form collectively the one party to the agreement, is a ques-tion which the other party has no right to ask. It is a point of internal order between Congress and those who undertook to act, and which they alone are competent to question, or decide. Congress, it is true, may *disavow* the retalia-tion. This will make it a wrongful act from the Beginning, and thereby render the Union, in the first instance, and the retaliating States ultimately, liable to make good the damage sustained by the adverse party, though the aggressor. But Congress have a right also to *avow* the act, if nothing else is wanting to make it rightful: or without either avowal or disavowal, to *demonstrate* to Great Britain, that, as to her, it was right. And this is what has been attempted in the answer under consideration.

"Shall this ground be abandoned? There is certainly room to suspect that Great Britain means to *come* forward with a demand of indemnification to her citizens for the debts pretended to have been lost through our wrong. If we have been guilty of a wrong, we must make good the losses it has occasioned. But if nothing more than a moderate and justifiable retaliation has taken place, we are liable for nothing. Will the Executive undertake to say that an unrea-sonable retaliation has taken place? to subject the Union, or the retaliating States to the demand of indemnification? to commit the nation by a language of extenuation, which is pleading guilty, when vindication is truth? If any respectable part of our citizens have regarded these measures as exceptionable, with respect to Great Britain, they have been misled either by the bold asser-tions of the opposite interest, or from a want of knowledge of the facts, or of industry to put them together, and to form a judgment for themselves. When-ever they shall know and consider them, they will condemn any complaisance we might now shew to their uninformed and premature opinions. I am there-fore of opinion that Great Britain cannot say we have done wrong in retarding in the moderate degree we have done, execution of some parts of the treaty, as an equivalent to what she had previously refused to fulfil on her part; that she cannot found on that any claim of indemnification for debts lost by lapse of time; and that the justifiable rights of our country ought not to be given up by those whom they have appointed and trusted to defend them where they may be justly defended."

fact, that Congress were inactive spectators of the Infractions which took place, because they had no effectual power to controul them? [15]

5 The truth of the position which seems to be admitted (Page 57) that the quality of *Alien Enemy* subsisted till the Definitive Treaty.[16] Does not an *indefinite cessation* founded too on a preliminary Treaty, put an end to the *State* of *War* and consequently destroy the relation of alien enemy. The State of War may or may not revive if points which remain to be adjusted by a definitive Treaty are never adjusted by such a treaty—but it is conceived that a definitive Treaty may never take place and yet the state of War and all its consequences be completely terminated.[17]

6 The expediency of grounding any argument on the supposition of either of the parties being in the *wrong* as in Page 65.[18] The rule

15. H is referring to Jefferson's statement: "That Congress had so far thought it best neither to declare, nor relinquish, the infractions of the other party, neither to give, nor refuse, their sanction to the retaliations by the four states." In the body of the report Jefferson lists five states (Virginia, South Carolina, Rhode Island, New Jersey, and Georgia) which had modified the conditions of debt recovery for British merchants. Jefferson commented on H's objections as follows: "4. the passage here alluded to is in the Recapitulation II. §3. It is struck out, and it stands now that Congress induced by assurances from the British court, &c. required from the States a repeal, &c."

16. In describing the opinion of a Georgia court, Jefferson had written: ". . . it is impossible to say that a treaty is become a law of the land as soon as it is provisionally signed only, & consequently to say that at the time Judge [George] Walton gave this opinion, the law of the land was repealed which denied to Alien enemies the right of maintaining suits." Jefferson modified this statement as follows: "And the Judge seems to have been of opinion that it was necessary the treaty should be *definitively* concluded, before it could become a law of the land, so as to change the legal character of an *alien enemy*, who cannot maintain an action, into that of an *alien friend* who may."

17. Jefferson's comment on H's fifth objection reads as follows: "5. I rather consider a preliminary Treaty as establishing certain heads of agreement, and a truce, till these and others can be definitively arranged; as suspending acts of hostility, but not changing the legal character of *enemy* into that of *friend*. However as this might be susceptible of a contradiction not worth our while to excite in this instance, I have struck out all affirmation of the position, and observed that whether Judge Walton was right or wrong in supposing that between the Preliminary and Definitive articles no subject of either party could maintain an action in the Courts of the other, the interval was so short, and this probably the only instance of an action essayed, that it is not worth an investigation."

18. In writing of the British complaint that American debtors had not paid interest on debts during the war, Jefferson had said: ". . . that it is a rule of natural, as well as municipal, law, that in questions de damno evitando, melior est conditio possidentis. If this maxim be just where each party is equally innocent, how much more so, where the loss has been produced by the wrong of the creditor?"

in construing Treaties is to suppose both parties in the right, for want of a *common judge* &c. And a departure from this rule in argument might possibly lead to unpleasant recrimination.[19]

The foregoing are the principal points that have occurred on one perusal. They are submitted without reserve. Some lesser matters struck which would involve too lengthy a commentary. Many of them merely respecting particular expressions. A mark thus + ⟨is⟩ in the margin of the places, which will probably suggest to the Secretary of State, on a revision, the nature of the reflections which may have arisen. It is imagined that there is a small mistake in stating that Waddington paid no rent.[20]

19. To H's sixth objection Jefferson made the following answer: "6. The word *wrong*, in the passage here alluded to §54. is struck out, and the word *act* substituted. We may say with truth that it was by their *act* we were hindered from paying interest, while, not qualifying it with epithet either of *right* or *wrong*, they are free to consider it as the former, while we do tacitly as the latter."

20. In answering this paragraph, Jefferson wrote: "Wherever the mark + has been found, and it's object understood, the passage has been corrected. They seem principally to have been affixed to those passages susceptible of being softened in the manner of expression. In some instances they were not understood. The mistake in the case of Wadington V Rutgers is corrected."

In section 41 of his draft, Jefferson had stated that Joshua Waddington had occupied Elizabeth Rutgers's brewhouse part of the time by permission of the quartermaster general and for the rest of the time by permission of the British commanding officer, "and during no part of it had he paid any rent." Jefferson deleted this section to accord with information which H sent to him in a letter dated April 19, 1792. Jefferson used H's letter of April 19 as Item No. 46 in the letter he wrote to Hammond on May 29, 1792.

From William Lindsay [1]

Collectors Office District of
Norfolk & Portsmo. [Virginia] 20 May 1792

Sir,

I have received Notice from Mr. James Wells that he has thought proper to resign his appointment of Surveyor for the Port of Smithfield, and also that of Port Inspector for the same place.

Colo. Parker has informed me he has recommended his Brother as a proper person to succeed Mr. Wells, who I doubt not (if appointed,) will justify the recommendation.

I am respectfully   Sir   Your Ob Serv   Wm. Lindsay Colr

Alexr. Hamilton Esqr
Secy of the Treasy.

ALS, George Washington Papers, Library of Congress.
  1. For background to this letter, see Josiah Parker to H, May 11, 1792; Edward Carrington to H, May 17, 1792.

From William Ellery

[*Newport, Rhode Island*] *May 21, 1792.* ". . . I wish to be favoured with your instructions respecting the case of the Brig Chance,[1] a Statemt. of which I sent to you on the 2nd. of Apl. last, with an explanation respectg. the Thermometer mentioned in my letter of the 9th. of the same month, and with your directions relative to the tare of Sugars mentioned in my letter of the 5th. of last March, when the important business of your office will permit it. Suffer me also to mention that I have acted as Superintendant of the Light House ever since the 11th. of Oct. 1790. and no allowance has been made to me for that Service, agreeably to the expectations your letter of the 27th. of April 1791 [2] induced me to entertain; And I have debited the United States for the money advanced for the Light-House; but no sums have been received by me in virtue of Warrants from the Treasy on account thereon by which the United States might be credited. . . ."

LC, Newport Historical Society, Newport, Rhode Island.
  1. See Ellery to H, April 2, 1792.
  2. Letter not found. On June 4, 1792, Ellery wrote to Tench Coxe, commissioner of the revenue: "Permit me . . . to mention to you that the Secry of the Treasy in a letter to me of the 27th April 1791 writes thus, 'Your disbursements as Superintendant of the Light-House, are to be kept & rendered separately; for which a commission will probably be allowed by the President, as in the case of the Massachusetts'" (LC, Newport Historical Society, Newport, Rhode Island). See also Ellery to H, July 18, November 11, 1791

To George Washington

Philadelphia May 21st 1792.

Sir,

I returned here yesterday from New Ark,[1] & find that nothing material has occurred in my absence.

There is nothing new except what is contained in the papers, and what I doubt not has been announced to you from the War Department—the Convention between Hamtramck and certain Tribes on the Wabash.[2]

With the most perfect respect and truest attachment, I have the honor to be &c.   Alexr. Hamilton.

LC, George Washington Papers, Library of Congress.
    1. H had left Philadelphia on May 13, 1792, to attend a meeting at Newark, New Jersey, of the directors of the Society for Establishing Useful Manufactures.
    2. On March 14, 1792, Major John F. Hamtramck of the First United States Infantry Regiment signed "Articles of Agreement with Wabash Indians," calling for a meeting of the Wabash chiefs and representatives of the United States at Vincennes to conclude a treaty of peace. The articles of agreement are printed in Carter, *Territorial Papers*, II, 374-75.

To Tench Coxe [1]

[Philadelphia] May 22d 1792

Sir

Pursuant to the 6th Section of the Act making alterations in the Treasury & War Departments,[2] I have concluded to commit to you the general Superintendence of the Light Houses and other establishments relating to the security of Navigation according to the powers vested in me by law.

Information will be given accordingly to the respective Superintendents who will be instructed to correspond in future with you, and take your directions.[3]

When the Presidents sanction is in any case requisite you will make report to me in order that the requisite submission to him may be made.

I am Sir &c   Alexr Hamilton

The Commissioner of the Revenue

LC, RG 26, Lighthouse Letters, Vol. 1, National Archives; copy, RG 26, Lighthouse Letters Received, "Segregated" Lighthouse Records, Hamilton, National Archives.
    1. On May 8, 1792, Congress abolished the office of assistant to the Secretary of the Treasury and established in its place the post of commissioner of revenue (1 *Stat*. 280). On the same day Coxe, who had been assistant to the Secretary of the Treasury, was appointed commissioner of revenue.
    2. Section 6 of "An Act making alterations in the Treasury and War Departments" provided that the commissioner of revenue should perform such

duties "as shall be directed by the Secretary of the Treasury" (1 *Stat.* 280 [May 8, 1792]).

3. See "Treasury Department Circular to the Superintendents of Lighthouses," May 22, 1792.

From Daniel Stevens [1]

[*Charleston, South Carolina, May 22, 1792.* On June 16, 1792, Tench Coxe wrote to Stevens: "The Secretary of the Treasury has delivered to me your letters to him of the 22nd. and 26th of May, and he has requested me to communicate to you the great satisfaction he feels at the success of your efforts to explain and render acceptable the duties on Spirits & Stills.[2] Your forbearance to prossecute the body of those persons, who have from want of due Consideration indiscreetly opposed the law, meets his approbation. It is wished that the deportment of the principal offender may be such as to render it prudent and safe to extend the same indulgence towards him, but this must depend upon his renouncing all refractory conduct, and convincing you of his sincere disposition to demean himself with due propriety in future. Should this temper be manifested by him, and should you not perceive any good reasons for prosecuting him, it may be well that he be treated with the same lenity." [3] *Letter of May 22 not found.*]

1. Stevens was supervisor of the revenue for the District of South Carolina.

2. These duties were imposed by "An Act repealing, after the last day of June next, the duties heretofore laid upon Distilled Spirits imported from abroad, and laying others in their stead; and also upon Spirits distilled within the United States, and for appropriating the same" (1 *Stat.* 199–214 [March 3, 1791]). The law had been substantially revised by "An Act concerning the Duties on Spirits distilled within the United States" (1 *Stat.* 267–71 [May 8, 1792]).

3. LC, RG 58, Letters of Commissioner of Revenue, 1792–1793, National Archives.

Treasury Department Circular to the Superintendents of Lighthouses [1]

Treasury Department May 22nd 1792

Sir,

Pursuant to the 6th Section of the Act making alterations in the Treasury and War Departments, I have concluded to commit to

Tench Coxe Esquire Commissioner of the Revenue, the general superintendence of the Light house and other establishments, relating to the security of navigation according to the powers vested in me by law.[2]

You will therefore be pleased to correspond in future with the said Commissioner of Revenue, touching all matters relating to the Light House establishment and take his directions thereon.

I am Sir   Your most obedt Servt   Alexander Hamilton

LS, to Jedediah Huntington, MS Division, New York Public Library; LS, to Benjamin Lincoln, RG 36, Collector of Customs at Boston, Letters and Papers re Lighthouses, Buoys, and Piers, 1789–1819, Vol. 1, National Archives; LC, RG 26, Lighthouse Letters Received, "Segregated" Lighthouse Records, Hamilton, National Archives.
   1. Huntington and Lincoln were both collectors of customs and superintendents of lighthouses.
   2. See H to Tench Coxe, May 22, 1792.

To William Seton

[*Philadelphia, May 23, 1792*. On May 28, 1792, Seton wrote to Hamilton: "Your kind letter of the 23d, I did not receive till after the last post for the week was gone out." *Letter not found.*]

Treasury Department Circular to the Collectors of the Customs [1]

Treasury Department
May 23. 1792.

Sir

I have to request, if in future you should have any *particular* communication to make to the Secretary of the Treasury, that you will designate Your Office upon the outside of your letters.

I am, Sir,   Your Obedt. Servant   A Hamilton

LS, The Turner Manuscript Collection at the Torrington Library, Torrington, Connecticut; LS, sold by Kingston Galleries, Inc., Lot 77, Catalogue No. 4.
   1. Although there is no addressee given on either copy of this circular letter, presumably it was addressed to the collectors of the customs as an amplification of the directions H gave in "Treasury Department Circular to the Collectors of the Customs," May 10, 1792.

From Thomas Willing

[*Philadelphia, May 23, 1792.* On May 23, 1792, Hamilton acknowledged the receipt of Mr. W Letter of today." *Letter not found.*]

To Thomas Willing

[Philadelphia, May 23, 1792]

Mr. Hamilton presents his Compliments to Mr. Willing incloses the rough draft of an agreement [1] comprising the ideas contained in Mr. W Letter of today.[2] If approved Mr. H will have it corrected & copied. If any alterations are desired Mr. W. will pleased to signify them. Mr. H is desirous of finishing the arranget as soon as may be.

May 23

AL, courtesy of the Trustees of the Boston Public Library.
1. The "rough draft" of this agreement has not been found, but for the final version see "Agreement with the President, Directors, and Company of the Bank of the United States," May 25, 1792.
2. Letter not found.

From Sylvanus Bourne

Boston May 24th 1792

Sir

Having been absent in the Country, it was not till yesterday, that I had the honour to receive your favr of the 10th Inst.[1]

I had (as you supposed) been previously informed of the issue of an affair, which tho' ultimately without your controul, had, I am confidant, the support of your most friendly exertions.[2] My letter to you of the 10th in a degree anticipated the present answer to yours of the same date. Taught by long experience the futility of indulging those pleasing hopes in regard to life, which my education has inspired me with, while they are opposed by relentless misfortune & dissapointments, I consent to accept, the only place, you can at present give me,[3] in confidence that "mens sibi conscia recti" may enliven the obscure path I am called to walk in, and serve as an antidote to the insiduous smiles of those who may enjoy more apparent fame.

I presume from the duty of the place you have assigned me that I shall be immediately subject to your directions & not subservient to the caprice of any clerks in the department: from this idea I derive solace.

Pressing as my situation is, I would still prefer the chance of contingent events, to the acceptance of a similar place with any one but you, my respected Sir—as I flatter myself yet to obtain (under the auspices of your kind patronage) some place more reputable & congenial to my wishes; provided the strength of these, may not beguile the weight of my pretensions.

Conscious that you cannot but view with Complacency the glow of a laudable ambition, I have not suppressed sentiments resulting from this source.

I have the honour to be with unequivocal Respect & Esteem   sir
Your most Obedt Humble servt   Sylva Bourne

PS. Some necessary arrangment of my affaires will unavoidably detain me 10 days or a fortnight in this town; for which I ask your kind indulgence.

ALS, Hamilton Papers, Library of Congress.
    1. Letter not found.
    2. Bourne had hoped that he would be appointed treasurer of the Mint. See Bourne to H, May 10, 1792.
    3. H had offered Bourne a clerkship in the office of the Secretary of the Treasury.

To William Seton

[*Philadelphia, May 24, 1792.* On May 28, 1792, Seton wrote to Hamilton: "I am honourd with your Letter of the 24th." *Letter not found.*]

Agreement with the President, Directors, and Company of the Bank of the United States [1]

[Philadelphia, May 25, 1792]

Agreement between Alexander Hamilton Secretary of the Treasury on behalf of the President of the United States of the one part and The President Directors and Company of the Bank of the United States of the other part—

Whereas in and by the Act intitled "An Act for raising a further sum of money for the Protection of the Frontiers and for other purposes therein mentioned" it is among other things enacted in the words following—"That the President of the United States be empowered to take on loan on account of the United States, from the President, Directors and Company of the Bank of the United States, who are hereby authorised and empowered to lend the same, from any other body politic or corporate within the United States, or from any other person or persons the whole or any part of the aforesaid Sum of Five hundred and twenty three thousand five hundred dollars to be applied to the purposes to and for which the same is above appropriated, and to be reimbursed out of the aforesaid Surplus of the duties by this Act imposed, which surplus is accordingly appropriated to the said reimbursment. Provided that the rate of Interest of such Loan shall not exceed five per Centum per Annum, and that the principal thereof may be reimbursed at the pleasure of the United States." [2]

And Whereas, The President of the United States by a Writing under his hand bearing date the seventh day of May in the year one thousand seven hundred and Ninety two did authorise the said Secretary of the Treasury to agree and contract with The President Directors and Company of the Bank of the United States, with any

D, signed by H and Thomas Willing, RG 59, Miscellaneous Letters, Letters of the Department of State, 1790–1799, National Archives.

1. For background to this document, see George Washington to H, May 7, 1792, and H to Thomas Willing, May 23, 1792.

2. This is a quotation of Section 16 of "An Act for raising a farther sum of money for the protection of the frontiers, and for other purposes therein mentioned" (1 *Stat.* 262 [May 2, 1792]).

other body politic or corporate within the United States or with any other person or persons for a loan or loans to the United States of any sum or sums not exceeding in the whole Five hundred and twenty three thousand five hundred Dollars to be advanced and paid in such proportions and at such periods as the said Secretary should judge necessary for fulfilling the purposes of the said Act, Provided that the rate of interest of such loan or loans should not exceed Five per Centum per annum and that the principal thereof might be reimbursed at the pleasure of the United States. And did thereby promise to ratify what the said Secretary should lawfully do in the premisses.

And Whereas the said President Directors and Company on the application of the said Secretary have consented to lend on account of the United States the aforesaid sum of Five hundred and twenty three thousand five hundred Dollars in conformity to the provision of the Act aforesaid.

Now Therefore these Presents Witness that it hath been agreed and it is hereby mutually agreed by and between the parties aforesaid as followeth to Wit—

First that The said President Directors and Company shall advance lend and pay on account of the United States the aforesaid sum of Five hundred and twenty three thousand five hundred Dollars, or so much thereof as may be required in the following installments and at the following periods respectively, namely One hundred thousand dollars on the first day of June next, One hundred thousand dollars on the first day of July next, One hundred thousand dollars on the first day of August next One hundred thousand dollars on the first day of September next, and the residue of the said sum of Five hundred and twenty three thousand five hundred dollars on the first day of January next which several sums shall be paid to the Treasurer of the United States upon Warrants issued from the Department of the Treasury according to Law and shall bear an Interest at the rate of Five per Centum per annum to be computed upon each of the said sums from the time of passing the same to the credit of the said Treasurer.

Secondly—that the Interest upon so much of the Loan aforesaid as may be advanced prior to the first day of January next shall be paid upon the said day and that thenceforth until the reimbursement of the principal sum which shall have been advanced and lent as aforesaid, interest shall be payable half yearly, that is to say upon the first day of July and the first day of January in each year.

Thirdly, That the surplus of the duties laid by the Act herein before mentioned shall pursuant to the true intent and meaning of the fifteenth Section of the said Act be well and truly applied, as the same shall accrue and be received to the reimbursement of the principal and interest of the monies which shall be advanced and lent as aforesaid and that until such reimbursement shall be completed, The Secretary of the Treasury for the time being shall cause half yearly returns of the amount of the said surplus to be laid before the said President Directors and Company for their information, as soon as may be after the expiration of each half year during the continuance of the said duties from the time of the commencement thereof until the said reimbursement shall be completed.

Provided always that the whole or any part of the monies which shall have been advanced upon the loan together with all arrears of interest thereupon to the time of such reimbursement may at any time whatsoever at the pleasure of the United States be reimbursed paid off and discharged.

And lastly—The said Secretary of the Treasury doth promise and engage That the President of the United States within two months from and after the date of these presents will in due form ratify and confirm the Agreement hereby made.[3]

In testimony whereof the said Secretary hath hereunto subscribed his hand and caused to be affixed the seal of the Treasury of the

3. At the end of this document the following confirmation of the agreement appears:

"Now Know Ye that I, having seen and considered the said agreement do hereby ratify and confirm the same and every part thereof: In Testimony whereof I have caused the seal of the United States to be affixed to these presents and signed the same with my Hand. Done at Philadelphia the fifth day of June in the Year of our Lord one thousand seven hundred and ninety two and of the independence of the United States, the sixteenth.

Go. Washington
By the President
Th: Jefferson"

(copy, RG 59, Miscellaneous Letters, Letters of the Department of State, 1790–1799, National Archives.)

United States and the said President Directors and Company have hereunto caused to be affixed the seal of the said Corporation. Done at Philadelphia the XXVth of May MDCCXCII.

Alexander Hamilton
Secretary of the Treasury
Thos. Willing Prest.

From Stephen Cross [1]

[*Newburyport, Massachusetts, May 25, 1792.* In a letter to Hamilton of October 18, 1792, Cross referred to "my letter of May 25th." *Letter not found.*]

1. Cross had been appointed collector of customs at Newburyport, Massachusetts, on August 3, 1789. On May 4, 1792, he was succeeded by Edward Wigglesworth.

From Charles Cotesworth Pinckney [1]

[*Charleston, South Carolina, May 25, 1792.* On June 25, 1792, Hamilton wrote to Pinckney: "I have duly received your letter of the 25th of May." *Letter not found.*]

1. Pinckney, who had served as a colonel in the First South Carolina Regiment during the American Revolution and had been a member of the Constitutional Convention, was at this time practicing law in Charleston, South Carolina.

To William Seton

Philadelphia
May 25. 1792

My Dear Sir
The Society for establishing useful manufactures, at their last meeting, resolved to borrow a sum of 5000 Dollars upon a pledge of deferred Stock.[1] Mr. Walker is impowered to negotiate the loan and I expect application will be made to the Bank of New York for it. I have a strong wish that the Directors of that Bank may be disposed to give facilities to this institution upon terms of perfect safety

to itself. I will add that from its situation it is much the interest of our City that it should succeed. It is not difficult to discern the advantage of being the immediate market to a considerable manufacturing Town. A pledge of public Stock will completely fulfil the idea of perfect security. I will add more—That in my opinion Banks ought to afford accommodation *in such cases* upon easy terms of interest. I think five ℔ Cent ought to suffice; for a direct public good is presented. And Institutions of this kind within reasonable limits ought to consider it as a principal object to promote beneficial public purposes.

To you My Dear Sir I will not scruple to say *in confidence* that the Bank of New York shall suffer no diminution of its *pecuniary faculties* from any accommodations it may afford to the Society in Question. I feel my reputation much concerned in its welfare.

I would not wish any formal communication of this letter to the Directors; but you may make known my wishes to such of them as you judge expedient.

With real esteem & great regard   D Sir   Yrs. Obed serv

A Hamilton

William Seton Esquire

ALS, Museum of the City of New York.
   1. At a meeting of the directors of the Society for Establishing Useful Manufactures, which H attended at Newark, New Jersey, on May 18, 1792, it was "Resolved that Benjamin Walker be authorized to negociate a Loan with the Bank of New York, or the Office of Discount and deposit of the Bank of the United States at New York, in behalf of the Society for establishing useful Manufactures, to the amount of Ten Thousand Dollars, on the best terms he can and that he deposit deferred Stock of the Society for the security of the same, for which purpose the Deputy Governor is hereby directed to execute a Power of Attorney under the common seal of the Society authorizing the said Benjamin Walker, to transfer so much of the deferred stock as will be necessary to accomplish the purposes aforesaid" ("Minutes of the S.U.M.," 38).

To Thomas Willing

Treasury Department
May 25. 1792

Sir

In conformity to my proposition accepted by the President Directors & Company of the Bank of the United States as expressed in their resolution of the 8th instant and to the desire of the Board signified in your letter of the 23,[1] I have caused an Agreement to be prepared, which having been first shewn to you[2] and approved, I have executed in two parts and now send them to you to be executed under the seal of the Corporation.[3] One of them you will please to have returned to me.

With very respectful consideration   I have the honor to be   Sir Your most Obedient & humble servant   Alexander Hamilton
Secy of the Treasury

Thomas Willing Esquire
President of the Bank of the UStates.

ALS, Historical Society of Pennsylvania, Philadelphia.
    1. Letter not found.
    2. See H to Willing, May 23, 1792.
    3. See "Agreement with the President, Directors, and Company of the Bank of the United States," May 25, 1792.

To Edward Carrington [1]

Philadelphia May 26th, 1792

My Dear Sir
    Believing that I possess a share of your personal friendship and confidence and yielding to that which I feel towards you—persuaded also that our political creed is the same on *two essential points*, 1st the necessity of *Union* to the respectability and happiness of this Country and 2 the necessity of an *efficient* general government to maintain that Union—I have concluded to unbosom myself to you on the present state of political parties and views. I ask no reply to what I shall say. I only ask that you will be persuaded, the representations I shall make are agreable to the real and sincere impressions of my mind. You will make the due allowances for the influence of circumstances upon it—you will consult your own ob-

JCH Transcripts.
    1. H had first met Carrington when they served with Arthur St. Clair as American commissioners for the exchange of prisoners in March, 1780. In 1785 and 1786 Carrington was a delegate from Virginia to the Continental Congress. In September, 1789, he was appointed marshal for the District of Virginia, and in March, 1791, he became supervisor of the revenue for the District of Virginia.

servations and you will draw such a conclusion as shall appear to you proper.

When I accepted the Office, I now hold, it was under a full persuasion, that from similarity of thinking, conspiring with personal goodwill, I should have the firm support of Mr. Madison, in the *general course* of my administration. Aware of the intrinsic difficulties of the situation and of the powers of Mr. Madison, I do not believe I should have accepted under a different supposition.

I have mentioned the similarity of thinking between that Gentleman and myself. This was relative not merely to the general principles of National Policy and Government but to the leading points which were likely to constitute questions in the administration of the finances. I mean 1 the expediency of *funding* the debt 2 the inexpediency of *discrimination* between original and present holders 3 The expediency of *assuming* the state Debts.

As to the first point, the evidence of Mr. Madisons sentiments at one period is to be found in the address of Congress of April 26th 1783, which was planned by him in conformity to his own ideas and without any previous suggestions from the Committee and with his hearty cooperation in every part of the business.[2] His conversations upon various occasions since have been expressive of a continuance in the same sentiment, nor indeed, has he yet contradicted it by any part of his official conduct. How far there is reason to apprehend a change in this particular will be stated hereafter.

As to the second part, the same address is an evidence of Mr. Madison's sentiments at the same period.[3] And I had been informed that at a later period he had been in the Legislature of Virginia a strenuous and successful opponent of the principle of discrimination. Add to this that a variety of conversations had taken place between

2. The draft of an "Address to the States, by the United States in Congress Assembled," in the handwriting of James Madison, may be found in the Papers of the Continental Congress, National Archives. It had been reported from a committee consisting of James Madison, H, and Oliver Ellsworth on April 26, 1783 (JCC, XXIV, 277–83).

3. In "Report Relative to a Provision for the Support of Public Credit," January 9, 1790, H had quoted the portion of the "Address to the States, by the United States in Congress Assembled" which stated that it would be impossible and unnecessary to discriminate among various creditors of the Government because, "If the voice of humanity plead more loudly in favour of some than of others, the voice of policy, no less than of justice, pleads in favour of all" (JCC, XXIV, 283).

him and myself respecting the public debt down to the commencement of the New Government in none of which had he glanced at the idea of a change of opinion. I wrote him a letter after my appointment in the recess of Congress to obtain his sentiments on the subject of the Finances.[4] In his answer there is not a lisp of his new system.[5]

As to the third point, the question of an assumption of the state Debts by the U States was in discussion when the Convention that framed the present Government was sitting at Philadelphia; and in a long conversation, which I had with Mr. Madison in an afternoon's walk I well remember that we were perfectly agreed in the expediency and propriety of such a measure, though we were both of opinion that it would be more adviseable to make it a measure of administration than an article of constitution; from the impolicy of multiplying obstacles to its reception on collateral details.

Under these circumstances, you will naturally imagine that it must have been matter of surprize to me, when I was apprised, that it was Mr. Madison's intention to oppose my plan on both the last mentioned points.

Before the debate commenced, I had a conversation with him on my report, in the course of which I alluded to the calculation I had made of his sentiments and the grounds of that calculation. He did not deny them, but alledged in his justification that the very considerable alienation of the debt, subsequent to the periods at which he had opposed a discrimination, had essentially changed the state of the question—and that as to the assumption, he had contemplated it to take place *as matters stood at the peace.*

While the change of opinion avowed on the point of discrimination diminished my respect for the force of Mr. Madison's mind and the soundness of his judgment—and while the idea of reserving and setting afloat a vast mass of already extinguished debt as the condition of a measure the leading objects of which were an accession of strength to the National Government and an assurance of order and vigour in the national finances by doing away the necessity of thirteen complicated and conflicting systems of finance—appeared to me somewhat extraordinary: Yet my previous impressions of the fairness of Mr. Madison's character and my reliance on his good will

4. H to Madison, October 12, 1789.
5. Madison to H, November 19, 1789.

towards me disposed me to believe that his suggestions were sincere; and even, on the point of an assumption of the debts of the States as they stood at the peace, to lean towards a cooperation in his view; 'till on feeling the ground I found the thing impracticable, and on further reflection I thought it liable to immense difficulties. It was tried and failed with little countenance.

At this time and afterwards repeated intimations were given to me that Mr. Madison, from a spirit of rivalship or some other cause had become personally unfriendly to me; and one Gentleman in particular, whose honor I have no reason to doubt, assured me, that Mr. Madison in a conversation with him had made a pretty direct attempt to insinuate unfavourable impressions of me.

Still I suspended my opinion on the subject. I knew the malevolent officiousness of mankind too well to yield a very ready acquiescence to the suggestions which were made, and resolved to wait 'till time and more experience should afford a solution.

It was not 'till the last session that I became unequivocally convinced of the following truth—"*That Mr. Madison cooperating with Mr. Jefferson is at the head of a faction decidedly hostile to me and my administration, and actuated by views in my judgment subversive of the principles of good government and dangerous to the union, peace and happiness of the Country.*"

These are strong expressions; they may pain your friendship for one or both of the Gentlemen whom I have named. I have not lightly resolved to hazard them. They are the result of a *Serious alarm* in my mind for the public welfare, and of a full conviction that what I have alledged is a truth, and a truth, which ought to be told and well attended to, by all the friends of Union and efficient National Government. The suggestion will, I hope, at least awaken attention, free from the byass of former prepossessions.

This conviction in my mind is the result of a long train of circumstances; many of them minute. To attempt to detail them all would fill a volume. I shall therefore confine myself to the mention of a few.

First—As to the point of opposition to me and my administration.

Mr. Jefferson with very little reserve manifests his dislike of the funding system generally; calling in question the expediency of funding a debt at all. Some expressions which he has dropped in my own presence (sometimes without sufficient attention to delicacy) will not permit me to doubt on this point, representations, which I have had from various respectable quarters. I do not mean, that he advocates directly the undoing of what has been done, but he censures the whole on principles, which if they should become general, could not but end in the subversion of the system.

In various conversations with *foreigners* as well as citizens, he has thrown censure on my *principles* of government and on my measures of administration. He has predicted that the people would not long tolerate my proceedings & that I should not long maintain my ground. Some of those, whom he *immediately* and *notoriously* moves, have *even* whispered suspicions of the rectitude of my motives and conduct. In the question concerning the Bank he not only delivered an opinion in writing against its constitutionality & expediency; but he did it *in a stile and manner* which I felt as partaking of asperity and ill humour towards me.[6] As one of the trustees of the sinking fund, I have experienced in almost every leading question opposition from him.[7] When any turn of things in the community has threatened either odium or embarrassment to me, he has not been able to suppress the satisfaction which it gave him.

A part of this is of course information, and might be misrepresentation. But it comes through so many channels and so well accords with what falls under my own observation that I can entertain no doubt.

I find a strong confirmation in the following circumstances. *Freneau* the present Printer of the National Gazette, who was a journeyman with Childs & Swain at New York, was a known anti-federalist. It is reduced to a certainty that he was brought to Philadelphia by Mr. Jefferson to be the conductor of a News Paper. It is notorious that cotemporarily with the commencement of his paper he was a Clerk in the department of state for foreign languages.[8] Hence a

6. See "Opinion on the Constitutionality of an Act to Establish a Bank," February 23, 1791.
7. For one such difference of opinion, see "Meeting of the Commissioners of the Sinking Fund," April 4, 1792, note 2.
8. Philip Freneau, editor of *The* [Philadelphia] *Freeman's Journal: or, the North-American Intelligencer* during the American Revolution, had been a frequent contributor to the [New York] *Daily Advertiser* published by Francis Childs and John Swaine. On August 16, 1791, Freneau was appointed clerk for foreign languages in the office of the Secretary of State, and the first issue of the [Philadelphia] *National Gazette*, of which he was editor, appeared on October 31, 1791.

clear inference that his paper has been set on foot and is conducted under the patronage & not against the views of Mr. Jefferson. What then is the complexion of this paper? Let any impartial man peruse all the numbers down to the present day; and I never was more mistaken, if he does not pronounce that it is a paper devoted to the subversion of me & the measures in which I have had an Agency; and I am little less mistaken if he do not pronounce that it is a paper of a tendency *generally unfriendly* to the Government of the U States.

It may be said, that a News Paper being open to all the publications, which are offered to it, its complexion may be influenced by other views than those of the Editor. But the fact here is that wherever the Editor appears it is in a correspondent dress. The paragraphs which appear as his own, the publications, not original which are selected for his press, are of the same malignant and unfriendly aspect, so as not to leave a doubt of the temper which directs the publication.

Again *Brown*,[9] who publishes an Evening paper called *The Federal Gazette* was originally a zealous federalist and personally friendly to me. He has been employed by Mr. Jefferson as a Printer to the Government for the publication of the laws; and for some time past 'till lately the complexion of his press was equally bitter and unfriendly to me & to the Government.

Lately, Col Pickering in consequence of certain attacks upon him, got hold of some instances of malconduct of his which have served to hold him in Check and seemed to have varied his tone a little.[10] I

9. Andrew Brown founded *The Federal Gazette, and Philadelphia Evening Post* on October 1, 1788. On April 1, 1790, the name of the paper was changed to *The Federal Gazette and Philadelphia Daily Advertiser.*

10. In an exchange of letters between Timothy Pickering, who had been appointed Postmaster General on August 19, 1791, and Brown, editor of *The Federal Gazette,* published in late January and early February, 1792, concerning the proposed postal rates for newspapers, Brown had criticized Pickering's calculations in support of the proposed rates as misleading and "a deviation from truth and candor (*The Federal Gazette and Philadelphia Daily Advertiser,* January 30, February 2, 3, 10, 1792; *Dunlap's* [Philadelphia] *American Daily Advertiser,* February 2, 9, 1792). In reply Pickering attempted to cast doubt on Brown's reputation for veracity by reprinting the following notice, dated March 2, 1786, which Eleazer Oswald had published in *The* [Philadelphia] *Independent Gazetteer and Agricultural Repository* on April 23, 1791:

"WHERE AS *I have caused reports to be circulated* that payments *had been* made by me to Jedediah Rogers, and *receipts for those payments* had been taken by me *from him,* in consequence of his having left in my hands a quan-

dont lay so much stress on this last case as on the former. There, I find an internal evidence which is as conclusive as can be expected in any similar case. Thus far, as to Mr. Jefferson.

With regard to Mr. Madison—the matter stands thus. I have not heard, but in the one instance to which I have alluded, of his having held language unfriendly to me in private conversation. But in his public conduct there has been a more uniform & persevering opposition than I have been able to resolve into a sincere difference of opinion. I cannot persuade myself that Mr. Madison and I, whose politics had formerly so much the *same point of departure*, should now diverge so widely in our opinions of the measures which are proper to be pursued. The opinion I once entertained of the candour and simplicity and fairness of Mr. Madisons character has, I acknowledge, given way to a decided opinion that *it is one of a peculiarly artificial and complicated kind.*

For a considerable part of the last session, Mr. Madison lay in a great measure *perdu.* But it was evident from his votes & a variety of little movements and appearances, that he was the prompter of Mr. Giles [11] & others, who were the open instruments of opposition. Two facts occurred, in the course of the session, which I view as unequivocal demonstrations of his disposition towards me. In one, a direct and decisive blow was aimed. When the department of the Treasury was established Mr. Madison was an unequivocal advocate of the principles which prevailed in it and of the powers and duties which were assigned by it to the head of the department. This appeared both from his private and public discourses; and I will add, that I have personal evidence that Mr. Madison is as well convinced as any man in the U States of the necessity of the arrangement which characterizes that establishment to the orderly conducting of the business of the Finances.

Mr. Madison nevertheless opposed directly a reference to me to

tity of goods in October last, *and that the said receipts were fraudulently taken from me by the said Jedediah*—this may certify, *that I* never paid any monies to the said Jedediah on account of the said goods *or otherwise,* and *that he has never* given me any *receipts for monies* paid him or for any other property delivered to him *whatsoever.*

ANDREW BROWN"

(*Dunlap's American Daily Advertiser,* February 9, 1792.)

11. William Branch Giles of Virginia was a leading spokesman for the "Republican interest" in the House of Representatives.

report *ways* & *means* for the Western expedition, & combatted *on principle* the propriety of such references.[12]

He well knew, that, if he had prevailed, a certain consequence was, my *resignation*—that I would not be fool enough to make pecuniary sacrifices and endure a life of extreme drudgery without opportunity either to do material good or to acquire reputation; and frequently with a responsibility in reputation for measures in which I had no hand, and in respect to which, the part I had acted, if any, could not be known.

To accomplish this point, an effectual train, as was supposed, was laid. Besides those who ordinarily acted under Mr. Madison's banners, several, who had generally acted with me from various motives, vanity, self importance, &c. &c. were enlisted.

My overthrow was anticipated as certain and Mr. Madison, *laying aside his wonted caution,* boldly led his troops as he imagined to a certain victory. He was disappointed. Though, *late* I became apprized of the danger. Measures of counteraction were adopted, & when the Question was called, Mr. Madison was confounded to find characters voting against him, whom he had counted upon as certain.[13]

12. Under "An Act for making farther and more effectual Provision for the Protection of the Frontiers of the United States" (1 *Stat.* 241–43 [March 5, 1792], three additional regiments were to be raised. During consideration in the House of Representatives of the additional expense which would be incurred by the expanded Army, a resolution was proposed which reads as follows: "Resolved, That the Secretary of the Treasury be directed to report to the House the *Ways and Means,* by which, in his opinion, the additional sums necessary for the public service ought to be raised" ([Philadelphia] *Gazette of the United States,* March 10, 1792). When this resolution was brought up for consideration on March 7 and 8, it provoked "warm and animated debate." Although Madison's remarks on this resolution are not recorded in the *Annals of Congress,* Theodore Sedgwick of Massachusetts summarized Madison's arguments in order to refute them. According to Sedgwick, Madison "had given in detail the several proceedings which ought to take place to obtain on one hand the benefit of the knowledge of the Secretary, and to maintain on the other the independency of the House. Thus, according to his plan, was the business to be pursued. The House was, in the first place, to call on the Secretary for a state of facts; it was then to resolve itself into a Committee of the Whole, to form opinions; these opinions were then to be referred to the Secretary, for him to report respecting them a systematic arrangement" (*Annals of Congress,* III, 439–40).

13. The resolution "That the Secretary of the Treasury be directed to report to this House his opinion of the best mode for raising the additional supplies requisite for the ensuing year" passed the House by a vote of thirty-one to twenty-seven (*Journal of the House,* I, 530–31).

Towards the close of the Session, another, though a more covert, attack was made. It was in the shape of a proposition to insert in the supplementary Act respecting the public Debt something by way of instruction to the Trustees "to make their purchases of the debt at the *lowest* market price." [14] In the course of the discussion of this point, Mr. Madison dealt much in *insidious insinuations* calculated to give an impression that the public money under my particular direction had been unfaithfully applied to put undue advantages in the pockets of speculators, & to support the debt at an *artificial* price for their benefit. The whole manner of this transaction left no doubt in any ones mind that Mr. Madison was actuated by *personal* & political animosity.

As to this last instance, it is but candid to acknowledge, that Mr. Madison had a better right to act the enemy than on any former occasion. I had some short time before, subsequent to his conduct respecting the reference, declared openly my opinion of the views, by which he was actuated towards me, & my determination to consider & treat him as a political enemy.

An intervening proof of Mr. Madisons unfriendly intrigues to my disadvantage is to be found in the following incident which I relate to you upon my honor but from the nature of it, you will perceive in the *strictest confidence*. The president having prepared his speech at the commencement of the ensuing session communicated it to Mr. Madison for his remarks. It contained among other things a *clause* concerning weights & measures, hinting the advantage of an invariable standard, which *preceded*, in the original state of the

14. On May 3, 1792, when "An Act supplementary to the act making provision for the Debt of the United States" (1 *Stat.* 281–83 [May 8, 1792]) was under discussion in the committee of the whole, "Mr. Madison moved to amend the section which relates to purchases of the public debt, by inserting the word 'lowest' before the words 'market price.' Considerable debate ensued on this motion. . . ." On the following day, "Mr. Madison's motion . . . was agreed to 24 to 23." When the bill was reported to the House later that day, the bill was passed as amended by the committee except for Madison's motion ([Philadelphia] *Gazette of the United States*, May 5, 1792). In the House, however, a section was added which appears as Section 8 of the act and which provides: "That all future purchases of public debt on account of the United States, shall be made at the lowest price, at which the same can be obtained by open purchase, or by receiving sealed proposals, to be opened in the presence of the commissioners, or persons authorized by them to make purchases, and the persons making such proposals" (1 *Stat.* 283).

speech, a clause concerning the Mint.[15] Mr. Madison suggested a transposition of these clauses & the addition of certain words, which I now forget importing an *immediate connection* between the two subjects. You may recollect that Mr. Jefferson proposes that the *unit of weight* & the *unit in the coins* shall be the same,[16] & that my propositions are to preserve the Dollar as the Unit, adhering to its present quantity of Silver, & establishing the same proportion of alloy in the silver as in the gold Coins. The evident design of this manoeuvre was to connect the Presidents opinion in favour of Mr. Jefferson's idea, in contradiction to mine, &, the worst of it is, *without his being aware of the tendency of the thing.* It happened, that the President shewed me the Speech, altered in conformity to Mr. Madisons suggestion, just before it was copied for the purpose of being delivered. I remarked to him the tendency of the alteration. *He declared that he had not been aware of it & had no such intention; & without hesitation agreed to expunge the words which were designed to connect the two subjects.*

This transaction, in my opinion, not only furnishes a proof of Mr. Madisons *intrigues,* in opposition to my measures, but charges him with an *abuse* of the Presidents confidence in him, by endeavouring to make him, without his knowledge, take part with one officer against another, in a case in which they had given different opinions to the Legislature of the Country. *I forbore to awaken the President's mind to this last inference;* but it is among the circumstances which have convinced me that Mr. Madisons true character is the reverse of that *simple, fair, candid one,* which he has assumed.

I have informed you, that Mr. Freneau was brought to Philadelphia, by Mr. Jefferson, to be the Conductor of a News Paper. My information announced Mr. Madison as the mean of negotiation while he was at New York last summer. This and the general co-

15. In his third annual message to Congress on October 25, 1791, Washington recommended "the carrying into immediate effect the resolution already entered into concerning the establishment of a Mint" (*GW*, XXXI, 403). On April 2, 1792, Washington approved "An Act establishing a Mint, and regulating the Coins of the United States" (1 *Stat.* 246–51).

16. H is referring to Jefferson's "Plan for Establishing Uniformity in the Coinage, Weights and Measures of the United States," July 4, 1790 (*ASP, Miscellaneous*, I, 13–20).

incidence & close intimacy between the two Gentlemen leave no doubt that their views are substantially the same.

Secondly As to the tendency of the views of the two Gentlemen who have been named.

Mr. Jefferson is an avowed enemy to a funded debt. Mr. Madison disavows in public any intention to *undo* what has been done; but in a private conversation with Mr. Charles Carroll (Senator), this Gentlemans name I mention confidentially though he mentioned the matter to Mr. King [17] & several other Gentlemen as well as myself; & if any chance should bring you together you would easily bring him to repeat it to you, he favoured the sentiment in Mr. Mercers speech [18] that a Legislature had no right to *fund* the debt by mortgaging permanently the public revenues because they had no right to bind posterity. The inference is that what has been unlawfully done may be undone.

The discourse of partizans in the Legislature & the publications in the party news-papers direct their main battery against the *principle* of a funded debt, & represent it in the most odious light as a perfect *Pandoras box.*

If Mr. Barnewell of St. Carolina,[19] who appears to be a man of nice honor, may be credited, Mr. Giles declared in a conversation with him that if there was a question for reversing the funding

17. Rufus King was a Federalist Senator from New York.

18. On March 30, 1792, John F. Mercer, a member of the House of Representatives from Maryland, said that although a majority of the present generation might bind themselves and "mortgage their own industry," nevertheless, "The grand and important question remains . . . Can they sell or mortgage the labor and industry of another generation—of posterity? . . . The God of Nature has given the earth to the living. . . . we have a right to the fruits of our own industry—they to theirs" (*Annals of Congress*, III, 504).

Madison, in a letter to Jefferson dated May 1, 1791, attributes this theory to Jefferson: "I send you herewith a copy of Priestley's answer to Burke which has been reprinted here. You will see by a note page 56 how your idea of limiting the right to bind posterity is germinating under the extravagant doctrines of Burke on that subject" (Hunt, *Writings of Madison*, VI, 47). See also "The Earth Belongs in Usufruct to the Living," Editorial Note, Boyd, *Papers of Thomas Jefferson*, XV, 384-91.

19. Robert Barnwell, a Federalist member of the House of Representatives from South Carolina, had served as a lieutenant in the South Carolina Militia during the American Revolution. He was a member of the Continental Congress in 1788 and 1789, and a member of the South Carolina Ratifying Convention.

system on the abstract point of the right of pledging & the futility of preserving public faith, he should be for reversal; merely to demonstrate his sense of the defect of right & the inutility of the thing. If positions equally extravagant were not publicly advanced by some of the party & secretly countenanced by the most guarded & *discreet* of them, one would be led, from the absurdity of the declaration, to suspect misapprehension. But from what is *known* any thing may be *believed*.

Whatever were the original merits of the funding system, after having been so solemly adopted, & after so great a transfer of property under it, what would become of the Government should it be reversed? What of the National Reputation? Upon what system of morality can so atrocious a doctrine be maintained? In me, I confess it excites *indignation* & *horror!*

What are we to think of those maxims of Government by which the power of a Legislature is denied to bind the Nation by a *Contract* in an affair of *property* for twenty four years? For this is precisely the case of the debt. What are to become of all the legal rights of property, of all charters to corporations, nay, of all grants to a man his heirs & assigns for ever, if this doctrine be true? What is the term for which a government is in capacity to *contract?* Questions might be multiplied without end to demonstrate the perniciousness & absurdity of such a doctrine.

In almost all the questions great & small which have arisen, since the first session of Congress, Mr. Jefferson & Mr. Madison have been found among those who were disposed to narrow the Federal authority. The question of a National Bank is one example.[20] The question of bounties to the Fisheries is another. Mr. Madison resisted it on the ground of constitutionality, 'till it was evident, by the intermediate questions taken, that the bill would pass & he then under the wretched subterfuge of a change of a single word "bounty" for "allowance" went over to the Majority & voted for

20. For Jefferson's position, see "Opinion on the Constitutionality of an Act to Establish a Bank," February 23, 1791. In a speech in Congress on February 2, 1791, Madison had opposed the charter of the Bank of the United States on the ground that such charters were unconstitutional because the Constitution "is not a general grant, out of which particular powers are excepted; it is a grant of particular powers only, leaving the general mass in other hands" (*Annals of Congress*, II, 1945).

the bill.[21] In the Militia bill [22] & in a variety of minor cases he has leaned to abridging the exercise of foederal authority, & leaving as much as possible to the States & he has lost no opportunity of *sounding the alarm* with great affected solemnity at encroachments meditated on the rights of the States, & of holding up the bugbear of a faction in the Government having designs unfriendly to Liberty.

This kind of conduct has appeared to me the more extraordinary on the part of Mr. Madison as I know for a certainty it was a primary article in his Creed that the real danger in our system was the subversion of the National authority by the preponderancy of the State Governments. All his measures have proceeded on an opposite supposition.

I recur again to the instance of Freneaus paper. In matters of this kind one cannot have direct proof of men's latent views; they must be inferred from circumstances. As the coadjutor of Mr. Jefferson in the establishment of this paper, I include Mr. Madison in the consequences imputable to it.

21. H is referring to "An Act concerning certain Fisheries of the United States, and for the regulation and government of the Fishermen employed therein" (1 *Stat.* 229-32 [February 16, 1792]). On February 6, 1792, during the debate in the House of Representatives on the question of bounties, Madison said: "I think, however, that the term 'bounty' is in every point of view improper as it is here applied. . . . For if, in the allowance, nothing more is proposed than a mere reimbursement of the sum advanced, it is only paying a debt; and when we pay a debt, we ought not to claim the merit of granting a bounty." After reiterating his views of the limited nature of the grant of specified powers in the Constitution and of the subversive nature of a broad interpretation of the "general welfare" clause, Madison indicated that he would vote for the bill if the wording was "so amended as to rest on the avowed principle of a commutation for the drawback" (*Annals of Congress*, III, 386-89).

22. H is presumably referring to "An Act to provide for calling forth the Militia to execute the laws of the Union, suppress insurrections and repel invasions" (1 *Stat.* 264-65 [May 2, 1792]). When this bill was in the committee of the whole, Madison had introduced a motion to modify the section giving the President authority to call forth the militia to execute the laws of the Union, suppress insurrections, and repel invasions. The newspaper account of this motion describes it as "A motion . . . by which the section was modified so as to restrict the exercise of this power, to the recess of Congress, and till ——— days after the next session shall commence" ([Philadelphia] *Gazette of the United States*, April 25, 1792). Section 2 of the act as passed reads in part as follows: "And if the militia of a state, where such combinations may happen, shall refuse, or be insufficient to suppress the same, it shall be lawful for the President, if the legislature of the United States be not in session, to call forth and employ such numbers of the militia . . . as may be necessary, and the use of militia . . . may be continued . . . until the expiration of thirty days after the commencement of the ensuing session" (1 *Stat.* 264).

In respect to our foreign politics the views of these Gentlemen are in my judgment equally unsound & dangerous. *They have a womanish attachment to France and a womanish resentment against Great Britain.* They would draw us into the closest embrace of the former & involve us in all the consequences of her politics, & they would risk the peace of the country in their endeavours to keep us at the greatest possible distance from the latter. This disposition goes to a length particularly in Mr. Jefferson of which, till lately, I had no adequate Idea. Various circumstances prove to me that if these Gentlemen were left to pursue their own course there would be in less than six months *an open War between the U States & Great Britain.*

I trust I have a due sense of the conduct of France towards this Country in the late Revolution, & that I shall always be among the foremost in making her every suitable return; but there is a wide difference between this & implicating ourselves in all her politics; between bearing good will to her, & hating and wranggling with all those whom she hates. The Neutral & the Pacific Policy appear to me to mark the true path to the U States.

Having now delineated to you what I conceive to be the true complexion of the politics of these Gentlemen, I will now attempt a solution of these strange appearances.

Mr. Jefferson, it is known, did not in the first instance cordially acquiesce in the new constitution for the U States; he had many doubts & reserves.[23] He left this Country before we had experienced the imbicillities of the former.[24]

In France he saw government only on the side of its abuses. He drank deeply of the French Philosophy, in Religion, in Science, in politics. He came from France in the moment of a fermentation which he had had a share in exciting, & in the passions and feelings of which he shared both from temperament and situation.

He came here probably with a too partial idea of his own powers, and with the expectation of a greater share in the direction of our councils than he has in reality enjoyed. I am not sure that he had

23. H is referring to the use made of Jefferson's views by the Antifederalists at the Virginia Ratifying Convention. See Boyd, *Papers of Thomas Jefferson,* XIII, 354–55.

24. Jefferson sailed from Boston for France on July 5, 1784, and returned to Virginia on November 23, 1789.

not peculiarly marked out for himself the department of the Finances.

He came electrified *plus* with attachment to France and with the project of knitting together the two Countries in the closest political bands.

Mr. Madison had always entertained an exalted opinion of the talents, knowledge and virtues of Mr. Jefferson. The sentiment was probably reciprocal. A close correspondence subsisted between them during the time of Mr. Jefferson's absence from this country. A close intimacy arose upon his return.

Whether any peculiar opinions of Mr. Jefferson concerning the public debt wrought a change in the sentiments of Mr. Madison (for it is certain that the former is more radically wrong than the latter) or whether Mr. Madison seduced by the expectation of popularity and possibly by the calculation of advantage to the state of Virginia was led to change his own opinion—certain it is, that a very material *change* took place, & that the two Gentlemen were united in the new ideas. Mr. Jefferson was indiscreetly open in his approbation of Mr. Madison's principles, upon his first coming to the seat of Government. I say indiscreetly, because a Gentleman in the administration in one department ought not to have taken sides against another, in another department.

The course of this business & a variety of circumstances which took place left Mr. Madison a very discontented & chagrined man and begot some degree of ill humour in Mr. Jefferson.

Attempts were made by these Gentlemen in different ways to produce a Commercial Warfare with Great Britain. In this too they were disappointed. And as they had the liveliest wishes on the subject their dissatisfaction has been proportionally great; and as I had not favoured the project, I was comprehended in their displeasure.

These causes and perhaps some others created, much sooner than I was aware of it, a systematic opposition to me on the part of those Gentlemen. My subversion, I am now satisfied, has been long an object with them.

Subsequent events have encreased the Spirit of opposition and the feelings of personal mortification on the part of these Gentlemen.

A mighty stand was made on the affair of the Bank. There was much *commitment* in that case. I prevailed.

On the Mint business I was opposed from the same Quarter, & with still less success.[25] In the affair of ways & means for the Western expedition [26]—on the supplementary arrangements concerning the debt except as to the additional assumption, my views have been equally prevalent in opposition to theirs.[27] This current of success on one side & defeat on the other have rendered the Opposition furious, & have produced a disposition to subvert their Competitors even at the expence of the Government.

Another circumstance has contributed to widening the breach. 'Tis evident beyond a question, from every movement, that Mr Jefferson aims with ardent desire at the Presidential Chair. This too is an important object of the party-politics. It is supposed, from the nature of my former personal & political connexions, that I may favour some other candidate more than Mr. Jefferson when the Question shall occur by the retreat of the present Gentleman. My influence therefore with the Community becomes a thing, on ambitious & personal grounds, to be resisted & destroyed.

You know how much it was a point to establish the Secretary of State as the Officer who was to administer the Government in defect of the President & Vice President.[28] Here I acknowledge, though I took far less part than was supposed, I run counter to Mr. Jefferson's wishes; but if I had had no other reason for it, I had already *experienced opposition* from him which rendered it a measure of *self defence*.

It is possible too (for men easily heat their imaginations when

25. See note 15.   26. See note 12.

27. For H's views on removing restrictions on the amount of state debts to be assumed, see "Report on the Public Debt and Loans," January 23, 1792.

28. No decision was reached on the question of Presidential succession in January, 1791, when the question was first raised. In February, 1792, in the debate in the House of Representatives on "An Act relative to the Election of a President and Vice President of the United States, and declaring the Officer who shall act as President in case of Vacancies in the offices both of President and Vice President," Egbert Benson's motion that the Chief Justice be the officer to fill the vacancy in the offices of President and Vice President was defeated. Giles's motion that the Secretary of State fill the vacancy was adopted after debate in the House, but the Senate refused to agree (*Annals of Congress,* III, 280–82, 302–03, 403–04, 417–18). In accordance with the proposals of the Senate, Section 9 of the act as approved on March 1, 1792, provided: "That in case of removal, death, resignation or inability both of the President and Vice President of the United States, the President of the Senate pro tempore, and in case there shall be no President of the Senate, then the Speaker of the House of Representatives, for the time being shall act as President of the United States until the disability be removed or a President shall be elected" (1 *Stat.* 240).

their passions are heated) that they have by degrees persuaded themselves of what they may have at first only sported to influence others—namely that there is some dreadful combination against State Government & republicanism; which according to them, are convertible terms. But there is so much absurdity in this supposition, that the admission of it tends to apologize for their hearts, at the expence of their heads.

Under the influence of all these circumstances, the attachment to the Government of the U States originally weak in Mr Jeffersons mind has given way to something very like dislike; in Mr. Madisons, it is so counteracted by personal feelings, as to be more an affair of the head than of the heart—more the result of a conviction of the necessity of Union than of cordiality to the thing itself. I hope it does not stand worse than this with him.

In such a state of mind, both these Gentlemen are prepared to hazard a great deal to effect a change. Most of the important measures of every Government are connected with the Treasury. To subvert the present head of it they deem it expedient to risk rendering the Government itself odious; perhaps foolishly thinking that they can easily recover the lost affections & confidence of the people, and not appreciating as they ought to do the natural resistance to Government which in every community results from the human passions, the degree to which this is strengthened by the *organised rivality* of State Governments, & the infinite danger that the National Government once rendered odious will be kept so by these powerful & indefatigable enemies.

They forget an old but a very just, though a coarse saying—That it is much easier to raise the Devil than to lay him.

Poor *Knox* has come in for a share of their persecution as a man who generally thinks with me & who has a portion of the Presidents good Will & confidence.

In giving you this picture of political parties, my design is I confess, to awaken your attention, if it has not yet been awakened to the conduct of the Gentlemen in question. If my opinion of them is founded, it is certainly of great moment to the public weal that they should be understood. I rely on the strength of your mind to appreciate men as they merit—when you have a clue to their real views.

A word on another point. I am told that serious apprehensions are disseminated in your state as to the existence of a Monarchical party meditating the destruction of State & Republican Government. If it is possible that so absurd an idea can gain ground it is necessary that it should be combatted. I assure you on my *private faith* and *honor* as a Man that there is not in my judgment a shadow of foundation of it. A very small number of men indeed may entertain theories less republican than Mr Jefferson & Mr. Madison; but I am persuaded there is not a Man among them who would not regard as both *criminal* & *visionary* any attempt to subvert the republican system of the Country. Most of these men rather *fear* that it may not justify itself by its fruits, than feel a predilection for a different form; and their fears are not diminished by the factions & fanatical politics which they find prevailing among a certain set of Gentlemen and threatening to disturb the tranquillity and order of the Government.

As to the destruction of State Governments, the *great* and *real* anxiety is to be able to preserve the National from the too potent and counteracting influence of those Governments. As to my own political Creed, I give it to you with the utmost sincerity. I am *affectionately* attached to the Republican theory. I desire *above all things* to see the *equality* of political rights exclusive of all *hereditary* distinction firmly established by a practical demonstration of its being consistent with the order and happiness of society.

As to State Governments, the prevailing byass of my judgment is that if they can be circumscribed within bounds consistent with the preservation of the National Government they will prove useful and salutary. If the States were all of the size of Connecticut, Maryland or New Jersey, I should decidedly regard the local Governments as both safe & useful. As the thing now is, however, I acknowledge the most serious apprehensions that the Government of the U States will not be able to maintain itself against their influence. I see that influence already penetrating into the National Councils & preverting their direction.

Hence a disposition on my part towards a liberal construction of the powers of the National Government and to erect every fence to guard it from depredations, which is, in my opinion, consistent with constitutional propriety.

As to any combination to prostrate the State Governments I disavow and deny it. From an apprehension lest the Judiciary should not work efficiently or harmoniously I have been desirous of seeing some rational scheme of connection adopted as an amendment to the constitution, otherwise I am for maintaining things as they are, though I doubt much the possibility of it, from a tendency in the nature of things towards the preponderancy of the State Governments.

I said, that I was *affectionately* attached to the Republican theory. This is the real language of my heart which I open to you in the sincerity of friendship; & I add that I have strong hopes of the success of that theory; but in candor I ought also to add that I am far from being without doubts. I consider its success as yet a problem.

It is yet to be determined by experience whether it be consistent with that *stability* and *order* in Government which are essential to public strength & private security and happiness. On the whole, the only enemy which Republicanism has to fear in this Country is in the Spirit of faction and anarchy. If this will not permit the ends of Government to be attained under it—if it engenders disorders in the community, all regular & orderly minds will wish for a change—and the demagogues who have produced the disorder will make it for their own aggrandizement. This is the old Story.

If I were disposed to promote Monarchy & overthrow State Governments, I would mount the hobby horse of popularity—I would cry out usurpation—danger to liberty &c. &c—I would endeavour to prostrate the National Government—raise a ferment—and then "ride in the Whirlwind and direct the Storm." That there are men acting with Jefferson & Madison who have this in view I verily believe. I could lay my finger on some of them. That Madison does *not* mean it I also verily believe, and I rather believe the same of Jefferson; but I read him upon the whole thus—"A man of profound ambition & violent passions."

You must be by this time tired of my epistle. Perhaps I have treated certain characters with too much severity. I have however not meant to do them injustice—and from the bottom of my soul believe I have drawn them truly and that it is of the utmost consequence to the public weal they should be viewed in their true colors. I yield to this impression. I will only add that I make no clandestine attacks on the gentlemen concerned. They are both apprized indirectly from myself of the opinion I entertain of their views. With the truest regard and esteem.

Receipt from William Pearce

[Philadelphia, May 26, 1792]

Received Philadelphia May 26. 1792 of Alexander Hamilton forty Dollars on account of the Society for establishing useful Manufactures.   Wm. Pearce

D, in the writing of H and signed by Pearce, Hamilton Papers, Library of Congress.

From William Short

[*Paris, May 26, 1792.* On June 28, 1792, Short wrote to Hamilton: "I had the satisfaction of announcing to you by a few lines written for that purpose only from Paris on the 26th of May, that a second loan at 4 p. cent had been contracted for." *Letter not found.*]

From Daniel Stevens

[*Charleston, South Carolina, May 26, 1792.* On June 16, 1792, Tench Coxe wrote to Stevens: "The Secretary of the Treasury has delivered to me your letters to him of the 22nd. and 26th of May." [1] *Letter of May 26 not found.*] [2]

1. LC, RG 58, Letters of Commissioner of Revenue, 1792–1793, National Archives.
2. See Stevens to H, May 22, 1792.

From Otho H. Williams

[*Baltimore, May 27, 1792.* On June 5, 1792, Hamilton wrote to Williams: "I have before me your letters of the 18th of March, 18th of April, 8th & 27th of May." *Letter of May 27 not found.*]

To ———

Treasury Department May 28th 1792

Sir,

Your letter of the 5th instant [1] has been received at the Treasury.

It will be impossible for me to give any opinion on the disatisfaction expressed by some of the Owners ⟨-⟩ing at your port respecting the former admeasurement ⟨of the⟩ir Vessels, until I am informed of the particular causes which have induced them to solicit a re-admeasurement.

I am with consideration   Sir,   your most humble Servt.

A Hamilton

LS, Bank of New York, New York City.
1. Letter not found.

Conversation with George Hammond [1]

[Philadelphia, May 28–29, 1792]

Accordingly within two or three days after the receipt of your Lordship's dispatch,[2] I waited upon Mr Hamilton. After some conversation upon other topics, I adverted to the sentiments expressed by the deputies of the six nations in their conferences with the President [3] (as mentioned in my dispatch No 21) relative to the neglect of them at the conclusion of the peace between Great Britain and the United States.[4] Mr Hamilton replied that he had not seen all the communications which had passed between the President and the Indians, but it was possible that the latter might have employed the kind of arguments to which I alluded. Upon this I said that this language and complaint of the Indian deputies had impressed me with an opinion that the present was a moment peculiarly favorable not only to the immediate restoration of peace, but to the future establishment of tranquillity in the northern part of this continent on a permanent basis. I added (as a sentiment of my own) that I thought a project might be devised which would conciliate all the clashing interests of the Indians, the United States, and the King's government of Canada, and bind them in one common system of harmony and reciprocal benefit. I then stretched out loosely the general outline of the proposition contained in your Lordship's dispatch, and enforced the numerous advantages that would arise from the adoption of it—the security that it would afford to the Indians by the removal of future grounds of complaint—the final arrangement of the subjects at present in discussion between our two countries—and the future prevention of any collision of interest between the subjects of the crown and the citizens of the United States, who would be thus separated from each other by the interposition of an intermediate territory, on which neither party would be allowed to form settlements.

Mr. Hamilton having heard me with great attention, did not attempt to enter into any discussion of the arguments I had alledged, but replied briefly and coldly, that he wished me to understand that any plan, which comprehended any thing like a cession of territory or right or the allowance of any other power to interfere in the disputes with the Indians, would be considered by this government as absolutely impracticable and inadmissible.[5]

D, PRO: F.O., Series 4, Vol. 15.

1. This conversation has been taken from Hammond to Lord Grenville, June 8, 1792, Dispatch No. 23.

2. The dispatch from Lord Grenville, the British Foreign Secretary, which was numbered "8" and dated March 17, 1792, was received by Hammond on May 26, 1792. In it Grenville renewed the offer of the British to mediate between the Americans and the Indians, an offer which Hammond had suggested to H in a conversation of December 15–16, 1791. Grenville also proposed that Hammond suggest to the Americans the desirability of creating a buffer state, occupied exclusively by the Indians, along the American-Canadian border. "The time and mode of bringing forward this particular Proposition," Grenville instructed the British Minister, "whether as part of your original Proposal, or in the course of any subsequent Discussions to which it may lead, must be left to your Discretion, guided by Circumstances on the Spot" (Mayo, *Instructions to British Ministers*, 25). In his letter to Grenville of June 8, 1792 (the same letter in which the above conversation with H was reported), Hammond discussed the reasons why the suggestion of the British Ministry for mediation and the creation of an Indian buffer state could not succeed. The United States Government, he said, was unalterably opposed to any such solution. Rather than formally propose Grenville's plan to the United States Government, Hammond reported that he had decided to discuss the plan with H unofficially. It was with this in mind that Hammond "waited upon Mr Hammond," and the above conversation ensued.

3. On March 13, 1792, a deputation of the Five Nations visited Philadelphia "for the purpose of attaching them to, and convincing them of, the justice and humanity of the United States; and also, to influence them to repair to the hostile tribes, in order to use their efforts to bring about peace. These

objects appeared to be effected, and they departed to carry them into execution. Besides abundant presents, fifteen hundred dollars, annually, were stipulated to these Indians by the President and Senate of the United States for the purpose of attempting to civilize them" (*ASP, Indian Affairs,* I, 229). See also Timothy Pickering to H, May 8, 1792.

4. Hammond in his Dispatch No. 21 to Grenville, dated June 8, 1792, stated: "The deputation of the Warriors of the Six Nations (whose arrival I announced in my dispatch No. 16) left this city about a month ago. I learn from good authority that, in some of their latest conferences with the President they regretted very feelingly the total inattention which had been manifested to their interests and preservation, in arranging the terms of the definitive treaty of peace between Great Britain and the United States. They said that so long as the Colonies remained under the dominion of Great Britain, the Indian Nations could always address themselves to the officers of that power for the explanation and redress of their grievances. But that since the establishment of the independence of the United States, they were now placed between two distinct and powerful Nations, neither of which seemed to take any decided interest in their protection or information: And that, thus situated, it was not surprising, that they should be exposed to the intrigues of artful individuals of both countries, who availed themselves of the passions or the ignorance of their Indian neighbors, to promote their own views of mischief or emolument. To these causes they principally attributed the present unfortunate hostilities between the Western Indians and the United States. They added that the continuance of the war was to them an object of serious concern, and that if the United States thought their services could be usefully employed for the purpose, they would readily exert their good offices with their Indian Brethren to effect the restoration of tranquility.

"I have been assured that these offers were accepted by this Government, and that, at the last conference, it was determined that some of the Chiefs should repair to the principal residences of the tribes now engaged in war, and communicate the terms upon which the United States would consent to a pacification. In consequence of this determination, four or five chiefs, selected for this object set off, about the beginning of last month, for Pittsburgh in order to prosecute their journey from that place, while the other members of the deputation proceeded on their return homeward.

"A short time after their departure, a Stockbridge Indian arrived here from Canada, who brought information that a general meeting of chiefs deputed from all the tribes of hostile Indians, was speedily to be held at French Creek for the purpose of consulting on their general interests, and of concerting the means of accommodating their disputes with the United States.

"Since that time information has been received from Major Hamtramck commanding at Post Vincennes on the river Wabash, dated the 30th of March last, and stating that he had concluded a pacific agreement with three of the principal divisions of the tribe of Wabash Indians, who have hitherto formed a very considerable branch of the Indian confederacy.

"The concurrence of these circumstances justifies in a great measure the public expectation that the disputes with all the Indian tribes may be amicably adjusted in the course of the ensuing summer. I learn from both Mr. Hamilton and Mr. Jefferson that the Government entertains the same opinion, which may perhaps be founded upon other corroborating facts that are not generally known." (MS Division, New York Public Library.)

5. On June 13, 1792, in Dispatch No. 25, Hammond wrote to Grenville: "The acceptance of the King's good offices in accommodating the disputes with the Indians is the sole ground on which such a negociation could be commenced, as would lead to the acquisition and establishment of the other

objects proposed. But my own personal conviction, the general (apparently well-founded) expectation of obtaining peace by other means, and the sentiments of Mr. Hamilton, all concur in influencing my belief, that a formal offer of the King's good offices, would, in the present moment, not only be instantly rejected, but would also excite considerable jealousy of the real views and wishes of his Majesty's government" (MS Division, New York Public Library).

From Tench Coxe

Treasury Department, Revenue Office, May 28, 1792. Encloses contract "for the digging and building of a well for the Use" of the Delaware lighthouse. Discusses "the causes of the extraordinary expence."

LC, RG 58, Letters of Commissioner of Revenue, 1792–1793, National Archives.

From Nathan Keais

Port Washingon [North Carolina] May 28, 1792. "I here inclose . . . Copys of Several bonds taken in consequence of the Contract . . . for staking the shoals and Channels within Ocracock Barr and Old topsail inlet. This I have done with all possible dispatch as the Stakes in and about Ocracock are principally down. . . ."

ALS, RG 26, Lighthouse Letters Received, Vol. "A," Pennsylvania and Southern States, National Archives.

To Henry Knox

Treasury department
28 May 1792

Sir

The Accountant for the departt. of War [1] having mentioned to me as on your part that it was requisite immediately to furnish to the officers on the recruiting service,[2] a further sum of money for that service and having suggested that some arrangement was necessary in relation to the transmitting of it to them—I have the honor to propose the following.

Let warrants issue by the Secy of war Countersign'd as the law requires [3] upon the Treasurer [4] in favor of the supervisor of the revenue within the State in which the recruiting officers are, specifying in it the names of the officers for whom the money is intended, and the Sum for each. Let these warrants be deposited wh. the Treasurer and let the Treasurer out of the monies which shall have been deposited in his hands for the Use of the war department remit in Bank post notes filled up in the name of the Supervisor the Amot of the warrant.

Let the *accountant* be Charged to inform the Supervisor of the officers to whom the money is to be paid the places where they are understood to be and the Sum to be paid to each, and let *him* also advise each officer of the amot which has been remitted for him and to whom. The requisite instructions from the Treasury to Secure the Cooperation of the Supervisors will be furnished. They will be directed 1st. on receipt of the money to send receipts for it by duplicates to the Treasurer 2d to advise the recruiting officers of its having come to hand & 3d to pay it to them, taking on themselves to forward it whenever it can be done with Safety.

The receipt of the Supervisor annexed to the Warrt. will be a Voucher to the Treasurer for the paymt, a Charge will be made in the Books of the Accountant to each Supervisor for the Sum remitted to him, from which he will exonerate himself by transmitting the receipts of the officers to whom he shall have paid the money who will then be Charged in the same Books wh. the amot paid to him respectively to be afterwards Accounted for.

At the foot you will find the names & places of abode of the Supervisors from Virginia to massachusetts inclusively. I understand [from] Mr Howell that the arrangement need not extend farther.

P.S.   In any Case in which you may deem it adviseable to send the money by a Special messenger a warrt. Can issue in favour of such messenger and a Charge in the Books of the Accountant raised against him to be discharged by the production of the officers receipts.

nath Gorham Esqe. Supervisor of the Revenue Boston. Massatts.

| John S Dexter | do | Providence R Island |
| John Chester | do | weathersfield Connecticut |

noah Smith	do	Bennington Vermont
Richd. Morris	do	New York New York
Aron Dunham	do	Trenton New Jersey
andrew Barrett	do	near Dover Delaware
Geo. Gale	do	Baltimore Maryland
*Edward Carrington	do	Richmond Virginia

* Joshua Wentworth Supervisor Portsmouth New Hampshire

Copy, RG 217, Miscellaneous Treasury Accounts, 1790–1894, Account No. 4459, National Archives.

1. Joseph Howell, Jr., was appointed accountant of the War Department on May 8, 1792, in accordance with "An Act making alterations in the Treasury and War Departments" (1 *Stat.* 279–81 [May 8, 1792]).

2. "An Act for making farther and more effectual Provision for the Protection of the Frontiers of the United States" allowed a bounty of eight dollars to every recruit enlisted under the act and two dollars to the recruiting officer for each recruit enlisted and mustered (1 *Stat.* 242 [March 5, 1792]).

3. Section 2 of "An Act making alterations in the Treasury and War Departments" reads as follows: "That the treasurer of the United States shall disburse all such monies as shall have been previously ordered for the use of the department of war by warrants from the treasury, which disbursements shall be made pursuant to warrants from the Secretary at War, countersigned by the accountant" (1 *Stat.* 280).

4. Samuel Meredith.

To Jeremiah Olney

Treasury Department May 28th 1792

Sir;

I am to acknowledge the receipt of your letter of the 10th Instant.

Whatever constructions may have been put upon the Act for regulating the coasting trade,[1] it is very certain that the law makes no provision for a second registry in the case as stated by you. It will be a natural conclusion therefore to suppose, that if any Ship or Vessel has been once registered agreeably to the forms prescribed by the Act, it supersedes the necessity of a second register unless some of the Casualties mentioned in the law have taken place.

I am with consideration   Sir   Your most humble Servt.

A Hamilton

Jeremiah Olney Esqr.
Collector Providence

LS, Rhode Island Historical Society, Providence; LC, RG 56, Letters to Collectors at Small Ports, "Set G," National Archives; LC, RG 56, Letters to the Collector at Providence, National Archives.

1. "An Act for Registering and Clearing Vessels, Regulating the Coasting Trade, and for other purposes" (1 *Stat.* 55–65 [September 1, 1789]).

From William Seton

[New York] 28th May 1792

Sir

I am honourd with your Letter of the 24th.[1] & have informed Messrs. Beach & Canfield,[2] that I will pay them the sum of 4350 Dollars upon their producing the receipt of Melancton Smith Esq.[3] for 5299 pair of Shoes—their receipt shall be worded as you direct.

I have now the honor to enclose the necessary Certificates for transferring the Stock I purchased as Agent for the United States [4] from the Books of the Commissioner of Loans to those of the Treasury vizt

Certificate N. 104. for 86790.^{65}⁄₁₀₀—6 ℔ Cents

Certificate N. 100 for 42409 ^{22}⁄₁₀₀—3 ℔ Cents

Certificate N. 297 for 14282.^{31}⁄₁₀₀—3 ℔ Cents

Certificate N. 105. for 12361 ^{30}⁄₁₀₀—Deferred Debt

Certificate N. 295. for 36108 ^{5}⁄₁₀₀—Deferred Debt

Making in the whole   86790.65.   —6 ℔ Cents

                        56691.53.   —3 ℔ Cents

                        48469.35   —Deferred

Agreeably to the returns I had the honor to make to you of the purchase by your orders on the 5th May instant.[5]

I am with the greatest respect   Sir   Your Obd Hble Serv

LC, Bank of New York, New York City.
1. Letter not found.
2. Nathaniel Beach and Abiel Canfield of Newark, New Jersey, furnished shoes for the Army.
3. Melancton Smith, who had been an Antifederalist member of the New York Assembly in the session from January to April, 1792, had a contract with the Government for supplying the troops at West Point.
4. See H to Seton, March 25, 26, 30, April 4, 12, 1792.
5. For Seton's account, dated May 5, 1792, see H to Seton, May 10, 1792, note 1.

From William Seton

New York 28th May 1792

My Dear sir

Your kind letter of the 23d,[1] I did not receive till after the last post for the week was gone out; I have seen Mr. Cutting [2] and informed him I was ready to pay the judgement against the Baron.[3] He said he would make out the Account & call upon me. The amount will be upwards of £500. As our Bank Stock is now only at 28 ⅌ Cent premium I think it will be better to have the Note of 1200 Dollars you enclosed to me, discounted, as before its period of payment I think the Stock will be higher. Mr. Troup [4] has endorsed it. I cannot however help expressing a regret, that the extreme delicacy of your feelings should induce you to part with a Stock so extremely more valuable than its present price in the Market.[5] In virtue of your Power of Attorney, I have signed the Books for all your Dividends —Vizt

Dividend on 1 Novr. 1790 . . . . Dolls . . .	26.25
Surplus Dividend 30 April 1791	186.
Dividend on 1 May 1791	26.25
Dividend on 1 Novr. 1791	52.50
Dividend on 1 May 1792	30.
Doll.	321.—

which Sum is carried to the credit of your Account, which was overdrawn before Dolls. 245 $^{72}/_{100}$—so that the ballance now due to you in Bank is Dolls. 75.$^{28}/_{100}$.

I trust you cannot doubt of the pleasure it will ever give me to obey your Commands—& how much you gratify my feelings by employing me in any way that I can testify the sincere respect & esteem with which I am Dear sir

Your Obliged Obed Hble Ser Wm Seton

ALS, Hamilton Papers, Library of Congress.
1. Letter not found.
2. Leonard M. Cutting was a New York City attorney.
3. In the Hamilton Papers, Library of Congress, is a bond signed by Baron von Steuben, dated January 18, 1790, in the amount of £700 18s. 11 1/4d.,

New York currency, payable with interest to Michel-Guillaume Jean de Crèvecœur (who sometimes referred to himself as J. Hector St. John), the well-
known author of *Letters from an American Farmer*, who had returned to
France in 1790. With this bond is a statement of the judgment of debt in the
Supreme Court of New York in the case of *Crèvecœur* v *von Steuben*. This
statement is in the writing of Cutting, who was attorney for the plaintiff, and
it reads as follows:
"On the *20th* October 1790 Settled the ballance due
which inclusive of Costs amounted to   £454.16.8 3/4
Wherein 7 pr Ct Interest is payable to this day   51.16.3 1/4
                                                Amount due   £506.13
5th June 1792 Recd: of Alexander Hamilton by the hands of William Seton
the sum of five hundred & Six pounds thirteen shillings the amount of the
above mentioned demand which Mr Hamilton had assumed to pay on behalf
of the abovementioned Defendt:"
    4. Robert Troup.
    5. At the time of the incorporation of the Bank of New York in 1791 H
owned one and one-half shares of stock in the bank. The stock's par value
was five hundred dollars.

Conversation with George Hammond [1]

[Philadelphia, May 29–June 2, 1792]

I have the honor of transmitting to your Lordship a representation
which I have received from Mr. Jefferson in answer to the statement
that I delivered to that Gentleman on the 5th of March last.[2]

The great quantity of irrelevant matter contained in this paper,
the positive denial of many facts, which I had advanced upon the
authority of the British agents and of other respectable persons in
this country, the unjustifiable insinuations thrown out with respect
to the mode of prosecuting the war, and to the conduct of his
Majesty's ministers subsequent to the peace, and the general acri-
monious stile and manner of this letter, all contributed to excite in
me considerable surprize.

Confidential   I therefore waited upon Mr Hamilton, and communicated to him
very freely my opinion of this extraordinary performance. This
Gentlemen treated me (as he has done upon every occasion) with
the strictest confidence and candour. After lamenting the intemperate violence of his colleague Mr Hamilton assured me that this
letter was very far from meeting his approbation, or from containing a faithful exposition of the sentiments of this government. He
added that at the time of our conversation the President had not had
an opportunity of perusing this representation: For having returned

from Virginia in the morning only on which it had been delivered to me,[3] he had relied upon Mr Jefferson's assurance, that it was conformable to the opinions of the other members of the executive government.[4]

D, PRO: F.O., Series 4, Vol. 15.

1. This conversation has been taken from Hammond to Lord Grenville, June 8, 1792, Dispatch No. 22.

2. Shortly after Hammond had presented his credentials as British Minister to the United States, Thomas Jefferson proposed that he and Hammond begin negotiations with an enumeration by each man of the treaty violations by the other country (see "Conversation with George Hammond," January 1–8, 1792, note 3). On March 5, 1792, Hammond submitted to the Secretary of State a detailed indictment of American refusal to fulfill the treaty obligations. Jefferson replied on May 29, 1792, with an extensively documented rebuttal. The exchange of letters and documents between Hammond and Jefferson is printed in *ASP, Foreign Relations*, I, 193–237.

3. Hammond was mistaken as to the time of Washington's return. The President returned to Philadelphia from Mount Vernon on May 28, 1792 (Freeman, *Washington*, VI, 358).

4. The letter of May 29, 1792, to Hammond was submitted by Jefferson not only to Washington for comment but also to James Madison, Edmund Randolph, and H. See Jefferson to Washington, May 16, 1792, and Jefferson to Madison, June 1, 1792 (Ford, *Writings of Jefferson*, V, 514–15; VI, 69). For H's comments to Jefferson on this letter, see H to Jefferson, May 20–27, 1792.

From Thomas Willing

[*Philadelphia, May 29, 1792.* On June 11, 1792, Hamilton acknowledged the receipt of Willing's "letter of the 29th of last month." *Letter not found.*]

From Edward Blake [1]

[*Charleston, South Carolina, May 30, 1792.* On June 18, 1792, Tench Coxe wrote to Blake: "Your accounts for the lighthouse . . . were delivered to me by the Secretary of the Treasury with your letter of the 30th May." [2] *Letter not found.*]

1. Blake was superintendent of the lighthouse at Charleston.

2. LC, RG 58, Letters of Commissioner of Revenue, 1792–1793, National Archives.

From William Duer [1]

[New York, May 30, 1792. The calendar summary of this letter reads as follows: "Much embarrassed by his engagement with Ohio Company." [2] Letter not found.]

1. Letter listed in "Calendar Summary of Philip Church and Alexander Hamilton Papers," Personal Miscellaneous, Box 6, Schuyler, MS Division, New York Public Library.
2. Duer's engagements with the Ohio Company as trustee of the Scioto Company were settled June 30, 1792 (DS, signed by Benjamin Tallmadge, American Antiquarian Society, Worcester, Massachusetts; Davis, Essays, I, 327; Archer Butler Hulbert, The Records of the Original Proceedings of the Ohio Company [Marietta, 1917] II, 23–24, 228–29). See also Benjamin Walker to H, December 28, 1790; William Playfair to H, March 30, 1791.

To William Ellery

[Philadelphia, May 30, 1792. On June 11, 1792, Ellery wrote to Hamilton: "I have recd. . . . your Letter of the 30th of the last month." Letter not found.]

From Thomas Jefferson

[Philadelphia] May 30, 1792. "Th: Jefferson presents his respectful compliments to the Secretary of the Treasury, and sends him the above extract [1] at the request of mr Short who, being unwell, wrote only a few lines to Th: J."

AL, letterpress copy, Thomas Jefferson Papers, Library of Congress; LC, RG 59, Diplomatic and Consular Instructions of the Department of State, 1791–1801, National Archives.
1. For the extract from William Short's letter to Jefferson of February 29, 1792, see Short to H, March 24, 1792, note 21.

From Thomas Marshall [1]

N York May 30th. 1792

Sir

'Tis with extreem regret I intrude upon your time, but will be as concise as possible, in short Sir, I respectfully solicit your Countenance to Benjm. Walker Esqr.[2] for the Loan, (upon my Bond) for 300 Dollars, for which I am perfectly willing to give legal Interest. The following are my reasons for this Solicitation—to keep my accounts even for at present I am 12 £ Dr. on my Books, and positively arising from no Extravagence, but from the Inadequacy of my Income to the expences attached to my Situation. My ⟨–⟩ and Turners will have within two Dollars a week as much as myself, which, all things Considered will render their places more beneficial than mine. For instance, a Turner of tolerable Capacity was engaged by me about two months back, being (from Sickness) much reduced, he solicited me to lend him 12 Dollars, and being afterwards unwel, the Debt amounted to 18. Dol. 7 Shillings, and on Monday Morning last the Man (at the suit of a Landlord at whose House he had boarded & Lodged) was sent to Jail. I shall in all probability loose the money for of Course the Society cannot notice it, but yet Sir, without doing what I never knew a Manufactoror do, I Cannot avoid the Danger to my other people. I have at least 20 Dollars advanced to them for the purpose of purchasing Tools, (for I agree with them to find their ⟨–⟩) and this I stop at so much per Week. I mean to remove into the Country next week, if possible previous to which I must supply myself several Necessaries my present Circumstance will not permit of. I will not longer intrude but hope that the above cited reasons will be sufficient to induce you to Comply from a Conviction of the propriety of the measure. I board at Mr. Robinson,[3] Builder, Verletenburgh Hill, and in Expectation of the favour of your Answer I remain respectfully Sir   Your Most Obedient   Humble Servent   Thomas Marshall

The Honble.
Alexr. Hamilton Esqr.

ALS, The Passaic County Historical Society, Lambert Castle, Paterson, New Jersey.

1. Marshall had been appointed by H to superintend the cotton mill of the Society for Establishing Useful Manufactures. See H to the Directors of the Society for Establishing Useful Manufactures, December 7, 1791.

2. Walker, a New York stockbroker, was a director of the Society for Establishing Useful Manufactures.

3. James Robinson was a New York City contractor.

To William Seton

[*Philadelphia, May 30, 1792.* On June 3, 1792, Seton wrote to Hamilton: "I have the honor to acknowledge the receipt of your letters of the 24th & 30th. May." *Letter of May 30 not found.*]

To Robert Ballard

Treasury Department
May 31. 1792.

Sir

In answer to your letter of the 20th. instant [1] I have to inform you that no provision for compensation to the Inspectors of the Revenue for Ports, has yet been made; But in consequence of greater latitude given to the President by the Act, concerning the duties on Spirits distilled within the United States,[2] the subject will be shortly under his consideration when your case will be duly attended to.

I am, Sir,   Your Obedt. Servant   Alex Hamilton

Robert Ballard Esqr.
Inspector of the Revenue for the
Port of Baltimore.

LS, Columbia University Libraries.
    1. Letter not found.
    2. Section 16 of "An Act concerning the Duties on Spirits distilled within the United States" provided: "That the President of the United States be authorized to make such allowances for their respective services to the supervisors, inspectors and other officers of inspection, as he shall deem reasonable and proper, so as the said allowances, together with the incidental expenses of collecting the duties on spirits distilled within the United States, shall not exceed seven and an half per centum of the total product of the duties on distilled spirits, for the period to which the said allowances shall relate, computing from the time of the act, intituled 'An act repealing after the last day of June next, the duties heretofore laid upon distilled spirits imported from abroad, and laying others in their stead, and also upon spirits distilled within the United States, and for appropriating the same,' took effect: *And provided also,* That such allowance shall not exceed the annual amount of seventy thousand dollars, until the same shall be further ascertained by law" (1 *Stat.* 270–71 [May 8, 1792]).

From Tench Coxe

Treasury Department, Revenue Office, May 31, 1792. "Prior to the recommencement of the building of the Light House on Bald Head,[1] I found it necessary to make an examination of that part of the work which has been executed under the direction of the Commissioners appointed by the Legislature of North Carolina:[2] and I do myself the Honor to state to you some ideas that have occured, together with the plan of proceeding, which appears most eligible in order, that you may be enabled to know the pleasure of the President thereon. First. The firmness of the ground on which the building stands, does not appear to be sufficiently ascertained. . . . Secondly. The foundation not being in any part of Stone, but entirely of brick and from its situation liable to be affected by salt moisture, there is some hazard of its being rendered too infirm in time by the crumbling of the Bricks to endure so great a Weight as the building above. . . . Third. By comparison with the light houses of Chessapeak, Delaware and New York the Walls of that at Bald head appear to be weak. . . . Fourth. The lanthorn is proposed to be Wood and without sufficient linings of Sheet Metal to guard against fire. On Account of these four objections I beg leave to suggest the following precautions additions to and variations from the original plan. . . . First. That an examination of the ground on which the building has been Commenced should be made by digging as near as will be safe a pit or hole down to the level of the foundation and below that level on one side, and another on the opposite side that if there be any want of firmness in the ground it may be discovered. . . . Second. It may be useful to erect some broad and firm butments of stone (if attainable) or of Brick to be laid with Stone lime within and without the building of the depth of the foundation and laid to the height of the level of the Earth. . . . Third. It will diminish the Comparative weakness of the Walls, if the masonry should be carried up to the height of Ninety feet instead of one hundred. . . . Fourth. The lanthorn should be secured from fire by a bed of mortar under the floor and by sheet copper, as the expence of an iron frame will not be within the Compass of the grant. . . ."

LC, RG 58, Letters of Commissioner of Revenue, 1792–1793, National Archives.

1. On April 2, 1792, "An Act for finishing the Lighthouse on Baldhead at the mouth of Cape Fear River in the State of North Carolina" became law (1 *Stat.* 246).

2. In 1783 commissioners were appointed in North Carolina under "An Act for facilitating the navigation, and regulating the pilotage of the several ports of this State." Additional appointments were made in 1784 under "An Act for regulating the Pilotage and facilitating the Navigation of Cape Fear River" and in 1789 by "An Act to Repeal Part of an Act, Entitled 'An Act to Explain an Act Directing the Duty of Naval Officers and all Masters of Vessels Coming into the Ports or Inlets of this State,' and to Amend the Navigation Law for Cape Fear River" (Clark, *State Records of North Carolina*, XXIV, 506, 591–92; XXV, 7).

From Tobias Lear

United States May 31st 1792.

By the President's command T. Lear has the honor to transmit to the Secretary of the Treasury the enclosed copy of a Letter from the Secretary of State to the President; [1] and to request that the Secretary of the Treasury will let the President know when the sum mention'd in the enclosed Letter will be conveniently ready for his order.

Tobias Lear
S.P.U.S.

LC, George Washington Papers, Library of Congress.

1. On May 30, 1792, Thomas Jefferson wrote to the President that Congress had appropriated fifty thousand dollars "to defray any expence which may be incurred in relation to the intercourse between the United States and foreign nations." He asked that the money be made available (LC, Thomas Jefferson Papers, Library of Congress).

From Jeremiah Olney

Providence, May 31, 1792. "Permit me to introduce to your Friendly Notice and Acquaintance the Bearrer Colo. Ephrm. Bowen [1] a Gentleman of Fair character and veracity, Connected in a Ginn & Rum distillery with Messrs Clark & Nightingale [2] of this Town, Merchants, He is bound to Baltimore and proposes on his arrival at Philadelphia to have an Interview with you on the Subject of a Seizure lately made at the former Place. . . ." [3]

ADfS, Rhode Island Historical Society, Providence.

1. During the American Revolution Ephraim Bowen had served as deputy quartermaster general.

2. The firm of John Clark and Joseph Nightingale.
3. The sloop *Ceres* and its cargo had been seized at Baltimore for fraud. The cargo of rum made in Rhode Island had been placed in West Indian casks "to do away [with] the prejudice that has heretofore opperated to the disadvantage of home distilled spirits, and . . . in order to promote the sale of it" (*Calendar of the General Otho Holland Williams Papers*, 262, 265).

To George Washington [1]

[*Philadelphia, May 31, 1792.*] ". . . the place of Keeper of the Light house on Thatcher's Island in the State of Massachusetts has become vacant by the death of Mr. Hustin.[2] The following persons are respectably recommended—Joseph Sayword—Henry White—Samuel Hustin, son of the deceas'd Keeper, and Rowe. . . ." [3]

LC, George Washington Papers, Library of Congress.
  1. For background to this letter, see Benjamin Lincoln to H, March 14, 1792.
  2. Samuel Houston.
  3. Sayward, White, and John Rowe were residents of Gloucester, Massachusetts.

From Wilhem and Jan Willink, Nicholaas and Jacob Van Staphorst, and Nicholas Hubbard

[*Amsterdam, May 31, 1792.* On August 3, 1792, Hamilton sent to George Washington "the copy of a letter of 31st May, just received from our Commissioners at Amsterdam." *Letter not found.*]

The Vindication No. I [1]

[Philadelphia, May–August, 1792] [2]

It was to have been foreseen, that though the virtuous part of those who were opposed to the present Constitution of the UStates while

ADf, Hamilton Papers, Library of Congress.
  1. Both J. C. Hamilton (*JCHW*, VI, 636) and Lodge (*HCLW*, III, 3) entitle this document "Vindication of the Funding System," but the title on the MS is "The Vindication No. I." Presumably H planned to publish this and the other three numbers in this series, but if he did so, the newspapers in which they appeared have not been found.
  2. This and the other three documents in this series were not dated by H. J. C. Hamilton printed them with no date and Lodge dated them "1791(?)." The summer of 1792, however, seems a more likely time for their composition, for parts of them are similar in content to both H to Edward Carrington, May 26, 1792, and H to George Washington, August 18, 1792.

in deliberation before the People would yield to the evidence which experience should afford of its usefulness and safety, there were of a certain character opponents, who as happens in all great political questions would always remain incurably hostile to it. That in the course of its administration, its greatest merits would be in the eyes of such men its greatest blemishes, its most brilliant successes to them occasions of bitter chagrin and envious detraction, its slightest mismanagements subjects of malignant exaggeration, its most trivial misfortunes the welcome topics of virulent accusation and insidious misrepresentation. With some men, the hardest thing to forgive is the demonstration of their errors—the manifestation that they are not infallible. Mortified vanity is one of the most corroding emotions of the human mind; one of the most inextinguishable sources of animosity and hatred.

It was equally to have been foreseen that personal disappointments, would be likely to alienate from the Govt some individuals who had at first advocated its adoption, perhaps from motives not the most patriotic or commendable; that personal rivalships and competitions would throw others into an opposition to its measures without much regard to their intrinsic merits or demerits, and that a third class would embrace the path of opposition as the supposed road to popularity & preferment, raising upon every colorable pretext the cry of "Danger to Liberty" and endeavouring to disseminate among the people false terrors & ill grounded alarms. Phœnomena like these have deformed the political horison and testified the depravity of mankind in all countries and at all times.

It was likewise to have been expected that among the well meaning friends of the Government, there would be a part competent to the proper management of the affairs of the Union, who sensible from experience of the insufficiency of the former system gave their assent to the substitute offered to their choice rather from general impressions of the necessity of a change than from an accurate view of the necessary compass of the authorities which ought to constitute it. When they came to witness the exercise of those authorities upon a scale more comprehensive than they had contemplated and to hear the incendiary comments of those who will ever be on the watch for pretexts to brand the proceedings of the government with imputations of usurpation and tyranny and the factious or indiscreet clamours of those who in and out of the legislature with too much levity torture the Constitution into objections to measures which they deem inexpedient, it was to have been expected, I say, that some such men might be carried away by transient anxieties and apprehensions and might for a moment add weight to an opposition which could not fail to grow out of other causes and the real objects of which they would abhor.

There is a yet another class of men, who in all the stages of our republican system, either from desperate circumstances, or irregular ambition, or a mixture of both, will labour incessantly to keep the government in a troubled and unsettled state, to sow disquietudes in the minds of the people and to promote confusion and change. Every republic at all times has it Catalines and its Cæsars.

Men of this stamp, while in their hearts they scoff at the principles of Liberty, while in their real characters they are arbitrary persecuting intolerant and despotic, are in all their harangues and professions the most zealous, nay if they are to be believed, the only friends to Liberty. Mercenary and corrupt themselves, they are continually making a parade of their purity and disinterestedness and heaping upon others charges of peculation and corruption. Extravagant and dissipated in their own affairs, they are always prating about public œconomy and railing at the Government, for its pretended profusion. Conscious that as long as the confidence of the people shall be maintained in their tried and faithful servants, in men of real integrity and patriotism, their ambitious projects can never succeed, they leave no artifice unessayed, they spare no pains to destroy that confidence and blacken the characters that stand in their way. Convinced that as long as order and system in the public affairs can be maintained their schemes can never be realised, they are constantly representing the means of that order and system as chains forged for the people. Themselves the only plotters and conspirators they are forever spreading tales of plots and conspiracies—Always talking of the republican cause, and meaning nothing but the cause of themselves and their party, virtue & Liberty constantly on their lips, framed usurpation and tyranny in their hearts.

There is yet another class of opponents to the Government & its administration, who are of too much consequence not to be mentioned, a sect of political Doctors—a kind of *Popes* in Government

—standards of political orthodoxy who brand with heresy all opinions but their own—men of sublimated imaginations and weak judgments pretenders to profound knowlege, yet ignorant of the most useful of all sciences, the science of human nature—men who dignify themselves with the appellation of Philosophers, yet are destitute of the first elements of true philosophy—Lovers of paradoxes, men who maintain expressly that Religion is not necessary to Society, and very nearly that Government itself is a nuisance, that Priests and Clergymen of all descriptions are worse than useless.

Such men the ridicule of any cause which they espouse and the best Witnesses to the goodness of that which they oppose have no small share in the clamours which are raised and in the dissatisfactions which are excited.

While the real object of those clamours, with the persons most active in propaging them, is opposition to the Government, the pretence is opposition to the administration of it. While they are straining every nerve to render it odious, they are profuse in their professions of attachment of it. To oppose avowedly the *work of the people* would be too barefaced. It would not accord with that system of treacherous flattery which is the usual engine of these pretended "Friends" but real "Betrayers" of the People. Circumstances require that the mode of attack should be changed. The Government is to be good if not excellent but its administration is to be execrable, detestable, a mere sink of corruption, a deep laid plan to overturn the republican system of the Country.

Suspicious of the most flagitious prostitution and corruption in office, of improper connections with brokers and speculations to fleece the community, of the horrid depravity of promoting wars and the shedding of human blood for the sake of sharing collusively in the emoluments of lucrative contracts, suspicions like these are if possible to be thrown upon men, the whole tenor of whose lives gives the lie to them, who before they came into office were never either *land*-jobbers or *stoc*[k] jobbers or jobbers of any other kind, who can appeal to their fellow citizens of every party and description to attest that their reputations for probity are unsullied; that their conduct, in all pecuniary concerns, has been nicely correct and even exemplarily disinterested, who it is notorious have sacrificed and are sacrificing the interests of their families to their public zeal, who whenever the necessity of resisting the machinations of the enemies of the public quiet will permit them to retire, will return poorer than they came into office, and will have to resume under numerous disadvantages, the pursuits which they before followed under every advantage. Shame where is thy blush, if detraction so malignant as this can affront the public ear. Integrity where is thy shield, where thy reward, if the poisonous breath of an unprincipled cabal can pollute that good name, which thou incessantly toiled to deserve!

People of America can ye be deceived by Arts like these? Will ye suffer yourselves to be cheated out of your confidence in men who deserve it most? Will ye be the dupes of hypocritical pretenders?

Think for yourselves. Look around you, consult your own experience. If any of you have doubts, listen calmly and dispassionately to the arguments and facts which in the course of the following numbers shall be opposed to the suggestions which would persuade you that the administration of your government has been in the aggregate weak or wicked or both!

The Vindication No. II [1]

First Version

[Philadelphia, May–August, 1792]

Among the measures in the course of the administration of the Government which have been most loudly inveighed against is the Funding System contained in the Act making provision for the Debts of the United States.[2] Against this measure, numerous objections have been urged, and, as is usual in similar cases, not in perfect con-

---

ADf, Hamilton Papers, Library of Congress.

1. In the margin of this MS, H wrote:

"Some preliminary observations however may not be improper.

"It is always to be remembered that the present Debt of the United States was contracted during the late war. It has neither been created nor added to by the present Government. Its administration is not chargeable with having produced it by ambitious schemes of conquest or glory. There is therefore no responsibility for its existence, no room for imputing blame on that account, unless indeed an abolition of the debt actual or virtual can be supposed to have been the duty of the Government.

"It is to be feared."

2. 1 Stat. 138–44 (August 4, 1790).

cordance with each other. These objections shall be stated and examined and it is confided that they will be shewn to be essentially destitute of foundation.

The first of them goes to the general principle of funding a debt, by which is to be understood the designating of certain definite funds and pledging them by a permanent law for paying the interest of the Debt until the principal shall be discharged.

This is represented as dangerous to Liberty by creating a monied interest too powerful for the other classes of the community and always devoted to the views of the Governing party and by multiplying taxes and tax gatherers the former depressing and humbling the people and fitting them for the yoke, the latter increasing the number of persons whose interest it is to promote the intentions good or bad of the existing Administration, promoting the accumulation of overgrown fortunes in destruction of republican equality as hurtful to the interests of the community, by inducing nations to enter too easily into War from the facility of carrying them on by establishing an undue preponderancy of the monied over the other classes of the community by substituting a spirit of speculation and gambling to the pursuits of useful industry encouraging idleness dissipation and luxury; and nourishing the pride insolence and power of a wealthy *few*.

Second Version [3]

[Philadelphia, May–August, 1792]

Of all the measures of the Government, that which has been most bitterly inveighed against is the Funding System contained in the Act making provision for the Debt of the United States.[4] As well for this reason, as on account of its superior importance, the objections which have been made to it are intitled to an examination in the first place.

It is a curious phœnomenon in political history (not easy to be parallelled) that a measure which has elevated the credit of the country from a state of absolute prostration to a state of exalted preeminence should bring upon the authors of it reprobation and cen-

3. ADf, Hamilton Papers, Library of Congress.
4. 1 *Stat.* 138–44 (August 4, 1790).

sure.[5] It is certainly what in the ordinary course of human affairs they could not have anticipated—they are even not chargeable with arrogance if they indulged from it the hope of credit & applause— and if the clamours which have been raised have truly proceeded as the clamourers assure us from patriotic motives, it must be confessed that they have the additional merit of Novelty and singularity. There must be something original in the passions as well as in the ideas of the sect to which they are attributable. It will be hardly possible not to believe that some mysterious work of political regeneration has begun to make its way in the world and that all those who have not been the subjects of it are in a state of pitiable darkness and error.

The two first points which in considering the funding system present themselves to attention are the *existence* and the *composition* of the Debt funded.

A person, who unacquainted with the fact should learn the history of our debt from the declamations with which certain news papers are perpetually charged would be led to suppose that it is the mere creature of the *present* government, for the purpose of burthening the people with taxes and producing an artificial and corrupt influence over them. He would at least take it for granted that it had been contracted in the pursuit of some wanton or vain project of ambition or glory. He would scarcely be able to conceive that every part of it was the relict of a War which had given independence and preserved liberty to the Country; that the present Government found it as it is in point of magnitude (except as to the diminutions made by itself) and has done nothing more than to bring under a regular regimen and provision what was before a scattered and heterogeneous mass.

And yet this is the simple and exact state of the business. The whole of the Debt embraced by the provisions of the funding system consisted of the unextinguished principal and arrears of interest of the debt which had been contracted by the UStates in the course of the late War with Great Britain and which remains uncancelled and the principal and arrears of interest of the separate debts of the respective States contracted during the same period; *which remained outstanding and unsatisfied; relating to sources and supplies for car-*

5. In the margin opposite this sentence H wrote the words "obloquy & reprobation."

rying on the War. Nothing more was done by that system, than to incorporate these two species of debt into one mass, and to make for the whole one general comprehensive provision.

There is therefore no Arithmetic no logic by which it can be shewn that the Funding system has augmented the aggregate of the debt of the Country. The sum total is manifestly the same; though the parts which were before divided are not united.

There is consequently no color for an assertion, that the System in question either created any *new* debt or made any *addition* to the *old*. And it follows that the collective burthen upon the people of the UStates must have been as great *without* as *with* the union of the different portions and descriptions of the Debt. The only difference can be that without it that burthen would have been otherwise distributed and would have fallen with unequal weight instead of being equally borne as it now is.

These conclusions which have been drawn respecting the new increase of the Debt proceed upon the presumption that every part of the public debt as well that of the States individually as that of the UStates was to have been honestly paid. If there is any fallacy in this supposition the inferences may be erroneous; but the error would imply the disgrace of the United States or of parts of them; a disgrace from which every man of true honor and genuine patriotism will be happy to see them rescued.

When we hear the epithets "vile matter" "corrupt mass" bestowed upon the public Debt and the owners of it indiscriminately maligned as the harpies and vultures of the community, there is ground to suspect that those who hold the language though they may not dare to avow it contemplate a more summary process for getting rid of debts than that of paying them. Indeed Charity itself cannot avoid concluding from the language and conduct of some men (and some of them of no inconsiderable importance) that in their vocabularies *creditor* and *enemy* are synonimous terms and that they have a laudable antipathy against every man to whom they owe money either as individuals or as members of the Society.

It has been said, that the sum of the Debt, to be ultimately provided for, has been artificially increased by the plan for the settlement of Accounts between the United & Individual States. This point will be most properly the subject of a distinct examination; as the Act for the settlement of accounts [6] is a distinct one from that which establishes the funding system. It will appear upon examination that there is no foundation for the assertion and moreover that the plan which has been adopted by the present Government for the settlement of Accounts is essentially a recapitulation of that which was adopted under the Confederation; [7] and which established principles which were not only equitable in themselves but could not have been reversed without an infraction of the public faith.

6. "An Act to provide more effectually for the settlement of the Accounts between the United States and the individual States" (1 *Stat.* 178–79 [August 5, 1790]).
7. For a discussion of the development of the policy for the settlement of state accounts under the Confederation, see E. James Ferguson, *The Power of the Purse* (Chapel Hill, 1961), 203–19.

The Vindication No. III

[Philadelphia, May–August, 1792]

My last number contained a concise and simple statement of facts tending to shew that the public Debt was neither created nor increased by the Funding system, and consequently that it is not responsible either for the existence or the magnitude of the Debt.

It will be proper next to examine the allegations which have been made of a contrary tendency.

In the first place it is asserted that the debt is greater than it ought to be, because from the state of depreciation in which the government found it a much less provision for it than that which was made might have sufficed. A saving of nearly one half it is said might have been made by providing for it in the hands of Alienees at least, at 8 or 10/ in the pound; who having come by it at a much less rate would have been well compensated by such a provision.

To a man who entertains correct notions of public faith, and who feels as he ought to feel for the reputation & dignity of the country, it is mortifying to reflect that there are partisans enough of such a doctrine to render it worth the while to combat it. It is still more mortifying to know that in that class are comprehended some men who are in other respects soberminded and upright, friends to order, and strenuous advocates for the rights of property.

ADf, Hamilton Papers, Library of Congress.

In reasoning upon all subjects it is necessary to take as a point of departure some principle in which reasonable and sound minds will agree. Without this, there can be no argument, no conclusion, in moral or political any more than in physical or mathematical disquisitions.

The principle which shall be assumed here is this—that the established *rules of morality and justice are applicable to nations as well as to Individuals;* that the *former* as well as the *latter* are bound *to keep their promises,* to *fulfil their engagements,* to *respect the rights of property* which others have acquired under contracts with them.

Without this, there is an end of all distinct ideas of right or wrong justice or injustice in relation to Society or Government. There can be no such thing as rights—no such thing as property or liberty. All the boasted advantages of a constitution of Government vanish in air. Every thing must float on the variable and vague opinions of the Governing party of whomsoever composed.

To this it may be answered, that the doctrine as a general one is true; but that there are certain great cases which operate as exceptions to the rule and in which the public good may demand and justify a departure from it.

It shall not be denied that there are such cases; but as the admission of them is one of the most common as well as the most fruitful sources of error and abuse it is of the greatest importance that just ideas should be formed of their true nature foundation and extent. To Minds which are either depraved or feeble, or under the influence of any particular passion or prejudice it is enough that cases are only attended with some *extraordinary circumstances* to induce their being considered as among the exceptions. *Convenience* is with them a substitute for *necessity,* and some temporary partial advantage is an equivalent for a fundamental and permanent interest of Society. We have too often seen in the United States examples of this species of levity. The treaties of the UStates the sacred rights of private property have been too frequently sported with from a too great facility in admitting exceptions to the maxims of public faith, and the general rules of property. A desire to escape from this evil was a principal cause of the Union which took place among good men to establish the National Government, and it behoved to friends to have been particularly cautious how they set an example of equal relaxation in the practice of that very Government.[1]

The characteristics of the only admissible exception to the principle that has been assumed are 1—*Necessity*. IId there being some intrinsic and inherent quality in the thing which is to constitute the exception, contrary to the Social Order and to the permanent good of society.[2]

Necessity is admitted in all moral reasonings as an exception to general rules. It is of two kinds, as applied to Nations—where there is want of ability to perform a duty and then it is involuntary, and where the general rule cannot be observed without some manifest and *great* national calamity.

If from extraordinary circumstances a nation is disabled from performing its stipulations, or its duty in any other respect, it is then excuseable on the score of inability. But the inability must be a real not a pretended one—one that has been experimentally ascertained, or that can [be] demonstrated to the satisfaction of all honest and discerning men. And the deviation ought to be as small as possible. All that is practicable ought to be done.

A nation is alike excuseable in certain extraordinary cases for not observing a right or performing a duty if the one or the other would involve a *manifest* and *great* national calamity. But here also an extreme case is intended; the calamity to be avoided must not only be evident and considerable, it must be such an one as is like to prove fatal to the nation, as threatens its existence or at least its permanent welfare.

War for instance is almost always a national calamity of a serious kind; but it ought often to be encountered in protection *even* of a *part* of the community injured or annoyed; or in performance of the condition of a defensive alliance with some other nation. But if such special circumstances exist in either case that the going to war would

---

1. In the margin opposite this sentence H wrote "Social order."
2. In the margin opposite this paragraph H wrote:
"Extreme necessity—
contrariety to Social order—
Mississippi ⎫
South Sea ⎬
40 for one" ⎭

eminently endanger the existence or permement welfare of the Nation, it may excuseably be foreborne.

Of the second class of exceptions the case of certain fœdal rights which once oppressed all Europe and still oppresses too great a part of it may serve as an example; rights which made absolute slaves of a part of the community and rendered the condition of the greatest proportion of the remainder not much more eligible.

These rights, though involving that of property, being contrary to the Social order and to the permanent welfare of Society were justifiably abolished, in the instances, in which abolitions have taken place, and may be abolished in all the remaining vestiges.

Wherever indeed a right of property is infringed for the general good, if the nature of the case admits of compensation, it ought to be made; but if compensation be impracticable, that impracticability ought to be an obstacle to a clearly essential reform.

In what has been said the cases of exception have been laid down as broad as they ought to be. They are cases of extremity—where these is a palpable necessity where some great and permanent national evil is to be avoided—where some great & permanent national good is to be obtained.

It must not be to avoid a temporary burthen or inconvenience, to get rid of a particular though a considerable one or to secure a partial advantage. A relaxation of this kind would tend to dissolve all social obligations, to render all rights precarious and to introduce a general dissoluteness and corruption of morals.

A single glance will suffice to convince that the case of the Debt of the UStates was not one of those cases which could justify a clear infraction of the fundamental rules of good faith and a clear invasion of rights of property acquired under the most unequivocal national stipulation. If there was any doubt before the real facility with which a provision for the debt has been made removes it; a provision which touches no internal source of revenue but the single article of distilled spirits, and lays upon that a *very moderate* duty.

But a history of the real state of the Debt when it was taken up by the Government will put the matter out of all doubt. This shall constitute the subject of my next number.

The Vindication No. IV

[Philadelphia, May–August, 1792]

The Debt proper or the original Debt of the UStates in its primary form may be classed under four general heads   I   the Old emissions of Continental money   II   The Loan office Debt contracted for monies lent to the Government   III   the army debt contracted for the pay and commutation of the army   IV   the debt of the five Great Departments as they are called in the resolution of Congress [1] being for services and supplies in the Marine Department, The Quarter Master's Commissary's cloathing and Hospital Departments. Emanations from these were the Registered Debt so denominated from new kinds of Certificates issued by the Register of the Treasury in lieu of the former evidences—Indents of Interest, being a species of paper payable to bearer which by different resolutions of Congress [2] were issued on account of arrears of Interest on the old Debt. The new emission money is not added to the enumeration because it was issued upon funds of the respective States with only a Guarantee of the UStates and falls perhaps most properly in the class of State Debts.

Of this original debt it appears by a statement of the Register of the Treasury published in   [3] not less than   in its first concoction belonged to Citizens of the States from Pensylvania to New Hampshire inclusively the remaining belonging to States from Maryland to Georgia inclusively in nearly the following proportions
    to Maryland
    to Virginia
    to N Carolina
    to S Carolina
    to Georgia
The reasons of this state of things are obvious. Until the   the principal theatre of the War had been in the States from Pensyl-

ADf, Hamilton Papers, Library of Congress.
  1. For an example of the use of the phrase "five great departments," see JCC, XXIX, 905.
  2. See, for example, JCC, XXVI, 312–13; XXIX, 743–50; XXXIII, 654.
  3. This and other spaces in this document left blank in MS.

vania North and after that period to the close of it the principal part of the enemy's force remained stationed at New York which obliged to the keeping upon the same quarter large bodies of troops, till the termination of the War.[4]

The natural consequence of this state of things was that a very large proportion of the means for carrying on the war, men money and other supplies were drawn from the States comprehended in the first division. They indeed possessed greater comparitive resources than the more Southern States & with only the same degree of zeal could furnish more to the common cause. Obvious causes always conspire to occasion larger aids to be drawn from the vicinity of the war than from more distant parts of the Country; and the main dependence of the UStates being credit a large debt was created in the scene from which the principal supplies came.

The use of this statement of the original distribution of the debt will appear hereafter.

A leading character of every part of the Debt is, that it was in its origin made alienable. It was payable to the *holder*, either in capacity of Assignee or bearer; far the greatest part of the latter description. The Contract therefore was, in its *very essence*, a contract between the Government and the *actual* holder.

A considerable part of the debt was consequently alienated by the first proprietors at different periods from its commencement down to the time of passing the funding Act.[5]

But there has been much exaggeration both as to the quantity alienated and as to the rates of alienation. The declamations on the subject have constantly represented far the greatest part of the debt in the hand of alienees and have taken the lowest price at which it ever was in the market, as the common standard of the alienation. The changes have been rung upon Two shillings and 6d. in the pound in all the arguments which have advocated a violation of the rights of the alienees.

Neither the first nor the last supposition is true.

As to the first point, namely the quantity of the debt alienated, there are no documents by which it can be satisfactorily ascertained, which of course gives full scope to imagination.

4. In the margin opposite this paragraph H wrote "Qr."
5. "An Act making provision for the (payment of the) Debt of the United States" (1 *Stat.* 138–44 [August 4, 1790]).

But there is an important fact which affords strong evidence that the quantity has always been much less considerable than has been supposed.

In the year   the State of New York passed a law [6] permitting the holders of Continental securities to bring them in and receive in exchange for them state securities upon certain conditions which were generally deemed for the advantage of the holders to accept. The same arrangement embraced an exchange of old state securities for new.

In the event of this exchange which was completed by the   it appeared that about   of the Debt remained in the hands of the original proprietors.[7]

It may be stated as a fact that there has always prevailed in the States North of New York a more firm confidence in an eventual provision for the Debt than existed in that state and it may be inferred that the alienation was still less in those states than in the state of New York.

In Jersey and Pennsylvania it is probable that the alienations were not more considerable in their degree than in New York. In Maryland they may be supposed to have been still less on account of that state having made a better provision for its debts than any other & having included in it Continental securities in the hands of its own citizens, by an exchange of Certificates.[8]

6. Sections LII through LV of "An Act for emitting the sum of two hundred thousand pounds in bills of credit for the purposes therein mentioned" concerned in part the assumption of Federal debt by the state of New York (*Laws of the State of New York*, II, 269–71 [April 18, 1786]).

7. At this point in MS H left a large blank space opposite which he wrote in the margin: "Alienations after this period."

8. During the Confederation period both the New Jersey and Pennsylvania legislatures had provided interest payments to their citizens who were creditors of the United States ("An Act for raising a Revenue of Thirty-one Thousand Two Hundred and Fifty-nine Pounds Five Shillings per Annum, for the Term of twenty-five Years, for the Purpose of paying the Interest and Principal of Debts due from the United States, agreeably to a Recommendation of Congress of the eighteenth Day of April, One Thousand Seven Hundred and Eighty-three, and for appropriating the same," *Acts of the Council and General Assembly of New-Jersey from the Establishment of the Present Government, and Declaration of Independence, to the End of the first Sitting of the eighth Session, on the 24th Day of December, 1783; with the Constitution prefixed. To which is Annexed, an Appendix, containing the Articles of Confederation of the United States, &c. With two Alphabetical Tables and an Index. Compiled under the Appointment of the Legislature, by Peter Wilson, A. M.* [Trenton: Printed by Isaac Collins, Printer to the State of New-Jersey, 1784], 363–77 [December 20, 1783]). Pennsylvania had assumed the United States

It is probable from information though not certainly known that a more considerable alienation in proportion had taken place in the States South of Maryland.

But making all due allowance for this and taking into the account that the principal part of the Debt was originally owned from Pensylvania North, the probability still is that the progress of alienation has been much less rapid than has been conjectured.

Nothing is more natural than a mistake on this point. The Dealers in the debt in the principal Cities appeared to be continually engaged in buying and selling large sums, and it has not been their fault generally to underrate the extent of their dealings. Thence it came to be imagined that the whole debt or the greatest part of it was in the market; whereas a small sum comparitively was sufficient to satisfy all the appearances. Bandied incessantly from hand to hand a few hundred thousand Dollars appeared like as many millions.

The best inquiries on the subject will lead to an opinion that there never was prior to the funding system three millions of Dollars of floating Debt in all the great Stock-Markets of the U States.

And the whole sum which had been acquired by foreigners was about   .

From all which it is very questionable whether ⅓ of the Debt in the hands of alienees at the time when Congress began to Deliberate concerning a provision for it would not be an ample allowance.

With regard to the terms of alienation they have varied from 20/ down to 2/6 in the pound.

----

debts owed to her citizens by issuing state "new loan" certificates in lieu of Continental certificates ("An Act for the Further Relief of the Public Creditors who are Citizens of this State by Receiving on Loan certain Debts of the United States of America and for Funding the Same for Paying the Annual Interest of Such Loans and the Interest of Certain Debts of this State Every Six Months," *Pennsylvania Statutes*, XII, 158–64 [March 1, 1786]). Maryland creditors of the United States were placed in a better position than those of either Pennsylvania or New Jersey, for that state's legislature not only assumed the United States debts owed its citizens but also made interest payable in specie rather than in bills of credit by an act of January 15, 1783 ("An Act proposing to the citizens of this state, creditors of congress on loan-office certificates, to accept this state for payment, on terms therein mentioned," *Laws of Maryland, Made and Passed at a Session of Assembly, begun and held at the city of Annapolis, on Monday the Fourth of November, in the year of our Lord one thousand seven hundred and eighty-two* [Annapolis: Printed by Frederick Green, Printer to this State, n.d.], Chap. XXV, Microfilm Collection of Early State Records, Library of Congress).

There are several considerable classes of alienees, who hold the debt at full or high values.

I   Those who advanced monies or furnished supplies to public officers upon Loan Office Certificates issued to those Officers in their own names. [An] example of this exists in the cases of purchases made during the War by public officers. Warrants from the Treasury would frequently be drawn in their favour upon the Commissioners of Loans who would often furnish loan office certificates in their own names in payment of those warrants. For these certificates the officers would sometimes procure the current paper in exchange and would transfer the certificates to those who advanced the money. In other cases they would pay for supplies in the certificates themselves which they would in like manner transfer. This is a very extensive case.

II   Those whose money has been placed in the funds by Trustees or Agents who took out certificates in their own names and afterwards assigned them to the true proprietors.

An instance of this was mentioned in the debates in Congress on the subject of a discrimination between original & present holders, and can be ascertained by any one who will take the pains to inquire. It was that of a Mr. Caldwell a respectable clergyman and zealous patriot in New Jersey, who acted for some time during the war in the capacity of Deputy Quarter Master.[9] In that capacity he frequently had money to pay to Individuals; which at their desire he would place in the Loan office for them, take certificates in his own name and afterwards transfer them to the persons whose money he had deposited.

There are likewise instances not a few of Trustees and Agents for absent persons and minors who placed the monies of those whom

9. The Reverend James Caldwell of Elizabeth was one of the local representatives appointed by Governor William Livingston of New Jersey under a resolve of the Continental Congress of June 29, 1779 (JCC, XIV, 783-85), to receive subscriptions for the Continental loan officer and transit the monies to the state loan office. At times the monies loaned were used for the quartermaster's department before they could be transmitted to the loan offices (JCC, XVIII, 832). On February 11, 1790, Elias Boudinot, during the debate in the House of Representatives over discrimination between original creditors and assignees, had used the example of local agents of the loan office or quartermaster departments to indicate the practical difficulty in distinguishing between original creditors and assignees (Annals of Congress, I, 1238).

they represented in the loan offices, took out certificates in their own names and afterwards transferred them to the parties intitled.

III Those who by laws of particular states were compelled to take certificates at the full value in payment of Debts.

A law of the State of New York passed in the year [10] obliged all persons who had resided within the British lines during the war to receive in satisfaction of their debts from those who had been without the lines, certificates.

IV Those who at different periods voluntarily received certificates in payment of Debts. This in some states is a very extensive case. From the precarious situation in which all persons were placed by the revolution whose property was merely personal it was no uncommon thing for creditors to receive from their Debtors certificates in payment of debts and this was almost always at high values.

Even since the peace compromises between Creditors and Debtors especially those whose fortunes had been injured by the War, in which Certificates were received at full value

10. In the margin opposite this blank space H wrote: "See the law." Section III of "An Act relative to debts due to persons within the enemies lines" provided "that it shall and may be lawfull for every defendant to pay in discharge of any debt so found due as aforesaid to such plaintiff as aforesaid, certificates or notes signed by any commissioner of loans of the United States, according to the value thereof as settled by the Continental scale of depreciation on certificates for money due on loan by this State according to the value thereof ascertained by law" (*Laws of the State of New York*, I, 500 [July 12, 1782]).

From Tobias Lear

United States June 1st 1792.

By the President's command T. Lear has the honor to return to the Secretary of the Treasury an Agreement between the Secretary of the Treasury on behalf of the President of the U. S. and the President, Directors & Company of the Bank of the U. S.,[1] which has been submitted to the President of the U. S., and to inform the Secretary of the Treasury that the said Agreement being made conformably to instructions given by the President to the Secretary for that purpose, the President approves the same.   Tobias Lear

S. P. U. S.

LC, George Washington Papers, Library of Congress.
1. See "Agreement with the President, Directors, and Company of the Bank of the United States," May 25, 1792.

To Ebenezer Tucker [1]

Treasury Department, June 1, 1792. Encloses warrant "from the Collector of Perth Amboy [2] to John Allen Smith appointing him Inspector of the Customs and Commandant of the Revenue Boat Patterson."

LC, RG 56, Letters to Collectors at Small Ports, "Set G," National Archives.
1. Tucker was surveyor of the port at Little Egg Harbor, New Jersey.
2. John Halsted was collector of customs at Perth Amboy, New Jersey.

From Wilhem and Jan Willink, Nicholaas and Jacob Van Staphorst, and Nicholas Hubbard

[*Amsterdam, June 1, 1792.* On September 19, 1792, Hamilton wrote to Willink, Van Staphorst, and Hubbard: "I have now to acknowledge the receipt of yours of the 1st. of June last enclosing your account current with the United States to that day." *Letter not found.*]

To Richard Harison [1]

[Philadelphia, June 2, 1792]

My Dear Sir

The Patents to the Ohio Company, in conformity to the Act,[2] were issued before the President went to Mount Vernon. I hope no inconvenience will have ensued. Mr. King having written to me on the same subject, I have sent him a rough sketch of the exterior line of the whole tract granted by the several Patents.

Yrs. sincerely   A Hamilton

Philadelphia June 2d. 1792

ALS, New-York Historical Society, New York City.
1. Harison was United States attorney for the District of New York.

2. "An Act authorizing the grant and conveyance of certain Lands to the Ohio Company of Associates" became law on April 21, 1792 (1 *Stat.* 257–58).

From Tobias Lear

[*Philadelphia*] *June 2, 1792*. ". . . The President approves of Joseph Sayword[1] to be Keeper of the Lighthouse on Thatchers Island, in the State of Massachusetts. . . ."

LS, RG 26, Lighthouse Letters Received, "Segregated" Lighthouse Records, Lear, National Archives; LC, George Washington Papers, Library of Congress.
    1. Joseph Sayward. See H to George Washington, May 31, 1792.

To Benjamin Lincoln

Treasury Department
June 2 1792.

Sir
    Your letter of the 4th of March remains yet to be answered.[1]
    The question there stated is in substance, whether a Citizen residing out of your state, coming to Boston, and there purchasing a Vessel, must *necessarily* take and subscribe the oath or affirmation required by law, *before the Collector of the District where such Citizen usually resides,* in order to obtain a certificate of Registry for such Vessel *from your Office.*
    I am of this opinion, it being conformable to the seventh section of the Coasting Act.[2] The design of the provision seems to be that the *identity* of the person who appears as owner, and his being a Citizen can be best known by the Collector of the District *where he resides.*
    Captain Sayward has been mentioned to the President as a Candidate for the Office of Keeper of the Light House on Thatcher's island, and I expect shortly to announce his appointment.[3]
    I am, with great consideration,   Sir, Your Obedt Servant
                                                        A Hamilton
Benjamin Lincoln Esqr.
Collector, Boston

LS, RG 36, Collector of Customs at Boston, Letters from the Treasury and Others, 1789–1809, Vol. 1, National Archives; LC, RG 56, Letters to Collectors at Small Ports, "Set G," National Archives; copy, RG 56, Letters to the Collector at Boston, National Archives.

1. H is referring to Lincoln's letter of March 14, 1792.
2. "An Act for Registering and Clearing Vessels, Regulating the Coasting Trade, and for other purposes" (1 *Stat.* 55–65 [September 1, 1789]).
3. Joseph Sayward. See Tobias Lear to H, June 2, 1792.

To Edmund Randolph

[*Philadelphia, June 2, 1792.* On June 21, 1792, Randolph wrote to Hamilton and referred to "your communication of the 2d instant." *Letter not found.*]

From Maria Reynolds [1]

[Philadelphia] Saturday Morning the June 2 [1792]

Dear Sir

I once take up the pen to solicit The favor of seing again oh Col hamilton what have I done that you should thus Neglect me Is it because I am unhappy But stop I will not say you have for perhaps you have caled and have found no opportunity to Come In at least I hope you have I am now A lone and shal be for afew days I believe till Wensday though am not sartain and would wish to se you this Evening I[f] poseble If not as soon as you can make It Convenent oh my dear freend how shal I pleade Enough what shal I say Let me beg of you to Come and If you never se me again oh If you think It best I will submit to It and take a long and last adieu   Mari

Col hamilton

for heaven sake keep me not In suspince Let me know yor Intention Either by a Line or by Catline.[2]

"Reynolds Pamphlet," August 31, 1797.
1. This letter is printed as document No. XVIII in the appendix of the "Reynolds Pamphlet," August 31, 1797.
For background to this letter, see Reynolds to H, December 15, 17, 19, 22, 1791, January 3, 17, March 24, April 3, 7, 17, May 2, 1792; H to Reynolds, December 15, 1791, April 7, 1792; Maria Reynolds to H, December 15, 1791, January 23–March 18, March 24, 1792.
2. H believed that this letter from Mrs. Reynolds proved "that it was not

her plan yet to let me off. It was probably the prelude to the letter from Reynolds . . . soliciting a *loan* of 300 dollars towards a subscription to the Lancaster Turnpike" ("Reynolds Pamphlet," August 31, 1797).

From James Reynolds [1]

[Philadelphia, June 3–22, 1792]

Sir

I am now under the necessity of asking a favour from you which if Can Oblige me with the loan of three Hundred dollars. it will be in my power to make five hundred Before the Next week is out. and if you Can oblege me with it. you may Rely on haveing of it again the last of Next Week. if I am alive and well. the use I wont it for is to Subscribe to the turn pike Road. there is a nomber of gentleman in town wants me to go up to Lancaster to Subscribe for them. no sir if you Can oblige as I want to leve town tomorrow morning and the books will be open for subscribing on monday morning Next. so that I shall have Little time to get there. you never Sir Can oblige me more than Complying with the above, please to let me know between this and 4 oClock if you dont I shant be able to go—from your Humble Sevt.   James Reynolds

Alexr. Hamilton Esqr.

"Reynolds Pamphlet," August 31, 1797.
   1. This letter is printed as document No. XIX in the appendix of the "Reynolds Pamphlet," August 31, 1797.
   For background to this letter, see Reynolds to H, December 15, 17, 19, 22, 1791, January 3, 17, March 24, April 3, 7, 17, 23, May 2, June 3–22, 1792; H to Reynolds, December 15, 1791, April 7, 1792; Maria Reynolds to H, December 15, 1791, January 23–March 18, March 24, June 2, 1792.

To James Reynolds [1]

[Philadelphia, June 3–22, 1792]

It is utterly out of my power I assure you 'pon my honour to comply with your request. Your note is returned.

"Reynolds Pamphlet," August 31, 1797.
   1. This letter was in answer to Reynolds to H, June 3–22, 1792. According

to H, this letter to Reynolds "demonstrates, that here was no concern in speculation on my part—that the money is asked as a *favour* and as a *loan*, to be reimbursed simply and without profit *in less than a fortnight*. My answer shews that even the loan was refused" ("Reynolds Pamphlet," August 31, 1797).

From William Seton [1]

Bank of N York
3rd. June 1792.

sir.

I have the honor to acknowledge the receipt of your letters of the 24th & 30th. May [2] agreably to the request contained in the former Messrs. Beach & Canfield of Newark have been paid the sum of four thousand three hundred and fifty Dollars, for which you have their receipt enclosed. The further payments shall be made to them as you desire upon the Certificates of Mr. Melancton Smith for the quantities of shoes they may deliver at the rate of 82⅔ Cents pr. pair.

I have the honour to be with the greatest respect   sir   Your obliged Obedt. Humb. servt.

Alexander Hamilton Esqr.
Secretary of the Treasury of the United States

LC, Bank of New York, New York City.
1. For background to this letter, see Seton to H, May 28, 1792.
2. Neither letter has been found.

[A Correspondent] [1]

[Philadelphia, June 4, 1792]

[Philadelphia] *Gazette of the United States*, June 4, 1792.
1. Part of the column devoted to correspondence in the June 4, 1792, issue of the *Gazette of the United States* is attributed to H by Philip Marsh ("Further Attributions to Hamilton's Pen," *The New-York Historical Society Quarterly*, XL [October, 1956], 353–54). No other evidence, however, of H's authorship has been found.

From William Ellery

[*Newport, Rhode Island*] *June 4, 1792*. "I have received your letter circular of the 22nd. of the last month and will correspond in future with the Commissioner of the Revenue touching all matters relating to the Light house establishment and take his directions thereon. . . ."

LC, Newport Historical Society, Newport, Rhode Island.

From Richard Harison

[*New York, June 4, 1792*. On June 26, 1792, Hamilton wrote to Harison: "I shall be mindful of the intimation in your letter of the 4th instant." *Letter not found.*]

Treasury Department Circular to the Collectors of the Customs

Treasury Department,
June 4th, 1792.

Sir,

The 17th section of the act, entitled, "An Act for raising a further sum of money for the protection of the frontiers, and for other purposes therein mentioned," having abolished the rate heretofore annexed to the livre tournois of France; [1] it becomes proper to give some general direction concerning the mode of estimating the value of goods imported from France.

It will be understood that the cause of this alteration in the law is the depreciated state of the Assignats, which now essentially constitute the current money of that country.

To distinguish therefore the natural and *real* from the artificial and *nominal* value of the goods imported is the point to be aimed at. To assist in doing this, it is easier to indicate some general criterions, than to establish a precise rule.

The criterions which have occurred are either 1st—The actual difference between specie and assignats at the *time* and *place* of exportation.

2d. The actual state of foreign *exchange* at the *time* and *place* of exportation.

3d. The prices of similar articles prior to the present revolution in France.

4th. An appraisement, as in the case of goods not invoiced according to the 36th section of the Collection Law.[2]

The first of these is the least to be relied upon. It was found in numerous instances in the course of the late war with Great Britain, that the comparative prices of goods in specie or paper did not correspond with the actual difference between them; and that they were otherwise artificially affected by the depreciation so as to vary from the natural standards of intrinsic value. The same thing is said to be remarked in France.

The second affords a better rule, though one, not free from objections. Commercial circumstances operate upon the rate of exchange; so as to render it an inaccurate test, of the intrinsic value of any circulating medium. As far as this rule is allowed to guide, the exchange with Amsterdam or London, must regulate the calculation.

The third is the best of the criterions mentioned, as often as it can be ascertained; and ought to be preferred. It is however not free from objection, as prices vary from causes, which ought to render the actual prices at the time of computation, the ground of it. But when they cannot be ascertained intrinsically, as in the present instance, no better substitute occurs.

The last rule is liable to some objections of weight. The appraisers it is obvious would want some certain guide as much as the officers. There are cases nevertheless in which a defect of competent lights otherwise may render it advisable to employ this expedient.

With these indications, it must be left to the respective Collectors to exercise a prudent discretion in the several cases, which will arise; combining a due regard to the public interest with a spirit of justice to individuals.

I wish them in the progress of the thing to note, wherever they have the requisite information, how nearly the three first rules correspond with each other in their results. This may furnish matter of useful observation.

It will be satisfactory to me to receive copies of the invoices which accompany the entries of goods from France; at least, Abstracts shewing articles and values—and the computations which are made towards ascertaining the duties.

Having observed an omission in some instances, in regard to the directions contained in my Circular of the 21st of September last, for cutting holes through all paid draughts of the Treasurer, cancelled certificates of registry and enrolments, when transmitted to this office, I must call your particular attention to this point for the future.

It appears also that the instructions relative to the transmission of cancelled certificates of enrolment, have in some instances not been complied with; probably under an idea that by the 22d section of the Coasting Act [3] such certificates were to be sent to the office of the Collector, whence they were issued. But the mode of transmiting them to the Treasury in the first instance, in order to their being sent from thence to the Collectors, is not conceived to be contrary to the act: And it is preferred, because it will save to the Collectors the expence of postage, which to many of the officers on account of their remote situation, would be an object of some consequence; you will therefore carefully observe the regulation.

Proof being before me, that the Register of the sloop Polly, of Chesterfield, was stolen from the master, in the month of December last; I desire in case discovery should be made of its having been fraudulently disposed of, or if it should again make its appearance in any way, it may be detained, and information given to me, the said sloop having been registered a-new at Bermuda Hundred. The certificate said to be stolen is No. 8, signed William Heth, Collector, Peter Peterson, Master, dated December 4th, 1789.

With consideration,   I am, Sir,   Your obedient Servant,

A Hamilton

LS, The Andre deCoppet Collection, Princeton University Library; LS, MS Division, New York Public Library; L[S], RG 36, Collector of Customs at Boston, Letters from the Treasury, 1789–1807, Vol. 4, National Archives; LS, Office of the Secretary, United States Treasury Department; LC, Essex Institute, Salem, Massachusetts; copy, United States Finance Miscellany, Treasury Circulars, Library of Congress; copy, RG 56, Circulars of the Office of the Secretary, "Set T," National Archives.

1. 1 *Stat.* 262–63 (May 2, 1792). See Benjamin Lincoln to H, May 12, 1792.
2. H is actually referring to Section 37 rather than Section 36 of "An Act

to provide more effectually for the collection of the duties imposed by law on goods, wares and merchandise imported into the United States, and on the tonnage of ships or vessels." For an explanation of the confusion in the numbering of the sections of this act, see H to Richard Harison, April 26, 1791, note 2. Section 37 reads in part as follows: "if any goods, wares or merchandise, on which duties are payable, shall receive damage during the voyage, or shall not be accompanied with the original invoice of their cost, it shall be lawful for the collector (and upon the request of the party he is required) to appoint one merchant, and the owner or consignee to appoint another, who being sworn or affirmed by the collector, well and truly to appraise such goods, shall appraise or value them accordingly, and the duties upon such goods shall be estimated agreeably to such appraisement or valuation . . ." (1 *Stat.* 166–67 [August 4, 1790]).

3. Section 22 of "An Act for Registering and Clearing Vessels, Regulating the Coasting Trade, and for other purposes" reads in part as follows: "whenever the property of such ship or vessel shall be changed in whole or in part, the person or persons who shall then be owner or owners, or one of them, shall make known such change to the collector of the district where he or they may reside, and such collector is hereby authorized and directed to grant a new certificate of the enrolment of such ship or vessel by her former name, to such owner or owners, upon his or their delivering up the former certificate, which shall be sent to the office of the collector from whence it was issued, to be cancelled . . ." (1 *Stat.* 61 [September 1, 1789]).

From Otho H. Williams

[*Baltimore, June 4, 1792.* On June 8, 1792, Hamilton wrote to Williams: "In answer to your letter of the 4th instant, concerning the Cutter, Active." *Letter not found.*]

From Otho H. Williams

Collector's Office, Balto. 4. June 1792

Sir

By The Act making further provision for the payment of the debts of the United States, it is, by the second section "enacted that an addition of ten ℔ Centum shall be made to the several rates of duties above specified and imposed, in respect to all goods, wares, and Merchandize which, after the said last day of December next, shall be imported in ships or Vessels *not* of the United States, except in the cases in which an *additional* duty is herein before specially laid on any goods, wares or Merchandize which shall be imported in such Ships or Vessels." [1]

As *all* the duties imposed by that act were *original* and had no reference to any other, I requested an explanation of the term "additional" and Mr Coxe [2] replied that it was to be understood "a greater or higher rate of duties;" and as such greater or higher rate of duties applied, in the first section of the law, to *Teas* only, It has been customary in this Office to add ten ℔ Centum to the several rates of duties on all merchandize, teas only excepted, imported in foreign Vessels.

By the "Act repealing, after the last day of June next, the duties heretofore laid upon distilled spirits imported from abroad" &c (passed at the third session of Congress) it is "enacted that after the last day of June next the duties laid upon *distilled spirits* by the act intitled "an Act making further provision for the payment of the debts of the United States" shall cease." [3]

Construing these two acts together my apprehension was, that altho' the second repealed the first, so far as it related to duties on *distilled spirits,* and substituted *other* duties thereon, yet the mode of ascertaining the sums to be collected, or of discriminating between domestic and foreign vessels, was not intended to be repealed, and consequently it has continued to be the practice in this Office to add ten ℔ Centum upon specific duties on distilled spirits imported in *foreign* vessels; and as the returns have been so passed at the Treasury I presume the same practice is universal throughout the department of the Customs.

The legallity of this practice, however has been very lately doubted here, and I have to request your opinion; and will be obliged to you, if you will be pleased to let me have it soon.

I am &c.   O H W. Collr

A Hamilton Esqr.

Copy, Maryland Historical Society, Baltimore.
1. 1 *Stat.* 181 (August 10, 1790).
2. Tench Coxe, commissioner of the revenue.
3. 1 *Stat.* 199 (March 3, 1791).

From Oliver Wolcott, Junior

Treasury Department, Comptroller's Office, June 4, 1792. "I have considered the question stated by Samuel Bayard Esq Clerk of the

Supreme Court of the United States . . . & am of opinion that charges for postage which may be incurred by him in executing his official duties can be properly allowed. . . . The Letters from Mr. Bayard to the several Clerks can be ⟨ma⟩rked as *paid* & the postage charged to him, to be settled quarterly with the Post Master & allowed in Mr. Bayards Accounts."

ADf, Connecticut Historical Society, Hartford.

From Jeremiah Olney

Providence, June 5, 1792. "I have received, under cover with several Acts of Congress, your circular Letters of the 21st. of February and the 10th of May. Due attention shall be paid to their contents. I have never had occasion to take any Bond of the kind mentioned in the latter. . . ."

ADfS, Rhode Island Historical Society, Providence.

To Otho H. Williams

Treasury Department   June 5th 1792

Sir

I have before me your letters of the 18th of March, 18th of April, 8th & 27th of May.[1]

I do not observe that it is stated how the Officers who were absent came to be so; so that I am at some loss to judge whether the absence was justifiable or not. I am however rather of opinion that their compensations follow their commissions, as *public Officers*, and that so long as they are retained in service they must be paid computing from the dates of their respective Commissions. It is at the same time proper matter of inquiry under what circumstances they were absent, in order that the propriety of their conduct may be judged of.

With regard to claims for compensation prior to the dates of Commissions, where any officers have been employed by authority in *performing any service*, in relation to the Cutter, an allowance not exceeding a Dollar ℔ day has been admitted by the Accounting Officers; and it is reported to me that a sum of 155 Dollars and eighty three Cents has been admitted in favor of Capt Gross.[2] If any *hands* were employed in aid, I presume due regard would be had to their case. But as to claims without special service on the ground of being retained, they will not be admitted.

If a contract cannot be effected, it is of necessity to subsist the Men in the other mode you mention as the only practicable one; but a contract even on higher terms than those heretofore limitted would be more agreeable to me. It ought to be so regulated as to secure the supply of the seamen in a satisfactory manner.

What however is necessary to render the Cutter useful must be done 'till what is desireable can be done.

Water and such were not contemplated as parts of the ration. They will be contingent charges, where they cannot be procured without expence. This however ought to be done as much as possible; and I should hope would be in the main practicable.

It was my intention to commit to you the business of supplies, equipment and repairs and the direction of the movements of the Cutter in conformity to the general instructions and indications which had been or might be given, without the necessity of a previous special reference to me in particular and ordinary cases. If any thing extra and out of the course of what may have been generally indicated should be contemplated, I should be glad to have it mentioned prior to the incurring of any extra expence.

As to additional sails and an additional boat they had better be deferred to be considered hereafter, when the expence of the first establishment is finally ascertained. I take it for granted the Cutter has now one good boat.

More hands than the law[3] provides for cannot of course be allowed.

Those who have had most to do with them remark in Masters of Vessels a strong disposition towards multiplying objects of expence. You will doubtless be upon your guard against this propensity when applications for new purposes are made.

Hitherto the Cutters in the Chesapaek have been of little utility. Under the powers you have as now explained to you I shall rely on your judgment, attention and zeal for rendering them as serviceable as they ought to be without being vexatious to the trade.

With great consideration   I am Sir   Your obedt Servant

A Hamilton

Otho H. Williams Esqr
Collector Baltimore

LS, Maine Historical Society, Portland; copy, Maryland Historical Society, Baltimore.

1. None of these letters has been found.
2. Simon Gross, master of the *Active*, the revenue cutter for Maryland.
3. Section 63 of "An Act to provide more effectually for the collection of the duties imposed by law on goods, wares and merchandise imported into the United States, and on the tonnage of ships or vessels" reads in part as follows: ". . . there shall be to each of the . . . cutters, one master, and not more than three mates, first, second, and third, four mariners and two boys" (1 *Stat.* 175 [August 4, 1790]).

From Benjamin Lincoln

Boston, June 6, 1792. "I mentioned to you under the 15 Feby last that we had put our hands on four hogs. N E Rum in old we[s]t India Casks. The matter came to trial yesterday. It was admitted that the rum was distilled in Portland but contended that the duties were duly paid. This being proved the spirits were acquitted. If these things can be practised with impunity a wide door will be opened through which frauds on the revenue may pass undetected. . . .[1] There was lately exported from this port a quantity of Coffe to Cadiz. On the arrival of the vessel there the Master discovered a new duty on the Coffee so heavy as to preclude the possibility of selling it without loss consequently did not land it. The exporter wishes to be exempt from paying a second duty on the Coffee. Can he be? If I do not receive particular instruction on the subject I shall receive the duty on the Coffee as in all other cases. . . ."

LC, Massachusetts Historical Society, Boston; LC, RG 36, Collector of Customs at Boston, Letter Book, 1790–1797, National Archives; two copies, RG 56, Letters from the Collector at Boston, National Archives.

1. For a similar problem, see Jeremiah Olney to H, May 31, 1792, note 3.

From Oliver Wolcott, Junior

T. D
C. Off June 6th 1792

Sir

The following occurrence has happened in relation to which I request your opinion.

Matthias Huysinga Misschert [1] in pursuance of a power of Attorney from Theodosus Gerhardus Bosch of Utrecht, has subscribed to the Loan proposed by Congress [2] about seventy thousand Dollars of Registered Debt, for which he requests Certificates of Funded Debt in the name of the said Bosch.

Previously to the time of subscription, the Credits of Bosch on the books of the Treasury had been attached at the suit of Paulus Kok.[3]

The question on which your opinion is requested is, whether the nature of Boschs credit with the United States can be changed while the claim of Kok is pending?

Yr hum &c

Honble
A. Hamilton Esq

ADf, Connecticut Historical Society, Hartford.
  1. Messchert was a Dutch merchant who lived in Philadelphia and traded with Germany.
  2. See "An Act supplementary to the act making provision for the Debt of the United States" (1 Stat. 281–83 [May 8, 1792]).
  3. See H to William Rawle, March 13, 1792.

To William Ellery

[*Philadelphia, June 7, 1792.* On July 10, 1792, Ellery wrote to Hamilton: "I have recd. your letters of the 7th 22nd. and 28th of the last month." *Letter of June 7 not found.*] [1]

  1. On June 25, 1792, Ellery wrote to Oliver Wolcott, Jr.: "I have . . . recd. a Letter from the Secry of the Treasy of the 7th of June in which he has manifested his consent to my purchase of the Scales and weights, and informs that he had instructed you in order to their being passed in my account" (LC, Newport Historical Society, Newport, Rhode Island).

To William Heth

My Dear Sir

The same cause which delayed my answering several of your Official Letters has postponed the acknowlegement of your three private letters of the 5.[1] 27 & 29th of February. The truth is, my situation hitherto has thrown upon me more business than it was possible for me to get through; and the intrigues of faction, to which I have been obliged to be attentive, have added not a little to my burthen. I hope from your friendship the proper allowances for my apparent neglect.

As to the question, which regards the permanency of the custom house at Bermuda Hundred [2]—as far as it turns on the point of having but one Port of entry in the State, you may be perfectly at your ease; but as it respects mercantile accommodation in relation to the best *position* in the district, I am really at a loss what to say to you. No formal representation has yet come from the Merchants on that point; but if it could be made appear that another situation was truly more convenient to them, City Point, Broadway or any other, it would probably be substituted—and even if they should become clamorous for another, on only colorable pretences, it might happen that an attention to popularity would produce a change.

You must therefore judge on this point from your own knowlege of circumstances and take your measures accordingly. The permanency of a Port of Entry *in your district* you may confide in.

The event will have relieved you from any anxiety on the subject of a certain exchange of office.[3] It could not have happened without your *ascertained* consent. I am ignorant whether there was any project of the kind—never having had any intimation of it but from yourself. I have however been witness to so many plots and counterplots so much intrigue and cabal in certain quarters, that I can wonder at nothing.

You speak of a Branch of the Bank at Richmond.[4] On this point I wish your confidential opinion. I take it for granted that it will not be long before a branch will be established either at Richmond Petersburg or Norfolk. I own that I have not data enough to judge which of these places ought to be preferred. *Deposits*, by Individuals are of very great importance to a Bank. In order to the enjoying of this advantage, it is necessary that the place where it is seated should have a considerable *mercantile circulating* Capital. This, Norfolk certainly has. Is it the case also with Richmond or Petersburgh & with which of them most? Where do the Merchants who carry on the business of your district principally *reside?* What is the course of its trade? What are the comparitive advantages of the several places?

As to your personal concerns, as far a[s] real esteem & friendship on my part can be of use to you, or can tend either to your *security* or advantage, you may firmly count upon it.

Farewell My D Sir   A Hamilton

W Heth Esqr.

ALS, Stanford University Libraries.
    1. Letter not found.
    2. See Heth to H, February 27, 1792.
    3. See Heth to H, February 29, 1792.
    4. See Heth to H, February 27, 1792.

To Edmund Randolph

[*Philadelphia, June 7, 1792.* On June 10, 1792, Randolph wrote to Hamilton and referred to "your favor of the 7 Instant." *Letter not found.*]

From Samuel A. Otis [1]

[*Philadelphia, June 8, 1792.* On June 8, 1792, Hamilton wrote to Otis: "I am to acknowledge the receipt of your favor of this date." *Letter not found.*]

    1. Otis, who was secretary of the Senate, was the younger brother of James Otis and the father of Harrison Gray Otis.

To Samuel A. Otis

Treasury Department June 8th: 1792

Sir,

I am to acknowledge the receipt of your favor of this date.[1]

Although it would afford me much pleasure to Contribute to your accomodation, yet in the present case I cannot consider myself at liberty to comply with your requisition, inasmuch as it is repugnant to the established usage of the Treasury. I am with Consideration Sir   Your Most Obedient Servant   A Hamilton

Samuel A. Otis Esquire

LS, RG 46, Second Congress, 1791–1793, Reports of the Secretary of the Treasury, National Archives.

1. Letter not found. Although the exact nature of Otis's request cannot be ascertained, it seems likely that he wished to transfer funds which were allotted to salaries for the Senate to the accounts used for his own and his staff's salaries. On November 19, 1792, Oliver Wolcott, Jr., wrote to Otis as follows:

"I find it necessary to request, that you will not discharge out of the money placed in your hands for the compensations of the Members of the Senate, the salaries and compensations due to yourself and to the clerks of your office. You will therefore render your own account, together with the accounts of the said persons at the end of each quarter, at the Treasury, that the whole may be included in one settlement, and payment thereof made to you." (LS, RG 46, Second Congress, 1791–1793, Reports of the Secretary of the Treasury, National Archives.)

Treasury Department Circular to the Collectors of the Customs

Treasury Department,
June 8, 1792.

Sir,

The 66, 67 and 68th sections of the Collection Law, make provision respecting the prosecution, receipt, appropriation and distribution of and for fines, penalties and forfeitures, under that act.[1] The provision is less precise and clear than could be wished, and may require legislative revision. In the mean time it is indispensable that some arrangement should be made and observed; consulting such indications as are to be found in the law, and pursuing the most convenient and orderly course.

The 66th section appears to contemplate the Collector, as the person, who is to direct, in the first instance, prosecutions for fines, penalties and forfeitures, and who is to *receive, distribute* and *pay* their proceeds.[2] This seems to be a leading idea, and one which will, most conveniently, guide the arrangement.

As incident to the duty of prosecuting, the paying of all expences incurred will belong to the Collectors. These expences being truly charges on the collection of the Revenue, will be properly paid out of the product of the duties, where they cannot be defrayed by the issue of the prosecutions.

As the Collector is to cause suits to be instituted, and, from official situation, must know the circumstances of each case, he can also best adjust these expences. The taxation, by the proper officers of courts, will guide as to the ordinary Court charges. A separate account must be stated of the charges attending each suit; and of the proceeds, that is, the value recovered, if any, and of the distribution. A form will be transmitted by the Comptroller.

The proceeds of forfeited vessels and goods, and the sums recovered, as for pecuniary fines and penalties, will naturally come, in the first instance, into the hands of the Marshals. These, they will pay over to the respective Collectors, who will pay the charges and distribute the net remainder.

Where judgment is rendered against the Public, or where, though in favour of the Public, *nothing* is or can be *received*, the plaintiff's costs and charges must be defrayed by the Collector out of the product of the duties.

Where judgment is rendered in favour of the Public, and something is both recovered and received, it is to be applied, in the first instance, towards the payment of expences. If not sufficient, the deficiency is to be paid out of the product of the duties. If more than sufficient, the moiety of the net surplus is to be accounted for to the Public by the Collector, as a specific fund, subject to special appropriation, and the other moiety is to be distributed among the parties entitled, as the law directs.

The same arrangement is to be observed with regard to penalties and forfeitures under the registering and coasting act.[3]

I am, with much consideration, Sir, Your obedient Servant.

A Hamilton

LS, to Philip Bradley, MS Division, New York Public Library; LC, to Samuel R. Gerry, Essex Institute, Salem, Massachusetts; L[S], to Benjamin Lincoln, RG 36, Collector of Customs at Boston, Letters from the Treasury, 1789-1818, Vol. 5, National Archives; LS, MS Division, New York Public Library; LS, Miss Eleanor C. Bishop, on deposit at Baker Library, Harvard University Graduate School of Business Administration; LS, Office of the Secretary, United States Treasury Department; copy, Buffalo and Erie County Public Library, Buffalo, New York; copy, United States Finance Miscellany, Treasury Circulars, Library of Congress; copy, RG 56, Circulars of the Office of the Secretary, "Set T," National Archives. The copy addressed to Bradley, Federal marshal for Connecticut, was enclosed in "Treasury Department Circular to the Marshals of the United States," June 8, 1792.

1. H is actually referring to Sections 67, 68, and 69 of "An Act to provide more effectually for the collection of the duties imposed by law on goods, wares and merchandise imported into the United States, and on the tonnage of ships or vessels" (1 *Stat.* 145-78 [August 4, 1790]). For an explanation of the confusion in the numbering of the sections of this act, see H to Richard Harison, April 26, 1791, note 2.

2. Section 67 reads in part as follows: ". . . the collector, within whose district the seizure shall be made, is hereby authorized and directed to cause suits for the same to be commenced and prosecuted to effect, and to receive, distribute and pay the sum or sums recovered, after first deducting all necessary costs and charges, according to law" (1 *Stat.* 176).

3. Section 21 of "An Act for Registering and Clearing Vessels, Regulating the Coasting Trade, and for other purposes" provided: "That all the penalties and forfeitures inflicted and incurred by this act, shall, and may be sued for, prosecuted and recovered in such courts, and be disposed of in such manner as any penalties or forfeitures inflicted, or which may be incurred for any offence committed against the United States, in and by an act, entituled, 'An act to regulate the collection of the duties imposed by law, on the tonnage of ships or vessels, and on goods, wares and merchandises, imported into the United States,' may legally be sued for, prosecuted, recovered and disposed of" (1 *Stat.* 60 [September 1, 1789]).

Treasury Department Circular to the Marshals of the United States

Treasury Department
June 8 1792

Sir

I herewith send you a copy of a Circular letter which I have this day written to the Collectors of the Customs. The arrangement therein suggested will conduce very much to the order of the business of the Treasury, and is presumed to be conformable with law. I feel a confidence that it will meet with the chearful co-operation of the several Courts and their respective Officers, and that the arrangement, itself, will be found well adapted to the security of all parties.

I am, Sir, with much consideration,   Your obedt Servant

A Hamilton

LS, Georgia Historical Society, Savannah.

To Otho H. Williams

Treasury Department
June 8. 1792.

Sir

In answer to your letter of the 4th instant,[1] concerning the Cutter, Active, I refer you to mine of the 5th.

With regard to the addition of 10 ℔ Ct to be made to the several rates of duties, in respect to all goods, Wares and Merchandizes imported in Ships or Vessels *not* of the United States, agreeably to the 2d Section of the Act "making further provision for the payment of the debt &ca," I am of opinion that your practice is consistent with the true construction of the laws. The same construction, it appears, has obtained generally in the Custom houses.[2]

I find, on a review of my correspondence, an opinion communicated to you in my letter of the 25th November 1789 to this effect "That you cannot register any Vessel whose husband or Acting Owner does not usually reside at or near some port within your District".

This opinion was given in answer to a question stated in your letter of the 14th November; [and was founded on the circumstances of the particular case;] [3] and by way of explanation I shall add, that I meant, you cannot register a Vessel under *such* circumstances, because you are not authorised *to administer the Oath* required by law, which must be taken before the Collector of the District in which such Owner or Ship's husband usually resides, as prescribed by the seventh section of the Act.[4] The design of the provision seems to be that the identity of the person, who appears as Owner, and his being a Citizen, can be best known by the Collector of the District where he resides. [The opinion given is therefore to be understood so as to admit of the exceptions resulting from the seventh Section.]

I am, with consideration, Sir, Your Obed Servant   A Hamilton

Otho H Williams Esqr
Baltimore.

LS, Columbia University Libraries.
1. Letter not found.   2. See Williams to H, June 4, 1792.
3. Material within brackets is in the handwriting of H.
4. "An Act for Registering and Clearing Vessels, Regulating the Coasting Trade, and for other purposes" (1 *Stat.* 56–57 [September 1, 1789]).

From William Heth [1]

[*June 9, 1792.* "The French Consul at Norfolk [2] has lately adopted a practice of taking the registers of vessels from such Masters belonging to his Nation, as called there to report on their passage to this district. If he has a right so to do, I shall not be surprized, if some Masters should depart from hence without paying tonnage." *Letter not found.*]

Extract, letterpress copy, Thomas Jefferson Papers, Library of Congress; extract, LC, Papers of the Continental Congress, National Archives.
1. This extract was enclosed in H to Thomas Jefferson, June 20, 1792.
2. Although Charles François Adrien le Paulnier, Chevalier d'Annemours, was French consul for Maryland and Virginia, Heth is presumably referring to Martin Oster, vice consul of France who resided at Norfolk at this time.

To Benjamin Walker [1]

[Philadelphia, June 9, 1792]

Dr. Walker

I enclose you a letter which I have received from Mr Marshall.[2] If you can with propriety accommodate him it will be well. I doubt not his embarrassements are real & his emoluments in proportion to his merit are small.

Yrs. sincerely   A Hamilton

June 9. 92
Benjamin Walker Esq

ALS, Passaic County Park Commission, Paterson, New Jersey.
1. Walker, a New York speculator and business associate of William Duer, was a director of the Society for Establishing Useful Manufactures.
2. Thomas Marshall to H, May 30, 1792.

To Otho H. Williams

Philad June 9. 1792

My Dear Sir

I feel myself not a little a delinquent in regard to a certain paper you forwarded it to me.[1] I will now explain the reasons of its non appearance. Though I thought it a merited & a very good reproof on certain folks as well as calculated to throw useful light on transactions interesting to the fame of our deceased friend—as the business depending was taking a favourable turn when I received your letter [2] —I doubted the expediency of starting any new Game; lest it should wound the pride and jar the nerves of more than the Individual meant to be chastised [3]—and so perhaps do harm to a cause we both wished to promote.

If things had continued in an unpromising train I should have been willing to have taken the chance of the publication. In me, it would have gratified feelings of more than one kind.

I at first intended to reserve the publication for the conclusion of the business, but then I doubted whether it was worth while to stir again the question. It could not serve the original purpose and it was not *necessary* to the fame of the General. That stands unassailable, with *success*.

If any *impressions* have fallen under your Notice, which induce you to think this last conclusion erroneous—the publication at this time will not be too late for that purpose.

Adieu My Dear Sir   Believe me always truly & affectionately Yrs

A Hamilton

P. S.   With your permission I will retain the paper as an interesting record of some particulars which were not before known to me.

Otho H Williams Esq

ALS, Maryland Historical Society, Baltimore.
1. See Williams to H, April 5, 1792, note 7.

2. The "business" which had taken "a favourable turn" was the action by Congress on a bill to indemnify Nathanael Greene's estate. On April 27, 1792, "An Act to indemnify the Estate of the late Major General Nathaniel Green, for a certain bond entered into by him during the late war" become law (1 *Stat.* 258).

3. H is referring to Thomas Sumter, a member of the House of Representatives from South Carolina. See Williams to H, April 5, 1792, notes 6 and 8.

From Fisher Ames [1]

Boston June 10th. 1792

Dear Sir

Those who percieve the arduous nature of your duties, ought to wish to aid you in executing them. Whether the auther of the *Path to Riches*,[2] had it in view to afford you such aid, or not, I think it fit to send you the work, as our political economy lies much within your department. You have found the path for our Country, and it is advancing in it, tho' you have not sought it for yourself.[3] To drop this obscure way of writing, I enclose Judge Sullivans pamphlet on Banks &c. The modest title page delights me. Where is the *upright* man to plead for a people? [4] Possibly this enquiry may be made by the people whom the auther so much desires to plead for. The fee expected for pleading is supposed to be the Chair of Governor.[5] Another view is suggested. A state Bank will afford a good field of speculation, of Which fame, that evil tongue says, many of the legislature were not unmindful at their last Session, when the Tontine was in discussion.[6] My friends tell me that the   [7] the Chair, the pride of state sovereignity   [8] Copy federal institutions and the thirst for speculations will move different parties, and produce some sort of bank [9] or Tontine project, and that resistance will be fruitless.

The inconsistent jargon of this pamphlet will make you smile. It will not amuse the many, nor instruct the few, but its bulk will deter many from reading it who will vote for a state Bank, presuming that there are arguments enough for it in that great Book.

All goes well in the State. The people really prosper, and what is more they know and say it, and give credit to the General Government & for the change they have witnessed. I feel persuaded they are perfectly well affected to good measures. I only fear that the high sense of honor in the paying duties is cooling. When money is in the case Merchants need watching. Mr Gore [10] mentions some facts which indicate the need of Vigilance.

I do not wish you to answer this. I would not write at all, if by doing it I should impose that task upon you.

I am dear Sir, with perfect esteem   Your most obt. humble servant.   Fisher Ames

JCH Transcripts.
   1. Ames was a Federalist member of the House of Representatives from Massachusetts.
   2. Written by James Sullivan, *The Path to Riches. An Inquiry into the Origin and Use of Money; and into the Principles of Stocks and Banks. To Which Are Subjoined Some Thoughts Respecting a Bank for the Commonwealth. By a Citizen of Massachusetts* (Boston, 1792) was a sustained attack on the policies of the Massachusetts Bank, the state's most important financial institution. A prominent Boston lawyer and politician, Sullivan had been a member of the Continental Congress in 1782 and a judge of probate for Suffolk County in 1788. In 1792 he was attorney general of Massachusetts.
   3. Ames is presumably referring to Sullivan's statement that "Solomon tells us that the rich have many friends; but our Secretary of the Treasury, by making others rich, has obtained [many]; and his reputation derives support, as well from the greatness of his character for enterprise, as from the pecuniary interest which so many rich men have in the support of it" (Sullivan, *The Path to Riches*, 45).
   4. Ames is paraphrasing the following verse which appeared on the title page of *The Path to Riches:*
         "Where is the upright man, with skill refin'd,
         To check their rage, and cure the public mind,
         With honest zeal, to plead *a People's cause,*
         And guard *their equal rights, by equal laws?*"
   5. Sullivan was an unsuccessful gubernatorial candidate in 1796 in Massachusetts.
   6. On June 11, 1791, the day following the opening of the session, the Massachusetts House of Representatives considered the desirability of a subscription to the Bank of the United States. The motion for a subscription was, however, rejected before the House of Representatives adjourned on June 18, 1791. On January 18, 1792, shortly after the session met again, the committee on the petition of William Tudor and others brought in "A Bill to incorporate sundry persons by the name of *The President and Trustees of the Boston Tontine Association.*" The agents of the Tontine Association were unable to obtain a charter. On March 5, 1792, "the petition of William Tudor Esqr & others praying to be incorporated for the purpose of establishing a Bank by the name of the President & Directors of the State Bank" was read in the Senate. The next day "The Hon: W Heath Esq: brought down the petition of Wm Tudor Esq: & others with a report of the joint Committee thereon that the petitioner have leave to bring in a bill for the purpose prayed for." Although both houses concurred, Tudor did not bring in a bill ("Journal of the House of Representatives of the Commonwealth of Massachusetts commencing 25 May 1791 ending 10 March 1792," 91, 103, 152, 288, 295, Microfilm Collection of Early State Records, Library of Congress).
   7. This space was left blank in MS with a note which reads: "defaced in original."

8. This space was left blank in MS with a note which reads: "defaced in original."

9. In the session which commenced in June, 1792, the Massachusetts legislature incorporated the Union Bank. The state subscribed to one-third of the new bank's stock (Bray Hammond, *Banks and Politics in America from the Revolution to the Civil War* [Princeton, 1957], 165).

10. Christopher Gore, who was the United States attorney for the District of Massachusetts, had resigned as director of the Massachusetts Bank on March 1, 1792.

From Edmund Randolph

Philadelphia June 10th. 179[2].[1]

sir.

In our conversation Yesterday we reduced the substance of your favor of the 7 Instant [2] to this question: Whether you ought, under any modification, to suspend the payment of Interest to a State, which is intitled under the 17th. section of the act "making provision for the debt of the United states," [3] to receive interest to the amount of the nonsubscribed deficiency; In trust for the nonsubscribing creditors of the State?

By the Same section it is provided, that this interest shall continue to be paid to a State, until there be a settlement of Accounts between the United States and It.

The loan is however again opened by the act of May the 8th. 1792,[4] from the first day of June 1792 to the first day of march 1793, on the same terms with the former loan.

If the first of march 1793 had now arrived, and the sum allotted to any State had been filled up by the subscriptions, that State woud cease to receive an Interest on any part of the allotted sum. For then there woud be no deficiency, nor any person Remaining, for whose benefit the trust was created. Under the Old Act indeed this interest would have been continued until the Settlement of accounts. But as it is manifest that this stipulation was made in contemplation of a deficiency; the very moment when that deficiency shall be removed, the groundwork of a state's claim to interest is removed also. To suppose, that congress granted this money to the States, whose limited complement was exhausted, would be to charge [5] them with a wanton loan from the Federal Treasury.

But I cannot assent to the propriety of Suspending the Payment of interest altogether until the 1st of March 1793. It may happen, that none of the creditors, who have hitherto refused to Subscribe, may be now inclined to Subscribe; and by the nonpayment their situation, which is intended to be equal to that of Subscribers may be renderd worse.

The strict line therefore woud be, as often as a quarters interest becomes due, to diminish the payment in proportion to the progress of the new subscription. But perhaps it would be more adviseable and be more satisfactory, if the deduction was to commence on the payment for the succeeding quarter. A quarter has something of the nature of an Integer; and the fixation of thirty days, the Interval between the Opening of the new subscription and the end of the present quarter, might favour of too much rigor.

I have the honor sir to be yr. mo. ob. serv.   Edm: Randolph

The Secretary of the Treasury

LS, RG 60, Copies of Opinions, National Archives.
1. This letter is misdated "1790."
2. Letter not found.
3. This section reads as follows: "*And be it further enacted,* That if the whole sum allowed to be subscribed in the debt or certificates of any state as aforesaid, shall not be subscribed within the time for that purpose limited, such state shall be entitled to receive, and shall receive from the United States, an interest per centum per annum, upon so much of the said sum as shall not have been so subscribed, equal to that which would have accrued on the deficiency, had the same been subscribed in trust for the non-subscribing creditors of such state, who are holders of certificates or notes issued on account of services or supplies towards the prosecution of the late war, and the defence of the United States or of some part thereof, to be paid in like manner as the interest on the stock which may be created by virtue of the said loan, and to continue until there shall be a settlement of accounts between the United States and the individual states; and in case a balance shall then appear in favour of such state, until provision shall be made for the said balance" (1 *Stat.* 143–44 [August 4, 1790]).
4. "An Act supplementary to the act making provision for the Debt of the United States" (1 *Stat.* 281–83).
5. In MS "change."

From William Ellery

[*Newport, Rhode Island*] *June 11, 1792.* "I have recd. your Letter inclosing sundry Acts of Congress,[1] and also your Letter of the 30th of the last month [2] respectg. the Brig Chance,[3] and have communicated the same and a State of the case to the Atty. of the District. . . .[4] By a letter from the Comptroller [5] of the 29th. of the last month it appears that I am not yet credited for the Scales & Weights I purchased for the Port of Bristol. Permit me to refer you to my Letter of the 19th. of last March, and to request that you would signify your approbatn of that purchase. . . . Permit me also to renew the wishes expressed in my letters of the 5th of March & 17th of April last for your directs. respecting the tare of Sugar &c.; and to ask for your directs relative to the Thermometer mentioned in my letter of the 9th. of April last."

LC, Newport Historical Society, Newport, Rhode Island.
1. "Treasury Department Circular to the Collectors of the Customs," May 10, 1792.
2. Letter not found.   3. See Ellery to H, April 2, May 21, 1792.
4. William Channing.   5. Oliver Wolcott, Jr.

From William Seton

New York 11th June 1792

My Dear sir

I now enclose you the Bond of Baron Steuben which I took up from Mr. Cutting with his receipt for £506.13 which I paid him.[1] I wished him to be more particular in the receipt, but he said you had already been informed of all the items that composed the Sum. Bank Stock still keeps from 26 to 28 ℔ Cent and therefore have not sold yours, as I am convinced it must rise, at least it ought to rise if People wish to purchase a Stock that will give them good interest for their money.

By the hands of Colo. Walker [2] I received your favour of the 25th May. It was accompanied with a Resolution of the Board of Directors of the Society for establishing Usefull Manufactures that he should negotiate a Loan for Ten thousand Dollars upon a pledge of Publick Stock.[3] Our Board immediately agreed to the Loan and to a charge of 5 ℔ Cent interest, only,—to be charged upon the Sum as drawn out of the Bank. It was taken up upon such a footing as you could have wished, & acceded to with the most earnest wish to promote the beneficial public purpose intended.

In the month of July last year, Mr Pearce the Manufacturer arrived here from Ireland.[4] He brought me Letters from Mr Digges [5] requesting my patronage &c & care of the Modells that he brought. I complied in every sense & receiving afterwards a Letter from the Secretary of State & Mr. Coxe [6] of what importance these Modells were, & directions how to forward them &c, I paid Mr. Pearce's passage & gave him Money to enable him to get to Phia. The modells I sent by my Son in Law Mr Vining.[7] For the Money I advanced to Mr. Pearce, which was 120 Dollars, I took his Note of hand, which I sent to Mr. Coxe [8] as Mr. Jefferson wrote me all charges would be thankfully repaid. However I have never yet been paid & Mr. Cox writes me that Pearces Note to me is in your hands. I take the liberty of Mentioning this, that it may not be forgot, as it was purely pro bono publico that I advanced the Money.

I am with the highest respect & esteem   Dear sir   Your obliged Obed Hbl Servt   Wm Seton

P.S.   your Letter was forwarded by the Packet.

Alexander Hamilton Esq

ALS, Hamilton Papers, Library of Congress.
    1. See Seton to H, May 28, 1792.
    2. Benjamin Walker.
    3. The resolution was dated May 18, 1792 ("Minutes of the S.U.M.," 38).
    4. See "Receipt from William Pearce," August 20, 1791.
    5. See Thomas Digges to H, April 6, 1792.
    6. Tench Coxe, commissioner of the revenue.
    7. On November 24, 1790, Anna Maria Seton was married to John Vining, a member of the House of Representatives from Delaware.
    8. On July 13, 1791, Coxe wrote to Thomas Jefferson: "I had the honor of your note by Mr Pearce and you may rely upon my attention to fix a man who appears of so much importance to the United States. He communicated with me very freely, and finding on my cautioning him about foreign seduction that he had been attacked in that way already at New york I have prevailed on him to deposit his articles at once in the patent office. . . . In consequence you will find enclosed an order, signed by him, to Mr. Seton to deliver the apparatus to such persons as you shall direct" (ALS, Thomas Jefferson Papers, Library of Congress).

Treasury Department Circular
to the Collectors of the Customs

Treasury Department,
June 11, 1792.

Sir,

Some misapprehension having arisen in regard to the provisions concerning Manifests, contained in the 9, 10, 11 and 12th sections of the Collection Law,[1] it becomes proper to enter into certain explanations—to convey the sense and expectations of this Department on the subject.

It occurs, in the first place, that these Manifests are only required, where vessels are owned in whole or part by *Citizens* or *Inhabitants* of the United States.[2] There is therefore, no hardship imposed on persons, who, from situation, are likely to be ignorant of the law.

Secondly. Though nothing is said in either of the above enumerated sections, that would not be satisfied, if the Manifests were *on board*, and ready to be delivered *upon the arrival* of a vessel within *four leagues* of the coast of the United States, whether they were made out at the place of departure, or at sea; yet it is clear, from express words in the 16th section, that they ought to be on board *at the time of the departure* of the vessel from the foreign port or place, at which her cargo was taken in. The general design of the provision, equally with the words alluded to, require this construction.

LS, to Jeremiah Olney, Rhode Island Historical Society, Providence; LC, to Samuel R. Gerry, Essex Institute, Salem, Massachusetts; L[S] (incomplete), to Benjamin Lincoln, RG 36, Collector of Customs at Boston, Letters from the Treasury, 1789–1818, Vol. 5, National Archives; LS, Office of the Secretary, United States Treasury Department; LS, The Andre deCoppet Collection, Princeton University Library; LS, Circulars of the Treasury Department, 1789–1814, Library of Congress; copy, Office of the Secretary, United States Treasury Department; copy, United States Finance Miscellany, Treasury Circulars, Library of Congress; copy, RG 56, Circulars of the Office of the Secretary, "Set T," National Archives.

1. "An Act to provide more effectually for the collection of the duties imposed by law on goods, wares and merchandise imported into the United States, and on the tonnage of ships or vessels" (1 *Stat.* 145–78 [August 4, 1790]).

2. Section 9 of the Collection Law required masters of United States vessels from foreign ports to have manifests of their cargo (1 *Stat.* 155–56).

If, therefore, it appears that no Manifests were on board at the time of the departure of the vessel from the foreign port or place, where her Cargo was taken in, it will become the duty of the officers to enforce the penalties of the act (which are found in the 10 and 12th sections) [3] subject to the powers of mitigation and remission, vested in the Secretary of the Treasury. Here will be room for a liberal attention to the difficulties which are natural to the first execution of new regulations.

The proviso to the 10th section is a further mean of giving an accommodating operation to the regulation; [4] taking care not to defeat the main design. If the Manifests have once been on board, and have been *lost* or *mislaid* without fraud or collusion; if they have been *defaced by accident*, or, if they are *incorrect*, through *mistake*, in each of these cases, the forfeiture is remitted, and the Collector is, in the first instance, the judge.

If any circumstances, therefore, required by the 9th section, are omitted—if any parcels of the cargo should not be included in the Manifests—if, upon the whole, the omission can be fairly ascribed to misapprehension, inadvertence, hurry or mistake, there is latitude to avoid a rigorous enforcing of the provision; and it is incumbent upon the Collector to make reasonable and due allowances, having regard to the usual course of business.

It has been suggested that it is impracticable to comply with some of the requisitions of the 9th section. That which respects the expressing of the marks and numbers of packages, in *words at length*, is particularly mentioned. [5]

On a review of these requisitions, understood as they ought to be, I do not perceive any real impracticability in any of them. That which requires the expression of marks and numbers, in words at length, is the most questionable of any, and it must be confessed, that where the *numbers* are unconnected, and the packages numerous, it might occasion a prolixity which would amount to an incon-

3. Section 10 provided for the forfeiture of the value of goods not included in the manifest; Section 12 provided a maximum penalty of five hundred dollars for failure to produce a manifest (1 *Stat.* 156, 157).

4. For the proviso contained in Section 10, see Charles Lee to H, January 11, 1792, note 2.

5. For Section 9, see Lee to H, January 11, 1792, note 2.

venience; but where the numbers are in succession, the execution
would be both simple and easy.

For example—

    20 Bales of Cotton,

P. S.

No. 1 to 20   +

G. which is the usual mode,

would be easily expressed thus:

    Twenty Bales of Cotton,

P. S.

No. *one* to *twenty*   +

G.

The marks would be expressed in both cases alike; because, on a
reasonable construction, it cannot be intended that marks, consisting
of *letters*, are to be expressed in *words;* still less, that mere characters,
which have no absolute signification, shall be so expressed; as, in the
example given, the +. The terms of every legal provision are to be
taken in a reasonable and practicable sense, and so as not to involve
impossibility or absurdity. If a literal execution be not practicable,
it must be approached as nearly as is practicable, pursuing the general intent, and securing a substantial conformity.

But there are cases, in which a provision, though not strictly impracticable, may be so inconvenient as to demand some degree of
relaxation. And where the question relates to collateral precautions
in Revenue laws, for the security of the Revenue, small deviations
from literal strictness may, with due circumspection, be admitted.
I will only observe that such deviations ought to be really necessary
ones—such, without which the essential course of business might be
disturbed, and oppression ensue—and ought to be as seldom, and as
little as possible.

A question occurs, as to the tenor of the oath prescribed by the
16th section, as it relates to the subject of Manifests. The Master or
Commander of the vessel is, in the cases in which Manifests are required to be on Board, to deliver them to the Collector to whom he
makes Report,—and to declare to the truth of them "as they ought
to be in conformity to the directions of the act."

It is to be observed that the precise form of the oath is not prescribed in the law—and is, therefore, left to be devised by those who are to administer it. It is of course to be so framed as to include whatever is directed to be included in it, and no more; but where general terms are used, the *particulars* which they appear, from the law, to be intended to comprise may be substituted. It would be dangerous, and might lead to unintentional perjury, to oblige a Master or Commander to swear that the Manifests, which he delivers, are, "as they *ought* to be, in *conformity* to the directions of the Act."

The declaration ought, therefore, to express, in *substance*, that the Manifests, produced and delivered, "contain a true, just and particular account of the cargo, which was on board the vessel at the time of her departure from the foreign port, (naming it) from which she *last* sailed for the United States, and that all matters and particulars, therein expressed, are true." What these particulars *ought* to be must be determined by the directions of the 9th section.

The evidence on which the law appears to rely, as to the fact of the Manifests being on Board at the foreign port of departure, is their being *ready* to be delivered, *upon demand*, at any time after the vessel arrives within *four leagues* of the Coast of the United States.

This, however, would not exclude the admission of other evidence, if there should be any other.

It is observable, that the Act speaks of one or *more* Manifests, in reference to the *same* vessel. This is to give greater scope to conform to circumstances. A part of the Cargo may be taken in at one port, and a Manifest made out there; another part, at another port, and another Manifest made out there. Or a Master may have supposed her loading complete, and prepared his Manifest, and he may afterwards take in other articles, and have to make a supplementary one—or there may be reasons of commerce for not including all the Cargo in one Manifest.

This regulation concerning Manifests is considered as of real importance to the Revenue. It will tend, by early ascertaining the true condition of vessels, to prevent plans for smuggling being concerted, after their arrival within the United States, and will be a considerable restraint upon the use of opportunities, which may present between the time of arrival upon the coast, and the final entry at the port of destination.

It is, therefore, expected that careful attention will be paid every where to its observance; with the qualifications, which have been indicated, to avoid any thing that might justly be deemed a grievance.

If the Merchants are made sensible that a compliance is expected, (and pains should be taken to inform them of what is expected) they can, without inconvenience, cause it to be effected by proper instructions to their Masters and Correspondents. A Manifest can surely be as well made out before the departure, as after the arrival of a vessel,—inaccuracies, in both cases, are to be expected, and due allowances made for them.

The 16th section of the Collection Law, considers the report of the Master as a distinct thing from the rendering of a Manifest.[6] But in every case the Manifest *may* constitute the principal part of the report, which may be annexed to the Manifest, with a reference to it; specifying such other particulars, required to be in the report, as may not be expressed in the Manifest. This will be a perfect compliance with the provision, and will save trouble.

With great consideration, I am, Sir, Your obedient Servant,

A Hamilton

6. The master of a vessel coming from a foreign port was required by Section 16 to make a report of his cargo within forty-eight hours and to deliver the manifest or manifests at the time of the report (1 *Stat.* 158–59).

From William Webb [1]

[*Bath, District of Maine, June 11, 1792.* On June 24, 1792, Hamilton wrote to Webb: "Your letter of the 11th instant was duly received." *Letter not found.*]

1. Webb was collector of customs at Bath, District of Maine.

To Thomas Willing

Treasury Department June 11th 1792

Sir

I have the honor to enclose for the *consideration* of the Board of Directors, the draft of an Agreement, for carrying into execution the

Eleventh Section of the Act, which incorporates the subscribers to the Bank of the united States.[1]

They will perceive that it is substantially in conformity to the suggestions, contained in your letter of the 29th of last month.[2] As far as there may be any difference in the manner, it is for the sake of pursuing with greater caution the letter of the law; which speaks of "*a subscription.*"

with respectful consideration   I have the honor to be   Sir   Your obedt Servt   Alexander Hamilton

P.S.   If any alterations appear proper The Board will please to suggest them.[3]

Thomas Willing Esqr
President of the Bank
of the United States

LS, RG 316, Letters donated by John D. Rockefeller, Jr., August, 1955, National Archives.
    1. For the provisions made by Section 11 of this act, see George Washington to H, May 9, 1792, note 1.
    2. Letter not found.
    3. The postscript is in the handwriting of H.

To William Seton

[*Philadelphia, June 12, 1792.* On June 25, 1792, Seton wrote to Hamilton: "I have made a long delay in answering your favours of the 12th. & 19th." *Letter of June 12 not found.*]

From Abishai Thomas

Philadelphia June 12th. 1792.

Sir

As Agent of the State of North Carolina I subscribed on Account of the loan to the United States proposed by Act of Congress of the 4th of August 1790 a Certificate or Receipt of James Green junr. late Treasurer of Loans in said State,[1] for 96,300 dollars of the emissions of May 20, 1777, and April 11th. 1778.[2] which had been deposited in his hands to be exchanged, which Certificate the Auditor[3] and Comptroler[4] have not admitted to be funded; I consider it therefore my duty to appeal to your decision, and to give you a concise statement of the transaction so as to place the business before you in its proper point of view. Mr. Green gave small Certificates to individuals for sums of money of the aforesaid emissions, which they brought in to be exchanged, pursuant to acts of Congress of the 2d. Jany. & 2d. July 1779.[5] these Certificates were taken up by the District Treasurers of North Carolina, whereby the state became the Assignee of the individuals. The treasurers on settlement of their Accounts with the Legislature deposited them in the hands of the Chairman of the Committee with whom they settled, and the Chairman by order of the General Assembly[6] delivered them to Mr. Green who gave one receipt for the whole amount, a duplicate of which is herewith sent. Now Sir, had the State kept possession of the original Certificates no difficulty would have occurred in the business, and I profess I see no just ground why there should as it now stands, for had the state been reimbursed in other money, or had She reclaimed and again received the Original Certificates, surely Mr. Green would have cancelled his receipt; upon the whole I am decidedly of opinion, that neither the one or the other ever did happen, that changing the face did not alter the nature of the obligation, and to sum up the whole, that the State of North Carolina has as indubitable a right to fund this paper as any other Certificate or evidence of public debt whatever, which is respectfully submitted, and your decision is respectfully solicited prior to the 16th. Inst.

I have the Honor &c. Ab. Thomas

Copy, North Carolina Department of Archives and History, Raleigh.

1. Thomas is referring to Green's position as commissioner of the Continental loan office in North Carolina, an office which he assumed on December 24, 1777 (Clark, *State Records of North Carolina*, XIII, 72). In North Carolina the Continental loan officer was often referred to as "Treasurer of Loans."

2. Section 3 of "An Act making provision for the (payment of the) Debt of the United States" included among the certificates which would be accepted in payment of subscriptions to the new Federal loans "Those issued by the commissioners of loans in the several states, including certificates given pursuant to the act of Congress of the second of January, one thousand seven hundred and seventy-nine, for bills of credit of the several emissions of the twentieth of May, one thousand seven hundred and seventy-seven, and the eleventh of April, one thousand seven hundred and seventy-eight" (1 *Stat.* 139 [August 4, 1790]).

3. Richard Harrison.
4. Oliver Wolcott, Jr.
5. See William Skinner to H, August 11, 1791, note 5. For the extension of time granted to North Carolina by Congress, see *JCC*, XIV, 795-96.
6. No resolution of the North Carolina House of Commons which clearly fits this description has been found. Under a resolution of October 20, 1779, however, Green redeemed the indents for "April and May money" then in the North Carolina treasury, and on Februry 12, 1781, the North Carolina House of Commons resolved that the indents for "April and May money" then in the hands of the state auditors should "be delivered by the Auditors to the Board of Trade the Better to enable them to supply our Delegates in Congress" (Clark, *State Records of North Carolina*, XII, 835; XVII, 782-83).

To Benjamin Lincoln

Treasury Department
June 13 1792.

Sir

⟨It appears by⟩ [1] a letter which I have received from ⟨the Collector of Bermuda⟩ Hundred [2] that Captain Silas ⟨Dogget, of the Ship George⟩ of Boston on clearing at his Office for a ⟨foreign port⟩ (Ostend) in May 1791, delivered up a trading license, issued at Boston, which, it is stated, was immediately transmitted to you, and a certificate of the delivery granted to Dogget. From Ostend the Captain returned to Boston; and being about to depart from thence to the District of Bermuda Hundred, he asked Mr Rice [3] for the trading license, which he had delivered up at Bermuda Hundred, and which, being found, *and not cancelled*, was given to him without his paying the Tonnage Duty; and that this identical license was again delivered up by the said Captain, on his clearing for Cadiz.

I communicate the circumstance to you, as the transaction was doubtless irregular; [4] the redelivery of the license, after a foreign voyage, being against the express letter of the law.[5]

Benjamin Lincoln Esqr.
Boston

L[S], RG 36, Collector of Customs at Boston, Letters from the Treasury and Others, 1789-1809, Vol. 1, National Archives; LC, RG 56, Letters to Collectors at Small Ports, "Set G," National Archives; copy, RG 56, Letters to the Collector at Boston, National Archives.

1. The material within broken brackets has been taken from the letter book copy.
2. No letter from William Heth concerning this problem has been found.
3. John Rice was deputy collector of customs at Boston.
4. The words "the transaction was doubtless irregular" are in the handwriting of H.
5. Section 30 of "An Act for Registering and Cleaning Vessels, Regulating the Coasting Trade, and for other purposes" reads in part as follows: "That if any ship or vessel having a license to trade or fish, for one year, shall within that time be destined to any foreign port, the master or commander of every such ship or vessel shall, before he departs from the United States, deliver such license to the collector of the port from whence he intends to depart; and it shall be the duty of such collector forthwith to transmit the license to him so delivered, to the collector of the district where the same was granted, who shall thereupon cancel every license . . ." (1 Stat. 63 [September 1, 1789]).

From Oliver Wolcott, Junior [1]

T. D
C. Off June 13. 1792

Sir,

The paper referred to by Abishai Thomas Esq. in his Letter dated the 12th instant, is merely a Rect. signed "*James Green Jr. Treas. Loan Office*" for a number of *indented Certificates* supposed to be then issued in pursuance of the resolutions of Congress of the 2d. of January & 2nd. of July 1779 in favour of a Chairman of a Committee of Accounts in North Carolina. The Rect. was given by Mr. Green, by order of the *General Assembly* for a deposit in his hands untill *further orders*. The manner in which the Rect. is expressed, and the character & office assumed by Mr. Green at the time of this transaction, evidently shew that he acted in the capacity of a *State* Officer.[2] This opinion is confirmed by the circumstance that no Credit has been passed for the deposit in question in Mr. Greens accounts as Commr. of Loans. There has not been the least evidence adduced that the indented Certificates were ever cancelled—the contrary is fairly to be inferred from the tenor of the Rect.—consequently if Mr. Thomas' claim should be admitted, the United States would be twice charged with the same debt.

It may also be observed that James Green had no authority to pass a Rect. which should be obligatury upon the United States as a debt; and if the contrary were true, still this Rect. could not be recd. on Loan as it answers none of the descriptions of evidences of debt, mentioned in the Act of Congress passed on the 4th of August 1790.[3]

It is my present opinion that the United States are in no respect bound by the rect. in question, but in case they are in any way affected, the operation of the Rect. ought to be determined by the Commrs. who are to settle the Accounts of the States with the United States.

I am &c

Hon
A H

ADf, Connecticut Historical Society, Hartford.
1. For background to this letter, see Abishai Thomas to H, June 12, 1792.
2. James Green had been one of the commissioners to receive state bills of credit in 1780.
3. For Section 3 of "An Act making provision for the (payment of the) Debt of the United States" (1 *Stat.* 138–44 [August 4, 1790]), to which Wolcott is referring, see Nathaniel Appleton to H, February 5, 1791, note 1.

To Abishai Thomas

Treasury department June 13th 1792
Sir

I referred your Letter of the 12th inst. to the Comptroller of the Treasury for the purpose of receiving from him the requsite information.

A copy of his answer [1] is inclosed.

I am clearly of opinion that the Certificate or receipt, in question, was inadmissible on the loan proposed by the Act of Congress, to which you refer.

With much consideration   I remain Sir   Your obedient servant
Alex Hamilton
Ab. Thomas Esquire
Agent for the State of N. Carolina

Copy, North Carolina Department of Archives and History, Raleigh.
1. See Oliver Wolcott, Jr., to H, June 13, 1792.

To William Gardner [1]

Philadelphia, June 14, 1792

Sir,

The Comptroller [2] has intimated to me that there are some expressions in a letter from you to him, indicating some disposition to resign, in consequence of the insufficiency of your compensation. The manner in which you have executed the duties of your office, has been so entirely satisfactory to me, that I shall regret your resignation not a little, and under this impression I am induced to recommend to you to wait the issue of another session. In a report which I made to Congress during the last session, I proposed an increase of your emoluments,[3] and I believe if it had not been for the lateness of the session, when the impatience of Individuals to get home, produced a disposition favorable to objections which tended to prevent the entering upon new business, an additional provision would have been made. The trust of a Commissioner of Loans is so very delicate and important, that it is impossible it can be long left in any state, without such a compensation as will secure a *worthy* and *adequate character* in the execution of it.

With much esteem, I am,   Your obedient servant,   A. Hamilton.

Wm. Gardner, Esq.

[New York] *Argus. Greenleaf's New Daily Advertiser*, July 31, 1798.

1. Gardner was appointed commissioner of loans for New Hampshire in December, 1790. In June, 1798, he was dismissed and replaced by John Pierce. In a letter dated July 13, 1798, addressed "To the impartial Public" and originally published in *The* [Portsmouth, New Hampshire] *Oracle of the Day*, Gardner attempted to vindicate his administration of the loan office. He stated that his term in office had been continued only at the special request of the Federal Government and for its convenience. Gardner also quoted part of the correspondence which he had carried on with the Treasury Department, including the letter from H printed above.

2. Oliver Wolcott, Jr.

3. See "Report on the Petitions of Jabez Bowen and William Gardner," February 29, 1792.

From Robert Purviance [1]

[*Baltimore, Maryland, June 14, 1792.* "The 21st. of last month, I was informed by three reputable Merchants of this place, that there had been landed from on board the Sloop Ceres, Jno. T. Child, Master, from district of New Port, a quantity of Rum, part of which was said to be West India, and that they had cause to believe that the same was Rum distilled within the United States. . . . I was fully convinced of the deception, and accordingly directed the Inspector to make a seizure of the whole of the rum under that description, and likewise to proceed without loss of time to seize on the Sloop. . . ." *Letter not found.*]

Extract, Maryland Historical Society, Baltimore.
1. Purviance was naval officer at Baltimore. For background to this letter, see Jeremiah Olney to H, May 31, 1792, note 2.
On June 4, 1792, Tench Coxe, in a letter to George Gale, supervisor of the revenue for the District of Maryland, marked "Confidential," wrote:
"A Communication has been made from Providence Rhode Island, relative to the Seizure of a parcel of Rum belonging to Messrs. Clarke Nightingale and Bowen, alleged to be Spirits distilled in the United States which has paid duty altho it is in Casks marked as containing foreign Rum and accompanied with certificates for foreign Rum. It is proper that you be confidentially informed that Mr. Bowen who goes on to Baltimore has admitted that and declared to the Secretary that the Spirits are of the distillation of the United States and that he alleges the duty has been paid.
"On this Case two points occur. In the first place, the claimants will have to prove the payment of the Excise, and the greatest care will be requisite in regard to the proofs of the identity of the rum seized and of that which they shall prove to have paid the duty. . . . Should the Claimants prove this to be American rum, which has paid the duty and which may afterwards have been shifted with mercantile Views only the penalty . . . of five hundred Dollars will be incurred for 'making use' of 'false' and 'untrue' Certificates.
"There has appeared in the course of this Business some disposition to take the ground of the Casks, certificates, and spirits being conformable, and to trust to the Jury's deciding on the quality of the Spirits, which (it seemed to be confided) is such as would prevent an unfavorable Verdi[c]t. This is intimated to put you on your guard. Should any such attempt be made you can rely on the Fact that the Spirits were distilled in the United States.
"It is not known whether this Seizure has taken place in the department of the Customs or the internal Revenue. If it should prove to be the former, a confidential communication of this letter will be necessary to General [Otho H.] Williams—as also to his or your Council." (LC, RG 58, Letters of Commissioner of Revenue, 1792–1793, National Archives.)

To William Short

Treasury Department
June 14 1792

Sir,

Your two letters of the 26th of January and 24th of March have come to hand since mine to you of the 7th of May.

For an answer to the first I believe I need do nothing more than refer you to former communications. On the latter some observations arise.

You will consider any suggestions which you may find in my letters concerning a rule for adjusting the value of the payments to France rather as hints than instructions. I must however repeat my wish that the point may be now settled. If left for future liquidation and brought to the seat of our Government considerations may be pressed which may embarrass a proper adjustment of the matter; though foreign to those which ought really to govern in such a case. There can be no juncture more favorable than the present for placing the affair upon an eligible footing.

The management of this matter as well as of every other which may concern the reimbursement to France remains with you. If in complicance with official usages, Mr. Morris's[1] instrumentality should be requisite, he will be instructed to co operate.

I shall learn with pleasure that the operation which you were meditating with Boyed and Keir has been carried into execution.[2]

That which you State as the only objection to it would not under the existing circumstances be of much weight. The pecuniary ability too of the parties and their connections would be a material security against some of the principal inconveniences, which were to be apprehended from the accumulation in question. And by creating *another* monied combination interested in the funds of the Country, it may even in some aspects, tend to render its credit less dependent on the speculations and resources of a small number of Individuals.

It will however be a very valuable ingredient in the arrangement, if it shall embrace an adjustment of the Indemnification to France for the depreciation of the Assignats. You will perceive that I am solicitous this point should in no event remain undetermined.

Your anxiety on the subject which closes your letter is natural but not necessary.[3] The situation you have been in is properly appreciated and that of your sucessor will be so likewise. You need not apprehend misconstruction either on the part of the Government or of the Community.

Accept my thanks for the continuance of your attention to the course of the Baltic Navigation,[4] and believe me always to be with sentiments of real consideration & esteem   Sir   Your obedt. Servant

Alexander Hamilton

William Short Esqr
Minister Resident
from the United States at the Hague

LS, William Short Papers, Library of Congress.
   1. Gouverneur Morris, recently appointed United States Minister Plenipotentiary to France, had arrived in Paris on May 6, 1792, to replace Short.
   2. See Short to H, March 24, May 14, 1792.
   3. See Short to H, March 24, 1792.
   4. See Short to H, December 30, 1791.

From Abishai Thomas [1]

Philadelphia 14 June 1792

Sir

I have duly considered your letter of the 13th with the Comptroller's answer to your reference to him of my letter to you of the 12th Inst.

The certificate or receipt in question *is in fact* what the Comptroller has only "supposed" it to be as may be fairly inferred from the face of the paper itself. The deposit being made *"until further orders"* does not in my opinion destroy the validity of the receipt, because nothing is adduced to shew that such further orders were issued and I am clearly of opinion such never were.

The idea suggested by the Comptroller that Mr. Green *"acted in the capacity* of a State *Officer"* is new to me, and I confess I cannot see any ground for that position. That he was an Officer of the United States at the time of this transaction is evident; indeed his signature and title affixed to the paper contended for is demonstrative of this, and the Treasury department have admitted the fact, by receiving on loan all other Certifica⟨tes⟩ issued by him, of the same description with those for which this receipt was given; which were presented for that purpose. Besides the State never had such an Officer, that came to my knowledge, and I believe if such had been established, I should have known it.

Mr. Green having died previous to the settlement of his accounts as Loan Officer, it is probable that no person can now explain fully the transaction, and as I have been informed his accounts are defective in other instances, I see no just cause why this should be selected as an article to be rejected for want of the formality of an item that such a deposit was made and that a corresponding credit existed to the State of North Carolina. Whether *"the indented Certificates were ever cancelled"* is a matter I cannot directly ascertain, but I conceive it improbable that they should again be put in circulation, no person had authority to withdraw them from the hands of Mr. Green except by order of the General Assembly, and if he held them uncancelled subject to such orders. It is probable they were destroyed among other papers which were buried to prevent their falling into the hands of the enemy.

It being obvious that Mr. Green was not a *state* officer, it follows that the United States are bound by his official acts, and the Comptroller's observation, that he *"had no authority to pass a receipt which should be obligatory upon the United States,"* is in my opinion a position untenable. The Comptroller himself has admitted the contrary by receiving on loan certificates signed by Mr. Green as before recited.

It is true that the paper in question does not literally "answer" any "of the descriptions of evidences of debt mentioned in the act of Congress passed on the 4th August 1790," but it is an acknowledgment of a deposit in the hands of an Officer of the United States of Certificates which *literally* do answer one of the descriptions recited in said act, as such I have claimed a right to fund it in behalf of the State of North Carolina. As such I yet hold the opinion that it ought to be received, and notwithstanding your having once decided against me, I have a presentiment that on giving the subject a candid discussion you will adopt my side of the question.

I have the honor to be,   Sir   Yr. obt. Servant   A. Thomas

Secretary of the Treasury

Copy, North Carolina Department of Archives and History, Raleigh.
1. Thomas did not send this letter to H on June 14, 1792. According to his report to the North Carolina legislature on November 22, 1792, Thomas "on reconsidering the matter thought it advisable to withold it until proper means were employed to ascertain whether the certificates in question might not yet remain uncancelled among the documents of the deceased Mr. Green, or if cancelled the documents might have been preserved which would ascertain the fact—or if the State had again reclaimed and got possession of the Certificates deposited, according to the right reserved, something might there be found to establish that position. The papers transmitted to the Treasury department by the representation of Mr. Green for the settlement of his Accounts as Loan Officer have been resorted to, nothing appears in them to throw any light on the transaction, and if documents cannot be procured by the interference of the legislature to place it in a proper point of view, the Agent is not without serious apprehensions that this sum will be lost to the State. The idea suggested by the Comptroller of the Treasury of submitting it to the decision of the Commissioners among our old claims, is incompatible with the opinion of the Agent whilst any other hope remains, and the Honorable the General Assembly may be assured that nothing within his power will be wanting to establish it on the ground he now holds" (ADS, North Carolina Department of Archives and History, Raleigh).
   A resolution passed by the North Carolina legislature at the end of December, 1792, reads as follows: "Resolved, That the agent, continue his exertions to have funded, the certificates of James Green Esqr. it being the clear and decided opinion of this General Assembly; that the validity of the debt is not destroyed, by the property being in the State" (DS, North Carolina Department of Archives and History, Raleigh).

To Jeremiah Wadsworth

Philadelphia June 14
1792

Dr Sir
   I sent you some days since the statement of monies received by me on account of Mr Church [1] & shall be glad to know it got safe to hand and has answered your purpose. It was as perfect as I could make it.
   Yrs truly   A Hamilton

J Wadsworth Esq

ALS, Connecticut Historical Society, Hartford.
1. John B. Church, an Englishman who had married Elizabeth Hamilton's

sister Angelica, and Wadsworth had been partners during the American Revolution and for some years after the peace. H was Church's attorney and business representative in this country.

To Lewis F. Delesdernier

Treasury Department
June 15. 1792.

Sir

I find by a remark, subjoined to one of your accounts, that you leave the monies, falling due on Bonds, in the hands of the Obligors, until a safe opportunity offers for Boston. This practice being against the express letter of the law must be forborn in future. It involves a responsibility, on your part, in as much as motives of safety would less exonerate you in cases where parties [1] should fail in their payments, after indulgence had been granted by you, than in a plain case of theft or robbery.

I conceive the safest mode of securing the public money would be to provide a small iron chest, which might be fastened to the floor; and if one that will answer the purpose can be procured upon reasonable terms I shall have no objection to the expence.

I am, Sir,　Your Obed Servant

Lewis F Delesdernier Esqr
Collector Passamaquody.

L[S], RG 36, Collector of Customs at Boston, Letters from the Treasury, 1789–1807, Vol. 4, National Archives.
1. The word "parties" is in the handwriting of H.

To John Langdon [1]

[*Philadelphia, June 18, 1792.* On June 28, 1792, Langdon wrote to Hamilton: "I was honor'd with your favor of the 18th. Inst. by post." *Letter not found.*]

1. Langdon was a New Hampshire merchant and United States Senator.

From Tobias Lear

[*Philadelphia*] *June 18, 1792.* Transmits "a letter from John Ritchie, Inspector of the 2d division in Maryland, to the President."

LC, George Washington Papers, Library of Congress.

To Otho H. Williams

Treasury Department
June 18. 1792.

Sir

I have this day decided upon the two cases of Zacharie Coopman and Company,[1] on behalf of Mr. Nichols, and of John Stump. In both I have remitted the interest of all parties, Upon the petitioner's paying for all actual and necessary disbursements. Duplicates of my decision go, by the mail of this day, to the Clerk of the District Court, at Baltimore.

I am, Sir, with consideration,   Your Obedt Servant   A Hamilton

Otho H Williams Esqr.
Baltimore.

LS, Columbia University Libraries.
    1. For a description of this Baltimore shipping firm and William's difficulties with it, see Williams to H, January 23, 1792.

To Otho H. Williams

Treasury Department
June 18th. 1792.

Sir

The Commissioner of the Revenue [1] has laid before me copies of three letters, one of the 3rd. of May from you to the Surveyor of

LS, Columbia University Libraries; copy, Maryland Historical Society, Baltimore.
    1. Tench Coxe.

Baltimore,[2] another of the 9th of May from him to you, and a third of the 7th of June from him, in capacity of Inspector of the Revenue for the port of Baltimore, to the Supervisor,[3] communicating the correspondence between you and him and stating certain embarrassments which had ensued in consequence of the opinion that the Inspectors of the Customs are not bound to perform the duty which has been assigned to them in relation to distilled Spirits.[4]

It is matter of regret that such a question has been pressed so far. It cannot certainly tend to the advancement of the public service to find its operations interrupted by a controversy between the officers respecting the limits of duty. It cannot promote the contentment of the Merchants with the laws of the Country if they are left to suffer in a manner, which they must ascribe either to want of proper arrangements, or to the deliberate non-execution of them. It cannot serve to impress respect for the authority of the Government, when it is understood that its immediate officers decline or evade a compliance with instructions, which have proceeded from the head of the proper department. It was to have been expected, that if doubts were entertained of the legality or propriety of those instructions, or of their true intent, these would have been first made known, by a representation of them to the source from which the instructions proceeded, not by hesitations in the execution, tending to embarrass the public source.

The appearance of the question has naturally led to a reconsideration of the grounds of the arrangements. The result is a confirmed conviction that it was right in its origin and ought to be carried into execution.

Three leading considerations led to it—one that where duties are closely allied and can be conveniently performed by the same

2. Robert Ballard was appointed surveyor of the customs at Baltimore on August 4, 1789, and inspector of the revenue for the port of Baltimore on March 8, 1792.

3. George Gale was supervisor of the revenue for the District of Maryland.

4. The "duty" of the inspectors "in relation to distilled Spirits" is described in "An Act repealing, after the last day of June next, the duties heretofore laid upon Distilled Spirits imported from abroad, and laying others in their stead; and also upon Spirits distilled within the United States, and for appropriating the same" (1 *Stat.* 199–214 [March 3, 1791]) and in "An Act concerning the Duties on Spirits distilled within the United States" (1 *Stat.* 267–71 [May 8, 1792]). See also the enclosure to "Treasury Department Circular to the Collectors of the Customs," May 26, 1791.

persons, it is most conductive to simplicity and order, that they should be so performed—another that the union of them would serve to avoid an unnecessary multiplication of officers—and a third that it was favorable to œconomy. Either none or smaller compensations for the new services would be requisite to persons who were previously in public employ and pay; and whose functions had an immediate connexion with the new ones to be executed.

Some if not all these considerations may be presumed to have influenced the Legislature in making special provision for constituting officers of the Customs, officers of Inspection, in cases in which it should be deemed adviseable.[5] The arrangement in question has therefore the recommendation of being conformable to this intimation of the Legislative sense.

No possibility of an interference of duties could operate as an objection to it. In general, it might be easily practicable to the ordinary inspectors of the Customs to perform the service; and if there are cases, in which from an extraordinary press of business, or other peculiar circumstances, the contrary happens, the remedy is an *occasional* and *temporary* appointment of *other* Inspectors. Their number is in the discretion of the Collector and their compensation being per diem, their appointments may be so likewise.

For the same reason (if the restriction in the Act concerning distilled spirits, as to the Article of expence, had not imposed a necessity of strict œconomy) [6] it could not have appeared a hardship on the Inspectors of the Customs to be required to perform the accessory duties which have been allotted to them. The law evidently contemplates a dollar and a quarter per day [7] as an adequate com-

5. The act of March 3, 1791, authorized the President "to appoint, with the advice and consent of the Senate, a supervisor to each district, and as many inspectors to each survey therein as he shall judge necessary." He was also authorized "in his discretion to appoint, such and so many officers of the customs to be inspectors in any survey of inspection as he shall deem advisable to employ in the execution of this act" (1 *Stat.* 200).

6. Section 58 of the act of March 3, 1791, placed a ceiling on the compensation paid to revenue officers. Total compensation could not exceed "seven per cent. of the whole product of the duties arising from the spirits distilled within the United States: . . . [provided] That such allowance shall not exceed the annual amount of forty-five thousand dollars, until the same shall be further ascertained by law" (1 *Stat.* 213).

7. Section 53 of "An Act to provide more effectually for the collection of the duties imposed by law on goods, wares and merchandise imported into the United States, and on the tonnage of ships or vessels" provided in part:

pensation for the services of those officers, and doubtless supposes that they are to be fully occupied. In every instance in which the time of employment might be prolonged, it would involve the advantage of additional compensation for the additional time.

It is to be observed that there is no precise delineation of the duty of an Inspector. It was clearly intended that he should perform all those lesser details which could not with convenience be enumerated; regulating himself by the directions of the Surveyor; who is himself under the direction of the Collector. There being no line drawn, there is the less room to say that this or that duty is not within the sphere of the office. Services analogous to those which constitute the general tenor of the duties of the officer may fairly be supposed to be of right demandable of him. And where they are not unduly burthensome, there is no just ground for complaint. It cannot therefore under all the circumstances of the case be admitted that the services required in the present instance are not legally obligatory on the Inspectors.

But if they were not, it would be incumbent upon them in point of general official propriety to acquiesce. And their not doing it would be a good reason for substituting others, who are better disposed.

Critical nicety about the boundaries of official duty (except where the rights of third persons are concerned) can only serve to embarrass the movements of Government. A spirit of refinement in this particular—a habit of recurring to the specific cases of duty defined in the laws to decide whether this or that instruction is to be executed would quickly clog the wheels of the public administration and throw it into disorder. There is a large chapter of undefined relative duties which appertain to every officer in every station. And the best general rule certainly is for each in his sphere to give all possible facility to the course of public business.

The door is always open to candid representation and discussion, where anything is required, which an officer may suppose to bear hard upon him whether it respect the quantum of compensation, the quantum of duty or any other matter. If any thing unreasonable

---

"To each inspector there shall be allowed for every day he shall be actually employed in aid of the customs, a sum not exceeding one dollar and twenty-five cents . . ." (1 Stat. 172 [August 4, 1790]).

is exacted and persevered in, an appeal lies to the highest authority, and if redress is not found there, the path is plain. The right course cannot be to give an example of disorder, by beginning with a non compliance with instructions.

If, as may have been the case, the mode of expression used, in the general instructions,[8] has led to a misapprehension of my meaning, what I have now said will remove the ambiguity. And I have the fullest reliance, that you will interpose with decision to cause the Inspectors of the Customs to perform the services, which have been required of them, in aid of the Inspectors of the Revenue, for the ports within your district.

With great consideration and esteem   I am   Sir   Your Obedient Servant   Alexander Hamilton

Otho H. Williams Esqr.
Collector, Baltimore.

8. See Section 2 and Section 8 of the enclosure to "Treasury Department Circular to the Collectors of the Customs," May 26, 1791.

From Jeremiah Olney

Custom-House,
Providence 19th June 1792.

Sir.

I have received your circular Letter of the 4th Instant. I will endeavor to comply with your Instructions in estimating the value of ad Valorem Goods which may be imported into this District from France; but I foresee difficulties in practicing the Third criterion, preferred by you, which appears to me essentially to involve the Fourth; for to ascertain the Prices of similar Articles prior to the Revolution, it will be absolutely necessary that they should be *seen* and *appraised* by competent Judges, the qualities of almost every Article being so various: this will be tedious, and expensive to the Consignees; and attended with considerable inconveniences and Loss in cases where the Goods especially if Glass or crockery Ware, are destined, not in the same Vessels, to other Ports or Places. You have Sir, decided so possitively against the First criterion, that without different directions, I shall never practice it; but the Second, requiring only a knowledge of foreign exchange, which may be always easily obtained, I cannot help wishing may yet be approved of by you as the principal, if not the sole, mode of estimating the value of Goods imported from France, and accompanied with Invoices. This would greatly facilitate the Business; and I imagine, would not be productive of Injury, either to the public or individuals, sufficient to counterbalance the inconveniences attending the practice of the Third criterion.

There have been Three or Four Enrolments, granted by me, transmitted from this Office, without a hole cut thro the name of the Collector, which was designedly omitted, in consequence of your circular Letter of the 2nd of Jany. last, in which the word *Enrolment* was not mentioned, tho' in every instance inserted in that of the 21st of September. However Sir, it shall not be omitted in future. The circumstance of the stolen Register shall be attended to.[1] I have the Honor to be &c.   Jereh. Olney Collr.

A. Hamilton Esquire
Secretary of the Treasury.

ADfS, Rhode Island Historical Society, Providence.
1. See "Treasury Department Circular to the Collectors of the Customs," June 4, 1792.

To William Seton

[*Philadelphia, June 19, 1792.* On June 25, 1792, Seton wrote to Hamilton: "I have made a long delay in answering your favours of the 12th & 19th." *Letter of June 19 not found.*]

To George Washington

Treasury Department, June 19, 1792. "The Secretary of the Treasury has the honor to submit to the President of the Ud. States a provisional Contract entered into between the Superintendent of the Delaware Lighthouse [1] and Abraham Hargis [2] for sinking a Well for the accomodation of that Light house. . . . The Secretary has delayed this communication under an impression that the allowance was excessive, and with a hope that something better might be done: but reputable workmen who have been consulted appear to be of opinion that the charge is not unreasonable, and no other person has been found disposed to undertake at a lower rate. . . ."

LC, George Washington Papers, Library of Congress.
   1. William Allibone. See Tench Coxe to H, May 25, 1792.
   2. Hargis was keeper of the Delaware lighthouse.

["C"] [1]

[Philadelphia, June 20, 1792]

[Philadelphia] *Gazette of the United States*, June 20, 1792.
   1. Philip Marsh has written: "On June 20th of the same year, when Hamilton, aroused by the attacks in Philip Freneau's *National Gazette*, was admittedly on the point of exposing the 'plot' to subvert the Constitution led, as he thought, by Jefferson, a strong indictment of that newspaper and its supporters as 'a faction,' signed 'C.,' appeared in Hamilton's favorite organ and in his style" ("Hamilton's Neglected Essays, 1791–1793," *The New-York Historical Society Quarterly*, XXXII [October, 1948], 289). No other evidence concerning H's authorship of this letter to the *Gazette* has been found

From Edward Carrington

Supervisors Office Dist. of Virga.
Richmond June 20, 1792

Sir
   By last post I received an Answer from Colo. Newton[1] to my enquiries concerning a successor to Mr. Wells[2] at Smithfield. He says that Mr. Copeland Parker is under the Character of an industrious attentive Man, and he thinks as proper a person for the Offices of Inspector & Surveyor as any to be engaged there. He also informs me that Colo. Lindsay has appointed him to Act during the vacancy. I have no kind of acquaintance with Mr. Parker, but suppose these recommendations as satisfactory as can be expected for that post.
   I have the Honor to be with the greatest respect &c.   Your Most ob sr.   Ed. Carrington
                                                    Supervisor D V.
Alexander Hamilton Esq.

ALS, George Washington Papers, Library of Congress.
1. Thomas Newton, Jr., was inspector of Survey No. 4 in Virginia.
2. James Wells. See William Lindsay to H, May 20, 1792; Josiah Parker to H, May 11, 1792; Carrington to H, May 17, 1792.

From Tench Coxe

Treasury Department, Revenue Office, June 20, 1792. Transmits "for the purpose of submission to the President a contract entered into between the Superintendent of the Delaware light House, piers &c. and Thomas Davis and Thomas Connaroe junior,[1] for the replacing of one of the piers which formed the harbour near Mud Island, which pier was carried away by the Ice at the Breaking up of the River Delaware in the last Spring." [2] Reports on reasons for high cost of repairing pier.

LC, RG 58, Letters of Commissioner of Revenue, 1792–1793, National Archives.
1. A copy of this contract may be found in RG 26, Lighthouse Deeds and Contracts, National Archives.
2. See William Allibone to H, March 13, 16, 1792.

To Thomas FitzSimons [1]

[Philadelphia, June 20, 1792]

Dear Sir

I return you Mr. Holkers [2] papers with the result of the examination which has been made by my direction.[3] As the thing at present appears to me I see no chance for Mr. Holker but in the final winding up of the arrangements concerning the public debt, when the existence or non existence of the certificates will be ascertained.

Yrs. with great esteem & regard　　　　　　　　A Hamilton

June 20
Thomas Fitsimmons Esq

ALS, RG 217, Segregated Documents, "Famous Names," Hamilton, National Archives.
1. FitzSimons was a member of the House of Representatives from Pennsylvania.
2. John Holker, a former inspector general of manufacturers in France, came to the United States in June, 1778. As marine agent of France in the United States, he purchased provisions for the French fleet and garrison at Santo Domingo. Although Holker is referred to as "consul of the King" as

early as 1779, his commission from France as consul general in New York, New Jersey, Pennsylvania, and Delaware was not forwarded to Congress until September 10, 1781 (Wharton, *Revolutionary Diplomatic Correspondence*, IV, 703). During the Confederation period, Holker was a charter subscriber to the Bank of North America, and with William Duer became involved in the financial affairs of Daniel Parker and Company. In privateering, government contracts, and other business ventures he was also associated with FitzSimons and Robert Morris (Robert A. East, *Business Enterprise in the American Revolutionary Era* [New York, 1938], 119, 123–25, 145, 200).

3. On February 20, 1816, Alexander Dallas, who was then Secretary of the Treasury, reported on a memorial of Holker. The memorial requested the renewal of $20,700 in loan office certificates which had been destroyed by fire on January 2, 1780. After a discussion of Holker's attempts to obtain a renewal of his certificates under the Confederation, Dallas's report states: ". . . on the 18th of February, 1792, the memorialist . . . formally applied to the Secretary of the Treasury for a renewal of the certificates, and was answered on the 20th of June following. . . . And this answer was accompanied with a note from the Comptroller of the Treasury [Oliver Wolcott, Jr.] stating that 'the memorialist did not comply with the resolution of Congress in advertising the certificates *immediately;* that, in some cases, no proper evidence was adduced that the certificates were advertised at all in the States in which they were issued; and that, in his opinion, the claim should be suspended until an arrangement of all the certificates, had been completed'" (*ASP, Claims*, I, 470). See "Report on Sundry Petitions," April 18, 1792, note 6.

To Thomas Jefferson

Treasury Department, June 20th: 1792.

Sir,

I enclose you an extract of a letter, lately received from the Collector of Bermuda hundred,[1] concerning a certain practice, which if persisted in, would interfere with the due execution of the laws; and would oblige to a line of conduct, that would involve in difficulties the French bottoms, which arrive in the United States.

To avoid both the one and the other, this communication is made, in order that a representation to the Minister of France,[2] may put a Stop to the procedure.

I have the honor to be   very respectfully   Sir,   Your obedt. servt.

A. Hamilton.

The Honorable
Thomas Jefferson. Esq
Secretary of State.

Copy, Thomas Jefferson Papers, Library of Congress; LC, Papers of the Continental Congress, National Archives.
    1. William Heth to H, June 9, 1792.   2. Jean Baptiste de Ternant.

From Otho H. Williams [1]

Ceresville [Maryland] 20th. June 1792

My Dear Sir

Your favor of the 9th relieved me from some degree of anxiety. I confess that, although I should not have any great objection to its being known that I had presumed to *write* in defence of the Character of a deceased friend, I would not that my private letter to you on the subject should fall into hands that might magnify my strictures on the conduct of some of the Members of Congress into a libel against the whole body. I doubted whether you had ever received it.

Your reasons for *deferring* the publication were politic; I would not myself have interupted the favorable dispostition of the legislature; but *I think* that at the close of the business Vindicator should have appeared with a little alteration and a short note giving the true reason for its not appearing sooner.

I know that the fame of our friend "stands unassailable with *success.*" But you, my Dr. Sir, do not seem to know that old *"impressions,"* and some of them made almost indelible by the envy which your own encomiums created,[2] are yet remaining; and that a few well authenticated facts only are necessary to their removal: and to give that Celebrity to His fame which is the best reward of his Virtues. Can it be forgotten, that the Country which he emancipated and the Men with whom He wrought that laborious task, were almost equally prejudiced against him? That the Government of South Carolina, which he restored by his wisdom and his Valor (its executive at least) opposed the authority which *he* derived from the head of the Union. That the Army (at least a great majority of the officers) censured him in effect for respecting a power put up by himself; while the half starved troops joined in the Cabal. Implacable emnities were the consequences. Besides he had personal enemies who assisted in blowing the Coals. The embers of envy are still alive; and altho' his *fame* will survive it suffers & his Friends must, and do, some times, *feel* the influence of those temporary prejudices. Among the most respectable, of my acquaintance, I know Men who entertain and who express doubts of the propriety of his conduct in respect to *"a certain affair."* [3] A particular friend, the Reverend Doctr. Allison,[4] who is a liberal and a well informed Man, & to whom I read the paper which I sent you expressed great obligations to me for removing suspicions which had long given him pain. He added that many of the facts which I had stated were new to him, and he was sure they would be to many. He pressed the *expediency* of the publication (But I [5] Submit it entirely to your discretion, having previously submitted it to your judgment). I destest controversy, particularly a literary one; I do not wear the Arms adapted to such kind of combat. But in such a cause and with truth and justice on my side I co[ul]d almost defy "the Devil & all his works." I am, affectionately Yrs   O H W

N. B   Indisposition, or rather a desire of improving my health, has induced me to retire for a few weeks to the Country.

ADf, Maryland Historical Society, Baltimore; AL (incomplete), Hamilton Papers, Library of Congress.
   1. For background to this letter, see Williams to H, April 5, 1792; H to Williams, June 9, 1792.
   2. See "Eulogy on Nathanael Greene," July 4, 1789; H to Ædanus Burke, April 1, 1790. Williams received information concerning H's controversy with Burke on April 18, 1790, from William Smith, a member of the House of Representatives from Maryland (*Calendar of General Otho Holland Williams Papers*, 213).
   3. Major General Nathanael Greene had been criticized for his conduct of the Battle of Camden, South Carolina, as well as for financial transactions entered into in connection with provisioning the troops. In "Vindicator," which Williams sent to H on April 5, 1792, Williams is primarily concerned with defending Greene's conduct at Camden. A draft of "Vindicator," which is partly in Williams's handwriting, is in the Hamilton Papers, Library of Congress.
   4. Patrick Allison was minister of the First Presbyterian Church of Baltimore from 1763 until his death in 1802.
   5. In MS the words "But I" are crossed out.

To Wilhem and Jan Willink, Nicholaas and Jacob Van Staphorst, and Nicholas Hubbard

[*Philadelphia, June 20, 1792.* On July 26, 1792, Hamilton wrote to Willink, Van Staphorst, and Hubbard: "You will herewith receive triplicates of my letters of the 7th. of May and 20th. ultimo." *Letter of June 20 not found.*]

To John Daves

Treasury Department, June 21, 1792. Requests "enquiries concerning fit Characters to serve as second and third Mates, in the Revenue Cutter on the North Carolina station."

Copy, RG 56, Letters to the Collector at New Bern, National Archives; copy, RG 26, Revenue Cutter Service Letters Sent, Vol. "O," National Archives; copy, Letters to Collectors at Small Ports, "Set G," National Archives.

From John Daves

New Bern [North Carolina] June 21, 1792. "I transmitted you in the month of February last [1] the description and dimentions of the Revenue Cutter built at Washington. . . . I should be thankful how soon her necessary Papers could be sent on, as she . . . will be ready for sea in a short time."

Copy, RG 56, Letters from the Collector at New Bern, National Archives.
1. Letter not found.

To Sharp Delany

Treasury Department, June 21, 1792. Requests "enquiries concerning a fit Character to serve as third mate in the Revenue Cutter on the Pennsylvania Station."

LS, Dr. Charles W. Olsen, Chicago, Illinois.

From John P. Mumford and Company [1]

New York, June 21, 1792. "Oliver Remington late of Jamestown on the Island of Conanicut, in the State of Rhode Island, was during the War, a Mate on board the Frigate Trumbull, James Nicholson Esqr Commander, in the service of the United-States. Since that period he has been lost at sea. His father Capt. Benja. Remington, intends claiming the balance due from the United States for his late Son's services, & has requested us to write you on the subject. He wishes a copy of Oliver Remington's Accot. as it stands on the Ship's Books, or in the proper Office, may be sent us. . . ." [2]

LS, RG 217, First Comptroller's Office, New York—Revenue and Miscellaneous, 1792–1815, National Archives.

  1. John P. Mumford and Company was a New York City mercantile house.
  2. On the cover of this letter H wrote: "Mr Woolcott will please to examine the fact & answer this letter in his own name."

From Edmund Randolph [1]

Philadelphia, June 21, 1792.

Sir,

I understand from your communication of the 2d instant,[2] that you do not wish my opinion upon any other point, than that which seems to have produced a schism between the Gentlemen of the New-York and Virginia bar. The former are interpreted to declare, that sixty Cents and no more are demandable by the Collectors for every entry of an inward Cargo directed to be made in conformity with the Coasting Act,[3] and for receiving of, and qualifying to, every manifest of vessels licensed to trade under that act. The latter, on the other hand, decide, that the Collectors may demand for every such entry sixty Cents, and for receiving of, and qualifying to, every such manifest sixty Cents.

It is natural to ask, whether this entry and this receiving of, and qualifying to a manifest be distinct services, or whether the latter be involved in the former.

Copy, RG 36, Collector of Customs at Boston, Letters from the Treasury, 1789–1818, Vol. 5, National Archives; copy, Circulars of the Treasury Department, 1789–1814, Library of Congress; LC, United States Finance Miscellany, Treasury Circulars, Library of Congress; copy, Essex Institute, Salem, Massachusetts.

  1. H enclosed this letter in "Treasury Department Circular to the Collectors of the Customs," July 22, 1792. For background to this letter, see William Heth to H, November 20, 1791, and Otho H. Williams to H, December 12, 1791. See also "Treasury Department Circular to the Collectors of the Customs," November 30, 1789, and Richard Harison and Samuel Jones to H, November 18, 1789.
  2. Letter not found.
  3. "An Act for Registering and Clearing Vessels, Regulating the Coasting Trade, and for other purposes" (1 Stat. 55–65 [September 1, 1789]).

I. The instances of entry are to be found in the 27th and 28th sections: [4] for example,

1. Where a vessel of 20 tons or upwards, licensed to trade not having ardent spirits exceeding 400 gallons, arrives from one district to another in the same state, or from a district in one state to a district in the next adjoining state, with goods of the growth or manufacture of the United States only.

2. Where such a vessel has received one of the duplicate manifests from the Collector or Surveyor of the port, at which the cargo was taken on board.

II. The Collectors are to receive and qualify to manifests in the following cases.

1. In the case of a Clearing Manifest under the 24th section.[5]

4. Sections 27 and 28 of "An Act for Registering and Clearing Vessels, Regulating the Coasting Trade, and for other purposes" read as follows:
"Sec. 27. *And be it further enacted*, That the master of every ship or vessel of the burthen of twenty tons or upwards, licensed to trade as aforesaid, not having on board rum or other ardent spirits, exceeding four hundred gallons, and arriving from one district to another in the same state, or from a district in one state to a district in the next adjoining state, with goods, wares or merchandise, of the growth or manufacture of the United States only, shall, within twenty-four hours, Sundays excepted, next after his arrival at any place or port where a collector or surveyor resides, and before any part of the cargo on board such ship or vessel be landed or unloaded, deliver to such collector or surveyor a manifest thereof, and shall make oath or affirmation before such collector or surveyor, that such manifest contains a true account of all the goods, wares and merchandise on board such ship or vessel, and thereupon shall receive from such collector or surveyor a permit to land or unload the same.
"Sec. 28. *And be it further enacted*, That in all other cases the master of every vessel of the burthen of twenty tons or upwards, licensed to trade as aforesaid, shall within twenty-four hours, Sundays excepted, next after his arrival at any port or place within the United States, where a collector or surveyor resides, and before any part of the cargo on board any such ship or vessel be landed or unloaded, deliver to such collector or surveyor the manifest thereof, authenticated before and received from the collector or surveyor of the port or place where the said cargo was taken on board, together with his permit to depart from the place of lading, whereupon it shall be the duty of such collector or surveyor to grant a permit to land or unload such cargo." (1 Stat. 63.)
5. Section 24 of the Coasting Act reads as follows: "*And be it further enacted*, That the master or commander of every ship or vessel bound to any foreign port, shall deliver to the collector of the district where such ship or vessel may be, a manifest of the cargo on board such ship or vessel, and on making oath or affirmation to the truth thereof, it shall be the duty of the said collector, to grant a clearance for such ship or vessel, and her loading; and if any ship or vessel bound to any foreign port, shall depart from the place of her loading without such clearance, the master, commander, consignee, or

2. Of returning one of the duplicate Manifests to the Master under the 25th section.[6]

3. So under the 26th section.[7]

4. Of a licensed vessel under the 27th section having particular cargoes.

5. Of all other licensed vessels under the 28th section not having particular cargoes.

III. The only example of receiving without qualifying to a manifest, is in the case of the duplicate Manifest, delivered at the port of destination.[8]

IV. Lastly, the Collectors are sometimes to receive and qualify to manifests, as in the 24th section, without granting an entry or permit:

In others they are to receive and qualify to manifests, and grant permits to proceed to the place of destination, as in the 25th and 26th sections:

In others they are to receive and qualify to manifests, and grant permits to unload, as in the 27th and 28th sections. I presume too that according to these two sections, an entry is to be made.

1. The result from hence is, that the receiving of and qualifying to, manifests under the 24th section, is a service standing by itself, and independent of, both entry and permit:

---

owner thereof, shall forfeit and pay the sum of two hundred dollars for every such offence" (1 *Stat.* 61).

6. Section 25 of the Coasting Act provides in part as follows: "That the master of every ship . . . licensed to trade between the different districts of the United States, having on board goods, wares or merchandise of foreign growth or manufacture, of the value of two hundred dollars, or rum or other ardent spirits exceeding four hundred gallons, and being bound from one district to another, shall deliver to the collector . . . duplicate manifests of the whole cargo . . . and . . . it shall be the duty of such collector or surveyor to return to the said master one of the said manifests, first certifying thereon that the same had been sworn or affirmed to, and delivered to him according to law, and also to grant to the said master a permit authorizing such ship or vessel to proceed to the place of her destination" (1 *Stat.* 61–62).

7. Section 26 of the Coasting Act gives similar instructions concerning manifests of ships carrying domestic products and reads in part as follows: "it shall be the duty of such collector or surveyor to return to the said master one of the said manifests, first certifying thereon, that the same had been sworn or affirmed to and delivered to him according to law; and also to grant to the said master a permit, authorizing such ship or vessel to proceed to the place of her destination" (1 *Stat.* 62).

8. Randolph is referring to Section 27 of the Coasting Act. See note 4.

2. The like service under the 25th and 26th sections is connected with a permit to proceed; and,

3. The like service under the 27th and 28th sections is connected with both an entry and a permit.

The three fees in the 31st section,[9] which claim our present attention, are

1. For every entry of an inward cargo directed to be made in conformity with the act, and for receiving of, and qualifying to every manifest of vessels licensed to trade, sixty cents:

2. For a permit to land goods of a foreign growth or manufacture, twenty Cents:

3. For every permit to proceed to the place of destination, twenty five Cents.

Now according to the Gentlemen of New-York, there is no fee for the first service because the entry and manifest do not concur; nor can there be any for the second and third, unless the fee for the permit and entry involve the receiving of and qualifying to a manifest, as a part of the act of granting a permit or entry; nor even then in the case of a permit for unloading, unless it be for unloading foreign goods. I must beg leave to differ from them for the following reasons:

Congress appear to have thought the receiving of, and qualifying to, a manifest, to be a work deserving of particular notice:

By thus noticing it, they indicate their sense, that it merits some allowance:

By placing it in the same sentence with the entry of an inward Cargo, it would seem to be implied that they both stand upon an equally respectable footing, and are entitled to an equal reward.

The law does not authorise an apportionment of the sixty cents between the two services; and without doing so the receiving of and qualifying to a manifest, must according to their doctrine, be often without emolument; that is when it is separated from an entry of an inward Cargo.

I am aware of some forcible objections—

1st Obj. The copulative *and* combines the two in one.

9. 1 *Stat.* 64.

Answ. If they be distinct things, the Copulative is more proper than the disjunctive. That they are so in some instances at least, has been shewn. It may be added, that unless they were considered as distinct, it was unnecessary to mention the receiving of and qualifying to the Manifest. Nay, when literal construction is pressed, does not the repetition of the word *for* give it the air of a new topick?

2d Obj. The Legislature have not united any two other services in the same sentence; although they might easily have thrown together the permit to land goods of foreign growth and manufacture, and the taking of a bond, each of which is assessed at twenty cents.

Answ. This circumstance is too slight to become a datum of reasoning; although probably the greater affinity between the two first services, than between the two last might have insensibly caused the junction of the former, and the severance of the latter.

3 Obj. The law annexes no fees to a permit for landing goods of the growth of the United States, and it may be as well presumed, that the Act in question was designedly omitted, as to a separate compensation.

Answ. This mode of argument can never be safe. On this occasion it is certainly erroneous; because the service is not omitted as in the case put, but is recognized as worthy of compensation.

Still, however, I must own, that this difficulty remains upon my mind. Manifests are often received and qualified to, when they are indispensable preliminaries to entries of an inward Cargo, and permits for which allowances are made. It strikes me as being right in itself, that Congress should have distinguished between manifests under different circumstances; and have established a fee for some, and excluded it from others. But their language is my guide. I cannot understand the same words in two different senses; nor can I degrade from a title to a fee that act, which they have thought proper to dignify with it. I must therefore say, that, in my judgment, the Collectors may demand sixty cents for every entry of an inward cargo, and sixty cents for receiving of and qualifying to every manifest of vessels, licensed to trade, under the Coasting law. I appeal also to the word "every," as illustrating and confirming this opinion.

I have the honor, Sir, to be, With great esteem, Your most obedient Servant, Edm. Randolph.

The Secretary of the Treasury.

To Joseph Whipple

[*Philadelphia, June 21, 1792.* On June 30, 1792, Whipple wrote to Hamilton: "I recd . . . your letter of the 21st instant." *Letter not found.*]

To Gaspard Joseph Amand Ducher [1]

[*Philadelphia, June 22, 1792.* On October 22, 1792, Ducher wrote to Hamilton: "J'ai reçu votre Lettre du 22. juin der." *Letter not found.*]

1. Ducher had been appointed French vice consul *ad interim* at Portsmouth, New Hampshire, in 1786, and in 1788 he was transferred to Wilmington, North Carolina. He returned to Paris in 1790, and for the next three years he sought to induce the French government to adopt a policy of encouragement to trade and navigation similar to that embodied in the English navigation laws (Frederick L. Nussbaum, *Commercial Policy in the French Revolution* [Washington, 1923], 14, 17, 35, 271-304).

To William Ellery

[*Philadelphia, June 22, 1792.* On July 10, 1792, Ellery wrote to Hamilton: "I have recd. your letters of the 7th 22nd. and 28th of the last month." *Letter of June 22 not found.*]

From Daniel Huger [1]

[June 22-25, 1792]

Dear sir

As it may be of some importance to the Federal revenue, relative to the excise [2] on whiskey, I take the liberty to inform you that during my Journey thro' Virginia, I learnt that it was customary with the North Carolinians to convey Large quantities of their distilled Spirits into that State, which, as privileged people, they Sold at a Cheaper rate than those of their Sister State could afford to do and of course had the preference. Some people at Halifax court House, in the Southern Border of Virginia, gave me this information, with expressions of doubt respecting the authority of their Federal officers to seize the Spirits so introduced; I roundly asserted that they were competent to it. Some hint from you to the Officers, might be useful on this Subject. All the Dominion seemed perfectly satisfied with excise and every thing done by their Government (except the appointment of Wayne to the Command of the Army) [3] 'till I got into G———s [4] & V———s [5] districts, and near their residence; where some few were rendered uneasy at the positive assertions of those Gentlemen that the union must be destroyed in less than ten years, by a Northern Faction. I wished to know if they had particularised any point or circumstance inducing such a decision; but could not find that they had. I then assured them that My penetration, must be very defective Indeed; for I cou'd with great Candour declare, that no faction had discovered itself to me from that Quarter; more apparently than from Virginia. The people of this State wou'd be perfectly Satisfied with the federal Government, if not misrepresented. I wish it were in my power to Say the Same of Sister N. Carolina; I fear that She is an Idle, Ignorant Wanton Jade.

Some time ago one of the excise Inspectors requested permission of a Distiller to gauge his Still; he opened the Door, let the officer in, turned the Key and kept him confined three Days on water only. He then very humanely, assured him that his life Shou'd not be in any danger, but he must submit to the mild punishment of having his Nose ground off at the Grindstone & the execution was prevented only by one of the Parties, whose heart happened fortunately, to possess a particle of humanity. I endeavored to persuade them that the Excise was the best Mode, by which we could raise a certain sum Necessary for the support of Government, that the Distillers cou'd not lose by it, and the Farmers undoubtedly wou'd gain; as it inhanced the price of their rye. The Latter seemed to attract some attention.

I am now writing in a Log House, consisting of one Small room, and in that room, with a Man, his Wife, and Seven Children I spent the last Evening and must this Day and night continue in the same N. C. paradise, by the Loss of one out of two Horses. And not Another in the Neighborhood, to be purchased, hired, or borrowed, to go twenty five Miles; which distance will, thank God, place me in So. Carolina.

I left Fayette [6] Yesterday, which was quite a treat to me after the dismal roads & accomodations of this State; It is a Lively, thriving Town, with two beautiful Streams Crossing in the very Center of it. This is Grove's [7] residence. He is a hospitable, Gentlemanly Man at his own Town, and wou'd be so every where, out of biting distance from Some Folkes. It is his opinion & that of Several other Gentlemen with whom I have had conversations, that the Scales will soon drop from the Eyes, and reconcile the Minds of the People here to the Excise. If you knew what satisfaction it gives me to transport my Mind from these to some Rational People, your Philanthropy wou'd I flatter myself, excuse the present intrusion in your Valuable time. by   Dear Sir   Yours respectfully

Dl: Huger
22 June 1792
No. Carolina

Mercers Speeches have reached S. Carolina and created great apprehensions in the Minds of some of My Constituents which I hope are now calmed.[8]

25. June.
Thank God in
So. Carlina

ALS, Hamilton Papers, Library of Congress.
1. Huger was a member of the House of Representatives from South Carolina.
2. An excise on distilled spirits was imposed by "An Act repealing, after the last day of June next, the duties heretofore laid upon Distilled Spirits imported from abroad, and laying others in their stead; and also upon Spirits distilled within the United States, and for appropriating the same" (1 *Stat.* 199–214 [March 3, 1791]) and amended by "An Act concerning the Duties distilled within the United States" (1 *Stat.* 267–71 [May 8, 1792]).

3. On April 11, 1792, Anthony Wayne was appointed a major general to succeed Arthur St. Clair, who had resigned from the Army.

4. William B. Giles, a resident of Amelia County, Virginia, was a member of the House of Representatives from Virginia and a leading opponent in the House of H's financial policies.

5. Abraham B. Venable, a resident of Prince Edward County, Virginia, was a member of the House of Representatives from that state and an outspoken critic of H's financial policies.

6. Fayetteville, North Carolina.

7. William Barry Grove was a member of the House of Representatives from North Carolina.

8. This is a reference to the opposition of John F. Mercer, member of the House of Representatives from Maryland, to the funding operations of the Treasury Department. Mercer was an outspoken critic of the use of Government funds to maintain the price of Government securities. See H to Edward Carrington, May 26, 1792, note 18.

To Tobias Lear

[*Philadelphia*] *June 22, 1792.* Encloses "a letter from Mr. Allibone,[1] which contains some explanations respecting the Well at Cape Henelopen."

LC, George Washington Papers, Library of Congress.

1. William Allibone was superintendent of lighthouses, beacons, buoys, public piers, and stakage for Cape Henlopen and Delaware.

On May 25, 1792, Allibone wrote to Tench Coxe: "Agreeably to your Instructions, I have herein enclosed a Contract with Abraham Hargis for Sinking and Building a Well for the use of the Light House upon Cape Henlopen having Reference to an estimate accompanying the same. The Original one which had been Exhibited to you, having in some small Instances been Reduced, and the present one corrected, I have also taken a Bond with one Sufficient Security in the Penal sum of Six hundred Dollars for the Performance thereof.

"The necessity of the case requiring that Mr Hargis Should proceed Imediately to the Business without waiting for the formality required by Law, You will be pleased to have the same presented to the president of the United States for Ratification as soon as may be Convenient." (ALS, RG 26, Lighthouse Letters Received, Pennsylvania and Southern States, National Archives.)

See H to George Washington, June 19, 1792.

From Tobias Lear

[*Philadelphia*] *June 22, 1792.* Transmits "the Contract made with Abraham Hargis for sinking a Well for the accomodation of the Delaware Lighthouse, which has received the President's approbation."[1]

LC, George Washington Papers, Library of Congress.
1. See H to George Washington, June 19, 1792; H to Lear, June 22, 1792; Tench Coxe to H, May 28, 1792.

On June 25, 1792, Tench Coxe wrote to William Allibone that the President's approval was stated as follows: "Approved June 22, 1792, with the reservation, that if all the materials mentioned . . . are not used in the work a proportional deduction shall be made from the sum stipulated" (LC, RG 58, Letters of Commissioner of Revenue, 1792–1793, National Archives).

To Gouverneur Morris

(Private) Philadelphia June 22d 1792

My dear Sir

Your three letters of the 21st of March, 6th and 10th of April have been received, and gave me great pleasure.

I accept your challenge to meet you in the field of mutual *confidential* communication; [1] though I cannot always promise punctuality, or copiousness. I will however do the best I can.

Will it not be a necessary preliminary to agree upon a Cypher? One has been devised for me, which though simple in execution is tedious in preparation. I may shortly forward it.

In the mean time, let us settle some appellations for certain official characters. I will call

The President	— Scavola
The vice President	— Brutus
The Secretary of State	— Scipio
The Secretary at War	— Sempronius
The Secretary of the Treasury	— Paulus
The Attorney General	— Lysander
Robert Morris	— Cato
Oliver Elsworth	— Virginius
Rufus King	— Leonidas
George Cabot	— Portius
Aaron Burr	— Savius
Richard Henry Lee	— Marcus
Monroe [2]	— Sydney
Ralph Izard	— Themistocles

Senators

Representatives	James Madison	— Tarquin
	Ames [3]	— Valerius
	Abraham Baldwin	— Hambden
	John Laurance	— Solon
	Mercer [4]	— Tacitus
	Murray [5]	— Livy
	Thomas Fitzsimmons	— Cicero
	Egbert Benson	— Cromwell
	Jeremiah Wadsworth	— Titius
	Jonathan Trumbull	— Quintus
	Giles [6]	— Chronus

You see, I have avoided characteristic Names. In my next you shall have a sketch of the general state of the country, its politics and parties.

I thank you for your calculations, as I will for every suggestion you shall make.[7] I shall seldom fail to get either a new idea, or a new application of an old one.

I shall endeavour to put in train, by this opportunity, the papers you advise to be sent, to the Russian Ambassador.[8]

If your courage is not put to the test by being put to *wear* what you have *won*, it will not be my fault.

Do you know enough of the catechism in the Vulgar Tongue to fulfil what you have lately undertaken?

Yrs sincerely   A H

P. S.   Do me the favour to have the inclosed delivered to the party.

Gouverneur Morris Esqr

Copy, Hamilton Papers, Library of Congress.
1. See Morris to H, March 21, 1792.   2. James Monroe.
3. Fisher Ames.   4. John F. Mercer.   5. William Vans Murray.
6. William B. Giles.   7. See Morris to H, April 6, 1792.
8. See Morris to H, April 10, 1792.

From Oliver Wolcott, Junior

T. D
C. Off June 22d 1792

Sir

I have the honour to enclose for your inspection a statement of the Loans recd. by the United States from the Government of France with a calculation of the Interest due thereon to the 1st. day of January 1792.[1] In this statement no notice is taken of the advances made at the Treasury of the United States or of the remittances by the Dutch Commissioners[2] on account of said Loans.

In the account transmitted by Mr. Short,[3] I observe that the following charges are made for advances to the United States which it is said the French Government has assumed to discharge.

	₶	s	d
By the Directors of the Powder Magazines	196.481.	.15.	3
By the Department of War	1.052.345:	11:	6
By the Administration for Clothing the Troops	134.065:	7.	6
By the Farmers General	846.770:	14	5
And for Interest on the above mentioned sums from Sept. 3d. 1783. to Decr. 31st. 1791 @ 5 ⅌ Cent	928.095.	0.	0
amounting to ₶	3.157.758.	0.	0

On those charges I think it proper to observe, that the Government of France, retained the sum of Five millions of Livres out of the Loan of ten millions,[4] to pay for certain articles of Cloathing and Military Stores which were ordered by Col. Laurens for the use of the United States.[5] It will appear from the inclosed account which has been extracted from the Books of Thomas Barclay[6] Comr. of Foreign Accounts, that the French Government has already recd. Credit for the two first mentioned sums, and that the third is a balance appearing due to the French Government on account of the excess of the supplies recd. above the Five millions which were retained out of the Loan.

To the claim for this balance of ₶ 134.065.[7] the United States have however a just right to oppose a much more considerable demand which remains to be liquidated between the two governments, for supplies furnished to the Marine of France, under the agency of Jno. Holker Esq. late Consul General.[8]

It is much to be desired that some arrangement for effecting a settlement should be soon concerted, and from the nature of the claim and the evidence by which it is to be supported, it is my opinion that it ought to be adjusted in this Country.

I had the honour to transmit to you on the 29th. of March, sundry documents relating to the claim of the Farmers General, as the balance of their account now appears to have been assumed by the French Government, it appears to be necessary to ascertain whether the Loan by the Farmers General was not comprehended as a part of the aid granted before the Treaty of February 1778, and if not so comprehended, to demand a disclosure of the person to whom one million of Livres which has not been brought to the Credit of the United States, was paid.[9]

I have &c

N. B.   It is supposed that the claim for supplies furnished the Marine of France may amount to about 200,000 Dollars.[10]

Hon A H.

ADf, Connecticut Historical Society, Hartford; two copies, William Short Papers, Library of Congress.

1. A copy of this enclosure may be found in RG 217, Oliver Wolcott's "Explanation of Accounts, 1792–1794," Comptroller of the Treasury, National Archives.

2. Wilhelm and Jan Willink, Nicholaas and Jacob Van Staphorst, and Nicholas Hubbard.

3. See William Short to H, January 26, 1792.

4. For a description of this loan, see Willink, Van Staphorst, and Hubbard to H, January 25, 1790, note 3.

5. In December, 1780, Lieutenant Colonel John Laurens was commissioned by Congress Envoy Extraordinary to France. He arrived in Paris in March, 1781, and succeeded in securing supplies for the United States.

6. On November 18, 1782, Congress had appointed Barclay commissioner to settle the accounts of the United States in Europe. Wolcott is referring to two ledger volumes of accounts which Barclay settled in Europe (D, RG 39, Foreign Ledgers, Public Agents in Europe, 1776–1787, National Archives).

7. This account appears on Folio 359 of the ledger containing foreign accounts settled by Thomas Barclay (D, RG 39, Foreign Ledgers, Public Agents in Europe, 1776–1787, National Archives).

8. For a summary of John Holker's business activities, see H to Thomas FitzSimons, June 20, 1792.

Some of the purchases which Holker made in the United States as marine agent of France were made through the commissary department under instructions from the Continental Congress (JCC, XVI, 251). Holker's account with the United States was not easily settled, for while he had been willing to pay when he had submitted his account to the Board of Treasury in July, 1780, he refused to make allowances for depreciation when Jeremiah Wadsworth, the commissary general of purchases, finally presented the account. The length of time that Wadsworth required to collect vouchers resulted in a loss through depreciation which according to the Board of Treasury amounted "at the lowest computation to half a million dollars" (JCC, XVI, 336–38; XVII, 606).

9. For an explanation of the difficulties surrounding the claim of the Farmers-General, see the introductory note to Wolcott to H, March 29, 1792.

10. In 1794 this account was stated as amounting to $183,119.36 (copy, RG 217, Miscellaneous Treasury Accounts, 1790–1894, Account No. 5878, National Archives). An adjustment in 1795 gave additional credit for old emissions paid by Holker and reduced the total to $156,539.89 (copy, RG 217, Miscellaneous Treasury Accounts, 1790–1894, Account No. 6855, National Archives).

To Tench Coxe

Treasury Department, June 23, 1792. Encloses "the contract between the Superintendent of the Delaware Light House and Abraham Hargis." [1]

LS, RG 26, Lighthouse Letters Received, "Segregated" Lighthouse Records, Hamilton, National Archives.

1. See Coxe to H, May 28, 1792; H to George Washington, June 19, 1792; H to Tobias Lear, June 22, 1792; and Lear to H, June 22, 1792.

From Henry Dufouer [1]

New York June 23d. 1792

Sir,

I am Again under the necessity of troubling you, and Appealing to your goodness of Heart to Excuse the Intrusion I make on your time while you Read this. It is long since I spent my last shilling relying on that Government for Bread by my Attachment to which I lost the place I held in the Customs & Obliged to behold Men in Office who would have waded thro' blood to Oppose it. I have the most perfect Relyance that you will provide for me because you have promised you would, not Only to me but to my friends. You may in the hurry of Business at times forget this but I am sure you Cannot break it, but my Good Sir, in the mean time I am in want. I am disturbed thereby both in mind & Body and am Often tempted to Despair. Excuse this Application. Do keep me in mind & my pray⟨ers⟩ shall Assend to Heaven for you⟨r⟩ Health & Happiness I am Sir   Your Verry humb. Servt.   Henry Dufouer

The Honbe. Alexander Hamilton Esqr.

ALS, Hamilton Papers, Library of Congress.
    1. According to a petition for the office of supervisor of the revenue for
New York which Dufouer sent to George Washington on March 7, 1793,
he had served in the customhouse at New York until 1776, when he "took a
decided part in the late Revolution." After the war he was appointed a "Land
and Tide waiter" at New York, a position which he held in 1792 ("The Petition of Henry Dufouer," 1793, George Washington Papers, Library of
Congress.)

[*To the* Gazette of the United States] ¹

[Philadelphia, June 23, 1792]

[Philadelphia] *Gazette of the United States*, June 23, 1792.
    1. Philip Marsh has written: "On June 23d, [John] Fenno printed, under
'Original Communications,' an unsigned but Hamiltonian threat at Republican
attacks on his measures" ("Hamilton's Neglected Essays, 1791–1793," *The
New-York Historical Society Quarterly*, XXXII [October, 1948], 290). Although this "threat" may be "Hamiltonian" in both style and content, no
conclusive evidence has been found that H was its author.

From Henry Lee

Richmond June 23d. 92

My dear sir.
    I cannot so well execute Mr. Randolph's ¹ desire as by enclosing
his letter to me. Whatever he has said in favor of Mr. Johnston ²
may be reckoned on with certainty.
    It has been a long time since I have heard from you, tho daily I
hear of you: commended by some, condemned by others—sometimes you are mounted to the skys on the wings of fame, again
whisked into the infernal pit.
    I have withdrawn myself from continental politics. My indiffer-
ence has begot an ignorance & both together have established an un-
interrupted calm in my breast. The State business furnishes me with
employment and ease & innocence accompany my execution of the
dutys of my station.³
    In love with every sweet nymph but not so far gone with any one
yet as to think of matrimony.⁴
    Sometimes I am interrupted by rumors of indian hostility but on
this score my fears decrease as the Secretary of War talks confi-

dently of peace. You never informed me how the horse suited you,[5] nor indeed have you dropt me a line In six months. The beautiful Miss Allen [6] I hear is still unpossessed. Present me to Mrs H.

    farewell, yours always   Henry Lee

ALS, Hamilton Papers, Library of Congress.
  1. David M. Randolph, marshal for the District of Virginia.
  2. On June 30, 1792, Randolph wrote to Thomas Jefferson suggesting the appointment of John W. Johnston as keeper of the lighthouse that was being constructed at Cape Henry, Virginia (ALS, George Washington Papers, Library of Congress).
  3. Lee was governor of Virginia.   4. Lee's wife had died in 1790.
  5. See Lee to H, October 18, 1791.
  6. Presumably Anne Penn Allen, one of the three daughters of James Allen of Philadelphia.

From Thomas Mifflin

[Philadelphia, June 23, 1792]

Sir.

By a late act of the General Assembly of Pennsylvania, provision is made,[1] among other things, for paying the nominal amount of the State Certificates, which are subscribable to the loan, proposed by Congress [2] to the State Creditors, "upon this condition, and not otherwise, that the State Creditors subscribe to that loan, and thereupon, *on or before the 1st day of July next*, transfer to the State Treasurer, for the use of the Commonwealth, the Certificates which they shall receive from The United States, in consequence of such subscription." [3]

The Comptroller General and Register General of the State,[4] have stated to me, that a difficulty occurs in the execution of this act; as, according to their information, the Certificates of The United States for the amount of the respective subscriptions of the State Creditors, will not be issued *until the 1st of March 1793*, and, of course, cannot be transferred to the State Treasurer for the use of the Commonwealth, at the period which the Legislature of Pennsylvania had prescribed, previously to the passing of the act of Congress, that extends the time for subscribing to the loan.[5]

Under these circumstances, I am induced to request, that you will, as far as you can with propriety, enter into an arrangement, to accommodate the State; and either direct the Certificates to be immediately issued (since there is no reasonable ground to suppose, that the amount of the subscription in pennsylvania will exceed the amount of the assumption); or give your sanction, to a transfer of the receipts, which the Loan-Officer issues, in the first instance, to the parties subscribing; so that, at the regular period, the certificates may be obtained, in the name and for the use, of the Commonwealth.

The readiness which you have shewn, on every occasion, to facilitate our fiscal operations, as far as they are connected with the Federal establishment, assures, me that no apology is necessary for this application, and increases the sincere respect, with which   I am, Sir, Your most obedt., Hble servt.   Thomas Mifflin.

Philadelphia,
June 23. 1792.

To Alexr. Hamilton,
Esqr., Secretary of the
Treasury, of The United States.

LC, Division of Public Records, Pennsylvania Historical and Museum Commission, Harrisburg; two copies, Division of Public Records, Pennsylvania Historical and Museum Commission, Harrisburg.

1. "An Act to Provide for Paying and Redeeming Certain Public Debts, and for Defraying the Expenses of Government," April 10, 1792, provided in part that "if congress shall, on or before the first day of July next, renew and again open the subscription to the loan heretofore proposed to the state creditors, or shall, in any other manner, and upon any other terms, provide for the assumption of the non-subscribed debts owing to such state creditors, the holder or holders of any certificate or certificates, subscribable to the subscription so renewed, or entitled to the benefit of such other provision, shall be entitled to have and receive the nominal value of the said certificate or certificates from the state treasurer, upon this condition, and not otherwise, that they shall and do subscribe to the loan so renewed, or acquiesce in the terms of such other provision; and thereupon, on or before the first day of July next, transfer to the state treasurer, for the use of the commonwealth, each and every the certificate and certificates which they shall receive from the United States in consequence of such subscription, or all and singular the interests and benefits to be derived from such other provision, together with the proper evidences thereof" (*Pennsylvania Statutes*, XIV, 309).

2. "An Act supplementary to the act making provision for the Debt of the United States" (1 *Stat.* 281–83 [May 8, 1792]).

3. Although the Pennsylvania act of April 10 had stipulated a deadline of July 1, Alexander Dallas, secretary of the commonwealth of Pennsylvania, gave public notice on May 16, 1792, that state certificates subscribed to the Federal assumption should be transferred to the state treasurer on or before the "first day of August next" (*Pennsylvania Archives*, 9th ser. [n. p., 1931], I, 394).

4. On June 22, 1792, in response to Mifflin's request, John Nicholson, comptroller general of Pennsylvania, and John Donnaldson, register general of Pennsylvania, wrote to Mifflin:

"The Act of the Legislature of *Pennsylvania*, entitled 'An Act for paying and redeeming certain public debts, and for defraying the expences of government,' provides that to entitle the holders, of such debt of this state, as is assumable by the United States, to payment therefor, they shall first subscribe the same to the loan of the United States, and on or before the first of July, 1792, transfer to the State-Treasurer for the use of the commonwealth, the certificate or certificates which they shall receive from the United States, in consequence of such subscription, or all and singular the interests and benefits to be derived from the provision which hath been made by the supplementary Act of Congress, passed at last sessions providing for the public debt.

"Under the said Act of Congress the certificates for the subscriptions made will not issue until March 1st, 1793, and consequently they cannot be transferred within the time limited above. The Loan-Officer on making the deposit of State debt grants a descriptive receipt therefor, conditional to return any, that may not be assumable—we have considered this subject, have consulted the Loan-Officer aforesaid, and obtained his concurrence, and are of opinion, that the best way will be to receive from the parties those certificates of deposit signed by Mr. [Thomas] Smith, examine the same, as to their being genuine certificates, and assumable, as well as the amount of principal and interest of such as are, till July 1st, 1792, and take a transfer to the Treasurer thereon, in such manner as the Loan-Officer agrees, shall enable him to issue the certificates on the first of March, 1793—according to the provisions of the Act of this State aforesaid.

"This plan is submitted for the approbation of your excellency." (Hogan, *Pennsylvania State Trials*, 215–16.)

5. The reopened subscription of state certificates was to be carried on in the manner provided by "An Act making provision for the (payment of the) Debt of the United States." Section 14 of this act provided, in case the subscription exceeded the sum allowed to any state, that ". . . the certificates and credits granted to the respective subscribers, shall bear such proportion to the sums by them respectively subscribed, as the total amount of the said sums shall bear to the whole sum so allowed to be subscribed in the debt of such state . . ." (1 *Stat.* 143 [August 4, 1790]). Since the sum allotted to Pennsylvania, however, was estimated to be greater by a million dollars than the total assumable debt in that state, there was, as Mifflin states, "no reasonable ground to suppose" that the provisions of Section 14 would be applicable to Pennsylvania. See Statement D of "Report on the Public Debt and Loans," January 23, 1792.

From James Reynolds [1]

Philadelphia 23d June. 1792.

Honnored Sir,

Your Goodness will I hope overlook the present application you will infenately Oblige me if you Can let me have the Loan of fifty dollars. for a few days. what little money I had I put into the turnpike Scrip. and I dont like to sell At the low advance the[y] are

selling at. at present. as its very low. if you Can Oblige me with that
much in the morning sir you shall have it in a short time again and
you Will very much Oblige your Humble and Obed. Serv.   J. R.

Alexr. Hamilton. Esq.

NB.   you will I hope pardon me in taking the liberty to Call to day.
but my Necessaty is such that it Oblige me to do it: sunday evening

"Reynolds Pamphlet," August 31, 1797.
    1. This letter is printed as document No. XX in the appendix of the "Reyn-
olds Pamphlet," August 31, 1797.
    For background to this letter, see Reynolds to H, December 15, 17, 19, 22,
1791, January 3, 17, March 24, April 3, 7, 17, 23, May 2, June 3–22, 1792; H to
Reynolds, December 15, 1791, April 7, June 3–22, 1792; Maria Reynolds to H,
December 15, 1791, January 23–March 18, March 24, June 2, 1792.

To William Short

Treasury Department
June 23rd. 1792.

Sir
    After closing my letter to you of the 14th. instant, the Comptrol-
ler, to whom I had submitted for examination the statement of the
French Treasury transmitted by you,[1] made some communications
to me on that subject, of which copies are here enclosed for your
information.[2]
    My own observations upon it must necessairly be reserved for
another opportunity, as Mr. Pinkney who will take charge of my
letters is to embark for London to day.[3]
    With consideration and esteem   I am Sir   Your Obedt. Servant
                                              Alexander Hamilton
Wm. Short Esqr.
Minister Resident of the United
States at the Hague.

LS, William Short Papers, Library of Congress; LS, marked "2nd," William
Short Papers, Library of Congress.
    1. See Short to H, January 26, 1792.
    2. See Oliver Wolcott, Jr., to H, June 22, 1792.
    3. The Senate had approved the appointment of Thomas Pinckney of South
Carolina as United States Minister Plenipotentiary at London on January 12,
1792 (Executive Journal, I, 96).

To Jean Baptiste de Ternant

Treasury Department
June 23d. 1792.

Sir

It has been heretofore understood between us, that the supplies furnished and payments made, or to be made, *within* the United States, on account of the debt due to France, should be liquidated according to the intrinsic par of the metals in the two Countries.[1]

It remains to settle what this par is, and to deduce from it the true value of a French livre in the legal Currency of the United States. I call that value Eighteen Cents and fifteen hundredths of a Cents, which is a small fraction in favour of the money of France.

To ascertain this I have pursued the following process.

I have supposed, first, as to your gold Coins, that thirty two louis d'ors, each of the value of twenty four livres ought to correspond with a mark of standard gold.[2]

But that, by reason of the *remedy of weight* they in fact weigh less, in proportion of fifteen grains per Mark.

And that, though your legal standard for gold is twenty two parts fine to two parts alloy, yet your real standard is $21\frac{22}{32}$ parts fine to $2\frac{10}{32}$ parts alloy on account of the *remedy of law*.

That a Mark or 4608 grains mark weight are equal to 3780 Grains troy weight. And, consequently, that a livre in your Gold Coins contains in fact, of fine Gold, 4 Grains & $433\frac{1}{10000}$ parts of a Grain troy weight.

Then as by a law of Congress of the last session for establishing a Mint,[3] 24 Grains & ¾ of a Grain troy weight of fine Gold are valued at a dollor or 100 Cents, it follows that a livre, in the gold Coins of France, corresponds with 17 Cents and $915\frac{1}{10000}$ parts of a Cent.

I have supposed, secondly, as to your silver Coins—

That Eight *pieces* of Six livres each and $\frac{9}{10}$ths of a *piece*, or in other words 49 livres & $\frac{8}{10}$ths. of a livre ought to weigh a Mark of standard silver.

But that by reason of the remedy of weight, they in fact weigh less, in the proportion of 36 grains per mark. And that, though your legal Standard for silver is 11 parts fine to 1 part alloy; yet your real standard is $10^2\frac{1}{24}$ parts fine to $1\frac{8}{24}$ parts alloy, on account of the *remedy of law*. And consequently the livre, in your silver Coins, contains in fact, of fine silver, 68 Grains & $^{25}\!\!/_{100}$ parts of a Grain troy weight.

Then, as by the law referred to, 371 Grains & $\frac{1}{4}$ of a Grain troy weight of fine Silver are valued at a dollar, or 100 Cents, it follows that a livre in the Silver Coins of France corresponds with 18 Cents & $^{3830}\!\!/_{10000}$ parts of a Cent.

The mean of which two values of the livre of France is, in the legal currency of the United States, something less than 18 Cents & $^{15}\!\!/_{100}$ parts of a Cent.[4]

This therefore is proposed as the rule or *principle* of liquidation. If there are any error of fact or calculation they of course will be to be rectified.

I have the honor to be with sentiments of respect and esteem   Sir Your Obedt Servant   Alexander Hamilton

The Minister Plenipotentiary
of France

LS, *Arch. des Aff. Etr., Corr. Pol., Etats-Unis*, Supplement Vol. 20; LC (French translation), *Arch. des Aff. Etr., Corr. Pol., Etats-Unis*, Supplement Vol. 10.

1. See H to Ternant, March 8, 1792.
2. H's discussion of the specie equivalent to the French livre follows closely the description which Jacques Necker had given of the standards of gold and silver coins (*A Treatise on the Administration of the Finances of France. In Three Volumes. By Mr. Necker. Translated from the genuine French Edition, 1784, by Thomas Mortimer, Esq.* [London: Printed at the Logographic Press, 1785]).
3. "An Act establishing a Mint, and regulating the Coins of the United States" (1 Stat. 246-51 [April 2, 1792]).
4. On the same day on which this letter was written, Oliver Wolcott, Jr., sent the following certificate to Ternant: ". . . a warrant was issued on the Treasurer of the United States dated the 21st. day of February 1792 for eight thousand three hundred and Twenty five Dollars in favour of Monsieur Jean de Ternant Minister Plenipotentiary of France which has been charged as a payment on account of the debt due by the United States to the Government of France and which being converted into Livres Tournois is estimated at Forty five thousand Livres" (copy, RG 217, Oliver Wolcott's "Explanation of Accounts, 1792-1794," Comptroller of the Treasury, National Archives).

To George Washington

Treasury Departmt. 23d. June 1792.

The Secretary of the Treasury respectfully submits to the President of the United States the Draft of an Agreement concerning the subscription on behalf of the U States to the Bank, agreeably to terms concerted with the Directors, in order that it may be considered by the President previous to it's execution.[1] The Secretary will wait upon the President for his Orders on Monday morning.

LC, George Washington Papers, Library of Congress.
1. See H to Thomas Willing, June 11, 1792.

From William Gardner

[*Portsmouth, New Hampshire, June 24, 1792.* On July 13, 1792, Hamilton wrote to Gardner: "I duly received your letter of the 24th ult." *Letter not found.*]

From Thomas Jefferson [1]

Philadelphia June 24. 1792.

Sir

I have the honor to inclose you the answer of the Minister of France [2] to the letter I wrote him on the subject of the complaint of the Collector of Bermuda hundred [3] against the French Consul at Norfolk,[4] whereby you will see that he undertakes to have the latter set right. I have not thought it necessary to reply to his observation that "Le Consul de Norfolk est sans doute obligé de maintenir les loix de France, aussi bien que le Collecteur de Bermuda hundred doit faire observer celles des etats-unis;" presuming he can only mean then the former do not interfere with the latter. The supremacy of the laws of every country within itself is too well known to be drawn into question. I shall take care however to note to him in conversation that the latitude of his expression, if taken in all it's intent, would render it erroneous. I have the honour to be with every sentiment of respect Sir Your most obedt & most humble servt   Th: Jefferson

The Secretary of the Treasury

ALS, letterpress copy, Thomas Jefferson Papers, Library of Congress; LC, Papers of the Continental Congress, National Archives.
  1. For background to this letter, see William Heth to H, June 9, 1792, and H to Jefferson, June 20, 1792.
  2. Jean Baptiste de Ternant's letter states that the laws of France require captains of French vessels to give their records to the French consul at their port of call. The letter also states, however, that the issue had been raised earlier at Philadelphia and New York and had been settled there to the satisfaction of the French consuls and the collectors of the customs at those ports (Ternant to Jefferson, June 23, 1792, letterpress copy, Thomas Jefferson Papers, Library of Congress).
  3. William Heth.
  4. Martin Oster was the French vice consul at Norfolk.

To James Reynolds [1]

[Philadelphia, June 24, 1792]

Inclosed are 50 dollars, they could not be sent sooner.

"Reynolds Pamphlet," August 31, 1797.
  1. This payment of blackmail was in response to Reynolds to H, June 23, 1792.

From James Reynolds [1]

[Philadelphia, June 24, 1792]

Received philadelphia 24th June. 1792 of Alexander Hamilton Esq. Fifty Dollars. which I promise to pay on demand to the said Alexr. Hamilton or Order as witness my hand.   James Reynolds

----

50 Dollars

"Reynolds Pamphlet," August 31, 1797
  1. This receipt is printed as document No. XX in the appendix of the "Reynolds Pamphlet," August 31, 1797.
  For background to this receipt, see Reynolds to H, June 23, 1792, and H to Reynolds, June 24, 1792.

To William Webb

Treasury Department
June 24 1792.

Sir

Your letter of the 11th instant [1] was duly received. In the case therein stated you were surely right in charging the Tonnage Duty upon granting a new license to the Vessel under the circumstances mentioned; which Tonnage cannot legally be refunded.

I am, Sir, Your Obedt Servant. A Hamilton

William Webb Esqr.
Bath.

LS, United States Finance Miscellany, Treasury Circulars, Library of Congress.
1. Letter not found.

To John Adams

Philadelphia June 25
1792

My Dear Sir

You will find enclosed your account, which I take the liberty to send, lest by not adverting to the state of it, some inconvenience might insue.

You are I presume aware, that Mr. Clinton is to be your Competitor at the next election.[1] I trust he could not have succeeded in any event, but the issue of his late election will not help his cause.[2] Alas! Alas!

If you have seen some of the last numbers of the National Gazette, you will have perceived that the plot thickens & that something very like a serious design to subvert the Government discloses itself.[3] With sincere respect & attachment I remain Dr Sir Yr. Obed ser A Hamilton

The Vice President [4]

ALS, Massachusetts Historical Society, Boston.

1. George Clinton was a candidate for Vice President. The electoral college, meeting on December 5, 1792, cast one hundred and thirty-two votes for George Washington, seventy-seven for Adams, and fifty for Clinton.

2. H is referring to the outcome of the New York gubernatorial election in which John Jay opposed the incumbent, George Clinton. See Philip Schuyler to H, May 9, 1792, note 4.

Even some of Clinton's supporters did not approve the decision of the majority of canvassers. Chancellor Robert R. Livingston wrote to Edward Livingston on June 19, 1792: "I find the determination of the canvassers occasions much uneasiness. I confess I could have wished that all the votes had been counted whatever might have been the event" (George Dangerfield, *Chancellor Robert R. Livingston of New York, 1746–1813* [New York, 1960], 263). On June 21, 1792, Thomas Jefferson wrote to James Madison: "It does not seem possible to defend Clinton as a just or disinterested man if he does not decline the Office, of which there is no symptom; and I really apprehend that the cause of republicanism will suffer and its votaries be thrown into schism by embarking it in support of this man, and for what? to draw over the anti-federalists who are not numerous enough to be worth drawing over" (Ford, *Writings of Jefferson*, VI, 89–90).

3. H is referring to the several anti-Administration letters printed in the [Philadelphia] *National Gazette*. These letters, which attacked the new excise tax, compared that tax to the taxes imposed under British rule. For example, one letter reads in part as follows: "The Spirited conduct of some good old whigs of 1775, in destroying the notification of the exciseman in Germantown, as *a disgraceful badge of slavery*, may convince our rulers that a free people will not be amused by financial palliatives. . . . The government of the United States in all things wishing to imitate the corrupt principles of the court of Great-Britain, has commenced the disgraceful career by an excise law, and during the last session of Congress attempted a *stamp duty* on cards, with a sanctified pretence to discourage gambling!" ([Philadelphia] *National Gazette*, June 18, 1792.)

4. Adams endorsed this letter: "Ansd. 4 Aug. 1792." Letter not found.

Agreement with the President and Directors of the Bank of the United States [1]

[Philadelphia, June 25, 1792]

Agreement between Alexander Hamilton Secretary of the Treasury of the United States, by virtue of authority from the President of the United States, on behalf of the United States, of the one part, and the President, Directors and Company of the Bank of the United States of the other part.

Whereas in and by the Act, intituled An Act to incorporate the Subscribers to the Bank of the United States,[2] it is among other things enacted in the words following "That it shall be lawful for the President of the United States, at any time or times, within eighteen months after the first day of April next, to cause a subscription to be made to the Stock of the said Corporation, as part of the aforesaid Capital Stock of Ten millions of Dollars, on behalf of the United States, to an amount not exceeding Two millions of Dollars; to be paid out of the monies which shall be borrowed by virtue of either of the Acts, the one entitled, An Act making provision for the debt of the United States; [3] and the other entitled, An Act making provision for the reduction of the public debt; [4] borrowing of the Bank an equal sum, to be applied to the purposes, for which the said monies shall have been procured; reimbursable in Ten years, by equal annual installments; or at any time sooner, or in any greater proportions, that the Government may think fit."

And whereas for carrying into execution the said provision, The President by writing under his hand bearing date the 9th day of May last past, did authorize the said Secretary to subscribe by one or more subscriptions on behalf and in the Name of the United States for such number of Shares of and in the Capital Stock of the said Corporation as together should amount to Two millions of dollars and the same to pay for out of any monies which have been or shall be borrowed by virtue of either of the Acts the one entitled "An Act making provision for the debt of the United States" and the other entitled "An Act making provision for the reduction of the public debt" and did further authorize the said Secretary to borrow of the said Corporation for and on account of the United States and equal sum, namely Two millions of Dollars to be applied to the same purposes for which the said Monies shall have been procured and to be reimbursable in Ten years by equal annual installments or at any time sooner or in any greater proportions that the Government may think fit; Provided that the Interest thereof should not exceed the rate of six per Centum per Annum; and did also empower the said Secretary to enter into and conclude with the said Corporation such contracts and agreements as should be necessary for fulfilling the purposes aforesaid promising to ratify whatever he should lawfully do in the premises.

Now therefore these presents Witness That it hath been agreed and it is hereby agreed by and between the parties aforesaid as follows, to Wit.

First—The said Secretary of the Treasury forthwith after the execution of these Presents shall pursuant to the authority to him given as aforesaid subscribe in some proper book at the said Bank in the name and on behalf of the United States for Five thousand Shares of and in the Capital Stock of the said Corporation.

Secondly—The subscription so to be made shall be deemed to have been made on the twentieth day of December last past and the said United States shall be deemed to have become on the said day and shall be proprietors of the said Five thousand shares of and in the said Capital Stock; subject to the conditions and agreements hereinafter specified.

Thirdly—The amount of the said Five thousand shares, namely two Millions of Dollars shall be payable in moieties, one moiety upon the day of the execution of these Presents, the other moiety on the first day of July next.

Fourthly—The said Corporation upon the payment of each of the said Moieties shall forthwith lend, advance and pay *a sum, equal to* such moiety to the United States to bear an Interest at the rate of six per centum per Annum; subject to the terms of reimbursement in the Act aforesaid specified.

Fifthly—As the dividend upon the said first moiety will begin to accrue on the said 20th day of December last past, the Interest upon the loan which shall be first made pursuant to the article next preceding, that is to say upon the principal sum of one Million of Dollars shall begin to accrue upon the said 20th day of December last, and the Interest upon the said Second loan of one million of Dollars shall begin to accrue upon the said first day of July next.

Sixthly—The interest upon the said loans shall be payable and paid half yearly, that is to say, the first half yearly payment shall be made on the first day of July next and thereafter a half yearly payment shall be made on the first day's of January and July in each year until the final reimbursement of the said Loans.

In testimony whereof The said Secretary hath hereunto subscribed his hand and caused to be affixed the seal of the Treasury of the United States, and the said President, Directors and Company have hereunto caused to be affixed the Seal of the said Corporation. Done at Philadelphia the Twenty fifth day of June in the year one thousand seven hundred and ninety two.   Alexander Hamilton

Secy of the Treasy [5]

Thos. Willing Prest.

Attest
John Kean Cashr.

D, signed by H and Thomas Willing, Historical Society of Pennsylvania, Philadelphia.

1. For a background to this document, see George Washington to H, May 9, 1792; H to Washington, June 23, 1792; and H to Thomas Willing, June 11, 1792.

2. 1 *Stat.* 191 96 (February 25, 1791).

3. 1 *Stat.* 138–44 (August 4, 1790).

4. 1 *Stat.* 186–87 (August 12, 1790).

5. The words "Secy of the Treasury" are in the handwriting of H.

From William Ellery

Colles Office [Newport, Rhode Island]
June 25th, 1792

Sir,

I have recd. your three Circular Letters of the 4th 8th & 11th. of this month; and shall pay due attention to the Explanations and directions contained in them.

By the 14 Sec: of the Act for registering and clearing vessels &c "if any ship or vessel after having been registered in pursuance of this act, shall in any manner whatever be altered in form or burthen" &c. "such vessel shall be registered anew by her former name" &c.[1] A figured head is put to a vessel after she has been registered: doth such alteration render it necessary that she should be registered anew? and if so, should the cause thereof be expressed in her new Register?

The master of a vessel of twenty tons or upwards licensed to trade between the difft. districts of the United States produces a certified manifest to the Collector of the District where she arrives: but has on board his vessel goods of foreign growth or manufacture, of less value than two hundred dollars, which are not mentioned in his manifest are such goods liable to seizure and forfeiture?[2]

Your answer to these questions will oblige me.

Agreeable to your direction[3] I have for sometime noted at the foot of my weekly returns the sum which would be wanted to pay off the drawbacks on distilled Spirits which would become due on the 26th of this month; but I have not yet received authority to borrow monies for that purpose. Permit me to request your attention to this matter.[4]

I am, Sir,   Yr. most obedt. servt.   Wm Ellery Coller

A Hamilton Esqr
Secry Treasy.

LC, Newport Historical Society, Newport, Rhode Island.
   1. "An Act for Registering and Clearing Vessels, Regulating the Coasting
Trade, and for other purposes" (1 *Stat.* 58–59 [September 1, 1789]).
   2. Ellery is referring to Section 29 of the same act, which provides in part
as follows: ". . . all goods, wares, and merchandise, of the value of two
hundred dollars or upwards, which shall be found on board any such ship or
vessel after her departure from the port where the same were taken on board,
without being contained in, and accompanied with such manifest . . . shall
be subject to seizure and forfeiture.
   "*Provided always,* That nothing herein contained shall be construed to
subject the master or owner of any ship or vessel licensed to trade as aforesaid, having on board goods, wares and merchandise of the growth and manufacture of the United States only . . . and bound from district to district in
the same state, or from a district in one state to a district in the next adjoining
state, to any penalty for having departed from the port of loading without
such permit and manifest, or to subject the said goods on board such ship or
vessel to seizure or forefeiture, in case they are not accompanied with a
manifest as aforesaid." (1 *Stat.* 63.)
   3. Letter not found, but see H to Jeremiah Olney, June 25, 1792.
   4. Ellery endorsed this letter "Answered." H's reply has not been found.

To William Ellery

[*Philadelphia, June 25, 1792.* On July 16, 1792, Ellery wrote to
Hamilton: "I have recd. your letter of the 25 of June last." *Letter
not found.*]

To Thomas Mifflin

Treasury Department
June 25 1792.

Sir
   I had this morning the honor of receiving your letter of the 23d
instant.[1]
   I would with pleasure concur in removing the difficulty you sug-
gest by anticipating the issuing of certificates for the debt of the
Commonwealth of Pennsylvania subscribed to the depending loan,

were I not apprehensive of embarrassment, in other cases, in which a similar anticipation might be urged on probable ground, but could not be complied with, with equal safety.

But I shall with pleasure co-operate in the alternative, which you suggest; by giving a sanction to a transfer of the receipts which the Loan Officer [2] issues to the parties subscribing; so that after the first day of March next, the Certificates, to be granted in lieu of those receipts, may issue in the name and for the use of the Commonwealth. To this it will be only necessary, that Receipts be lodged with the proper Officer of the State accompanied by competent transfers or assignments, and that notice be given of those which shall have been so deposited prior to the first of March next.

With very sincere and high respect I have the honor to be Sir, Your Mo. Obedt and humble Servant.   Alexander Hamilton

His Excellency Thomas Miflin Esqr

LS, Division of Public Records, Pennsylvania Historical and Museum Commission, Harrisburg.
1. See also Oliver Wolcott, Jr., to H, June 25, 1792.
2. See H to Thomas Smith, June 8, 1791, for H's instructions concerning the issue of these receipts from the Pennsylvania loan office.

To Charles Cotesworth Pinckney

Philadelphia June 25. 1792

My dear Sir

I have duly received your letter of the 25th of May,[1] by duplicates, with the first and second of a set of bills of Exchange for £ 200 sterling, received by you on account of Mr. Church's [2] bond.

Your former remittance of £ 300 Carolina money was also received and I thought had been acknowledged; but I find by your letter that this was not done. It is not easy for me to give you an idea of the distractions incident to my situation, which alone could account to you for so singular an omission. I shall however rely on your friendship for a proper interpretation of the delay.

It is mortifying to me not to be able now to answer your enquiry concerning my opinion on the points you mention to have been stated to me; your letter having been either mislaid or forwarded to

Mr Church and the particulars having escaped my recollection. I must ask you to take the trouble to restate them and you may rely on a speedy answer.

With the truest esteem and most real regard, I remain Dear sir Your Obedt. Servant.   A Hamilton

Charles C Pinckney Esqr

LS, The Turner Manuscript Collection at the Torrington Library, Torrington, Connecticut; LS, Mr. Pierce Gaines, Fairfield, Connecticut; copy, Mr. George T. Bowdoin, New York City.
  1. Letter not found.   2. John B. Church.

To Edmund Randolph

[*Philadelphia, June 25, 1792.* On June 26, 1792, Randolph wrote to Hamilton and referred to "your communication of yesterday." *Letter not found.*]

From William Seton

New York 25th. June 1792.

Dear Sir
    I have made a long delay in answering your favours of the 12th & 19th.[1] owing to not being able to meet with Col. Walker to settle the Bill for 300 Dollars.[2] He has just sent me word that he will call up & pay it tomorrow. The amount will then be past to your Credit in Bank. I shall watch a favorable opportunity for the disposal of your Stock [3]—at present it does not go beyond 27 or 28 ⅌ Cent advance. I am much obliged to you for your promise respecting My advance to Mr. Pearce the Manufacturer,[4] but am sorry you should have any trouble in the business. Our Direction are informed of your Sentiments respecting the Loan to the Manufactoring Society.[5] Be assured My Dear Sir, they have so much confidence in any measure pointed out by you, & take so much pleasure in promoting your Views, which they are all well convinced are ever intended for the public good, that by complying with your wishes, they have not

even an opportunity of retaliating the obligations this Institution is under to you. Of mine, personally, I shall [say] nothing, but that I am with the highest respect   Dear sir   Your Obliged Ob Hu Serv

Wm Seton

Alexr. Hamilton Esqr

ALS, Hamilton Papers, Library of Congress.
1. Neither letter has been found.
2. See Thomas Marshall to H, May 30, 1792.
3. See Seton to H, May 28, 1792.   4. See Seton to H, June 11, 1792.
5. See H to Seton, May 25, 1792, and Seton to H, June 11, 1792.

Treasury Department Circular to the Collectors of the Customs

Treasury Department,
June 25th, 1792.

Sir,

As it is probable that doubts may arise, in regard to the construction of the fifth section of the Act, entitled, "An Act for raising a farther sum of money for the protection of the frontiers, &c." [1] that is, whether the additional Ten per centum, mentioned in the said section, relates only to the former rates of duties, laid by the Act "making farther provision for the payment of the debt of the United States," [2] or to those imposed by the first recited Act, I think it necessary to communicate my sentiments upon the subject in a circular letter.

I am of opinion (in which the Attorney General, who has been consulted concurs) that the rates of duties prescribed by the Act "making farther provision for the payment of the debt of the United States," must govern the addition of ten per centum.

To elucidate this by an example, it would stand thus:
Madeira wine of the quality of London particular,
   by the former Act is subject to a duty of . . 35   cents.
But wines of that description being by the Act, for
   raising a farther sum of money, &c. liable to a duty
   of 56 cents, add the difference 21
                                   —————
                                 56   cents.

If imported in ships or vessels not of the United

States, 10 per centum are to be added to the first

rate, which is 3½

The Amount of the duties payable in this case would

be per Gallon . . . . 59½ cents.

It has been suggested that there is a diversity in practice in expressing in the Registers of vessels their respective lengths, which is attended with some disadvantage. To remedy this, it is my desire, that the *actual length* "from the fore part of the main stem to the after part of the stern post" be expressed in each Register as the length of the vessel—not the remainder of that length, after deducting 3/5th of the breadth, as is sometimes practiced.[3]

The twelfth section of the Act, entitled, "An Act to establish the Post-Office and Post-Roads within the United States,"[4] is deemed to contemplate no other ships or vessels than those arriving from abroad.

Previous to the adoption of the constitution of the United States, by Rhode-Island,[5] the duty of fifty cents per Ton was in a variety of instances paid upon vessels of that state, trading between different districts, for want of coasting licenses, pursuant to the twenty third section of the Act for registering and clearing vessels, regulating the coasting Trade and for other purposes.[6] Applications have been made for a return of the extra-duties in such cases. I am of opinion that the fourth section of the Act, entitled, "An Act imposing duties on the Tonnage of ships or vessels"[7] extends to ships and vessels of North-Carolina [8] and Rhode-Island, prior to the respective periods of their adoption of the Constitution.

With consideration, I am, Sir, Your obedient Servant,

A Hamilton

L[S], to Benjamin Lincoln, RG 36, Collector of Customs at Boston, Letters from the Treasury, 1789–1807, Vol. 4, National Archives; LS, Office of the Secretary, United States Treasury Department; LS, Rhode Island Historical Society, Providence; LS, MS Division, New York Public Library; LS, Estate of Stuart Chevalier, Pasadena, California; LC, to Samuel Gerry, Essex Institute, Salem, Massachusetts; copy, RG 56, Circulars of the Office of the Secretary, "Set T," National Archives; copy, United States Finance Miscellany, Treasury Circulars, Library of Congress.

1. Section 5 of this act reads as follows: "*And be it further enacted*, That the addition of ten per centum made by the second section of the 'act making farther provision for the debts of the United States,' to the rates of duties on goods, wares and merchandise, imported in ships or vessels not of the United States, shall continue in full force and operation, after the said last day of June

next, in relation to the articles herein before enumerated and described" (1 *Stat.* 260 [May 2, 1792]).

2. 1 *Stat.* 180–82 (August 10, 1790). Otho H. Williams had raised this question. See Williams to H, June 4, 1792, and H to Williams, June 8, 1792.

3. Section 44 of "An Act to provide more effectually for the collection of the duties imposed by law on goods, wares and merchandise imported into the United States, and on the tonnage of ships or vessels" reads in part as follows: "That to ascertain the tonnage of any ship or vessel, the surveyor . . . shall . . . take the length thereof from the fore part of the main stem to the after part of the stern post above the upper deck; the breadth thereof at the broadest part above the main wales, half of which breadth shall be accounted the depth of such vessel, and shall then deduct from the length three fifths of the breadth, multiply the remainder by the breadth, and the product by the depth, and shall divide this last product by ninety-five, the quotient whereof shall be deemed the true contents or tonnage of such ship or vessel" (1 *Stat.* 169 [August 4, 1790]). See Benjamin Lincoln to H, March 21, 1792, and H to ———, May 28, 1792.

4. Section 12 of this act reads as follows: "*And be it further enacted,* That no ship or vessel, arriving at any port within the United States, where a post-office is established, shall be permitted to report, make entry or break bulk, till the master or commander shall have delivered to the postmaster, all letters directed to any person or persons within the United States, which, under his care or within his power, shall be brought in such ship or vessel, other than such as are directed to the owner or consignee: but when a vessel shall be bound to another port, than that, at which she may enter, the letters belonging to, or to be delivered at the said port of delivery, shall not be delivered to the postmaster at the port of entry. And it shall be the duty of the collector or other officer of the port, empowered to receive entries of ships or vessels, to require from every master or commander of such ship or vessel, an oath or affirmation, purporting that he has delivered all such letters, except as aforesaid" (1 *Stat.* 235–36 [February 20, 1792]).

5. Rhode Island had ratified the Constitution on May 29, 1792.

6. 1 *Stat.* 61 (September 1, 1789).

7. Section 4 of this act reads as follows: "Be it therefore further enacted, That in all cases in which the said foreign duty shall have been heretofore paid on ships or vessels of the United States, whether registered at the time of payment or afterwards, restitution thereof shall be made, and that no such foreign duty shall hereafter be demanded on the said ships or vessels" (1 *Stat.* 136 [July 20, 1790]).

8. North Carolina had ratified the Constitution on November 21, 1789.

From Oliver Wolcott, Junior

Treasury Department, Comptroller's Office, June 25, 1792. "I have considered the proposition stated in . . . Governor Mifflins Letter to you dated the 23d. instant, and can discover no objection to an arrangement being made, for permitting transfers to the Commonwealth of Pensylvania, of the sums which have been subscribed in the State Certificates. If this is done the Commonwealth will be intittled to receive the Certificates of Funded Debt which may be issued therefor subsequent to the first day of March next. . . . it may be proper to limit the permission which may be given in such manner, that the right in a State to subscribe Certificates, which have been redeemed or discharged, be not conceeded."

ADf, Connecticut Historical Society, Hartford.

To Henry Glen

Treasury Department
Philadelphia June 26. 1792

Sir

Your letter of the 10th of May duly came to hand.[1]

When Mr. Van Ingen[2] was in Philadelphia on your business[3] he communicated to me his errand—and though the constitution of the department refers the settlement of Accounts exclusively to the Auditor and Comptroller, I interfered so far as to converse particularly with the latter Officer, and it appeared to me that the difficulties, which remained, were insurmountable.

As the matter was fully & particularly explained to Mr. Van Ingen, it is unnecessary to enter into any explanation here.

But if there is any point on which you are desirous of further light I would advise you to write Oliver Woolcott Esquire Comptroller of the Treasury who I doubt not will give you speedy and full information.

With consideration and esteem   I am Sir   Your obedient servant

Alex Hamilton

Henry Glen Esquire
Albany

ALS, from the original in the New York State Library, Albany.
1. Letter not found.
2. William Van Ingen, a resident of Schenectady, New York, was Glen's son-in-law.
3. In the Hamilton Papers, Library of Congress, an unaddressed letter from William Barber, dated June 15, 1791, reads as follows: "I do well recollect while I was employed in settling claims against the united States by individuals of the State of New York and within the time limited by congress for exhibiting the same, That *Henry Glen* Esqr demanded from me a settlement of a claim for certain supplies and services furnished the Indian department by himself and sundry other individuals inhabitants of the said State, And I declined a settlement of the same. . . ."

From Catharine Greene [1]

New York 26 June 1792.

My Dear Sir

The bearer Mr Miller [2] will wait on you to learn the particulars of the transaction with Mr Royal Flint [3] respecting the Certificate I obtained from Baron Glausbeck.[4] I beg you will consider him as My particular friend and any information you can give on this or any other Subject relating to the affairs of My unfortunate family, who, as he will inform You (are all on float again) will greatly oblige your sincerly affectionate, Cathe Greene

ALS, Hamilton Papers, Library of Congress.

1. H had been an effective advocate for payment of the claim of Major General Nathanael Greene's widow, Catharine, against the United States. See "Report on the Petition of Catharine Greene," December 26, 1791. "An Act to indemnify the Estate of the late Major General Nathaniel Green, for a certain bond entered into by him during the late war" became law on April 27, 1792 (1 *Stat.* 258).

2. Phineas Miller was the tutor of the children of Nathanael and Catharine Greene. In 1796 Miller became Catharine Greene's second husband.

3. Royal Flint, a New York City businessman, had been engaged in the Army supply business during the American Revolution and was later appointed a commissioner under the Continental Congress to settle accounts in the state of Massachusetts.

4. By a resolution of the Continental Congress of February 3, 1784 (*JCC,* XXVI, 65), the services of foreign officers during the American Revolution were recognized as a debt of the United States. By an act of September 29, 1789, entitled "An Act to allow the Baron de Glaubeck the pay of a Captain in the Army of the United States" (6 *Stat.* 1), Glaubeck had been added to the list of foreign officers.

Because of debts owed to General Greene by Glaubeck, Flint and William Duer proposed to purchase from Glaubeck rights to the payments which the Government was to make to Glaubeck and to pay the difference between the purchase price and the Government payments to the general's widow. On this understanding, sometime before July 28, 1790, a certificate for the baron's claim was issued by the Treasury Department to Flint as attorney for Catharine Greene. Duer and Flint actually purchased rights to the baron's pay, not from Glaubeck, but from a third party who had obtained the rights for an inconsiderable sum and was willing to part with them for very little. Duer and Flint apparently retained the difference between the purchase price and the nominal value which they charged against the payments to be made to Catharine Greene. H had evidently helped to prepare Flint's power of attorney in the belief that the whole transaction had been undertaken for the benefit of Greene's widow. In May, 1793, H's part in this transaction formed the basis of a charge made by Andrew Fraunces, a former Treasury Department clerk, that H had speculated in Government debts while Secretary of the Treasury (Fraunces to H, May 16, 1793).

To Richard Harison

Philadelphia June 26. 1792

Dear Sir

I shall be mindful of the intimation in your letter of the 4th instant[1] repecting Mr. Mc Comb;[2] so that you may be secured.

Your account some how or other has remained unsettled. The Comptroller has promised to have it speedily finished. This done, the money shall be paid without delay.

With great esteem and regard   Dear Sir   Your obedient servt

Alex Hamilton

Richard Harrison Esquire

ALS, New-York Historical Society, New York City.
    1. Letter not found.
    2. John McComb, Jr., was the contractor for erecting a lighthouse at Cape Henry, Virginia.

To William Heth

Private   [Philadelphia] June 26, 1792

Dear Sir

This accompanies an official letter.[1] I acknowlege, I doubt the accuracy of the opinion of the Attorney General on the last point.

A law is not to be so *litterally* construed as to involve *absurdity* and *oppression*. The legislature might *reasonably* restrain its officers from future *buying* and *selling* of stock, but could not *reasonably* prevent their making a disposition of property, which they had previously acquired according to the laws of their country.[2]

At the same time for greater caution I should in my own case follow the strict interpretation.

All my property in the funds is about 800 Dollars 3 per Cents. These, at a certain period, I should have sold, had I not been unwilling to give occasion to cavil.

The restriction itself, as it respects the officers of the Treasury, and I rather think the commissioners of loans, is a wise & unexceptionable one. But the propriety of its further extension is not obvious, and I doubt whether it will be lasting.[3] The act passed in a prodigious hurry.   A H

Copy, Hamilton Papers, Library of Congress.
  1. See Edmund Randolph to H, June 26, 1792.
  2. Regulations concerning conflict of interest were coeval with the establishment of the Treasury Department. A change in the law, which had apparently provoked Heth's question, was made during the spring of 1792. These regulations were changed again in March, 1793.
  Section 8 of "An Act to establish the Treasury Department," applicable only to the six major officers appointed by the act, provided in part: "That no person appointed to any office instituted by this act, shall directly or indirectly be concerned or interested in carrying on the business of trade or commerce, or be owner in whole or in part of any sea-vessel, or purchase by himself, or another in trust for him, any public lands or other public property, or be concerned in the purchase or disposal of any public securities of any State, or of the United States, or take or apply to his own use, any emolument or gain for negotiating or transacting any business in the said department, other than what shall be allowed by law; and if any person shall offend against any of the prohibitions of this act, he shall be deemed guilty of a high misdemeanor, and forfeit to the United States the penalty of three thousand dollars, and shall upon conviction be removed from office, and forever thereafter incapable of holding any office under the United States" (1 *Stat.* 67 [September 2, 1789]).
  On May 8, 1792, Section 12 of "An Act making alterations in the Treasury and War Departments" provided: "That the restriction on the clerks of the department of the treasury so far as respects the carrying on of any trade or business, other than in the funds or debts of the United States or of any state, or in any kind of public property, be abolished, and that such restriction, so far as respects the funds or debts of the United States, or of any state, or any public property of either, be extended to the commissioner of the revenue, to the several commissioners of loans, and to all persons employed in their respective offices, and to all officers of the United States concerned in the collection or disbursement of the revenues thereof, under the penalties prescribed in the eighth section of the act, intitled 'An act to establish the treasury department,' and the provisions relative to the officers of the treasury department, contained in the 'Act to establish the post-office and post roads,' shall be and hereby are extended and applied to the commissioner of the revenue" (1 *Stat.* 281).
  3. H's doubts concerning the permanence of this provision of the 1792 act proved to be justified. Section 6 of "An Act supplementary to the act, entitled, 'An act to provide more effectually for the collection of the Duties imposed by law on Goods, Wares and Merchandise, imported into the United States, and on the Tonnage of Ships or Vessels'" repealed that part of the 1792 provision which prohibited the revenue officers of the Treasury Department from selling Federal and state securities (1 *Stat.* 337 [March 2, 1793]).

To Thomas Jefferson

[Philadelphia, June 26, 1792]

Mr. Hamilton presents his respectful compliments to Mr. Jefferson & requests to be favoured with a copy of his Report concerning the distillation of Fresh from Salt-Water.[1]

June 26. 1792

AL, Harvard College Library.
1. A joint resolution of the Senate and House of Representatives of May 8, 1792, stipulated: "That the Secretary of the Treasury cause to be provided, for the use of the several collectors in the United States, printed clearances, on the back whereof shall be a printed account of the methods, which have been found to answer for obtaining fresh, from salt water, and of constructing extempore stills, of such implements, as are generally on board of every vessel, with a recommendation, in all cases, where they shall have occasion to resort to this expedient for obtaining water, to publish the result of their trial in some gazette, on their return to the United States, or to communicate it for publication, to the office of the Secretary of State, in order that others may, by their success, be encouraged to make similar trials, and be benefited by any improvements or new ideas which may occur to them in practice" (1 *Stat.* 286). The resolution accorded with a proposal made by Jefferson in his report of November 21, 1791, entitled "Plan for Converting Salt Water into Fresh" (*ASP, Miscellaneous*, I, 44–45).

To William Maxwell

Private

Philadelphia June 26
1792

Dear Sir

Your letter of the 27 of March was duly received[1] and has been communicated to the President.

The information and the observations it contains prove that you have not forgotten your old Trade.[2] They have been well received by the President.

With great esteem and regard I remain Dear sir Your obed. Ser't   A Hamilton

General Maxwell

JUNE 1792   575

Copy, New Jersey Historical Society, Newark.
1. Letter not found.
2. Maxwell's "old Trade" was soldiering. Before the American Revolution
he served in the British army and took part in several major actions during
the French and Indian War. He remained in the British army until 1774 as a
colonel in the commissary department. He was a brigadier general in the
Continental Army from October, 1776, to July, 1780.

To the Officers of the Massachusetts Line

Philadelphia June 26. 1792

Gentlemen

I have received your circular letter of the 28 of February last.

I consider it as addressed to me, in the capacity of a fellow soldier,
and in that capacity, I now acknowlege and answer it.

Respect for you, Gentlemen, and for those, on whose behalf, you
write, does not permit me to be silent—and, in replying, the frank-
ness which is due to you and them, and, which is not less due to my
own character, forbids me to dissemble

My judgment does not accord with the views which are announced in your letter. A perseverance in them will not, I believe,
be productive of any advantage to the parties, and may, I fear, be
attended with some public inconveniences, which, I am persuaded,
they would regret.

I also have made sacrifices *with* the army, and, what is less known,
for the army. I feel, that I love those who remain, of that respectable
band, and that no one can be more solicitous than myself for their
welfare. I trust therefore they will do justice to my motives on the
present occasion.

With very respectful consideration   I have the honor to be   Gentlemen   Your most obedient & most humble serv

William Heath ⎤
J Brooks   ⎥
H Jackson   ⎥
W Eustis   ⎬ Esquires
Jos Crocker   ⎥
Thomas Edwards⎦

ADf, Hamilton Papers, Library of Congress.

To Jeremiah Olney

Treasury Department June 26th. 1792

Sir,

In answer to your letter of the 19th ultimo I have to inform you that the instruction with regard to the Notice to be given to other Collectors in cases where Bonds are put in Suit, is meant to be general, within the Limits of my Circular letter of the 6th of February last.

I am Sir   Your obedt Servant   A Hamilton

Jereh Olney Esqr
Collector Providence

LS, Rhode Island Historical Society, Providence; copy, RG 56, Letters to the Collector at Providence, National Archives; copy, RG 56, Letters to Collectors at Small Ports, "Set G," National Archives.

From Edmund Randolph [1]

Philadelphia June 26th. 1792

Sir

In answer to your communication of yesterday,[2] on the case of Col. Heth the Collector of Bermuda Hundred, I have the honor to inform you, that his enquiries demand different solutions.

The contract, made before the passing of the law,[3] to which he alludes, may be consummated on the 2nd day of January next without impropriety. For the restriction on Collectors, on the disposal of public securities must be future in its operation, and he may be well said to have disposed of them *before* the existence of that restriction.

I am also well satisfied that it is too severe in itself, that Congress should have intended to preve⟨nt⟩ the Collectors from disposing at any time of their public debt acquired before the passage of the law. But how can I bend the word "disposal" unqualified, as it is? [4] Could I fin⟨d⟩ a construction which ⟨wou⟩ld accommodate them, and not set principle at defiance, I would embrace it. But not knowing, where I should stop, I cannot enter upon this uncertain field; and must therefore conclude, that the Collectors are prevented by that law from disposing of *any* public securities whatsoever, *subsequent* to the date of its commencing in force.

I have the honor, Sir, to be   Yr. mo. ob. serv.   Edm. Randolph

The Secretary
of the Treasury

Copy, Hamilton Papers, Library of Congress.
1. For background to this letter, see H to William Heth, June 26, 1792.
2. Letter not found.
3. "An Act making alterations in the Treasury and War Departments" was approved on May 8, 1792.
4. Randolph is referring to Section 8 of "An Act to establish the Treasury Department" (1 *Stat.* 67 [September 2, 1789]). See H to Heth, June 26, 1792, note 2.

From Jean Baptiste de Ternant

Philade. 26 Juin 1792.

Mess.

J'ai recu la lettre du 23 de ce mois par laquelle vous me comuniquez le résultat de votre travail sur la fixation de pair intrinséque de nos especes respectives, pour servir de regle à la liquidation des objets fournis et des sommes payés ou à payer ici par votre gouvernement à compte de sa dette envers la france. Je desirerois que ce principe de liquidation recut son application en france, et que les comptes de vos fournitures, et avances en argent y fussent définitivement arretés. Si, comme je n'en doute pas votre gouvernement y consent, je transmettrai auplutot à ma cour la lettre que vous m'avez fait l'honeur de m'addresser, et au moyen des instructions qui seront donnés en même tems à votre Ministre à Paris [1] les comptes s'y regleront définitivement entre lui et notre gouvernement.

Le M. d f. p. l. E. U.   T

au secretaire de la
tresorerie des Etats
Unis.

LC, *Arch. des Aff. Etr., Corr. Pol., Etats-Unis,* Supplement Vol. 20.

1. Gouverneur Morris had been appointed United States Minister Plenipotentiary to France in May, 1792.

To Jean Baptiste de Ternant

Treasury Department
June 26. 1792

Sir

In answer to your letter of this date, it is only necessary for me to say that it is perfectly agreeable to this Government, that the principle of liquidation, to which you refer should receive its application in France, and that the accounts for supplies and advances of money should be there definitively fixed. I am authorised by The President to say that instructions will accordingly be sent to our Minister at your Court.

I have the honor to be   With real respect & esteem   Sir   Your obedient servant   Alexander Hamilton

The Minister Plenipotentiary of France

ALS, *Arch. des Aff. Etr., Corr. Pol., Etats-Unis,* Supplement Vol. 20; copy, *Arch. des Aff. Etr., Corr. Pol., Etats-Unis,* Supplement Vol. 20.

Treasury Department Circular to the Collectors of the Customs in Massachusetts

Treasury Department
June 26th. 1792

Sir,

It appears from a Return of the Office of discount & deposit of the United States Bank at Boston, that many of the Collectors in your State make their remittances to that institution; discontinuing the former mode of paying into the Bank of Massachusetts. This transfer of payment from one Bank to the other, having never been directed by me, is irregular and requires explanation.

As it was however my intention that such an arrangement should take place at a certain time, I have to desire that the practice already adopted may henceforth be continued.

I am, Sir, Your obedient Servant A. Hamilton

LC, to Samuel Gerry, Essex Institute, Salem, Massachusetts.

To George Washington

Treasury Department, June 26, 1792. Submits "a Report of the Commissioner of the Revenue on the subject of a certain Pier to be erected in the River Delaware." Also submits "the Contract provisionally entered into between the Superintendant of the Delaware Lighthouse &c. and Thomas Davis and Thomas Connaroe Junior, as the best thing practicable." [1]

LC, George Washington Papers, Library of Congress.
1. See Tench Coxe to H, June 20, 1792.

From Tench Coxe

Treasury Department
Revenue Office June 27th. 1792.

Sir,

Among the Cases, which have been brought before the Auditor of the Treasury [1] and myself in consequence of the 7th. Section of "the Act making Alterations in the Treasury and War Department" [2] is one in which the Secretary at War is the Claimant.[3] In a conference with the Auditor it appeared to Us a matter of doubt whether the Case is within the meaning of the law, and I do myself the honor to make a statement of it to you, for the purpose of obtaining the Attorney Generals opinion on the subject. The Auditor does not join me on the occasion, being necessarily absent.

Not long after the organization of the present general Goverment, the Secretary at War rendered an account to the late Auditor of the Treasury (Oliver Wolcott Junr. Esquire, the present Comptroller) who on the 11th. day of June 1790 (after deducting the items now claimed) transmitted the same certified to the late Comptroller [4] for his Decision thereon. On the 19th. of the same Month the said late Comptroller admitted the Settlement, and certified the same to the Register, as appears by his certificate inscribed in the ordinary manner and form, on the report of the Auditor.

By the proviso to the 5th. Section of the Act of September 1789 establishing the Treasury Department,[5] any person whose Account has been audited and who is disatisfied with the settlement of the Auditor for the time being, may appeal against it to the Comptroller within six months. The enclosed original paper of the 31st. December 1790 was presented to the Auditor of the Treasury. The date, it will be perceived, is more than six Months after the Auditors settlement. It is affirmed by the Claimant that he was unacquainted with the determination taken by the officers of the Treasury upon his account, tho' it is stated by him and appears from the records of the two offices, that in March 1790, he was apprized by the Auditor of his intention to reject the items in Question, and that both he and the Auditor had Communications with the late Comptroller, on the merits of the Claim in that Month before the late Auditors settlement and the late Comptrollers admission thereof. It does not appear by the records of the Treasury that any communication of the settlement, or of the admission of it, was made by the late Comptroller although it was common for that officer to make a communication of his decision to the party in writing. Every thing of the Nature of an appeal which is before us, is above stated. The Question on which the Attorney Generals opinion is desired is *whether this Claim of the Secretary at War can be legally taken up and decided upon by the officers named in the 7th. Sectn. of the Act making alterations in the Treasury and War Departments.*

It may be proper to mention, Sir, that the papers came to us without a statement and report of the Auditor upon enquiring for which the papers and proceedings above mentioned were procured. If the proceedings of the late Auditor shall appear to have been duly acted upon by the late Comptroller, we conceive the case cannot be deemed to be one of those contemplated by the Legislature, because the old report of the Auditor will appear to be disposed and there will be no Auditors report in the new Case. But if it shall appear to the Attorney General that the Auditors report in the former case bars his taking it upon the present application, then a very important Question will remain to be determined, viz whether we are to take up the matter on the old or new application. Because if it be on the latter it results that after a rejection by the Auditor and Comptroller of one or more Items in the account of a Claimant, those items may be reconsidered and admitted by the officers of the Treasury Department. The Question however upon which it is material for us to be informed is that already stated.

I have the honor to be, with the most respectful Attachment, Sir, Your most obedient Servant   Tench Coxe.

The honble. the
Secretary of the Treasury.

LC, RG 58, Letters of Commissioner of Revenue, 1792–1793, National Archives.
1. Richard Harrison became auditor of the Treasury Department on November 29, 1791.
2. Section 7 of this act reads as follows: "*And be it further enacted*, That in every case of an account or claim not finally adjusted, upon which the present comptroller of the treasury, as auditor, may have decided, it shall be the duty of the commissioner of the revenue, and of the auditor of the treasury, finally to adjust the same, and in case of disagreement between the said commissioner and auditor, the decision of the attorney general shall be final" (1 *Stat.* 281 [May 8, 1792]).
3. Henry Knox's claim against the Government, which was for "travelling expenses for various journeys on public service during the years 1785 and 1786," amounted to $610.31. See Richard Harrison and Tench Coxe to H, August 2, 1792.
4. Nicholas Eveleigh.   5. 1 *Stat.* 66–67 (September 2, 1789).

From Tench Coxe

Treasury Department, Revenue Office, June 27, 1792. Encloses "a contract between the Superintendant of the Delaware light House [1] and Benjamin Price for two mooring Chains for two of the Beacon boats stationed in the bay of Delaware."

LC, RG 58, Letters of Commissioner of Revenue, 1792–1793, National Archives.
1. William Allibone.

[To the Gazette of the United States] [1]

[Philadelphia, June 27, 1792]

[Philadelphia] *Gazette of the United States*, June 27, 1792.
1. Philip Marsh states that the defense of the Bank of the United States which was published under "Original Communications" was "apparently"

written by H ("Hamilton's Neglected Essays, 1791–1793," *The New-York Historical Society Quarterly*, XXXII [October, 1948], 291). On June 29, 1792, Thomas Jefferson wrote to James Madison: "The present will cover [John] Fenno of the 23d & 27th. In the last you will discover Hamilton's pen in defence of the bank, and daring to call the republican party *a faction*" (Ford, *Writings of Jefferson*, VI, 95). No additional evidence that H was the author of this article has been found.

To Joseph Hiller

Treasury Department
June 27 1792.

Sir

I have yet to reply to your letter of the 19th Ultimo,[1] concerning American Rum, which may have been exported, and re-imported for want of sale.

The penalties against the landing of articles, which have been entered for exportation, are not understood to apply to the bringing back of articles, which have actually and bona fide been *at* a foreign port; but to relanding before going to a foreign port.

Difficulties might however arise in such cases from the twelfth Section of the Act, entitled "An Act concerning Duties on Spirits distilled within the United States." [2] But should the case happen without premeditation the forfeiture would doubtless be remitted, on returning the drawback, or paying the Duties. All Spirits not marked and certified would of course be deemed foreign Spirits.

I am, Sir, Your Obedt Servant   A Hamilton

Joseph Hiller Esqr.
Salem.

LS, MS Division, New York Public Library.
    1. Letter not found.
    2. Section 12 of this act reads as follows: "*And be it further enacted*, That after the last day of June next, no distilled spirits shall be brought into the United States, from any foreign port or place in any cask or vessel, which shall have been marked pursuant to any law of the United States concerning distilled spirits, on pain of forfeiture of the spirits so brought, and of the ship or vessel in which they shall be brought" (1 *Stat.* 270 [May 8, 1792]).

To Benjamin Lincoln

Treasury Department
June 27 1792.

Sir

I have before me your letter of the 6th instant. I refer you to the 45th Section of the Act, commonly called the Excise law,[1] where you will find a penalty of five hundred Dollars, for making use of *untrue* certificates. This Section would be applicable in the case you state, as the certificate accompanying the Rum must be deemed *untrue* relatively to the article.

I am of opinion that, though there may be a hardship in the case, you cannot dispense with the duty on the Coffee upon re-importation.

With great consideration, I am, Sir,

Benjamin Lincoln Esqr.
Boston.

L[S], RG 36, Collector of Customs at Boston, Letters from the Treasury, 1789–1807, Vol. 4, National Archives; copy, RG 56, Letters to the Collector at Boston, National Archives; copy, RG 56, Letters to Collectors at Small Ports, "Set G," National Archives.

1. "An Act repealing, after the last day of June next, the duties heretofore laid upon Distilled Spirits imported from abroad, and laying others in their stead; and also upon Spirits distilled within the United States, and for appropriating the same" (1 *Stat.* 199–214 [March 3, 1791]).

From Tench Coxe

Treasury Department, Revenue Office, June 28, 1792. Discusses the advantages and disadvantages of "three contracts for Stakeage in the rivers and Bays of North Carolina from the port of Beaufort inclusively to the northern part of Albemarle sound."

LC, RG 58, Letters of Commissioner of Revenue, 1792–1793, National Archives.

To William Ellery

[*Philadelphia, June 28, 1792.* On July 10, 1792, Ellery wrote to Hamilton: "I have recd. your letters of the 7th 22nd. and 28th of the last month." *Letter of June 28 not found.*]

To John Fitzgerald [1]

[*Philadelphia, June 28, 1792.* On the envelope of a letter from Fitzgerald to Hamilton, dated November 21, 1791, Hamilton wrote: "Ansd June 28." *Letter not found.*]

1. Fitzgerald, a resident of Alexandria, Virginia, had served as an aide-de camp to George Washington during the American Revolution.

From William Heth

Bermuda Hundred [Virginia] 28th June 1792

Dear Sir

Your very friendly & polite favor of the 7th Inst; was received—unsealed—a day or two ago in Richmond with sundry official letters. I beg, my dear Sir, that you will accept of my sincere thanks for the condescending attention which you have paid to my private concerns, and for your assurances of friendship.

The business & system of banks, being but new in this country, I have never thought much on the subject, and am therefore, not sufficiently informd, to say, whether a branch of the national bank would answer in Virginia, or not; but at your request, the following loose observations, are, with great deference communicated.

The trade of this State is carried on chiefly with foreign capital. Those engaged in it, hardly deserve the name of Merchants, being the factors, agents, and Shopkeepers of the Merchants, and Manufacturers of G Britain, and their business to dispose of the goods of that, for the produce of this Country, and remit it to the order of

ALS, Hamilton Papers, Library of Congress.

their principals; with whom, the profits of the trade, of *course* centre. And *this commerce,* is so divided, that it will be extremely difficult to find unanimity enough, to fix upon the place for establishing the bank. Richmond, Petersburg, Norfolk, & perhaps, *Alexandria,* may contend for this *honor* (Tho, at a meeting of the Merchants from the two first on the subject of moving this Office, it was admitted that Richmond shd be the place), and fixd as it must be, at one of these places, it would occasion such chagrin and disappointment to the others, that, if they did not approve, they would not co-operate in the measure. The trade of Petersburg, at present, exceeds that of Richmond—but both, are infinitely greater than that of Norfolk, the latter, being confined chiefly to the W. Indies—and tho' to a stranger, or to yourself—Judging from what he *sees*—and you from the Collectors returns—it may appear greater, yet I know it to be otherwise; insomuch that, perhaps threefourths of the goods enterd at Norfolk, are imported by the Merchants of Petersburg, Richmond & other parts *up* the country; to whom Norfolk is only a convenient Interpot for sometimes discharging and loading Vessels. Certain Vessels are enter'd *there* because I am Collector *here.* The produce which swells the Returns of exports from Norfolk, are Shippd by Merchants in the Upper Districts. Lumber, & Naval Stores, are almost every thing it furnishes. So that, it may with great propriety be said, that those, who carry on the business of Norfolk, reside in the upper Country, as do those in Petersburg & Richmond, who carry on the business of this District. For these reasons, & also, from its exposed, and remote situation from the heart of the Country, it does not by any means appear to be the proper place, nor is it possible that any man can recommend it to you; if possessd of one grain of candor, or information. The last of these objections applies equally to Alexandria.

Tho' the Trade of Petersburg, is at present greater than Richmond, and, infinitely more so than any in the State, I should nevertheless, give the preference to the latter; because its situation is more central and convenient for business. Being the seat of government, where the assembly *always* meet, where all public-Offices are kept, where the supreme courts are always held, it occasions a great and continual intercourse with all parts of the State. The number & *wealth* too of its inhabitants are greater, & it is increasing more rapidly, than any other place in the Country; and when the canal is completed, of which, there is now a flattering prospect,[1] and a good navigation brought to the place, it will most unquestionably draw to it, a considerable part of that trade which now goes to Petersburg. And when the canal that is opening between the waters of Elizabeth river and N. Carolina is finishd,[2] it will still lessen, if not *ruin* the trade of Petersburg.

Tho' I have no doubt in my own mind as to the most proper place, for fixing the bank; yet, I have very great doubts of its answering in this State at present (for my convenience as a public Officer, I wish it). If the principal object is discount, I question much, whether it will defray its expences. For the reasons already given, there is no considerable mercantile, circulating Capital; and there are but few monied men in the Country: consequently, the deposits in Specie will be inconsiderable. And the Merchants, or those who carry on the trade, having no attachment to the country, no fixd, or permanent residence in it, or any visible property except their goods and debts, discount will be uncertain; and cannot with propriety be carried to any extent, with this description of people.

But an opinion—tho' I conceive an erroneous one—has prevailed here, that the constitution of the Bank admitted of other deposits than specie. If so, Tobacco offers in this State, a very safe and good deposit. It is not perishable; at least, when of good quality, and properly put up, it will keep sound for years, and be improv'd by age. It is brought to public warehouses for Inspection, and there kept for a certain time free of Storage, and at the risk of the State. So that, the risk the bank would run by receiving it as a deposit, and giving notes for ⅔ds of its current specie value, with liberty to sell at 60 to 90 days, if not taken up, would be, their Notes returning upon them before that time, and in case the Tobacco should be destroyd, waiting untill repaid by the State. The first might be obviated by issuing their notes payable at 60 to 90 days after date— and the last, by an Insurance, by which, in case of loss they might recover of the underwriters, who would stand in the place of the

1. The James River Company was constructing a canal which would connect Richmond with tidewater.
2. The canal was to be built by the Dismal Swamp Canal Company, which had been organized in 1791.

bank, and obtain restitution from the State. The redemption of the Tobacco should be by specie only to be paid into the bank. The deposits in Tobacco would be considerable, and the bank Notes wd acquire such an extensive circulation, that numbers would be lost, and the circulation so slow, that vast advantages would result to the bank from the use of the Money.

It would facilitate, and greatly promote the circulation of their notes, if the bank could obtain an act of the Legislature here, for depositing the funds of the State in the bank, and making the taxes receivable in bank-notes. It would be farther necessary to give the bank power of proceeding in a summary manner in recovering payments of discounted bills. Upon the whole I think *the Trade* of this Country should agree upon the proper place for fixing the bank, should give assurance of their hearty union in its support, and at the same time that it should receive the *countenance and protection* of the State, before a branch is fixd here otherwise it might give rise to Such an opposition, as would defeat the end. And, in my humble opinion, the *last* essential, would be difficult to obtain unless some leading influential members of our legislature, should become Stockholders in the bank. One of the most able consel in this country, has already given it as his opinion, that a branch of the bank *cannot* be established in Virginia, if it demands, or receives an higher Interest than 5 ℀ Cent. Besides, the operations of the government hath by no means been pleasing to the people of this country—on the contrary, the friends to it are daily decreasing. Some of the highest in rank, and ability among us, & who supported it in our convention, are now extremely dissatisfied, and loud in abusing its measures, while some others, of equal fame, only express their chagrine and disappointment in private to those, who joind them in wishing to see the government establishd.

Thus my dear Sir, have I given you my confidential opinion, agreeably to your request, and, with a freedom of remark & observation, unfetterd by restraint, or reserve.

The business of the Customs being but little in this District at this Season of the year, and having some things of importance to myself to attend to, in Winchester and Philadelphia, this summer; I propose leaving this for a few weeks, as soon as possible in the ensuing month, after my quarterly accounts are closed; by which time, I hope there will be but little money on hand, and there is no prospect of any business to render my attendance necessary. Besides, private business, which hath been neglected ever since my coming into Office, my constitution has been so much affected by the great application which I paid to the duties of my Office, and constant attendance at this unhealthy place for the first two years, that I find it absolutely necessary to spend some time in the upper country this summer.

It will be the middle of August perhaps before I reach Philadelphia, when I hope to find you so much at leisure, as to be able to attend to observations on the revenue laws, which I have long forborne to make, from a persuasion that, if *every* Collector had been as troublesome to you on that score as I have, it would have employd your *whole* time to have read our letters, and directed answers. So that, instead of feeling any surprise at not receiving answers to such parts of my letters as appeard to *me* to require immediate notice I have only *wonderd* how you got through the great load of business, which hath been thrown upon your shoulders.

I am Dear Sir with the sincerest Esteem & friendship Yrs

W. Heth

Colo. A Hamilton.

To Rufus King

Philadelphia
June 28. 1792

My Dear King

I have not, as you will imagine, been inattentive to your political squabble.[1] I believe you are right [2] (though I have not accurately examined) but I am not without apprehension that a ferment may be raised which may not be allayed when you wish it. Tis not to be forgotten that the opposers of Clinton are the real friends to order & good Government; and that it will ill become them to give an example of the contrary.

Some folks are talking of Conventions and the Bayonet.[3] But the case will justify neither a resort to first principles nor to violence. Some amendments of your election law and possibly the impeachment of some of the Canvassers who have given proofs of *premeditated* partiality will be very well[4]—and it will answer good purposes to keep alive within proper bounds the public indignation. But beware of extremes!

There appears to be no *definite declared* objects of the momements on foot[5] which renders them the more Ticklish. What *can* you do? What do you *expect* to effect?[6]

Yrs. affectly   A Hamilton

Rufus King Esq

ALS, New-York Historical Society, New York City.

1. H is referring to the controversy in New York over the decision of the board of canvassers in the contested 1792 gubernatorial election. See Philip Schuyler to H, May 9, 1792, note 4; H to John Adams, June 25, 1792, note 2.

Before the committee of canvassers made its report on June 12, 1792, it had requested the opinions of King and Aaron Burr, United States Senators from New York, on the legality of canvassing the votes of Otsego, Clinton, and Tioga counties. King's opinion supported the eligibility of the votes of all three counties, while Burr opposed the admission of the Otsego County ballots. Both opinions are printed in *The* [New York] *Daily Advertiser* of June 18, 1792, together with the opinions of the majority and minority of the canvassers. The same issue carried a notice of a meeting of the "Friends of Liberty" who opposed the rejection of the Otsego and Clinton votes. The meeting adopted several resolutions condemning the decision of the majority of canvassers and approved a committee of correspondence to communicate with similar committees in other counties "and to devise such measures as may be best calculated to support the rights of the people" (*The* [New York] *Daily Advertiser*, June 18, 1792).

2. H is referring to King's answers to the questions submitted to him and to Burr by the committee of canvassers. The questions that were submitted read as follows:

"1st. Was Richard R. Smith the sheriff of the county of Otsego when he received and forwarded the ballots by his especial deputy?

"2d. If he was not sheriff, can the votes sent by him be legally canvassed?

"3d. Can the joint committee canvass the votes when sent to them in two parcels, the one contained in a box, and the other contained in a paper or separate bundle? Or

"4th. Ought they to canvass those sealed in the box and reject the others? . . .

"Ought the votes of Tioga to be canvassed? . . .

"Ought the votes of Clinton to be canvassed?" (*The* [New York] *Daily Advertiser*, June 18, 1792.)

In reply to these questions King gave the following opinion:

"OTSEGO

"It may be inferred from the constitution and the laws of the state, that the office of sheriff is held during the pleasure of the council of appointment, subject to the limitation contained in the 26th section of the constitution. The sheriff may therefore hold his office for four years, unless within that period a succession shall have been appointed, and shall have entered upon the execution of the office. The term of four years from the appointment of R. Smith not having expired, and B. Gilbert not having entered upon the execution of the office before the receipt and delivery of the votes by R. Smith to his deputy—I am of opinion that R. Smith was then lawfully sheriff of Otsego.

"This opinion is strengthened by what is understood to be practice—namely, that the office of sheriff is frequently held for more than a year under one appointment.

"R. Smith's giving notice to the council of appointment, of his disinclination to be re-appointed, or his acting as supervisor, cannot in my opinion be deemed a resignation or surrender of his office.

"Should doubts, however be entertained, whether R. Smith was *lawfully* sheriff when he received and delivered the votes to his deputy, the case contains facts which in another view of the subject are important. It appears that R. Smith was apointed sheriff of Otsego on the 17th Feb. 1791, and afterwards entered upon the execution of his office—that no other person was in the execution of or claimed the office after the date of his appointment, and before the time when he received and delivered the votes of the county to his deputy; that during that interval, R. Smith was sheriff or the county was without a sheriff; that R. Smith during the election, and when he received and delivered the votes to his deputy, continued in the actual exercise of the shrievalty, and that under color of a regular appointment. From this statement, it may be inferred, that if R. Smith, when he received and delivered the votes to his deputy was not *dejure*, he was *defacto* sheriff of Otsego.

"Though all the acts of an officer de facto may not be valid, and such of them as are merely voluntary and exclusively beneficial to himself, are void, yet such acts as tend to the public utility, and such as he would be compellable to perform, such as are essential to preserve the rights of third persons; and without which they might be lost or destroyed, when done by an officer *de facto*, are valid.

"I am therefore of opinion, that admitting R. Smith, when he received and delivered the votes to his deputy was not *de jure* sheriff, yet that he was *de facto* sheriff, and that he receiving and delivering of the votes, being acts done under color of authority, tending to the public utility, and *necessary* to the carrying into effect the rights of suffrage of the citizens of that county, they are, and ought to be deemed valid; and consequently the votes of that county may lawfully be canvassed.

"2d Question—The preceeding answer to the first question, renders an answer to the second unnecessary.

"3d and 4th Questions—The sheriff is required to put into one box every inclosure delivered to him by an inspector, appointed for that purpose by the inspectors of any town or district, and for omitting to put any such enclosure into the box, he is liable to prosecution; but in case of such omission, the votes put into the box and seasonably delivered into the Secretary's Office, may, notwithstanding such omission, be lawfully canvassed; and equally so, whether the omitted enclosure be kept back or sent forward with the box to the Secretary's office. I am therefore of opinion, that the votes contained in the box may lawfully be canvassed; but that those contained in a separate packet, from considerations explained in the depositions, and distinct from the objection of not being included with the box, cannot be lawfully canvassed.

"CLINTON

"The deputy having no interest in the office of sheriff, but being merely the sheriff's servant, it does not seem to be necessary that the evidence of his being employed or made deputy should be a deed or an instrument in writing, though the latter would be proper, yet a deputy may be made by *parol*—I am therefore inclined to the opinion, that the votes of Clinton may be canvassed.

"TIOGA

"The sheriff is one who executes an office in person or by deputy so far at least as the office is ministerial when a duty is required of the sheriff eo nomine, he may execute it in person or by deputy; but if the deputy appoints a deputy, it may be doubted whether ordinary the acts of the last deputy are the acts of the sheriff: The present instance is an extreme case; had the duty been capable of being performed within the county, the sheriff or another deputy could have performed: Here the deputy being in the execution of his duty, and without the county is prevented by the act of God from completing it, the sheriff could not appoint, and the deputy undertakes to appoint a deputy, to finish his duty, who accordingly does so. The election law is intended to render effectual the constitutional right of suffrage, it should therefore be construed liberally, and the means should be held in subordination to the end.

"In this case it may reasonably be doubted, whether the canvassers are obliged to reject the votes of Tioga."
(*The* [New York] *Daily Advertiser*, June 18, 1792.)

3. In the June 15, 1792, issue of *The Daily Advertiser* a letter signed "Gracchus" proposed that meetings of electors in all the counties and committees of correspondence should be arranged. "Gracchus" concluded: "Such measures, adopted with ardour, and prosecuted with firmness, will, I trust, have the desired effect; if not, and the ordinary powers of legislation, should prove an incompetent remedy for rescuing the people from an usurped authority; the same powers which established the constitution, must in the last resort convene for its preservation." In the following issue another writer stated: "To remedy the abuse I sincerely hope *violent* measures will not become necessary" (*The* [New York] *Daily Advertiser*, June 15, 16, 1792).

4. William Willcocks, a constant and outspoken opponent of the "governor of Mr. Burr and the canvassers," suggested in a letter of June 13, 1792: ". . . although *trifles* will not rouse large bodies to a Sion, or even reflection, an attack upon a privilege which is the *basis* of political security, will be soon severely felt, end long remembered, and a wise community will pursue with ardor, every mode of relief, consistent with the peace and good order of society. . . . The prevailing sentiment is, that . . . [the canvassers] ought to be impeached—I hope and believe they will" (*The* [New York] *Daily Advertiser*, June 15, 1792).

5. The heated, but indefinite, character of the opposition to the canvassers' decision is suggested by the resolutions approved by the meeting of the "Friends of Liberty" on June 18, 1792. The resolutions concluded that electors from each county in the state should unite "in an application to the legislature at their next meeting, for a redress of the injury which has been done to the rights of the people" and that committees of correspondence should "devise such measures as may be best calculated to support the rights of the people" (*The* [New York] *Daily Advertiser*, June 19, 1792).

6. On a page attached to this letter King wrote: "I have had no agency in promoting the measures adopted respecting the decision of the Canvassers. I have however felt the utmost indignation."

From John Langdon

Portsmo. [New Hampshire] June 28th. 1792

Sr.

I was honor'd with your favor of the 18th Inst.[1] by post; by which I see, Mr. Church[2] supposes he was not one of the Owners of the Ship Portsmouth,[3] at the time she was in France, in which he will find himself Mistaken, when he recollects, that he Came to this place with Mr. Moore[4] and Mercer[5] and Recd. his proportion of a very Valuable Prize, called, the New Duckinfield, which was Captured, by the Portsmouth; in the very Cruise, in which these expences, on the Ship were incurr'd; and at the same time signed, an Agreement and Direction, as one of the owners, of the Portsmo. to me, to fit out the Ship for another Cruise; there were also some small matters bro't from France, in the Portsmouth, which he recd. his proportion of; Therefore there could be no doubt of his being an Owner that Cruise, as myself and the other Owners Consider'd and delt with him as such.

Inclosed is list of the Owners of the Armed Ship Portsmo, with the proportion each held. Mr. Archibald Mercer of New Jersey one of the Owners, and with whom Ive Settled will be able to give you full information Touching this Affair

I think Mr. Church purchased his part of the Ship latter part of the year 1777.

You'll please Recollect the reason why this was not Settled in Course; The Demand was not, known till some time since the peace took place. I have the honor to be with highest Esteem & Respect. Sr. your most Obt. Servt.   John Langdon

Hon.
A. Hamilton.

ALS, Hamilton Papers, Library of Congress.
    1. Letter not found.
    2. John B. Church. H handled Church's business affairs in the United States.
    3. A letter of marque had been granted to the *Portsmouth*, a New Hampshire ship, on June 7, 1777. The owners were listed as "John Langdon and others, Portsmouth" (*Naval Records of the American Revolution*, 420).

4. Either Patrick or Philip Moore of Philadelphia, both of whom were engaged in extensive privateering during the American Revolution.

5. Archibald Mercer, a New Jersey businessman and the deputy governor for the Society for Establishing Useful Manufactures.

From Tobias Lear

Philadelphia, June 28, 1792. "By the President's command T. Lear has the honor to return. . . . a contract, with his approbation subjoined, between the Superintendant of the Delaware Lighthouse &c. and Thomas Davis & Thomas Connaroe. . . ." [1]

LC, George Washington Papers, Library of Congress.

1. See Tench Coxe to H, June 20, 1792, and H to George Washington, June 26, 1792.

From William Short

The Hague June 28, 1792

Sir

I have the honor of resuming from this place my correspondence with you which has been lately suspended by my change of place & circumstance.[1] My late letters & particularly those to the secretary of State will have shewn by what cause so long a space of time has elapsed between my appointment & my arrival here. I am anxious that it should be seen that there was no activity wanting on my part to comply with the will of government in this instance. It was not made known to me until the 7th of May.[2] I immediately took measures which I hoped would enable me to set out on the 26th of the same month—my departure was however unavoidably deferred some days longer. Then being forced to pass through England from the circumstances of the moment & in the hope of rendering my

ALS, letterpress copy, William Short Papers, Library of Congress.

1. Short had been appointed Minister Resident to The Hague in January, 1792.

2. Gouverneur Morris had written to Short from London on February 10, 1792, informing him of an official communication received in the British capital concerning Morris's nomination by Washington as Minister Plenipotentiary to France and Short's nomination as Minister to The Hague (Morris, *Diary of the French Revolution*, II, 363-64). Short's official letter of appointment, however, was delivered to him by Morris on the latter's arrival in Paris.

arrival here more direct & perhaps more early, it was not until the 15th inst. that I got to this place.

I found here your letter of Nov 30. 91. I have since recieved from Amsterdam yours of April 2. 10 & 16. 92. I received at Paris those which you had done me the honor to write me previously in the course of the present year. Mine to you have been dated Jan. 26. March 24. April 22. 25. May 14. 26.[3]

Before taking up the subjects of your several letters as relative to the business at Amsterdam I will briefly report what has been mentioned in mine as relative to matters at Paris, in order that in quitting them I may leave with you as clear an idea as I can of the then situation. They are principally as follows.

1. Depreciation on payments made to France: I have already had the honor of informing you of my announcing your intention on this subject on the reciept of your letter—my reasons for considering it necessary to do so—& my applying this intention to payments to be made in future.[4] Those made on the Antwerp loan only come within this description as yet. You have been informed also how it became indispensable to avoid risk to the U. S. & loss of time to make these payments at Antwerp to a person there authorized by the French government who gave his receipts expressed in florins & marking the exchange at the date of each payment.[5] I have frequently mentioned to you also that the basis on which the depreciation should be calculated, being known & therefore no inconvenience being to be apprehended from a short delay, & having every reason to believe that the person who was to represent the will of government permanently at Paris either was or soon would be designated, I thought it most advisable under every consideration to leave so delicate a subject to his care.[6] The event having manifested the propriety of my not taking this business on myself—I delivered to Mr. Morris my correspondence from Antwerp with the commissaries on the subject, & urged his settling it without delay, on account of the situation of the present government, with whom it was evidently better to regulate the value of assignats than with any other.

3. Letter of May 26, 1792, not found.
4. See H to Short, September 2, 1791; Short to H, November 22, 1791, January 26, March 24, May 14, 1792.
5. See Short to H, January 26, March 24, May 14, 1792.
6. See Short to H, March 24, April 22, 25, May 14, 1792.

He was fully sensible of this—but mentioned two causes of delay 1. a letter he had recd from the Sec. of State from which there appeared an intention to throw the depreciation on France [7]—2. his not having been admitted reguarly to deliver his credentials,[8] & his not chusing to do anything previously. I hope that ere this he will have recieved some further explanation from the sec. of State which will enable him to proceed—& that the other cause of delay will have ceased also as he informed me previously to my leaving Paris that the day was fixed for his having his audience of the King—& that he will have adjusted the business of depreciation with the French government, although I have as yet no letter from him announcing it. I am waiting for it with some impatience in order to re-commence the payments from Amsterdam, making the proper reservations for your draughts.

2. Prospect of paying off the French debt by a single operation— I have mentioned to you several alteratives which I thought the increasing credit of the U.S. would present to their choice. That which appeared to me to merit unquestionably the preference was the offer of the house of Boyd & Kerr,[9] supported by La Borde [10] & connected with Hope [11] of Amsterdam. I spoke of this subject particularly in my letter of March 24. You will see there by what means it was delayed. Whilst the exchange continued regularly declining, they would have contracted without hesitation & with the prospects of considerable gain. Before the arrival of Mr. Morris at Paris, a rise in the exchange as unaccountable as unexpected took place wch would have rendered such a contract at least unprofitable & probably ruinous to the houses which would have contracted.

7. See Short to H, May 14, 1792, note 18.
8. Morris explained the delay in presenting his credentials in a letter to Jefferson, dated June 10, 1792. The pertinent section reads as follows: "As Mr Short remained here until the second instant, and was better acquainted with the current transactions, I relied on him for the communication of them. He informed you, that we obtained an interview with M. Dumouriez on the fifteenth of May. In this interview he told me, that he thought it was best I should be presented to the King immediately, but yet my first audience did not take place until the third of this month. He apologised for this delay, as proceeding from the state of public affairs, which kept him continually occupied and agitated" (Sparks, *Gouverneur Morris*, II, 176).
9. See Short to H, March 24, 1792.
10. Jean Joseph, Marquis de Laborde, banker to Louis XV.
11. Henry Hope, head of an Amsterdam banking firm.

The new minister also of the department of finance,[12] being much versed in the business of exchange & supposed to employ artificial means of influencing it, no house chose to risk such an enterprize under such circumstances. I informed Mr. Morris of the subject, & he will no doubt make a proper use for the U.S. of such an opportunity if it should again present itself. The Minister who was most feared by the bankers who wished to undertake this business & who indeed were the only ones competent to it, from the funds they had at command, has been lately displaced. I know not how far this may encourage them to renew their offers. I shall ever consider it as a misfortune that they were not formerly closed with—but I don't doubt you will feel Sir, that the motives which I formerly had the honor of mentioning to you as influencing me in wishing for delay, were fully legitimate.

3. Application of a part of the debt to France, to succour S. Domingo as proposed by the minister of marine. My letters from Amsterdam & Paris will have informed you of the origin & progress of this business [13]—& by what means I have been brought on to suspend the application of the first 4. per cent loan towards remittances to France, in hopes of its being converted into supplies to be purchased in the U. S. for succours to S. Domingo. The decree of the assembly was at length passed. I had agreed with the minister that you should hold 800,000 dollars at his disposition for these purchases, writing to you at the same time to draw for that amount at Amsterdam. My letters of April 22. & 25 & May 14 will have informed you how this business was delayed—& for what reasons—& also how in consequence of your letter of March 21. it was determined to hold that loan at your disposal instead of longer engaging the 800,000 dollars to the Minister of Marine. It was considered that the delay which he had as[k]ed & the sums already applied in America towards the demands of S. Domingo, would furnish Mr. Morris with fully sufficient reasons for considering the promise I had made, as no longer in force. I have not as yet heard from Mr. Morris what

12. Short was probably referring to Etienne Clavière, who had been appointed Minister of Finance on March 23, 1792, and was replaced on June 13, 1792, by François Beaulieu.
13. See Short to H, December 28, 1791, January 26, March 24, April 22, 25, May 14, 1792.

JUNE 1792 597

has been done in this business—but am persuaded there will have been no difficulty in it.

4. Favorable prospect for the U.S. from the disposition of the ministry as to the decrees relative to American commerce—& from the ministry's having then for the first time a majority in the assembly. Although this does not immediately concern the American debt, yet as I mentioned it to you in a former letter I cannot avoid here touching it again for the last time. I must beg you to recollect the consideration which induced me to mention it to you in my letter of March 24 as well as what I then said respecting it. Since then that ministry have fallen out among themselves—lost the majority which they had in the assembly & consequently the force they exercised on the Monarch. They have been accordingly successfully dismissed although they were always probably unworthy of the confidence of the nation & certainly never enjoyed that of the King, yet if they could have supported themselves & kept the majority they first had in the assembly, I am fully persuaded they would have annuled the late hostile decrees to the commerce of the U.S. & this as well from the principles of the leading members of the ministry, as from their wish in general to counteract the proceedings of the former assembly, which wore a disposition that had become very popular in this. The destruction of this ministry has hastened a crisis in France, the most severe that has yet happened. It is probable that the system of absolute anarchy ⟨- - -⟩ which has been growing up there for some time would in the course of things have brought it on. The post not having since arrived here (stopped as it is supposed either at Paris or on the way) we only know from a single letter sent by express that the mob had broken into the King's Palace, & unopposed by the national guard had offered every insult to his person—armed with pikes on which the general devise was the death of the King. It is certain that he & his family were totally at their disposal & everyone trembles to learn the fate of this most unfortunate monarch—thus abandoned & delivered up to the fury of a race of miscreants which it was hoped the lights of the present age had dissipated in this civilized part of the world. Government will certainly receive much earlier & fuller information of this melancoly & alarming scene from their minister

at Paris. I should not have mentioned it to you but for its connexion with what I had formerly said respecting the abolition of the late decrees respecting the commerce of the U States the late ministry possessing the majority of the assembly.[14]

In the re-examination of your several letters which are now before me unanswered—the first circumstance which occurs as necessary to be taken notice of is the part of your letter of Nov. 30. relative to what I had said respecting the commencement of re-imbursements to the 1st of this month. It was an error into which I had been led by the bankers at Amsterdam. They gave me to understand it at a time when I was urging the excess of our means above our wants of money—& when they wished me to believe the contrary. I had not examined the contract & was pleased when I found it was an error.

I recieve Sir with an heartfelt satisfaction the expressions of your letter of April 2 relative to my exertions at Amsterdam in reducing the interest on the loan at that time to 4. p. cent. If my exertions in France to serve my country & give satisfaction to the government by whom I was employed there have been less successfully faced yet I must beg leave to repeat to you Sir assurances that it was not through want of zeal or efforts on my part. I feel much pleasure in persuading myself that your knowledge of the spirit which prevailed there, & the operations which naturally proceeded from the order of things then existing, will enable you to attribute the effects to their true causes—& convince you that nothing on our part could have arrested the torrent of innovation which prevailed during my residence there charged with the interests of the U. S.—& have protected, much less extended, the privileges of our commerce, in opposition to the cabals & private intrigues of interested individuals which ever gave—ever must govern such assemblies.

What you are pleased to say Sir with respect to the satisfaction with which the intelligence of the result of my exertions at Amsterdam was received by the President & the pleasure it gave to the public at large cannot but be doubly pleasing at this moment in particular.

14. This paragraph refers to the fall of the Girondin Ministry, which had come into power in March, 1792.

I shall communicate to Mr. Morris an extract of your letter of April 2 respecting the adopting a rule for liquidating the payments to France—referring you to what I have said above on that subject.

Nothing has been done at Antwerp since my letter informing you that M de Wolf [15] had suppressed a part of the loan at 4.½ p. cent on the condition of being supplied with bonds at 4. p. cent. I expect him here soon & will inform you of the result of our conference. He is very devious & thinks his exertions entitle him to be employed in a new loan at 4. p. cent. Mr. Morris also is an advocate in favor of it & from his superior knowledge & degree of confidence placed in him by government, his opinions are necessarily entitled to much weight. What you say on the other hand with respect to holding out the idea of confining the loan at Amsterdam in some measure counteracts this.[16]

I observe what you say in your abovementioned letter with respect to your intended draughts. The two & an half million which you there speak of, you may draw for as soon as you please. In order that there may be no misunderstanding or delay on this subject—it will be well to mention to you that a part of the loans already made will suffice to answer your draughts. I had the satisfaction of announcing to you by a few lines written for that purpose only from Paris on the 26th of May, that a second loan at 4. p. cent had been contracted for.[17] It is now going on. The 800,000 dollars I formerly mentioned to you on account of the minister of marine, to be drawn for, & afterwards as being to be held at your disposition, I shall consider as making a part of the 2½ million of guilders you mention in your letter of April 2, unless you direct the contrary in some future letter. Taking care therefore that the bankers shall be provided to answer your draughts for 2½ million

15. See Short to H, March 24, 1792.
16. See H to Short, April 2, 1792.
17. Letter not found. The Holland loan of 1792 had been authorized by H in his letter to Short of March 21, 1792. The loan "was drawn for three millions of guilders ($1,200,000), at 4 per cent. interest, to run for eleven years, then to be redeemable in five equal annual payments of 600,000 guilders each. The commission and charges amounted to 5 per cent, with an additional charge of 1 per cent. on the interest received and paid" (Bayley, *National Loans*, 26). The contract for this loan, dated August 9, 1792, and Washington's ratification, dated November 5, 1792, may be found in RG 59, Records Relating to Foreign Accounts, 1782–1797, Letters, Accounts, and Contracts, National Archives.

of florins, so as with ½ million already drawn for to complete the 3 millions, I shall as soon as I hear from Mr. Morris direct them to proceed in their payments to France—the sums which they have already on hand having accumulated to a much greater degree & remained much longer idle that I would have wished, for the reasons which have been mentioned to you in my several letters. There will be no risk in applying a considerable part of the cash now intended towards the French debt & counting on future entries to answer a part of your draughts. It would be well therefore to inform me as nearly as you can of the times at which they will be made.

Your letter of April 10 informs me of payments made or to be made in America on account of the French debt. I observe they are expressed in dollars. Would it not be proper that your minister at Paris should be informed of them as well as the rate at which the dollar is to be converted into livres tournois? It would be advantageous probably if it were to be settled by the same rule by which he shall settle the payments made in florins if you have not already fixed it.

The information contained in your letter of April 16. was highly satisfactory. The bankers at Amsterdam seemed to think that the impression made there by the fluctuation of the funds in America was too partial & momentary to render it necessary to publish any thing respecting it. They apprehended it ought rather do harm & as my own opinion was similar I have not done it—& therefore kept your letter for my own satisfaction & to enable me to meet such observations as I may hear made on the subject. I do not apprehend that the state of things in France require any thing to be said there either respecting the business. Still for greater security I shall in consequence of what you say send a copy of your letter to Mr. Morris. I have the honor to be Sir, with the accustomed sentiments of attachment & respect your most obedient & humble servant.

                                                      W Short
Alexander Hamilton Secretary of the Treasury, Philadelphia

To George Washington

Treasury Department, June 28, 1792. Submits "copy of a Report of this date from The Commissioner of the Revenue,[1] on the subject of certain provisional contracts, which have been entered into for the stakeage of certain waters in North Carolina."

LC, George Washington Papers, Library of Congress.
1. See Tench Coxe to H, June 28, 1792.

From Otho H. Williams

Ceresville [Maryland] 28 June 1792

Sir.

A necessary attention to my health required my leaving Baltimore, for a time, and occasions my writing to you from the vicinity of Frederick town.

I have just received your letter, dated the 18th Inst: relative to certain communications by the Commissioner of the Revenue,[1] comprehending a letter from me of the 3d. of May last, to the Surveyor of the district of Baltimore.[2]

It is matter of very great surprize to me that what occurred on the subject alluded to should be represented to you as "a controversy, between the officers, respecting the limits of duty." I am still more surprized that you should think it justifiable to remonstrate in a strain of rebuke which I know is unmerited.

My letter to the Surveyor was occasioned by a representation of some of the Inspectors that they had been employed by him in the department of the Revenue in marking of Casks,[3] & in such laborious & servile parts of the duty as they considered as degrading, and which they apprehended proceeded from pique and resentment. That they were detached from their particular duty as Inspectors of the Customs, & that they were not qualified, or *requested* to qualify,

ADf, Maryland Historical Society, Baltimore; copy, RG 53, "Old Correspondence," Baltimore Collector, National Archives.
1. Tench Coxe.
2. Robert Ballard. See H to Williams, June 18, 1792.
3. Section 13 of "An Act repealing, after the last day of June next, the duties heretofore laid upon Distilled Spirits imported from abroad, and laying others in their stead; and also upon Spirits distilled within the United States, and for appropriating the same" provided that the officers of inspection should mark the "casks, vessels and cases" of spirits (1 *Stat.* 202 [March 3, 1791]). For Treasury regulations concerning the administration of this section of the act, see the enclosure to "Treasury Department Circular to the Collectors of the Customs," May 26, 1791.

as the Excise law required that they were even obnoxious to penalty by law [4] for acting as they had been desired and that they had no promise or expectation of indemnification or reward.

I gave no immediate, or direct, answer to this representation. In fact I did not answer to it at all; But wrote a line to the Surveyor containing, it is true, my opinion relative to their being employed in the revenue department which I conceived to be strictly agreeable to law and therefore not capable of being construed as contradictory to the Instructions of the secretary of the Treasury; [5] For, although the Instructions direct the employing of Inspectors of the Customs as Inspectors of the revenue, as it appeared to me that the Legislature contemplated the *expediency* only of such a measure I could not imagine that a *necessity* was intended to be created, and an obligation imposed, without an alternative, by the mode of executing the Law.

The intimate connection between the departments, and the ambiguity of the "large chapter of undefined relative duties which appertain to every officer in every Station" made me conscious of my responsibility and more particularly attentive to my own Station. I saw the "possibility of an interference of duties" which you deny; I saw that the men whom I had selected, for integrity as well as for abilities, to perform duties, which ought not to be committed to unworthy or ignorant persons, might be engaged in a department wherein I had no controul; and that the Department under my particular superintendence must occasionally be supplied by such as I could pick up: and such as might be picked up by any one else and for any other purpose. Men proper for the service are not to be commanded at an hours warning. I saw too, while I was actually under this embarrassment, and the Government in greater hazard of being rendered odious than it otherwise might have been that those men who had devoted themselves to the service were in a situation to receive "Either none or smaller compensations" than

4. Section 6 of the same act provided for a penalty of two hundred dollars for officers appointed under the act who failed to take an oath before commencing their duties or failed to send a copy of the oath to the comptroller of the Treasury within three months after commencing their duties (1 *Stat.* 200).

5. Williams is referring to instructions given in the enclosure to "Treasury Department Circular to the Collectors of the Customs," May 26, 1791.

the law allowed for the performance of duties for which they were especially appointed.

Upon recollection, Sir, it will occur to you that the form required by the Comptroller (whose instructions in respect to forms you have directed me to obey) [6] for *Inspectors* accounts is *for services on board of certain Vessels;* and although (upon my representation of the necessity of often employing them otherwise, and the allowance by Law being for *"days service in aid of the customs"*) the Comptroller was pleased to dispense with that form, he yet insists on their accounts being Stated *in detail.* It was not provided for and it was impossible for me to conceive the propriety, even if it might be admitted at the treasury, of charging the Customs with expences incidental to the Revenue. By law & by my instructions I could pay *only* for services in aid of the former; and, in fact, respecting Services in aid of the latter I could have no official information.

I claim the merit, if it is such, of being prompt in the performance of my duty, and of not being disposed to *"hesitate in the execution of the laws."* No officer is less *"disposed to embarrass the public service"* or *"clog the wheels of administration."* I have given no *"example of disorder."* My letter to the Surveyor was to *prevent* disorder; and to suggest to him the propriety of obviating in his double capacity, those objections which had been strengthened if not created, by his manner of enforcing instructions of which no legal intimation had given the least anticipation. It occured at a time of an extraordinary stress of business, when all the time of all the Inspectors was necessarily taken up in attending on and discharging of Vessels. Could I have apprehended that at such a time or at any time, the business of the Customs was to be retarded by that of the Revenue; or that, if additional aid was necessary, it was material to the Govert. by which department it was procured? There were Officers enough in one department, and it never occurred to me that

6. See "Treasury Department Circular to the Collectors of the Customs," February 17, 1790. In a circular to the collectors of the customs, dated June 8, 1792, Oliver Wolcott, Jr., comptroller of the Treasury, advised: "You are desired hereafter to state in your Quarterly Account current, the Salaries of Surveyors or other officers of the Customs which are or may be payable in your District; the mode now generally adopted of charging them in the Abstract of payments to Inspectors, &c. being found by experience to be inconvenient" (LS, Office of the Secretary, United States Treasury Department).

it was my duty to create more in order to supply the other, in which the power of Creation is by law made adequate to its occasions.

When this affair is properly understood it will appear that all the embarrassments which did actual occur proceeded not from any "spirit of refinement or critical nicety about the boundarys of Official duty" in the Officers of the Customs.

I am much pained by the unexpected necessity of defending myself against the imputation of being the Author of them; and I feel not a little, Sir, from your suggestion that the Inspectors not performing duties required of them, *whether legally obligatory on them or not*, would be a good reason for substituting others.

The men at present employed as Inspectors have, most of them, been long in the service of their Country—some of them in much more respectable stations than at present. One of them had the honor to serve early in the first Congress, and several of them, through the whole of the late War, as Officers in the army. Want of a just requital of former services in respect to some of them may be assigned as the cause of their present humble condition.

I shall inform them, as I have heretofore done, that not only in the particular line of their duty as officers of the Customs, but in relation to the Revenue department, and in every other situation wherein it is in their power to promote the execution of the laws, and support the Government of the United States, it is a duty incumbent on them to do it. I will inform them also that it is your opinion that as Inspectors of the Customs they are bound to obey the orders of the Inspector of the Revenue, as such, and that obedience is expected of them. But I do not engage myself to dismiss them if they should demur to an opinion in which I cannot myself implicitly acquiesce. I believe that the officers as well as the departments were intended to be distinct. The Legislature otherwise wod. not have made a special provision for constituting officers of the one to be officers of the other,[7] as if to reconcile a seeming incompatibility; but wod. have assigned the same duties at once or directed it to be done.

Confirmed as I am in this opinion before I became the instrument of what I must consider as injustice to deserving men I will appeal

7. See H to Williams, June 18, 1792, note 5.

to that highest authority to which your letter refers. "If redress is not found there, the path" (you are pleased to tell me) "is plain." To me it is very plain. Believe me, no sense of dishonor is attached to my idea of a private Station. Neither disgrace nor distress will attend me. But to others the path may not be equally plain and smooth. Thorns and difficulties may lie in their way; even the terrors of poverty may assail them, and force a compliance with directions right or wrong. This necessity, in my opinion (for I cannot abandon the privilege of thinking) would be an aggravation to the oppression, and I can not apprehend that the compulsive expedient which you recommend will be insisted upon. It would eventually destroy every degree of respectability and render the Inspectors unworthy of that confidence which must necessarily be reposed in officers of even the lowliest denomination.

Sure I am that if, when the Surveyor of Balte. was appointed Inspector of the Revenue he had said, as he reasonably might have done, that all his time and talents were necessarily engaged in discharging the duties of the first office, he would not have been told, "Sir, you must do this, and without compensation too, or—*the path is plain.*"

The analogy will not be questioned; nor can I conceive how any officer, who holds his Commission at pleasure, and who does not depend on popular consequence for support, can expect to be at all times exempt from a similar coercion.

Concerned as I certainly am in this question I will endeavour to acquit myself with that stedfast fidelity to the Government, the dignity of which is not independent of the Virtue of its officers, which, in all events, will insure me the quiet of my own conscience and the approbation of those who judge with information, candor and liberality.

I am, Sir, your most obedient, and most Humble Servant

O. H. Williams

A Hamilton Esqr Secy of the Treasury

To Tench Coxe

Treasury Department
June 29 1792.

Sir

The President having approved of the contract between the Superintendent of the Delaware Light House &ca. and Thomas Davis and Thomas Connaroe,[1] for erecting a pier in the River Delaware, the papers relating to that object are herewith returned, in order that the business may be proceeded upon.

I am, with great consideration,   Sir,   Your Obedt Servant

Alexander   Hamilton

Tench Coxe Esqr.
Commissioner of the Revenue.

LS, Connecticut College Library, New London, Connecticut.
  1. See Tobias Lear to H, June 28, 1792.

To Thomas Jefferson

Treasury Department
June 29th 1792

Sir

In consequence of the letter, which you sent me from Mr. Short,[1] I find it will be convenient to draw on the Commissioners in Holland[2] for the sum which is required pursuant to the third Section of the Act intitled "An Act making certain appropriations therein specified."[3]

I therefore propose the following arrangement that the Treasurer draw bills, in your favour, for a sum in guilders equal to fifty thousand dollars; that you give him an acknowlegement for these bills, as a purchase for the use of your department; promising to pay the amount when you shall be furnished with money for that purpose from the Treasury, pursuant to the abovementioned Act.

This will, consistently with the course of the Treasury, put you in possession of the requisite sum, for the next packet; and will avoid the necessity of a loan 'till the occasion for an application of the amount of the bills *here* shall occur, acording to the destination of that fund.

This arrangement being merely with a view to Treasury convenience and œconomy will not I presume appear liable to any objection. Should it not, it shall be immediately carried into effect.

I have the honor to be, very respectfully Sir   Your most Obedient servt   Alexander Hamilton

The Secretary of State

ALS, James Madison Papers, Library of Congress.
  1. See William Short to H, April 22, 1792.
  2. Willink, Van Staphorst, and Hubbard.
  3. Section 3 of this act reads as follows: "*And be it further enacted,* That a sum of fifty thousand dollars in addition to the provision heretofore made be appropriated to defray any expense which may be incurred in relation to the intercourse between the United States and foreign nations, to be paid out of any monies, which may be in the treasury, not otherwise appropriated, and to be applied under the direction of the President of the United States who, if necessary, is authorized to borrow, on the credit of the United States, the said sum of fifty thousand dollars" (1 *Stat.* 285 [May 8, 1792]).

To Tench Coxe

Treasury Department, June 30, 1792. Returns "contracts for the stakeage of certain waters in North Carolina" which have received the President's approbation.[1]

LS, RG 26, Lighthouse Letters Received, "Segregated" Lighthouse Records, Hamilton, National Archives.
  1. See H to George Washington, June 28, 1792.

To John Jay

Philadelphia June 30. 1792

My Dear Sir

The bearer of this is Lt Colonel Toussard, a French Officer, who lost his arm in our service during the late war.[1] He is now Lt Colonel of the *Regiment Du Cape*,[2] and lately from St Domingo with his family. Being desirous of purchasing some lands in our State, he is setting out on a journey to N York and has requested a line introducing him to you. This I readily comply with, as he is generally esteemed a man of real worth.

The attentions you may shew him will oblige   Dr Sir   Yr. Affect & Obed serv   A Hamilton

Chief Justice Jay

ALS, courtesy of the Alexander Hamilton Bicentennial Commission.
  1. Lewis Tousard had served as a captain of artillery and later as aide-de-camp to Lafayette during the American Revolution. After he was wounded at Rhode Island in 1778, the Continental Congress granted him a life annuity. At the end of the war he held the rank of lieutenant colonel by brevet.
  2. The Regiment du Cap-Français was to be disbanded under a decree of the National Assembly of France of September 29, 1791. The reorganization of the colonial special regiments did not take effect in Santo Domingo until December, 1792. Tousard returned to Santo Domingo and was sent back to France in the fall of 1792 with other officers of the Regiment du Cap-Français under suspicion of counterrevolutionary activities. In 1793 he fled from France to join his family in the United States.

From Tobias Lear

[*Philadelphia*] *June 30, 1792.* Transmits "three Contracts entered into for the stakage of certain waters in North Carolina, which have been submitted to the President of the United States & have received his approbation." [1]

LC, George Washington Papers, Library of Congress.
  1. See H to Tench Coxe, June 30, 1792.

To John Lowell [1]

[*Philadelphia, June 30, 1792.* On July 12, 1792, Lowell wrote to Hamilton: "I recd. your letter of the 30th: of June last." *Letter not found.*]

  1. Lowell was United States judge for the District of Massachusetts.

To William Short

Treasury Department
June 30. 1792.

Sir
I have before me your letter of the 22nd. of April last.

As I doubt not the details of the projected mangement will leave sufficient latitude, as to time, to avoid embarrassment to the Treasury, it cannot but be satisfactory.

A bill has been drawn in favour of the Secretary of State on our Commissioners for One hundred and twenty three thousand, seven hundred and fifty Guilders,[1] which, together with the Five hundred thousand, of which you were advised by my letter of the 2nd. of April last will constitute part of the fund which may be reserved for the arrangement in question. I shall forbear any further drafts 'till I am advised of its completion.

You will no doubt take care to retain a competent sum for the payment of the Interest, which shall be payable during the present year on the Dutch and Antwerp Loans.

With much consideration I have the honor to remain Sir Your obedient servant   Alexander Hamilton

William Short Esqr.
Minister Resident at the Hague.

LS, William Short Papers, Library of Congress; LS, marked "Duplicate," William Short Papers, Library of Congress. A copy of this letter was enclosed in H's "Report on Foreign Loans," February 13, 1793.
1. See H to Thomas Jefferson, June 29, 1792.

To Benjamin Walker

[*Philadelphia, June 30, 1792.* Letter listed in dealer's catalogue. *Letter not found.*]

ALS, sold by Stan V. Henkels, Jr., December, 1892, Catalogue No. 694, Item 221.

From George Washington

[Philadelphia, June 30, 1792]

For carrying into execution the provisions of the third section of the Act intitled, "An Act making certain appropriations therein specified," passed the Eight day of May in this present year.[1]

I do hereby authorise you the said Secretary of the Treasury in the name and on the credit of the United States to borrow of any body or bodies politic, person or persons whomsoever the sum of Fifty thousand Dollars; and to enter into such Agreements for the reimbursement thereof as shall be needful and proper; hereby promising to ratify whatever you shall lawfully do in the premises.

In testimony whereof I have hereunto subscribed my hand at the City of Philadelphia the thirtieth day of June in the year One thousand seven hundred and ninety two.   G: Washington

LC, George Washington Papers, Library of Congress.
1. Section 3 of this act reads as follows: "*And be it further enacted,* That a sum of fifty thousand dollars in addition to the provision heretofore made be appropriated to defray any expense which may be incurred in relation to the intercourse between the United States and foreign nations, to be paid out of any monies, which may be in the treasury, not otherwise appropriated, and to be applied under the direction of the President of the United States who, if necessary, is authorized to borrow, on the credit of the United States, the said sum of fifty thousand dollars; an account of the expenditure whereof as soon as may be, shall be laid before Congress" (1 *Stat.* 285 [May 8, 1792]).

From Joseph Whipple

Portsmouth, New Hampshire, June 30, 1792. "I recd. by the post last evening your letter of the 21st instant.[1] Soon after the receipt of your letter of the 4th of February last,[2] I wrote you under date of the 28th of that Month and transmitted the Name of Benjamin Gunnison as a Suitable person in my opinion for first Mate of the Scammel. . . . I now beg leave to renew my nomination of Mr. Gunnison. . . ."

LC, RG 36, Collector of Customs at Portsmouth, Letters Sent, 1792–1793, National Archives; copy, RG 56, Letters from the Collector at Portsmouth, National Archives.
1. Letter not found.   2. Letter not found.

To John Bayard, Elisha Boudinot, and Nicholas Low [1]

[Philadelphia, June, 1792]

Gentlemen

I have had a full conversation with General Schuyler [2] on the subject of the several propositions which have been under consideration respecting the location of the buildings for the Manufactory.[3] My original impressions on the point have been confirmed by the subsequent examination & I now entertain no doubt that the most adviseable course is to abandon for the present the idea of a Canal and to erect the necessary buildings near the Great Falls.

It is not clear to me that the advantages of pursuing the Canal-plan would at any rate compensate the difference of expence; but I think it very evident that to attempt it in the first instance would disable the company from prosecuting with adequate means the subsequent arrangements necessary to the Manufactory.[4]

As to the location of the District or Township I think it ought to comprehend the *little Falls* and the *head of the Navigation* of the Passaick and ought to embrace both sides of that River the whole distance between those two points. As to the rest the more compact it is & consequently the more ⟨near⟩ly [5] in a Square the better. Many local ⟨circum⟩stances unknown to me must decide ⟨the precise⟩ form. I once thought it might be well to take three Miles by twelve on the Passaick; but on further reflection I see no solid advantage in such an extension in length and there will be an obvious convenience in a more compact form. The police of the district in particular can be much better regulated.

Permit me to suggest that as soon as the location is made a Meeting of the Directors ought to be called at a *very short* day. Many things press & much will depend on going forward henceforth with ardor & dispactch. With very great esteem & consideration I am Gentlemen Your obedient servant   Alexander Hamilton

Messrs Bayard Low &
Boudinot

ALS, New Jersey Bank and Trust Company, Paterson, New Jersey; copy, Hamilton Papers, Library of Congress.

1. This letter was written to Bayard, Boudinot, and Low in their capacity as directors of the Society for Establishing Useful Manufactures. At a meeting of the directors of the society at Newark, New Jersey, at which H was present, on May 18, 1792, it was resolved that the operations of the society should be carried on at a place to be named Paterson which should be "located upon the Waters of the River Passaick." It was further resolved that "Mr: Low Mr: Bayard and Mr: Boudinot or any two of them be, and they are hereby authorized to locate the said Town within the limits in the foregoing Resolution, and to make purchases of such Lands as they shall deem requisite for the purposes of the Society, and to employ such surveyor or other Persons under them as they shall deem proper" ("Minutes of the S.U.M.," 37).

2. Philip Schuyler, H's father-in-law.

3. The committee, consisting of Bayard, Boudinot, and Low, reported at a meeting on July 4, 1792, of the directors of the Society for Establishing Useful Manufactures. The committee's report reads in part as follows: "That on the 29th of May last, they went to the Great Falls of Passaick accompanied by General Schuyler and several other Gentlemen well acquainted with the Country and the nature of Water Works in general, That they went over the ground for some Miles round, employed proper persons to make surveys and levels, That they found it practicable to take the Water from above the great falls carry it by Canals across the Country and empty it again into the River at several Places between the falls and Acquackanack . . ." ("Minutes of the S.U.M.," 42–43).

4. The committee report of July 4, 1792, states that the desired canals "in all probability would cost more than the funds of the Society would at Present Warrant" and that "upon consulting with Colo. Hamilton, They judged it most prudent to fix the principal Seat of the factory at the Great falls and accordingly made a purchase of certain Lands described in a Map marked A . . ." ("Minutes of the S.U.M.," 43).

5. Words within broken brackets have been taken from the copy in the Hamilton Papers, Library of Congress.

From Thomas Marshall [1]

[New York, June, 1792]

Sir

The Men, Women, and Children employ'd in the Above Mill (in the preparing and Spinning Departments) will be at least 150. And the Weight of Twist Spun will not fall short of 768 lbs of No 20's pr. Week. When the Mill is Completed it will be Indispensibly Necessary to have in Constant Employ, A Clock Maker, a Turner, a Joiner, and a Smith and Striker. On the Onset the Number of Trademen must be proportionate to the Expedition which is wishd for in Completing the Works. [2]

AL, The Passaic County Historical Society, Lambert Castle, Paterson, New Jersey.

1. H, on behalf of the Society for Establishing Useful Manufactures, had appointed Marshall to superintend the society's cotton mill. See H to the Directors of the Society for Establishing Useful Manufactures, December 7, 1791, and H to Marshall, May 30, 1792.

2. This letter was accompanied by estimates supplied by Marshall on the cost of erecting a cotton mill and of supplying that mill with machinery.

On May 18, 1792, at a meeting of the directors of the Society for Establishing Useful Manufactures at which H was present, it was resolved that "Mr. Marshall be directed to prepare as speedily as he can, machinery for a Mill of eight Drums for the use of the Cotton Manufacture" ("Minutes of the S.U.M.," 38).

On July 5, 1792, at a meeting of the directors of the society which H attended, it was resolved "that a Cotton Mill of Eight Drums and that for the Building of the same and providing the requisite Machinery the sum of fifteen thousand Dollars be appropriated, which Cotton Mill shall be of the following description Vizt. 55 by 32 feet to be built of Stone . . ." ("Minutes of the S.U.M.," 46).

INDEX

COMPILED BY JEAN G. COOKE